New York City

New York City

Paul Karr

Interior photography by the author and Kim Grant

SECOND EDITION

THE COUNTRYMAN PRESS — WOODSTOCK N.Y.

The Countryman Press ✳ Woodstock, Vermont

DEDICATION

For my lovely girl, my wonderful family, and my remarkable friends.

We welcome your comments and suggestions. Please contact Explorer's Guide Editor, The Countryman Press, P.O. Box 748, Woodstock, VT 05091, or e-mail countrymanpress@wwnorton.com.

ISBN-13: 978-0-88150-758-4
ISBN-10: 0-88150-758-X
ISSN 1545-6099

Cover and interior design by Bodenweber Design
Cover photograph by Patrick Batchelder
Text composition by PerfecType, Nashville, TN

Maps by Moore Creative Designs © 2003 The Countryman Press with the exception of the New York City Subway Map on cover and pages 10 and 11 © Metropolitan Transportation Authority. Used by permission. Subway and bus map current as of July 2006. Service is subject to change. For information about current service, go to www.mta.info or pick up a current subway map at any subway station booth.

Published by The Countryman Press, P.O. Box 748, Woodstock, Vermont 05091

Distributed by W. W. Norton & Company, Inc., 500 Fifth Avenue, New York, NY 10110

Printed in the United States of America

10 9 8 7 6 5 4 3 2 1

EXPLORE WITH US!

This is the second edition of *New York City: An Explorer's Guide,* full of interesting neighborhood attractions, fine- and casual-dining experiences, and hotels large and small. I have also given you the savvy you will need to drive into the city, cope with the vast and sometimes confusing public transit system, park your car or hail a taxi, check in, improvise a sightseeing tour, obtain theater or other event tickets, and make a reservation for dinner.

WHAT'S WHERE IN NEW YORK CITY

In the beginning of this book you'll find a short alphabetical listing of some of the highlights of New York City—everything from practical information on subway cards to the latest on no-smoking areas, cab fares, and street food. You'll also find out where the best city views are and how to sit in the studio audience for a live television taping, among other things.

LODGING

New York City offers up tens of thousands of hotel rooms on a given night, but not all of them are exactly what you want for your vacation. I've winnowed through the mountain of choices and made my selection of lodgings based on their intrigue, merit, history, and convenience, then tried to described them as fully as possible. Some are very, very expensive, while others are surprisingly affordable; I have stayed away from listing any dirt-cheap lodgings, boardinghouses, or hostels. (If you want those, buy another guidebook.) A few very well known hotels are absent from this book for a variety of reasons, and some fairly obscure ones have been included. Often I have included suite hotels, because they are very convenient for families. I can state with confidence that the lodgings listed herein are, as a group, clean and decently run—I'd stay there if I were visiting. In fact, I have.

To help you sort through the options, I have separated the city's lodgings into several categories. In roughly descending order of average room price, they are *Luxurious Hotels* (over-the-top, grandiose establishments—New York's finest); *Expensive Hotels* (pricey and elegant); *Boutique Hotels* (a new breed of interesting, artistically designed hotels that provide unique New York–style experiences usually at a usually premium price); *Business Hotels* (high-quality, straightforward offerings, with work desks and good Internet access); *Affordable Hotels* (less luxurious offerings good for those on a budget); *Inns* (country-style inns, often with antique furnishings, duvets, and the like); and *Bed & Breakfasts* (usually quite simply furnished rooms, with an included breakfast in a common dining room).

Prices: Though I have tried to be accurate as of press time (2006), prices can and do change each year. The price ranges here are to be taken as a snapshot in time and general guideline only; always confirm the price of a hotel room when booking. Restaurant entrée price ranges are likely to be consistent with those listed here.

Smoking: New York City enacted a tough new antismoking ordinance in spring 2003, eliminating smoking from most indoor public areas. Hotels normally reserve floors and/or certain rooms for smokers, though some of the city's inns and bed & breakfasts enforce strict no-smoking policies. See *What's Where in New York City* for more details on the ordinance.

RESTAURANTS

In each chapter you will note a distinction between *Dining Out* and *Eating Out*. The *Dining Out* establishments tend to be more expensive and formal, while *Eating Out* sections list eateries that are more casual and inexpensive.

KEY TO SYMBOLS

❧ **Special value.** The blue-ribbon symbol appears beside selected lodgings, restaurants, and attractions that combine quality with moderate prices.

✐ **Child-friendly.** The crayon symbol appears beside lodgings, restaurants, and activities of special interest to those traveling with children.

& **Handicapped access.** The wheelchair symbol appears beside lodgings, restaurants, and attractions that are handicapped accessible.

🐾 **Pets.** The dog-paw symbol appears beside lodgings that accept and cater to pets.

Any comments should be sent to Explorer's Guide Editor, The Countryman Press, P.O. Box 748, Woodstock, VT 05091; or e-mail countrymanpress@wwnorton.com.

CONTENTS

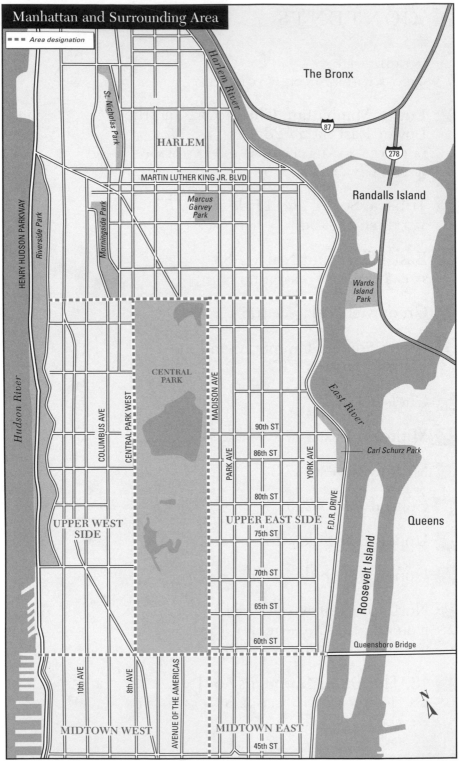

Manhattan and Surrounding Area

- - - *Area designation*

The Bronx

Harlem River

St. Nicholas Park

HARLEM

MARTIN LUTHER KING JR. BLVD

Marcus Garvey Park

Morningside Park

HENRY HUDSON PARKWAY

Riverside Park

Randalls Island

Wards Island Park

CENTRAL PARK

MADISON AVE

COLUMBUS AVE

CENTRAL PARK WEST

East River

Hudson River

90th ST

86th ST

PARK AVE

YORK AVE

Carl Schurz Park

80th ST

UPPER WEST SIDE

UPPER EAST SIDE

F.D.R. DRIVE

75th ST

Queens

70th ST

65th ST

Roosevelt Island

60th ST

Queensboro Bridge

10th AVE

8th AVE

AVENUE OF THE AMERICAS

N

MIDTOWN WEST

MIDTOWN EAST

45th ST

© The Countryman Press

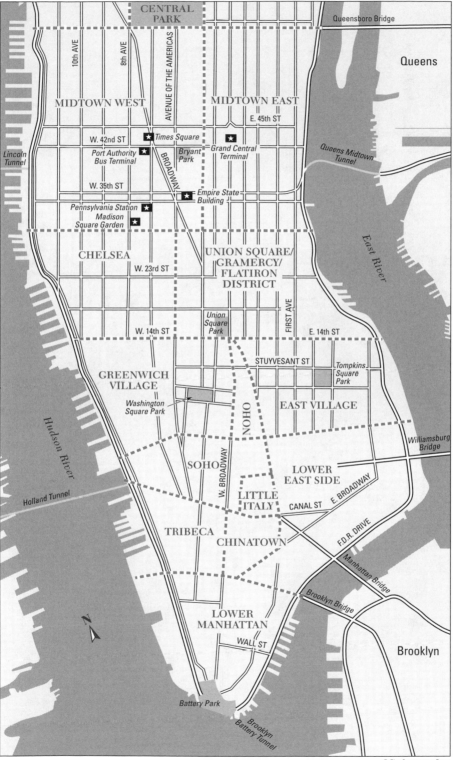

© The Countryman Press

MTA New York City Subway
with bus, railroad, and ferry connections

Metropolitan Transportation Authority

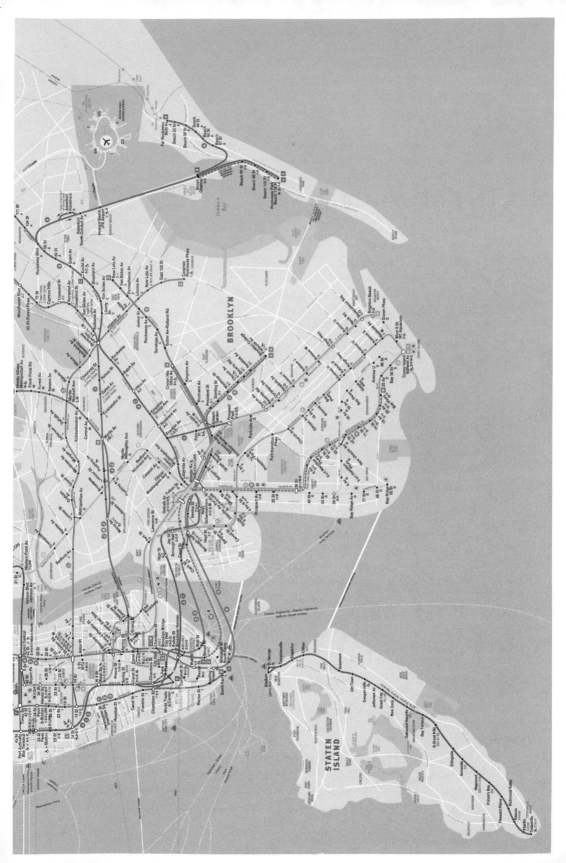

INTRODUCTION

The Big Apple. There isn't another city like it on earth.

All the clichés, all the movies, all the hype—only here, it seems, do they actually ring true. If anything, New York City is *more* than you expected.

What other place brings to mind such a rapid-fire series of cultural associations? The glittery ball descending upon Times Square as the year's final stroke of midnight approaches. A theater curtain rising. The crack of a bat at Yankee Stadium. Lovers gliding around Rockefeller Center's tiny oval skating rink. *Breakfast at Tiffany's.* King Kong dangling off the edge of the Empire State Building. Tom Hanks and Meg Ryan making eyes at each other as rival bookstore owners. *Law & Order* and *NYPD Blue* cops busting down a door in some Lower East Side dive. Frank Sinatra belting out a tune. A horse-drawn carriage in the snow in Central Park.

And, indelibly, the tear-streaked, ash-covered faces of firemen and rescue workers confronting, and then excavating, the ruins of the World Trade Center disaster.

Where else, too, can you find such an assortment of pocket neighborhoods, running the gamut from gritty but upward-trending Harlem to the boho/seedy Lower East Side, from past-its-trendy-moment SoHo to the coolly upper-crust Upper East Side to newly white-hot Tribeca, and beyond? Then there are the Outer Boroughs, places like Brooklyn, Queens, and Staten Island: They were once boring bedroom boroughs but have now become increasingly interesting places to live, work, play, or just visit.

This guidebook will attempt to lead you to a few of the places, tastes, and experiences that make New York such a distinctive wonder. Some are so famous that tourists who speak not a word of English can point the way to them. Others are so obscure that I'd wager many New Yorkers don't have a clue they even exist. Before leading you there, however, it's fair to ask: Just how did the city *get* this way, anyhow?

As most American junior high school students know (or are supposed to), the lower tip of Manhattan Island represented the original European settlement of what is now New York City. Before that, the same students learn, a band of Native Americans had roamed it, selling its land rights to a Dutchman for the equivalent of something less than $30 in beads and wampum. But this shorthand version doesn't really tell the full history. In fact, a patchwork of Native tribes occupied Manhattan, their fates and compositions shifting with each successive battle. They were savvy: All told, they sold its rights not once but multiple times to various Europeans willing to pay a price. Pretty sly. The Algonquins who made the land deal were nowhere near the first residents of the island—they were simply the ones who happened to be encamped there at the moment of Dutch colonization.

In fact, eons before black-clad *artistes* would arrive, the city had already achieved a certain unaffected cool: It had been covered for 100,000 years (give or take a few thousand) with a mile-high pack of ice, just as was the rest of New York and New England. When the great glaciers retreated, they left scrapings (still visible on the bedrock of Central Park), and a mixed forest of hardwoods and conifers eventually grew up in place of the retreating ice. The present-day outlines of Manhattan and its surrounding islands and bodies of water began to emerge; animals began to roam the woods, fish and shellfish filled the fresh-water rivers and saltwater bays surrounding it; and—soon and surely enough—indigenous peoples came to live.

It was only a matter of time before European ships, heady with the lust for conquest and acquisition, would arrive to transform the place from a sylvan island of rich fishing grounds and moderate strategic consequence to the cross-roads of the modern world economy.

The Italian explorer Verrazano appears to have been the first European to lay eyes on Manhattan; incredibly, however, he didn't set foot on the island, nor did he linger. Henry Hudson (sailing on behalf of the Dutch) further explored the river that would take his name, and his employers quickly realized its potential. In 1626 Peter Minuit made his famous $24 land swap, and he and his fellow Dutch farmers and traders swiftly gained the first true toehold here, establishing a series of settlements at the lowermost tip of the island as well as others up-island and in Brooklyn, across the East River. (The word *brooklyn* is Old Dutch for "broken land," tribute to the outcroppings and hills that characterize parts of the borough; Harlem is named for the small Dutch port city of Haarlem.)

The Dutch occupation of the area was impressive, but short lived; in 1664 expansion-minded English arrived by ship, seizing control of New Amsterdam (as it was then called) from the Dutch, and began remaking the trading town over in their own image. Up went Trinity Church and signs proclaiming the city NEW YORK after the northern English city of that name. Beneath a tree on Wall Street assembled the first traders of what would become the New York Stock Exchange. For a century the British would rule the roost and steadily grow and organize the city, even as the American Revolution raged. The Brits held out until 1783 before capitulating, and the victorious Americans made New York the new nation's first capital until 1790.

New York's fate as a future center of commerce and progressive politics was sealed, and the next decades brought change after rapid change. The Erie Canal was built, bringing a world of commerce down the river to New Yorkers' doors. The vast, loosely organized lands and blocks of the island north of Canal Street were divided into grids of avenues and streets with a military precision that al-lowed easier navigation (the street plan survives to this day). Central Park was laid out. Far uptown, farms and estates were cleared from the woods and marshes— and the transit system formerly known as the IRT (and now known as the MTA) began extending the city's reach toward them. The causes of women's rights, workers' rights, and abolition all began to blossom. The first waves of foreign immigrants—Irish and Italians, mostly—began pouring into Ellis Island to help build the newly muscular metropolis.

A World's Fair was hosted; the city's first major museum (the Met) threw open its doors; Madison Avenue, Wall Street, and Fifth Avenue began developing their distinctive personalities. Crime bosses and syndicates rose and fell on the wings of scandal. The Great Depression struck a blow to the city, but it was not a lasting one; the Empire State Building and Chrysler Building had both gone up within two years of the stock market crash, and they remain the city's two most recognizable buildings to this day. Throughout it all, fresh immigrants continued to arrive, each successive group bringing another interesting shade to the ever-more-complex patchwork cultural quilt that New York had, by now, become.

Not all was rosy in Gotham, however. After the postwar economic boom times of the 1950s, the 1960s and 1970s saw the city's soaring fortunes crashing back to earth. Inflation, unemployment, drugs, the sex trade, and rampant crime shook the metropolis and drained life from it; it would take decades to reverse these trends. Still, the World Trade Center's design and construction, completed in the spring of 1973, were a signal that New York would not easily relinquish its title of the world's leading city. The 1980s were marked by dizzying stock market gains and real estate speculation, along with all the sordid excesses that come with enormous newfound wealth. The emergence of deal makers such as Donald Trump and Leona Helmsley, their fates diverging wildly, were just a few of many, many subplots during this heady, at times unsettling, period.

New York has achieved a comfortable blending of assets. It is exhibit A in the case for America as melting pot. Crime is down; business, despite a precipitous drop immediately after the terrorist attacks on the World Trade Center of September 11, 2001, is up. Fine restaurants and boutique hotels open with regularity. And the city's collective arts offerings remain the world's best: Broadway's theaters, the Metropolitan Museum of Art, the Guggenheim, and the assorted music, opera, and dance organizations under the auspices of Lincoln Center (which went up in 1959, controversially replacing a slum neighborhood) alone would outshine any other major city's artistic arsenal, but these are simply the tip of the iceberg. Factor in the galleries of SoHo and 57th Street, museums such as the Whitney and the American Museum of Natural History, Harlem's growing cultural pride, summer plays and music performances in Central Park, a thriving poetry and music scene, and some of the finest independent-film houses in the nation, and you'll never spend a night in your hotel room wondering what to do for the evening.

What's been sung by Sinatra, then, can also be said of the traveler, because once you've seen New York, in a sense you've seen the whole world in microcosm; you could never travel abroad in your lifetime, and yet still know something of Jewish religion, Eastern European pastry, Chinese history, Japanese fashion, English punk, French high cuisine, Brazilian dance, Austrian coffee shop life, and Italian opera—not to mention a great deal more about American food, music, and art than you ever did before—and you might even see a movie star walking the same streets, acting like a regular person, in the process.

It was true then, and it's still true today: If you can make it here, you can make it (vicariously, at least) anywhere.

WHAT'S WHERE IN NEW YORK CITY

AIRPORT TRANSPORTATION From JFK airport to Midtown, a taxi ride will cost a flat fee of $45 plus tip and tolls; it's best to contact a private limousine or car service (consult a phone book) for the ride back, because it costs roughly the same fare but offers more comfort. From LaGuardia airport, the taxi ride costs $20–30 plus tolls and tip.

AREA CODES for Manhattan are 212 and 646; for outer boroughs like Brooklyn, Queens, and the Bronx, the area codes are now 78 and, sometimes, 347. Then there is the mysterious 917 area code, which was originally used for mobile phones and pagers but now increasingly pops up in business listings as a land-line prefix too.

BOOKS Barnes & Noble is the undisputed king of reading material in New York; in a world where Amazon and Borders are gobbling up the small cities, B&N stands tall. Check out the locations near Lincoln Center (at 66th Street and Broadway), on the Upper West Side (at 82nd Street and Broadway), and in Midtown (on Third Avenue, near 52nd Street).

Paul Karr

Smaller, locally owned bookstores are scattered throughout New York, especially thick in Greenwich Village and the NYU area but also in pockets of Midtown.

COFFEE It's easy to find coffee in New York, but New Yorkers must not be too fussy about their joe because, quite frankly, the options in this city could be better. Starbucks are ubiquitous, of course, with prominent locations scattered throughout the city; there are big ones near Lincoln Center and Rockefeller Center; inside Barnes & Noble bookshops; on Spring Street in SoHo; on Broadway, Seventh Avenue, and 56th Street in Midtown East; and lots of other places, too. The coffee is only so-so, though there are plenty of pricey permutations—seasonal eggnog latte, sweetish caramel Frappuccino—to tempt you, and a decent assortment of sweets (scones, brownies, and so forth) for accompaniment. As an alternative, the local chain New World Coffee serves a decent, if unspectacular, brew at fewer locations around the city. Hotel restaurants serve brews at too-high prices (at a nice one, it can run you $10 or more for a cup).

Really, it's best to look instead for an authentic Italian café such as the Upper East Side's Via Quadronno (see chapter 10) for the best cup. If it's a *Friends*-like atmosphere you're seeking rather than superior beans, find a hip coffeehouse like SoHo's Café Café (see chapter 2) and settle into a couch or corner table.

DEPARTMENT STORES There's really only one neighborhood you need visit if you're here to find department stores: Midtown East, specifically Fifth Avenue between East 60th and East 49th streets. Here you can find Henri Bendel, Saks Fifth Avenue, Bergdorf Goodman, and the Japanese department store Takashimaya, among others. (You'll also find Tiffany & Co., Cartier, and Bulgari, three of the world's most famous jewelers, along this stretch.) A few blocks west, at Lexington Avenue between East 59th Street and East 60th Street, is the giant Bloomingdale's.

Farther downtown, taking up an entire block of West 34th Street between Broadway and Seventh Avenue, the midrange store Macy's has operated its flagship store for decades; it's a good place to get a souvenir of New York without paying an arm and a leg.

That about covers it for the big-name stores. Other prime shopping areas include SoHo (particularly Spring Street, Prince Street, Broadway, and West Broadway) for hip, arty, and overpriced stuff; Chinatown for cheapy kitschy souvenirs, knockoff watches, jewelry, perfumes, and the like; Chelsea and the West Village for fine antiques; and the East Village for Bohemian furniture, crafts, and vintage clothing.

HOT DOGS AND PRETZELS Street vendors are legend in New York. You'll find them on any busy downtown street corner at lunchtime, and around town in locales such as Central Park and the shopping districts.

NEON If it's bright lights you want, Times Square is still the center of the action—the first place most visitors go when visiting New York, and undeniably its most stimulating sight. The

Paul Karr

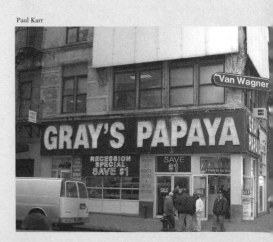

square and its surrounding side streets are more appealing than ever thanks to a decade of city and police crackdowns on the drug dealing, crime, and adult theaters that once surrounded the district and depressed its character.

PARKING If you've chosen to drive into the city, parking can be incredibly vexing and expensive. There are certainly plenty of parking lots and garages, and plenty of ways to park like a resident.

Garages are everywhere, but they're expensive—anywhere from $20 a night in a so-so neighborhood to more like $40 a night in an upscale one. There's also no guarantee you can find a spot in a choice garage at a peak time: In Midtown that means weekdays during the day, and anywhere else it means whenever a special event such as a ball game or concert has driven up demand. Many hotels have worked out arrangements with nearby garages for $25–30 per night. If you're just coming on a day trip, many garages and lots offer early-bird specials; if you enter after 10 AM and leave by 6 PM, you can often park for less than $10 total.

One more thing: In New York, parking is tight and garages and lots are creative with space. That means it's very often necessary to give up your keys to a parking lot attendant, who will wedge the car into a spot—then hang on to your keys (and access to your car) for the duration of your stay. Locals have gotten used to it, and of course they don't leave valuables in their trunks, but if this situation makes you uncomfortable you will either have to swallow hard and accept it or spend hours looking for a true self-park lot. If you do, of course,

it's probably a good idea to bring valuables to your hotel and secure them in a safe if one's available—at good-class business hotels, one usually is.

Parking on the street requires a lot of savvy, luck, and the ability to decipher a complex web of parking regulations posted on signs that are not always obvious and sometimes contradict each other. The various perils include parking on residents-only streets or during residents-only hours; parking during street-sweeping hours; parking near fire hydrants, which are not always streetside or obvious; parking in hotel loading zones or in front of concealed garages; and parking during rush-hour or heavy-traffic daytime hours. Then there are special events, such as movie and television shoots and parades, which sometimes alter the equation further.

If you come to the city regularly, you might eventually get the hang of it, but you're almost certain to get an expensive ticket during your education. It's really best to consult with your hotel in these situations.

PUBLIC RESTROOMS It's not easy to find a decent public restroom in a pinch in Manhattan, but it's not impossible, either; the considerable numbers of cafés, coffee shops, restaurants, and hotels offer plenty of possibilities. In Midtown, make a beeline for a reliably big chain hotel and look for public restrooms toward the back. In the Times Square area, find a burger chain or hotel bar. On the Upper West Side, look for a deli; on the Upper East Side, duck into a department store or late-hours wine bar—you may need to descend stairs to find the holy grail. SoHo's got coffee shops; Chinatown, eateries; Wall

Street, a McDonald's. Fifth Avenue's department stores and some upscale jewelry stores also possess very nice facilities, as do museums—though of course you must buy a ticket to get access.

SMOKING AREAS Believe it or not, as of April 1, 2003, smoking was banned from almost all of New York's public areas; with very few exceptions, this means every hotel, restaurant, and bar above a certain size is smoke-free. This is either very good or very bad news, depending on whether or not you're a smoker. Citywide, enforcement has been largely effective (save a few ugly confrontations and sneaky bars), and the smoke-free experiment seems mostly to be working.

SUBWAYS New York's subway system ($2 a ride at press time, though this may change) is among the world's oldest, and sometimes it still feels that way: Despite recent upgrades to the MTA system and renovation of the car stock, some cars remain dirty, poorly air-conditioned, and smelly, with poor announcement-sound quality, while others are newly manufactured in Japan and almost as comfortable. It's hit or miss, really.

Paul Karr

To find a station, consult the listings in this book. I have listed the nearest available station or stations for all hotels, restaurants, and attractions. When in doubt, ask a local; they're usually all too happy to direct you to the nearest subway station, often only a block or two away.

Tokens are no longer accepted on the subway (as of 2003), and have been replaced by the MetroCard®. MetroCard vending machines, available at the stations, accept debit cards as well as credit cards and cash. Buses accept MetroCard and exact change (no bills or pennies). If you purchase $10 or more of MetroCard, a 20 percent bonus is added to the card (for instance, pay $10 and you'll receive $12 in value on the card, pay $20 and you'll get $24 in value on the card, etc.). With pay-per-ride MetroCards, you can transfer from a subway to a bus or from a bus to a subway for free within two hours of use; with unlimited-use cards, transferring from subway to bus or from bus to subway is unlimited. One-, seven-, and thirty-day unlimited-ride MetroCards are also available. You can get a free map of the subway system in the terminals; you'll need it, because the city's color-coded lines are a bit complicated to the uninitiated. Agents can usually help you find the right line and platform.

Bear in mind that certain trains (the B train, for example) run only on weekdays or during rush hours, and that express trains (the A and Q trains, for example) stop only at busy express stations. If you need to get to a local station, such as 23rd Street (the heart of Chelsea), Prince Street (the heart of SoHo), or 66th Street (Lincoln Center), you must take a local train. The best strategy is to take an express train as far as possible, then switch to the slower local train—usually you can do it cross-platform—but if you have any doubt at all, simply take the local train; it might take longer, but you're guaranteed that the train won't whiz past the correct station.

Also remember that each platform has two choices, often between "uptown" (north, toward higher street numbers) and "downtown" (south, toward Lower Manhattan and lower street numbers). Trains headed toward Queens and Brooklyn usually are going south through Lower Manhattan and then east; trains heading for the Bronx or Harlem are going north. There are few crosstown trains, so use a bus to get across town swiftly.

Still confused? Try to get to the Times Square station at 42nd Street—more of the city's lines converge here than anywhere else, and there are usually plenty of policemen and transit employees around who know the right directions.

To cut the cost of traveling, buy 1-day or 1-week passes if you'll be in town for a while.

TAXIS Hailing a taxi in New York City is both amazingly easy and devilishly difficult, depending on a wealth of factors that might or might not include the prevailing weather conditions, time of day, a cabdriver's individual mood, the doorman's lung power, and your own personal hailing technique.

The best place to hail a taxi is certainly outside a hotel; head for the nearest big one, where drops will occur by the minute. If there isn't a hotel available, head next for the local version of restaurant row. On the Upper West Side and Upper East Side, taxi business is slow during weekdays and daytimes, so you can

Paul Karr

almost surely catch a ride within a few minutes. But weekend nights are tough going, as hordes head uptown for dinner or drinks. In Midtown, taxis stream up and down the avenues all day long; at rush hour, however—when the well heeled are getting out of work, heading for dinner reservations, or doing a bit of shopping—it can be next to impossible to get a ride. Prepare for a free-for-all with the surprisingly aggressive madames and messieurs.

In Lower Manhattan and the West Village, the situation is trickier—the winding warrens of streets are cab-unfriendly, and most drivers won't go any farther into the muck than they need to do to make a drop. The East Village is laid out in a grid, but cabbies don't head here quite as often, as the mixture of locals doesn't exactly guarantee big tippers.

You have the right to argue with a cabbie over route choice and driving speed, but generally speaking cabdrivers are fair and as speedy as humanly possible—nobody, after all, can clairvoyantly predict each instance of New York gridlock in time to avoid it. If you ever feel in danger, of course, get out; if you feel the cabbie has stiffed you, don't tip anything and take note of the medal number (on the back of the driver's seat) for later reference—let the driver know you can (and should) complain to the city taxi board as soon as possible. If the bill seems high for a 10-block ride, remember that when you're stuck in traffic the cost quickly mounts—and you're all but obliged to tack on a 10–15 percent tip, too (though it is by no means required). Also remember, always, to get a receipt as you exit the cab; should you leave something behind in the taxi, that little slip of paper is perhaps your only chance of locating it later.

TELEVISION SHOWS There are two ways to get a ticket to one of the many live television tapings that take place in New York each day before live studio audiences. You can either write, in advance, for tickets—some very popular programs use a lottery system—or simply show up on taping day and hope for cancellations or standby tickets.

Late Night with Conan O'Brien (212-664-3056) is taped at NBC Studios, located at 30 Rockefeller Plaza (50th Street at Sixth Avenue), Tuesday through Friday at 5:30 PM. You need to call the NBC ticket hotline (above) for a ticket (maximum order: 4 tickets), and you can only order once

every six months. Or, show up before 9 AM to inquire about unclaimed standby tickets (which do not guarantee admission). Come to the studio by 5 PM if you have standby tickets. You must be 16 or over to attend tapings.

The *Late Show with David Letterman* (212-975-5853 or 212-247-6497) is taped at the Ed Sullivan Theater, located at 1697 Broadway at the corner of West 54th Street, Monday through Thursday at 5:30 PM. There's sometimes a second taping at 8 PM Thursday. Enter a request online at www.cbs.com, or show up at the theater Monday through Friday from 9:30 AM to 12:30 PM or weekends 10 AM to 6 PM. If you can't do that, call the ticket line between 11 AM and noon for unclaimed or standby tickets—and remember to get in line at the theater 45 minutes early.

Saturday Night Live (212-664-4000) is taped at NBC Studios, located at 30 Rockefeller Plaza (50th Street at Sixth Avenue), at 11:30 PM certain Saturdays; there's a dress rehearsal at 8 PM. To get a ticket, you must write well in advance to NBC, and they will hold a lottery. Failing that, show up around 7 AM on taping day at the 49th Street entrance to the studio. If you somehow snag a standby ticket (which doesn't guarantee admission), get to the studios good and early that night—an hour and a half ahead isn't too early. You can pick from a ticket to the dress rehearsal or the 11:30 live taping.

If you can't manage to secure tickets to any of those three shows, head instead for the General Motors Building across from the Plaza Hotel and Central Park (it's the building containing toy store FAO Schwarz) early one weekday morning. CBS's *The Early Show* films live through a window in

Kim Grant

front of a sea of corny signs (HI TO LAURIE IN LITTLE ROCK or maybe O'BRIENS FROM NATICK LUV 'TEK—SOX RULE!), and anchors or weathermen sometimes wander through the crowd outside to do impromptu interviews. The same thing goes for *The Today Show,* NBC's daily smile-fest, whose studios reside in Rockefeller Center, and the show sometimes shoots stand-ups from the famous ice rink and other outdoor public areas.

TREES Central Park is by far New York's greenest patch, and a walk, bike, jog, or buggy ride here is the quickest way to escape the din of Manhattan; certain upper reaches of the park actually feel wild. Reach the park by strolling north along Fifth Avenue to 59th Street, or, from Times Square, head north along Broadway until you reach Columbus Circle; the park is directly across the circle.

Other good spots to find trees include Tompkins Square Park, the Brooklyn Botanic Garden, and Brooklyn's Prospect Park.

VIEWS The archetypal New York view is from the 86th-floor observation deck of the Empire State Building (see chapter 8), which has reopened after its closure in the wake of the September 11 tragedies. Rockefeller Center, located about 20 blocks north of the Empire State Building, has also opened a great new observation deck. There are other ways to see the sky-line, too: Try the rooftop bar or pool of a Midtown hotel such as the Penin-sula, Novotel, or Le Parker Meridien (see chapter 8); the panoramic view from the Brooklyn Heights Prome-nade (see chapter 13); or a scenic boat ride from the southern tip of Manhattan such as the Staten Island Ferry (see chapter 13).

Lower Manhattan, Chinatown, and the Lower East Side

1

LOWER MANHATTAN, CHINATOWN, AND THE LOWER EAST SIDE

It's almost unbelievable to think so, but for most of recorded history there were no significant permanent human settlements north of Canal Street. New York City was essentially confined to the 30 or so short blocks stretching from Canal down to the narrow southern tip of the island until the mid-1800s, when boom times and wave after wave of immigration forced developers and manufacturers to quickly build up adjacent areas such as Chelsea, SoHo, Gramercy Park, and the Village. It was just a matter of time before this growth continued to spread up and out, horizontally and vertically, until nearly every corner of the island of Manhattan had been filled.

But it all started here; though they're mostly gone from the city today, Dutch and other European bankers and traders get all the credit. The remarkably multicultural New Netherland colony was nothing like it looks today; instead, it resembled a quiet corner of Amsterdam or Venice, with placid canals and bridges interlacing the islands, farms, windmills, and gardens. A fort (built in 1624, of which no trace remains) stood guard at the southern tip of Manhattan, and a defensive wall extended along the northern boundary of what was then quite a small area. Thus protected, the hodgepodge of seamen, importers, exporters, bankers, traders, and speculators assembled here could carry out the business of shaping a new capitalist economy.

Chinatown and Manhattan's so-called Lower East Side have historically been quite different in character from each other, and from the financial area I've described above, but recently these two adjacent neighborhoods have begun to resemble one another more and more as Chinatown continues expanding east, trimming away at the Lower East Side's formerly Eastern European character.

On the other hand, the East Side has been newly discovered by trendy young folks who once haunted the East Village (from which it is separated by Houston Street). This has meant a flurry of New American restaurants, tapas bars, and hip clubs, although the actual streets and buildings of this district remain drab and a bit seedy.

LOWER MANHATTAN

Many of the financial fortunes of the rest of this island are still made or broken here in Lower Manhattan. But the area's character has completely changed from that idyllic Dutch trading colony of so long ago. Today Lower Manhattan is a mixture of high-rise office buildings and leftover historic structures from a much earlier time—places like Trinity Church, Fraunces Tavern, the Customs House building, and Federal Hall, which are a delight to come upon amid the windy, shadowed canyons of steel and concrete. Everything is faster down here, you'll notice—the walking, the talking, the shop service—because that's the way the movers and shakers like it.

For the purposes of this guidebook, I have defined Lower Manhattan as everything south of Chambers Street and the Brooklyn Bridge's Manhattan side. The district takes in some of Manhattan's most important sites: Wall Street, Battery Park, the renovated South Street Seaport complex, the ferry that takes you to the Statue of Liberty and Ellis Island (both of which I have included in this chapter), and—of course—Ground Zero, the somber remainder of what were once two of the world's very tallest, most densely occupied buildings. Designs have been approved for a new World Trade Center complex, but they're still being wrangled over and it will be a good while before they're realized. In the meantime, come and remember.

GETTING THERE The Financial District and Lower Manhattan are very well served by public transit—how do you think all those bankers and traders get here from their homes in New Jersey, Connecticut, Long Island, and the Upper East Side? (Actually, some of them take helicopters to work, but that's another matter.) Anyhow, the tightly packed streets and lack of parking make driving here a very bad idea.

By car: There's no easy way to get here by car, and little chance of parking once you do. Chinatown and Tribeca are your best bets for parking, but even in these areas a spot can be elusive—and you'll still need to hike a ways to these attractions. Still, if you must drive, take either the FDR (East Side) Drive or Broadway south.

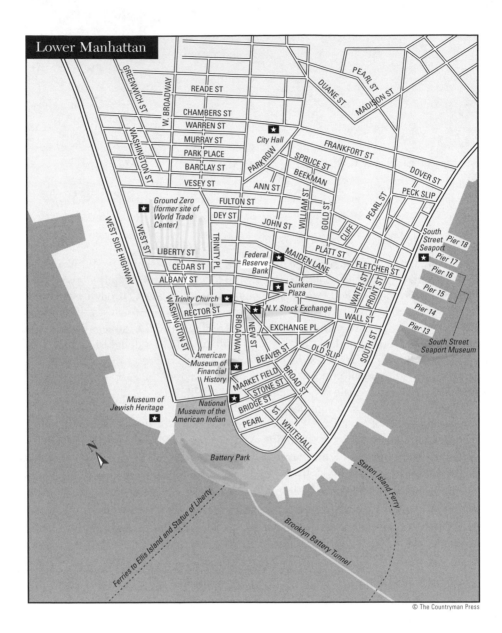

Lower Manhattan

© The Countryman Press

By subway: Numerous subway lines stop in Lower Manhattan. From the Upper West Side or Midtown West, take the A, C, E, N, R, W, 1, 2, or 3 train downtown. From the Upper East Side or Midtown East, take the 4, 5, or 6 train downtown. From the Rockefeller Center area, you'll need to change trains at West 4th Street or Broadway–Lafayette. To reach the World Trade Center site, take an E train to World Trade Center (the final stop heading downtown) or an N, R, or W train to Cortlandt Street. To reach Wall Street and its many attractions, take a 2, 3, 4, or 5 train to Wall Street. And to reach South Ferry (the ferry to the Statue of Liberty), take a 1 train (get into one of the front five cars) to South Ferry; a 4 or 5 train to Bowling Green gets you fairly close, also, but the 1 is a better choice.

By bus: Relatively few bus lines penetrate Lower Manhattan, mostly because the city's regular grid structure breaks down here and negotiating a bus around the tight corners would be something of a nightmare. But there are a few options. From anywhere on the East Side, the 15 bus runs all the way down Second Avenue to South Ferry, then back up First Avenue; the 1 bus runs along Fifth Avenue and Madison Avenue all the way to South Ferry (stopping at Wall Street along the way). From Midtown West and Times Square, the 6 bus also runs all the way to South Ferry, stopping at Wall Street en route. And the 20 bus is useful because it stops closer to the World Trade Center and Battery Park areas than the others; catch it in Times Square, along Seventh Avenue below Times Square, or along Broadway up to Lincoln Center.

GETTING AROUND The 20 bus is handy, as it makes a loop of Lower Manhattan along Vesey Street (eastbound) and Chambers Street (westbound), stopping near many of the main sites described below.

✳ To See

HISTORIC SITES ♿ **Ellis Island** (212-269-5755 or 1-866-STATUE-4), between Jersey City, New Jersey, and Manhattan. Ferry: from Battery Park (subway: 4 or 5 train to Bowling Green, or 1 train to South Ferry) each half hour, 8 AM–4 PM. Open daily 9 AM–5:15 PM summer, rest of the year 9:30 AM–5:15 PM. Contrary to

THE FATE OF MILLIONS OF IMMIGRANTS WAS DETERMINED IN ELLIS ISLAND'S GREAT HALL.

Kim Grant

popular belief, Ellis Island—which is either in New York or New Jersey, depending on whom you ask—is *not* the site of the Statue of Liberty (see below), though it's very close to it. Rather, this was the port of immigration for millions of travelers seeking a better life in America between 1892 and 1954. Their answers to the immigration officers' grilling determined their fates—and the fates of their families. Most made it through safely, though nearly all remembered the mixed trepidation and elation they felt as they waited in the Great Hall for their interviews. Today you can find a three-floor museum that wonderfully captures the immigrant experience through artifacts, journals, photographs, and other materials, a Wall of Honor commemorating 600,000 immigrants' names (and counting), and a research library where you can check for the records of your own forebears. The island visit and museum are free, although the ferry ride ($11.50 for adults, $9 for senior citizens, $4.50 for children 3–17) is not. Remember that new security regulations forbid backpacks and any other large packages on the ferry; you will be inspected before boarding. Contact the Circle Line (number above) for tickets.

Ground Zero, between Vesey and Liberty streets, from Church to West streets. Subway: E train to World Trade Center, or N, R, or W train to Cortlandt Street. Viewing area open daily 9 AM–9 PM. The most somber, and popular, destination in a post-9/11 New York City, the former site of the World Trade Center towers can no longer be seen from a ticketed viewing platform. Instead, a viewing area has been laid out along Liberty Street from Church Street/Trinity Place to Greenwich Street or Washington Street. All that remains now of the two huge, 110-story towers destroyed by jet collisions is an enormous, empty 16-acre space, though a design for a replacement structure has been selected. There is also a memorial wall along four blocks of Church Street, stretching from Liberty Street to Vesey Street; the steel fence with fiberglass memorial panels approximates the area where so many spontaneous memorials sprung up immediately after the disaster. The best place to get a view of the site, however, might be across West Street from the adjacent Winter Garden in the World Financial Center (212-945-2600). The garden's 45,000-square-foot glass atrium, arched ceiling, marble floors, 16 live palm trees, and grand staircase—most of it severely damaged in the attacks, and since restored—do seem a bit excessive, given the bleak empty space nearby. But its large window provides an excellent view onto the towers' ghostly footprint, and entry is free. Reach the Financial Center by carefully crossing busy West Street at Vesey, West Thames, or Chambers streets.

♿ **Statue of Liberty** (212-363-3200 or 212-269-5755), Liberty Island between Jersey City, New Jersey, and Manhattan. Ferry: from Battery Park (subway: 4 or 5 train to Bowling Green, or 1 train to South Ferry) each

A SEPTEMBER 11 MEMORIAL

Paul Karr

half hour, 8:30 AM–4:30 PM summer, less frequently 8:30 AM–3:30 PM rest of the year. Open daily 9:30 AM–6 PM in summer, rest of the year daily 9:30 AM–5 PM. The Statue of Liberty must be the single most recognizable symbol of New York City. This 150-foot-tall copper-and-iron sculpture by Frédéric-Auguste Bartholdi (with help from Gustave Eiffel) took more than 20 years to complete, then was shipped in pieces by France as a gift to the United States in time for the 110th anniversary of its independence. Before the statue arrived, America needed to raise considerable funds to pay for the 150-foot base, and it took quite an odyssey of fund-raising; eventually, however, the monies were secured—publisher Joseph Pulitzer played a major role—and the statue was unveiled to the public in 1886. Today Lady Liberty stands regally thrusting her gold torch to the skies, unmistakably French in carriage yet undeniably American now. She is heavy with numerical symbolism; nothing is random. Her crown's 25 windows represent the known precious stones in Bartholdi's time, while its seven rays represent the continents of the earth. The book she holds is incised with the date of American independence. Emma Lazarus's poem, inscribed into the base, speaks perfectly to an America that welcomed tens of millions to its shores during the 19th and early 20th centuries:

> Cries she
> With silent lips. "Give me your tired, your poor,
> Your huddled masses yearning to breathe free,
> The wretched refuse of your teeming shore.
> Send these, the homeless, tempest-tost to me,
> I lift my lamp beside the golden door!"

Ironically, after the events of September 11, 2001, the interior of the statue was closed to the public due to security concerns. The upper levels of the statue remain closed to the public, but the second-floor museum in the pedestal re-opened in 2004. Concealed within the huge pedestal is a lobby area where visitors could once view Bartholdi's original torch—age forced it into retirement in the 1980s, when a new one was cast. And of course, you could previously ascend hundreds of steps to the crown and its unparalleled views of the city. At least you can console yourself with the knowledge that the sculptor never intended for the public to enter or climb the statue—his proposal was that it be filled with sand for stability—and, in fact, it is best perceived coming closer and closer from the ferry as you're approaching it, just as millions of immigrants did.

To be brutally honest, all the new security has made a trip to the statue less pleasant than ever; there's a constant military presence, bomb searches, and long waits at each step. All this tension in the air might be a bit uncomfortable for kids. But if you do go—and it's certainly worth seeing, despite the waiting times, even with the family—I'd recommend skipping the interior statue tour (except the museum) entirely, as you don't see all that much anymore and you need to reserve a block of 'entrance time' in advance of coming. Instead, savor a view of Lady L by strolling around the island around it. Entrance to Liberty Island is free, although the ferry ride ($11.50 for adults, $9 for senior citizens, $4.50 for children 3–17) is not. You may not bring a backpack or any large package onto the ferry, and you may be searched before boarding it.

MUSEUMS ♿ **Museum of Jewish Heritage** (212-509-6130), 36 Battery Place (in Battery Park City). Subway: N, R, W, or 1 train to Rector Street. Open Sunday through Thursday 10 AM–5:45 PM (Wednesday to 8 PM), Friday 10 AM–3 PM (5 PM in winter). Meant to be a kind of living memorial to the Holocaust, this Battery Park museum unveiled a new wing in spring 2003. Its documentaries, home movies, diaries, feature film archive, and objects fulfill that mission admirably—as do special exhibitions on topics such as Jewish life in France and portraits of East European Jewish life during the 1930s. One show highlighted photographs and other objects from the World Trade Center attacks. Admission costs $10 for adults, $7 for senior citizens, $5 for children.

♿ **National Museum of the American Indian** (212-514-3700), 1 Bowling Green between Broadway and State Street. Subway: 4 or 5 train to Bowling Green, 1 train to South Ferry, or N, R, or W train to Whitehall Street. Open daily 10 AM–5 PM, until 8 PM Thursday. Housed within Lower Manhattan's grandiose, seven-story Beaux-Arts-style U.S. Customs House, this museum—also known as the George Gustav Heye Center, for the collector who assembled most of its holdings—is a serious collection and research archive of the continent's Native peoples. The permanent holdings here include stone carvings, masks, painted hides, Plains Indian bonnets, ceramics and artifacts from Central and South America, carved jade from the Maya, Amazonian feather work, and a great deal more—though some of this collection is slowly being shifted to another branch of the museum outside Washington, D.C. Recent special exhibits have showcased the influences of Oaxacan culture; photographs of Caribbean Native peoples; and the arts and crafts of Mexico's states. The museum, which is affiliated with the Smithsonian Institution, is entirely free of charge.

♿ **South Street Seaport Museum** (212-748-8600), South Street at Fulton Street at Piers 15 and 16. Subway: 2 or 3 train to Wall Street or Fulton Street, A or C train to Broadway–Nassau, J, M, or Z train to Fulton Street, or 4, 5, or 6 train to Brooklyn Bridge–City Hall. Open Tuesday to Sunday 10 AM–6 PM April through September, Friday to Monday 10 AM–5 PM the rest of the year. Tied into the port's nautical theme, this museum restores, displays, and explains seagoing vessels; there are eight here at present along the so-called Street of Ships, including the wooden, steam-powered tugboat the *W. O. Decker* (built in 1930 to service the Newtown Creek inlet of the East River; you can book a ride on it around the harbor) and the enormous four-masted tall ship the *Peking*, which was launched from Germany in 1911—with 350-foot masts and a 300-foot-long steel hull, still one of the largest vessels ever to ply the seas. The museum also offers several galleries of exhibits relating port history—they are organized to highlight marine artisans and a children's section, among other areas—as well as a research library that can be visited for genealogical purposes by appointment. Admission costs $8 per adult, $6 seniors, $4 children 5–12.

FOR FAMILIES ✒ ♿ **New York Unearthed** (212-748-8753), 17 State Street between Pearl and Whitehall streets. Subway: 1 train to South Ferry, 4 or 5 train to Bowling Green, or N or R train to Whitehall Street. Open Monday through

Friday *by appointment only*. Part of the South Street Seaport complex (see *Markets and Public Spaces*), though a bit removed from it, New York Unearthed teaches visitors—especially kids—about the 6,000 years of natural and human history revealed through the various excavations, both industrial and archaeological, that have taken place in Manhattan. Dioramas and artifacts explain the city's history, while downstairs you can watch archaeologists piecing together, researching, examining, and cataloging freshly recovered items. Among the interesting facts: Residential backyards often reveal some of the most interesting finds. The museum and site are free, but are open only on weekday afternoons.

CHURCHES **St. Paul's Chapel,** Broadway at Fulton Street. Subway: E train to World Trade Center, N, R, or W train to Cortlandt Street, or 4, 5, J, M, or Z train to Fulton Street. Museum open Monday through Saturday 10 AM–6 PM, Sunday to 4 PM. Built in what was then a field in 1766, this stone Georgian chapel of Trinity Church (see below) was designed to resemble London's graceful St. Martin-in-the-Fields; it saw George Washington and other notable citizens kneel at its pews—beneath 14 cut-glass chandeliers and a painting of the Great Seal of the United States—during the two years in which New York City served as America's capital. But the chapel took on a new significance in the aftermath of September 11, 2001, when thousands of workers ate, slept, and suited up here during eight months of cleanup operations at the World Trade Center—whose towers had stood almost directly across the street from it. Church volunteers played an enormous supporting role in this effort, and the new chapel exhibit Out of the Dust—about Ground Zero rescue workers and the volunteers who helped them restore body and spirit—is open daily 10 AM–6 PM (Sunday until 4 PM). The church and museum are both free to enter.

&. **Trinity Church** (212-602-0872), 74 Trinity Place at Broadway and Wall Street. Subway: 4 or 5 train to Wall Street, or N, R, W, 1, or 9 train to Rector Street. Church open Monday through Friday 7 AM–6 PM, Saturday 8 AM–4 PM, Sunday after the 11:15 AM service. Welcome center open Monday through Friday 10–11:45 AM and 1–2:30 PM, Saturday 11:30 AM–2:30 PM. Museum open Monday through Friday 9–11:45 AM and 1–3:45 PM, Saturday 10 AM–3:45 PM, Sunday 1–3:45 PM. This anachronistic Gothic Revival church, whose dignified 300-foot spire is tucked among Lower Manhattan's skyscrapers, is an Episcopal house of worship whose founding dates to 1697. The present Gothic Revival structure, however, was the third church to be built on the site; designed by Richard Upjohn and built of reddish sandstone, its doors were intended to reflect Ghiberti's in Florence. Free tours take place daily at 2 PM, and there's a small museum as well. The pretty, secluded church graveyard between Rector Street and Broadway contains notable graves such as those of Alexander Hamilton and Robert Fulton; nearby is St. Paul's Chapel (see above), which played a major role in the World Trade Center cleanup effort. Far uptown, Trinity's larger cemetery—part of what was once John James Audubon's farm in Harlem, between 153rd and 155th streets and bisected by Broadway—contains many more famous graves; see chapter 12 for more information.

DOLLARS AND SENSE American Numismatic Society (212-571-4470), 96 Fulton Street at the corner of William Street. Subway: 2, 3, J, M, or Z train to Fulton Street or A or C train to Broadway–Nassau. Open to the public Monday to Friday 9 AM–5 PM. If you're nuts about coins, visit ANS, which collectors formed in 1858 and which moved to lovely new four-story headquarters (a former bank) in Lower Manhattan in 2004; an exhibition hall is planned by 2007 or 2008. Its carefully kept collections include a silver Roman coin dating from 112 BC, a bronze Roman coin from Nero's time (around AD 65), a zinc-plated American penny from the World War II years of copper rationing, and a number of silver peace medals minted by the Jefferson, Lincoln, and other administrations for use in negotiations with Native American tribes. The ANS also hosts periodic events in the city, including a 2002 exhibition at the Federal Reserve Bank (below), a public forum on numismatics, and a World's Fair of Money. Admission is free.

♿ **Federal Reserve Bank** (212-720-6130), 33 Liberty Street at Nassau Street, Williams Street, and Maiden Lane. Subway: 2, 3, 4, or 5 train to Wall Street or Fulton Street, or J, M, or Z train to Fulton Street. Open Monday through Friday 8:30 AM–5 PM. Money exhibit open 10 AM–4 PM. Perhaps even more important than Wall Street in terms of national and global economics, the "Fed" (as it's known) rarely merits dinner-table conversation. Yet within the walls of this block-long Italianate building in the Financial District sits one of the world's most important financial institutions. It is one of 12 local reserve banks that make up the nation's central banking entity, and its officers alone have the power to create monetary policy—the printing of currency, the increasing or holding steady of the nation's total supply of dollars, the setting of lending rates, the sale of U.S. dollars to foreign banks when needed (which affects exchange rates), and the storage of nearly priceless quantities of gold and securities notes in vaults. A big job.

Visitors will glimpse this activity, though the tour is understandably a bit sketchy on the technical details. A new exhibit, Drachmas, Doubloons, and Dollars: The History of Money, which opened here in January 2002 and will run through 2007, is more accessible: It brings together rare examples of coins and bills from the American Numismatic Society's vast collections (see above), which span 3,000 years of currency. Unfortunately, you cannot simply drop by the Fed; visits must be scheduled in advance—the bank recommends calling at least a month before your visit, and there's no guarantee you'll get a spot even then. If successful, once here you will be searched with metal detectors first; no large packages are allowed inside. There are five tours daily, at 9:30 AM, 10:30 AM, 11:30 AM, 1:30 PM, and 2:30 PM. A tour takes approximately 1 hour; you'll need to clear tight security, and leave all packages and cameras behind. Note that there is wheelchair access from the Maiden Lane entrance.

♿ **Museum of American Financial History** (212-908-4519 or 1-877-98-FINANCE), 28 Broadway between Exchange Place and Beaver Street. Subway: 4 or 5 train to Bowling Green, J, M, or Z train to Broad Street, or 1, R, or W train to Rector Street. Open Tuesday through Saturday 10 AM–4 PM. This small museum, housed inside Alexander Hamilton's former law office, is appropriately right

Kim Grant

THE NEW YORK STOCK EXCHANGE IS THE WORLD'S LARGEST EQUITIES MARKET.

across from the animated bull statue for which this neighborhood is famous. The museum has explained the history of Wall Street and America's financial institutions since 1988. Past exhibits have included a look at rare American currency, a history of the Nobel Prize, displays of piggy and other banks, the life of J. Pierpont Morgan, the importance of the Erie Canal, a look at financial journalism, and the history of the Wells Fargo Bank.

& **New York Stock Exchange** (212-656-5168), 20 Broad Street at Exchange Place and Wall Street. Subway: J, M, or Z train to Broad Street, or 2, 3, 4, or 5 train to Wall Street. Amazingly, this powerhouse of an institution got its start as a group of two dozen or so traders gathering beneath the branches of a buttonwood tree two blocks east to haggle privately over various commodities. From that humble beginning in 1792, it has grown into the world's largest equities market—and one that is a good deal more difficult to gain admission to now. On a typical day, some 200 million shares of stock might change hands, much of it done by computer but a great deal still also done by the knots of frenzied traders and specialists screaming out purchase and sales orders in the "pit." There is actually an order to this chaos, though it isn't visible to the casual observer: Each computerized workstation takes bids only on certain stocks. Too bad you can only see the outside; the action—including the ceremonial ringing of the bell by famous sports, show business, and other personalities—was, until September 11, visible from a visitors gallery; that gallery and the visitors center, however, are now closed for security reasons.

Wall Street, from Broadway to South Street. Subway: 2, 3, 4, or 5 train to Wall Street, or J, M, or Z train to Broad Street. This short street has made and broken more fortunes than you could possibly count. There really was once a wall here— it was built of logs, for a year, to keep the British out of Lower Manhattan— but to stroll it today is to find an urban street framed by banks, a luxury hotel, houses of exchange, and a church. Among the important sites located along or just off Wall Street are Federal Hall, the New York Stock Exchange (see above), the lovely District Hotel (see *Lodging—Business Hotels*), and Trinity Church (see *Churches*). Don't forget to touch the nose of sculptor Arthur de Modica's huge bronze statue of a bull, either, at one end of the street—it's at the corner of Broadway—for good luck: Thousands before you already have.

MARKETS AND PUBLIC SPACES ✍ ♿ **South Street Seaport,** South Street at Fulton Street, at Piers 16 and 17. Subway: 2 or 3 train to Wall Street or Fulton Street, A or C train to Broadway–Nassau, J, M, or Z train to Fulton Street, or 4, 5, or 6 train to Brooklyn Bridge–City Hall. Open Monday through Saturday 10 AM–9 PM, Sunday 11 AM–8 PM. These 12 square blocks of cobbled streets, historic buildings, and shops and restaurants occupy what was once America's busiest, most important port facility. You're walking over three centuries of maritime history; activity peaked during the mid-1800s, as the Erie Canal brought the world's goods to New York's door and spurred the city's growth into the world's most distinctive metropolis. At that time the port brimmed over with a salty mixture of sailors, open-air food stalls, oyster shuckers, cake vendors, and much more; it fell into decay by the early 20th century, but a restoration effort has resulted in the juxtaposition of older structures with the predictable chain stores such as Gap, Godiva, Victoria's Secret, Coach, and Ann Taylor. Despite this commercialism, it's still a good place to simply wander with the kids—with good views of the Brooklyn Bridge and riverboats as a bonus, a *Titanic* memorial, and the architecturally pleasing Federal-style buildings of Schermerhorn Row reminiscent of a more dignified time.

Sunken Plaza, Chase Manhattan Plaza, at William Street between Cedar and Pine streets. Subway: 2, 3, 4, or 5 train to Wall Street or J, M, or Z train to Broad Street. Architect Isamu Noguchi's 1964 public space of seven huge Japanese stones and miniature waterfalls looks different from different angles. For another view, enter the Chase Manhattan Building and proceed down to the plaza's bottom level. Across the plaza lies French sculptor Dubuffet's giant, 45-foot-high multimedia *Four Trees* composed of metal, plastic, and fiberglass.

✳ Green Space

Battery Park, between State Street and New York Harbor. Subway: 1 train to South Ferry or 4 or 5 train to Bowling Green. Not to be confused with Battery Park City, the vast housing complex in the Hudson River just north of it, this green space has unparalleled views of the harbor, islands, statue, boats, and so on. There's a great deal of public art here, as well as the Castle Clinton complex where you must buy tickets for ferries to Ellis Island and the Statue of Liberty. As press time the park was also the temporary home to Fritz Koenig's damaged sculpture *Sphere,* which had stood in the plaza between the twin towers of the World Trade Center until the attack; its scarred face is a kind of touchstone for the entire September 11 experience.

✳ Lodging

LUXURIOUS HOTEL Ritz-Carlton New York (212-344-0800 or 1-800-241-3333; fax 212-344-3801), 2 West Street in Battery Park at Battery Place. Subway: 4 or 5 train to Bowling Green. Sure, it's a chain hotel, but you'd be hard pressed to find a luxury hotel in Manhattan with better views than this one, which opened in early 2002—delayed by the September 11 tragedies—with about 300 rooms, including 44 suites. The views of the harbor and Lady Liberty are matchless, especially from the terrace bar (see Rise under *Bars and Clubs*). And they really pile on the luxe touches here: Witness a water sommelier who offers a selection of bottled waters tailored to your body type and health condition (pregnant women might get a San Pellegrino rich in calcium, for example). Order a special bath romance package, and your maid will sprinkle rose petals in the tub and prepare a hot bath while you're out of the room. There's a health club, of course, and the hotel's upscale restaurant 2 West is outstanding. Double rooms here generally begin around $600 per night, and suites begin around $750 per night—but you can sometimes find weekend specials when prices plunge as "low" as $300 or $375 per night.

BUSINESS HOTELS ✄ **Embassy Suites Hotel New York City** (212-945-0100 or 1-800-362-2779; fax 212-945-3012), 102 North End Avenue at Vesey Street. Subway: E train to World Trade Center, or N, R, or W train to Cortlandt Street. This all-suite property reopened in May 2002 after 8 months closed in the wake of the September 11 tragedies. Yes, it's a chain hotel, but the more than 460 spacious two-room suites are ideal for those with families—each has a pull-out sofa, microwave oven, kitchenette, and business-hotel amenities such as dataport, fax machine, worktable, free high-speed Internet access, and safe. Kids will also enjoy the on-site 16-screen multiplex theater and shopping area, while a 14-story atrium gives views of the Hudson River. The hotel dining isn't bad, either: Cooked breakfast is included free, and there are Chinese, sushi, Mexican, and American family restaurants as well. The upscale restaurant in the group, Unity, is decorated in a patriotic theme created as a response to September 11; it serves lunch weekdays and dinner daily. Suites here generally range from approximately $200 to 350.

Millennium Hilton (212-693-2001; fax 212-571-2316), 55 Church Street at Fulton Street. Subway: E train to World Trade Center, or N, R, or W train to Cortlandt Street. This towering hotel stands right beside Ground Zero (west-side rooms look directly down into the hole still left from the September 11 tragedy.) It reopened in May 2003, a pretty quick recovery from the damage. They pack in 565 sleek rooms here, including 102 suites—all with 42-inch plasma-screen televisions, CD players, and two-line cordless phones. There's a glassed-in heated indoor lap swimming pool with potted trees. In-hotel dining can be had at the third-floor eatery Church & Dey (open for three meals daily, it features seafood), and there's both a cool little bar in the lobby called Liquid Assets and a Starbucks coffee shop. As an added bonus, this hotel is situated practically across the street from the popular Century 21 discount clothing shop. Rooms range from about $350 to $500 per night for a double.

New York Marriott Financial Center (212-385-4900 or 1-800-228-9290; fax 212-227-8136), 85 West Street between Albany and Carlisle streets. Subway: N, R, W, 1, or 9 train to Rector Street. Damaged in the terrorist attacks of September 11, 2001, this 38-story tower hotel was back up and running within months with a new lobby and renovated rooms. Its 500 or so units are equipped with business-class amenities such as a two-line phone, desk, speaker phone, and even (in some) wet bar and high-speed Internet access. Newspapers are delivered to the rooms; there's a health club, spa, florist, and business center on the premises; and the hotel can even provide a secretary should you really need one. Interestingly, the hotel restaurant (Roy's) serves Hawaiian fusion meals, making it worth a look. Rates range from $250 to $500 per night.

∂ **Wall Street District Hotel** (1-877-667-9541 or 877-667-9540; fax 212-232-7800), 15 Gold Street at the corner of Platt Street. Subway: 2 or 3 train to Fulton Street. This modern hotel is a kind of high-tech mecca—they really push the fact that this was the first hotel in the city to have high-speed T-1 Internet access, and the bottom 17 floors actually come with PCs running office software. It's a good bet not only for the newness (it was constructed in 1999) but also for the family-friendly touches such as Nintendo games, big rooms, and a health club. Staff will patch calls to your room through to your cell phone; there's a special "laptop safe," and the big work desks with ergonomic chairs are a welcome break from boutique-hotel-ville. On the club-level "SMART" floor you can even use the hotel's laptops and printers and get a free shoeshine. The lobby looks like that of a much fancier hotel, and there's a business center. Other nice touches include big bathrooms, interesting showers, and cleverly concealed ironing boards—somebody's been listening to business travelers. The San Marino restaurant offers Italian dining on-site. Rates can vary from the $200-per-night range up to $350 or so per night.

AFFORDABLE HOTELS *✿ ∂* **Best Western Seaport Inn** (212-766-6600 or 1-800-HOTEL-NY; fax 212-766-6615), 33 Peck Slip between Front and Water streets. Subway: 2 or 3 train to Fulton Street. What would you expect from the self-proclaimed "world's largest hotel chain"? Well, probably anything but a restored brick warehouse with a nice lobby, touches of historic charm, and some rooms containing whirlpools and/or balconies with views of the Brooklyn Bridge. Yet that's just what this Best Western offers. All 72 rooms have hair dryer, refrigerator, VCR, Nintendo games, and coffeemaker. Who cares if they're as cookie-cutter as those at any other Best Western? You're not all that far from the major attractions in the area, even if the other listings in this chapter are closer. Rates generally run about $220–300 per night, a little steep for a chain hotel certainly—but winter and other specials can drop them lower, sometimes even as low as $150 per night.

✳ Where to Eat

DINING OUT Bayard's (212-514-9454), 1 Hanover Square between Pearl and Stone streets. Subway: 2 or 3 train to Wall Street, or N or R train to Rector Street. Open Monday through Saturday for dinner 5:30–10:30 PM. Long a favorite of Wall Street types, Bayard's serves simple and pricey (but delicious) Continental cuisine in a beautifully restored restaurant of nicely spaced tables, mahogany, brass, chandeliers, original art, and classy maritime decor. Start with chef Eberhard Müller's lobster salad, crab salad, smoked cod salad, sautéed foie gras with peaches, or caviar, then continue with main courses of roasted monkfish, sole meunière, steamed halibut, rack of lamb, strip steak, braised veal, or roast chicken; everything is fresh, and much of it's raised on Müller's own gentleman's farm. Finish with almond cake, apricot compote, champagne sorbet, a Grand Marnier parfait, or one of the good soufflés. The whole prix fixe will run you $60–$95, but it's money well spent if you're downtown and want to have a good time. Jacket and tie are required of men.

🐟 **Bridge Café** (212-227-3344), 279 Water Street at the corner of Dover Street. Subway: 4, 5, or 6 train to Brooklyn Bridge–City Hall or J, M, or Z train to Chambers Street. Open Monday through Friday for lunch 11:45 AM–4 PM and for dinner 4–11 PM, Saturday for dinner only 5 PM–midnight, Sunday for brunch 11:45 AM–4 PM and for dinner 4–10 PM. A sort of Manhattan counterpart to Brooklyn's River Café, which sits beneath the opposite supports of the gorgeous Brooklyn Bridge, the smallish, friendly Bridge Café has become the paper pusher's after-work unwinding spot of choice. Tucked literally right beneath the Manhattan side of the bridge, the alehouse-looking room actually plates medium-to-upscale meals such as grilled jumbo shrimp, steamed mussels, grilled brook trout paired with zucchini and mango salsa, or buffalo steak with mashed potatoes. The $20 brunch has become less adventurous over time but still includes a daily market catch in chili, lime, and horseradish aioli with greens. The power clientele might be under the illusion they're having a burger at a local beer joint like one of the guys, but when you're paying $20 or more a pop for lamb tenderloin in Merlot sauce or a crisped cut of Atlantic salmon—and one of the guys is the former mayor of the city—it's hard to maintain that working-class illusion. These folks claim this is the oldest restaurant in New York still operating in its original location, so they must be doing something right.

Fraunces Tavern and Museum (restaurant, 212-968-1776; museum, 212-425-1778), 54 Pearl Street at the corner of Broad Street. Subway: N or R train to Whitehall Street. Open Monday through Friday for lunch 11:30 AM–3 PM and dinner 4:30–9:30 PM, Saturday for lunch until 5 PM. Inside a historic brick house/tavern where George Washington ate, drank, and bade his courageous army farewell, kitchen staff produce wonderfully unadorned American meals—the sort you might find in a (fancy) Boston diner. Ponder that farewell address in the Queen's Head Tavern, all those years ago, over starters of pan-fried oysters, and grilled duck sausage. Then move on to entrées ($16–38) such as burgers, stuffed lobster tail, rack of lamb, prime rib with potato pancakes, or something from the tavern menu—it lists pot roast, steaks, chops, poultry, roast turkey, chicken potpie, and meat loaf, among other New England favorites. Finish with upscale versions of down-home desserts like butterscotch bread pudding, pumpkin cheesecake, blackberry cobbler, or strawberry shortcake.

The 14 Wall Street (212-233-2780), 14 Wall Street (31st floor), between Broad Street and Broadway. Subway: 4 or 5 train to Wall Street. Open Monday through Friday for breakfast 7–9:30 AM, for lunch 11:30 AM–2:30 PM, and for dinner 5–7:30 PM. It's hard to imagine a restaurant with a better front-porch view than this one. The top (that's the 31st) floor of J. P. Morgan's townhouse offers standout vistas of the harbor, Statue of Liberty, Verrazano Bridge, Staten Island, and, well, Brooklyn from most of its five dining areas (the Street Room is best). It serves power breakfasts and power lunches to a seriously suit-and-tie crowd, and long luxurious French dinners of steak, chicken, and fish afterward—but this place also conceals a very good three-course prix fixe deal at dinnertime, when you can get out of here for a steal. The à la carte menu is much fuller, with starters of foie gras with apple chutney, a lobster-shrimp crêpe, and smoked salmon and main courses of seared scallops, Peking duck breast with dried cherries, oak-planked salmon, roast duck with an orange-cranberry sauce, filet mignon with Vidalia onions, yellowfin tuna, and rack of lamb Moroccan-style, among

others. The tasty desserts include a chocolate mousse served with honeyed pears and a small flourless chocolate cake, lemon mousse packed into millefeuilles, hot-chocolate truffle cake, apple gratin with almond cream, and sorbets and ice cream.

MarkJoseph Steakhouse (212-277-0020), 261 Water Street at Peck Slip. Subway: 2 or 3 train to Fulton Street. Open Monday through Thursday 11:30 AM–10 PM, Friday to 11 PM, Saturday for dinner only 5–11 PM. This South Street Seaport–area chop house is raising eyebrows downtown among the power set with its strong steak dinners, wine list, and unruffled decor; some are wondering if it might join the ranks of New York's handful of elite steak houses (Sparks, Michael Jordan, Peter Luger, and the like) before long. Lunchtime consists of burgers and sandwiches in addition to the signature steaks, but dinner is really where the meat takes center

A SNACK SHOP ALONG LOWER BROADWAY
Paul Karr

stage. There are plenty of soups, salads, and seafood appetizers, but go straight for the steak—$40–60 per person, and well worth it. Like so many other steak houses, they charge extra for side dishes; baked potatoes, broccoli, and the like will ding you for $7.50–10 apiece. There are also a few fish entrées on the menu, but don't get those. You want steak.

EATING OUT ❀ **Kitchenette** (212-267-6740), 80 West Broadway at the corner of Warren Street. Subway: A, C, 1, 2, 3, or 9 train to Chambers Street. Open Monday through Friday 7:30 AM–10 PM, weekends 9 AM–10 PM. When in Tribeca and tired of dressing up for the likes of Nobu, do as the locals do: Head on over to Kitchenette for some good ol'-fashioned grub that's somewhat reminiscent of that served in, say, a Vermont diner. However, the kitchen here is playing to Manhattan tastes and has to be a bit more sophisticated for the tough breakfast crowd. This is the sort of place where a wedge of pie and a coffee are the rule, not the exception; where you can order breakfast any time of day (or night) and the (hopefully gum-snapping) waitress won't bat an eyelash. Think French toast or egg dishes and you're getting the picture, and they serve them all day long—kind of like being in college again, where you could roll out of bed at 2 PM and scare up some breakfast. The atmosphere is decidedly downscale given the neighborhood, too. Sound boring? It's not, really. Standards are relatively high, ingredients are fresh and even sometimes innovative. Even dinner's a blast, from the pot roast to chicken-and-biscuits to crabcakes to turkey BLTs. Do yourself a favor and breakfast or lunch here on weekdays, after the early-morning or noontime rushes; weekend brunch is a zoo, if a tasty one.

✳ Entertainment

FILM Battery Park Stadium 16 (212-945-4370), 102 North End Avenue at Vesey Street. Subway: E train to World Trade Center or N, R, or W train to Cortlandt Street. Located inside the Embassy Suites Hotel, this is your only blockbuster-film bet in Lower Manhattan, and quite out of the way. The theater shows all the usual Hollywood hits.

BARS AND CLUBS Rise (212-344-0800), 2 West Street in Battery Park at Battery Place. Subway: 4 or 5 train to Bowling Green. Open Monday through Saturday 5:30 PM–midnight. All right, it's a hotel bar in a chain hotel. But the 14th-floor views here are nearly matchless, save perhaps those from twice-as-high 14 Wall Street Restaurant (see *Dining Out*). This bar is characterized by blond wood, big windows, and slightly expensive drinks. Yet the bar snacks and sweets are actually quite good, and—again—repeat to yourself: *It's all about the view.*

CHINATOWN

It has been estimated that half of New York's 300,000 or so Chinese live in the Chinatown neighborhood, and that half of those still do not speak a word of English. A quick walk down Mott Street, Mulberry Street, or Canal Street will confirm that Chinese is the primary language of signs and street talk.

In this book, I have remained conservative with my definition of Chinatown, keeping it quite small, even though it has spread east into the Lower East Side and north into Little Italy. Here, it is everything between wide, busy Canal Street and Chambers Street, stretching east from Broadway to the curving Bowery (which is known as Park Row south of Worth Street).

GETTING THERE Chinatown is centered just south of Canal Street, so getting there usually means reaching one of the various stations splayed out along that street.

By car: From the west side of town, take Broadway all the way south to Chinatown. Or use West Street to Spring Street, turn right onto Canal Street, and work your way east through the heart of Chinatown. From the east side of town, one of the handiest ways to get here is by taking Bowery, a Lower Manhattan renaming of Third Avenue—which becomes two-way below 23rd Street. (Coming from the north, you'll need to take another avenue to 23rd Street first.)

By subway: From Times Square, Midtown West, Fifth Avenue, Union Square, or SoHo, take an N, R, W, or express Q train to Canal Street. From Midtown East, the NYU area, Union Square, or the Upper East Side, take the 6 train to Canal Street. From the Lower East Side, take the J, M, or Z train to Canal Street. You can also reach the area by taking a 4, 5, or 6 train to the Brooklyn Bridge–City Hall station or a J, M, or Z train to Chambers Street and walking north.

By bus: From the Upper East Side, Midtown East, the Gramercy–Flatiron area, and the East Village, the 103 bus runs south down Lexington Avenue and north along Third Avenue to Bowery, on the eastern side of Chinatown. The only other useful bus is the 1 bus, which runs down Fifth Avenue and then Broadway from Midtown East, Greenwich Village, and SoHo. It runs north again along Lafayette, Park Avenue South, and Madison Avenue.

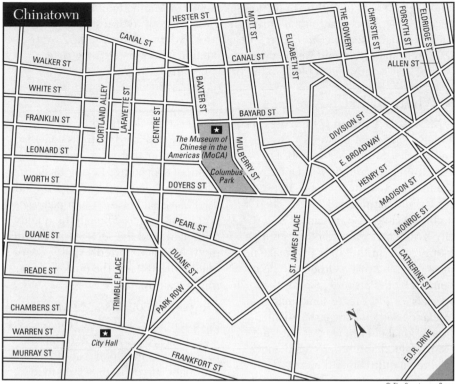

✳ To See

MUSEUM **The Museum of Chinese in the Americas (MoCA)** (212-619-4785), 70 Mulberry Street (second floor) at the corner of Bayard Street. Subway: J, M, N, R, Z, or 6 train to Canal Street. Open Tuesday through Thursday, noon–6 PM, Friday noon–7 PM, and weekends noon–6 PM. This little-known museum in the heart of Chinatown documents this important cultural segment's contributions not only to New York but to the Western Hemisphere as well. The central exhibit is Where Is Home?, a collection of artifacts and narratives explaining the spread of Chinese people throughout the Americas—the migration process, religion, and the role of women are some of the topics explored—and a new exhibition of Chinatown's attempts to recover from the events of September 11, 2001. There are also some quite interesting temporary exhibitions, such as an exploration of Chinese-American musical performers and a history of one successfully emigrated silk-merchant family; additional materials are available for sale at the small museum store. Admission costs $3 for adults, $1 for seniors and students, and is free for children under 12.

✳ Green Space

Columbus Park, along lower Mulberry Street between Bayard and Worth streets, isn't exactly green and wild, but its playgrounds and benches do make for a rare quiet place for sitting in the lower reaches of Manhattan. And the park becomes the focus of attention during the Chinese New Year festivities early each February (see *Special Events*). Reach the park by taking a J, M, Z, or 6 train to Canal Street and walking east on Canal to Mulberry, turning right (south), and continuing a block to the park on your right.

✳ Where to Eat

DINING OUT Canton (212-226-4441), 45 Division Street between Bowery and Market Street. Subway: B, D, or Q train to Grand Street. Open Wednesday to Sunday noon–10 PM, Friday and Saturday to 11 PM. There's no finer Cantonese restaurant in the city, say some locals; who cares if it's a lot pricier than the dives that make up most of Chinatown? Others are disappointed by the attitude. Go for the specials, or just create something freelance and challenge the talented, professional chef to work it out from fresh seafood and other ingredients. (There's a quite limited menu.) The hostess is legendary around the neighborhood. Just be prepared for sticker shock post-meal—and bring enough cash; they don't take credit cards.

Grand Sichuan (212-625-9212), 125 Canal and the Bowery. Open daily 11 AM–10:30 PM. Subway: J, M, N, Q, R, W, Z, or 6 train to Canal Street. The top Szechuan place in town, probably—and spawn of a million soundalikes, most of which are completely unrelated—Grand Sichuan has been doing the fiery regional food (dumplings, noodles, stir-fries, and so forth) better than anyone else for a long while now. They don't take credit cards, either.

Peking Duck House (212-227-1810), 28 Mott Street between Park and Pell streets. Subway: J, M, N, Q, R, W, Z, or 6 train to Canal Street. Open Sunday to Thursday, 11:45 AM–

10:30 PM, weekends to 11 PM. As might be expected, patrons come to this place for that most revered of Chinese specialties, Peking duck: crispy, succulent, melt-in-your mouth duck, layered between thin pancakes and hoisin sauce. Though the quality of a meal (and the service) on a given night here is reportedly spotty, everyone comes to taste the duck and you might want to, too.

Ping's (212-602-9988), 22 Mott Street between Mosco and Pell streets. Subway: J, M, N, Q, R, W, Z, or 6 train to Canal Street. Open daily 10 AM–midnight. If you're on a "see-food" diet, Ping's is your place: You can pick out what swims in tanks and have it cooked. Cantonese-style fish and seafood dishes take center stage here; the sauces and fried meals are generally good, as is the weekend dim sum. It's a bit pricier than most of the places along Mott Street, but that won't insulate you from the chaos that comes along with any Chinatown-locals' favorite. Consider that to be part of the experience.

EATING OUT Goody's (212-577-2922), 1 East Broadway at Chatham Square, between Catherine and Oliver streets. Subway: J, M, N, Q, R, W, Z, or 6 train to Canal Street. Open weekdays 11 AM–10:30 PM, weekends to 11 PM. Outstanding Shanghai-style soup dumplings (filled with broth, meat, and vegetables), braised fish, and noodle soups are just a few of the highlights here at Goody's. Steamed buns are another favorite, but don't come for fancy dining.

❧ **House of Vegetarian** (212-226-6572), 68 Mott Street between Bayard and Canal streets. Subway: J, M, N, Q, R, W, Z, or 6 train to Canal Street. Open daily 11 AM–11 PM. A favorite vegetarian place wedged in amongst the chaos of Mott Street, House of Vegetarian specializes in "mock" meats—*seitan* or tofu crafted into a reasonable facsimile of beef, pork, chicken, or seafood, adulterated with Chinese sauces and liberally sided with veggies. Some dishes don't even pretend to be meat: They simply lay on the peppers, broccoli, and the like in fresh and spicy preparations. Meals here are quick and cheap (you'll almost certainly pay less than $10), but credit cards are not accepted.

Joe's Shanghai (212-233-8888), 9 Pell Street between Bowery and Mott Street. Subway: J, M, Z, or 6 train to Canal Street. Open daily 11 AM–11 PM. There's only one place in town, so far as I know, to get the best *bao* (a dumpling filled with hot broth and meat), and this is it. Therefore, you need to swallow a dose of typical Chinatown-style ambience—which means a far-from-serene atmosphere —and the noise and bother of eating elbow to elbow with a sometimes vocal crowd of fellow diners. But the reward is a hot squirt of delicious soup, combined with succulent pork or seafood, and a bite of dumpling, too . . . a great experience for the un-initiated. They also do a great *mapo* tofu, drunken crabs, and other dishes too. I really like this place, which is constantly packed. If you can't make it to Lower Manhattan for a look, there's another, more subdued —or snobby, depending on your opinion—location in Midtown at 24 West 56th Street (212-333-3868) and two more in Queens.

A CHINATOWN STREET SCENE

Kim Grant

New York Noodle Town (212-349-0923), 28 Bowery at the corner of Bayard Street. Subway: J, M, Z, or 6 train to Canal Street. Open daily 9 AM–3:30 AM and weekends to 4:30 AM. Besides the namesake noodles, this eatery serves a variety of good grilled and fried meats and excellent soft-shell crabs, and it's open until quite late at night—after 4 AM on weekends! That alone makes it worth a visit, although I wouldn't make a habit of visiting this desolate-by-night neighborhood on foot at this hour. In any case, note that (like many other Chinatown joints) this place does not accept credit cards.

🍲 **Pho Viet Huong** (212-233-8988), 73 Mulberry Street between Bayard and Canal streets. Subway: J, M, N, Q, R, W, Z, or 6 train to Canal Street. Open daily noon–10 PM. No, it's not Chinese, but Chinatown's best Vietnamese bite is well worth seeking out. This big place is a temple to beef, prepared in many delicious ways, yet it would be a mistake to skip over the great noodle soups, shrimp specials, hot pot–style dishes, curries, and—of course—spring and summer rolls. They know how to cook healthily, and prices are unbelievably low. Check out the small courtyard if you feel like dining outside. Yes, they do deliver to some areas of the city.

Saigon Banh Mi (212-941-1541), 138-01 Mott Street. Subway: J, M, or Z train to Bowery or B or D train to Grand Street. Open Tuesday to Sunday. This place is something else, a hole-in-the-wall where you can dig into an authentic Vietnamese *banh mi* sandwiches of meat, sauce, and a bit of vegetable. The French influence comes in the baguette enveloping it. Don't forget a Vietnamese iced coffee. You can feed three diners with a $10 bill here, and many locals do: It's quickly gaining a small cult following among city foodies.

Sweet-n-Tart Café (212-964-0380), 20 Mott Street between Pell Street and Worth Street. Subway: J, M, Z, or 6 train to Canal Street. Open daily 10 AM–midnight, weekends from 9 AM. This place has zero atmosphere, and it always will, but it's awfully fun if you want a quick and inexpensive sampling of chaotic Chinatown. Tucked low on a typically busy, crazy C-Town street, this eatery features an array of fruity blended drinks and a menu of cafeteria-style snacks that you'd go *really* crazy for if you were from Hong Kong—dim sum dumplings, flavorful pork, shrimp, and chicken tidbits, and the like. There's another location at 76 Mott Street, between Bayard and Canal streets and a third in Queens.

COFFEE AND SNACKS 🍲 🍦 **Chinatown Ice Cream Factory** (212-608-4170), 65 Bayard Street between Elizabeth and Mott streets. Subway: J, M, N, Z, or 6 train to Canal Street. Open daily 11 AM–11 PM, weekends to 11:30 PM. Some say this hole-in-the-wall deep in the heart of Chinatown makes the city's best ice cream; whether you agree or disagree with that assessment, one thing's for certain—it makes the city's most *unusual* ice creams, and locals like the place well enough that it's been here for a quarter century now. Where other ice cream outfits stop at coconut or green tea and call it an exciting day, Chinatown Ice Cream forges bravely ahead toward the taste frontier with worthy experiments such as red bean, lychee, taro, and more. Try a taste for free before committing to something serious; on the other hand, if you're really wild about something and don't expect to get back here soon (and you have access to a big freezer), you can buy a big tankard of most flavors. Note that the shop does not accept any credit cards.

Saint's Alp Teahouse (212-766-9889), 51 Mott Street between Bayard and Canal streets. Subway: J, M, N, Q, R, W, Z, or 6 train to Canal Street. Open daily 11 AM–11:30 PM. This place has become wildly popular among local Chinese for the "bubble teas"–iced green teas with milk and pearls of tapioca floating in it. The huge straw you get is just big enough

to suck one pearl through. They also do a nice variety of hot teas, Chinese snacks, and sweets, but the tea's the thing here—everybody orders it.

✳ Special Events

Late January–early February: **Chinese New Year** (212-226-1330). The Chinese community's annual New Year's celebrations in New York include a looping parade that begins at Columbus Park (see *Green Space*), then heads up Mulberry Street to Canal Street, turns down Mott Street, and follows East Broadway, Market, and Division streets and Bowery before finishing in the park. There's also a 2-day festival in Columbus Park.

THE LOWER EAST SIDE

Below Houston (pronounced *HOUSE-ton*) Street, you enter the Lower East Side—a neighborhood that is old and full of character, yet lacks focus. (The Bowery, for example, a street once synonymous with punk music and urban decay, is slowly spiffing up and transforming itself into a neighborhood-of-the-moment—with the higher rents and fancy new restaurants that come with the territory.) Parts of this district are still dirt cheap and dirt poor, and parts still reflect the area's Jewish heritage, but interspersed within you can also now find a sudden injection of luxe.

In this book I have defined the Lower East Side as a large area just south of the East Village—everything from Houston Street south to the Brooklyn Bridge and west from the East River to Bowery (also called Park Row). Anything else in this area south of the bridge, I have covered in the Lower Manhattan chapter; anything west of Bowery/Park Row I consider Chinatown if it is below Canal Street, Little Italy if it is between Canal Street and Kenmare Street, and Nolita (part of SoHo) if it is between Kenmare Street and Houston.

GUIDANCE Surprisingly, there is a kind of tourist information center in the Lower East Side. The **Visitor Center** (212-226-9010 or 1-866-224-0206) at 261 Broome Street—it's at the corner of Orchard Street, a short block from Allen Street—is open daily 10 AM–4 PM. The closest subway station is the Bowery station on the J, M, and Z lines, though they cannot be reached from uptown; from there, take an F train to Second Avenue and walk four blocks south of Houston to Broome Street.

GETTING AROUND *By car:* Getting to the Lower East Side by car is similar to reaching Chinatown, the East Village, or SoHo: First you must get to Houston Street via Broadway, Second Avenue, West Street, or the FDR (East Side) Drive, then work across on Houston.

By subway: Subway service to this big neighborhood is quite limited, and many of the most interesting parts are very far from stations. This has helped preserve the area's character, but it makes for tiring traveling. From Midtown, take either an F train to Second Avenue or Delancey Street or a V train to Second Avenue. From Lower Manhattan, take a J, M, or Z train to Bowery or Essex Street.

The Lower East Side

© The Countryman Press

There is also a shuttle service from the West Village and NoHo; take this S train from West 4th Street or Broadway–Lafayette to Grand Street.

By bus: Most local bus service here is very localized: The 9 bus runs to and from Union Square, the 14 bus runs up to 14th Street and then goes crosstown through Union Square and the West Village, the 21 bus runs crosstown along Houston Street, the dividing line between SoHo and the West Village. The only truly useful long-distance buses in these parts are the 101, 102, and 103 buses running north and south along Bowery, Lexington Avenue, and Third Avenue, and the 15 bus, which travels north and south on a similar route (but along First and Second avenues) through the East Village, the Gramercy Park area, Midtown East, and the Upper East Side.

✳ To See

SYNAGOGUE ♿ **Eldridge Street Synagogue** (212-219-0888), 12 Eldridge Street between Canal Street and Division Street. Subway: B or D train to Grand Street, 6, N, or R train to Canal Street, or F train to East Broadway. Now in the shadow of the Manhattan Bridge, this was the first synagogue built in America by Eastern European Jews, during the massive wave of immigration during the late 19th century; sadly, it closed for worship half a century ago, as the neighborhood's character and composition changed, but it's still open for tours and concerts. The nonprofit Eldridge Street Project has taken up slowly the task of restoring the synagogue, focusing on the lovely stained-glass work and unusually intricate facade.

MUSEUM ♪ **Lower East Side Tenement Museum** (212-431-0233), 90–97 Orchard Street at the corner of Broome Street. Subway: F train to Delancey Street, or J, M, or Z train to Essex Street. Open Tuesday through Sunday 11 AM– 5:30 PM. This, for my money, is one of Manhattan's more intriguing museums— rather than celebrate high art, it celebrates the humble origins, day-to-day lives, and departures of hundreds of former African American, Irish, Italian, and other tenants of this building, whose surrounding neighborhood was once the city's poorest. Themed tours explore such topics as the history of immigrants working New York's garment industry, the Great Depression, and the individual families who struggled to live here. In addition, interesting art exhibits explore such topics as the building's restoration, the layers of wallpaper accumulated through its history, the conditions that immigration detainees face even today, and the effect of housing code policies on New York's urban makeup. Note that you must book a guided tour to visit the museum; you can also get a combination ticket of tours.

✳ Green Space

Sara Delano Roosevelt Park, along Forsyth Street and Chrystie Street from Houston Street to Canal Street. Subway: F train to Second Avenue, J, M, or Z train to Bowery, or B or D train to Grand Street. This narrow park extends seven short blocks between wide cross streets, and is testament to local action and activism: A group of Lower East Side residents banded together to form the park association in the 1990s. It's a welcome break from the general grayness of the row houses in this part of the city.

✳ Lodging

AFFORDABLE HOTELS **Howard Johnson Express** (212-358-8844; fax 212-473-3500), 135 East Houston Street between Allen Street and Forsyth Street. Subway: L train to Second Avenue, J, M, or Z train to Bowery, F, V, or S train to Broadway–Lafayette, or 6 train to Bleecker Street. Opened in February 2002, this is exactly what you would expect it to be: a bland, six-floor chain property with cookie-cutter rooms. It is also, however, the first true hotel in eons to open in either the East Village or the Lower East Side, and as such it deserves a look. No, it isn't as close to SoHo as they'd like you to think. Room rates are usually around $180–230 per night (occasionally as high as $260), and the 46 rooms have two-line phone.

Off SoHo Suites Hotel (212-979-9808 or 1-800-633-7646; fax 212-979-9801), 11 Rivington Street between the Bowery and Chrystie Street. Subway: J, M, or Z train to Bowery, or F or V train to Second Avenue. The second largest hotel in this neighborhood, Off SoHo offers two levels of comfort: You can check into a smallish economy suite of two twin beds, and gamble that the next room might go unoccupied (the bathrooms are shared). Or go for a "deluxe" suite, which adds a full kitchen, private bathroom, pullout sofa, two-line phone, voice mail, satellite television, iron and ironing board—and the choice of a queen bed. Economy suite rates start at $99, while the suites with private bathroom cost $119–279 each. All rooms have color television and air-conditioning, and there's a small café and tiny fitness center if you wish to work out. Note that this hotel isn't really located near the best sections of SoHo.

✳ Where to Eat

The Lower East Side is in a great deal of flux right now. New restaurants are popping up, closing down, and swapping chefs faster than I can keep track. The best advice I can give is to simply wander down Orchard and Clinton streets (during the daytime) and see what's new.

EATING OUT aKa Café (212-979-6096), 49 Clinton Street between Rivington and Stanton streets. Subway: F train to Delancey Street. Open Monday through Friday 6 PM–midnight, Saturday 11 AM–4 PM for lunch and 6 PM–midnight for dinner, Sunday 11 AM–4 PM. This former retail store has been dressed up with potted plants and a you-see-it-all kitchen serving excellent daily soups and tapaslike dishes. It's run by the same folks who brought you wd-50 (see

below). The small plates here incorporate many of the deli ingredients from the surrounding neighborhood; the lamb's tongue sandwich with almond butter is legend among locals in the know, and there are inventive mixed drinks to go along.

Katz's Delicatessen (212-254-2246), 205 East Houston Street at the corner of Ludlow Street. Subway: F train to Delancey Street, or J, M, or Z train to Essex Street. Open daily 8 AM–10 PM, Friday and Saturday to 3 AM. Right on busy Houston Street, and very easy to drive past if you are driving a car, Katz's turns out to be one of New York City's most famous Jewish delicatessens. The food is classic for the

THE OFF SOHO SUITES HOTEL OFFERS TWO LEVELS OF ACCOMMODATIONS IN THE LOWER EAST SIDE.

Kim Grant

form: You can get any number of treats here, from egg creams to blintzes. I always go simple here, like savvy diners, and munch on split, char-grilled beef hot dogs, huge hand-carved meat sandwiches, or a knish, then guzzle Dr. Brown's soda or a glass of deli-brewed beer afterward.

Schiller's Liquor Bar (212-260-4555), 131 Rivington Street at the corner of Norfolk Street. Subway: J, M, or Z train to Bowery. Open Monday to Thursday 11 AM–1 AM, Friday to 3 AM, Saturday for brunch 10 AM–4 PM and then 6 PM–3 AM, Sunday same but closes at 1 AM. From man-with-magic-touch Keith McNally (of Balthazar fame; see "SoHo") comes this fabulous bar that's a combination of glamorous and down-and-dirty. How did he do that? In any case, this is the Lower East Side's best place to get a drink. But that's not all. Thanks to the kitchen (same supervising chefs as Balthazar), it makes a serious run for culinary honors, too, with fun yet inexpensive stuff like Welsh rarebit swapping licks on the menu with toffee pudding, stir-fries, pastas, thick sandwiches, the usual *steak frites,* and great brunch items (the doughnuts have a quiet local following). There's even a kids' menu; it's everything your neighborhood bar wants to be—plus the good food.

DINING OUT 71 Clinton Fresh Food (212-614-6960), 71 Clinton Street between Rivington and Stanton streets. Subway: F train to Delancey Street. Open Sunday to Thursday 6–10:30 PM, weekends to 11:30 PM. In this small space that's always packed, young chef Wylie Dufresne first made his stand on suddenly hip Clinton Street. Dufresne has moved on (see

below), but the top-rank—and fun—food remains. In winter, start with Tasmanian ocean trout tartare with pickled mustard seeds and pine nuts, squid-ink gnocchi, and a foie gras gussied up with bitter chocolate bits, candied orange, lemon thyme, and almond milk. Move on to poached hake with caramelized tofu, striped bass with mission figs, warmed salmon gravlax, pork jowls with mint and beans, loin of venison with chanterelles, or a cocoa ravioli. But dessert is the most fun: Try whatever's on, such as a bay leaf panna cotta with blueberry soup and candied fennel, or warm chocolate cake with a peanut butter ganache. Want more? Go for the $60 tasting menu ($85 with wines). Note: At press time the restaurant's chef and owner was considering closing it. Check ahead.

wd-50 (212-477-2900), 50 Clinton Street between Rivington and Stanton streets. Subway: F train to Delancey Street. Open daily 6–11 PM, except to 10 PM Sunday. Like a manic food scientist, Wylie Dufresne uses this Clinton Street space as his laboratory, partnering in ownership with the great Jean-Georges Vongerichten. Expect the unusual—right out of the gate, you might pick from options incorporating fried mayonnaise, mussel-olive oil soup, foie gras with candied olives . . . and those are just a few of the *starters.* Entrées range all over the map too, but once again juxtapose exciting (or just plain odd) flavor combinations with tried-and-true main dishes. Thus, rack of lamb, short ribs, scallops, and trout are spiked by eggplant-raisin purees, celery noodles, swiss cheese consommés, whiskey-flavored caramel sauce, and the like. The little wine list is fabulous, as well.

COFFEE AND SNACKS The Dough-nut Plant (212-505-3700), 379 Grand Street between Essex and Norfolk streets. Subway: F train to Delancey Street, J, M, or Z train to Essex Street, or B or D train to Grand Street. Open Tuesday through Sunday 6:30 AM–5 PM. These big, yeasty, sweet dough-nuts are far and away the best in New York, and this is where they're made with wholesome, partly organic, somewhat healthy ingredients. You can choose from chocolate, nut, vanilla, raspberry, and other flavors depending on what's cooking. There are only about two seats in the place, though, and no parks nearby, so don't plan on eating in. Too busy to make it all the way down here to never-never land? No problem. Many coffee shops and specialty food markets around Manhattan now stock them, including Oren's Daily Roast on the Upper East Side and in Grand Central Terminal, Zabar's on the Upper West Side, and Higher Grounds in the East Village—though they'll jack up the price. Here they cost about $1.75 each (yes, each); in a market or at a coffee shop, they might cost as much as three bucks.

Il Laboratorio del Gelato (212-343-9922), 95 Orchard Street between Delancey and Broome streets. Subway: B or D train to Grand Street, or J, M, or Z train to Bowery. Open daily 10 AM–6 PM. Owner Jon Snyder, who comes from an ice cream family and founded the popular Ciao Bella gelato company (now stocked throughout New York supermarkets) while still a pup, opened this bright, clean shop near the Tenement Museum (see *To See—Museum*) in 2002. Though its purpose is partly to serve as a facility where local restaurateurs can experi-ment with new gelato ideas off-site (the workers wear lab coats), there's also a small retail operation. Try inno-vative ice cream flavors like chocolate Kahlúa, prune Armagnac, apple Calva-dos, fig, mascarpone, and green tea, or sorbets such as grapefruit, champagne, black grape, peach, passion fruit, and kiwi—what you can order will depend, though, on what's been made that week. You can also get pints of more standard flavors like coffee, hazelnut, almond, chocolate, and vanilla at some New York markets.

✳ Entertainment

PERFORMING ARTS VENUE Henry Street Settlement (212-598-0400), 466 Grand Street at the corner of Pitt Street. Subway: F train to Delancey Street, or J, M, or Z train to Essex Street. Also known as the Abrons Arts Center, the venerable Henry Street Settlement—founded back in the late 1800s to help expose impoverished local residents to high art—actually contains three distinct stages. There's a recital hall, the Harry de Jur Play-house (which seats more than 300), and a small, less comfortable experi-mental theater, as well as an outdoor space for summertime shows. In addi-tion to theater, the facility showcases folk musicians, opera, modern dance, and other performances.

MUSIC VENUES Bowery Ballroom (212-533-2111 or 212-260-4700), 6 Delancey Street at the corner of Bowery. Subway: J, M, or Z train to Bowery. An eclectic mix of quality rock, blues, folk, bluegrass, and world acts take the stage here in the heart of the Lower East Side—expect anything from Apples in Stereo to the Afrobeat Orchestra, with the likes of bluesman

Joe Jackson and folkie Dar Williams showing up, too.

CBGB–OMFUG (212-677-0455), 313 Bowery at the corner of Bleecker Street. Subway: 6 train to Bleecker Street, or F or V train to Second Avenue. Still punk after all these years. Just steps from the Amato Opera, CBGB remains as down-to-earth (or down-at-heel) as ever—fans brought mementos and flowers here to mourn the death of Queens punk singer (and local legend) Joey Ramone in 2001. With a good sound system and a mix of gratingly loud acts with names like Kill by Inches, Dog Food, and Unsane, this is definitely a place to *avoid* if you're seeking quiet. Still, there's a jazz lounge on site that gets high marks for its freestyle jams.

The Living Room (212-533-7235), 154 Ludlow Street between Stanton Street and Rivington Street. Subway: L train to First Avenue. The best spot on the East Side to catch unknown acoustic and folk acts is The Living Room, where at least two—and often four or five—acts take the stage each and every night. It's astonishing how many singers perform here in a typical year, and although you've never heard of any of them, you might one day. There is no cover; a $5 donation to the artists is suggested.

FILM Landmark Sunshine Cinema (212-330-8182), 143 East Houston Street between Eldridge and Forsyth streets. Subway: L train to Second Avenue, or J, M, or Z train to Bowery. A combination museum–screening room, Sunshine shows a surprisingly good mixture of flicks: Robert Altman's *A Prairie Home Companion,*

a film about Australian aborigines, Almodóvar's latest, even the Hollywood big release *Adaptation.* They sometimes do special midnight screenings of campy 1980s and 1990s films for those who came of age during those strange decades.

CLUB Happy Ending (212-334-9676), 302 Broome Street between Eldridge and Forsyth streets. Subway: J, M, or Z train to Bowery, or B or D train to Grand Street. Set in a drab kind of secondary Chinatown east of the better-known one, this bar gets my vote for wackiest in Manhattan. From the front, during the daytime, there's just an ugly tin door and a mysterious sign in Chinese (with a phone number that no longer works). But persevere, because this former Chinese "health spa"—and, to put it delicately, that meant the gentlemen customers received a different sort of workout—has been converted into a very hip place. Downstairs, in private booths where the men used to receive steam treatments (and more), you can rent a table for your pals and drink beneath showerheads. There's also now a small menu of bar snacks, and they're much better than what you might expect.

✳ Selective Shopping

FOOD AND DRINK The covered **Essex Street Market** at 120 Essex Street (at the corner of Delancey Street) makes a good first stop. Check out the stalls of fruits, vegetables, meats, and specialty foods, and the house restaurant.

Russ & Daughters (212-475-4880), 179 East Houston Street between Allen and Orchard Streets. Subway:

F train to Second Avenue. Open Monday through Saturday 9 AM–7 PM, Sunday 8 AM–6 PM. This fourth-generation business is well worth tracking down when in the East Village or Lower East Side. It sells lots of Jewish treats such as smoked salmon, caviar, bagels, cream cheese, and sweets, but it's the herring they're most famous for—lots and lots of permutations of herring, gleaned from the world over. If you're crazy for salty fish, absolutely come down and take a look and chat with the friendly shop staff; they'll make sure you go home with exactly what you came for.

Tribeca, SoHo, and Little Italy

2

TRIBECA, SOHO, AND LITTLE ITALY

The areas known as Tribeca, SoHo, and Little Italy are instantly recognizable to even the casual tourist. Yet few visitors spend much time in these areas; they are far from the throb of Midtown, with an industrial character that conceals the truly interesting cultural, artistic, and culinary changes going on within them at any one time.

Tribeca, in particular, is finding itself in the spotlight right now—both for its proximity to the former World Trade Center towers (it was more devastated, economically, than any other city neighborhood by the towers' destruction) and its remarkable resilience, evidenced by a number of new, excellent restaurants.

SoHo and Little Italy are each a bit different from what you might expect. SoHo, thought of as a small, arty district, is in fact bigger and more commercial than you likely think; you need a thick wallet to survive here. And Little Italy has been shrinking for years, from a once thriving area down to a tiny pocket—one street, really—of dubious lineage. Most of the city's Italian community has long since moved to the Outer Boroughs and beyond. Still, it's worth a look if you're already in SoHo; the two neighborhoods are almost touching each other, and 5 minutes of walking takes you from one to the other. Don't neglect Nolita (North of Little Italy) in your wanderings, either: It's a hot new area for those seeking a slightly grittier SoHo.

TRIBECA

The so-called Triangle Below Canal Street (TriBeCa) is a small area, but it's getting bigger—in terms of cachet, anyway. Robert De Niro has an office here, and John F. Kennedy Jr. and his wife lived in the neighborhood until a plane crash tragically took their lives. The once industrial district's warehouses are swiftly being transformed into superexpensive loft apartments, condominiums, eateries, and specialty shops. There are no significant historical sights worth seeing in this small pocket area, and there's little to do other than dine—but that, you can certainly do, at some of the city's best restaurants. Think of it as a culinary field trip.

For the purposes of this guidebook, I have defined Tribeca as the blocks between Canal Street and Chambers Street, from Broadway west to the Hudson River.

GETTING THERE Tribeca isn't on the way to anywhere but is nevertheless fairly easy to reach both by car and via a few subway lines.

By car: From uptown, either take the West Side Highway to Spring Street, then head south beyond Canal Street, or use Seventh Avenue—it changes names to become Varick Street and then West Broadway as it passes through Tribeca. From the east side of town, head downtown on the FDR (East Side) Drive to Grand Street, then cut south on Bowery to Canal Street; use Canal as a cross street until you reach the west side of town. When you can see the river, you're there.

By subway: From Times Square, the Upper West Side, or Lower Manhattan, take the 1 train to Canal Street (the bottom of SoHo) or Franklin Street or Chambers Street (for Tribeca); you can also take the 2 and 3 express trains to Chambers Street from the same locations and from Brooklyn. From SoHo, the Upper West Side, Eighth Avenue, the West Village, or Lower Manhattan, you can also take an A or C train to Canal Street or Chambers Street. Or take the E express train from Fifth Avenue, Port Authority, or the World Trade Center site to Canal Street.

By bus: The 20 bus is most convenient, because it passes through the heart of Tribeca going both north and south. Catch it from the World Trade Center

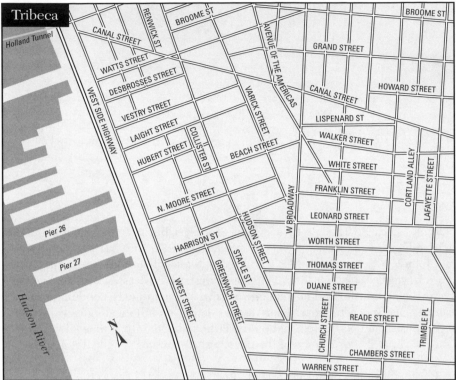

Tribeca

© The Countryman Press

site area on Vesey Street, or along Hudson Street, Seventh Avenue, and Eighth Avenue in the West Village, Chelsea, Midtown West, and the Upper West Side as far north as Lincoln Center. From the East Village or SoHo, you can use the crosstown 21 bus, which traverses Houston Street as it connects the two neighborhoods.

✳ Lodging

BOUTIQUE HOTEL ✦ **Tribeca Grand Hotel** (212-519-6600 or 1-877-519-6600; fax 212-519-6700), 2 Sixth Avenue between Walker and White streets. Subway: 1 train to Franklin Street, or A, C, or E train to Canal Street. At the moment this is Tribeca's only recommended lodging option, though that should change soon as the burgeoning area begins to spawn additional development. The surrounding streets and exterior may each look bleak and unfriendly, but inside is concealed a hotel as hip as the industrial-chic neighborhood within which it stands. The wedgelike building features a heated entryway with a too-cool-for-his-own-good doorman; inside, the huge and high lobby leads to a minimalist reception, a sleek, softly lit bar and lounge, and a more formal restaurant. The 200 or so rooms, although certainly decorated in fine materials, may not be as luxe or large as you might expect for these prices—you're paying for location and attitude, not museum-quality digs. At least they're well lit. Business amenities such as fax machine, cordless phone, Internet access via the television, small TV in the bathroom, Bose radio/CD player, and VCR in the rooms are all standard. The seven penthouse suites add more luxuries, a living room with modern furniture, and better views. Rates range from $350–600 per night for double rooms, and run to around $700 for suites (but up to $1,500 per night for the penthouse suites).

✳ Where to Eat

DINING OUT Bouley (212-964-2525), 120 West Broadway between Duane and Reade streets. Subway: A, C, 1, 2, or 3 train to Chambers Street. Open daily for lunch 11:30 AM–3 PM and dinner 5–11:30 PM. One of New York's better-known restaurateurs, David Bouley started this place as a makeshift bakery while he assembled an empire of eateries around town to replace his former four-star Bouley. Wouldn't you know it? Bouley's plans never quite panned out, but his former bakery—converted into a fullblown, low-key restaurant with the same name as the original—is now one of the city's best, a tour de force of updated French cooking with plenty of Asian and New American accents. You can dine on lunches or dinners of Maine lobster, roast chicken, rack of lamb, roast venison, coriander-crusted duckling, or chicken steamed in buttermilk, pairing them with appetizers such as sashimi, smoked trout, or steamed sea urchins. You might also find Kobe steak from Japan on the card. The tasting menu, at $90 per person, is a bit fuller and more inventive: seafood in a phyllo

or potato crust for an appetizer, wild squab with foie gras, fruit soup or the chocolate soufflé for dessert. Reservations are not only advised but also essential—even with the expansion of table space in this place after the bakery closed, it's still not all that large.

Chanterelle (212-966-6960), 2 Harrison Street at the corner of Hudson Street. Subway: 1 train to Franklin Street. Open Monday 5:30–10 PM, Tuesday through Saturday noon–2:30 PM and 5:30–11 PM. This fine French restaurant, run by chef David Waltuck and wife Karen, is one of the city's best: An eclectic menu is thoughtfully considered, carefully cooked, and then served in a calming room of soft lighting, chandeliers, and drapery. After starting with foie gras, wild mushroom consommé, oysters, grilled sausage, or veal carpaccio, move on to entrées such as cumin-crusted tuna with lemon and leeks, Maine sea scallops with duck fat and basil, noisettes of organic pork, rack of lamb with a cumin-salt crust, or grilled breast of duck. Finish with a bitter chocolate tart sided with banana-malt ice cream, a pineapple napoleon with lime-coconut sorbet, or the inventive sampler plates of chocolate or caramel

Paul Karr

desserts. It is expensive (the tasting menu is priced at $125 per person), but well worth it; put this on any short list of French eateries to consider during a brief visit to the city.

City Hall Restaurant (212-227-7777), 131 Duane Street between Church Street and West Broadway. Subway: A, C, 1, 2, or 3 train to Chambers Street. Open Monday through Friday for lunch noon–4 PM and dinner 4–11 PM, Saturday for dinner only 5:30–11 PM. In an age of modern, slickly styled rooms, City Hall's elegance is refreshing. Housed inside a cast-iron 19th-century building, Henry Meer's second effort has the look of a steak house from 100 years ago with its checkered floors, soft lighting, propeller fans, curved banquettes, and high ceilings. Start with lobster-ginger bisque, tuna tartare, or some P.E.I. mussels, then continue with a straightforward main course ($19–38) such as peppered tuna steak, lamb with curried onion rings, Maine lobster, Dover sole, a Delmonico steak with Maytag blue cheese, or chateaubriand or prime rib for two. The lighter entrées and sandwiches here are particularly appealing—a salmon club, a crab omelet, a seared-tuna salad, a sweet potato baked with cinnamon and nutmeg. Finish with chocolate soufflé, apple cobbler, or New York–style cheesecake with amaretto cream.

🐟 **Danube** (212-791-3771), 30 Hudson Street at the corner of Duane Street. Subway: A, C, 1, 2, or 3 train to Chambers Street. Open daily 5:30–11:30 PM. David Bouley, he of the on-and-off-again Bouley (see above), scored a big hit in 2000 with the opening of this Austrian-themed Tribeca restaurant. There's plenty of interior

decor here that Klimt might recognize, not to mention rich tapestries and banquettes, solid wooden tables, and mod lighting fixtures throughout the oddly shaped room. Meals run to traditional Wiener schnitzel, slow-roasted meats, soups, stews, sturgeon with potatoes, beef cheeks in wine, port-glazed venison, and intriguing desserts of berries and even flowers. But he also tries new twists on seafood (lobster with sunchoke, honey-glazed duck, bass with mushroom tortellini might make appearances) that seem less New Austrian than New American. Certain dishes must be ordered in advance, such as beef Kavalierspitz, squab and truffles in an artichoke heart, Kaiser schmarrn (a kind of dessert pancake with roasted plums, huckleberries, and ice cream inside), and Austrian poppy seed soufflé—all with very traditional garnishes and sauces you might not find elsewhere on this side of the Atlantic—but these are the most interesting things on the menu, so think about trying them. The superb wine list introduces Americans to the wonderful and underappreciated wines of Austria and Hungary.

Duane Park Cafe (212-732-5555), 157 Duane Street between Hudson Street and West Broadway. Subway: A, C, 1, 2, or 3 train to Chambers Street. Open Monday through Friday for lunch noon–2:30 PM and dinner 5–10 PM, Saturday for dinner 5:30–10:30 PM, Sunday for dinner 5–9 PM. This upscale neighborhood eatery has been a winning addition to Tribeca's already crowded restaurant card. The $20 prix fixe lunch begins with salad or roasted red peppers, then moves to veal Milanese, roast fish, or homemade tagliatelle with a tuna ragout, and finishes with homey desserts such as strawberry-mango shortcake or peach-blueberry crisp. The à la carte menu is good, too, with starters like scallop-crab cakes, corn-fried oysters, lobster spring rolls, and pastas and entrées of halibut, seared tuna, a seafood sauté, and roast chicken; desserts include chocolate cake, apple cobbler, plum strudel, and pear-grape crisp paired with interesting custom-made ice creams. Dinner closely parallels the lunch menu but adds heftier fare such as cider-glazed pork chops, pan-roasted bass filet, salmon Wellington, peppery beef tenderloin with an oxtail risotto cake, Long Island duckling, and roast rack of lamb with spaetzle. Keep an eye on this place.

Montrachet (212-219-2777), 239 West Broadway between Walker and White streets. Subway: A, C, or E train to Canal Street, or 1 train to Franklin Street. Open Monday through Thursday for dinner 5:30–10:30 PM, Friday for lunch noon–2:30 PM and dinner 5:30 PM–11 PM, and Saturday for dinner 5:30–11 PM. Restaurateur Drew Nieporent's first solo effort in the city—the first in what would become a very healthy string of Nieporent successes—Montrachet opened in 1985 and still showcases French cooking at its finest. The interior design here could certainly use a freshening, as 1980s-style pastels and earth tones are no longer the rage—but nobody ever complains. In a city of world-class French food, Montrachet stands nearly shoulder to shoulder with the likes of Ducasse.

Begin with a starter such as a bowl of English pea soup with jalapeños, sautéed frog legs with coriander, Maine crab with fennel, apple, tan-

gerine, and green peppercorn gelée, or seared Hudson Valley foie gras with a strawberry chutney; then segue to a main course of organic black risotto, smoked lobster à la Biscayenne, striped bass with green asparagus and fava beans, halibut baked in a fig leaf, rack of lamb with rosemary sauce, or côte de boeuf with spring onions and wild mushrooms. Finish with a cheese plate or fondue, or a decadent Grand Marnier soufflé, crème brûlée, or chocolate-hazelnut bombe. The wine list is among the city's best devised, featuring (unsurprisingly) Montrachet vintages; *Wine Spectator* magazine awarded the restaurant a Grand Award in 1994, the highest possible accolade for a restaurant's wine list. This all comes very, very expensively; but ask about prix fixe lunches and dinners, which can be a surprisingly reasonable way to experience the menu.

🍴 **Next Door Nobu** (212-334-4445), 105 Hudson Street at the corner of Franklin Street. Subway: 1 train to Franklin Street. Open Monday through Thursday for dinner 5:45 PM–midnight, Friday and Saturday to 1 AM, Sunday to 11 PM. In a smaller room than its adjacent forebear Nobu (which spawned it in 1998; see below), wildly popular Next Door Nobu is no longer just a poor cousin. This place manages to deliver a superb dining experience at less expensive (though still not inexpensive) prices. The decor is soothing, with reed mats on the walls and the same view of Tribeca's industrial streetscape. Note, however, that this place is first come, first served—they don't take any reservations—which could be a plus or a minus, depending on whether you end up at a table or in a long line.

The cuisine? It's kicky, befitting the founder's South American influences: spicy miso chips with tuna or scallops, *toro* (tuna belly) tartare, Nobu-style ceviches, tuna *tataki* with *ponzu* sauce; sashimi, salmon-skin, pasta, and lobster salads; yellowtail sashimi with jalapenos; and *tiradito*. . . and these are just the *cold* dishes.

Nobu (212-219-0500), 105 Hudson Street at the corner of Franklin Street. Subway: 1 or 9 train to Franklin Street. Open Monday through Friday for lunch 11:45 AM–2:15 PM and dinner 5:45–10:15 PM, weekends for dinner only 5:45–10:15 PM. One of the most famous restaurants in New York almost since the moment it opened in 1994, Nobu takes sushi to dizzying heights where it's rarely been before. But this place may not be for everyone. This is superexpensive (it's not unusual to spend $100 per person here) and supersophisticated food, and you've got to twist arms or plan way ahead to get a table here; don't plan on blowing into town on vacation and catching a cancellation, because that's just not going to happen.

Why not? Head chef Nobuyuki Matsuhisa's kitchen turns out amazingly inventive raw fish and cooked dishes blending Japanese and Peruvian influences (Matsuhisa formerly lived in Peru, Argentina, Alaska, and California, among other places); expect sashimi, ceviches, the signature cod with miso, and a range of cooked dishes—even faux pasta fashioned of raw squid—combining Japan with South America to an exciting effect you would never have dreamed up on your own. For a real splurge, order the *omakase* (chef's choice) meal of the day, for $80 to $120 per person and up. The decor is as modern,

clean, and spare as you might expect, with lots of blond wood and birch trees giving a natural, almost Scandinavian feeling to the place; the back room is more formal than the front. If you simply cannot arrange a reservation, or are alternately trying to save a few dollars for a splurge elsewhere, try Next Door Nobu (see above), which does indeed adjoin Nobu and serves a different menu at much lower—if not exactly *low*—prices.

The Odeon (212-233-0507), 145 West Broadway between Duane and Thomas streets. Subway: 1 or 2 train to Franklin Street, or A, C, or 3 train to Chambers Street. Open Monday through Friday noon–2 AM, weekends from 11 AM. One of a growing number of semiformal, semicasual French American bistros in New York, this one gets lots of late-night action from the clubbing crowd. That doesn't mean the kitchen is slipping, though—entrées such as *steak frites* and chicken rise above the usual standard around town for these oft-cooked dishes; brunch is excellent, too. The Odeon may have seen its heyday a decade or two ago, but the food here is still very special and the art deco room is a kick.

Tribeca Grill (212-941-3600), 375 Greenwich Street at the corner of Harrison Street. Subway: 1 or 9 train to Franklin Street. Open Monday through Saturday 11:30 AM–5 PM and 5:30–11 PM, Sunday for brunch to 3 PM and for dinner to 10 PM. Right on the ground two floors of Robert De Niro's impressive, pathbreaking Tribeca Film Center, this is one of *the* places to eat steak with Manhattan's swish crowd inside a renovated former coffee factory. (Some of the investors include folks like Christopher Walken,

Bill Murray, and Mikhail Baryshnikov.) Needless to say, you never know when some sunglasses-wearing star might pop in—but come here for the food, too. De Niro teamed up with star city restaurateur Drew Nieporent in 1990 to open the restaurant beneath, and they'll certainly grill you a steak. But you can also get fish and other meats at this high-ceilinged, fun (if expensive) place. Desserts are justly lauded as well. Can't snag a table? Hit the beautiful mahogany-topped bar for a drink. Wine isn't a bad choice—this place purports to house the world's largest selection of Châteauneuf du Papes.

EATING OUT ✄ **Bubby's** (212-219-0666), 120 Hudson Street at the corner of North Moore Street. Subway: 1 train to Franklin Street. Open Monday through Thursday 8 AM–11 PM, Friday and Saturday to midnight, Sunday 9 AM–10 PM. In no way does this Lower Manhattan stalwart serve top-drawer food, but if you are looking for caloric comfort food (and some odd concessions to fusion influences), you can find reliable choices such as burgers and fries, mac and cheese, barbecue, shakes, lasagna, pancakes, big pieces of pie (Bubby's original began life as a cottage-industry pie business), and the like here. Kids are treated like royalty, so families especially like this place. There's now a second location in the DUMBO neighborhood of Brooklyn, beneath the Manhattan Bridge.

Il Mattone (212-343-0030 or 212-343-1210), 413 Greenwich Street at the corner of Hubert Street. Subway: A, C, E, or 1 train to Canal Street. Open Monday through Wednesday 11 AM–10 PM, Thursday and Friday

11 AM–11 PM, Saturday 5–11 PM. One of the least-pretentious places in the neighborhood, Il Mattone serves dynamite pastas, grilled items, and brick-oven pizzas in a trattoria space that's classic Tribeca—pressed-tin ceilings, brick walls, wide doors. It's the sort of place where the owner's kids might drop by and romp around after hours. Yet the cooking is surprisingly classy; the meal starts with rugged yet airy peasant bread and a cube of butter. The eponymous Il Mattone pizza is a winner, with its sausages, pepperoni, perfectly roasted red peppers, and fresh mozzarella all obviously chosen and prepared with care. Soups, such as broccoli with pastini and parsley, change daily, and selections of straightforward pasta dishes are also well done. Other menu items ($10–26 each) include grilled tuna, veal chops, breaded chicken or veal cutlets, panini, Italian salads, and shrimp.

SNACKS ✄ **Bazzini's** (212-334-1280), 339 Greenwich Street at the corner of Jay Street. Subway: A, C, 1, 2, or 3 train to Chambers Street. Open daily 8 AM–8 PM, except Friday to 3 PM. This storefront started out doing just one thing, for a long time, and doing it better than anyone else in Manhattan: roasting nuts and dishing 'em up to appreciative hordes of Tribeca-area types. Of course, that was more than a century ago, before anyone coined the hip term for the neighborhood—before Tribeca decomposed, and before it mysteriously retrendified before our very eyes. Anyhow, the operation has since expanded to include a range of specialty foods you can't get just anywhere in this part of downtown. You can grab a sandwich, salad, or soup if you want. But I'd still opt for something simple and snacklike.

✳ Entertainment

MUSIC VENUE Knitting Factory
(212-219-3006), 74 Leonard Street between Broadway and Church Street. Subway: 1 train to Franklin Street, N or R train to Canal Street, or A or C train to Chambers Street or Canal Street. This venerable alternative-music haunt has been presenting cutting-edge jazz, folk, world music, and other uncategorizeable genres for years. Events at the four separate venues could include anything from an avant-garde film festival and a group of Irish tenors to a disk jockey contest or a Van Morrison tribute. Tickets usually range $10–20 per person.

BARS AND CLUBS Bubble Lounge
(212-431-3433), 228 West Broadway between Franklin and White streets. Subway: 1 train to Franklin Street. Open Monday through Thursday 5 PM–2 AM, Friday and Saturday to 4 AM. This Tribeca bar specializes in the bubbly—champagne, that is. You can sample 40 different kinds by the glass here, or one of a dozen designer cocktails made with the sparkling wine. Don't feel like that? Vodka lovers can try one of eight designer martinis. Snacks to go along with the drinks include sweets, sushi, oysters, cheese plates, and caviars. There's live music Monday and Tuesday nights. Needless to say, the crowd's beautiful and well heeled.

The Liquor Store Bar (212-226-7121), 235 West Broadway at the corner of White Street. Subway: 1 train to Franklin Street. This is one of Tribeca's friendliest neighborhood bars, occupying the site of a small former liquor store but now considerably brightened up. They pack 'em in for happy hour and beers, and you can either stand by the windows or sit outside on the street during good weather.

✳ Special Events

Late April–early May: ♪ **Tribeca Film Festival** (212-941-2400 or 1-866-941-FEST), various locations. Actor Robert De Niro helped create this new festival, which made its debut in spring 2002 to help Lower Manhattan recover from the economic blow created by September 11. It has already staked its claim as a major American film festival by serving as the premiere location for such films as *Stars Wars: Episode II, Poseidon* and *Insomnia,* and there is an all-day family film component as well. Check the festival's Web site (www.tribeca filmfestival.org) each April for specific details of scheduling, films, lectures, and venues.

SOHO

$\mathcal{S}$ oHo is defined as south of Houston (Street), and for the purposes of this book I consider it to be everything between Canal Street and Houston Street—a relatively small area, but one packed with dining, galleries, shops, and bars—and west from Lafayette to the Hudson River.

A former manufacturing district, SoHo is distinctive for its architecture of tall, beautiful cast-iron buildings. The area enjoyed a second life beginning in the 1960s as a haven for artists snapping up the cheap-rent industrial loft spaces in these buildings and renovating them in modern furnishings. Those same low rents went stratospheric during the 1980s and 1990s. Things have since cooled off a bit, and chain stores have moved in—eroding the area's character somewhat. Most of the shops, bars, galleries, and hotels here today are very pricey; you get the feeling a lot of famous people live here, surfacing at night when their limos spirit them to secret, members-only bars.

An important subdivision of SoHo is the tiny, so-called **Nolita district** (for North of Little Italy), which extends four blocks east from Lafayette Street to Bowery and three blocks north of Kenmare Street up to Houston Street. Tiny these 12 square blocks may be, but they make up a kind of SoHo East that's perhaps the city's hottest neighborhood right now as funky clothing boutiques, garden bistros, wine bars, jewelry shops, expensive loft apartments, and movie stars rapidly move in. (In this book I have included Nolita's restaurants and other listings alongside the SoHo listings, rather than separating them into another section, because you can easily walk the four blocks between the two neighborhoods.)

NoHo, on the other hand, is different: the area just north of SoHo and Nolita, beginning on the north side of Houston Street. I have covered this equally small, equally fascinating wedge of a neighborhood in the East Village chapter (see chapter 3).

GETTING THERE *By car:* From the West Side, take the West Side Highway to Spring Street and turn east. From the east side of town, you might try the FDR (East Side) Drive to Avenue C, which runs down to Houston Street. Bowery is also useful for getting here; take Third Avenue south from 23rd Street. Or you can simply take Broadway from uptown until you pass through SoHo. Parking in SoHo is hit or miss: Sometimes (on weeknights or weekend mornings, for

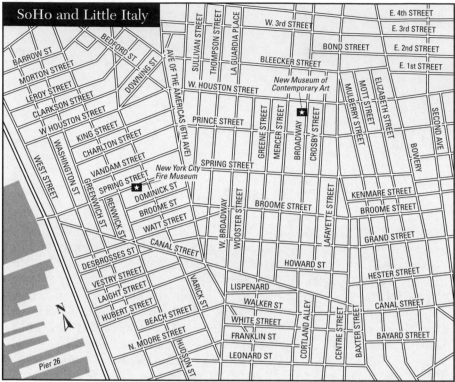

New Museum of Contemporary Art

New York City Fire Museum

© The Countryman Press

instance) it can be ridiculously easy. On weekends after about noon in good weather, or on Friday and Saturday nights, it can be thankless.

By subway: It's easy to reach SoHo by subway. From Midtown, Times Square, Fifth Avenue, or Union Square, take an N, R, or W train to Prince Street. From Harlem, the Upper West Side, Port Authority, Midtown West, the West Village, Lower Manhattan, or Tribeca, take a C or E train to Spring Street. From the Upper East Side, Grand Central Terminal, Midtown East, or Gramercy Park, take a 6 train to Spring Street. Or from Rockefeller Center, Fifth Avenue, the East Village, or the Lower East Side, take an F or V train to Broadway–Lafayette and cross Houston Street.

By bus: The best ways to get here from uptown by bus are by taking either the 1 bus southbound along Fifth Avenue or a 6 bus southbound from Seventh Avenue (north of Times Square), Times Square, or Broadway south of Times Square. Both stop along Broadway in the heart of SoHo. The 21 bus is useful as a crosstown bus along Houston Street.

✳ To See

& **New York City Fire Museum** (212-691-1303; www.nycfiremuseum.org), 278 Spring Street between Hudson Street and Varick Street. Subway: C or E train to Spring Street or 1 or 9 train to Houston Street. Open Tuesday through

Saturday 10 AM–5 PM, Sunday to 4 PM. Inside a solid stone 1904 firehouse, this museum is particularly relevant in the aftermath of September 11. It holds one of the nation's largest collections of fire equipment, old fire engines (including horse-drawn, steam-powered, and gas-powered vehicles), pump trucks, hoses, buckets and helmets, and a good deal of fire-related history. You'll learn what the "rattle watch" was, study the evolution from vintage to modern fire gear, and see the Jaws of Life in action. Admission is by donation; they suggest $5 for adults, $2 for senior citizens and students, $1 for children under 12.

✳ Lodging

BOUTIQUE HOTELS ♪ **Mercer Hotel** (212-966-6060 or 1-888-918-6060; fax 212-965-3838; www.mercerhotel .com), 147 Mercer Street at the corner of Prince Street. Subway: N, R, or W train to Prince Street, F, V, or S train to Broadway–Lafayette, or 6 train to Bleecker Street. Owner André Balazs, he of the star-frequented Chateau Marmont in Hollywood, has picked a simple idea here: to show guests a bit of the SoHo loft experience in six stories of quiet luxury. Movie stars and other celebs have quickly taken to it. Once you've found the entrance (it's quite low-key), check in on the Mercer's ground floor among stacks of library books. The rooms upstairs are quite large, done in modern furniture, rich woods, and tasteful beige, white, and black interiors; the tiled bathrooms are as fancy as you'd expect—in fact, they're even sexy, from the lighting to the oversized tubs in many to romantic extras. Toiletries come from a Swedish cosmetics store right down the block. The 75 rooms also contain fashion magazines, VCR, fax, computer, three phones each, fast T-1 connections, Dean & DeLuca snacks, personal telephone numbers and business cards, city and international newspapers, *and* video game consoles— just like a local's apartment might. The exposed brick, iron, and wooden floors add to the postindustrial feeling. They've even thought about families here: You can obtain a crib and toys. Service is impeccable throughout, and the hotel restaurant, Mercer Kitchen, is one of superstar chef Jean-Georges Vongerichten's (see *Dining Out*). There's even a secret basement bar accessible only to hotel guests. Double rooms begin at about $440 per night, while suites can run $700 to 1,100 per night . . . or more.

🐾 **SoHo Grand Hotel** (212-965-3000 or 1-800-965-3000; fax: 212-965-3244), 310 West Broadway between Grand and Canal streets. Subway: A, C, E, or 1 train to Canal Street. Opened in 1996, this ultracool boutique hotel tries to play it young—but it's actually the oldest of the three hip hotels in SoHo. The obligatory black-clad staff and concierges (you'll also find this uniform at the Mercer, 60 Thompson, and Tribeca Grand hotels) busily work the phones and street trying to keep the pampered clientele happy; in winter giant heat lamps keep the covered taxicab waiting area comfortably warm. Pets are heartily welcomed— floors are decorated with lots of cast-iron dogs, and you can order a meal for your pooch. For humans, the 370 rooms are a bit like miniature art galleries and feature Frette linens, work desk, CD player (you can rent CDs),

Internet access via television, and modern-industrial furniture and lighting—comfortable and chic, though not overly luxurious. Bathrooms feature locally made Kiehl's toiletries, and each room comes with a mini guidebook to the surrounding SoHo area. The second-floor Grand Bar is a great place for a drink (see *Entertainment—Bars and Clubs*). Rooms begin at about $315 per night and climb from there to the $700 range. If you're in a romantic mood, inquire about the "Seduction in Soho" package ($300–$500 per night), which serves up two glasses of champagne, chocolate-dipped berries, drinks at the bar, and late checkouts.

60 Thompson (212-431-0400; fax 212-431-0200), 60 Thompson Street between Broome and Spring streets. Subway: C or E train to Spring Street. This 12-story boutique hotel opened in January 2001 and quickly set a new standard for coolness in SoHo. Most of the 100 rooms have good views of the surrounding area, and all have marble bathroom and fireplace, big sink and tub, white Frette bedcovers and linens, plush pillows, tastefully concealed CD/DVD player, and high-speed Internet cables. The suites add wrought-iron balconies with even better views of SoHo, and the very expensive Thompson Loft is a duplex penthouse with a private roof deck and garden, stone fireplace, and four-poster king bed. Double room rates begin at around $375 per night but are sometimes much higher, up to about $700 per night.

AFFORDABLE HOTEL & **Holiday Inn Downtown** (212-966-8898 or 1-800-465-4329; fax 212-966-3933), 138 Lafayette Street between Canal Street and Howard Street. Subway: J, M, N, Q, R, Z, or 6 train to Canal Street. This Holiday Inn doesn't pretend to be anything other than what it is—an amazing deal considering that it's less than half a dozen blocks from SoHo and rooms that cost three to four times as much. It offers more than 225 reasonably priced, business-class rooms, some of them quite large and nicely designed. Views and decor are nothing to write home about, but the place is certainly clean and well maintained. One warning: The surrounding neighborhood gets very hectic during the day (especially weekends), and then very empty and spooky late at night. The Asian restaurant in the lobby might be the only one open when you're hungry. Double room rates range $169–269 per night in summer, but sometimes dip as low as $140 per night during slower periods; junior suites generally cost $270–400 per night.

✳ Where to Eat

DINING OUT Aquagrill (212-274-0505), 210 Spring Street at Sixth Avenue. Subway: C or E train to Spring Street. Open daily noon–3 PM for lunch, 6–11 PM for dinner, Sunday to 10:30 PM. Among Manhattan's seafood restaurants, this one in a hip corner of SoHo might be the biggest fish of all. The standout here is the oyster bar, considered by many the city's finest—choose from several dozen varieties, if you know your oysters—but the regular menu doesn't drop off in quality one bit, from appetizers such as seared river scallops through entrées such as scampi and grilled, fried, and roasted fish, to good desserts. The dining room, which is not so much an elegant one as a hip-

and-hoppin' one, is usually packed. As a bonus, service here is better than terrific; you'll never let yourself be either ignored or harried by a New York waiter again after experiencing the staff's professionalism. Not surprisingly, Aquagrill is so highly regarded that reservations are essential.

Balthazar (212-965-1414), 80 Spring Street between Broadway and Crosby Street. Subway: 6 train to Spring Street. Open Monday through Friday 7:30–11:30 AM for breakfast, noon–5 PM for lunch, 6 PM–1:30 AM for dinner, weekends 7:30 AM–3:30 PM for brunch and from 5:30 PM for dinner. This is one of my favorite places in SoHo, indeed New York; after just a few years, it is already firmly established as a place of top-flight dinner, lunches, brunches, baked goods, and service in short, a nearly perfect establishment that's never become too full of itself despite a sometimes star clientele. Owner Keith McNally has created a Parisian-style brasserie with a wonderful bar (topped in zinc, of course), calm booths and tables, and art deco touches. Brunch is just wonderful, among New York's best, and even breakfast during the week is surprisingly good, likely miles better than that served at your hotel. But dinner is the real star—the seafood tower is legendary—and it isn't priced through the stratosphere, either. Finally, absolutely do not miss the cranberry-pecan or other specialty nut breads sold at the bakery next door: Take one back to the hotel for breakfast.

Blue Ribbon (212-274-0404), 97 Sullivan Street between Prince and Spring streets. Subway: C or E train to Spring Street. Open Tuesday through Sunday 4 PM–4 AM. Related to the renowned West Village bakery and the sushi joint just down the street (see below), Blue Ribbon serves lively New American meals of chicken, duck, steak, and the like in a happy little room that's seemingly always packed with neighborhood folks. Since it's open until 4 AM, top city chefs sometimes drop by here late at night to chat and chew. But there are no reservations taken—unless maybe your name is Jean-Georges—so plan on lining up and waiting at peak dinner hours.

Blue Ribbon Sushi (212-343-0404), 19 Sullivan Street between Prince and Spring streets. Subway: C or E train to Spring Street. Open daily noon–2 AM. A tiny, sunken spot just a few steps away from the popular Blue Ribbon restaurant (to which it is closely related), this eatery proffers

SOHO BUILDING DETAIL

Paul Karr

excellent sushi in an exemplary setting. Diners lucky enough to snag a
spot in the evening lineup grab
phones and wait outside for their
summons, then penetrate a sensuous
warren of dining spaces, grottoes, and
low wooden tables. The sushi is very
good, too, and it's pricey.

🍴 **Country Café** (212-966-5417), 69
Thompson Street between Broome
and Spring streets. Subway: C or E
train to Spring Street. Open Monday
through Thursday 5–11 PM, Friday
11 AM–11 PM, Saturday and Sunday
from 10 AM. Owned by a French chef,
this little bistro off the main SoHo
shopping drag is an authentic and
low-key French restaurant with a
sunny decor and feel—plus some nice
African and Middle Eastern twists
(she grew up in Morocco). Expect
meals of chicken, steak, pâté, seafood
stews, and similar fare at very reasonable prices; lunch, especially, is a bargain, and there's a longish weekend
brunch as well.

Cub Room (212-677-4100), 131 Sullivan Street at the corner of Prince
Street. Subway: C or E train to Spring
Street. Open Monday to Wednesday,
11 AM–2 AM, Thursday to Saturday to
4 AM. Named for a mythically exclusive club in the Bette Davis film *All
About Eve,* the Cub Room is a combination of hip SoHo corner joint and
fine-dining experience; it was also
owner Henry Meer's first venture on
his own after years cooking at some of
the city's eateries. (Meer has since
opened a second establishment, the
City Hall Restaurant in Lower Manhattan; see *Dining Out* in "Tribeca.")
As befits SoHo, the Cub Room's
streetside lounge hops late into the
night with the hip and the beautiful,
while serious diners retreat to a qui-

eter back room to sample the cuisine
of Meer's handpicked executive chef
Craig Samuel—who did time at
French restaurants around the city
and in Spain before coming here to
head up the kitchen.

Lunch is a relatively simple affair of
pasta, seafood, and steak, while dinner
entrées (priced $18–28 each) consist
of such choices as skate in a shiitake
crust, salmon Caesar salad, roasted
monkfish, pot roast with cabbage and
spaetzle, seared scallops with short
ribs and cream sauce, steak with filet
mignon, cognac, and green peppercorn sauce, and signature soufflés;
you might also find lobster fricassee,
sweetbreads, and berry tarts, depending on the season. There's also a
brunch menu of salads, risotto, pasta,
pancakes, smoked salmon, and potato
latkes with eggs and bacon. If you're
coming with a group, inquire about
the private dining room—14 seats at
a rich wooden table, a wall of exposed
brick, and a fireplace create a cozy
and secluded atmosphere. If you reserve it, you must order from a set of
four- to seven-course tasting menus
costing $65–80 per person. Too rich
for your blood? In winter the adjacent
café (see Cub Room Café under *Eating Out*) offers the outstanding bargain of a prix fixe dinner from 6 PM
until closing.

Kittichai (212-219-2000), 60 Thompson Street between Broome and
Spring streets. Subway: C or E train
to Spring Street. Open Monday
through Friday 7–11 AM for breakfast,
noon–2:30 PM for lunch, 6–11 PM for
dinner; Saturday same breakfast and
lunch hours but 5:30 PM–midnight;
Sunday 5:30–10 PM for dinner. This
new hotel restaurant (inside the ultra-
hip 60 Thompson Street property)

brings upscale Thai to town. Chef Ian Chalermkittichai (hence the name) formerly cooked at the Four Seasons in Bangkok, and here he goes right for the jugular with Thai tapas dishes like fish cakes with chutney, a ceviche of diver scallops and caviar wrapped in egg nest, or crispy jasmine rice crackers with relish, and thrilling main dishes such as seared sirloin with black bean and whiskey sauce, loin of lamb with eggplant, foie gras, and Thai pesto, braised cod in lime-coriander broth, crispy fish with basil, wok-fried chicken with cashews and chiles, honey-glazed duck, or a clay pot of prawns with vermicelli noodles. Desserts are even more exciting: The night's offerings might include a lime tart with coconut ice cream and palm syrup, a white chocolate–jackfruit parfait, flourless chocolate cake and cherry compote in Thai red wine syrup, a 'Thai ice cream sundae,' or a fruit satay with chili salt crystals. This place looks like a definite up-and-comer with staying power: it's doing something nobody else is, in a lovely spare Rockwell Group–designed space.

🍴 **L'École** (212-219-3300), 462 Broadway at the corner of Grand Street. Subway: N, R, W or Q train to Canal Street, or 6 train to Spring Street. One of the city's best dinner-time deals, L'École occupies a suitably hip corner room on the southern fringes of SoHo. Tucked among news-stands, home furnishings stores, and clothiers, the French Culinary Institute's house restaurant serves $24 prix fixe lunches and $35.50 four- and five-course prix fixe dinners. What's the catch? None, really—your meals are prepared by student chefs-in-training, so there is always the risk that some-one's having an off night (sorry, "learning experience") at your expense. But most diners agree that the young Bocuses deliver quality.

The three-course lunch is served weekdays 12:30–2:30 PM and changes daily: You might find leek and potato soup, ragout of venison in cranberry, pepper, and red wine sauce, apple Charlotte with a cider foam, a trio of crème brûlées, baked scallops, roast duck with lime sauce, Grand Marnier soufflé, a seafood chowder or lobster bisque, short ribs braised in red wine, or leg of lamb. The four-course dinner, served Monday through Wednesday 6–7:30 PM (the five-course dinners are served 8–9:30 PM), and Thursday through Saturday from 5:30 PM, begins with an hors d'oeuvre and a salad, then serves an entrée and concludes with dessert. You might start with soup, pâté, a vegetable terrine, a caramelized onion tart, or a potato galette with smoked salmon, then continue with a main course such as seafood and vegetables simmered in a saffrony lobster broth; Maryland crabcakes with red pepper coulis; a grilled fillet of tuna; organic roast chicken with fries; sautéed duck and confit of duck with berry sauce; venison stew with mushrooms, chestnuts, and cranberries; rack of lamb; or steak. Dessert is usually something simple and satisfying, such as a warm-served chocolate cake with espresso sauce, a crisp apple tart with vanilla ice cream, or crème brûlée. The five course dinner menu is served daily (the restaurant is closed Sunday) 8–9:30 PM, for the same price—it varies daily, but approximates the lunch menu. Whichever meal you choose, however, be very sure to make reservations. This place is deservedly popular.

Le Jardin Bistro (212-343-9599), 25 Cleveland Place between Kenmare and Spring streets. Subway: 6 to Spring Street. Open daily for lunch noon–3 PM, and for dinner 6–10 PM. This little, slightly hard-to-find French restaurant is one of my favorites in Manhattan—not because it's got a star-power chef or a five-star menu, but simply because it's extremely romantic, and the food is really good, and sometimes that's all you want in a place. There's a small front dining room, but in warm weather there's only one place you want to be: in the back garden, where arbor vines interlace above your head and appreciative couples murmur to each other as waitstaff pour flutes of champagne and glasses of house wine. Order a salade Niçoise, tuna tartare, mussels, steak, or any of the other French bistro meals the kitchen successfully pulls off with understatement and skill; finish with the good profiteroles or crème brûlée, and be glad you picked it.

❧ **Mercer Kitchen** (212-966-5454), 99 Prince Street at the corner of Mercer Street. Subway: C or E train to Spring Street, or N or R train to Prince Street. Open daily 7 AM–midnight, to 1 AM Friday and Saturday. A boisterous hotel restaurant that fronts über-hip Prince and Mercer streets, Mercer Kitchen is Jean-Georges Vongerichten's new project. He serves French and New American lunches and dinners ($20–$35 each) of roast chicken, Alsatian tarts, roast cod, grilled and pan-seared skate and salmon, designer pizzas, steak, rack of lamb, tender braised short ribs in a pot—in short, more of the same sort of well-prepared cuisine you can now find anywhere in the city, only it's conceived more brilliantly and cooked more skillfully here. The dining-room design features several communal tables and open kitchens nearly surrounding the diners; while you watch, the chefs toss salads, work the wood-burning pizza oven, roast chickens, fish, and lobster in a rotisserie, and bake tarts and cakes for dessert. The prix fixe lunch is a good deal, and this is one of the very few top-rung restaurants in the city that serve breakfasts daily—the waffles and smoked salmon bagels are as divine as anything else. There's even a separate tea bar with two dozen custom-blended teas and tea-based desserts to try.

EATING OUT Alidoro (212-334-5179), 105 Sullivan Street between Prince and Spring streets. Subway: C or E train to Spring Street. Open Monday through Saturday 11:30 AM–6 PM. You can do much worse in SoHo than grabbing a focaccia at this brisk little sandwich shop, run in fine Italian style; though the ran-a-very-tight-ship original owner has recently passed the mantle (that is, he sold the place), it's still pretty good. They've got every sort of Italian bread, cold cut, cheese, and pickled vegetable at the ready. They don't take credit cards here, though; that would only slow down the operation.

Cub Room Café (212-677-4100), 131 Sullivan Street at the corner of Prince Street. Subway: C or E train to Spring Street. Open Monday through Friday noon–2:30 PM for lunch and 6–10 PM for dinner, weekends 11 AM–4 PM for brunch. This café serves a lighter, less expensive menu than its next-door parent Cub Room (see *Dining Out*), though it's not inexpensive by any means. The menu leans

Paul Karr

ALFRESCO DINING IN SOHO

toward meat, fish, salads, and sandwiches. In winter the café serves a $20 prix fixe dinner from 6 PM until closing time.

Fanelli's (212-226-9412), 94 Prince Street at the corner of Mercer Street. Subway: N, R, or W train to Prince Street, F, V, or S train to Broadway–Lafayette, or 6 train to Bleecker Street. Open Monday through Saturday 10 AM–2:30 AM, Sunday 11 AM–12:30 AM. When you first spy the neon sign of this bar-trattoria, plunked down right in the middle of some of SoHo's trendiest blocks, you might think it's a classy place. Well, you might be in for a bit of a surprise. If you've shopped way past your credit limit, however, you might be pleasantly surprised: That's because the place dishes up simple, cheap Italian food—washed down with beers that are actually reasonably priced (as many people come here for the drinks as for the food)—in an absolutely unpretentious atmosphere. You're as likely to run across an earthy Irish waitress just getting off work as you are a fashion victim or *artiste* from one of the surrounding lofts.

Honmura An (212-334-5253), 170 Mercer Street between Houston and Prince streets. Subway: F, V, or S train to Broadway–Lafayette, N, R, or W train to Prince Street, or 6 train to Bleecker Street. Open Tuesday for dinner only 6–10 PM, Wednesday and Thursday for lunch noon–2:15 PM and dinner 6–10 PM, Friday and Saturday to 11 PM, Sunday to 9:15 PM. An offshoot of a Tokyo restaurant, this one cooks just one thing—handmade soba (buckwheat) noodles—but does them better than anyone else in the city; they've got nothing to hide here, as evidenced by the you-see-it-all-happening udon area, where chefs work the noodles into shape, steep their masterworks in a variety of broths, and combine them with innovative small dishes.

Kelley and Ping (212-228-1212), 127 Greene Street between Prince and Houston streets. Subway: N, R, or W train to Prince Street, 6 train to Bleecker Street, or F, V, or S train to Broadway–Lafayette. Noodles rule at this small and fun SoHo eatery with the cool interior design (you may forget you're in Manhattan and believe you're in Asia for a while). It's small enough that you might occasionally have to stand up while waiting for a table, but the good and inexpensive noodles, dumplings, and other menu choices make it all well worth the wait. Wash it down with a sweetly flavored coffee or tea.

Le Pain Quotidien (212-625-9009), 100 Grand Street at the corner of Mercer Street. Subway: A, C, E, J, M, N, Q, R, W, Z, 1, or 6 train to Canal Street. Open daily 7:30 AM–7:30 PM. Belgian brasseries were briefly all the rage in New York, but their moment has cooled off considerably; only the hardy survive. Belgian bakeries, on the other hand, seem to be booming: At least two upscale mini chains are spreading like wildfire around the city. One of them is Le Pain Quotidien, which began in Paris and Belgium and took Gotham by storm. The SoHo location offers a big, pleasing room that's brightly track lit and high ceilinged; at long communal unpainted wooden tables, *artistes* and their kids tuck into a menu of egg dishes, breads, sandwiches, brioche, *pain au chocolat,* and a soup of the day. Not to mention NYC's best croissant. The baker's basket is an outstanding deal; for $6.50, you can sample half a dozen breads with butter and jam; just remember that you may only order it— and eggs—before noon weekdays, or 2 PM weekends.

The sandwich selection is top quality, featuring such tasty bites as ham on dark bread with three mustards, roast beef with a caper mayonnaise, beef carpaccio, and Brie with nuts, while the daily specials might include a curried chicken sandwich, a tuna salad sandwich made with Dijon mustard, or tofu-seaweed salad with miso dressing. There are also meat and cheese platters for bigger appetites; if you're hankering for something sweet, go for the buttery, crispy Belgian waffle, which is served without syrup (but conceals a delightful layer of crystallized sugar within)—it's sublime as a snack. Don't have time for a meal? Order the same sandwiches for $2–3 less at the take-out counter, and don't forget to toss in some pear galettes, a slice of chocolate cake, or something racked on the wall—a bottle of extra-virgin olive oil or some Belgian chocolate bars, for instance. They make terrific, classy gifts.

Lombardi's (212-941-7994), 32 Spring Street between Mulberry and Mott streets. Subway: 6 train to Spring Street. Open Monday through Friday 11:30 AM–11 PM, to midnight Saturday, to 10 PM Sunday. Sadly, the terrific little bakery that Lombardi's once operated next door is no longer here—their doughnuts were among my favorite in town—but the main restaurant remains. This is said to have been New Yawk's very *first* coal-oven pizzeria, which is saying something, and the pies here are still good enough to justify a trip: Among the city's legion of pizza joints, the brick oven here holds it own. Friendly staff serve up matchless pies with charred thin crusts, sweet fresh tomato sauce toppings, and good cheese. They don't hold back on the garlic, either.

❧ **Snack** (212-925-1040), 105 Thompson Street between Prince and Spring streets. Subway: C or E train to Spring Street. Open Monday to Saturday noon–10 PM, Sunday to 9 PM. The size of a postage stamp, and horned into out-of-the-way Thompson Street (which is fast becoming a very hip corner of SoHo), this tiny restaurant doesn't look like much from the outside. Snack has only *three* tables, but it delivers a taste-and-value punch inside; the kitchen serves up such good Greek cuisine that Snack is nearly always full. Think lamb, chicken dishes, salads—all affordable, and served with a smile. Good luck grabbing a seat near mealtime.

Spring Street Natural Foods (212-966-0290), 62 Spring Street at the corner of Lafayette Street. Subway: 6 train to Spring Street, or N or R train to Prince Street. Open daily 9 AM–11:30 PM, Sunday from 10:30 AM. Possibly New York's most popular health food eatery, this corner restaurant squeezed into a nebulous area between SoHo, Nolita, and Chinatown has been going strong for a quarter century. Look for lots of rice dishes, dairy- and egg-free salads, local fish, Middle Eastern foods, sandwiches, and pastas.

Thai Angel (212-966-8916), 141 Grand Street between Crosby Street and Lafayette Street. Subway: J, M, N, Q, R, Z, or 6 train to Canal Street. Open Monday through Saturday 11:30 AM–10:30 PM, Sunday noon–10:30 PM. This Thai restaurant doesn't pop up on the radar of either guide books or many locals, but it's still a good choice when you're tapped out from SoHo shopping and need a break before continuing on to hectic Chinatown. The cheap pad Thai is a good effort, and the grilled pork-and-papaya salad is delicious, too. There are plenty of dishes heavy on the sig-

nature Thai ingredients of basil, curry, and chile peppers, as well as a short menu of seafood items such as Angel Crispy Shrimp (sautéed in Thai chili paste, broccoli, and basil), seafood soup, and scallops.

Zoë (212-966-6722), 90 Prince Street between Broadway and Mercer Street. Subway: 6 train to Spring Street, or N, R, or W train to Prince Street. Open Tuesday through Friday for lunch noon–3 PM and dinner 6–10:30 PM, Friday and Saturday for brunch 11:30 AM–3 PM and dinner to 11 PM, Sunday for brunch 11:30 AM–3 PM and dinner to 10 PM. Lots of shoppers pass by this Prince Street storefront on their way to SoHo's many cosmetics counters and fashion stores, but Zoë is an attractive and affordable lunch, brunch, or dinner stop. The wine list features some 250 selections, the room is filled with custom-made Tuscan fixtures, marble, columns, and tiles, and the wooden doors open out in summertime. Dinner entrées ($18–28) come from a wood-burning grill and oven in the open kitchen—mostly of pizza, roasted and grilled meats, and pastas—but things really get busy during the weekend brunch; it's one of SoHo's best-kept brunch secrets (Balthazar—see *Dining Out*—can hardly be classified as a secret), but locals know. So come early if you're planning to sample it.

COFFEE AND SNACKS Bari (212-431-4350), 529 Broadway at the corner of Spring Street. Subway: N or R train to Prince Street, or 6 train to Spring Street. Open daily 7 AM–8 PM. The ground floor is mostly artist types and Japanese tourists sipping cappuccino and pastries, but the real action is up on the second floor. You can get

JACQUES TORRES' CHOCOLATE HAVEN

a great view of the SoHo scene from up here—all while sipping the same coffee drinks—and at night elegant Italian dinners are served out of the same upstairs space; they're surprisingly good.

Café Café (212-226-9295), 470 Broome Street at the corner of Greene Street. Subway: 6 train to Spring Street, or N, R, or W train to Prince Street. Open daily 8 AM–7 PM. One of several SoHo coffeehouses tucked into the side streets, this bilevel space sees a lot of local artists—and a few guidebook-toting foreign tourists—dropping in for a quick cup of coffee and a brownie, a blended juice drink (steeply priced at $6.50 each), or a lunch salad while leafing through a leftover newspaper or one of the free fashion magazines. The bottom level features some communal benches and tables where you'll overhear talk of fashion, art installations, and the like; upstairs is more private, with narrow tables and counters for gazing into space or meeting with friends.

Ceci-Cela (212-274-9179), 55 Spring Street between Lafayette and Mulberry Street. Subway: 6 to Spring Street. Daily 7 AM–10 PM. When they're looking for a romantic, buttery bite of French pastry, locals flock to this tiny-looking Nolita dessert spot—and you should, too. Every sort of authentically delectable *pain au chocolat,* croissant, quiche, and turnover you can imagine has been crafted here by real French bakers for your snacking enjoyment; the bakery also serves a small but tasty selection of sandwiches. A seat in the back room, if scored, makes the perfect place to try out the day's offerings.

Eileen's Special Cheesecake (212-966-5585), 17 Cleveland Place between Centre and Kenmare streets. Subway: 6 train to Spring Street. Open Monday through Friday 8 AM–10:30 PM, weekends 10 AM–6 PM. Eileen's makes one of the best cheesecakes in Manhattan, and if you can find her shop you'll likely agree. Tucked on a hard-to-find corner near nothing noteworthy, it's worth seeking out.

Jacques Torres Chocolate (212-414-2462), 350 Hudson Street, one block south of Houston. Open Monday through Saturday, 9 AM to 7 PM. Sunday from 10 AM to 6 PM. The Manhattan storefront outlet of the chocolatier's Brooklyn factory. (See "The Outer Boroughs.")

✳ Entertainment

FILM Film Forum (212-727-8110), 209 West Houston Street between Sixth Avenue and Varick Street. Subway: 1 train to Houston Street, or C or E train to Spring Street. Documentaries rule the roost at the Film Forum; if you enjoy PBS, this is your New York theater. Look for left-wing political commentary, Middle Eastern intrigue, and the like. You might also look out for special programs such as, for example, a Robert Altman retrospective or a showing of a classic film.

THEATER/PERFORMING ARTS
HERE Arts Center (212-647-0202), 145 Sixth Avenue between Broome and Spring streets. Subway: C or E train to Spring Street. Since 1993, this SoHo company has drawn on the work of a range of resident performing groups and artists to put on some rather avant-garde (and Obie award-winning) productions. The mission: to encourage independent, talented artists who frankly might have no other respected place to hang a shingle if it weren't for HERE. That's no knock on them, of course; kudos to the center's Supported Artist Program for giving them a venue. HERE doesn't just do theater, either—one night, you might walk in to find, say, a chamber music group playing some new composition.

The Wooster Group (212-966-9796), 33 Wooster Street between Broome and Grand streets. Subway: A, C, E, 1, or 9 train to Canal Street. Based out of its own Performing Garage space on Wooster Street, this repertory company tours widely abroad when not home practicing experimental new pieces in SoHo; the works fuse classical work with dance,

art, and mythology. You never know what you're going to get. Recent work has included *Brace Up!* (a new take on Chekhov's *Three Sisters*) and *To You, The Birdie!* (a translation and update of Racine's *Phèdre,* using hidden cameras and other modernist art techniques).

BARS AND CLUBS Fanelli's (212-226-9412), 94 Prince Street at the corner of Mercer Street. Subway: N, R, or W train to Prince Street, F, V, or S train to Broadway–Lafayette, or 6 train to Bleecker Street. Known as SoHo's one sure bet for value-priced Italian food served in quantity, this is also a great place to tip one back with a cast of characters ranging from black-clad, slumming photographers and models to blue-collar, working-class heroes.

Grand Bar at the SoHo Grand (212-965-3000), 310 West Broadway between Grand Street and Canal Street. Subway: A, C, E, or 1 train to Canal Street. Super-ritzy—just like the hotel within which it resides—the Grand Bar isn't for the timid; this is a place to see, be seen, pay exorbitant

ART-HOUSE FILM MECCA IN SOHO

Paul Karr

prices for drinks, and exchange cell phone numbers, all while pretending not to care about the entire sordid process.

MUSIC VENUE Jazz Gallery (212-242-1063), 290 Hudson Street between Dominick and Spring streets. Subway: C or E train to Spring Street, or 1 train to Houston Street. A nonprofit cultural center and exhibition space with "memberships" since 1995, the Jazz Gallery opens all its shows for the general public. There are two sets each night, at 9 PM and 10:30 PM; admission costs $12 to $15 per set. Summertime brings occasional weekend shows on a boat in the Hudson River.

PUBLIC ART *The Broken Kilometer,* 393 West Broadway between Spring and Broome streets. Open to the public Wednesday to Sunday, noon–6 PM

except closed 3–3:30 PM. Walter De Maria's sculpture is laid out in a prime SoHo loft space and consists of 500 polished brass rods, each exactly 2 meters in length and about 2 inches in diameter (total length: 1 kilometer), arranged in a precise geometric fashion beneath stadium-style lighting. Free to visit, it is administrated by the Dia Center for the Arts (212-989-5566), a fascinating, challenging organization currently hunting for a new space in the Meatpacking District (it already maintains a museum in the Hudson River valley town of Beacon, and for decades occupied a large space in Chelsea.)

The New York Earth Room, 141 Wooster Street between Houston and Prince streets. Open to the public Wednesday through Sunday, noon–6 PM (except closed 3–3:30 PM). Also by Walter De Maria, the Earth Room

SOHO STREETSCAPE

Paul Karr

is literally a room full of soil, sculptured (or so they say). The earth covers the space to a depth of 22 inches—and the room is 3,600 square feet! It is also free.

✳ Selective Shopping

BOOKSTORE **Housing Works Used Books Cafe** (212-334-3324), 126 Crosby Street between Houston and Prince streets. Subway: F, V, or S train to Broadway–Lafayette, N or R train to Prince Street, or 6 train to Bleecker Street. You'll have to hunt to find this coffee shop, tucked into a cool industrial backstreet landscape of warehouses and iron fire escapes. But once inside, you'll find plenty of used books in a suitably musty atmosphere, plus coffee, tea, and snacks. It's the sort of place you'd imagine local poets come to read their latest scribblings—and they do. The twist here is that all profits go to an AIDS hospice organization nearby.

FOOD AND DRINK **Dean & DeLuca** (212-226-6800), 560 Broadway at the corner of Prince Street. Subway: N or R train to Prince Street. Open daily 10 AM–8 PM, Sunday to 7 PM. This gourmet food emporium is one of New York's classiest, and its SoHo location has the good sense to offer a short menu of upscale bakery items, sandwiches, simple entrées, good strong espresso, and great hot chocolate made from a mixture of French chocolate and milk. The chocolates section is outstanding, and you'll find top-shelf imported items—French and Danish butter, Swiss yogurt, English clotted cream, not to mention cookies, jams, coffees, smoked fish, and other things you never thought you'd find here. There's also a section of cookbooks and cookware in the back.

Italian Food Center (212-925-2954), 186 Grand Street at the corner of Mulberry Street. Subway: J, M, N, Q, R, W, Z, or 6 train to Canal Street, or B or D train to Grand Street. Open daily 8 AM–7 PM. One of the better Italian delis downtown, the Italian Food Center serves great, famously long sandwiches at rock-bottom prices. Or pick up supplies (flatbread, cheese, olives, a drink) for your impromptu picnic.

✳ Special Events

Late January: **Outsider Art Fair** (212-777-5218), 295 Lafayette Street near the corner of Houston Street. Subway: F, V, or S train to Broadway–Lafayette, or 6 train to Bleecker Street. Inside the Puck Building, this annual show was expanded to 3 days in 2003 due to its growing popularity. More than a decade old, it seeks to show contemporary art by outsiders—nontraditional artists such as amateurs, self-taught artists, and the mentally ill—by some of the nation's most respected dealers of this sort of art. The fair has not been without controversy; some feel it exploits the artists, rather than celebrating them. Admission costs $15 per day.

LITTLE ITALY

Little Italy is so much smaller than it once was that quite frankly it deserves little time on a Manhattan itinerary. (See map on page 66.) However, if you're really wanting to try an espresso and some authentic Italian bakery treats, by all means come here on your way to Chinatown, SoHo, or the Lower East Side.

GETTING THERE *By car:* Getting to Little Italy is similar to getting to Chinatown or SoHo—use Canal Street or Houston Street.

By subway: It's easiest to reach Little Italy by taking a 6 train from the Upper West Side, Midtown East, Union Square, or NoHo to either Spring Street or Canal Street. From Lower Manhattan or the Lower East Side, you can take the J, M, or Z train to Bowery or Canal Street.

By bus: Little Italy is poorly served by bus routes. The only real way to get here by bus is to take a 103 bus south from the Upper East Side or Midtown East along Lexington Avenue to Bowery.

✳ Where to Eat

Any night of the week, you'll run a gauntlet along Mulberry Street of aggressive maître d's and waiters hoping to lure you in. Most of these Italian joints are nothing special at all; the fascination they hold for the strolling tourists is something of a mystery. While the area's eateries are more or less interchangeable in terms of both quality and price (middling on both counts), there are a few spots that poke slightly above the crowd.

DINING OUT Angelo's of Mulberry St. (212-966-1277), 146 Mulberry Street between Grand and Hester Streets. Subway: J, M, Z, or 6 train to Canal Street. Open Tuesday to Sunday noon–11:30 PM, Friday and Saturday to 12:30 AM. Angelo's is big and busy, and they certainly play to the crowds, but ignore the huckstering and the fanfare; the pastas with tomato sauces and veal parmigiana here are pretty decent, good enough to keep the place in business more than a century (so far).

Il Cortile (212-226-6060), 125 Mulberry Street between Canal and Hester Streets. Subway: J, M, Z, or 6 train to Canal Street. Open daily noon–

midnight, weekends to 1 AM. Definitely a cut above the other contenders along this stretch of Mulberry Street, Il Cortile specializes in better-than-average chops and other veal dishes, as well as the usual pastas and other Italian entrées such as octopus, lamb, and sole. Antipasti are good, too. It's a little more expensive, sure, but you can eat outdoors in the warmer weather, one of your very best seating options in this neighborhood, and they sometimes do mini–dinner theater events on slow midweek nights. The service here, however, definitely leaves something to be desired, especially when they're really busy.

🐌 **Il Fornaio** (212-226-8306), 132A Mulberry Street between Grand and Hester Streets. Subway: J, M, Z, or 6 train to Canal Street. Open daily 11 AM–11 PM. This is not the fanciest place on the street, and isn't the most touristy. It might fall right beneath your radar. But consider it if you're in the mood for a low-key, authentically Italian meal; big plates of red-sauced pasta are the rule and reason for coming, but even the other dishes and sauces (such as capellini with lobster meat) are worth sampling. And prices here are remarkably reasonable, given those at other places along Mulberry.

Il Palazzo (212-343-7000), 151 Mulberry Street between Grand and Hester Streets. Subway: J, M, Z, or 6 train to Canal Street. Open daily noon 11 PM, Friday and Saturday to midnight. Touristy but dependable, Il Palazzo serves sturdy pasta dishes and sandwiches on good bread, as well as pricier full meals. The food is excellent compared with other places around the neighborhood—try a

melon and prosciutto, stuffed artichoke, or calamari appetizer, followed by a pasta and a good chicken or veal dish—and the leafy outdoor patio is a big plus. However, as with most of its fellow eateries in Little Italy, service here isn't exactly presented with a smile. It's more like a rush. Lunch is an especially affordable bargain.

🐌 **Pellegrino's** (212-226-3177), 138 Mulberry Street between Grand and Hester Streets. Subway: J, M, Z, or 6 train to Canal Street. Open daily noon–11 PM, weekends to midnight. More of a those-who-know spot than many others along Mulberry Street, this Italian eatery behind a pink-and-white awning veers away from red sauces. Instead, the chef forks up tasty fresh pastas (try the linguine), lasagna, and shrimp and chicken entrées (like chicken with asparagus and mozzarella), finishing meals with sweets such as tiramisu and chocolate mousse. You can also order authentic country dishes such as stracciatella (Italian egg-drop soup), carpaccio, and gnocchi. Prices are reasonable considering the portion sizes (especially at lunch), and the service isn't bad. It's one of my favorite lesser-known places in the area.

Taormina's (212-219-1007), 147 Mulberry Street between Grand and Hester Streets. Subway: J, M, Z, or 6 train to Canal Street. Open daily noon–11 PM. Don't necessarily come here for the food—though it is good—but rather come here because Taormina's was a (former) favorite hangout of organized-crime honchos like legendary boss John Gotti (he ate here once a week at a reserved table) and Anthony ("Tony Pep") Trentacosta. Those days are said to be past.

Expect loads of good filling Sicilian fare and a real family feel (in the wholesome sense, I mean). This place is lots chummier than most.

Umberto's Clam House (212-431-7545), 386 Broome Street between Mott and Mulberry Streets. Subway: J, M, or Z train to Bowery, or 6 train to Spring Street. Open daily 11 AM–4 AM. It has a murderous past—a mob boss was gunned down at the original location—but today Umberto's serves big meals of lasagna, antipasti, pasta, steak, lobster, shrimp, seafood, and fish to the masses. Celebrities are sometimes spotted here.

EATING OUT Noop! (646-613-8890), 365 Broome Street between Elizabeth and Mott Streets. Subway: J, M, or Z train to Bowery, or 6 train to Spring Street. Open Monday through Saturday 11 AM–10 PM. When you're cruising the Chinatown–Nolita area in search of a quick munchie, Noop! makes a surprising detour—a place where you can get a sweet fruity drink (such as lychee nectar, kumquat lime juice, honey lemonade, or a frothy tea), a bowl of soup, a dim-sum-like appetizer of dumplings or lobster ravioli, even just a cheeseburger. Note that they do not accept credit cards here. There's also a small array of linguine plates, rice dishes, side dishes (fried fish with creamed corn; Korean short ribs), and Asian desserts. I have no idea what the unifying theme of this place is, but if it stays in business—opening hours seem to be irregular, and it's not exactly easy to find—it might in time develop a cult following.

COFFEE AND SNACKS Ferrara Bakery & Café (212-226-6150), 195 Grand Street between Mott and Mulberry Streets. Subway: J, M, Z, or 6 train to Canal Street, or 6 train to Spring Street. Open daily 8 AM–midnight, Saturday to 1 AM. When you see Ferrara's neon sign, you're gazing upon Little Italy's most distinctive landmark: This bakery, which threw open its doors more than a century ago, continues to crank out reliable coffee, baked goods, and gelati to an unending queue of admirers and tourists. They also serve panini, espresso, and small pizzas. The interior, with its café tables and genuinely Italian stand-up bar, are authentic and appealing.

✳ Special Events

September: **Feast of San Gennaro,** along Mulberry Street. Subway: J, M, Z, or 6 train to Canal Street. This 11-day party of grilled sausages, tacky booths, and general Italiana takes over part of Mulberry Street each September.

East Village and NoHo 3

EAST VILLAGE AND NOHO

Manhattan's East Village—and its sibling neighborhood, the Lower East Side (see chapter 1)—have seen nothing short of a remarkable turnaround in recent years. Once tenement housing for the city's immigrant poor, the neighborhood is suddenly hipper than it can handle.

It wasn't always this way. Believe it or not, this was once prime real estate. The area was originally a large farm, the home of Manhattan's director; that farm ("Bouwerie Number One") was linked to the banks and trading houses of Lower Manhattan by the street now known simply as Bowery during that brief period of the mid-17th century when the Dutch ruled the roost in Manhattan.

Some of New York's richest families built mansions in the East Village during the boom times of the 1800s. But changing demographics and cheap real estate in the area soon conspired to turn it and the Lower East Side into a fast-growing, overcrowded neighborhood of immigrants packed into poor-quality tenement housing. Since then it's been a long, strange trip. Counterculture, social protest, Irish pub life, punk rock, the arts, and now upscale fusion cuisine and lounge-bars all took root here first, and those influences now make this the city's most interesting—if hard-to-pinpoint—district. Despite its apparent scruffiness, it is now one of the hot restaurant neighborhoods of the moment in New York. Everyone—from upscale places, to hole-in-the-walls serving burgers and hot dogs, to just about anyone with a new concept—seems to be muscling in, going toe to toe in the process with Jewish and Russian delis that had already been slugging it out here with each other for more than a century.

For the purposes of this book, I have defined the East Village as everything east of Broadway, from 14th Street to the north to Houston Street to the south.

The adjacent, oddly shaped NoHo (north of Houston) neighborhood is also important to bear in mind—many interesting eateries are located here. The section takes in Astor Place and once grungy but newly hip Bond and Great Jones streets, among others.

EAST VILLAGE

The East Village was long a district of Italian, Eastern European, and other immigrants, but it looks almost nothing like that today. Only on Second and Third avenues do you find traces of the past.

It's in Alphabet City—an area east of First Avenue, beginning with Avenue A at Tompkins Square Park—where this part of the city gets particularly interesting. Madonna lived down here in 1978 when she (and the area) were much more down on their luck, but today twentyish techno and hip-hop deejays and IT professionals hobnobbing in French cafés mingle with Spanish families, clubbers, postpunks in spiked hair and leather, fashion mavens, and Japanese youth scarfing down the city's cheapest sushi.

Indeed, this has become Manhattan's best neighborhood for cheap eats; you won't believe how much you can get away with spending, even for a good and big meal, here—often $10 per person or less for dinner. Other pockets of the neighborhood are thick with Indian food, Ukrainian delis, sake bars, and antiques.

GETTING THERE *By car:* Getting here from the north is relatively straightforward: Use Second Avenue, which heads south into the neighborhood. You can also take the FDR (East Side) Drive to the 23rd Street area, where you exit and funnel onto Avenue C and pass within two blocks of Tompkins Square. Turn right and head west to park closer to the action. From the west side of town, use the West Side Highway (which becomes Tenth Avenue), Seventh Avenue, Fifth Avenue, or Broadway to get south. You can cut crosstown on 23rd Street or 14th Street, though smaller cross streets may be more useful. Remember that the even-numbered streets head east, toward the East Village.

By subway: The East Village is a little difficult to reach by subway. The easiest way to get here is to take a 6 train from the Upper West Side, Grand Central Terminal, Midtown East, Gramercy Park, or Lower Manhattan to Astor Place and walk west along St. Marks Place (East 8th Street). From Times Square and Midtown, the N, R, and W trains also stop at 8th Street–NYU, but a few blocks west of Astor Place; again, walk west on 8th until you hit the numbered and lettered avenues. From 14th Street stations such as Union Square, you can also

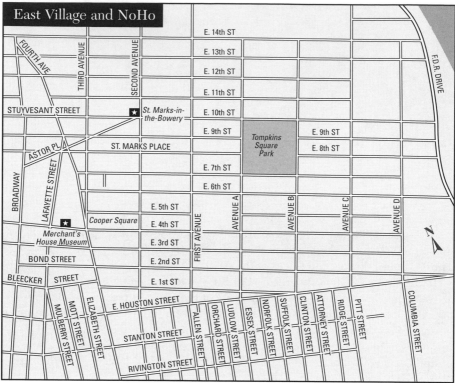

take an L train to First Avenue and then walk south half a dozen blocks. Or take an F or V train from Midtown or West Village to Second Avenue and walk north from Houston Street.

By bus: Crosstown buses serve this area much better than uptown and downtown lines do, and might be useful to get you to a subway station. The 8 bus shuttles back and forth along 8th Street and, in the East Village, 10th Street. The 14 bus dips into the neighborhood before shuttling along 14th Street all the way west to the Hudson River. The 21 bus shuttles along Houston Street. Uptown service is limited to the 15 bus, which travels far uptown along First Avenue and Second Avenue to and from the Upper East Side. And the 9 bus runs along Avenue B to Union Square.

✳ To See

CHURCH St. Marks-in-the-Bowery (212-674-6377), 131 East 10th Street at the corner of Second Avenue. Subway: 6 train to Astor Place, or L train to Third Avenue. The core of this church—created for Manhattan governor Peter Stuyvesant (who is buried here with his family)—is older than much of Manhattan: It dates back to 1799. The steeple was added in 1828, the portico 30 years later, and it has since become a very activist church, advocating on behalf of the poor and gays and lesbians. Its history as a performance space is legend; many of the great writers of the 20th century have given readings here, the top dancers in the world have danced here, famous playwrights have workshopped their work here, and Andy Warhol even screened some of his experimental films here. Oh, and it's also said to be haunted—by more than one ghost.

✳ Green Space

The East Village's **community gardens** are the city's best. To see a particularly rich concentration, walk east through Tompkins Square and emerge at East 9th Street; there are two gardens at this corner. Turn right and walk south down Avenue C to East 7th Street, turning right again—halfway down the block there's another large garden. Continue along East 7th to Avenue B, make a right, and walk one block to East 6th Street. At this corner there's yet another one, perhaps the finest of the lot—an oasis of flowers, plants, water, birds, and butterflies. It's open to the public only for limited hours, however, as are some of the others.

Tompkins Square Park, East 7th Street to East 10th Street, between Avenues A and B. Subway: L train to First Avenue, or 6 train to Astor Place. One of New York's most fascinating parks to people-watch in, Tompkins Square has seen a long, tumultuous history. It was created in the 1830s (around the same time as Washington Square Park, in central Greenwich Village) and named for a former New York governor who was also elected to two terms as vice president of the United States (1817–1825). Protests began almost immediately, and have never really stopped—the 1960s saw plenty of Woodstock-style acts jamming here before blissed-out crowds, and as recently as 1991 there were major confrontations between police and locals in the park—but the current midnight curfew has virtually eliminated the squatting and riots that once prevailed. Central Park architect Frederick Law Olmsted had a small hand in the square's redesign; today it is intriguingly surrounded by attractive town houses on one side, Avenue A's craziness on another, and the beginnings of a Spanish neighborhood on a third.

✳ Lodging

AFFORDABLE HOTELS East Village Bed & Coffee (212-533-4175), 110 Avenue C between East 7th and East 8th streets. Subway: L train to First Avenue. A bit grittier looking than its former companion property (see below), Anne Edris's European-style Bed & Coffee guesthouse is indeed cheaper but still decent. The brick-walled, wooden-floored rooms ($105–120 double, none with private bathroom) in the apartment building are decorated in treehouse, Mexican, Afghani, chalet, French, and British themes. There is also a common kitchen area and lounge, a tiny flag-stoned garden, and high-speed Internet access. It's a bit like being part of the cast of *Friends*, only in a much smaller place (and without the witty banter). Check out the fantastic lighting fixtures, constructed by the "in-house electrician" from used bottles. Now isn't that just *so* East Village?

Second Home on Second Avenue (212-677-3161; fax 212-677-3161), 221 Second Avenue between East 13th and East 14th streets. Subway: L train to Third Avenue, or N, Q, R, W, 4, 5, or 6 train to 14th Street–Union Square. Very close to Union Square, Carlos Delfin's Second Home accommodation service offers six rooms in an attractive 19th-century town house; the living-room suite—the biggest—is huge, with a Persian rug, leather couch, and French doors leading into an airy bedroom. Other rooms (lacking private bathrooms) are also clean, feature solid wooden floors, and are nicely furnished in Caribbean, tribal, Peruvian, and other themes, but are occasionally pint sized. Each room comes with air-conditioning, a phone (local calls are free), color cable television, and a radio; suites add VCR and CD player. There's also a kitchen nook on the premises with dishwasher, refrigerator, and small dining table, shared among all the guests. Double rooms cost $100–110, while the suites —which have private bathrooms— cost $175–195. Ring bell 1 through the red door when you get there.

✳ Where to Eat

DINING OUT **Jewel Bako** (212-919-1012), 239 East 5th Street between Second and Third avenues. Subway: 6 train to Astor Place. Open Monday through Saturday 6:30–10:30 PM. Beneath an interesting bamboo ceiling in a pint-sized dining space, Jewel Bako puts out what might be the East Village's best sushi—in fact, some patrons claim it's some of New York's best. You can either go with the chef's daily personal choice of the freshest (called an *omakase* meal), which is very expensive, or order à la carte.

🍴 **Jules Bistro** (212-477-5560), 65 St. Marks Place (East 8th Street) between First and Second Avenues. Subway: L train to First Avenue, or 6 train to Astor Place. Open Monday through Friday for lunch noon–5 PM and dinner 5:30 PM–1 AM, Friday to 2 AM, Saturday for brunch 11 AM–4 PM and dinner until 2 AM, Sunday for brunch 11 AM–4 PM. An authenti-

Kim Grant

cally French bistro of wine, music, and good affordable food, this is a sleeper choice amid the grunge and chaos of St. Marks Place. For lunch or brunch ($7–16 per entrée), you can start with escargots, onion soup, or pâté, then continue with *steak frites,* a salad, poached salmon, steamed mussels, a *croque-monsieur,* or a plate of charcuterie; side orders include several good gratins. One good way to sample the dinner menu is to try the excellent $20 pretheater prix fixe deal of a beet-and-greens salad, fish stew, onion soup, or liver terrine appetizer; a bouillabaisse, hangar steak with risotto, tender beef bourguignon, or lamb shank stew main course; and dessert of chocolate cake, ice cream, or chilled crème brûlée with a wonderfully crisp, caramelized crust. The à la carte menu adds a daily roast fish, swordfish steak, southwestern French casserole of pork sausage and duck, roast suckling pig, and duck à l'orange. Brunch is also a popular draw. There's jazz (live or piped over the sound system) each night of the week, and a sidewalk terrace besides, both further enhancing the feeling of just having stepped off a Paris street.

Zakuro (212-505-5624), 143 Second Avenue at the corner of East 9th Street. Subway: 6 train to Astor Place. Open daily 5:30–11 PM. It almost never opened, but this smart new sushi joint on a busy Second Avenue corner incorporates unexpected French touches into the usual sushi lineup: Brie packed into rolls with the salmon, grilled steaks, chestnuts, and French red wines.

EATING OUT A Salt & Battery (212-254-6610), 80 Second Avenue between East 4th and East 5th streets.

Subway: F or V train to Second Avenue. Open daily 11 AM–10 PM. The daughter of a great West Village fish-and-chips shop (see chapter 4), this location offers the same fried seafood, the same unhealthy side dishes, and the same Brit inclination, plus a bigger selection of eats thanks to a breakfast option on the menu.

Avenue A Sushi (212-982-8109), 103 Avenue A between East 6th and East 7th streets. Subway: 6 train to Astor Place, or F or V train to Second Avenue. Open Sunday through Thursday 5 PM–2 AM, Friday and Saturday until 3 AM. This one-of-a-kind eatery combines decent sushi with the novelty of disco-like strobe lights and a giant flickering television screen with Japanese TV playing in continuous loops. It's more a club—an experience, really—than a fine-dining establishment, and you can get much better sushi at Jewel Bako (see *Dining Out*), but if you want to feel like you're one of the young East Village crowd it's one of the best places to start.

B&H Dairy Restaurant (212-505-8065), 127 Second Avenue between East 7th Street and St. Marks Place (East 8th Street). Subway: 6 train to Astor Place, or F or V train to Second Avenue. Open daily 7 AM–10 PM. This old-fashioned Jewish restaurant carries absolutely no meat on the menu—just soups, snacks, and cheese-filled items that are purportedly all good for you. (Rumor has it the name means "Beauty and Health.") This is food of a disappearing style, and extremely inexpensive.

Blue 9 Burger (212-979-0053), 92 Third Avenue between East 12th and East 13th Streets. Subway: L, N, Q, R, W, 4, 5, or 6 train to 14th Street–Union Square. Open daily noon–

midnight. This popular burger shop on Third Avenue close to Union Square offers amazingly cheap burgers, shakes, and fries in a place of absolutely zero decor—the chairs look like something out of an elementary school from 30 years ago, but who cares? The meat is fresh (never frozen), made to order, and perfectly grilled; the potatoes are diced and peeled right on the premises; the food comes fast; and there are three kinds of shakes. And an entire meal costs less than $5 if you just order a burger and a cola. Don't expect anything resembling class or decor, but do expect some of the cheapest burgers in the city to taste better than you'd expect. Note: They don't take credit cards. Not that you'd need one.

Crif-Dogs (212-614-2728), 113 St. Marks Place between Avenue A and First Avenue. Subway: 6 train to Astor Place, or L train to First Avenue. Open daily noon–midnight Sunday through Wednesday, until 2 AM Thursday, until 4 AM Friday and Saturday. The other participant in Alphabet City's hot hot-dog rivalry (see Dawgs on Park, below)—and it *is* a rivalry, make no mistake about that—Crif-Dogs wins by a nose with better wieners, better toppings, a more relaxed atmosphere. The house smoked dog is tasty, a grilled all-beef frank snaps when you bite it, and the combination dogs available include the chihuahua (with bacon, avocados, and sour cream), a chili dog, a "sourcheese dog" of pickles and melted cheese, a bacon-wrapped BLT dog, and a good veggie dog with jalapeños and other grilled vegetables. It's very in tune with the oddball, slightly punk feel of the neighborhood, a bit friendlier than the other place—and they make

great burgers and shakes here, too, if you're somehow tired of perfectly grilled and fried hot dogs. You might even see a *real* dog here.

Dawgs on Park (212-598-0667), 178 East 7th Street between Avenues A and B. Subway: 6 train to Astor Place, or L train to First Avenue. Open Monday through Thursday 9 AM–11 PM, Friday and Saturday 9 AM–3 PM, Sunday 10 AM–10 PM. One of two big-name frank joints that duke it out in the vicinity of Tompkins Square Park, this is the slightly more upscale of the two, serving meat and vegetarian dogs with fancy accoutrements. There are also a few other oddball items such as Frito pies (a messy, inexpensive Tex-Mex snack built around corn chips), but stick with the wieners.

Dojo (212-674-9821), 24–26 St. Marks Place between Second and Third Avenues. Subway: 6 train to Astor Place. Open daily 11 AM–midnight, Friday and Saturday until 1 AM. One of what seem like numerous downscale Japanese eateries with sidewalk tables spaced out along a few blocks of St. Marks Place between Astor Place and Tompkins Square Park, Dojo has held its own for decades as a healthy East Village fueling-up stop. Expect stir-fried meals, chicken, tofu, rice, and the occasional burger, all delivered in a hectic atmosphere but at dirt-cheap prices.

🍲 **Flor's Kitchen** (212-387-8949), 149 First Avenue between East 9th and East 10th streets. Subway: 6 train to Astor Place, or L train to First Avenue. Open Sunday through Thursday 11 AM–11 PM, Friday and Saturday until midnight. Right on busy First Avenue, this little place epitomizes the best virtues of an ethnic eatery. It's bright, cheery, clean, and affordable, the food is both unique and tasty—and the cooking and atmosphere rise far above the hole-in-the-wall level; only the complete lack of pretense prevents this place from becoming a hot spot for the beautiful people. The kitchen cooks up a menu of inexpensive native soups, stews, *arepas* (corn cakes filled with meat) with sauce, handmade empanadas, shredded beef, grilled steak, chicken, and fish—and many entrées won't run you much more than about $5 per plate (though some cost as much as $13). Plus Flor's serves hearty breakfasts of eggs, coffee, and fried plantains. Accompany your meal with fresh corn pancakes and a glass of fresh mango or passion fruit juice, hot chocolate, or *guarapo* (sugarcane) served with lemon to cut the sweetness; dessert should be *quesillo* (similar to flan), rice pudding, *dulce tres leches cake,* or a piece of coconut pie. In an East Village already full of interesting places, this is truly one of the most unusual. There's now a second location at 170 Waverley Place in the West Village, as well.

Gnocco (212-677-1913), 337 East 10th Street between Avenues A and B. Subway: L train to First Avenue. Open Monday to Friday 4 PM–midnight, weekends 11 AM–4 PM. Gnocco, where all the chefs come straight from Italian cooking schools, is fast gaining a local following as a great place for a light meal or a snack; the signature dish here is the one the eatery is named for—a *gnocco* is a fried dough appetizer, topped with carpaccio-thin slices of meat. Simply delicious. You can also order a range of pasta dishes, such as *tubetti* with bacon; a cut of pork tenderloin; or

tuna. There's a list of wines and a set of pasta dishes and other entrées as well. However, the restaurant does not accept credit cards.

Kai Kai (212-420-5909), 131 Avenue A between St. Marks Place and East 9th Street. Subway: 6 train to Astor Place. Open Monday through Saturday noon–11 PM, Sunday for dinner only 5–11 PM. Everyone goes for the pad Thai at this busy, reliable Avenue A snack shop, where you can even eat alone at one of the tiny tables and watch the world go by—they won't care. The lunch bargain is a great deal for $4.50 (usually red curry chicken, *massaman* curry chicken, vegetarian pad Thai, or vegetarian red curry plus a rotating special such as stir-fried glass noodles with mushroom, onion, carrot, and scallion), and they've got good salads of grilled shrimp, spicy squid, and peanuty greens. Thai dumplings, skewers of chicken satay, and fish cakes make great starters, but really it's the pad Thai ($5–8) you should try as the main course; get it made with chicken, shrimp, crab, or even—wow—lobster, a great idea. Finish with an unusual dessert: There are only two choices, but both are very interesting—chicken puff pastry with onion and potato, or sticky rice with banana and black bean, wrapped inside a banana leaf.

Mama's Food Shop (212-777-4425), 200 East 3rd Street between Avenues A and B. Subway: F or V train to Second Avenue. Open Monday to Saturday 11 AM–10:30 PM. This East Village standard has attracted a loyal local following for its low prices (all entrées are $8) and rib-sticking meals of fried chicken, grilled chicken, salmon, meat loaf, and ribs. Each comes with one side dish such as dynamite mashed potatoes, macaroni and cheese, coleslaw, or honey-glazed sweet potatoes; you can purchase additional sides (broccoli with roasted garlic, say, or maybe couscous) for just $1 a throw. Desserts are also impressive—banana cream pie, a sweet daily cobbler, and big chocolate chip cookies, to mention just three. Only trouble? Get there too late and they might have run out of food; they only cook a certain quantity of it each day, and the good stuff's often gone long before the closing hour. (Of course, with more than a dozen side dishes each night, it's still unlikely you'll go home hungry.) If there's a particular dish you really want to try, simply get there early enough to ensure you won't be shut out. On nights when you don't have time for a full meal, cross the street and check out the offerings at the lighter-fare Stepmama instead (see below).

Old Devil Moon (212-475-4357), 511 East 12th Street between Avenues A and B. Subway: L train to First Avenue, or N, R, Q, W, 4, 5, or 6 train to 14th Street–Union Square. Open Monday through Friday, 5–11 PM, Friday to midnight, Saturday and Sunday for brunch 10 AM–4 PM and dinner 5 PM–midnight. This is the ultimate kitschy East Village eatery, with yard-sale decor, bright lights and bits of tinsel, even a Lionel train tooling around the bar; if you can handle the stimulation, the menu consists of hearty all-American portions of catfish, brisket, chops, ribs, po' boys, steak smothered with shrimp, and the like ($10–18), with side dishes of corn bread, mashed potatoes with gravy, macaroni and cheese, black-eyed peas, and more; the $10 early-bird dinner special—which includes a salad and dessert—is an outstanding deal. Brunch consists of the usual egg dishes and hotcakes, but also catfish, burgers, homemade biscuits, a Sicilian frittata, even hot cider in wintertime. It's not at all highbrow, but worth a look if you're craving something filling and offbeat. And of course they have beer—are you kidding?

Organic Grill (212-477-7177), 123 First Avenue between East 7th Street and St. Marks Place (East 8th Street). Subway: F or V train to Second Avenue, L train to First Avenue, or 6 train to Astor Place. Open Monday to Friday noon–10 PM, weekends from 10 AM. In a cute pastel storefront nearly lost amid the hubbub that is First Avenue, the Organic Grill dishes up some of the city's healthiest grub using organic, local, and artisanal products—even down to the wines and beers. Lunch or dinner might be roasted hummus, a big salad—the house specialty is citrus-marinated *arame* and *hijiki* over mesclun—omelets, veggie burgers, barbecued *seitan*, grilled eggplant caponata, or the $14 "macro meal," which includes a pot of tea, a bowl of miso soup, rice, marinated tofu, and other healthy stuff. On Saturday and Sunday the brunch items ($4–14 each) run to egg-and-tofu scrambles, French toast, waffles (with a maple-tofu whip, of course), eggs Benedict (served with a tofu hollandaise), or a "TLT": tempeh bacon, lettuce, tomato, and sprouts.

Paul's (212-529-3033), 131 Second Avenue between St. Marks Place (East 8th Street) and East 7th Street. Subway: 6 train to Astor Place, or L train to Third Avenue or First Avenue. Open Monday through Thursday 11 AM–midnight, Friday and Saturday 11 AM–1 AM. Depending on who you are, this place either has great kitschy atmosphere or none at all. Simply put, Paul's is an altar built to the hamburger. Sure, you can order other stuff here—turkey burgers, Philly cheesesteaks, fried chicken, and fish fillets—but the half-pound beef burgers ($4–9 each, extra for fries, lettuce, and tomatoes) are what you want; get anything from a simple cheeseburger to a burger on an English muffin to a chili burger, or go all the way with an Eastsider burger—a bacon cheeseburger with ham, mushrooms, tomatoes, and onions. A fried egg sandwich is a good breakfast choice, and there are plenty of fun side dishes such as gravy fries, onion rings, baked beans, and even garlic bread. Wash it down with a shake, a frosted (a shake with extra ice cream), or a root beer. (Disclosure notice: While confusion is understandable, I do not own this restaurant. Disclosure notice: wish I did.)

Stepmama (212-228-2663), 199 East 3rd Street between Avenues A and B. Subway: F or V train to Second Avenue. Open Monday through Sunday 11 AM–10 PM. The quicker version of Mama's Food Shop (see above), this is more a place for getting a take-out sandwich on the run—and once again everything is cheap and simply done. Tuck into a yummy sandwich ($3–7) of grilled chicken, roast turkey, grilled tuna, grilled catfish, egg salad, eggplant, or even portobello mushrooms, roasted garlic, and Brie (for fancy-food eaters). Or try the surprisingly popular potato-fennel soup, which is said to be good for upset stomachs. Any sandwich can be made with jerk sauce, too. There's always chicken soup, half-pound burgers, corn dogs, and a daily salad; even the drinks are fun—try pineapple limeade, ginger iced tea, Orangina, or a root beer.

Veselka (212-228-9682), 144 Second Avenue near the corner of East 9th Street. Subway: 6 train to Astor Place, or L train to Third Avenue. Open 24 hours. It's just a Ukrainian coffee shop, perched on sometimes bleak but fast-becoming-hip Second Avenue, and gets very mixed reviews; still, Veselka makes an interesting detour in your culinary wanderings. Expect heavy food—pierogi, blintzes, sausages, pancakes—and plenty of it for lunch, dinner, or brunch. The all-hours policy means you'll occasionally encounter a weird mix of club refugees, punk wannabes, and elderly Jewish folks speaking languages you couldn't possibly have studied in college.

Yakitori Taisho (212-228-5086), 5 St. Marks Place near the corner of Second Avenue. Subway: 6 train to Astor Place, or N or R train to 8th Street. Open daily 6 PM–3:30 AM. There are few places more authentically Japanese and fun than this crazy one—a sunken, unkempt bar where clumps of Japanese kids and tourists come to drink cheap beer, wolf down skewers of grilled meat, and just generally yuk it up. It's so much fun you can't believe you're in New York. Just don't expect elbow room or white-glove service.

Zum Schneider (212-598-1098), 107 Avenue C at the corner of East 7th Street. Subway: F or V train to Second Avenue, or L train to First Avenue. Open Monday through Thursday 5 PM–2 AM, Friday and Saturday to 4 AM, Sunday 1 PM–1 AM. Stumble onto this corner joint late at night, and you just might think you'd turned a dark corner in Munich and found a miraculous watering hole waiting to slake your thirst; it's that authentic. A genuine beer hall—except for the hip,

20-something all-American set frequenting it, that is—Zum Schneider serves a couple of dozen brews from all over Germany, plus a typically German bar menu of sausages, chops, and the like. If you're crazy for Deutsche beers (and you should be), make the trek out here.

COFFEE AND SNACKS Alt. Coffee (212-529-3333), 137 Avenue A between East 9th Street and St. Marks Place (East 8th Street). Subway: 6 train to Astor Place. Open daily 8 AM– 1:30 AM, Friday to 3 AM, weekends from 10 AM. This alternative coffee shop right across from Tompkins Square Park has a Bohemian feel throughout—think dogs, kaftans, unmade couches—and there are also a couple of computer terminals (not always working, mind you) available to check e-mail on the run. It's a good place for would-be Beat poets to scribble meaningful lines about the Tao while time slowly passes in a haze of coffee-fueled good feeling.

Café Pick Me Up (212-673-7231), 145 Avenue A between East 9th Street and St. Marks Place (East 8th Street). I'm not sure whether the name of this coffee shop refers to caffeine content or a singles meet-market, but either way it's an enormously popular and comfy place where locals meet, greet, drink, do homework on a laptop, and otherwise relax right across the street from Tompkins Square.

De Robertis Pasticceria (212-674-7137), 176 First Avenue between East 10th and East 11th streets. Subway: L train to First Avenue or 6 train to Astor Place. Open Monday noon– 11 PM, Tuesday to Sunday 9 AM– 11 PM. De Robertis been around for a century now (since 1904), so they

must be doing something right—and, in this case, "something right" means top-grade cannoli, biscotti, and coffee served to an always-changing mix of East Village students, artists, professors, hipsters, and professionals.

♠ **Ninth Street Espresso** (212-358-9225), 700 East 9th Street at the corner of Avenue C. Subway: L train to First Avenue. Open daily 7 AM–7 PM. There are few neighborhood coffee shops around better than this little one, Ken Nye's place perched a block off Tompkins Square Park. It's actually on the national radar for the owner's high-quality espresso and the coffeemaking tools and techniques he's constantly developing. Local folks, bike couriers, poets, hipsters, cops, dogs, unemployed playwrights, and the occasional lost tourist know that you can get top-rank espresso, superb doughnuts, and a range of other beverages, pastries, and light meal items here. Staff are super-friendly; it's a good place to have a sip and consider East Village life.

Juicy Lucy's (212-777-5829), 85 Avenue A between East 5th and East 6th streets. Subway: F or V train to Second Avenue. Open Monday through Friday 8 AM–10 PM, Saturday 10 AM–10:30 PM, Sunday 10 AM–9 PM. This tiny, colorful Cuban-themed café is just the place on Avenue A for a quick pick-me-up, whether that takes the form of a strong espresso shot (with an orange-slice kicker); a *café con leche;* a powerful mixed juice, energy drink, or smoothie; or one of the great Cuban or turkey sandwiches, wraps, or breakfasts of Cuban toast, cream cheese, and guava jelly. Nothing on the menu costs more than $6, and most of the items cost a great deal less.

Panya (212-777-1930), 10 Stuyvesant Street between Third Avenue and East 9th Street. Subway: 6 train to Astor Place, or L train to Second Avenue. Open Monday through Friday 7:30 AM–8:30 PM, weekends 8 AM–8:30 PM. If you're suddenly in the mood for the sort of special baked treats you can only get in Japan, Panya's the place for you. The exceptionally friendly staff serve tiny Japanese doughnuts, rolls, slices of green tea cake, green tea tiramisu, chestnut cream cake, potato croquettes, and the like. They also bake croissants, pumpkin cupcakes, brownies, Danish, and loaves of French bread, and they fix up sandwiches (including yakisoba and ham). Sip green tea, espresso, chai, Thai tea, refreshing barley tea, fruit soda, or juice; in summer they also make frozen sorbet- and shaved-ice-like concoctions. Everything costs $1–4.

Room 4 Dessert (212-941-5405), 17 Cleveland Place near the corner of Kenmare Street. Subway: 6 train to Spring Street. Open Monday to Thursday, 6 PM–midnight, Friday and Saturday to 1 AM. Pastry chef Will Goldfarb cut his teeth in a pretty unusual place: as sidekick to rash *experimenteur* Paul Liebrandt. As such, his inventions at this new dessert-only shop are outlandish yet delicious: for $7–12 per plate, you dig into to cheese plates, ice creams, cotton candies, jellies, and more in carefully orchestrated "flights" of desserts. Maybe everything won't be to your liking, but then again you'd hard-pressed to ever have this much fun at dessert again in your life. Quality wines, teas, and designer cocktails accompany.

Veniero's (212-674-7070), 342 East 11th Street between First and Second Avenues. Subway: L train to First Avenue or 6 train to Astor Place. Open daily 8 AM–midnight. A busy and popular East Village standby since 1894 (it even predates the nearby De Robertis, which is saying something), Veniero's does Italian pastries such as cannoli, sfogliatelle, and millefoglie better than most others in the city. They also sell truffles, cheesecake, gelati, tartufi, spumoni, and the like; wash it down with an espresso or cappuccino, or order one of their kicked-up coffees infused with a shot of anisette—or liqueur of your choice.

✳ Entertainment

THEATERS Classic Stage Company (212-677-4210), 136 East 13th Street between Third and Fourth avenues. Subway: 4, 5, 6, N, L, or R train to 14th Street–Union Square. This well-respected company operates a 180-seat theater just off Union Square; its mission statement claims that it "creates theater that looks forward by looking back." The company has garnered a number of off-Broadway awards for its productions of such classically inspired plays as *Antigone*, *The Mysteries*, and *Voyage Around My Room*.

Kraine Theater/Red Room (212-206-1515), 85 East 4th Street near the corner of Second Avenue. Subway: F or V train to Second Avenue. In the pretty, 100-seat Kraine Theater space, the newish Horse Trade Theater Group—which also operates the St. Marks Theater—presents a program of short festivals and other avant-garde work. The Red Room, housed on the same site, is even more experimental.

La MaMa E.T.C. (212-475-7710), 74A East 4th Street between the

Bowery and Second Avenue. Subway: F or V train to Second Avenue, or 6 train to Astor Place or Bleecker Street. A decaying brick front conceals three well-respected theaters, all founded by Ellen Stewart. Tickets generally run $12–20 per person.

♿ **New York Theatre Workshop** (212-780-9037 for information, 212-460-5475 for tickets), 79 East 4th Street between Second Avenue and the Bowery. Subway: 6 train to Astor Place. This attractive theater shucked its "tiny and experimental" label when the breakout play *Rent* opened here and began to attract a wider audience that eventually became a tremendous bigger-venue smash. Now it's one of the places producers—and fans—go to see what's fresh and new around the city.

♿ **Orpheum Theatre** (212-307-4100), 126 Second Avenue between East 7th Street and St. Marks Place (East 8th Street). Subway: 6 train to Astor Place. Once a hugely successful Yiddish-language theater, the Orpheum has seen a tremendous second life as an off-Broadway star thanks to the successful nine-year run of the trash-can-lid-banging, broom-swishing, pail-ringing cast of *Stomp,* which continues to play here. Tickets cost $30–60.

P.S. 122 (212-477-5288), 150 First Avenue between East 9th and East 10th streets. Subway: L train to First Avenue or 6 train to Astor Place. That's *Performance Space* 122. For more than 15 years, this public-school-turned arts space has been commissioning and presenting a wide variety of music, video, film, and theatrical work such as *Matt & Ben,* Mindy Kaling and Brenda Withers's hilarious sendup of Hollywood's golden boys of the moment, which they wrote and in which they also starred. But the same season also saw David Neuman's *Sentence*, in which Neuman's troupe strung together a series of sometimes odd, but always fascinating, dance sequences and dialogues.

♿ **Theater for the New City** (212-254-1109), 155 First Avenue between East 9th and East 10th streets. Subway: 6 train to Astor Place, L train to First Avenue, or N or R train to 8th Street. Four stages occupy this simple, big space that resembles a bunker from the outside; depending on the production, you might find yourself packed into a tight, small crowd or spreading out with several hundred other theatergoers. Several small companies rotate use of the space, and it has gained acclaim (and a Pulitzer Prize) for the quality of the writing that has taken its stages. This is also the location of the annual Lower East Side Festival of the Arts (see *Special Events*).

ARTS VENUE **St. Mark's Church in-the-Bowery** (212-674-6377), 131 East 10th Street at the corner of Second Avenue. Subway: 6 train to Astor Place. This church is much more than a church: For years it has been an eclectic performance space where poets read, dancers dance, and singers sing. Don't expect liturgical chants—many of the events and artists here have an international background or an activist tinge.

MUSIC VENUE **5C Café** (212-477-5993), 68 Avenue C at the corner of East 5th Street. Subway: F train to Delancey Street, or J, M, or Z train to Essex Street. Here in the nether reaches of Alphabet City, a café serving coffee, juice, smoothies, and pastries—part of the 5C Cultural Center—also showcases low-key jazz at the early hour of 5 PM each night. With just a $8 cover charge, this is an unbelievable deal—and you'll be out by dinnertime.

READINGS Nuyorican Poet's Café (212-505-8183), 236 East 3rd Street between Avenues A and B. Subway: 6 train to Astor Place or Bleecker Street. Latino and "slam" poetry made this place famous; the occasional film is screened here, too.

FILM AND MOVIES Anthology Film Archives (212-505-5181), 32 Second Avenue at the corner of East 2nd Street. Subway: F or V train to Second Avenue. This terrific little theater—formerly a courthouse—operates according to the idea that great independent films must be viewed and re-viewed many times; accordingly, it screens up to three films daily, often collections of work by little-known new directors or documentaries such as *Hidden Wars of Desert Storm* and *War Photographer.* There are two venues—the 200-seat Courthouse Theater and 66-seat Maya Deren Theater—as well a huge repository of documents pertaining to independent film. Tickets cost about $8 for adults, $5 for seniors and students.

CC Village East (212-529-6799), 189 Second Avenue at the corner of East 12th Street. Subway: L train to Second Avenue. This movie theater shows second-run or little-noticed but quality films, for about $11 per adult (discount for seniors).

Cinema Village (212-924-3363), 22 East 12th Street at Third Avenue. Subway: L train to Second Avenue, or N, R, 4, 5, or 6 train to 14th Street–Union Square. Like Village East, this theater also screens second-run and lesser-known releases. Tickets cost about $9 per adult, about half that for children and seniors.

BARS AND CLUBS McSorley's Old Ale House (212-473-9148), 15 East 7th Street between Second and Third avenues. Subway: F or V train to Second Avenue, N or R train to 8th Street, or 6 train to Astor Place. Open Monday through Saturday 11 AM–1 AM, Sunday noon–1 AM. This East Village staple is a great stop for a burger and a beer, but also for loads of Irish-pub atmosphere. The place comes by its history honestly: Some believe it's the oldest continuously operating pub in Gotham.

✳ Selective Shopping

Numerous **punk clothing shops** cluster along St. Mark's Place (East 8th Street) between Second and Third avenues, places with names like Trash & Vaudeville, Search and Destroy, and Religious Sex. If you're in the market for tattoos, piercings, or the sort of black, ripped fishnet clothing that looks like Halloween (or a Ramones tailgate party) year-round, come here. Slightly more respectable **used vintage clothing shops** congregate nearby, a few blocks east (toward Tompkins Square Park) on a stretch of St. Mark's between Avenue A and First Avenue; look for places with names like Physical Graffiti, Trash, Starfish & Jelli, and Consignment City, though these basement-level shops are quickly being crowded out by the raft of gourmet food markets, dessert shops, and other upscale spots that seem to have taken over the East Village almost overnight.

An active **flea market** operates at the corner of Avenue A and 11th Street on Saturday; here you'll find every sort of trash or treasure, depending on your taste. Expect plenty of used women's clothing, cowboy boots, furniture, bad 1980s CDs, and the like. The ethos here isn't so much punk as it is "vintage kitsch."

BOOKSTORE **St. Mark's Bookshop** (212-260-7853), 31 Third Avenue at the corner of East 9th Street. Subway: 6 train to Astor Place. Open Monday through Saturday 10 AM–midnight, Sunday from 11 AM. Right at the busy corner of Third Avenue and East 9th, St. Marks is a local institution and a wonderful place to pop in on a rainy day for an hour or two. You won't find a chain-store mentality here, but rather shelves and shelves of intelligent journals, magazines, under-the-radar poetry chapbooks, graphic design and photography books, essays and social critiques by the likes of Noam Chomsky, philosophy books, and other hard-to-find titles.

PRINTS **Pageant Print Shop** (212-674-5296), 69 East 4th Street between Bowery and Second Avenue. Subway: J, M, or Z train to Bowery. Open variable hours. After 5 years on hiatus, this print shop (which appeared in the Woody Allen film *Hannah and Her Sisters* while in its previous location) has reopened with a big collection of some 15,000 items. Run by two sisters,

it features anything from wonderful botanical prints to vintage lithographs, maps, views, ads, and postcards.

✳ Special Events

Late May: **Lower East Side Festival of the Arts,** early May at the Theater for the New City, 155 First Avenue between East 9th and East 10th streets. Subway: 6 train to Astor Place, L train to First Avenue, or N or R train to 8th Street. This annual festival celebrates the wacky, quirky personality of New York's funkiest neighborhood.

August: **Charlie Parker Jazz Festival** (973-377-6565), Tompkins Square Park at the corner of Avenue A and St. Marks Place (East 8th Street). Subway: L train to First Avenue, or 6 train to Astor Place. This festival has put on free jazz for 10 years. One Sunday in late August, a series of jazz players and combos takes the stage at Tompkins Square Park for a 5-hour jam beginning at 2 PM.

August: **Annual New York International Fringe Festival** (212-279-4488; www.fringenyc.org). For 2 weeks in August each year, this festival spreads over venues across downtown NYC, and especially the Lower East Side. Show tickets cost $15 each; one can also buy passes for multiple shows or days (Fiver Pass to Lunatic Pass). Billed as the largest theater festival in North America, it's an opportunity to see just about any kind of performance work you can imagine, from more than a dozen countries and a dozen states. The popular Broadway show *Urinetown, the Musical,* began at the Fringe; the festival also sponsors panel discussions and workshops.

NOHO

oHo (North of Houston) isn't a big area, yet it's very well known among young New Yorkers. (See map on page 86.) Some of the city's coolest addresses—Bond St, Indochine, the giant Tower Records shop, the Great Jones Café, the home of the Blue Man Group—have somehow wedged themselves into the district.

In this book, I have defined NoHo as a strip extending north from Houston Street to East 14th Street between Broadway, Bowery, and Fourth Avenue—a skinny area that begins just a few blocks wide, and then becomes even skinnier—just a block wide at Union Square.

GETTING THERE *By car:* Getting here from the north is the same as getting to the East Village. Broadway heads directly south into the neighborhood. Or you can take the FDR (East Side) Drive to the 23rd Street area, where you exit and funnel onto Avenue C; turn right at 14th Street. From the west side of town, use the West Side Highway (which becomes Tenth Avenue), Seventh Avenue, Fifth Avenue, or Broadway to get south. Then drive crosstown on 23rd Street or 14th Street, or a smaller cross street with an even number. Parking in NoHo can be difficult.

By subway: NoHo is bookended by Houston Street and Astor Place, so it's easy to reach by public transit. From the Upper West Side, Grand Central Terminal, Midtown East, Gramercy Park, or Lower Manhattan, take a 6 train to Astor Place or Bleecker Street. From Times Square and Midtown, the N, R, and W trains stop at 8th Street–NYU, two short blocks west of Astor Place. Or take an F, V, or S train from Midtown or the West Village to Broadway–Lafayette.

By bus: From the west side of town, the 6 bus travels south along Seventh Avenue and Broadway to NoHo; from the east side, the 1 bus (along Fifth Avenue and Park Avenue South) and the 2 and 3 buses (both along Fifth Avenue) also head south to NoHo. Crosstown buses are also useful here. The 8 bus shuttles back and forth along 8th Street and, in the East Village, 10th Street. The 14 bus dips in the neighborhood before shuttling along 14th Street all the way west to the Hudson River. The 21 bus shuttles along Houston Street.

✳ To See

MUSEUM Merchant's House Museum (212-777-1089), 29 East 4th Street between Cooper Square (the Bowery) and Lafayette Street. Subway: 6 train to Bleecker Street or Astor Place, N or R train to 8th Street, or F, V, or S train to Broadway–Lafayette. Open Thursday through Monday noon–5 PM. This slim, three-story brick Federal and Greek Revival building appears out of nowhere on East 4th Street. The interior decor of this 1832 building was left almost completely unchanged for a full century by the eccentric merchant family who lived there; the seven rooms contain what is, essentially, a snapshot of the early 19th century—including the family's own furniture, dishes, clothes, and all the rest of the articles of daily life. There's also a fine garden open in good weather. Admission to the house tours costs $8 for adults, $5 for students and seniors; on weekdays, you have to walk yourself around, but on weekends guided tours leave each half hour.

PUBLIC SPACE Astor Place, junction of East 8th Street, Lafayette Street, Fourth Avenue, and Cooper Square. Subway: 6 train to Astor Place or N, R, or W train to 8th Street–NYU. This intersection of roads is a favored gathering place for legions of New York University students thanks to its chain coffee shop, subway station entrance, and Kmart department store. On a small green island amid the traffic stands the sculpture called *The Alamo* (created in 1967 by artist Tony Rosenthal and more commonly known as *The Cube*)—a giant, heavy steel cube that perches delicately on one point, and rotates when a little force is applied to it. Just down the short street also known as Astor Place there's a bookstore.

✳ Where to Eat

DINING OUT Bond St (212-777-2500), 6 Bond Street between Broadway and Lafayette Street. Subway: F, V, or S train to Broadway–Lafayette, or 6 train to Bleecker Street. Open Monday through Saturday 6 PM–midnight, Sunday 6–11 PM. This expensive, posh restaurant immediately grabs your attention upon entry: The entrance looks like a catwalk, you'll feel like a luminary, and the waitresses are extremely attractive, too. The dining rooms are hip enough to qualify for club status; though this restaurant's in-moment has already passed, the occasional celebrity still flits in for a private meal. Entrées, priced at $20–25 each, run mainly to sushi. It can still be almost impossible to get a reservation at times here, so inquire about having a drink at the bar—you can eat there, too.

Five Points (212-253-5700), 31 Great Jones Street between the Bowery and Lafayette Street. Subway: F, V, or S to Broadway–Lafayette, or 6 train to Bleecker Street. Open Monday through Saturday noon–3 PM and 6 PM–midnight, Sunday for brunch 11:30 AM–3:30 PM and until 10 PM for dinner. Great Jones Street isn't exactly the best-looking street in New York—in fact, it looks a little ragged. But this pretty townhouse entrance conceals a fine restaurant with a splendidly tranquil interior decor characterized by light and water. Dinner consists mainly of grilled and oven-charred meats, while the good brunch is a NoHo draw.

Indochine (212-505-5111), 430 Lafayette Street between Astor Place and East 4th Street. Subway: 6 train to Astor Place, N or R train to 8th Street, or F, V, or S train to Broadway–Lafayette. Open daily 5:30 PM–midnight, until 12:30 AM Friday and Saturday. The fish and shellfish shine at this French-Vietnamese restaurant, where a pretty clientele dines on entrées that don't cost too much ($12–20 each, generally). The green interior of palm leaves evokes a tropical outpost, and the great spring rolls set the stage for a meal of small plates of seafood.

EATING OUT Acme (212-420-1934), 9 Great Jones Street between Broadway and Lafayette Street. Subway: 6 train to Bleecker Street, F, V, or S train to Broadway–Lafayette, or N or R train to 8th Street. Open daily 11:30 AM–11:30 PM, weekends to 12:30 AM, Sunday to 10:30 PM. This dinerlike Cajun eatery, tucked away on a short, grubby street of good eats, gets the prize for truth in advertising: "An okay place to eat. A great place to drink," declares the menu, and that is more or less true. The food is unspectacular, nowhere near as good as at the home-cookin' Great Jones Café (see below) right across the street. Trouble is, Great Jones is often mobbed; this makes a decent second choice when you need to fuel up, offering filling brunch specials (eggs, fish, browned potatoes, mimosas) and regular dishes that are unspectacular but caloric—the gumbo could be a lot better, but they do know how to fry a catfish in

cornmeal. The atmosphere is pretty good, with bottles of hot sauce lining the walls before an appreciative local crowd.

🦐 **Cooper 35 Asian Pub** (212-375-9195), 35 Cooper Square (Bowery/Third Avenue) at the corner of East 6th Street. Subway: N, R, or W train to 8th Street, or 6 train to Astor Place. Open Monday through Friday 4 PM–12:30 AM, weekends noon–2:30 AM. It's all about the food at this NYU-area eatery, whose menu—and interior decor—wavers uncertainly between lowbrow and highbrow. Once a Mediterranean place, it's now Asian—which the chef was and is. The kitchen mixes and matches entrées such as snapper, shrimp, and lobster, there are salad choices, and there's a pretty covered outdoor garden area for dining in warm weather. There's a club-like atmosphere at night, what with fruit-flavored martinis and private parties. But the incredible prix fixe dinner deal here is the don't-you-miss-it bargain, among the city's best deal in terms of value: It gives you a glass of wine, soup, salad, crabcakes ("better than before" report staffers), and dessert . . . for just $15!

Emerald Planet (212-353-9727), 2 Great Jones Street between Broadway and Lafayette streets. Subway: F, V, or S train to Broadway–Lafayette, or 6 train to Bleecker Street. Open Monday through Friday 9 AM–9:30 PM, Saturday noon–9:30 PM, and Sunday noon–7 PM. Wraps came and went pretty quickly, but energetic Emerald Planet is still standing thanks to a good assortment of freshly made offerings (and the nearby presence of New York University). Among the stars are the

Barcelona, with its paella-type filling of grilled shrimp, chicken, onion, peppers, and saffron; the New Orleans, with shrimp, mango salsa, and caramelized and green onions; and others reminiscent of Japan, Vietnam, Jamaica, India, Mexico . . . and Texas. There are also drinks—including those of the alcoholic variety, and a good selection of smoothies and energy drinks—soups, salads, side dishes (like a zippy ginger coleslaw), and cute desserts.

❧ **Great Jones Café** (212-674-9304), 54 Great Jones Street between Bowery and Lafayette Street. Subway: F, V, or S train to Broadway–Lafayette, or 6 train to Bleecker Street. Open Sunday through Thursday 5 PM–midnight, Friday until 1 AM, Saturday and Sunday also for brunch 11:30 AM–4 PM. Hard to find, and apparently grubby from the outside, the dingy orange Great Jones Café turns out to be one of the city's most interesting Cajun eateries. Best bets include such standards as po' boys (sandwiches of fried oysters or a rotating variety of other fillings between thick bread); jambalaya; gumbo; grilled rib-eye steaks; barbecued ribs; smothered pork chops; chicken roasted with honey-pecan glaze; and the always packed and noisy $8.95 weekend brunch of omelets, pancakes, and the like. The unpretentious (read: somewhat cramped) bar is wildly popular at all hours, too, with youthful types from the surrounding East Village neighborhood—perhaps because drink prices here are surprisingly reasonable. Elvis would have liked this place.

NoHo Star (212-925-0070), 330 Lafayette Street at the corner of Bleecker Street. Subway: 6 train to Bleecker Street, or F, V, or S train

to Broadway–Lafayette. Open Monday through Friday 8 AM–midnight, weekends 10:30 AM–midnight. This can't-miss place, on a busy corner of Lafayette Street, beckons you with its distinctive star and then surprises you with a host of unusual eats and late hours. The food here's a good bit fancier (and also more expensive) than it appears from the restaurant's exterior; try upscale burgers or sandwiches from the American menu, or a fresh stir-fry from the Chinese side.

✳ Entertainment

THEATERS Astor Place Theatre (212-254-4370), 434 Lafayette Street between Astor Place and East 4th Street. Subway: 6 train to Astor Place. This 300-seat theater is currently home of the Blue Man Group, the dynamic performance troupe made famous by a series of computer-chip ads; tickets to experience the bald blue trio's mixture of theater, percussion, paint, and other antics cost $55–65.

Bouwerie Lane Theatre (212-677-0060), 330 Bowery between Bond Street and Great Jones Street. Subway: 6 train to Bleecker Street, F or V train to Second Avenue, or S train to Broadway–Lafayette. Originally built as a bank in the 19th century, this pleasant, smallish (140-seat) theater is today home to the resident Jean Cocteau Repertory Company, which presents an interesting collection of productions of both classic and new works such as Chekhov's *Uncle Vanya*.

45 Bleecker Theater (212-253-7017 or 212-253-9983), 45 Bleecker Street between Bowery and Lafayette Street. Subway: 6 train to Bleecker Street, or F, V, or S train to Broadway–Lafayette. This theater, roomier than you'd expect, hosts innovative small off-

Broadway productions (sometimes with big names attached) such as the Bob Balaban–directed *Exonerated* about death-row prisoners or a play about RFK.

Joseph Papp Public Theater/New York Shakespeare Festival (212-539-8500), 425 Lafayette Street between Astor Place and East 4th Street. Subway: 6 train to Astor Place or N or R train to 8th Street. This theatre complex has presented a highly impressive lineup of award-winning productions over the past 35 years, including such Broadway-bound hits as *Hair*, *A Chorus Line*, *That Championship Season*, and the more recent *Take Me Out*. Founded in 1954 by Papp as the Shakespeare Workshop, the Public Theater's dramatic space opened in 1967 on Astor Place in the former Astor Library. It's also the site of the popular Joe's Pub music venue (see "Music Venue"), and is also known for putting on the free star-studded Shakespeare in Central Park at the Delacorte Theater (offerings include other works than just the bard's; see Central Park listings). It also offers intensive summer Shakespeare workshops.

OPERA 🎔 **Amato Opera Theatre** (212-228-8200), 319 Bowery between East 2nd Street and Bleecker Street. Subway: F or S train to Broadway–Lafayette, F train to Second Avenue, or 6 train to Bleecker Street. A family-owned, pint-sized opera house? You bet. Sally and Tony Amato's creation still presents the classic chestnuts (*Madame Bovary*, *La Bohème*, *The Barber of Seville*), as well as rarely seen works from Verdi and other composers, in an intimate setting just as it has done since 1948. As a bonus, about once a month the theater pres-

ents shorter versions of famous operas aimed at kids and families; these performances begin at 11:30 AM, last only 90 minutes in total (because kids are restless, right?), and cost just $15 per person.

MUSIC VENUE 🎔 **Joe's Pub at the Public Theater** (212-539-8777 or 212-239-6200), 425 Lafayette Street between Astor Place and East 4th Street. Subway: 6 train to Astor Place, or N or R train to 8th Street. Once a library, the Public Theater opened as performance space in the late 1960s. Today it contains no fewer than six spaces, including the famous Joe's Pub (a cabaret room hosting poetry readings, comedians, musicians, and musicals).

READINGS **Bowery Poetry Club** (212-614-0505), 308 Bowery at the corner of Bleecker Street. Subway: F train to Second Avenue, or 6 train to Bleecker Street. Along this desolate section of the Bowery, improvisational poetry is making a comeback. Readings are held nightly—sometimes costing $5–15 per person—and there is also a variety of poetry classes, drumming nights, comedy benefits, and poetry slam competitions.

FILM ♿ **Regal Union Square Stadium 14** (212-253-6266), East 13th Street at the corner of Broadway. Subway: L, N, Q, R, W, 4, 5, or 6 train to 14th Street–Union Square. Blockbuster films are screened here.

✳ Selective Shopping

BOOKSTORE **Strand Book Store** (212-473-1452), 828 Broadway at the corner of 12th Street. Subway: F, L, N, Q, R, W, 4, 5, or 6 train to

14th Street. Open Monday through Saturday 9:30 AM–10:30 PM, Sunday from 11 AM. This famous corner bookstore with the handsome face is the last remnant of what was once a long Booksellers' Row along Fourth Avenue in NoHo. The store, founded in 1927, still offers tons of selections— "18 miles of books," by their count— and they'll even rent or sell books to interior designers by the foot! There's also an annex at 95 Fulton Street in Lower Manhattan (212-732-6070).

FOOD AND DRINK Astor Wines & Spirits (212-674-7500), 12 Astor Place at the corner of Lafayette Street. Subway: 6 train to Astor Place, or N or R train to 8th Street. Open Monday through Saturday 9 AM–9 PM. Inside the same building as Kmart, this is one of the area's best places to grab wine, sake, or liquor. The "top 10 under $10" deal is perfect for NYU students—but you can take advantage of it, too. Regular tastings, promotions, and lectures add to the fun.

Greenwich Village

4

GREENWICH VILLAGE

Once little more than a marsh, and later the site of lucrative tobacco fields, Greenwich Village began building up as far back as the late 1600s, when the British took over what had been Dutch land. A kind of grid plan was laid out early on—well before Midtown's larger right angles were drawn up and plotted—but the neighborhood didn't really take off until the 1800s, when thousands of Lower Manhattan residents began moving north to the Village to escape the crowds.

Since that time it has attracted a concentrated mix of musicians, artists, and poets—not to mention Italian restaurants and cafés. New York University joined the Village in the 1830s, and its large, diffused campus—with more than 30,000 students, many of them resident in the neighborhood—has given the area a fresh shot in the arm. During the 1960s and 1970s this was *the* city headquarters for Beat poetry, folk music, Zen, street-corner philosophy, war resistance . . . and experiments with consciousness-altering substances.

The Village has gone considerably more upscale since the 1980s, a change that has dampened the district's Bohemian character somewhat but also brought a number of very famous resident actors and musicians to its confines (not to mention Ed Koch and the six perky sitcom characters on television's *Friends*). There are few harder tickets in town than a town house, condo, or great apartment here—everybody wants one, preferably on a tree-lined street. To see the best of the West Village's townhouse architecture, try strolling in the vicinity of Jane Street; West 10th, 11th, and 12th streets, between Fifth and Sixth avenues; the tight-knit warren of Bank, Barrow, Bedford, Charles, Grove, Morton, and Perry streets; or St. Luke's Place.

One of the more intriguing corners of this neighborhood in recent years has been the so-called Meatpacking District, a triangle of cobblestoned streets and industrial buildings that once served (and still do) as the chief entry port, storage area, and processing center for the tons of raw beef shipped into New York each year. Today the area is much better known for its weird juxtaposition of art spaces and delivery vans, late-night bistros and early-morning garbage trucks, pork packers and hip Asian restaurants. You have been warned.

If all that's a bit much for you, head instead for Bleecker Street. This is a good jumping-off point for the jazz clubs, record stores, coffee shops, and general funkiness that continue to make the Village one of New York's most intriguing

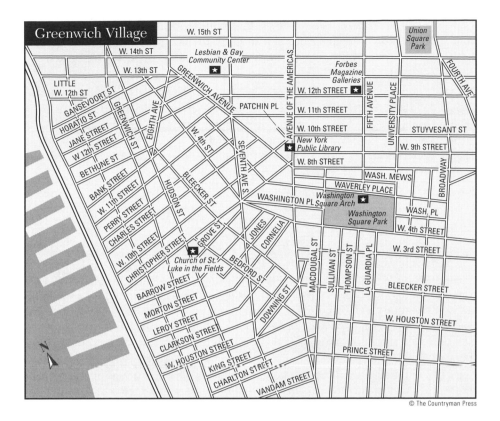

Greenwich Village

W. 15th ST

W. 14th ST

Lesbian & Gay Community Center ★

Union Square Park

W. 13th ST

GREENWICH AVENUE

Forbes Magazine Galleries

W. 12th STREET ★

LITTLE W. 12th ST

GANSEVOORT ST

PATCHIN PL

AVENUE OF THE AMERICAS

FIFTH AVENUE

UNIVERSITY PLACE

HORATIO ST

W. 11th STREET

JANE STREET

W. 4th ST

W. 10th STREET

STUYVESANT ST

EIGHTH AVE

W. 12th STREET

New York Public Library ★

W. 9th STREET

BETHUNE ST

SEVENTH AVE S.

GREENWICH STREET

W. 8th STREET

BROADWAY

BANK STREET

WASH. MEWS

HUDSON ST

WAVERLEY PLACE

W. 11th STREET

BLEECKER ST

WASHINGTON PL

Washington Square Arch ★

WASH. PL

PERRY STREET

Washington Square Park

CHARLES STREET

GROVE ST

JONES

CORNELIA

W. 4th STREET

CHRISTOPHER STREET

W. 10th STREET

★

MACDOUGAL ST

SULLIVAN ST

THOMPSON ST

LA GUARDIA PL

W. 3rd STREET

Church of St. Luke in the Fields

BEDFORD ST

BARROW STREET

BLEECKER STREET

MORTON STREET

DOWNING ST

LEROY STREET

W. HOUSTON STREET

CLARKSON STREET

W. HOUSTON STREET

PRINCE STREET

KING STREET

CHARLTON STREET

VANDAM STREET

N

© The Countryman Press

neighborhoods. If you've got time for only a quick tour, Bleecker—where a Bohemian influence predominates—is a good place to soak up the Village's general craziness. Wander down to the corner of MacDougal Street and you'll find yourself awash in a sea of camera-clicking tourists, Italian cafés, guitar stores, comedy clubs, Irish bars, used-record and vintage-clothing stores, and small folk and rock music clubs. West 4th Street is also good slice-of-Village life.

To sample the grunge, artiness, and culture of the Village, head for a short length of 8th Street from Broadway west to Sixth Avenue. Along the way you'll pass a tacky stretch of fast-food and cut-rate leather shops, then increasingly nice town houses, pocket fashion shops exhibiting the latest cutting-edge creations of small designers, and guitarist Jimi Hendrix's Electric Ladyland Studios. Afterward you can wander a block or two south and sit in Washington Square Park, contemplating all that you've seen—the strangeness, the counterculture, the row-house architecture, the pulse of what feels almost like a certain city—while buskers busk, dogs romp, and students sun.

GETTING THERE Take care not to get lost here; the West Village is one of Manhattan's most confusing neighborhoods—at one point crooked West 4th Street actually intersects West 12th Street.

By car: The area is easily accessible via the avenues; from uptown, Seventh Avenue and Greenwich Avenue run south through the heart of the West Village, while Broadway and Fifth Avenue run south through the heart of Greenwich Village.

By subway: The key station here is the big West 4th Street station, which can be reached via many subway lines. From SoHo, Lower Manhattan, Times Square, or the Upper West Side, take an A, C, or E train. From Rockefeller Center, Fifth Avenue, or the Lower East Side, take an F or V train. You can also reach the neighborhood by taking a 1 or 9 train from the Upper West Side, Times Square, or Lower Manhattan to Christopher Street.

By bus: The 5 and 6 buses run through the Village from both uptown and downtown; the 20 bus runs through the West Village, going north along Hudson Street and south along Seventh Avenue.

✳ To See

MUSEUM ♿ *Forbes* **Magazine Galleries** (212-206-5548), 60 Fifth Avenue at the corner of 12th Street. Subway: F, L, or V train to 14th Street, or N, R, Q, W, 4, 5, or 6 train to 14th Street–Union Square. Open Tuesday, Wednesday, Friday, and Saturday 10 AM–4 PM. One of Malcolm Forbes's legacies has been this outstanding free museum of his collections, which has been housed on the ground floor of *Forbes* magazine's headquarters since the mid-1980s. Though the amazing exhibit of a dozen Fabergé imperial Easter eggs has been sold (it was one of the world's largest such personal collections), there's also a substantial collection of jewelry, hundreds of toy boats, and more than 10,000 miniature soldiers—not to mention rare items from former U.S. presidents (a copy of Lincoln's Emancipation Proclamation) and some intriguing early sets of the board game Monopoly.

OUR LADY OF POMPEII CHURCH,
GREENWICH VILLAGE

Paul Karr

CHURCHES Judson Memorial Church (212-477-0351), 55 Washington Square South near the corner of Thompson Street. Subway: A, C, E, F, S, or V train to West 4th Street–Washington Square. This eye-catching brick church was founded in 1890 by preacher Edward Judson—with the help of Rockefeller and Astor money—as a progressive force to advocate for the city's growing immigrant class through education, health care, and similar programs. From those beginnings, it has also grown into something of a cutting-edge arts venue (you can experience dance, theater, music, art, and literary work here) as well as a center for peace activism, women's rights work, and the like. The design, by noted 19th-century architect Stanford White, is frankly a mishmash of Greek, Romanesque, Renaissance, and other elements, but the main building is undeniably solid and impressive; the attached tower—which reminds one of Italian campaniles—was added shortly afterward as low-cost housing for the poor. Judson was able to convince sculptor Augustus Saint-Gaudens to design some interior marble relief work, and artist John LaFarge did the stained-glass work.

The Church of St. Luke in the Fields (212-924-0562), 487 Hudson Street between Grove and Christopher streets. Subway: 1 or 9 train to Christopher Street. One of the prettier churches in the lower reaches of New York. Built in 1822, St. Luke's was long Catholic in denomination but has been Episcopal since 1976. A 1981 fire sadly gutted much of the church, but within 4 years it had been restored to something like its former glory; today the parish is well known in the local neighborhood for its AIDS work. There's a nice garden behind the church gate.

HISTORIC BUILDINGS ♿ **New York Public Library** (Jefferson Market branch) (212-243-4334), 425 Sixth Avenue between West 9th and West 10th streets. Subway: A, C, E, F, V, or S train to West 4th Street. New York's most whimsical and interesting-looking library stands directly (and distinctively) across Sixth Avenue from two gourmet food markets, coffee shops, and restaurants galore. Central Park designer Calvert Vaux built the library as a brick-and-stone courthouse in 1877, constructing a fire tower and adding a set of distinctive smaller turrets, pitched roofs, and arched, stained-glass windows. During the late 1960s the structure, by then empty, was converted into the West Village's main library.

Perry West (173 Perry Street and 176 Perry Street, at the corner of West Street). Subway: 1 or 9 train to Christopher Street. This pair of 16-story glass towers by modernist architect Richard Meier opened for business in 2003 just steps from Hudson River Park, and they're already among the most-talked-about buildings in Manhattan. Condos here are some of the city's hottest new

JEFFERSON MARKET, A DOWNTOWN BRANCH OF THE NEW YORK PUBLIC LIBRARY

Paul Karr

addresses (Calvin Klein and Nicole Kidman each reportedly shelled out millions for digs here), and a superstar-chef restaurant has opened in the lobby of #176. Some locals love the towers, which reflect gorgeous sunlight from the riverside, while others decry the contrast between the nearly see-through materials and height and the low-rise, reddish and brownish brick town houses for which the West Village is so famous. The back side of these buildings, as well, doesn't match the aesthetic of the glassy west facades. Meier is the architect who previously converted a Bell Telephone facility into the famous Westbeth artists space in the 1960s.

HISTORIC SITE *Gay Liberation*. Christopher Park, Seventh Avenue South between Christopher Street and Grove Street. Subway: 1 train to Christopher Street. These realistic bronze sculptures of two same-sex couples by George Segal were moved to Christopher Park—not nearby Sheridan Square Park, as it's sometimes mistaken for—in the heart of the Village's most famously gay street in 1991. A pair of women sit holding hands on a bench, while two men stand close together upright in the park. They're quite close to the former site of the Stonewall Inn, where city police clashed violently with gay and lesbian protesters in June 1969 after a raid on the gay bar at 51 Christopher. (Less historically significant, the statues also served as a backdrop for a scene in the Adam Sandler film *Big Daddy*.)

GAY & LESBIAN RESOURCES **New York City Lesbian, Gay, Bisexual, & Transgender Community Center** (212-620-7310), 208 West 13th Street between Greenwich and Seventh avenues. Subway: 1, 2, or 3 train to 14th Street, A, C, or E train to 14th Street, or L train to Eighth Avenue. Open Monday to Friday, 9 AM–10 PM. This former high school serves as kind of nerve center for Manhattan's gay and lesbian communities, specializing in the development of programs to fight substance abuse, educate gays and lesbians about AIDS, and treat those affected by its devastating toll. The center also operates a lending library, encourages gay and lesbian voter turnout, functions as a meeting place for activist and other groups, and curates a museum and archive. Its social programs include bingo, dances, talks, and exhibits. The meeting room—formerly a bathroom—decorated with Keith Haring murals is worthy of a visit alone; it's one of the few remaining places in the city where you can see original Haring public art.

NEIGHBORHOODS **Meatpacking District,** Gansevoort to West 15th Street. Subway: A, C, or E train to 14th Street, or L train to Eighth Avenue. One of New York's most intriguing and distinctive public spaces wasn't created by a plan at all, but rather by the forces of history and commerce. The so-called Meatpacking District, which stretches roughly from West 15th Street down to Gansevoort Street between Eighth and Tenth avenues, is a gritty mélange of meat trucks hauling carcasses late at night, neon, cobblestones, garbage, hip clubs, weird street characters, cool murals, bistros, and art galleries. It all finally comes together at the roughly pentagonal point where West 12th Street, Ninth Avenue, and Greenwich Street merge in a tense standoff; you can imagine a futuristic, *Mad Max* sort of duel taking place here. This district's out of the way, off the beaten track, and hardly beautiful, but for sheer atmosphere day or night it is a great spot to visit for a few minutes while in the nearby West Village. As a bonus, there are plenty of quality eateries such as Florent and the Little Pie Company (described in this chapter) within a stone's throw.

New York University (212-998-4636). Information center, 40 Washington Square at the corner of Wooster Street. Subway: N or R train to 8th Street, 6 train to Astor Place, or A, C, E, F, V, or S train to West 4th Street. Founded in 1831, NYU continues to dominate Greenwich Village and pump fresh life through its arteries each autumn: Its student body numbers more than 48,000 today (not

Paul Karr

THE WASHINGTON MEWS AT NEW YORK UNIVERSITY

all of them attend the Village campus, however). Some of the university occupies pretty, turn-of-the-20th-century brick buildings; much of it, however, is modernist and frankly jarring in contrast with the neighborhood's character—a point that has been sorely contended over the years by locals each time NYU plans a new structure. It's worth noting that two residence halls on Bleecker Street were designed by architect I. M. Pei, and the complex also includes a very large sculpture by Picasso.

✳ Green Space

🐾 **Washington Square Park,** between West 4th Street, Waverly Place, MacDougal Street, and University Place. Subway: A, C, E, V, or S train to West 4th Street. A distinctive thick marble arch (sometimes hidden behind fences while under repair) marks this huge rectangular park, plunked down almost right under the nose of NYU. Once an execution and burial ground (thousands of bodies lie beneath it), the park knew a brief moment of high-society cachet: Henry James's novel *Washington Square* marks that brief historic moment when New York's highest fliers lived around the square. Gradually it lost its luster, however, and became in time a gathering place for NYU students (NYU opened its doors just 4 years after the park was designated and opened to the public, and thus the two have been inexorably linked and entwined ever since), political activists, and the down-and-out. The square is sometimes still a bit dangerous at night when sketchy characters wander through, but most of the visitors today are simply idling students, sunning faculty, an amusing variety of local chess players, wannabe Beat poets, or guitar-strummers, and Frisbee-tossing dog owners. Expect impromptu jam sessions of "Proud Mary" and the like—with crowd participation—lots of 1960s-era tie-dyes, and lots of dogs: in short, a much more Bohemian crowd than the ones at, say, Madison Square Park or Gramercy Park.

✳ Lodging

BOUTIQUE HOTEL **Hotel Gansevoort** (212-206-6700 or 1-877-426-7386; fax 212-255-5858), 18 Ninth Avenue at West 13th Street. Subway: A, C, or E train to 14th Street, or L train to Eighth Avenue. This ambitious new project by Henry Kallan's boutique hotel group—responsible for some of Manhattan's most interesting properties, including the Giraffe, Library, and Elysée Hotels—is a 13-floor hotel, the first in the heart of the newly hip Meatpacking District. (Other hotels are scrambling to play catch-up.) From architect Stephen Jacobs and interior designer Andi Pepper (the same team responsible for the Library and Giraffe hotels), the new building is clad in zinc, canopied, many windowed, and marked by changing colored columns of light. Fully one-third of the rooms have a balcony, while the 20 corner suites are larger than average—they have living rooms. But every room offers high-speed Internet connections, two-line phones, and hair dryers, among other amenities. Sheets of translucent glass replace the usual boring hotel doors; bathrooms feature steel industrial-chic sinks but also Italian marble. The 45-foot rooftop garden and pool (with underwater music) are hot spots to mingle, and a full-service spa, three-level bar, and Japanese restaurant ratchet up the pleasure factor additionally. Rates range from $435 and up for double rooms to $675 and up for suites (but the duplex penthouse

is a cool $5,000 per night); check for frequent package deals.

AFFORDABLE HOTEL **Washington Square Hotel** (212-777-9515 or 1-800-222-0418; fax 212-979-8373), 103 Waverly Place between MacDougal Street and Sixth Avenue. Subway: A, C, E, F, V, or S train to West 4th Street. This nine-story, 160-room hotel on a townhouse-lined street kitty-corner from Washington Square Park, can't be characterized as a luxury hotel even if the lobby—of iron-work and marble—looks nice. In fact, as a former 1960s and 1970s hangout of boho crooners like Bob Dylan and his ilk, it's understandably lowbrow and low service. Still, you'll hear few complaints about these prices: Rooms come with minimal furnishing that is certainly adequate, and some have views of the square. Surprisingly, there's a small exercise room as well. Double rooms—with television in each—cost a lot more than they used to (figure around $200 a night), but a continental breakfast is included with all room rates and at least the location's good; jazz packages, combining a stay with nights at local clubs, are also offered.

BED & BREAKFASTS **Abingdon Guest House** (212-243-5384; fax 212-807-7473), 13 Eighth Avenue between Jane Street and West 12th Street. Subway: A, C, E, 1, 2, 3, or 9 train to 14th Street. This guesthouse—actually

a series of rooms inside two walk-up 19th-century town houses—is the West Village's best deal. It's upscale enough to feel comfortable even on a business trip (you'll feel like a resident of your very own Village apartment, actually), but it won't break your bank. Best of all, a stay brings modern conveniences you don't normally find in an inn—phone with answering machine, free local calls, hair dryer, air-conditioning, white-noise machine, cable television, daily maid service, and the like. Each of the nine rooms has been decorated with unique
character and good design sense: The quiet, green-themed Garden Room's queen bed is accentuated by a love seat, brick fireplace, and classy oval mirrors, plus views of a small, attractive garden courtyard. The Ambassador Room is bigger, with a four-poster king bed, love seat, kitchenette and wet bar, sitting area, and big tiled bathroom. The Martinique Room's four-poster comes with a canopy. (Upper-floor rooms offer fewer creature comforts but very high ceilings.) Most rooms cost $170–190 double occupancy, with the Ambassador costing around $245 per couple; bear in mind that there's no elevator, and that smoking is not permitted in either of the guesthouse buildings.

Larchmont Hotel (212-989-3333; fax 212-989-9496), 27 West 11th Street between Fifth and Sixth avenues. Subway: L, N, Q, R, S, W, 4, 5, or 6 train to 14th Street–Union Square, or F or V train to 14th Street. One of the cheapest decent hotels in the city, the Larchmont occupies a six-floor town house on an attractive little tree-lined street right off Sixth

Avenue's fancy-food shops, coffee shops, and restaurants. As for the hotel, though, it's not fancy at all—all the rooms share smallish bathrooms on the hall—but management does deserve some credit for keeping the place clean and trying to make the experience as pleasant as possible, outfitting the simple rooms with conveniences such as air-conditioning, slippers, robes, writing desk, and the like. Furnishing is minimal (think wicker), phones are provided, there's a sink in each room and a shared kitchen on each floor, and continental breakfast is included with the room rates; small libraries of books are also provided. On the other hand, guests might sometimes cross paths with building residents (it isn't just a hotel). Rooms cost just $99–135 double occupancy—weekends cost the most—with a surcharge for fax use, hair dryers, and umbrellas.

✳ Where to Eat

The Village contains an almost uncountable number of bistros, bars, taverns, diners, coffee shops, and fine restaurants—I could easily have written an entire guidebook covering them alone. Though they are by no means comprehensive, here are some of my choices for the finest dining, eating, and snacking experiences in this complex, fascinating section of the city.

DINING OUT **Babbo** (212-777-0303), 110 Waverly Place between MacDougal Street and Sixth Avenue. Subway: A, C, E, V, or S train to West 4th Street. Open Monday through Saturday 5:30–11:30 PM, Sunday 5–11 PM. Ponytailed superstar chef Mario

Batali, he of the television cooking programs and a small string of successful eateries around the city, opened this West Village star to express the country cuisine of Italy. Many devoted New Yorkers feel this is one of the city's best restaurants, and they might be right. In yellow-washed rooms touched up with subdued, elegant furnishings, start with one of the antipasti such as marinated fresh sardines, steamed cockles in red chiles and Thai basil, spicy quick-fried calamari in soup, or grilled octopus in a spicy limoncello vinaigrette. Primi (first courses of pasta, priced around $17–20 each) might include Batali's amazing goat cheese tortelloni with dried orange and wild fennel pollen, some goose liver ravioli, gnocchi with braised oxtail, or beef cheek ravioli with squab liver and truffles; his secondi (priced around $23–29 each) are more rib sticking, yet still complex and mature, from osso buco to grilled

quail to lamb chops. Some of the dishes even border on the dreamy, such as the kicky lamb sausages with mint "love letters" and a puree of sweet peas. To get a broader feel for the kitchen's reach, splurge on one of the tasting menus—one centers on pasta, one leans toward the more traditional Italian country cooking, and both are revelations. Finish with chocolate hazelnut cake, gelati, budino, or *semifreddo,* and thank your stars you were able to somehow book a table.

Da Silvano (212-982-2343), 260 Sixth Avenue between Bleecker Street and Houston Street. Subway: A, C, E, F, V, or S train to West 4th Street, or 1 train to Houston Street. Open daily noon–11:30 PM. This rustic, brick room (augmented by the cute and very popular sidewalk tables) draws famous faces galore for Silvano Marchetto's Tuscan and Florentine fare. Translation: Don't expect red-sauce and meatballs, but something much more spectacular (not that there's anything wrong with meatballs). A meal here begins with an appetizer such as grilled sausage with broccoli, crostini, carpaccio, or grilled shrimp. The first courses of pasta feature such things as penne with meat sauce or hot pepper sauce; *taglierini* (thin noodles) with sausage, cream, and peas in a tomato sauce; or rigatoni with a cream and tomato sauce of smoked bacon. Main courses run to items like veal chops, veal scaloppine, lobster, grilled steak with green peppercorns, osso buco, sautéed calf liver, and veal tripe. The wine list—it almost goes without saying—is fantastic. And if Jack Nicholson or Liv Tyler happens to show up at the next table, well, that's just icing on the cake.

WEST VILLAGE APARTMENTS

Paul Karr

Il Cantinori (212-673-6044), 21 East 10th Street between Broadway and University Place. Subway: L, Q, W, 4, 5, or 6 train to 14th Street–Union Square, or N or R train to 8th Street. Open Monday through Friday for lunch noon–2:30 PM, daily for dinner 5:30–11 PM. Actually closer to the East Village than the West Village, this pioneering upscale restaurant took the city's Italian cuisine in a completely new and different direction well before Mario Batali showed up. Today Il Cantinori still attracts a crowd of Hollywood lights, fashion designers, and models to its romantic room (which manages quite nicely to stand in for a Tuscan country farmhouse). The menu runs to the usual array of pastas, sausages, carpaccio, osso buco, chops, bistecca Fiorentina, game meats—only these things weren't the norm, not at all, when the place opened way "back" in 1983. Even if the food has slid, the fabulo vibe hasn't. Note that reservations are required.

Il Mulino (212-673-3783), 86 West 3rd Street between Sullivan and Thompson streets. Subway: A, C, E, V, or S train to West 4th Street. Open Monday through Friday for lunch noon–2:30 PM and dinner 5–11 PM, Saturday for dinner only. Almost everyone in the Village seems to feel that this is among the top two or three Italian restaurants in the entire city, so expect to pay a pretty penny and to need a reservation—actually, you may not be able to *get* a reservation for dinner, so try for lunch if you can't. Oh, the food is wonderful and not so complicated as to be unapproachable—scampi, risotto, and veal are some of the standbys—while staff are extremely dapper and profes-

sional. Question, though: How come they never answer the phone?

Knickerbocker Bar and Grill (212-228-8490), 33 University Place at the corner of East 9th Street. Subway: N or R train to 8th Street. Open Tuesday through Thursday 11:45 AM–1 AM, Friday and Saturday until 2 AM, Sunday until midnight. This wood-paneled room with plenty of Gotham memorabilia sees an elite, educated, often famous crowd of actors, writers, and others coming for live music, chef Jason Bunin's grilled steaks and other very good meals, and atmosphere. For lunch, start with yellowfin tuna sashimi, escargots, grilled chorizo with mesclun, or fried oysters with horseradish crème fraîche, then move on to a crabcake sandwich, an oyster po' boy, a Cuban sandwich, grilled lamb tenderloin, or braised short ribs (entrées about $7–15). Or just go for the famous steaks ($30). The dinner menu (entrées about $15–30) adds paella, seared scallops, pasta dishes, a rib plate, duck breast, pork chops, and the like. Thursday through Saturday nights there's live jazz, with a small cover charge after 9:45 PM. You want pedigree? Charles Lindbergh inked his deal to fly the ocean at the marble bar. And yes, that really is a Hollywood star wearing sunglasses at the next leather booth.

🐟 **Mary's Fish Camp** (646-486-2185), 64 Charles Street at the corner of West 4th Street. Subway: A, C, E, F, V, or S train to West 4th Street, or 1 train to Christopher Street. Open Monday through Saturday for lunch noon–3 PM and dinner 6–11 PM. It's a little hard to find, but Mary's is one of the Village's top seafood restaurants and possesses an extremely pleasing atmosphere on top of it. Owner Mary

Redding, who helped create the good Pearl Oyster Bar (see below) before a nasty split with her partner, has done a bang-up job of melding New England–style seafood with New York cool in this tiny corner joint. Go for the lobster—prepared either as a classic summertime lobster roll (my preference), as a whole boiled crustacean, in a potpie, or as a set of cold "knuckles" (chunks) in butter. Or if that's not your fancy, try something else nautical such as the clam chowder, conch chowder, oysters, scallops, or grilled snapper. Just want a sandwich? Mary's serves both a standard fried cod sandwich and one of peekytoe crabmeat. Afterward, desserts are sweetly down-home and simple, with nothing fancy at all about them to throw you off-kilter after the pleasingly rich seafood flavors of the main course. Mary's look is deliberately downscale, but don't let this fool you; the real characters come out of the woodwork at night, when the place gets even more packed (if that is possible) and takes on a happening feel. Yet the final bill will be surprisingly reasonable—entrées cost $7–24. You could pay much, much more in New York for food not half this good.

Mi Cocina (212-627-8273), 57 Jane Street at the corner of Hudson Street. Subway: A, C, or E train to 14th Street, or L train to Eighth Avenue. Open Monday through Thursday for dinner 5:30–10:45 PM, Friday until 11:45 PM, Saturday and Sunday from 4:30 PM, also Sunday for brunch 11:30 AM–2:45 PM. Almost everyone agrees that this redbrick corner restaurant serves New York's best upscale Mexican food, and it has done so since 1991. Jose Hurtado Prud'homme—he of roots in both the state of Veracruz and Guanajato— fires up a kitchen that's much more diverse than the usual beans-and-rice joint. Right from the get-go, appetizers show off Prud'homme's inventiveness and ability to introduce and interpret his native cuisine: Try a *caracoles* stew of snails in tomato, garlic sauce, and wine; small empanadas filled with beef, raisins, and olives; or the special guacamole recipe. Main courses include chicken cutlets marinated in lime, oregano, and agave tequila, shrimp in a tomato-wine-chipotle sauce, and mole poblano enchiladas from a family recipe. (There's also a healthy selection of margaritas and tequilas with which the uneducated can wash it all down.) The decor is right: Fun wooden chairs sport bright Aztec back designs, and masks and original Mexican art hang on the walls. And brunch (a buffet deal)—which includes huevos rancheros, enchiladas, and fajitas, of course—also reaches out to embrace regional specialties such as *chilaquiles*, Mexican omelets, tripe soup, banana pancakes with caramelized goat milk, and *cazuela de calabacitas* (a zucchini casserole of corn, onions, tomatoes, and poblano chiles).

North Square (212-254-1200), 103 Waverly Place (West 7th Street) between MacDougal Street and Sixth Avenue. Subway: A, C, E, F, V, or S train to West 4th Street. Open Monday through Friday for breakfast 7:30–11 AM, lunch noon–3:30 PM and dinner 5:30–10:30 PM, Saturday for lunch from 12:30 and dinner, Sunday for brunch 11:30 AM–4 PM and dinner. The Washington Square Hotel's North Square restaurant (formerly known as C3) serves three meals daily. Lunch and dinner entrées are New American but lean toward Latin American influences. Lunch might be a seafood paella or some pan-seared shrimp and scallops with couscous and a coconut sauce. For dinner, start with a grilled sausage plate (of Hudson Valley sheep cheese, *merguez*, marinated onions and tomatoes, and garlic bread); tuna tartare; a kicky lobster-and-artichoke tamale (with chili sauce and crème fraîche); or the foie-gras-and-mushroom ravioli. Then segue to interesting dinner entrées such as grilled arctic char, pan-roasted lobster, grilled quail, cioppino, spice-rubbed grilled pork chops, a tortilla-crusted snapper with corn flan and pear butter, saddle of lamb, roast chicken with quinoa salad, or some simple egg noodles with vegetables, pesto, feta, and lemon oil. The popular Sunday jazz brunch offers all the usual suspects (eggs, Canadian bacon, challah French toast), but also a few surprises such as pumpkin-pecan pancakes, chicken quesadillas, a citrus-cured salmon plate, and seared lobster and shrimp cakes. Lunch entrées cost $7–15, while dinner items run $14–25 each.

One If By Land, Two If By Sea (212-228-0822), 17 Barrow Street (between Seventh Avenue South and West 4th Street). Subway: 1 train to Christopher Street. Open daily for dinner 5:30–11 PM. Located inside the oldest building in Manhattan that contains a restaurant, this is the city's single most romantic eatery—little wonder that it's hard to get a table. The place is so debonair that there's no real sign at all, just a sign on the outside of a pretty carriage house with the street number (17) and a small posted menu; tables are decked with fresh roses, chairs are formal and

comfortably worn, fireplaces crackle and glow. To the tinkling ivories of a pianist, perhaps over a drink at the bar (see *Bars and Clubs*), you look over the menu—there's only a choice of a three-course prix fixe, in several incarnations—and select from among appetizers of raw seafood, gnocchi, foie gras, or mushroom tart.

Then you settle into your table in one of the handsome rooms (one facing a garden, one facing the little street, one on an upper level) while executive chef Gary Volkov (formerly of FireBird) brings out his artful entrées. They could include beef Wellington, arctic char, crisped Muscovy duck served with figs, artichokes, and lemon sauce, seared sea scallops with a cauliflower risotto, spice-roasted monkfish, smoked rack of pork, and rack of lamb. For dessert, you must choose again—crème fraîche panna cotta (with passion fruit sorbet), spiced pumpkin brioche, chocolate fondant with cherry ice cream, chocolate soufflé, or perhaps a cheese plate. Few go home unbewitched. The house is steeped in American history, too: Star-crossed Aaron Burr once owned the estate to which it belonged (in fact, he used this building as a carriage house for his horses), as did John Jacob Astor, before the original mansion here was renovated, gutted, and relocated.

❧ **Pastis** (212-929-4844), 9 Ninth Avenue at the corner of Little West 12th Street. Subway: A, C, or E train to 14th Street, or L train to Eighth Avenue. Open daily 9 AM–2 AM, weekends until 3 AM. All-night Parisian-style bistros are all the rage in New York these days, but owner Keith McNally (he of the wonderful Balthazar bakery-brasserie in SoHo) gets it right more often than the others with Pastis. Here, food isn't sacrificed for atmosphere, yet it's all affordable, filling, and quite delicious. The menu mostly runs to pleasingly simple $10–15 meals of *steak frites, croque-monsieur,* and the like, though you can also order more expensive entrées such as leg of lamb. Expect to see a familiar famous face from time to time, too, and don't miss the brunch—it's much better than it has to be, with plenty of seafood choices taking center stage.

Pearl Oyster Bar (212-691-8211), 18 Cornelia Street between Bleecker and West 4th streets. Subway: A, C, E, F, V, or S train to West 4th Street. Open Monday through Friday for lunch noon–2:30 PM and dinner 6–11 PM, Saturday for dinner only. A kind of upscale Maine fish shack, Pearl's is most renowned around the Village for the tiny bar that gives it its name. And indeed, you can find some of the city's freshest oysters here. But being relegated to a table isn't such a bad fate, really; you can slurp clam chowder or P.E.I. mussels, crack lobsters, and fork up tender grilled fish here, too— or just gorge yourself on the many small plates. Owner and chef Rebecca Charles (formerly of Maine's White Barn Inn) sought to duplicate the colors and flavors of the southern Maine coast, and she's done that with her lobster rolls, whole lobsters sided with corn pudding, pan-roasted sea scallops, and blueberry crumble pie. You also can go with fancier items such as smoked salmon with johnnycakes and crème fraîche; everything's good, and you won't break the bank.

❦ **Philip Marie** (212-242-6200), 569 Hudson Street at the corner of West 11th Street. Subway: 1 train to Christopher Street. Open Tuesday through Friday noon–11:30 PM, Saturday and Sunday 10 AM–4 PM and 5– 11:30 PM. Chef John Greco, who once cooked at legendary Italian restaurants San Domenico and Torre di Pisa, runs the kitchen at this red-painted, New American corner bistro. Together with his wife (her middle name is Marie, hence the name), Greco turns out filling and delicious lunches of grilled tuna, pasta, burgers, steak sandwiches, and meat loaf, and dinners starting with smoked fish, crab-cakes, fried green tomatoes, and fresh cheese-nut-fruit salads with good homemade dressings leading into entrées of lobster ravioli, big chicken potpie, steaks, chops, planked salmon, lamb, and more. There's jazz several times weekly, and a super-romantic single wine table in the cellar where you and your loved one can partake of a four-course, completely private candlelit meal for about $175. Folks book this room up months (even a year) in advance for popping the question and the like, though, so don't waltz in expecting it to be available.

Sushi Samba 7 (212-691-7885), 87 Seventh Avenue at the corner of Barrow Street. Subway: 1 train to Christopher Street. Open daily noon–2 AM, Sunday to midnight. Immortalized on the popular HBO series *Sex and the City,* this multicolored place is becoming legendary for its outrageous combination of top-shelf sushi (even Japanese diners proclaim it tops, which tells you something) and Latin American food and music: All things considered, it's got to be one of New York's most entertaining eateries. Once you've worked past the sofas in the waiting area, you'll find a modern interior; as Latin music is piped over the PA, you begin with fruity cocktails if you like, then move on to the amazingly fresh raw fish. No matter what you get (tuna and yellowtail sashimi are terrific choices, as is the four-fish sampler), the chef will pick out the day's best for you—among some of the finest in the city, according to devotees. Latin-inclined diners can veer over to the good ceviches, either in the form of a tasting platter or à la carte (choices include octopus in Dijon mustard and miso and lobster in mango and lemon juice). Other Latino entrées include sea bass and mahimahi—or you could wait until Sunday for the justifiably famous "samba brunch." Desserts are all Latin and mostly outstanding: Try mango mousse, a chocolate tamale, coconut panna cotta with mango coulis, or roasted bananas. In summer a rooftop patio opens for dining, ratcheting up the fun even further (as if this place needed it), and the backlit bar is very cool as well. It's not an inexpensive place to dine, however, so bring the plastic. There's another location in the Gramercy Park–Union Square area (see chapter 5).

Tomoe Sushi (212-777-9346), 172 Thompson Street between Bleecker and West Houston streets. Subway: 1 train to Houston Street. Open Wednesday through Saturday for lunch 1–3 PM and dinner 5–11 PM, Monday and Tuesday for dinner only. Just half a block from the official SoHo line (Houston Street), this tiny sushi joint is unbelievably popular among the local professionals who fill the surrounding town houses and apartment buildings; any night of the week you might find a line of surprisingly patient New Yorkers waiting on the sidewalk. Inside, the enormous

hunks of raw fresh fish take center stage. This certainly isn't the fanciest place in New York to eat sushi, but ask a local—it's simply one of the best.

Wallsé (212-352-2300), 344 West 11th Street at the corner of Washington Street. Subway: 1 train to Christopher Street. Open daily for dinner 5:30 PM–midnight, weekends for brunch also 11:30 AM–3 PM. Austrian cuisine is fast becoming a star in Manhattan, and few do the style as well as Wallsé's Kurt Gutenbrunner. You can expect to find Wiener schnitzel and other wheels-on-the-road Viennese specialties on the menu, of course, but the chef also displays a surprisingly light and creative hand with the fish plates, meat salads, and his dessert menu. Think of it as New Austrian, and be glad you gave it a whirl.

EATING OUT A Salt & Battery (212-691-2713), 112 Greenwich Avenue between West 12th and West 13th streets. Subway: A, C, or E train to 14th Street, or L train to Eighth Avenue. Open daily 11 AM–10 PM. Missing Great Britain? New York's top fish-and-chips shop sits right next to an affiliated storefront selling tea and other British goods. The chippie—which seems actually to be staffed by Aussies at times, but no matter—fries up perfectly coated codfish and haddock cuts, sides them with thick fries (the "chips"), then pours you a British beer if you want one in a minuscule space of just a few stools. Other menu choices include a giant battered banger; the horrible-sounding (but semihealthy) deep-fried beets; a combo plate of fried scallops, shrimp, and cod; or potato dabs. Wash 'em down with an apple Tango soda, a Boddingtons beer, or a bubblegum-flavored and hopped-up can of IRN BRU soda from Scotland. Finish with the fried Mars bar. Really. There's now a second location in the East Village (see chapter 3), too, with a larger menu.

Blue Ribbon Bakery (212-337-0404), 33 Downing Street at the corner of Bedford Street. Subway: A, C, E, V, or S train to West 4th Street, or 1 train to Houston Street. Open daily noon–midnight, weekends 11:30 AM–2 AM. Run by the same Bromberg brothers who operate Blue Ribbon and Blue Ribbon Sushi in SoHo, this amazing brick bakery dishes up much more than just bread (although the bread and cookies *are* quite good). You can order moderate or expensive—but always delicious—snacks, small plates, and meals such as a cheese selection, duck, steak tartare, innovative sandwiches, and smoked fish. Weekend brunch here is a true

CAFFE TORINO ON WEST 10TH STREET

Paul Karr

Village event set to throbbing dance music, but since the bakery won't take reservations you'll need to arrive early to snag a seat; everyone and his or her roommate wants to be here, too. There's even a small and hip bar with good European import beers on tap.

Café Loup (212-255-4746), 105 West 13th Street between Sixth and Seventh avenues. Subway: F, V, 1, 2, or 3 train to 14th Street, or L train to Sixth Avenue. Open weekdays for lunch noon–3 PM and dinner 5:30–11:30 PM, dinner only until midnight Saturday, brunch only noon–3:30 PM Sunday. In an everlastingly popular French bistro—one that actually feels classy and roomy, for a change—chef Lloyd Feit cooks with organic produce and fresh ingredients. Entrées, priced $12–20 apiece, run to delicate fish dishes, steaks, and upscale burgers, as well as more authentically French country meals. The dimly lit room sometimes sees famous faces from the neighborhood dropping by for a bite.

♣ **Caffe Torino** (212-675-5554), 129 West 10th Street between Greenwich Avenue and Seventh Avenue South. Subway: A, C, E, F, V, or S train to West 4th Street, or 1 train to Christopher Street. Open daily for dinner 5 PM–midnight. One of the Village's best dinner deals can be found in this little café, whose kitchen serves up uninspired but satisfying northern Italian fare.

Cent'Anni (212-989-9494), 50 Carmine Street between Bedford and Bleecker Streets. Subway: A, C, E, F, V, or S train to West 4th Street. Open Monday through Friday for lunch noon–2:30 PM and dinner 5–11 PM, weekends for dinner only 5–11 PM. This tiny but very good trattoria serves Italian food to crowds of appreciative locals, who come for pastas but also for Italian country cooking such as steaks, stews, and game dishes. Just don't expect a lot of room to spread out.

🦞 **Chez Brigitte** (212-929-6736), 77 Greenwich Avenue between Bank Street and Seventh Avenue South. Subway: A, C, E, 1, 2, 3, or 9 train to 14th Street, or L train to Eighth Avenue. Open daily noon–10 PM. This tiny place just keeps turning out great French comfort food for the people at a fraction of what the big stars are charging for much fancier, harder-to-decipher food, and although you'll never be surprised or awed here, it's still a legend among Village regulars. Owner Brigitte Catapano, a native of Marseilles, France, founded this place in 1958, vowing to keep prices low and meals hearty; though she's passed on, the same ethos prevails in a shoe-box-sized space (it seats just 11) that occasionally requires creativity and cooperation from the patrons. The menu's quite simple in reach— just omelets; spaghetti; various beef, veal, and chicken stews; salads; hearty sandwiches (basically stews packed into French bread); and a changing daily special of turkey, pork chops, leg of lamb, or veal in white wine. The outstanding-value $8 full lunch specials include soup or salad, potatoes, a beverage, and a choice among beef stew, veal stew, roast chicken, chicken parmigiana, fillet of sole, and several other meaty entrées.

Chumley's (212-675-4449), 86 Bedford Street between Barrow Street and Grove Street. Subway: 1 train to Christopher Street. Open Monday through Thursday 4 PM–midnight,

Friday and Saturday noon–1:30 AM, Sunday 3 PM–midnight. This is such a locals' place that *both* of its entrances, around the corner from each other, are unmarked! Once you step down into the dining room, however, it's clear that the neighborhood appreciates it. Brunch is the big draw, with a $13 prix fixe that gets you a choice of scrambled, poached, or fried eggs (with smoked salmon, if you like), a big burger with all the fixings, eggs Benedict, or an omelet—plus one drink, a beer or cocktail if you want.

🦞 **Corner Bistro** (212-242-9502), 331 West 4th Street at the corner of Jane Street. Subway: A, C, or E train to 14th Street, or L train to Eighth Avenue. Open daily 11:30 AM–4 AM, Sunday from noon. New Yorkers rarely agree on much of anything, but nearly all those who've made the burger rounds of the city seem to agree on this: Corner Bistro, a neon-marked eatery on a corner of pretty Jane Street, cooks the best burger in Manhattan. That's why there can be a long line of hip local Villagers snaking through the packed restaurant almost anytime—even late on a Sunday night—drinking cocktails or longnecks to pass the time. Don't bother with anything on the menu but the thick $5 hamburgers, accompanied by a cold draft.

Deborah Life Love Food (212-242-2606), 43 Carmine Street between Bedford Street and Bleecker Street. Subway: A, C, E, F, V, or S train to West 4th Street. Open Tuesday through Sunday, 11 AM–11 PM. Never-predictable chef-owner Deborah Stanton has come back to New York (and earth) with this down-home eatery in the West Village. Expect middle-American staples such as pork chops, meat loaf, sandwiches, burgers and fries, fruit pies, and the like—but always cooked with a bit of an upscale or world-cuisine twist and an eye toward health.

DoSirak (646-336-1685), 30 East 13th Street between Fifth Avenue and University Place. Subway: L, N, Q, R, W, 4, 5, or 6 train to 14th Street–Union Square. Open Monday through Saturday noon–10:30 PM, Sunday from 5 PM. This Japanese-run place serves a very unusual menu, half of it completely based on sweet potatoes (which are far more appreciated—and creatively used—in that country than they are here), the other half focused on simple and cheap Korean dishes, most featuring noodles. They don't take credit cards.

Florent (212-989-5779), 69 Gansevoort Street between Greenwich and Washington streets. Subway: A, C, or E train to 14th Street, or L train to Eighth Avenue. Open daily 24 hours. You have to work (or pay a cabbie) to find this out-of-the-way Meatpacking District bistro-diner, but once here you'll drink in a scene that goes around the clock. Good basic—and surprisingly inexpensive—French meals like decent *steak frites* or fat mussels, paired with bottles of quite affordable wine, form the backdrop; but the real reason to come is for the conversations surrounding your dining table. Whether it's the overdramatic waitstaff, the street and club life filtering in at all hours (on weekends the place often gets busier after midnight), or the aspiring modelette waiting out her next photo shoot with a cigarette, you'll find it a mighty interesting slice of New York. Note that they do *not* accept credit cards.

Garage Restaurant & Café (212-645-0600), 99 Seventh Avenue South at the corner of Grove Street. Subway: 1 train to Christopher Street. Open daily noon–4 PM and dinner 5 PM–1 AM, Friday and Saturday until 2 AM. Yes, this Village standby is housed in a former garage—but the space was also a former off-Broadway theater that launched the careers of a number of Hollywood stars. It's since been retrofitted into a hip, bistro-type eatery of exposed rafters, red leather banquettes, brick walls, wooden floors, a balcony, and a fireplace; locals come for the nightly jazz and weekend jazz brunches (there's never a cover charge), or to sip cocktails or one of more than a dozen microbrewed beers at the bar. Dinner entrées, priced around $10–26 apiece, are straightforward: lobster sandwiches, grilled steaks and fish dishes, scampi, rigatoni with Italian sausage, and the like. The lunch menu, with items priced around $14–20 each, is shorter and simpler but does include *steak frites.* There's also a raw bar here. The inexpensive jazz brunch features vanilla-bean-flavored French toast (with optional macadamia nut, coconut, and rum butter) and the usual assortment of eggs, omelets, and burgers.

Gray's Papaya (212-260-3532), 402 Sixth Avenue at the corner of 8th Street. Subway: A, C, E, F, V, or S train to West 4th Street. Open 24 hours. There's no better hot dog in the West Village than the cheap ones grilled up by this Gray's Papaya branch, an offshoot of the frank chain that began uptown and has slowly spread. This location does a pretty brisk all-day business serving locals, tourists, and even the occasional panhandler; scrumptious onions and other toppings add a kick to the already terrific wieners, while fruity papaya, orange, pineapple, and coconut drinks only enhance the experience. Understandably, though, the countermen here cannot accept credit cards; they're too busy barking orders, taking cash, and keeping the line moving to wait for Mr. Visa.

Greenwich Village Bistro (212-206-9777), 13 Carmine Street between Bleecker Street and Sixth Avenue. Subway: A, C, E, F, V, or S train to West 4th Street. Open daily 10 AM–11 PM, Friday and Saturday until midnight. More than just a bistro, the GVB features a surprisingly light-on-its-feet menu: the $5–12 lunch menu includes anything from meat loaf or Texas barbecue to burgers and even Japanese breakfasts of salmon, egg, rice, nori, and pickled plum; wash it all down with a milk shake or an egg cream. Dinner is more elaborate. But what really sets the place apart from some other bistros in the area is the acoustic and jazz music schedule; check ahead for the night's performance.

Hog Pit BBQ (212-604-0092), 22 Ninth Avenue at the corner of 13th Street. Subway: A, C, or E train to 14th Street, or L train to Eighth Avenue. Open Monday 5 PM–4 AM, Tuesday through Sunday noon–4 AM. For down-home barbecue in Manhattan, there are few better options than the Hog Pit, which is appropriately located in a semigrungy industrial neighborhood. Expect Harley riders, truck drivers, and a fair share of Manhattanites who only *wish* they drove trucks and rode Harleys. Go for the ribs or fried chicken, and don't forget a bottle of the cheapest possible beer. Needless to say, there's no dress

code—in fact, you might get tossed out *for* wearing a tie.

Home (212-243-9579), 20 Cornelia Street between Bleecker Street and West 4th Street. Subway: A, C, E, F, V, or S train to West 4th Street. Open daily 11:30 AM–4 PM and 5–10 PM. At Home you'll find hearty country meals of chicken, steak, and fish tricked up, as is the trend these days, with specially made sauces and toppings. It's high-grade comfort food, extremely well done. The interior decor here is soothing (it really does look something like a farmhouse), too, though hardly spacious.

❧ Hudson Corner Café (212-229-2727), 570 Hudson Street at the corner of West 11th Street. Subway: A, C, or E train to 14th Street, or L train to Eighth Avenue. Open Monday through Thursday noon–11 PM, Friday until midnight, Saturday 11:30 AM–midnight, Sunday 11:30 AM–10 PM. The Hudson Corner Café is sort of like a diner—a really, really good diner where the kitchen actually cares about the food it's putting out on the tables. It's big, uncomplicated food, but tasty nonetheless—think meat loaf (regrilled after cooking, as is becoming the fashion in New York), pork chops, and the like. It's also a great place to watch the world go by.

❧ 'ino (212-989-5769), 21 Bedford Street between Downing Street and Sixth Avenue. Subway: 1 or 9 train to Houston Street. Open Monday through Friday, 9 AM–2 AM, Saturday and Sunday 11 AM–2 AM. Little 'ino isn't one of Mario Batali's side projects, but it's almost one: The proprietor is Batali's coconspirator at Lupa (see below). And this tiny eatery is very good at doing what it does—serving panini and other Italian-style sandwiches to appreciative knots of Villagers. You can get anything from a cured-ham sandwich to a vegetable or a chocolate sandwich, and while the prices might be a bit high, you'll never go back to your hotel hungry or unsatisfied. Also don't miss a glass of wine or a quick shot of quality espresso, preferably bolted down Italian-style while standing up.

☙ **John's Pizzeria** (212-243-1680), 243 Bleecker Street at the corner of Jones Street. Subway: A, C, E, F, V, or S train to West 4th Street, or 1 train to Christopher Street. Many a New Yorker proclaims this pizzeria to be the city's very best, and its distinctively charred brick-oven pies have been a staple of Village life since the 1920s. Woody Allen shot a scene here for his film *Manhattan.* All you want is a whole pizza, divided among good friends, and maybe a beer. There are now other locations in Midtown West, the Upper West Side, and the Upper East Side, but this one—if not the fanciest—is still the original and best.

La Lanterna Caffe (212-529-5945), 131 MacDougal Street between West 3rd and West 4th streets. Subway: A, C, E, F, V, or S train to West 4th Street. Open daily 10 AM–3 AM, Friday and Saturday until 4 AM. An Italian coffee shop serving coffees, pastries, and gelati until the late, late hours, La Lanterna also cooks sandwiches and light meals. The menu options here include minestrone and other soups, house-made bruschetta, and salads ($6–10) of smoked chicken or smoked duck with mixed greens; a daily quiche; crostini and *panini* sandwiches (including one of *bresaola* beef, goat cheese, and vodka); a selection of pizzas ($8–10) ranging from

simple margheritas to one topped with chili con carne; calzones; and tasty beef and fish carpaccio.

Le Gamin (212-673-4592), 132 West Houston Street between MacDougal and Sullivan streets. Subway: 1 train to Houston Street. Open daily 8 AM–midnight. One of two West Village incarnations of this superpopular bistro chain, Le Gamin serves food leaning toward French—crêpes are probably the most popular thing on the menu—but also does a brisk business in fancy salads and other delicate, tasty meals. The food is astonishingly low priced given the quality, but bear in mind that they do not accept credit cards here. There's another branch very nearby at 27 Bedford Street, between Downing and Houston streets (212-243-2846).

☙ **Lupa** (212-982-5089), 170 Thompson Street between Bleecker and Houston streets. Subway: A, C, E, F, V, or S train to West 4th Street, or 1 train to Houston Street. Open daily for lunch noon–3 PM and dinner 5–11:30 PM. If you're too intimidated by chef Mario Batali's high-priced, culinarily challenging other restaurants, head here instead. Batali has helped create a Rome-style eatery that manages to convey a wonderful range of Italian flavors and experiences, at a much more reasonable price, for the masses. Antipasti include a wide range of treats such as octopus in ink, preserved tuna, citrus-cured sardines, and mortadella. For the first and second courses, fork up a cheese plate or one of the wonderful pasta dishes, following them with striped bass, warm salmon, or crispy duck for lunch, perhaps saltimbocca, tuna, luxurious ricotta gnocchi, or "devil's chicken" at dinnertime. Finish with an inventive dessert such as roasted plum bruschetta, wild fennel pollen panna cotta, or spiced dates with mascarpone (or just go with a cheese plate and some espresso). There's a full list of sweetish dessert wines, too, of course, and pay special attention to the *piatto del giorno* (daily special plates), which might include a whole roasted fish, grilled sardines, fried salt codfish, lamb sausage, or gnocchi. Note that it's very hard to get a table here, so reserve early.

Moustache (212-229-2220), 90 Bedford Street between Barrow and Greene streets. Subway: 1 train to Christopher Street. Open daily noon–11 PM. This eatery serves some of the city's best cheap Middle Eastern food (such as hummus and tabouleh), as well as unique pita bread pizzas; finish with the strong house coffee.

Otto Enoteca and Pizzeria (212-995-9559), 1 Fifth Avenue at the corner of East 8th Street. Subway: N, R, or W train to 8th Street. Open daily 11:30 AM–11:30 PM. Celebrity chef Mario Batali has practically cornered Manhattan's fine-dining Italian market, and—as if that weren't enough—now he's going downmarket. This fun eatery near NYU features grill-cooked exotic pizzas (including one topped with strips of lard, another with potato) and other savory Italian snacks and antipasti. There's a daily bruschetta special, too. The dining room is handsome and serves authentic Italian (which will feel strange to diners raised on red-sauces and calamari), but I like the marble-topped bar for a glass of wine and some quick bites. Batali has also tried his hand at one of his favorite desserts, gelato, and it's superb (see *Coffee and Snacks*). This is a fun place to experience a cool restaurant without spending a mint; just be prepared for the slight strangeness of the pizzas.

Paradou (212-463-8345), 8 Little West 12th Street between Ninth Avenue and Washington Street. Subway: A, C, or E train to 14th Street, or L train to Eighth Avenue. Open weekdays 6 PM–midnight, weekends from noon. Another wine bar in the far West Village? Yes, but this one's actually somewhat distinctive for its regional (as in the south of France) snacks—delicious sandwiches, cold cuts, and the like—at affordable prices. They've got outdoor dining, too.

✤ **Peanut Butter & Co.** (212-677-3995), 240 Sullivan Street between Bleecker Street and West 3rd Street. Subway: A, C, E, F, V, or S train to West 4th Street. Open daily 11 AM–9 PM, weekends until 10 PM. Most of the "entrées" at this hip little dinerette, it seems, are peanut butter themed, from the obligatory sandwiches (though in several dozens variations that go way beyond PB&J) to scrumptious desserts. There are other comforting diner-type staples as well—burgers, shakes, stuff you'd have found in your lunchbox in 1975—and while you'll pay more than you did at Mom's (six bucks for a sandwich?), Mom probably didn't make 'em until 10 at night.

Petit Abeille (212-741-6479), 466 Hudson Street between Barrow and Grove streets, and also at 400 West 14th Street at the corner of Ninth Avenue (212-727-1505). Subway: 1 train to Christopher Street. Open Monday through Saturday 7:30 AM–11 PM, weekends 9 AM–11 PM. Belgian mussels-and-fries bistros were briefly white hot in Manhattan, but the trend seems to have quickly cooled off. The mini chain Petit Abeille remains standing, however, perhaps thanks to the enduring quality of its offerings—cones of crispy fries, mussels, salmon, steak, all cooked on an open grill. Naturally there are plenty of Belgian beers to choose from, and there's plenty of French and Dutch (or is it Flemish?) flying through the air. You'll also find locations in Chelsea and Lower Manhattan.

Piccolo Angolo (212-229-9177), 621 Hudson Street at the corner of Jane Street. Subway: 1 train to Christopher Street, or A, C, or E train to 14th Street. Open Tuesday through Saturday 5–11 PM, Saturday until midnight, Sunday 4–9:30 PM. This little brick corner restaurant (hence the name; it means "little corner" in Italian) has a solid repeat clientele of area West Villagers who come back time and again for the midpriced northern Italian cuisine. You might not catch the specials the first time your waiter or waitress races through them. Thankfully, though, the cuisine here stays the home-cooking course—you'll find garlicky lasagna, spicy shrimp, good chicken dishes, rich rabbit, and meaty pasta Bolognese. Desserts are equally well done. This place is always packed, always noisy—which is both an upside (it testifies to the place's fiercely local clientele and popularity) and a downside if you're looking for a quiet romantic date.

⚘ **Pó** (212-645-2189), 31 Cornelia Street between Bleecker and West 4th streets. Subway: A, C, E, F, V, or S train to West 4th Street. Open Wednesday through Sunday for lunch 11:30 AM–2:30 PM, Tuesday through

Saturday for dinner 5:30–11 PM, Sunday for dinner 5–10 PM. Mario Batali no longer runs this renowned Tuscan eatery, but it's still top rate and a surprisingly good dining deal whether you go à la carte or with the prix fixe. Start with the fresh, white-bean-topped bruschetta, then try spicy linguine with clams and pancetta, *pappardelle,* or perhaps one of the exemplary salads of roasted beets. The few outdoor tables are wonderful in good weather.

Spice (212-982-3758), 60 University Place between East 10th and East 11th streets. Subway: L, N, Q, R, W, 4, 5, or 6 train to 14th Street–Union Square. Open daily 11:30 AM–11 PM. This Asian chain is known around Greenwich Village for its extremely fresh and affordable Thai food, with price-conscious $6 lunch specials including a choice of spring rolls, dumplings, fritters, or salad plus an entrée and rice. Choose from pad Thai, rice noodles with basil, bean sauce, and eggs, a ginger-pineapple sauté, and more. For dinner start with Thai crêpes of peanut, chicken, and chili sauce, satay, or a coconut-chicken soup; the entrées, priced $7–16 each, run to curries, spicy duck, shrimp in a clay pot, grilled chicken, fried whole fish seasoned with tamarind or ginger, and tofu with peanut sauce. The fun rice choices to accompany your meal include "6 o'clock train spicy fried rice" and the entrée-sized, Phuket-style pineapple-fried rice (it comes with chicken, shrimp, and squid).

⚘ **Tanti Baci** (212-647-9651), 163 West 10th Street between Seventh Avenue South and Waverly Place. Subway: A, C, E, F, V, or S train to West 4th Street, or 1 or 9 train to Christopher Street. Open daily

11 AM–11 PM. These two sister Italian cafés in the West Village serve downright tasty pasta dishes, salads, and coffee, all at a realistic price. There's another location at 135 Seventh Avenue South, between Charles Street and West 10th Street (212-727-8333).

Tartine (212-229-2611), 253 West 11th Street at the corner of West 4th Street. Subway: 1, 2, or 3 train to 14th Street. Open daily 9:30 AM–10:30 PM. Too tight, too busy, and too French—in other words, just like a million other places in the Village. Tartine's popularity just won't wane; witness the nearly perpetual lines. The softly lit interior is weirdly decorated, while food wavers between nearly great (the more French, the better, generally speaking) and extremely average. The Sunday brunch is an especially tough ticket, even more so if you're craving one of the four or five tiny sidewalk tables in good weather. Though they don't take credit cards, their prices are surprisingly moderate, which may help explain Tartine's loyal clientele.

Tavern on Jane (212-675-2526), 31 Eighth Avenue at the corner of Jane Street. Subway: A, C, or E train to 14th Street, or L train to Eighth Avenue. Open Monday through Friday noon–1 AM, from 11 AM weekends. This isn't a fancy place at all; in fact, it's more like the West Village's version of *Cheers*, a corner joint where regular folks drop by to hang out and nosh. The menu is straightforward but offers good bar food and bistro fare such as burgers, plus grilled tuna sandwiches and the like.

Tea & Sympathy (212-807-8329), 108 Greenwich Avenue between West 12th and West 13th streets and between Seventh and Eighth Avenues. Subway: A, C, E, 1, 2, or 3 train to 14th Street, or L train to Eighth Avenue. Open Monday through Friday 11 AM–10:30 PM, weekends from 9:30 AM. This extremely tiny tea spot—right next door to the fish-and-chips shop run by the same ownership (see A Salt & Battery, above)—serves classic British fare ranging from the plebeian (shepherd's pie, bangers-and-mash, a deep-fried "Scotch" egg) to fancier, more expensive items. The high tea each afternoon, with all the trimmings, is quite popular. Don't expect loads of elbow room here, but do be prepared for the occasional brush with famous movie stars—even non-British ones—who love this place for some reason.

COFFEE AND SNACKS Café Figaro (212-677-1100), 184 Bleecker Street at the corner of MacDougal Street. Subway: A, C, E, F, V, or S train to West 4th Street. Open daily 10 AM–2 AM, Friday and Saturday to 4 AM. Once a famous hotbed of alternative thought and poetry, Café Figaro—with its outdoor tables—rose from the ashes and is again a popular gathering spot for locals, with a genuinely French atmosphere. Meals are uncomplicated (if unspectacular); coffee, croissants, sweets—and the time to linger over them—remain the main draw.

Caffe Dante (212-982-5275), 79 MacDougal Street near the corner of Bleecker Street. Subway: A, C, E, F, V, or S train to West 4th Street, or C or E train to Spring Street. Open daily 10 AM–2 AM, Friday and Saturday until 3 AM. Caffe Dante has been here a long time, gets the Italian-café decor just right (tiny tables, prints of Italy), and serves one of the better cups of espresso in New York. In addition to a range of coffee drinks, sweets, and liqueurs, the gelato is good, and the kitchen serves excellent sandwiches of fresh mozzarella, cured meat, and roasted vegetables as well as some light meals. The coveted sidewalk tables always go fast.

Cones (212-414-1795), 272 Bleecker Street between Jones and Morton streets. Subway: A, C, E, F, V, or S train to West 4th Street. Open Sunday through Thursday 1–11 PM, Friday and Saturday 1 PM–1 AM. This relative newcomer makes some of New York's dandiest ice creams, gelati, and sorbets, and they're never too sweet. The Argentinean owner whips up satisfying dishes and waffle cones of fruit flavors such as blueberry, apple, banana, and mango, as well as rich more conventional dark chocolate and an unusual white chocolate. Many locals and critics have already pegged this as the city's best.

French Roast (212-533-2233), 78 West 11th Street at the corner of Sixth Avenue. Subway: A, C, E, F, V, or S train to West 4th Street. Open 24 hours. Villagers seem to love this little corner café–coffee shop more than just about any other, even if the meals and coffee are far from the city's best French fare. In front of big windows and silvered mirrors, in a completely Left Bank atmosphere, regulars sip cups of café au lait or dig into French bistro fare or brunches, with a view of busy Sixth Avenue. And that's why you come: to rent your little window on the human parade.

Grey Dog's Coffee (212-462-0041), 33 Carmine Street between Bedford and Bleecker streets. Subway: A, C, E, F, V, or S train to West 4th Street, or 1 train to Houston Street. Open daily 6:30 AM–11:30 PM. More than just a bright-colored, Bohemian coffee shop (although it is that), Grey Dog's also serves rudimentary breakfasts, excellent soups, and better-than-they-have-to-be lunches.

Little Pie Company (212-414-2324), 407 West 14th Street between Ninth and Tenth avenues. Subway: A, C, or E train to 14th Street, or L train to Eighth Avenue. Open Monday through Friday 9 AM–8 PM, Saturday and Sunday 10 AM–8 PM. Pies on the fringe of the Meatpacking District? Indeed: All they do here is make pies, but they make some pretty terrific ones, from richly fruity pies to sour cream stunners to classics like good old apple. And yes, you can order— and eat—by the slice.

Magnolia Bakery (212-462-2572), 401 Bleecker Street at the corner of West 11th Street. Subway: 1 train to Christopher Street. Open Monday noon–11:30 PM, Tuesday through Friday 9 AM–11:30 PM, until 12:30 AM Friday, Saturday from 11 AM. Everyone in the West Village seems to show up here at one time or another, even late at night, for a taste of Magnolia's legendary cupcakes and other baked treats.

Otto Enoteca and Pizzeria (212-995-9559), 1 Fifth Avenue at the corner of East 8th Street. Subway: N, R, or W train to 8th Street. Open daily 11 AM–11:30 PM. Mario Batali's pizzeria and wine-tasting bar serves what is already some of the city's best gelato. Go for a taste of chocolate, caramel, lemon, or one of the others—and finish, of course, with a shot of espresso. The beautiful marble bar is a nice place to try it.

Porto Rico (212-477-5421), 201 Bleecker Street between MacDougal Street and Sixth Avenue. Subway: A, C, E, F, V, or S train to West 4th

Street. Open Monday through Saturday 9 AM–9 PM, Sunday noon–7 PM. Peter Longo knows coffee. City connoisseurs know that his small chain of roasteries (all located in Manhattan's hipper districts) produce good-value, yet tasty, beans—beans that become even more of a value during periodic sales. He's also got plenty of imported coffees, and you can sip a cup on-site when you need a pickup. This location has been in the family since 1907.

✳ Entertainment

THEATERS **Actors Playhouse** (212-463-0060), 100 Seventh Avenue South between Barrow and Grove streets. Subway: 1 train to Christopher Street. Long a Village off-Broadway standard, the Actors Playhouse makes up with creativity in production what it lacks in creature comforts: These tight quarters have a venerable history of presenting important work.

& **Bank Street Theatre** (212-633-6533), 155 Bank Street between Washington and West streets. Subway: A, C, or E train to 14th Street. More a kind of arts campus than just a theater—it's part of the Westbeth Arts Complex—the Bank Street hosts small independent productions.

Barrow Street Theatre (212-239-6200), 27 Barrow Street at the corner of Seventh Avenue. Subway: 1 train to Christopher Street. There are about 200 seats at this centrally located West Village theater, home to The Drama Dept. company. Its productions include the fetching *Shanghai Moon*, about romance and intrigue in the Far East.

& **Cherry Lane Theater** (212-989-2020), 38 Commerce Street between Barrow and Bedford streets. Subway: 1 train to Christopher Street. Down

at the end of a quaint side street and nicely renovated in recent years, the Cherry Lane was founded by the young Maine poetess Edna St. Vincent Millay during the 1920s and once showcased important work by the likes of Pinter and Beckett. Today it's known for avant-garde off-Broadway works.

Jane Street Theatre (212-924-8404), 113 Jane Street at the corner of West Street. Subway: A, C, or E train to 14th Street. Inside a once historic hotel, the Jane Street holds almost 300. They sell snacks during shows.

& **Minetta Lane Theatre** (212-420-8000), 18 Minetta Lane between Sixth Avenue and MacDougal Street. Subway: A, C, E, F, V, or S train to West 4th Street. Tucked away on cute Minetta Lane, this surprisingly big (seating more than 400) and popular West Village theater puts on such interesting shows as *Tuesdays with Morrie*, a play based on the Mitch Albom book about his aging, wise mentor.

13th Street Repertory Theatre (212-675-6677), 50 West 13th Street between Fifth and Sixth avenues. Subway: F train to 14th Street. Inside a typical Greenwich Village town house, the 13th Street's small stage hosts such productions as *A Christmas Carol*.

MOVIES AND FILMS **Angelika Film Center** (212-995-2000), 18 West Houston Street at the corner of Mercer Street. Subway: F or S train to Broadway–Lafayette, or N or R train to Prince Street. This is one of New York's very best theaters; if you enjoy alternative films, make a trip. Features could include a striking film such as Atom Egoyan's *Ararat* or Gus van Sant's experimental *Gerry*, screened as early as 11 in the morning or as late as 12:30 in the morning. The lobby café opens at 10:30 AM sharp if you want to grab a pre-previews bite.

Quad Cinema (212-225-8800), 34 West 13th Street between Fifth and Sixth avenues. Subway: F, L, N, Q, R, W, 4, 5, or 6 train to 14th Street. An amazing range of quality foreign and independent films are prevalent at this four-screen theater, which has a ferociously loyal clientele (including former mayor Ed Koch). Expect documentaries, intriguing imports, and small-release projects by big-name stars; no matter what's playing, it's sure to be thought provoking. Tickets cost $10 for adults, $7 for senior citizens and children 5–12; children younger than 5 cannot enter.

JAZZ CLUBS 🦞 **Arthur's Tavern** (212-675-6879), 57 Grove Street at the corner of Seventh Avenue South. Subway: 1 train to Christopher Street. This might be my favorite jazz club in the city, for a few reasons—it's not too full of itself, it's got pedigree (it is the longest-operating jazz club in Manhattan, open since 1937), the music's great . . . and there's no cover charge at all! Anything from Japanese jazzers to Dixieland might be playing the small room, once called the "Home of the Bird" for its association with Charlie Parker. There's live jazz 7–9 PM Tuesday through Saturday and Dixieland-style jazz 8–11 PM Sunday and Monday nights; blues and R&B acts take over the stage late-night until around 3 AM.

Blue Note (212-475-8592), 131 West 3rd Street between MacDougal Street and Sixth Avenue. Subway: A, C, E, F, V, or S train to West 4th Street. It's sometimes hard to believe this legendary jazz club is less than a quarter century old. Jazz stars play a consecutive week here, giving you a chance to catch multiple gigs if you really enjoy a performer; covers range $5–40, depending on who's playing. Sure, it may seem huge, overhyped, and over-touristed at times, but the big stars do play here and the weekend jazz brunches are a bargain: food plus really good jams from artists you don't know . . . yet.

Garage Restaurant & Café (212-645-0600), 99 Seventh Avenue South at the corner of Grove Street. Subway: 1 train to Christopher Street. Open daily noon–4 PM and dinner 5 PM–1 AM, Friday and Saturday until 3 AM. If you can't catch the Saturday or Sunday jazz brunch here, check the weekly jazz schedule—Monday is big-band night, Tuesday through Thursday features a rotating lineup of combos, and weekends feature early vocalist shows and (more uptempo) late-night band sets. Some pretty big names sometimes drop by.

North Square Lounge (212-254-1200), 103 Waverly Place (West 7th Street) between MacDougal Street and Sixth Avenue. Subway: A, C, E, F, V, or S train to West 4th Street. The Washington Square Hotel's lounge, formerly known as C3, still maintains a jazz brunch Sunday despite the recent change in name. There's also a schedule of other jazz performances through the week.

Smalls (212-929-7565), 183 West 10th Street near the corner of Seventh Avenue South. Subway: 1 train to Christopher Street, or 2 or 3 train to 14th Street. Opens daily at 10 PM; Friday and Saturday at 7 PM. This jazz club is legendary around the Village for its inexpensive (for Manhattan) cover charge, late-night (10 PM and 1 AM) sets, and jams that actually last until dawn on weekends. A pretty regular cast of musicians shows up each week.

Village Vanguard (212-255-4037), 178 Seventh Avenue South at the corner of West 11th Street. Subway: 1 train to Christopher Street, or 2 or 3 train to 14th Street. Founded in 1935 by Max Gordon, this is the center of the Village jazz scene—and has been for ages, since a day when it saw all the leading lights of jazz (Charles Mingus, John Coltrane, Thelonius Monk, Miles Davis) pass through its doors. Today there are two sets nightly, beginning at 9 PM and 11 PM; weekends sometime bring a third, late set around 12:30 AM. The cover charge is steep—$30 Sunday through Thursday, $35 Friday and Saturday—with a supplement sometimes also charged for big-name players. Note that there's no kitchen, so eat before you get here—and don't talk during sets. They don't like it.

OTHER MUSIC VENUES **The Bitter End** (212-673-7030), 147 Bleecker Street between LaGuardia Place and Thompson Street. Subway: A, C, E, F, V, or S train to West 4th Street. Perhaps the city's oldest rock club (it opened in 1961), the Bitter End once played host to famous folkies galore. You may never have heard of the acts playing here, but you might recognize them someday later when they've hit the big time; catch them now, at a fraction of the cost.

BARS AND CLUBS **Baggot Inn** (212-477-0622), 82 West 3rd Street between Thompson Street and Sullivan Street. Subway: A, C, E, F, V, or S

train to West 4th Street. Open Monday through Saturday 11 AM–3 AM, Sunday noon–2 AM. Downstairs from the Boston Comedy Club, this cellar bar brings Irish hospitality to the Village in the form of a small convivial room, long communal tables, good beers and wines, and plenty of music—a bluegrass jam session each Wednesday night, for example. There's no cover; NYU students therefore love the place.

Chumley's (212-675-4449), 86 Bedford Street between Barrow Street and Grove Street. Subway: 1 or 9 train to Christopher Street. Open Monday through Thursday 4 PM–midnight, Friday to 2 AM, Saturday from 10 AM, Sunday 1 PM–1 AM. A former speakeasy, with the design features to match (ask a bartender about it), atmospheric Chumley's is one of the in places if you're a writer or just admire good writing; famous pens have rested here for decades, and this was once a hotbed for alternative social thought. The decor is absolutely charming—fireplaces, wooden floors, heavy solid tables for serious drinking (or drafting poetry), shaggy dogs lounging around—and the jazz keeps the groove mellow. They serve meals as well (see *Eating Out*).

Meet (212-242-0990), 71–73 Gansevoort Street between Greenwich and Washington streets. Subway: L train to Eighth Avenue, or A, C, or E train to 14th Street. A few years back there were few West Village–Meatpacking spots trendier than this one—every famous model in town seemed to be here. Fame is ephemeral, however, and Meet is no longer the city's spot-du-jour. Instead, it's merely a combination Mediterranean restaurant and pickup joint. The advantage to its moment having passed, of course, is that regular folks can now get in—but once here you'll contend with outrageously priced tapas-style small plates. At least they have live jazz, with no cover charge, on Wednesday nights. It's a better idea to stick to the interesting mixed drinks.

One If By Land, Two If By Sea (212-228-0822), 17 Barrow Street (between Seventh Avenue South and West 4th Street). Subway: 1 train to Christopher Street. This upscale restaurant (see *Dining Out*) may be frequently booked full with romancing or celebrating couples, but the small attached piano bar is always open for business if you can snag a seat. It opens daily at 4 PM, though competition for the small banquettes can

THE WHITE HORSE TAVERN IN GREENWICH VILLAGE ONCE HOSTED DYLAN THOMAS.
Kim Grant

seem fierce. Seven barside seats await the runners-up in the sweepstakes.

Rhône (212-367-8440), 63 Gansevoort Street between Greenwich Street and Washington Street. Subway: A, C, or E train to 14th Street, or L train to Eighth Avenue. Open weekdays 5 PM–4 AM, weekends from 1:30 PM. This wine bar, next to the all-night bistro Florent, reaches for a hip crowd with more than three dozen good red and white wines and an appropriately Franco overload of attitude.

White Horse Tavern (212-989-3956), 567 Hudson Street at the corner of West 11th Street. Subway: 1 train to Christopher Street, or A, C, or E train to 14th Street. Open daily 11 AM–2 AM, until 4 AM Thursday through Saturday. More atmospheric once upon a time than it is today, the White Horse acquired almost legendary status when the talented Welsh poet (and alcoholic) Dylan Thomas drank himself into a stupor here one night in 1953; by the next evening he was dead. They're trying to recapture that era, when this was the haunt of tormented poets, artists, writers, and deadbeats, but it's not exactly working—tourists and 20-somethings are far more likely to show up here today to drink inside or at the little sidewalk patio. Still, it's worth a stop if you're a literary buff.

✳ Selective Shopping

BOOKSTORES Biography Bookshop (212-807-8655), 400 Bleecker Street near the corner of West 11th Street. Subway: A, C, or E train to 14th Street, or L train to Eighth Avenue. Just as the name says, this bookstore features lots of biography, autobiography, letters, and the like.

Partners & Crime (212-243-0440), 44 Greenwich Avenue across from the corner of Charles Street. Subway: 1 train to Christopher Street. Mystery books are the specialty here, with plenty of rare and unusual books and author visits. The store sometimes even hosts atmospheric live readings, in the manner of old radio shows.

Three Lives & Co. (212-741-2069), 154 West 10th Street at the corner of Waverly Place. Subway: 1 train to Christopher Street. Villagers love this place—named after Gertrude Stein's novel—for its fiction, theology, and other sections.

FASHION Diane von Furstenberg the Shop (646-486-4800), 385 West 12th Street at the corner of Washington Street. Subway: A, C, E, or L train to 14th Street. On the edge of the Meatpacking District, this jewel box–like shop features gossamerlike dresses.

FOOD AND DRINK Jefferson Market (212-533-3377), 450 Sixth Avenue between East 10th and East 11th Streets. Subway: A, C, E, F, V, or S train to West 4th Street. Open daily 8 AM–9 PM, except Sunday to 8 PM. Jefferson Market is considered by many Villagers to be the superior store for all the same items you'd get at the other place: cured meats, steak, imported pasta, produce, and the rest. Prices aren't really much different here, but you might detect a difference in the level of customer service—and you'll certainly have a little more room in which to negotiate your shopping basket.

MUSIC Bleecker Bob's (212-475-9677), 118 West 3rd Street between Sixth Avenue and MacDougal Street. Subway: A, C, E, F, V, or S train to West 4th Street. Quite possibly the model for *Seinfeld* record store Bleecker Bob's, this Village legend makes up in its selection of wax (vinyl records—remember those?) what it lacks in organization and professionalism.

Bleecker St. Records (212-255-7899), 239 Bleecker Street between Sixth Avenue and Carmine Street. Subway: A, C, E, F, V, or S train to West 4th Street. This store has one of the Village's better collections of hard-to-find listening in all genres, especially bluesy and folksy music. This is a great antidote when you're tired of huge record stores.

Generation Records (212-254-1100), 210 Thompson Street between Bleecker Street and West 3rd Street. Subway: A, C, E, F, V, or S train to West 4th Street. Generation is one of the better Village new-and-used-record stores; if you can get past the occasionally scary-looking staff and record covers, you'll find plenty of surprises. Needless to say, the selection is heavy on punk and heavy stuff—but they've got classic rock, too, and even some folk and world music. The used section, of course, is a mixed bag but is worth looking through.

Union Square, Gramercy, and the Flatiron District

5

Kim Grant

UNION SQUARE, GRAMERCY, AND THE FLATIRON DISTRICT

Though difficult to characterize or even define, the amorphous Union Square–Gramercy Park–Flatiron District neighborhood simply must be seen. (I have used 14th Street and 30th Street as my arbitrary cutoffs; others may disagree.) It's here that some of Manhattan's most stylish photographers and modeling agencies set up shop; the buildings, the clothes, and the shops all have style; and a new wave of restaurants has moved in lately, making it one of the city's hottest dining areas.

Union Square is easy to find: It's at the confluence of 14th Street, Broadway, and Park Avenue South (an upscale renaming of what really should be called Fourth Avenue). The square—which is actually a three-block-long oval—anchors the neighborhood's pricey bistros and restaurants, staffed by the young and the beautiful and owned by celebrity chefs. Daytime brings the city's best green-market to the square; by night, the area morphs into a theatrical and clubgoers' paradise, and scads of NYU students filter up here to shop at huge big-block stores or nosh in fusion and sushi eateries.

Small, pretty Gramercy Park lies just north of Union Square, between Park and Third avenues and between East 20th and East 21st Streets. Over time the largely residential blocks and side streets north and south of the park between the avenues—once marshlands (*Gramercy* is almost Dutch for "crooked swamp")— have also become loosely known by the designation of Gramercy Park. The graceful architecture of the town houses here—built when a genius 19th-century developer drained the marsh, built a private park, and instantly created cachet— rivals any of the city's finest, and there were probably more famous New Yorkers born and raised in this neighborhood than anywhere else in the city. (This tradition continues, by the way; actress Julia Roberts owns an apartment on the park.)

Finally, the distinctively slim Flatiron Building rises at the corner of Broadway and Fifth Avenue, across the street from big Madison Square Park and several more impressive skyscrapers. The neighborhood to the south and east of the building, along Fifth Avenue and between Fifth and Sixth avenues, is known as the Flatiron District. Formerly industrial, it has in recent times harbored some of the more interesting publishers, writers, creative artists, photographers, modeling shops, ad shops, print shops, and new restaurants in New York, not

© The Countryman Press

to mention plenty of upscale chain stores purveying Italian fashion and the like. Ironically, many such stores are located in renovated department stores built in the 1800s. In some senses its lofts, nooks, crannies, and industrial bent make it the new SoHo. It is also the worthy successor to the old Ladies' Mile, the stretch of Broadway connecting Madison Square with Union Square, which is today full of chain retailers but brimmed over at the turn of the 20th century with some of New York's finest jewelers, hatters, and clothiers.

For the purposes of this book, I have drawn a line of demarcation at 30th Street; attractions north of that street, I have included in "Midtown East" (see chapter 7) if they are east of Fifth Avenue, or in "Chelsea" (see chapter 6) if they are west of Fifth Avenue. Attractions south of 14th Street are divided into two chapters: Those west of Broadway, I have included in "Greenwich Village" (see chapter 4), while those east of Broadway are described in "Lower Manhattan, Chinatown, and the Lower East Side" and "East Village and NoHo" (see chapters 1 and 3).

GETTING THERE Union Square is more than just one of New Yorkers' favorite parks—it's also a major transit hub. Beneathground lies a huge subway station reachable from almost anywhere in the city via the L, N, Q, R, W, 4, 5, and 6 trains; get off at 14th Street–Union Square.

By subway: From the East Village or West Village, get here by taking an L train. From Times Square, Midtown East, or Lower Manhattan, take the N, Q, R, or W trains here. From Lower Manhattan, NYU, Grand Central Station, Midtown East, or the Upper East Side, take a 4, 5, or 6 train to get to Union Square Station. Gramercy Park is more easily reached by taking a 6 train to the 23rd Street station. You can walk nine blocks from Union Square to the Flatiron Building and surrounding district, or take an N, R, or W subway car to the 23rd Street station, which surfaces on the street right beneath the distinctive structure (if you can't see it, you're probably standing right in front of it); all three lines pass through Union Square on their way south to SoHo and Lower Manhattan and north to Times Square and Midtown East.

By bus: The 1, 2, 3, and 5 buses run up and down Fifth Avenue and Park Avenue in this neighborhood and are good for getting north and south to points not well served by the subway. To get crosstown (that is, east and west) on 14th Street or 23rd Street—the two main arteries in this part of the city—it's easy: Just take a 14 or 23 bus.

By car: Reach this area via the FDR Drive (also known as the East Side Drive), exiting at either 23rd or 14th Street (you'll need to take Avenue C for a few blocks first). It's almost impossible to park in this area, because of both congestion and the residential neighborhoods' Byzantine parking rules, though you'll occasionally find metered spots—along avenues such as Fifth Avenue and Park Avenue South—or free-for-all spots on side streets near Irving Place or Gramercy Park. Overnight, good luck.

UNION SQUARE

Paul Karr

✷ To See

Union Square, running from East 14th to East 17th streets between Broadway and Fourth Avenue (Park Avenue South), is the central hub of this neighborhood. Long a site of left-wing and populist political protest, Union Square—which is really more oval than square—is today one of New York's hottest outdoor gathering spaces (if such a thing is possible). Its history has seen demonstrations against everything from the Civil War to Sacco and Vanzetti's executions. The square has served as a parade ground for Civil War troops, and its surrounding streets have been the tramping grounds of Andy Warhol and his set; headquarters for labor unions created to fight for the rights of garment workers on Seventh Avenue; and former department-store headquarters of such heavyweights as Tiffany & Co. and FAO Schwarz. (The square also became a central point for services and memorials in the wake of the World Trade Center tragedies in September 2001.) Plenty of restaurants, clubs, hotels, and chain stores surround Union Square, around which traffic roars all day long; what would the statues of Gandhi and George Washington think? The southern border (14th Street) is mostly distinguished by the big Virgin Megastore, a good place to stay warm, grab a coffee, or browse cutting-edge music, and a massive Whole Foods natural foods store. The northeast corner sports the W New York–Union Square hotel, with a good lobby lounge. The western edge of the square (and the side streets running west from it) are where some of the hippest, most expensive bars and restaurants in the city are located.

MUSEUM Museum of Sex (212-689-6337), 233 Fifth Avenue at the corner of 27th Street. Subway: N or R train to 23rd Street. Open Sunday through Tuesday and Thursday 11 AM–6:30 PM, Friday and Saturday until 8 PM. This new Flatiron-area museum is surprisingly tasteful, explaining and chronicling the history and intrigue of sexual matters in a mostly forthright and frank manner. Sections and exhibits illuminate such pressing matters as the history of prostitution, birth control, the sexual revolution, deviant sexuality, and so forth. Admission costs a hefty $14.50 per person ($1 discount for seniors, though I doubt many show up); children under the age of 18 cannot enter.

HISTORIC SITE Theodore Roosevelt Birthplace (212-260-1616), 28 East 20th Street between Broadway and Park Avenue South. Subway: N, R, or 6 train to 23rd Street, or L, Q, W, 4, or 5 train to 14th Street–Union Square. T. R. was the only native New Yorker ever elected president, and he may hold the title for a while longer yet. (Think about it: Five of the last six elected U.S. presidents have been Southerners.) The young Roosevelt lived at this location on East 20th Street until age 14; though the original home is no longer extant, the attractive brownstone standing on the site is partially furnished from the original structure, and additional furnishings were later donated by the Roosevelt family. You must book one of the 40-minute tours to visit the home; while waiting, inspect the good little museum on the first floor, holding newspapers, photos, and other mementos that flesh out Roosevelt's full life of governance, policymaking, armed service, big-game hunts (the animal heads upstairs testify to that), and philanthropy. The house is open daily except Monday, 9 AM–5 PM; it costs $3 per adult.

FARMER'S MARKET ✐ Union Square Greenmarket, Union Square. Subway: L, N, W, 4, 5, or 6 train to 14th Street–Union Square. New York's

THE UNION SQUARE GREENMARKET

Paul Karr

best farmer's market is the large, active, and colorful Greenmarket in stalls lining the northern and western sides of Union Square on Monday, Wednesday, Friday, and Saturday. The city's top chefs and their minions never miss it, and you, too, are sure to find some sort of cheese, shellfish, herb, milk product, or craft you've never seen before in your life, courtesy of the artisanal producers who drive into town from the surrounding rural tristate area. These vendors have real personality and talent. Come Saturday morning for the best selection, and come early— the action starts around 7 AM, and the best produce is often gone by noon. And bring the kids.

✳ Green Space

Gramercy Park, between Lexington Avenue and Irving Place at East 20th and East 21st streets. Subway: 6 train to 23rd Street. This park was built in 1831, bringing Lexington Avenue to an end and gating itself off from the masses; today it's the lone London-style private park in New York City. This means only residents of the surrounding streets get one of the prized keys that open those gates, behind which lie cultivated gardens. These same residents must have had some sort of pull—the four short streets surrounding the park have been renamed Gramercy Park North, South, East, and West, and are lined with beautiful town houses, a hotel, and a restaurant. (Note to the wise: Hotel guests of the Gramercy Park Hotel—see *Lodging—Affordable Hotels*—also get access. It's probably your only chance at an inside look at this small, leafy enclave of society.)

✐ ✿ **Madison Square Park,** from East 23rd Street to East 26th Street between Fifth and Madison avenues. Subway: N, R, or W train to 23rd Street. If it seems strange and confusing that Madison Square Garden isn't located here on its namesake square, but instead way over on the west side of town near Penn Station, take heart: The Garden once was located here, along with a bevy of luxury hotels, financial institutions, and fine restaurants. Today the surrounding area is notable mostly for the profusion of interesting urban architecture surrounding it, including the dramatically copper-topped New York Life building, whose octagonal spire was inspired by an English cathedral; the blocky MetLife building (said to have been built as the original base for the Empire State Building); and of course the famously trim Flatiron Building. The park, named for President James Madison, was renovated and reopened to the public in June 2001. It features a reflecting pool, dog run, and plenty of statues and benches. The park is especially popular on weekends, when well-heeled local parents dress down and bring their kids to a central playground featuring good swings, play areas, and a kind of fun waterwheel.

✳ Lodging

BOUTIQUE HOTELS Hotel Giraffe (212-685-7700 or 1-877-296-0009; fax 212-685-7771), 365 Park Avenue South at the corner of East 25th Street. Subway: 6 train to 23rd Street, or N, R, or W train to 23rd Street. Owner Henry Kallan supposedly named this extremely pleasant hotel for his favorite animal, but safaris aren't really the overarching theme here; instead, the place strikes a terrific balance between the new breed of modern business hotels taking over Manhattan (the W, the SoHo Grand, and their like) and the friendlier classic boutique hotels such as the Elysée and Library operated by the same ownership. The tranquil lobby's 15-foot ceiling features an interesting lighting trick to simulate the passage of light during a day; its tall windows and classy curtains enhance the feeling of having stumbled into an oasis amid Park Avenue's chaos. It's candle-lit at night.

There are just 73 rooms in all here (21 are beautiful suites), in the superior or deluxe categories; all sport Art Moderne colors and forms evoking the 1920s and 1930s, blond wood closets and tables, high ceilings, velveteen upholstered chairs and ottomans, and black-and-white photographs. These are not your standard business-hotel rooms, but rather a touch classier—fluted wineglasses, sleek bathrooms with lit vanity mirrors, and plenty of other touches. Beds are draped in satin bedcovers then topped with leather headboards. The deluxe rooms add French doors opening onto a small, European-style balcony, while suites also add a living room. There's a concierge to help plan excursions and obtain tickets, two bars frequented by dot-commers and entertainment types from the surrounding office buildings, a rooftop garden accessible only to guests, and a healthy selection of newspapers to read—not to mention video and compact disk libraries, complimentary gym passes, and a business center.

A fine continental breakfast is served daily, as are complimentary snacks of espresso, biscotti, fruit, and cookies. Then, each weekday 5–8 PM, a complimentary champagne, wine, and cheese service is offered in the lobby to the sounds of a live piano player (take it in your room if you like). Double room rates here begin at $260, while suites begin at $430 but climb as high as around $2,500 per night for the outstanding penthouse—which comes with its own Steinway grand piano, fireplace, and private garden.

W New York–Union Square (212-253-9119 or 1-877-946-8357; fax 212-253-9229), 201 Park Avenue South at the corner of East 17th Street. Subway: L, N, Q, R, W, 4, 5, or 6 train to Union Square–14th Street. Unsurprisingly given all the creature comforts, it's hard to get a room here at one of the W's showpiece New York projects. The hotel occupies the Guardian Life building, a Beaux-Arts granite-and-limestone structure built in 1911; the grand staircase is very impressive, and architect David Rockwell supervised the conversion to boutique-hotel

W NEW YORK—UNION SQUARE HOTEL

Paul Karr

nirvana. A down-to-earth motif pervades throughout—there's a patch of turf with flat stones in the lobby, and natural materials are employed wherever possible. The big lobby contains gaming tables, high, arched windows on the square, and topiary walls. Though some rooms are a bit smallish, all feature high-speed Internet access, fax machine, VCR, big work desk, unusual bed coverings, handsome headboards, velvet chairs, and a box of snacks. Union Square Park is just steps away, and if you're staying inside the hotel, Rande Gerber's Underbar (see *Entertainment—Bars and Clubs*) is a candlelit, stylish space of banquettes and private, curtained-off areas. Superchef Todd English's Olives NY restaurant (see *Dining Out*) is this W's fine-dining entry. Double rooms begin around $279, while suites start around $500.

INN Inn at Irving Place (212-533-4600 or 1-800-685-1447; fax 212-533-4611), 56 Irving Place between East 17th and East 18th streets. Subway: N, Q, R, W, 4, 5, or 6 train to 14th Street–Union Square. No sign marks New York's top bed & breakfast, but savvy travelers book this inn on Gramercy Park months in advance when they're coming to town. If you crave a luxurious townhouse experience as an antidote to business hotels or hip boutique lodgings—and don't mind paying top dollar—you, too, should try to snag one of just 12 rooms and suites in the two elegant 1834 town houses that make up the lodgings. (You'll have to compete with some pretty famous actors, actresses, and models, though.)

The two brownstones underwent 3 years of renovations and were unveiled as an inn in 1994. Each guest room is uniquely furnished with antique four-poster queen bed, fireplace, armchair and ottoman, mirrors, beautiful coffee table, rich carpeting, and other period antiques, plus modern touches such as multiline phone, hair dryer, air-conditioning, Internet access, climate control, CD player, and VCR; the bathrooms sport pedestal sink, brass fixtures, and Frette linens. The more expensive suites add elegant sitting areas. A delicious continental breakfast is included, of course: tea, scones, and the like served in a breakfast room—or in *your* room, if you prefer, along with your complimentary copy of *The New York Times*. The inn's tearoom, Lady Mendl's (see *Where to Eat—Coffee and Snacks*), serves high tea daily using antique teapots and fine china, and you'll also find a lounge, a light-meals café, and a fine-dining restaurant on the premises. Double room rates begin at $325 and run up to $495; note that the inn does not accept children under the age of 12.

AFFORDABLE HOTELS Carlton Arms (212-679-0680 or 212-684-8337), 160 East 25th Street at the corner of Third Avenue. Subway: 6 train to 23rd Street. Don't let the name deceive you into believing this is a luxury property; Carlton Arms is, at best, a lowbrow—all right, downbeat—pick in an area possessing few hotels to speak of, and it's definitely not for everyone. (The place was once a shelter and halfway house for addicts.) At times it seems more like a dormitory than a hotel: The majority of the 55 rooms share bathrooms, none has television or telephone, and furniture is sparse and a bit tatty. (Only upside: They've finally installed air-conditioning.) Room and wall decor is as amazingly—all right, disturbingly—free-form as an acid trip gone awry. Please, please inspect your room *before* checking in; all are quite different from each other, and yours might contain anything from a trick light switch that triggers music and moving art, to plush children's toys, to designer scarves draped across the walls. If you enjoy bizarre art or bad surprises, however, you might love it. Double room rates range $87–100 per night.

The Gershwin (212-545-8000; fax 212-684-5546), 7 East 27th Street between Fifth and Madison avenues. Subway: N, R, or W train to 28th Street. The word *funky* doesn't even begin to describe this unusual—and unusually artsy—13-floor hotel parked in a slightly bland neighborhood just north of Madison Square. The blocky Greek Revival facade seems regal from the exterior, and in no way prepares you for the wackiness within. But in no other New York hotel will you find an autographed Warhol soup can (the owner is an avid collector of the late artist's work), for example, while the lobby is a mishmash of modern furniture. Prices are rock-bottom for Manhattan—figure as little as $99 for a double room—but you'll have to compromise a bit on comfort and amenities: Some of the 150 rooms share bathrooms, and while the decor and furniture may be artistically endearing (walls are painted wild shades of yellow or green) and kitschy, they never approach luxury-level comforts. (Some lack television.) It's difficult to generalize here, though, because you never know exactly what you'll get until you see a room—some of the dozen or so big suites have

wood floors, rich rugs, and potted trees. The suites, it should be noted, are nicer (and considerably more expensive—up to $329 per night). Where this hotel does succeed without qualification is in the culture department. A regular series of poetry readings, comedy, jazz, and other performances keep things hopping—the watchword here is *fun*—and the clientele is refreshingly diverse (in sharp contrast with that of many other Midtown hotels). Two terminals in the lobby allow guests to check e-mail; there's an art gallery next door; in summer the rooftop terrace becomes the site of social gatherings; and 2-night packages allow visitors to sample local clubs and galleries. If you're *really* on a budget, the hotel also maintains an extensive hostel section with some of the city's best dormitory bunks.

Gramercy Park Hotel (212-201-1061), 2 Lexington Avenue at the corner of East 21st Street. Subway: 6 train to 23rd Street. Note: At press time, this hotel was closed for renovations and expected to reopen in summer 2006. Newly recast by uber-cool hotelier Ian Schrager, the place is sure to get a minimalist whitewash; expect industrial-steel sinks, white walls, and not a stick of wood in your room. The big hotel, right across the street from private Gramercy Park, was once a midpriced gem, and it may remain so (Schrager's other New York hotels are not famously expensive). The place certainly has history on its side: John F. Kennedy Jr. lived here as a boy, Babe Ruth frequented its bar, and Humphrey Bogart was married in the rooftop garden. There will be far fewer than the original 500 rooms (some are being converted to luxury

Kim Grant

THE GRAMERCY PARK HOTEL OFFERS GUESTS ACCESS TO EXCLUSIVE GRAMERCY PARK.

apartments) in two buildings. No word on whether the hotel bar, where director Cameron Crowe shot scenes from *Almost Famous*, will remain. The real kick, though, *is* that guests are expected to get access to super-private Gramercy Park (see *Green Space*).

Hotel 17 (212-475-2845; fax 212-677-8178), 225 East 17th Street between Second and Third avenues. Subway: L train to Third Avenue, or N, Q, R, W, 4, 5, or 6 train to Union Square–14th Street. One of the city's most unusually decorated hotels, sitting behind a great art deco entrance, the 17 is also one of this area's hit-or-miss choices. It's no wonder they offer weekly rates for the 125 or so already cheap rooms (most share bathrooms on the hall, and all lack telephone), though there are a few more expensive suites. Rates range from about $90 to $120 for a room sharing a

bathroom, $120–150 for a room with its own private bathroom. The hotel's sole redeeming values would appear to be the rooftop pool and the extremely wild decor, which lured director Woody Allen here to film *Manhattan Murder Mystery*.

✳ Where to Eat

DINING OUT **Blue Smoke** (212-447-7733), 116 East 27th Street between Lexington Avenue and Park Avenue South. Subway: 6 train to 28th Street. Open Sunday through Wednesday 11:30 AM–11 PM, Thursday through Saturday to 1 AM. If you like making the scene but also crave barbecue from time to time, you'll enjoy a visit to Blue Smoke. Lunch consists of ribs cooked in an apple-wood smoker, or an assortment of plates—brisket with mashed potatoes and onions, smoked organic chicken, pan-fried catfish with squash and okra. Dinner could be ribs again (either babyback, St. Louis–style, or salted and peppered); or try one of the bolder offerings such as barbecued lamb shoulder with pepper dip and green beans or rib-eye steak with onion rings. The jukebox, however, is anything but that of a typical juke joint—Bob Dylan comingles with Björk, the Rolling Stones, and The Meters. I love the interior, which features a sunlit back room great for brunch or nighttime; a bar with an especially good assortment of beers from around the world; and front tables on the street. Craving some smoky jazz? Don't worry: There's also a club, Jazz Standard, right downstairs (see *Entertainment—Music Venues*).

Blue Water Grill (212-675-9500), 31 Union Square West at the corner of East 16th Street. Subway: L, N, Q, R, S, 4, 5, or 6 train to Union Square–

14th Street. Open Monday through Saturday 11:30 AM–midnight, Sunday 10:30 AM–midnight. Massive columns and imposing marble (the building was once a bank) announce one of Union Square's trendiest eateries, where seafood rules the roost and attitude is everything. Pardon me if it isn't quite what it once was, but it's still good enough—and a great place to swap business cards, too. Oysters on the half shell are a dependable starter, as is a lobster and shrimp spring roll and tuna tartare, while sushi can be ordered as both a main course and an appetizer. A rotating selection of grilled and roast fish entrées and specials constitutes much of the rest of the menu, with rich and inventive sauces and side dishes. Finish with fruit dipped in chocolate fondue; everyone else does. There's also a quietly pleasant jazz bar in the basement where the superrich crowd kicks back a bit, and coveted sidewalk seating right across from Union Square. This place remains wildly popular, so getting a table at the last minute is problematic—try to book ahead.

Casa Mono (212-253-2773), 52 Irving Place between East 17th and East 18th streets. Subway: N, Q, R, W, 4, 5, or 6 train to 14th Street–Union Square. Open daily 11:30 AM–2:30 PM for lunch and 5:30 PM–midnight for dinner. Inside the lovely Inn at Irving Place block (*see Lodging—Inn*), the unstoppable Mario Batali (he of Pé, Otto, Babbo, Lupa, etc.) tackles Spanish tapas. Well, it's not just tapas ($3–15 apiece), though there's a lot of that: squid croquettes, sweetbreads, duck eggs. But these are hardly light snacks, and you also have access to a range of heftier grilled meats, as well as interesting preparations of duck, lamb, and even boar—Batali fans

know by now to look for these things. He's also set up a bar next door, Bar Jamón, which is more casual and features cold cuts and cheeses served up bar-style in a space so tiny you're practically standing in the kitchen. But after a few glasses of wine you won't care—and yes, you will feel practically transported to Spain. The name, by the way, means "house of the monkey"—whatever that's supposed to mean.

Coffee Shop (212-243-7969), 29 Union Square West at the corner of 16th Street. Subway: L, N, Q, R, W, 4, 5, or 6 train to Union Square–14th Street. Open Monday 7 AM–2 AM, Wednesday through Saturday to 5:30 AM. Coffee Shop, marked with a sign saying simply that, may not look like much from the outside, but it's one of the very hottest spots in hip Union Square. (It's also the noisiest restaurant in the city, according to a *New York Post* investigation.) Owned

TRENDIER-THAN-TRENDY BAR "COFFEE SHOP" ON UNION SQUARE

Paul Karr

and largely staffed by models—which guarantees a fabulous-looking server, as well as clientele—this nearly round-the-clock eatery turns out to serve much more than coffee; it features (rather spicy) Brazilian diner cooking. Expect lots of meat and seafood cooked South American–style, such as *ropa vieja* (shredded beef), steak, strong coffee, and sweet desserts. The cocktails here are as fun as you'd expect them to be, and there's peppy live music to accompany the wildly popular brunch on weekends; but late at night is really the best time to see this place in its element. If you're staying in the area, drop by in the wee hours.

Craft (212-780-0880), 43 East 19th Street between Broadway and Park Avenue South. Subway: N, R, W, or 6 train to 23rd Street. Open daily 5:30–10 PM, weekends until 11 PM. Chef Tom Colicchio (who also supervises the kitchen at Danny Meyer's Gramercy Tavern; see below) is trying a daring concept with this newish Flatiron-area restaurant, which opened in 2000, a kind of high-cuisine mix-and-match idea. It works like this: Assisted by the professional waitstaff, you first choose a basic type of food (meat, fish, shellfish, pasta), then choose a cooking style (braising, perhaps?), some vegetables, and a dessert category; you leave the rest to Colicchio's *chef de cuisine,* Damon Wise. (You could once choose from a range of sauces as well, but that was deemed too complex for the diners.) He'll create something unusual and satisfying, from some of the freshest greens, cheeses, shellfish, and fish in the city—always presented in minimal, unadorned fashion that truly brings

out the flavors of, say, a very freshly harvested diver scallop. In particular, this kitchen goes for the foods of small, artisanal producers with good results. If it's too challenging to envision what might result from your choices, simply go with the chef's tasting menu—expensive, yes, but worth it, and desserts here are quite memorable. (Pastry chef Karen DeMasco won the 2005 James Beard award for Outstanding Pastry Chef.) The room (a former printing building) is striking and the concept, if getting a bit creaky, still deserves a try for its sense of improvisation.

Eleven Madison Park (212-889-0905), 11 Madison Avenue at the corner of East 24th Street. Subway: N, R, W, or 6 train to 23rd Street. Open daily for lunch 11:30 AM–2 PM and dinner 5:30–10:30 PM. How many restaurants did Danny Meyer open in this neighborhood, anyway? Union Square Café, Gramercy Tavern, Blue Smoke . . . and this one, the most elegant and romantic of them all. How romantic? Huge, 35-foot windows in the art deco bank building look onto the big park across the street; the interior (it was the bank's lobby) is decorated with plenty of touches that remind you just how much a meal will cost here. The menu also succeeds brilliantly, as chef Kerry Heffernan's French cuisine—mostly fish and game dishes—shines, accompanied by interesting side dishes and appetizers such as a squash-apple risotto and red pepper flan, a good wine list, and dynamite chocolate soufflés. The setting is so warm, and service so good, that I'd call this one of the city's top two or three restaurants for a significant celebration such as an anniversary.

Giorgio's of Gramercy (212-477-0007), 27 East 21st Street between Broadway and Park Avenue South. Subway: N, R, W, or 6 train to 23rd Street. Open weekdays for lunch 12:30–3:30 PM and for dinner 5–10:30 PM, Saturdays for dinner only 5–11 PM, Sunday for dinner only 5–10 PM. No, the chef isn't named Giorgio, but this Italian restaurant—known almost exclusively to locals—serves top-rate shellfish, pastas, and grilled fish. The interior is especially romantic, good for a quiet dinner with a loved one.

Gotham Bar & Grill (212-620-4020), 12 East 12th Street between Fifth Avenue and University Place. Subway: N, Q, R, W, 4, 5, or 6 train to 14th Street–Union Square. Open Monday through Friday for lunch noon–2:30 PM and for dinner 5:30–10:30 PM, Saturday for dinner only 5–11:30 PM, and Sunday for dinner only 5–10:30 PM. The original home of so-called tall food, Gotham chef Alfred Portale's baby continues its tradition of piling the lobster tails, vegetables, pieces of meat, whatever, as high and artistically on the plate as humanly possible. Is it homage to the city's sky-scrapers? Who knows. You'll find this conceit either fetching or annoying, but you'll never quibble at the food, which has held its own in the upper echelon of New York's fancy eateries for a quarter-century now in a room of narrow tables, billowy "parachute" lighting, and discreet booths. (In 2002 the restaurant walked away with the prestigious James Beard Foundation's award for top U.S. restaurant.)

Expect a lunch menu of chicken foie gras, cured salmon, grilled fish, duck risotto, and rack of lamb (or simply go for the prix fixe menu of a daily soup, a main course of salmon or *pappardelle* with braised duck, and chocolate cake or sorbet). Dinner might consist of goat cheese ravioli, seafood salad, or scallop soup to start and spiced duck breast, roast squab, peppercorn steak, or the famously vertical Maine lobster tails as a main course. Desserts are truly outstanding—try such winners as the vanilla crème brûlée sided with raspberry beignets, peanut-butter-and-grape napoleon (an upscale peanut butter and jelly sandwich), a milk chocolate caramel cake, or the mission fig tart. A huge wine list, well priced (look for a $20 half-bottle or the three-glass specials), accompanies everything; dress up if you're coming, though, because almost everyone else does. If you haven't, though, don't fret: Try to get a seat at the bar—there's no shame in it. You'll receive the same great service, dine from the same menu, and even get a special maple-wood tray off which to neatly eat your skyscraping meal.

Gramercy Tavern (212-477-0777), 42 East 20th Street between Broadway and Park Avenue South. Subway: N, R, or 6 train to 23rd Street. Open Monday through Thursday for lunch noon–2 PM and dinner 5:30–10 PM, Friday and Saturday to 11 PM. Danny Meyer's New American star is one of the city's top bites, bar none, well worth a splurge—and a splurge it will be. Start with the knowledgeable staff explaining chef Tom Colicchio's award-winning menu of grilled and braised meats, roast chicken, roast fish, spice-rubbed lobster, fresh root vegetables and herbs, lamb, wonderful salt-baked salmon, and much more. The compositions are often adventurous: braised or grilled bacon (a Colicchio favorite ingredient) with figs, for instance, or tuna tartare augmented by apples and horseradish. Desserts must also rank among New York's finest; the night's offerings might include a coffee meringue ice cream sandwich, a chocolate mousse paired with mint ice cream, molten chocolate cake, a tangy green apple *tarte Tatin,* or choices from the astonishingly deep list of cheeses.

Order à la carte; the prix fixe tasting menu is fine but doesn't showcase all the best entrées. If you're trying to conserve funds, come for the prix fixe lunch, which is still not cheap at $36 per person. Better yet, if dinner is a must (and it should be), remember that there are two dining rooms here—the tavern room nearer the street serves a more affordable menu, at tables and a bar, than the more formal dining room in back does. This room is a good place for a quicker, more informal meal of stew, a signature bacon dish, or something else. Just remember: Everyone in New York knows about the tavern, and you'll be hard pressed to get a table or seat at the bar last-minute.

Japonica (212-243-7752), 100 University Place at the corner of East 12th Street. Subway: L, N, Q, R, W, 4, 5, or 6 train to Union Square–14th Street. Open Monday through Friday noon–10:30 PM, Saturday noon–11 PM, Sunday noon–10:30 PM. NYU kids dining on parental credit and local models alike pop into this low-lit, slickly designed sushi fusion restaurant on busy University Place. They dig into pricey lunch and dinner menus of tempura and obscenely huge sushi rolls—but it's not just about quantity here; some of the cuts of fish are a good deal more inventive than what you'll find elsewhere in town—beneath tropically themed walls. Lunch entrées run about $15–20 each, and dinners can easily start at $35 per person for a main course, so save it for a splurge and dress in stylishly casual clothing—not only your date but the masses of streetwalkers on University Place will see you lounging on your banquette through the big windows. If you're traveling in a big group, try to reserve the big table (there's only one); it seats 10.

Kitchen 22 (212-228-4399), 35 East 22nd Street between Broadway and Park Avenue South. Subway: N, R, W, or 6 train to 23rd Street. Open Monday through Thursday for dinner 5–10 PM, Friday and Saturday to 11 PM. New York native Charlie Palmer—who formerly cooked at Brooklyn's River Café, then opened Aureole at the age of 28—has downscaled the prices and the complexity of the menu for this Gramercy Park–area eatery, and it's much the better for it. Bargain hunters need look no farther than here for terrific food from a name chef at affordable prices. A narrow place on a nondescript stretch of street, Kitchen 22 turns out to have a sleekly modern, bistro interior. The solid prix fixe meals are the only thing on the menu; the three-course $25 dinner is a real bargain price, especially given the quality. Start with a squash-apple soup, marinated seafood salad, salmon tartare, or beef carpaccio, then move on to a main course such as fennel-crusted salmon, roast chicken with porcini risotto, or lentil-dusted mahimahi. Finish with a piece of pecan pie, some tiramisu, a chocolate dessert, a hazelnut terrine, or rum-caramelized pineapple.

Mesa Grill (212-807-7400), 102 Fifth Avenue between 15th and 16th streets. Subway: L, N, Q, R, W, 4, 5, or 6 train to Union Square–14th Street. Open Monday through Friday for lunch noon–2:30 PM and dinner 5:30–10:30 PM, Saturday for brunch 11:30 AM–3 PM and dinner 5:30–11 PM, Sunday for brunch 11:30 AM–3 PM and dinner 5:30–10:30 PM. New York foodies remember precisely the moment in 1991 when Bobby Flay's Mesa Grill shook up the city's culinary landscape with a miniature earthquake that signaled the arrival of southwestern cuisine. Flay—now a celebrity with his own TV show, cookbook, and endorsement deals—was one of the first big-league chefs to find a way to fuse the tastes of the American Southwest (blue corn, chipotle, anchos, tamales, tomatillos, and so forth) with the ethos of New American cuisine (rare and seared fish, pairings of soft main-course meats with crispy side dishes, fancy chocolate desserts, and less-is-more styling). Above all he goes for complex, spicy flavors that leave the taste buds singing afterward.

Lunch could start with a lamb-ancho taco, chicken *posole* soup with plantains, or a blue corn pancake filled with duck and habanero sauce, then continue with a chile pork tenderloin sandwich, chicken and sweet potato hash, grilled shrimp, or a chile relleno. The dinner menu adds entrées such as charcoal-grilled snapper, beef short ribs with polenta, salmon with chili sauce, and spicy steaks, pork loin, shrimp, and swordfish, while brunch might run to tequila-smoked salmon, a peppy grilled chicken breast with fries, steak-and-egg tortillas, or Mexican cinnamon French toast. Flay's formula obviously struck a nerve and remains just as much a success today—just sit down and try to hear yourself talking among the boisterous, overjoyed crowds of diners filling this fun room every single day of the week. It's still one of the most enjoyable and exciting places to challenge your palate in town.

Olives NY (212-353-8345), 201 Park Avenue South at the corner of East 17th Street. Subway: L, N, Q, R, W, 4, 5, or 6 train to 14th Street–Union Square. Open daily for breakfast 7–10:30 AM, lunch noon–2:30 PM, and dinner 5:30–10 PM. Inside the modern W New York–Union Square hotel, Olives is the New York branch of Boston chef Todd English's growing American empire. His cuisine comfortably cruises a gamut of New American, Italian, and Mediterranean—think high-class steaks, lamb, and fish, inventively presented without being too challenging—cooked in wood-fired ovens and on the grill. There are plenty of wines to accompany everything, and the sleek two-story, wooden-floored space is decorated with bright colors and Oriental rugs; banquettes have great views of Union Square or the open kitchen, depending on which one you're more interested in watching. Despite aspirations to greatness, the food here is not among the best in the city, and sometimes goes overboard with the spicing, sweetening, or oil. Still, desserts are outstanding and legitimately worth an order.

Pipa (212-677-2233), 38 East 19th Street between Broadway and Park Avenue South. Subway: L, N, Q, R,

W, 4, 5, or 6 train to 14th Street–Union Square. Open weekdays noon–3 PM for lunch and 6–11 PM for dinner, Friday to midnight, weekends 11 AM–4 PM for brunch and for dinner to 11 PM Saturday, to 10 PM Sunday. Douglas Rodriguez's candlelit, gorgeously decorated tapas restaurant, improbably lodged in an upscale home furnishings store, has made a splash with its exciting menu of paella, flatbreads, soups, casseroles, bits of seafood and shellfish, cheeses . . . and lots of garlic. Individual tapas plates here cost $5–10, so the price of a meal can quickly escalate—but at least you'll enjoy the ride, even before trying one of the dreamy desserts such as smooth custard or a crunchy fried doughnut. The brick-walled, chandeliered space (the restaurant has been designed by the same folks who operate the store) alone is worth a visit.

Sushi Samba Park (212-475-9377), 245 Park Avenue South between East 19th and East 20th streets. Subway: 6 train to 23rd Street. Open Monday through Saturday 11:45 AM–1 AM, Thursday through Saturday until 2 AM, Sunday from 1 PM. Smaller than its counterpart in Greenwich Village (see chapter 4), this Sushi Samba is more for the business crowd. But it serves the same enchanting mixture of Brazilian-Latino food and sushi, featuring superfresh fish, a great raw bar, and outstanding people-watching. Try anything from the amazing long menu of ceviches or *tiraditos* (a lovely glass sampler plate of four is definitely the best way to go); a main course such as the good lobster tempura roll with peanut sauce, sea bass, striped bass, pan-seared salmon, rich duck with coffee sauce, *churrasco samba*, or steamed mahimahi; and classy

desserts of simple, strong flavors—I like the molten chocolate cake sided with chocolate sorbet, green tea ice cream, and a crisp cookie. You'll thrill to the taste of a piece of salmon in onion-citrus froth or lobster with mango. Don't forget a potent *mojito* or other rum-based Brazilian cocktail in a tall glass.

Union Square Café (212-243-4020), 21 East 16th Street between Fifth Avenue and Union Square. Subway: L, N, Q, R, W, 4, 5, or 6 train to 14th Street–Union Square. Open Monday through Saturday for lunch noon–2:15 PM and dinner 5:30–9:45 PM, weekends until 10:45 PM. The first in hot owner Danny Meyer's empire of New York restaurants, the Union Square Café is widely accepted as one of the city's top two or three eateries today, in the same rarefied air as Gramercy Tavern (see above) and Nobu. However, today the menu bears the stamp of owner-chef Michael Romano as much as it does of Meyer: Pastas cooked in richly flavored, silky sauces; grilled and seared fish; and game cooked with plenty of herbs dominate the menu. Everything is good and hearty, whether it's simply a roast chicken or suckling pig, or a creation such as a shepherd's pie made with lobster meat.

Service in the handsome, cherry-floored room is absolutely flawless, and the decor isn't stuffy at all—this is an amazingly comfortable place to eat one of the country's best meals (upscale garlicky potato chips are actually on the menu as an appetizer, and they're very popular). Union Square isn't even all that expensive alongside some of its fellow top-ranked New American and French restaurants in town. However, the flip side to this coin is that so much consistent success has made this an almost impossible place to get a table; try to book very far in advance if you possibly can.

Veritas (212-353-3700), 43 East 20th Street between Broadway and Park Avenue South. Subway: N, R, or 6 train to 23rd Street. Open Monday through Saturday 5:30–10:30 PM, Sunday 5–10 PM. Anyone who cares about such things knows that Veritas boasts the city's best vino list, an incredible selection of some 2,700 wines assembled by the capable hands of owner Gino Diaferia, rising young chef Scott Bryan (formerly of Bouley and other top kitchens), and wine expert Tim Kopec. Michelin puts it this way: "Veritas spells paradise for oenophiles." But Bryan's food keeps pace with the wine—and the hype. The simple and dependable $76 prix fixe dinner might start with sweetbreads, tuna tartare, lobster salad, or foie gras, then move on to braised short ribs, organic roast chicken, seared diver scallops, a piece of pepper-crusted venison, pan-roasted cod, roast lamb, strip steak, veal, or saddle of lamb. Wondrous desserts from pastry chef Dalia Jurgensen could include a strawberry rhubarb crumble with toasted almond ice milk and candied ginger, a chocolate soufflé with caramel ice cream, a warm *tarte tatin* with macadamia nut brittle and butter rum sauce, a maple crème caramel with candied pecans and sour cherry sauce, a ricotta or Meyer lemon tart, or a honey-grapefruit sorbet. But it all comes back to the wine—anything from an affordable sip (many wines here are available by the glass) to a $20,000 bottle of an exceedingly rare vintage.

Chat 'n' Chew (212-243-1616), 10 East 16th Street between Fifth Avenue and Union Square West. Subway: L, N, Q, R, W, 4, 5, or 6 train to 14th Street–Union Square. Open daily 11:30 AM–midnight, weekends from 10 AM. There's no pretense here; this is diner-style Americana cooking all the way, anything from a peanut butter sandwich to a BLT to good fried chicken, burgers, and grilled cheese—all at reasonable prices. You might not feel like you're in New York City anymore, but sometimes even locals need to get away without getting away.

City Bakery (212-366-1414), 3 West 18th Street between Fifth and Sixth avenues. Subway: L, N, Q, R, W, 4, 5 or 6 train to 14th Street–Union Square. Open Monday through Saturday 7:30 AM–7 PM, Sunday 9 AM–6 PM. There must be a million salad bars in New York City; every last convenience store on the Upper West Side seems to operate one, entire chains have sprung up based on the buffet–salad bar concept, and the quality is highly variable. But you haven't really tasted a New York salad bar until you've worked your way downtown to the City Bakery, an unassuming two-story cafeteria tucked on a side street in the Flatiron District near Union Square. Owner Maury Rubin is legendary among celebrities, models, and the like for his fresher-than-fresh greens, dressings, sandwiches, and soups (served on the ground floor) and more filling hot meals (served on the second level); just be prepared for a little sticker shock—you'll be paying top dollar per pound for the quality, and they don't accept plastic. The homemade desserts here don't have gourmet aspirations; they're simply some of the most satisfying brownies, cakes, cookies, and pies you'll eat in New York. Yes, it's expensive, but when you don't feel like a fancy lunch this is a great choice: all things considered, one of the city's top delis . . . serving what is possibly New York's best hot chocolate.

craftbar (212-780-0880), 900 Broadway between 19th Street and 20th Street. Subway: N, R, W, or 6 train to 23rd Street. Open Tuesday to Saturday noon–2:30 PM for lunch and 5:30–11 PM for dinner, Sunday and Monday to 10 PM. An offshoot of the adjacent upscale eatery (Tom Colicchio's Craft; see *Dining Out*), this is a more affordable eatery with pressed *panini* sandwiches, fried snacks, rice balls, chicken soup, a good bar, a decent wine list, and late hours. There are also a few daily specials such as lasagna, fried fish, pasta with duck sauce, and lamb well worth trying. Desserts come from same Craft-y kitchen: fritters with ice cream, chocolate tarts. Standards are every bit as high here as they are next door, and service is terrific, too; you'll save money and time on nights when you don't feel like a 2-hour culinary marathon. Note that they do not take reservations.

Eisenberg's Sandwich Shop (212-675-5096), 174 Fifth Avenue between West 22nd and West 23rd streets. Subway: N or R train to 23rd Street. Open Monday through Friday 6 AM–8 PM, Saturday 8 AM–4 PM. There are so many Jewish delis in New York that it's easy to fall into the trap of thinking they're all the same; they're not. This one is better than most, and specializes in sandwiches ranging from the dainty (tuna salad) to meaty (great

Reubens). They've also got soups and side dishes. No matter what you order, though, absolutely don't forget to order an egg cream to wash it all down.

Friend of a Farmer (212-477-2188), 77 Irving Place between East 18th and East 19th streets. Subway: N, Q, R, W, 4, 5, or 6 train to 14th Street–Union Square. Open Monday through Thursday 8 AM–10 PM, Friday to 11 PM, Saturday and Sunday from 9:30 AM. I love this place precisely because it dares to be nothing more than a middle-America kind of place amid a sea of upscale restaurants in the surrounding area. You're going to get nothing more complicated than Mom's chicken, turkey, roast beef, apple pie, and the like. Oh, there might be a few fancy touches—fresher vegetables than those you'd get at the A&P, an exotic-looking mushroom here, a fresher-than-expected bread there. After all, this isn't a diner in the backwoods of Vermont; a few concessions had to be made to New York tastes. But all in all, it's a refreshingly simple place. The delicious brunch is wildly popular here, too; come early on weekends (the line forms fast and gets long) if you're really intent on trying it.

Mizu Sushi (212-505-6688), 29 East 20th Street between Broadway and Park Avenue South. Subway: N, R, or 6 train to 23rd Street. Open Monday through Friday for lunch noon–3 PM and dinner 5–11:30 PM, Saturday for dinner only 5–11:30 PM. This sushi joint, located on the same precious block as famous Gramercy Tavern (see *Dining Out*), puts out a full slate of sushi rolls, sushi, sashimi, maki, and combinations thereof. The fish isn't cheap, but it's not overly expensive, either. There are also hot meals such as tempura, teriyaki, soba and udon noodles, *tonkatsu* (pork cutlet), and salmon, and snacks like *shumai* (dumplings), *yakitori,* and *edamame* (steamed soybeans). All desserts and drinks are likewise authentically Japanese.

COFFEE AND SNACKS Lady Mendl's (212-533-4466), 56 Irving Place between East 17th and East 18th streets. Subway: N, Q, R, W, 4, 5, or 6 train to 14th Street–Union Square. Open Wednesday through Friday for tea 3–5 PM, Saturday and Sunday for tea 2–4:30 PM. Lady Mendl's bring another touch of class to the Inn at Irving Place (see *Lodging—Inn*), as if the place needed it. You can order only one thing here—a grand, five-course high tea—and you must reserve it in advance, but in this part of town nobody does the form better. Don't come wearing jeans and sneakers.

✳ Entertainment

THEATER/PERFORMING ARTS

Repertorio Español (212-889-2850). Performances at Gramercy Park Theatre, 138 East 27th Street between Lexington and Third avenues. Subway: N, R, or W train to 28th Street. After waiting out a fresh renovation of its theater, this company began a new run of shows in August 2003. The company was founded in 1968 by producer Gilberto Zaldivar and artistic director René Buch as a way of bringing the finest Latino playwrights, productions, and actors to Manhattan audiences. The company moved to the Gramercy Park Theatre in 1972. All Spanish productions here

are presented with simultaneous infrared English translations, allowing non-Spanish-speaking patrons to enjoy the performances silently and unobtrusively; you can see such classic plays as *Don Quijote y Sancho Panza,* but also cutting-edge work such as *Vieques,* a prize-winning comedy by new playwright Jorge González about American military forces on the island of Puerto Rico. Tickets cost $20–45.

Union Square Theatre (212-505-1700), 100 East 17th Street at the corner of Park Avenue South. Subway: L, N, W, 4, 5, or 6 train to 14th Street–Union Square. This two-story, 500-seat theater just off the square is home to LAByrinth Theater Company productions such as the affecting play *Our Lady of 121st Street,* about a nun's death that reunites a group of old friends at a Harlem funeral home, and *Slava's Snow Show.*

Vineyard Theatre (212-353-4466), 108 East 15th Street between Irving Place and Union Square East (Park Avenue South). Subway: L, N, W, 4, 5, or 6 train to 14th Street–Union Square. This great off-Broadway theater in the basement level of the Zeckendorf Towers apartment building seats about 120 but packs a punch. Its company has staged such intriguing works as the singing-puppet comedy *Avenue Q* (about life after college for New Yorkers without a job) and *How I Learned to Drive*

MUSIC VENUES Irving Plaza (212-777-6800), 17 Irving Place at the corner of East 15th Street. Subway: L, N, W, 4, 5, or 6 train to 14th Street–Union Square. This Union Square–area club puts out one of the most interesting schedules in town—everything from folkies like Kasey Chambers and Susan Tedeschi to modern rock acts like Toad the Wet Sprocket and Better Than Ezra; the Mink DeVille Band; 1980s rock band Concrete Blonde; and even Super Diamond, the Neil Diamond tribute act. Tickets start at around $20 per person. Blockbuster acts like U2 and Prince have even been known to drop in very occasionally and play unannounced sets.

Jazz Standard (212-576-2232), 116 East 27th Street between Lexington and Park avenues. Subway: 6 train to 28th Street. Part of Danny Meyer's barbecue restaurant Blue Smoke (see *Dining Out*), this club is a good place in the neighborhood to catch live jazz along with a beer and a plate of ribs.

ABRAHAM LINCOLN IN BRONZE, UNION SQUARE PARK

Paul Karr

Most show tickets cost $20–25; sets begin nightly at 7:30 and 9:30 PM, with a third late show on Friday and Saturday nights kicking off around 11:30 PM.

FILM Loews 19th Street East (212-50-LOEWS, ext. 858), 890 Broadway at the corner of East 19th Street. Subway: N or R train to 23rd Street, or L, Q, W, 4, 5, or 6 train to 14th Street–Union Square. Hollywood hits are shown here, but occasionally a sleeper film as well.

BARS AND CLUBS Underbar (917-534-5913), 201 Park Avenue South at the corner of East 17th Street. Subway: L, N, Q, R, W, 4, 5, or 6 train to Union Square–14th Street. Open 4 PM–3 AM. Inside the hip W New York–Union Square hotel (see *Lodging—Boutique Hotels*), this quiet bar designed by Rande Gerber imposes a dress code—doormen will likely scrutinize every inch of you for coolness before admission.

✳ Selective Shopping

ANTIQUES The ShowPlace (212-633-6063), 40 West 25th Street between Broadway and Sixth Avenue. Subway: N, R, or W train to 23rd or 28th Street. Some galleries open Monday through Friday 10 AM–6 PM, all floors open weekends 8:30 AM–5:30 PM. This is the Flatiron District's under-one-roof antiques facility, a three-floor complex of stalls operated by a mixture of itinerant and established dealers—more than 130 in all, selling Asian art, European antiques, glass, antique jewelry, art deco and art nouveau pieces, and silver, among other items. There's an espresso bar on the premises.

HOME FURNISHINGS ABC Carpet & Home (212-473-3000), 38 East 19th Street, and 888 Broadway. Subway: L, N, Q, R, W, 4, 5, or 6 train to 14th Street–Union Square. ABC is one of the most remarkable stores in the city—far more interesting, in many ways, than a temple to excess like Saks or Bloomingdale's, and it stands head and shoulders above some other pretty good home furnishings shops in the area of Broadway and 20th Street. The upscale store has trolled the world for the interior items New Yorkers just have to have: anything from Kashmiri silk or fine linens to Venetian handblown chandeliers, luxury beds, Tibetan chests, French armoires, and Chinese cabinetry, all chosen with a collector's eye and much of it custom-made for the store. Entire sections of this 350,000-square-foot emporium— which is actually spread out over two facilities standing face-to-face across Broadway—are devoted to statuary, lighting, carpets (naturally; there's a whole building full), electronics, and garden supplies, among other essentials.

Chelsea 6

CHELSEA

Originally a mostly British residential settlement, Chelsea knew a brief heyday as a center for the arts—theaters and an opera house were in vogue for a time, and local developer Clement Clark Moore put some grace and order into the area when he began developing rows and rows of town houses in the mid-19th century. The first motion-picture companies were actually based here before heading west to California in search of larger spaces and sets. Soon other business began moving uptown to Times Square as well, and Chelsea was forced to adapt. It chose to utilize its position near the Hudson River piers to transform the area into a heavily industrial district of fur and flower merchants, garment factories, and fashion-design cutters. There's an intense history of struggle between the owners of those garment firms and their workers; labor unions got their start here, as did the American socialist and communist movements.

Today Chelsea has reinvented itself anew as cultural capital: Some of the city's most interesting galleries, antiques shops, restaurants, and clubs are located here among the fine old Georgian and Victorian homes and town houses and renovated warehouses. It is the heart of the city's gay and lesbian population, a distinction the West Village once held all to its own. It's worth noting that many of the shops and businesses here are gay- or lesbian-owned; this remains the city's most vital gay and lesbian quarter, and you'll find the familiar rainbow flag in abundance.

For the purposes of this guidebook, I have become a little generous with my definition of Chelsea: Herein, it's everything west of Sixth Avenue to the Hudson River, from the north side of 14th Street up to 30th Street.

GETTING THERE Chelsea is off the beaten track—one reason, perhaps, for its sometimes zany character.

By car: It's easy to get here, if a little time consuming. From uptown just take the West Side Highway until it runs out, then continue down Twelfth Avenue. From Midtown, work your way across to the west side of town on an odd-numbered cross street as soon as you can and then take a south-traveling avenue (Broadway, Seventh, Ninth, Eleventh, Twelfth); if you're very far east, use Second Avenue to get south first, then cut across on an odd-numbered cross street.

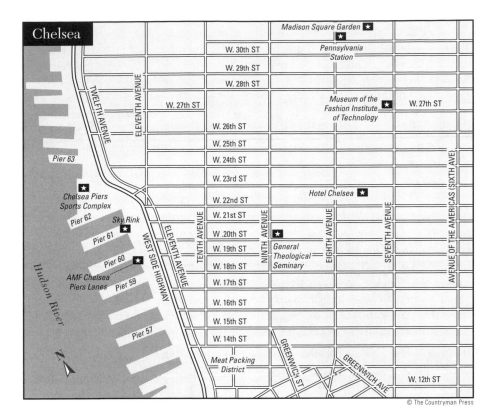

Chelsea

Madison Square Garden ★

W. 30th ST

Pennsylvania Station

W. 29th ST

W. 28th ST

TWELFTH AVENUE

ELEVENTH AVENUE

W. 27th ST

Museum of the Fashion Institute ★ of Technology

W. 27th ST

W. 26th ST

W. 25th ST

Pier 63

W. 24th ST

W. 23rd ST

AVENUE OF THE AMERICAS (SIXTH AVE)

★ Chelsea Piers Sports Complex

W. 22nd ST

Hotel Chelsea ★

Pier 62   Sky Rink ★

W. 21st ST

Pier 61

WEST SIDE HIGHWAY

ELEVENTH AVENUE

TENTH AVENUE

W .20th ST

NINTH AVENUE

★

EIGHTH AVENUE

SEVENTH AVENUE

Pier 60 ★

W. 19th ST

General Theological Seminary

AMF Chelsea Piers Lanes   Pier 59

W. 18th ST

Hudson River

W. 17th ST

W. 16th ST

W. 15th ST

Pier 57

W. 14th ST

N

Meat Packing District

GREENWICH ST

GREENWICH AVE

W. 12th ST

© The Countryman Press

By subway: Your options are limited to Seventh and Eighth avenues; for the multitude of galleries, restaurants, and clubs west of Eighth Avenue, you'll simply have to hoof it or find a bus to get you closer (not an easy task). To get to Seventh Avenue, take the 1 train to 28th Street, 23rd Street, or 18th Street. The 2 and 3 express trains stop at 14th Street and Seventh Avenue. To get to Eighth Avenue, take the C or E train to 23rd Street or down to 14th Street (near the Meatpacking District); the A express train also stops at 14th Street and Eighth Avenue.

By bus: The 20 bus travels uptown and downtown along Eighth Avenue, Seventh Avenue, and Broadway to and from the Upper West Side. You can also catch a 10 bus from uptown—this bus takes a similar route, stopping just short of Chelsea at 31st Street.

GETTING AROUND Crosstown transportation in Chelsea is limited to just the 14 bus, which shuttles to and fro along 14th Street, and the 23 bus, which does the same along 23rd—a street that is one of the hubs of the action and a good introduction to Chelsea.

✳ To See

There's no better way to get a quick taste of Chelsea than by hightailing it down to West 23rd Street and simply exploring. The prime block to see is between Seventh and Eighth avenues, where a Bohemian character begins to take hold: Here you'll find the Hotel Chelsea (see *Lodging—Affordable Hotels*), the headquarters of the Communist Party USA, the island's oldest YMCA, a public library branch, a European-style french-fry-and-hot-dog take-out place, *and* every manner of street character. Patti Smith and Robert Mapplethorpe lived upstairs of what is now a good Thai restaurant at No. 206.

The next blocks west are a mishmash of galleries, movie theaters, tatty hotels, apartment buildings, and restaurants, not to mention the beginnings of the giant, odd Penn South housing projects constructed for Garment District workers in the 1960s. (The buildings and plaza do successfully interrupt the rigid Manhattan grid plan for about four blocks north, and are worth a quick look if you're on foot.) West of Tenth Avenue, beyond the off-off-Broadway theaters, bars, and more apartments, there's a small park and then the huge Chelsea Piers Sports Complex (see *To Do—Indoor Sports*). This same complex of buildings on the river also houses television studios, stages, and production companies, including the one that produces the *Law & Order* programs.

Just five blocks away is 28th Street, nearly as interesting for its juxtaposition of the Flower District (see *Neighborhoods*), the Fashion Institute of Technology (see *Museums*), and the former Tin Pan Alley music publishing district (see *Neighborhoods*).

MUSEUMS **Chelsea Art Museum** (212-255-0719), 556 West 22nd Street between Tenth and Eleventh avenues. Subway: C or E train to 23rd Street. Open Tuesday through Saturday noon–6 PM, Thursday to 8 PM. This is a minor museum, certainly, but nonetheless its shows—such as an exhibit of crime photography and a group showing based around the idea of open space—may intrigue you on a rainy day. The squat red facility is operated by the Miotte Foundation, and thus dedicates some of its exhibit space to founding father Jean Miotte; its stated mission is to present the art of artists who might not otherwise find a venue. Admission costs $6 for adults, $3 for students and senior citizens.

The Museum at FIT (212-217-7642), Seventh Avenue at the corner of West 27th Street. Subway: C or E train to 23rd Street, or 1 or 9 train to 28th Street. Open Tuesday through Friday noon–8 PM, Saturday 10 AM–5 PM. Not only is the Fashion Institute of Technology's museum a great bargain (it's free of charge), but few New Yorkers have been here—so this is a chance to see something many locals haven't. Holding an important collection of costumes and textiles, the museum aims to document the history of fashion and explain its cultural contexts. You'll also find intriguing exhibits on, for instance, Scaasi's evening gowns, Italian fashion, and women's fashions in turn-of-the-20th-century Paris; periodic talks and seminars explore such topics as "The Femme Fatale." This is definitely a one-of-a-kind, only-in-New-York experience.

New Museum of Contemporary Art (212-219-1222), 556 West 22nd Street
at Eleventh Avenue. Subway: C or E train to 23rd Street. Open Tuesday through
Saturday noon–6 PM, Thursday to 8 PM. This little-known museum, recently
relocated to Chelsea, is heavy on digital and multimedia art from artists you
might never have heard about, and also offers readings and thought-provoking
installations and exhibitions. Admission costs $6 for adults, $3 for students and
senior citizens; it's $3 for adults Thursday night, and always free for anyone
under age 18.

NEIGHBORHOODS **Cushman Row,** 406–418 West 20th Street between Ninth
and Tenth avenues. Subway: C or E train to 23rd Street. These are not actually
some of the many, many town houses built by Chelsea developer (and poet)
Clement Clark Moore during the 19th century. Instead, they were erected by
Don Alonzo Cushman—and they are considered the city's finest examples of
Greek Revival rowhouse architecture.

Flower District, West 28th Street between Sixth and Seventh avenues. Subway:
1 train to 28th Street. For more than 100 years, some of America's biggest florists
have operated out of this stretch of 28th Street. There aren't any actual retail
stores here now, and more vendors get squeezed out by new development or
suburban competition each year. (In fact, the vendors' association is trying to
move elsewhere and create a new flower district—but, reportedly, it can't find
affordable real estate anywhere.) So see it now, while it still exists. This is a ves-
tige of the old New York.

Tin Pan Alley, 28th Street between Broadway and Seventh Avenue. Subway:
N, R, or W train to 28th Street. This was once the original heart of New York's
music publishing business, before it all moved uptown—along with the theaters,
which also once dotted this neighborhood—to the Times Square area and the
Brill Building. Songwriters and publishers would hire musicians (including a
teenage George Gershwin) to play tunes to woo passersby, and the racket supposedly inspired the colorful name. Today, though, it's a mostly disused area, an
adjunct to the miniature wholesale fur district stretching along 29th Street a
block north.

HISTORIC SITES **General Theological Seminary** (212-243-5150), 175 Ninth
Avenue at the corner of West 20th Street. Subway: C or E train to 23rd Street.
Library open Monday through Thursday 8 AM–11 PM, Friday to 10 PM, Saturday
9 AM–7 PM, Sunday 3–10 PM. This 19th-century Episcopal campus is off-limits to
the general public, including the St Mark's Library—which holds an impressive,
world-class collection of Latin Bibles and other religious materials, and regularly
exhibits such holdings as material from the poet T. S. Eliot. It's something of a
pity that you must have either a card from another theological association or a
special letter or permission to visit this resource. The campus architecture is
equally interesting, featuring a chapel with a tall campanile and examples of
Gothic Revival structures.

✹ To Do

INDOOR SPORTS ✍ **Chelsea Piers Sports Complex,** 23rd Street at the Hudson River. Subway: C or E train to 23rd Street. This enormous sports complex is great for a cold or rainy day—New Yorkers go nuts over it, because there's so much to do no matter what the weather's doing. At the popular **Golf Club** (212-336-6400) on Pier 59, open 6 AM–midnight in summer, slightly shorter hours in winter, you can rent clubs, learn from a teaching pro, or simply hit out into the Hudson (don't worry—a net not a fish, will catch the balls). Free lessons are offered Saturday and Sunday mornings (8–10 AM). Another tip: During off-peak hours you can get more swings per dollar.

In the **Field House** at Pier 62 (212-336-6500) you can climb fake rocks, take swings in a batting cage (10 balls for $2), or shoot hoops on a basketball court for $8 an hour. There's a big set of bowling lanes, **AMF Chelsea Piers Lanes,** between Piers 59 and 60 (212-835-2695); the 40 lanes cost $7 per person per game plus $4.50–5.50 per person for shoe-rental fees, and the action is sometimes jazzed up by fog, glow-in-the-dark pins, and the like. They offer good family-of-four deals (soda and popcorn included, pizza optional), too.

The **Sky Rink** at Pier 61 (212-336-6100) is the place to skate; it cost $11 per adult or $8.50 per youth or senior—and skates and helmets cost about $9 extra per session to rent.

Muscles getting tired? The **Spa at Chelsea Piers** (212-336-6780) on Pier 60 offers a variety of treatments and packages weekdays 9 AM–9 PM, Saturday to 6 PM, and Sunday 10 AM–7 PM. Pier 60 also features a **roller hockey rink** (212-336-6200), which opens for the summer in April. (Local leagues continue play at the rinks through the winter.)

✹ Lodging

BOUTIQUE HOTEL Maritime Hotel (212-242-4300; fax 212-242-1188), 363 West 16th Street at the corner of Ninth Avenue. Subway: 1 train to 14th Street. This massive hotel was designed to look like an ocean liner, in finest art deco style, and it does. Sort of. (Rooms on the Hudson River side each have porthole windows.) There's a reason why—this was once the head office of the National Maritime Union. But there the comparison ends; inside, this is no ship's cabin, but rather a yachtlike ride. The expensive rooms are equipped with flat-screen TVs, Wi-Fi, gorgeous beds and bathrooms, and the like. No wonder movie and music stars prowl the halls regularly, hitting the twin hip hot spots of the moment without even leaving hotel grounds: an exclusive Japanese basement bar (Hiro; big names often close it for private parties) and the upscale Japanese eatery Matsuri. In warmer weather, there's an expansive outdoor terrace overlooking the west side: Sun yourself and try to pretend you're in Malibu, not Ninth Avenue.

BUSINESS HOTEL Hampton Inn Chelsea (212-414-1000; fax 212-647-1511), 108 West 24th Street between Sixth and Seventh avenues. Subway: F, V, or 1 train to 23rd Street. Chelsea's first modern business hotel has 144 rooms and offers free breakfasts and free local phone calls, just as other properties in the Hampton Inn chain do. Double rooms in peak season start at around $180–190 per night.

INN ☙ **Inn on 23rd** (212-463-0330 or 1-877-387-2323; fax 212-463-0302), 131 West 23rd Street between Fifth and Sixth avenues. Subway: F, V, or 1 train to 23rd Street. This little red 19th-century town house is little known among tourists seeking big-box hotels, but it's actually a very good choice if you're seeking a smaller-scale experience in the Chelsea neighborhood. Annette and Kenneth Fisherman, formerly gallery owners and art collectors from Long Island, moved to the Apple in 1998 with their family to renovate the town house. Now the 14 spacious rooms in the self-described urban B&B—a kind of hybrid business hotel and B&B—are each simply but tastefully furnished in different motifs such as French Provincial, Victorian, Bamboo, 1940s, 1950s, Cabin (with leather sofa and armchair), Skylight (with a skylight, exposed brick walls, and chandeliers), and a large suite consisting of a handsome living room and separate bedroom, furnished with an antique globe, daybed, skylight, and views of the Empire State Building. (Most of these antiques and furnishings came from the former Long Island home.)

All units come with newly installed private bathroom, satellite television, queen or king bed, two-line phone with dataport, plush towels, and blackout shades and double-glazed windows to keep out noise and light. The owners happily provide cribs, CD players, and VCRs on request. Local phone calls, faxes, photocopies, elevator rides, and great advice about the neighborhood? They're all free.

There's also a fully stocked honor bar, a guest refrigerator and freezer, and an included breakfast that's good right down to the little touches—the coffee comes from top small-scale importer Porto Rico, the tea from Harvey and Sons. Double room rates start at $219 per night, while the suite begins at around $329 per night.

AFFORDABLE HOTELS **Chelsea Inn** (212-645-8989 or 1-800-640-6469; fax 212-645-1903), 46 West 17th Street between Fifth and Sixth avenues. Subway: F or V train to 14th Street, L train to Sixth Avenue, or L, N, Q, R, W, 4, 5, or 6 train to Union Square–14th Street. Definitely on the lower end of the scale, the Chelsea is just a smidgeon better than youth-hostel-style accommodation: Rooms in the brownstone do have a rather simple kitchenette, as well as phone, coffeemaker, safe, television, and air-conditioning. Only a few come with their own private bathroom, however—everyone else will be sharing. Rooms are clean and sparsely furnished with a mishmash of furniture, their wall murals painted by art students. The hotel's quite close to Chelsea's nightlife as well. Rooms with shared bathrooms go for $89–139 each; the double room rates range $139–197, and the one- and two-bedroom suite $159–279.

☙ **Chelsea Lodge and Suites** (212-243-4499; fax 212-243-7852), 318 West 20th Street between Eighth and Ninth avenues. Subway: C or E train to 20th Street, A train to 14th Street, or L train to Eighth Avenue. This attractive three-story brownstone owned by a husband and wife is a relatively new Chelsea entry, offering air-conditioned, plainly furnished rooms of wood and parquet floors, pleasant wallpapers, and private showers (bathrooms are shared and located on the hallways of each floor). All the beds here are smallish doubles, but the owners clearly care about what they're doing; there's a television in each unit and small chocolates to greet you, and the entire place is very well kept up. It's definitely a cut above the other budget-priced lodgings in Chelsea. There aren't any room phones, but at prices this low ($99–$115 double per night) you might not care. All in all, it's a great bargain if you're keen on visiting Chelsea or the nearby Meatpacking District and want to stroll back home along a pretty block at the end of each day.

The hotel also offers four suites in another brownstone nearby—only these are more spacious, and come outfitted with tall windows, brand-new marble bathroom with pedestal sink, kitchenette, comfy queen bed, couch, dresser, VCR, art prints on the walls, a phone (local calls are free), and a jack to plug in your laptop modem. Two of these suites face the street, two face a private garden, but all cost the same: $195 per night for double occupancy. And, yes—the rooms have air conditioning.

Chelsea Savoy Hotel (212-929-9353 or 1-866-929-9353; fax 212-741-6309), 204 West 23rd Street at the corner of Seventh Avenue. Subway: 1 train to 23rd Street. This place is nothing fancy to look at, either inside or out, but it's actually one of the few hotel options central to Chelsea's most interesting parts. And the 90 or so rooms, if as uniformly bland as a Motel 6, seem clean and well-enough kept—they even come with standard motel amenities like phone, dataport, miniature refrigerator, and television. Queen-bedded rooms cost $135–250 per night; rooms with two double beds cost up to $250, while single occupancy can cost as little a $99 per night; king rooms are a bit more expensive. There's a midpriced restaurant in the lobby area, as well as a sitting room where you can watch the world (Chelsea-style) go by.

Hotel Chelsea (212-243-3700; fax 212-675-5531), 222 West 23rd Street between Seventh and Eighth avenues. Subway: C, E, or 1 train to 23rd Street. Known widely in the city as the "Chelsea Hotel." Part residence, part history lesson, part funky hotel, the Chelsea is for those with a sense of adventure; no other New York accommodation brings together the city's artiest elements and presents them to the casual visitor in such brash fashion. Built in 1884 as the city's first cooperatively owned apartment building, the 12-story Chelsea was New York's tallest building for more than 15 years. The co-op failed and was converted into a hotel, which soon began attracting notable writers

THE HOTEL CHELSEA

Paul Karr

to stay, or even live, within its walls: Mark Twain, O. Henry, and Edgar Lee Masters at first, Thomas Wolfe, Dylan Thomas, and Arthur C. Clarke later. A raft of associated painters, poets, musicians, thinkers, dancers, actors, and other artists who would become world famous—Bob Dylan, Willem de Kooning, Robert Mapplethorpe, William Burroughs, Jane Fonda, Arthur Miller, Joni Mitchell, Sarah Bernhardt, and the French photographer Henri Cartier-Bresson, among many others—all followed. Today there are still many resident artists here, and some have lived here for more than a quarter century. The rooms? Depending on which one you get, they're either nothing special or quite interestingly decorated: Pete Hamill lived in the French-decorated No. 822 for several years, and Bon Jovi shot a video there; film companies like No. 603; and so on. All include cable television and private bathroom, and some (but not nearly all) now also include high-speed Internet access. Double rooms cost $175–300 per night, while suites cost $300–350; the hotel also has a number of single rooms. But it's the residents who really make the place what it is—if you stay, try to get to know them a little.

BED & BREAKFAST Colonial House Inn (212-243-9669 or 1-800-689-3779; fax 212-633-1612), 318 West 22nd Street between Eighth and Ninth avenues. Subway: C or E train to 23rd Street. One of Chelsea's best lodging bargains caters unabashedly to an almost exclusively gay clientele. Former record executive Mel Cheren renovated his mid-19th-century brownstone and installed clean, brightly designed rooms with full or

queen bed, exposed brick, and lots of rainbows; a self-serve continental breakfast in the bright little breakfast area is included as part of a night's stay, and you can check e-mail at the lobby's Internet terminal. This isn't your father's B&B, though—you'll get an eyeful both on the walled-in, clothing-optional rooftop lounge in warm weather and Cheren's superb little gallery of his own artwork in any weather. Economy rooms (with smaller bed and shared bathrooms) cost $85–105 per night, standard rooms (with queen bed, again sharing bathrooms) cost $104–130 per night, and deluxe rooms—those with private bathroom—go for $135–150 per night.

✳ Where to Eat

DINING OUT Bottino (212-206-6766), 246 Tenth Avenue between West 24th and West 25th streets. Subway: C or E train to 23rd Street. Open Tuesday through Saturday for lunch noon–3:30 PM and for dinner 6–11 PM. Way over on Tenth Avenue, Bottino serves outstanding upscale Italian fare in a former hardware store retrofitted by architect Thomas Leeser. (Wine is racked on the old wooden shelving.) Lunch items range from salads to tuna tartare to antipasto; pasta dishes include spaghettini with clams, and penne with smoked prosciutto; other choices include hearty *ciabatta* sandwiches and grilled salmon with salsa verde, green beans, and potatoes. Dinner entrées ($10–28) are simply but skillfully prepared— think grilled steaks, rack of lamb, a roast rabbit loin with basil, pine nuts, grilled polenta, and tender sautéed zucchini, or rigatoni served with eggplant, peppers, tomato, and ricotta. The banquettes, the bar, and the modern Barcelona chairs all speak to a clientele that's here to eat and be seen (head for the back garden if you're the shy sort); several galleries are located on the premises, explaining the preponderance of art and antiques dealers you'll find dining here.

da Umberto (212-989-0303), 107 West 17th Street between Sixth and Seventh avenues. Subway: F or V train to 14th Street, 1 train to 18th Street, or L train to Sixth Avenue. Open Monday through Friday for lunch noon–3 PM and dinner 5:30–11 PM, Saturday for dinner only 5:30–11:30 PM. Comfortable Italian food in a simple room is the name of the game at da Umberto, and chef Umberto Assante delivers by rolling out the veal chops, pasta dishes with tasty sauces (many featuring mushrooms), a terrific *bistecca alla fiorentino,* and some exemplary Italian desserts. It's an expensive place to dine, to be sure, but locals seem to like this place very, very well.

Old Homestead (212-242-9040), 56 Ninth Avenue between West 14th and West 15th streets. Subway: A, C, or E train to 14th Street, or L train to Eighth Avenue. Open Monday through Thursday noon–11 PM, Friday to 1 AM, Saturday 1 PM–1 AM, Sunday 1–10 PM. It might not be New York's very best or poshest steak house, but it's one of its most atmospheric—and definitely the city's oldest—and that counts for something. The unmistakable neon sign announcing this place (in the heart of the Meatpacking District, where else?) gives the first hint that you're in on a local secret New Yorkers have enjoyed for more than a century. All you need to know is this: Get steak, preferably a porterhouse for two.

Don't bother with the superfluous side dishes, appetizers, or seafood entrées. Japanese tourists will be mighty impressed by the fact this is one of the very few places in New York where you can get an authentic Kobe steak, from steers that are massaged and fed beer daily—now, that's living. Skip the full steak (it's very, very expensive), the $41 burger of Kobe beef, and the newer Kobe beef hot dog, but try a sampler of it if you're curious.

Porters New York (212-229-2878), 216 Seventh Avenue between West 22nd and West 23rd streets. Subway: 1 train to 23rd Street. Open daily 11 AM–midnight, weekends until 2 AM. Once a straightforward power-lunch sort of steak house, Porters has revamped itself in recent years to become a bit more of a bistro; it still seems out of step with the times, which isn't necessarily a bad thing. You can still order the good signature porterhouse steak from nattily attired waiters—and menu tabs are still high—and yet you can now also choose from such items as roast sea bass, roast Colorado rack of lamb, breaded and pan-fried sea scallops, a changing rotation of soufflés (including chocolate), and Riesling-cooked pear tarts. The room is pleasantly, sedately decorated in art deco trim and heavy woods. There's a large wine list as well.

❦ **The Red Cat** (212-242-1122), 227 10th Avenue between West 23rd and West 24th streets. Subway: C or E train to 23rd Street. Open daily for dinner 5:30–11 PM, Friday and Saturday to midnight, Sunday to 10 PM. Locals and artists are absolutely crazy about this neighborhood restaurant along the no-man's-land that is Tenth

Avenue; chef Jimmy Bradley's New American and Mediterranean fare is served in a careful, uncloying room of wood and fine china. Start with appetizers such as ravioli, char tartare, fried sardines, pan-roasted scallops on a salad, foie gras, or a Gorgonzola-stuffed pear. The short menu of main courses might consist of monkfish paired with a duck stew, crisped skate wing, grilled pork chop, pan-fried trout, or a simple shell steak in Cabernet sauce with Yukon gold potatoes. Finish with one of the outstanding desserts such as a maple crème brûlée (served with apricot and cardamom scented biscotti), a peanut butter mousse made with milk chocolate ganache, a strawberry tart, a pistachio *semifreddo* with chocolate sauce, a tasting of house-made sorbets, or *tarte Tatin* for two.

EATING OUT **Cast Iron Café** (212-462-2244), 641 Sixth Avenue between West 19th and West 20th streets. Subway: F or V train to 23rd Street, or L train to Sixth Avenue. Open Monday through Friday 6 AM–7 PM, weekends 9 AM–7 PM. A good spot for a quick lunch, the Cast Iron features a menu of quality baked goods and breads, reasonably priced designer pizzas, and soups and sandwiches. The interior space is quite interesting to dine in, too.

Empire Diner (212-243-2736), 230 Tenth Avenue at the corner of West 22nd Street. Subway: C or E train to 23rd Street. Open 24 hours. Tucked way over here on Tenth Avenue, the Empire is a singular Chelsea landmark—*the* place to nosh late-night after clubs, or to fire up a middle-of-the-night breakfast. There's more than meets the eye here, however, because this place must cater to its upscale neighborhood clientele with fresher-than-usual ingredients. The menu has some almost Continental flourishes that take it beyond the requisite burgers and fries (though those are fine, as well).

F&B (646-486-4441), 269 West 23rd Street between Seventh and Eighth avenues. Subway: C, E, or 1 train to 23rd Street. Open Tuesday through Saturday noon–11 PM, Sunday and Monday to 10 PM. HAVE A GÜDT DAY! proclaims the sign on your way out, and you probably will after eating at this narrow, easy-to-miss shop tucked among the neon of West 23rd Street. F&B (the name stands for "*frites and beignets*") is a glorious little pocket of Europa right in the heart of Chelsea, one part Scandinavia, one part Belgium, and one part . . . Coney Island? Perhaps. The featured items here are hot dogs prepared more ways than you would have thought possible—the Great Dane is a pork wiener topped with pickles and mayonnaise, for example—sided with good *pommes frites* (Belgian fries), a selection of Brussels-style dipping sauces such as curry ketchup and pesto, and a lemonade or other drink. Or just go for the Bare Bones, a beef dog dolled up with any combination of pickles, relish, onions, ketchup, and mustard you like. You can also order even more unusual items such as Swedish meatballs, salmon dogs, and sweet potato fries. And the Viking (a fish-filet sandwich with horseradish and diced tomatoes) is both scrumptious *and* cheap, one of my favorite quick meals in the city. For dessert, try a trio of little round beignet doughnuts—pick from apple or cheese (I like the apple)—dusted with confectioner's sugar. They even serve good imported beers and hard cider like Duvel, Leffe, Paulaner, and Woodchuck, and keep happy hours where a bottle of imported brew costs just two bucks: a price unheard of in New York. Ignore the staff's dourness and you'll be fine.

The Half King (212-462-4300), 505 West 23rd Street near the corner of Tenth Avenue. Subway: C or E train to 23rd Street. Open daily 9 AM– 3:30 AM. Co-owned by journalist Sebastian Junger, who struck gold with his book *The Perfect Storm,* this Irish bar serves a rather ordinary bistro sort of menu: salads, sandwiches, chili, fish dishes, pasta, burgers, steaks, macaroni and cheese, and the like. There are a few concessions to Ireland in the kitchen, however— a beef-Guinness casserole, shepherd's pie, and an Irish breakfast including black-and-white pudding among them.

La Luncheonette (212-675-0342), 130 Tenth Avenue at the corner of West 18th Street. Subway: A, C, or E train to 14th Street, or L train to Eighth Avenue. Open Monday through Friday for lunch noon– 3:30 PM and dinner 6–11 PM, weekends noon–10:30 PM. That's "la" luncheonette as in Left Bank, not "LA" luncheonette as in Left Coast. This tiny place is as unprepossessing as a French restaurant can be, and has struggled mightily through various economic tosses and turns; it's hard to find, quiet, affordably priced, and underappreciated. But it's also still open, a credit to the owners. The French country food is good, hearty, and uncomplicated: steak with creamy sauce, cassoulet, liver, rabbit stew, trout, various preparations of gourmet mushrooms . . . there may be few sur-prises, but the quality of a meal is uniformly high. And you won't bust your bank account eating here.

Le Gamin (212-243-8864), 183 Ninth Avenue at the corner of West 21st Street. Subway: C or E train to 23rd Street. Open daily 8 AM–midnight. When you're looking for an affordable French lunch, brunch, salad, soup, or light dinner—or even just a coffee— it's hard to beat Le Gamin, which has spread to become a successful little chain anchored in some of the city's hippest quarters. This Chelsea location is the most bustling. They don't accept credit cards, however.

Le Singe Vert (212-366-4100), 160 Seventh Avenue between West 19th and West 20th streets. Subway: 1 train to 18th Street. Open Monday noon– 4 PM, Tuesday through Friday for lunch noon–4 PM and dinner 5:30 PM– midnight (Monday to 11 PM, Friday to 1 AM), weekends for brunch 11:30 AM–4 PM and dinner 5:30–11 PM (Saturday to 1 AM). From the owner of Jules Bistro in the East Village (see chapter 3) comes another thoroughly French bistro. This time Georges Forgeois has named his eatery for a bar in Senegal, decorated it like a bistro in Lyon, and then commissioned an artist from West Africa to paint the bathrooms; as usual, then, it's a truly international project. The oyster bar here is quite popular, as are the appetizers and entrées ($12–20 each) of steak tartare, lamb, onion soup, duck, cassoulet, salade Niçoise, seared skate, mussels with fries, and the like. Of course, there are lots of wines by the glass.

❦ **Pepe Giallo to Go** (212-242-6055), 253 Tenth Avenue between West 24th and West 25th streets. Subway: C or E train to 23rd Street.

Open Monday through Saturday 11 AM–11 PM, Sunday 4–10:30 PM. Yes, all they make is standard Italian meals, but they do it better than most in New York—and though the prices are quite reasonable, the Italian owners don't skimp on anything here. The result is one of New York's sleeper midrange places for red-sauce fare. Dig into pastas with a cream, meat, or pink sauce, a fish entrée, a veal plate, or any of the other big and rich meals. Finish with desserts of fruit tart, tiramisu, or panna cotta; in good weather be sure to check out the back patio, a fun area to hang out while dining.

COFFEE AND SNACKS **Rue des Crêpes** (212-242-9900), 104 Eighth Avenue between West 15th and West 16th streets. Subway: A, C, or E train to 14th Street, or L train to Eighth Avenue. Open daily 11 AM–10 PM. This is a good, Parisian-like spot to sample real buckwheat crêpes of either the meal or dessert variety; only difference is, in Paris you'd buy 'em right out on the street from a sharp-eyed guy working the griddle. Here you can settle in with a coffee and soak up the atmosphere.

✳ Entertainment

THEATERS **Atlantic Theater Company** (212-645-1242 for information, 212-239-6200 for tickets), 344 West 20th Street between Eighth and Ninth avenues. Subway: C or E train to 23rd Street. Housed in the former St. Peter's Episcopal Church—built as a Gothic Revival church in the mid-19th century—this theater company founded by playwright David Mamet is known for putting on small but ambitious, high-quality productions in an attractive, small space.

& **Irish Repertory Theatre** (212-255-0270 for information, 212-727-2737 for tickets), 132 West 22nd Street between Sixth and Seventh avenues. Subway: F, V, or 1 train to 23rd Street. Founded in 1988, this theater company is dedicated exclusively to presenting the classic and new works of Irish and Irish American playwrights such as Oscar Wilde, Frank McCourt, and Sean O'Casey. Tickets for performances generally run $35–40 each.

PERFORMING ARTS VENUES **Dance Theater Workshop** (212-924-0077), 219 West 19th Street between Seventh and Eighth avenues. Subway: A, C, E, 1, 2, or 3 train to 14th Street, or L train to Eighth Avenue. Founded in 1965 as a collective of choreographers, DTW offers an extremely varied selection of modern dance programs and performances—and the big, modern headquarters here at the Bessie Schönberg Theatre show rehearsals off to pedestrians and give better sight lines to those attending performances. Ticket prices vary.

Joyce Theatre (212-242-0900), 175 Eighth Avenue near the corner of West 19th Street. Subway: 1 train to 18th Street. This art deco dance theater, formerly a movie house, presents quality work from such cutting-edge American and international companies as the Ballet Hispanico, Dance Brazil, the John Goode Performance Group, and Ballet Tech.

The Kitchen (212-255-5793), 512 West 19th Street between Tenth and Eleventh avenues. Subway: A, C, or E train to 14th Street, or L train to Eighth Avenue. This combination art gallery–performance space—which started out in SoHo—showcases the very cutting-edge work of artists who often turn out to be major cultural forces. (Philip Glass, Eric Bogosian, Peter Greenaway, Robert Mapplethorpe, and Laurie Anderson all got their starts here, among others.) In 1985 the organization moved to this converted icehouse in Chelsea.

FILM AND MOVIES Clearview Chelsea

(212-777-FILM, ext. 597), 260 West 23rd Street between Seventh and Eighth avenues. Subway: C, E, 1, or 9 train to 23rd Street. Straightforward Hollywood hits are screened here.

Clearview Chelsea West (212-777-FILM, ext. 614), 333 West 23rd Street between Eighth and Ninth avenues. Subway: C or E train to 23rd Street. An alternative to the formula fare at the nearby Clearview cinema (see above), Chelsea West screens a slightly more interesting mix of movies.

BARS AND CLUBS Bungalow 8

(212-629-3333), 515 West 27th Street between Tenth and Eleventh avenues.

CHELSEA CLEARVIEW CINEMA ON WEST 23RD STREET

Paul Karr

Subway: C or E train to 23rd Street, or 1 train to 28th Street. Open 10 PM–4 AM in winter, 8 PM–4 AM in summer. It's almost impossible to believe that a hip club lies behind the facade of this abandoned storefront, in a formerly industrial section of Chelsea (take a cab if you're not driving). But hip it is: The interior looks like a bungalow from Fiji or the Caribbean. Drinks are expensive, the crowd is beautiful, the late-night vibe is laid back—if you can get in, that is (it might require an invitation from a regular).

Glass (212-904-1580), 287 Tenth Avenue between 26th and 27th streets. Subway: C or E train to 23rd Street, or 1 or 9 train to 28th Street. Open 5 PM–2 AM weekdays, 5 PM–4 AM Thursday through Saturday. This is still one of New York's hot (and coolest-looking) clubs, with the likes of Calvin Klein making regular appearances—though the industrial exterior by day hardly shows off that fact. At night, however, the corrugated-tin storefront rolls up to reveal an exquisite front done in special glass that fogs up. Inside, some of New York's A-list hobnobbers and fashion models titter over drinks. There's also a garden area.

The Half King (212-462-4300), 505 West 23rd Street near the corner of Tenth Avenue. Subway: C or E train to 23rd Street. Open daily 9 AM–3:30 AM. The 30-foot bar and private lounge in this far-West Chelsea bar are both good places to quaff a hand-pulled Harp, Guinness, or other brew, but methinks the $6-per-glass price is a bit steep.

This Irish bar-restaurant features readings every Monday night by a noted author.

✷ Selective Shopping

Chelsea is jam-packed full of interesting furniture stores, antiques dealers, and purveyors of cutting-edge clothing and accessories, and even acceptable branches of gigantic chain retailers. Sixth (Avenue of the Americas) and Seventh avenues, in the vicinity of West 23rd Street, are the best places in Manhattan to shop in the big chain stores such as Old Navy, Bed Bath & Beyond, Filene's Basement, Best Buy, and the like without the hurry or hustle of Fifth Avenue: Here you'll find the usual merchandise, except it's displayed in wider aisles inside beautiful old buildings.

For gay- and lesbian-oriented shopping, go west, young man (or woman): Try strolling Eighth and Ninth avenues, or the cross-streets such as 14th, 17th, and 18th as they cut west from Seventh to Eighth, Ninth, and Tenth avenues; the farther west you get, the more outrageous.

BOOKSTORE **Books of Wonder** (212-989-3270 or 1-800-207-6968), 16 West 18th Street between Fifth and Sixth avenues. Subway: N, R, or W train to 23rd Street, or L, Q, 4, 5, or 6 train to 14th Street–Union Square. Open Monday through Saturday 10 AM–7 PM, Sunday noon–6 PM. This is the best children's bookstore in Chelsea, and one of the best in the city—the staff really care about the books. It's almost like the one Meg Ryan owned in *You've Got Mail;* some say, in fact, that the film was based on the bookshop—though this can't be strictly true, because the film was a remake of a 1940 Jimmy Stewart film, and this shop opened (in a different location) in 1980. Anyhow, the special touches here include a whole special section devoted to L. Frank Baum's Oz books. There are regular readings, signings, story hours, and book release parties (for the Harry Potter books, for example).

DEPARTMENT STORES **Loehmann's** (212-352-0856), 101 Seventh Avenue at the corner of West 16th Street. Subway: 1, 2, or 3 train to 14th Street or 1 train to 18th Street. Open Monday to Saturday, 9 AM–9 PM, Sunday 11 AM–7 PM. A kind of higher-end Filene's Basement, this is a great place to find your favorite midlevel and top-end labels (Donna Karan, Calvin Klein, Versace, and so forth) at amazing prices. The secret? New York's fashion tastes swerve so quickly that perfectly good overstock is often left in the dust of the change of seasons; Loehmann's swoops in and rescues the good stuff for those who don't want or need to pay the got-to-have-it-now original prices. Unusually, the store is equally strong in both women's and men's wear (tucked in the basement); the chic brands are housed on the uppermost floor. This was formerly the original location of the Barneys department store.

FASHION **Alexander McQueen** (212-645-1797), 417 West 14th Street between Ninth and Tenth avenues. Subway: A, C, or E train to 14th Street or L train to Eighth Avenue. Open Monday to Saturday 11 AM–7 PM, Sunday 12:30–6 PM. One of two prominent Brits alighting on West 14th Street (see Stella McCartney, below), former Givenchy designer McQueen here showcases his slightly outrageous British couture and boots in a weird interior that's either 1975 . . . or 2525.

Barneys Co-op (212-826-8900), 236 West 18th Street between Seventh and Eighth avenues. Subway: 1 train to 18th Street. Open Monday to Friday, 11 AM–8 PM, Saturday to 7 PM, Sunday noon–6 PM. Here's where plenty of the city's hip young fashion students, models, and gay men go for their street wear: the poorer cousin of megawatt department store Barneys. It's a great place to drop $200 on a pair of sneakers, $250 on a pair of vintage-look jeans, and another $200 on a tight-fitting mesh shirt that's been carefully ripped by its designer to simulate wear, throw them on, and stroll out the door—preferably with latte in hand—pretending you just rolled out of your SoHo loft in the outfit. The young, attractive staff will greet you by (and remember your) first name.

Comme des Garçons (212-604-9200), 520 West 22nd Street between Tenth and Eleventh avenues. Subway: C or E train to 23rd Street. Open Tuesday to Saturday 11 AM–7 PM, Sunday noon–6 PM. In the heart of Chelsea's burgeoning gallery district, Comme des Garçons's only American store starts you off with a kind of art-installation entrance (it has to be seen to be appreciated) and never gets any closer to normalcy. Japanese founder Rei Kawakubo, who had no formal fashion training, opened the first shop in 1969 in Tokyo; her unique zoot suit–style designs soon caught the world's attention, and the brand has since carved out a niche around the globe for its unique designs, which feature splotches and patches of light and dark hues, misplaced buttons and pockets, and a somewhat unisex quality. Perhaps it's still 1969 here: Everything is a little outrageous in color,

cut, or pattern, so don't come here if you're looking for anything remotely traditional, or—for that matter—friendly customer service. You won't find either here.

Jeffrey NEW YORK (212-206-3928), 449 West 14th Street at the corner of Tenth Avenue. Subway: A, C, or E train to 14th Street or L train to Eighth Avenue. Open daily 10 AM–8 PM. Jeffrey Kalinsky started his own high-end shoe empire in Atlanta (he formerly traveled the world rooting out hip shoes for Barneys), but he's been an even bigger hit in Manhattan. This is positively one of the coolest shops in the city, still focused on designer shoes—come here first if you're intent on dropping a bundle on a high-end pair—yet also now carrying women's wear and (a few) menswear labels from Prada to Gucci to Helmut Lang, plus lesser-known discoveries. And the staff? Helpful to the point of being almost too helpful, they never let you feel out of place.

Stella McCartney (212-255-1556), 429 West 14th Street between Ninth Avenue and Tenth Avenue. Subway: A, C, or E train to 14th Street or L train to Eighth Avenue. Open Monday to Saturday 11 AM–7 PM, Sunday 12:30–6 PM. Everyone knows who she is—Sir Paul and Linda's daughter, of course—but this designer has taken the Meatpacking District/Chelsea set by storm, and may have staying power. Her north-side-of-14th Street showroom is an eyebrow-raising place that's worth a look for the interior alone: Yes, that's a reflecting pool, and the walls are indeed tiled. If it all seems a bit much, concentrate instead on the former Chloe designer's clothes—pricey T-shirts, dresses, jeans, and skirts that retain both a delicate and a cutting-edge look. (It's perhaps as close to London fashion as you'll get on a trip to Manhattan.) And there's no leather to be found here, only high-quality look-alike materials; Linda would have been proud. Two tips: Try not to ogle when the big stars waltz in with their entourages, and don't bother affecting an English accent. It'll get you nowhere with the sales "assistants."

FOOD AND DRINK 🍴 ✆ **Chelsea Market** (212-243-5678), 75 Ninth Avenue between West 15th and West 16th streets. Subway: A, C, E, or L train to 14th Street. Open Monday through Friday 8 AM–8 PM, weekends 8 AM–10 PM. Manhattan's biggest food court, occupying the ground floor of a former cookie and cracker factory, holds an amazing selection of artisanal bakeries, pastry shops, soup stalls, wine merchants, and other purveyors of specialty and gourmet foods. Chelsea Market is so good that it's worth listing the full card of vendors; bear in mind, though, that this lineup can and does change frequently. **Eleni's Cookies** (212-255-7990) bakes cookies; the **Chelsea Wine Vault** (212-462-4244) is one of the city's better vendors of vintages; **Fat Witch Bakery** (212-807-1335) turns out delicious breads and pastries despite the name, as does **Sarabeth's** (212-989-2424). **Ronnybrook Farm** (212-741-6455) sells flavored milk from its dairy, while **Jimmy's Gelato** (no phone) is a good, recently installed stand. **Amy's Bread** (212-462-4338), **Ruthy's Bakery** (212-463-8800), **Frank's Butcher Shop** (212-242-1234), **Hale & Hearty Soup** (212-255-2400), and the **Manhattan Fruit Exchange** (212-989-2444) vend self-evident products.

Other stalls here purvey newspapers and magazines, flowers, Thai groceries, wicker baskets for picnics or gifts, sushi, even modern furniture and quality cooking and kitchenware items.

Interestingly, the upper floors are occupied by some pretty heavy-duty corporate customers: Major League Baseball's Web site operations, Oprah Winfrey's Oxygen Media Company, the NY1 television network so many New Yorkers turn to for the latest dish, The Food Network's offices and studios (including "Kitchen Stadium"), and the Oxygen women's television network, among others.

GALLERIES Chelsea has become such a hot spot for up-and-coming art galleries that there isn't one Gallery District here—there are four or five, and trying to recommend individual galleries for inspection swiftly becomes an exercise in futility. The formerly drab, industrial-looking blocks out in the western reaches of West 25th and West 26th streets between Tenth and Eleventh avenues hold the richest concentration; the same areas of West 22nd and West 27th streets are also quickly developing, and restaurants and shops are following.

Two of the more famous names in this area are the **Fischbach Gallery** (212-759-2345), at 210 Eleventh Avenue between West 24th and West 25th streets, and the **PaceWildenstein** (212-929-7000) at 534 West 25th Street between Tenth and Eleventh avenues. Take the C or E train to both. But there are dozens—perhaps hundreds—more, and it all depends on your personal taste in art. Check listings in papers such as the *Village Voice* for some idea of who's showing where. Also consult the Web site www.westchelseaarts.com.

MUSIC **Jazz Record Center** (212-675-4480), 236 West 26th Street between Seventh and Eighth avenues. Subway: C or E train to 23rd Street, or 1 train to 23rd Street. The acknowledged center of the jazz record universe in the city isn't in the West Village; surprisingly, it's down here in Chelsea, and owner Fred Cohen has also carefully stocked a good selection of vintage recordings, rarities, and jazz-related memorabilia. And yes, he has compact disks, too.

VINTAGE FASHION **Lucille's Emporium** (212-691-1041), 127 West 26th Street between Sixth and Seventh avenues. Subway: F, V, or 1 train to 23rd Street. Vintage treasure chest of the stars, Lucille asks downright amazing prices for her quality haute couture fashions, used furniture, antiques, and books. It's miles better than you would have any right to expect a thrift-store-type shop to be.

Housing Works Thrift Shop (212-366-0820), 143 West 17th Street between Sixth and Seventh avenues. Subway: 1 or 9 train to 18th Street. Open Monday to Friday 10 AM–7 PM, Saturdays 10 AM–6 PM, and Sundays noon–5 PM. Talk about a great cause: The proceeds from this Chelsea thrift shop go towards AIDS service, prima- rily to homeless minority New Yorkers afflicted with the disease. And you can find amazing bargains here on brand-name clothing, furniture, and home items once owned by real, live New Yorkers; the store windows are surprisingly clever and sleek-looking. Bundle a trip here together with one to Loehmann's (see Department Stores) and Barney's Co-op (see Fashion), both of which are literally right around a corner from here—and bring luggage with wheels. You'll almost certainly be gleefully toting something back to your hotel. There are now also additional branch Housing Works thrift shops in Greenwich Village, Flatiron, the Upper East Side, and the Upper West Side; for an updated list, see the organization's Web site, www.housingworksauctions .com.

✳ Special Events

September: **The Kitchen Neighborhood Street Fair** (212-255-5793), West 19th Street between Tenth and Eleventh avenues. Subway: A, C, or E train to 14th Street, or L train to Eighth Avenue. This annual street festival takes over a block of West 19th Street for African drumming, salsa music, performance art, puppet shows, modern dance, hip-hop, and more. It's very cutting edge and youth oriented.

Midtown East 7

Midtown East

E. 61st ST

E. 60th ST — Roosevelt Island Aerial Tramway ★ — Queensboro Bridge

E. 59th ST

THIRD AVENUE

E. 58th ST

E. 57th ST

Sony Wonder Technology Lab ★ — E. 56th ST

SECOND AVENUE

FIRST AVENUE

SUTTON PLACE

E. 55th ST — ★ Central Synogogue

PARK AVENUE

E. 54th ST

★ Citigroup Center — E. 53rd ST

E. 52nd ST

LEXINGTON AVENUE

E. 51st ST

■ St. Patrick's Cathedral — E. 50th ST

BEEKMAN PL.

E. 49th ST

E. 48th ST

E. 47th ST

FIFTH AVENUE

MADISON AVENUE

VANDERBILT AVENUE

E. 46th ST

E. 45th ST

E. 44th ST — United Nations ★

East River

E. 43rd ST

Grand Central Terminal ★ — ★ Chrysler Building — E. 42nd ST

Bryant Park ★ — E. 41st ST

N.Y. Public Library — E. 40th ST

MURRAY HILL — E. 39th ST

E. 38th ST

E. 37th ST

E. 36th ST

★ — E. 35th ST

Pierpoint Morgan Library — E 34th ST

★ — E. 33rd ST

Empire State Building — E. 32nd ST

PARK AVENUE SOUTH

Heliport

E. 31st ST

E. 30th ST

E. 29th ST

E. 28th ST

E. 27th ST

© The Countryman Press

MIDTOWN EAST

For the purposes of this book, I have defined Midtown East as everything from the east side of Fifth Avenue east to the East River, from 30th to 59th streets. This neighborhood is world famous for many reasons. Madison Avenue is renowned for its advertising agencies; the shopping here is legendary (at Tiffany, Saks, Bloomingdale's, and the like); and the towering Empire State and Chrysler buildings are among the world's best known. For many visitors, *this* is New York.

The vast majority of the area is in fact simply known as Midtown East. To the south, the neighborhood known as Murray Hill runs along a stretch of Lexington, Park, and Madison avenues south from Grand Central Terminal to around 34th Street; though it carries its own name and identity, it's a mainly quiet, almost boring area of pretty town houses. Lots of diplomats live here—though in recent years an influx of boutique hotels and their associated bars have ratcheted up the hipness of the area somewhat.

Other mini-neighborhoods in this district include Kips Bay, Turtle Bay, and Sutton Place, all in the vicinity of First Avenue. East 41st Street is one of New York's most concentrated Japanese neighborhoods.

GETTING THERE Your key to getting here is to remember three words: *Grand Central Terminal,* which was built in the mid-19th century (and rebuilt in 1913) to handle commuter and long-distance trains to the city. It remains one of New York's single greatest achievements of transit, people-watching, public space, dining diversity, and historic preservation and renovation. The station is the jumping-off point for many of the hotels, restaurants, and sights discussed herein.

By subway: Get to Grand Central Terminal from Times Square by taking the handy S train shuttle, or from the Upper East Side or Lower Manhattan via the 4, 5, and 6 trains (the 6 stops everywhere and is slower, while the other two are quick express trains). From other points, you will likely need to change trains at Times Square.

By car: Travel in Midtown by car is a bit of a nightmare. Traffic is usually congested (except on weekends, when it's tolerable). Parking is a disaster Monday through Saturday, and although there are numerous small underground garages scattered on side streets throughout the neighborhood, they are very, very expensive—you'll be shocked when you run up a $30 tab for 5 hours of shopping and dining. If you have brought a car, consider parking it outside the city (or at least in another neighborhood). If you park on the street, pay very careful attention to the Byzantine parking laws posted on various signs—often you cannot park until 7 PM on a street, or can park there only 1 or 2 days a week, or some such other thing.

✳ To See

BIG BUILDINGS Chrysler Building, Lexington Avenue at the corner of East 42nd Street. Subway: S, 4, 5, 6, or 7 train to 42nd Street–Grand Central. Save for the Empire State Building, perhaps no other building in New York is more recognizable than the Chrysler—and none is more distinctive. William van Alen designed the structure as a kind of nod to the shapes and forms prevalent in the auto giant's then current line of automobiles. There are plenty of art deco touches throughout the 1,000-foot-plus building, culminating in the pyramidal spire with its layers of "spikes" that look a bit like the rays of Lady Liberty's crown. Unfortunately, you cannot explore the building within (except the lobby, which is worth a detour for its art deco interior details), but it's always a treat to look up and gaze upon it from somewhere in the city when you need an orienting point.

GRAND CENTRAL TERMINAL OFFERS FINE PEOPLE-WATCHING.

Kim Grant

Grand Central Terminal (212-340-2210 for events, 212-532-4900 for commuter train schedules, 212-712-4500 for lost and found), East 42nd Street at the corner of Park Avenue. Subway: S, 4, 5, 6, or 7 train to 42nd Street–Grand Central. Open daily 5:30 AM–1:30 AM. New York's commuter train hub was once its long-distance train connection to the rest of North America. Built by Cornelius Vanderbilt in the mid-19th century, it was rebuilt in 1913 and somehow integrates local subway lines, trains from Connecticut and suburban New York, and a wealth of attractive food and shopping options without seeming obtrusive. In fact, it's downright beautiful today thanks to the 1997 renovation that saw the great hall considerably polished up. The deep blue sky on the high, high (12-story) vaulted ceiling shines with the constellations of a star map. Sculptures on the exterior further add to the station's intrigue. Inside, several balconies hold food courts and eateries from lowbrow to fine dining (the bottom level offers the most choice), a giant newsstand stocks papers and magazines from around the world, and a fresh market (see *Selective Shopping—Food and Drink*) holds cases of fine cheese, seafood, meat, fish, and other specialty products. There are also some 50 shops tucked into the various passages, hallways, and concourses. Near the stationmaster's office, the Brooklyn-based New York Transit Museum maintains a small annex showing such exhibits as a series of classic art-deco-influenced railroad posters; the free museum is open weekdays 8 AM–8 PM, weekends 10 AM–6 PM. You can even take a free guided tour of the station Wednesday and Friday at 12:30 PM. The Transit Museum Annex also contains a store. Meet at the terminal information booth Wednesday or in front of the station on East 42nd Street Friday to take the tours.

Even if you don't need to eat or take a train, try to visit the station—it is probably the best place in Manhattan for people-watching if you can find a quiet place from which to look. Pretzel vendors on the sidewalk, hurrying businessmen and businesswomen with briefcases, commuting families, tourists with suitcases, airport buses discharging recharged vacationers, dazed-looking wanderers and tour groups, policemen and military men in fatigues warily eyeing the crowd for security risks, giant train schedule boards flipping as they mark the comings and going of a another workday . . . now, *this* is New York.

✄ ﾠ **United Nations** (212-963-TOUR), entrance at the corner of First Avenue and East 46th Street. Subway: S, 4, 5, 6, or 7 train to 42nd Street–Grand Central, or E or V train to Lexington Avenue–53rd Street. Tours weekdays from 9:30 AM– 4:45 PM, weekends 10 AM–4:30 PM; closed weekends in January and February, plus some holidays. The world's often controversial meeting place—whose meeting rooms take center stage whenever there is talk of potential war— occupies a heavily guarded slablike tower in far-east Manhattan marked by the flags of its member nations. It is an essential visit for anyone concerned with global politics and development. The UN was built on 18 acres of East River frontage purchased by Rockefeller, and it began operating in 1945; since 1952 the general public has been allowed to tour most of the complex. When you visit, you're traveling into another country—actually, no country at all. The UN prints its own postage, maintains its own post office, and is not part of the United States. Anyone can visit the Visitors' Lobby of the General Assembly Building for free, where you can view exhibitions on UN themes. Fuller tours of the UN led by nattily attired guides leave each half hour and last from 45 minutes to an hour; they cost $12 for adults, $8.50 for senior citizens, $8 for students, and $6.50 for children 5–14. (Children younger than age 5 cannot visit; springtime brings scads of school groups from around the world.) The tour ends at the huge, semicircular General Assembly Hall, then at the public area where the post office sells the special stamps and a bookstore and gift shop also operate.

FOR FAMILIES ✄ ﾠ **Sony Wonder Technology Lab** (212-833-8100 for information, 212-833-5414 for reservations), Madison Avenue at East 56th Street. Subway: E or V train to Fifth Avenue–53rd Street, or N, R, or W train to Fifth

Avenue–59th Street. Open Tuesday through Saturday 10 AM–5 PM, Sunday noon–5 PM. Kids love Sony's unabashedly commercial—but undeniably entertaining—Midtown complex. Visitors are briefed on the history of communication, greeted by a remarkable talking robot, then turned loose to create music videos, watch movies in a high-definition theater, and be amazed by various other technological wonders. All entrancing enough—though, for my money, if this is the future it's a bit insular what with real live New York passing by the windows all day long. I'd rather be out there than in here. In any case, the experience is entirely free—and, as a result, wildly popular. Show up early for a ticket; get there right at opening time on busy days.

♿ **St. Patrick's Cathedral** (212-753-2261), Fifth Avenue at the corner of 50th Street. Subway: E or V train to Fifth Avenue–53rd Street. Open daily 7:30 AM–8:30 PM. Huge St. Pat's is the largest Catholic-owned cathedral in the nation (though uptown, near Columbia, there's a bigger cathedral; see chapter 12). Designed by James Renwick to resemble the amazing Gothic Dom (cathedral) in Köln, Germany, this church features a pair of 33-story spires that were added a few years after the main body was finished. Enter the huge bronze doors and visit the church any day of the week; Mass services are held daily, and you can also view stunning sculptures, statues, carvings, and other artworks. It is nearly the equivalent of a quick museum visit.

ST. PATRICK'S CATHEDRAL

Kim Grant

LIBRARY ♿ **Morgan Library & Museum** (212-685-0610, gallery 212-685-0008), 29 East 36th Street between Madison and Park avenues. Subway: 6 train to 33rd Street, or S, 4, 5, or 7 train to 42nd Street–Grand Central. Open Tuesday through Thursday 10:30 AM–5 PM, Friday 10:30 AM–9 PM, Saturday 10 AM–6 PM, Sunday 11 AM–6 PM. Originally the private library of financier Pierpont Morgan, this library is wonderful not only for its collection of rare manuscripts and art but also for its architecture and gardens. Among the many items here are extensive collections of medieval and Renaissance papers and illuminated manuscripts; rare stone tablets and amulets from ancient Mesopotamian rulers and lands; and art from the likes of Degas, Pollock, Rubens, and even William Blake. The library shows artworks and manuscripts during special exhibitions throughout the year. The library reopened in the spring of 2006 with an enlarged space, a lovely new garden cafe, and increasingly public-friendly exhibits; this is a place, after all, holding three Gutenberg Bibles and manuscripts by Dickens and Twain. It's open daily except Mondays and admission is $12 for adults, $8 for seniors, students, and children under 16.

✳ Lodging

LUXURIOUS HOTELS ✐ **Four Seasons** (212-758-5700 or 1-800-332-3442; fax 212-758-5711), 57 East 57th Street between Madison and Park avenues. Subway: 4, 5, or 6 train to 59th Street, or N, R, or W train to Fifth Avenue–59th Street. Very close to both Fifth Avenue and Central Park, New York's tallest hotel (52 stories) delivers a luxury punch and classic art deco architecture courtesy of no less than I. M. Pei, who designed the entire limestone structure. The cavernous, three-story-high lobby is beyond grandiose, with its exotic wood and stone—great for people-watching (to the sounds of a live pianist), and the first tip-off that rooms and services here will be over-sized for once rather than trimmed down and minimalist. No wonder stars love the place.

Upstairs, every one of the high-ceilinged 300 rooms and 60 suites is unusually large, decorated in blonds and muted whites; their huge sycamore-and-Florentine-marble bathrooms possess deep, quick-filling tubs, dressing areas, and outstanding views of Manhattan. Even the simplest "moderate" rooms here are huge, with enormous king bed, beautiful wood inlays, big television, comfortable sycamore armchair, and padded silk walls; superior rooms add an oval wood desk, while deluxe rooms have big sofa, suite-sized floor space, and better views of 57th and 58th streets. Each bedroom also contains a Bose radio–CD player, leather work chair, down pillows, duvets, a mini bar, terry-cloth bathrobes, and several two-line phones; the silk curtains are covered by sliding shades, operated electronically from a bedside console. Most rooms have king beds, fitted with fine Italian linen sheets, and about 20 even come with their own private furnished terrace—get one if you can—while some rooms also contain a microwave for heating up quick snacks. The one-, two-, and three-bedroom suites on the hotel's upper floors are extremely expensive even by New York City standards but come with such splurge-worthy extras as, for example, a Jacuzzi with a direct view of Central Park, the Chrysler Building, or the Empire State Building; a dining room seating six; and a four-poster sycamore bed.

Guest services are extensive—a spacious health and fitness facility includes a whirlpool, sauna, and steam rooms, with a masseur or masseuse on call and a full-service spa. The business center has faxes, a postage machine, photocopying, delivery services, even translators and secretaries on call and a travel desk; there are also goodies for children, free shoeshines, a limousine service, a newsstand, clothes pressing, umbrellas, and babysitters. Laptops, cell phones, and VCRs can be rented to enhance the experience of being in the office even further. Staff are extremely professional—they meet each morning to discuss individual guest histories and needs—and there's twice-daily maid service.

The hotel's New American restaurant, FiftySevenFiftySeven, (see *Dining Out*) is a prime place to observe an early-morning New York power breakfast or power lunch, while a lobby lounge offers additional chances to get out of your room—should you actually want to do that. When you're paying room rates like this, however, you might want to soak up every available second behind the closed doors. Double room rates at the hotel range from around $585–865, while suite rates generally begin at about $1,000 and run up to as much as $2,000 per night.

Hotel Elysée (212-753-1066 or 1-800-535-9733; fax: 212-980-9278), 60 East 54th Street between Madison and Park avenues. Subway: E or V train to Fifth Avenue–53rd Street or 6 train to 51st Street. This little 99-room hotel is a great hideaway in Continental style, and the staff are unbelievably friendly—another reason this is one of my very favorite New York City hotels. (If you come, too, you'll be in good company: Previous big-name visitors have included Tennessee Williams and Ava Gardner, among others.) Right off busy Madison Avenue, its lobby is an oasis of French calm done in marble and wood. The place's reputation is that of a quiet, low-profile refuge with outstanding service and facilities, where celebrities can—and do—duck in for a few nights to be themselves without the fuss, or paparazzi, of more famous hotels.

All guest rooms are decorated with reproduction antiques and fitted with VCR, voice mail, and fax, while the lovely marble-floored bathrooms are bigger than expected, with comfortable tubs and English toiletries. Some rooms come with patio, kitchenette, or even a big tiled solarium and terrace (ask ahead) with tables looking out over Midtown's offices and high-rises. If you're really feeling flush, book the Piano Suite: The handsome Steinway was donated by Victor Horowitz, and its rooms are furnished with plush couches and French chairs. You can take your included continental breakfast—one of the best I've had in the city, with tasty dried fruits, chocolate croissants, and nut muffins, among other choices—as well as all-day-and-night complimentary tea, coffee, and cookies in the Club Room. Its leather sofa, rich red carpeting, and street views lend it a quietly convivial atmosphere. For more sophisticated fare, the adjacent, renowned Monkey Bar (see *Entertainment—Bars and Clubs*) is back in good form, serving fine meals and fancy drinks. Or you can order room service from the restaurant without ever leaving your lair. Double room rates range from around $345–365, while suites range from around $425–525 (the Piano Suite is about $1,000 per night).

The Kitano (212-885-7000 or 1-800-KITANO-NY; fax 212-885-7100), 66 Park Avenue at the corner of East 38th Street. Subway: 6 train to 33rd Street. If you're craving a thoroughly Japanese lodging experience, come here. On a quiet stretch of Park Avenue, the Kitano operates 149 rooms (including 18 suites) in an 18-story building once owned by Rockefellers but now operated by Japanese management. The lobby features a bronze dog sculpture by Fernando Botero. The rooms are just what you'd expect: quiet, simply furnished in solid woods, packed with no-nonsense business amenities (two-line phones, fax machines) and quality art and photography throughout. There are also tea makers, green tea, and heated towel racks. Some rooms have a hot tub; also inquire about a more luxurious corner room if you can afford it. Dining and drinking options here include an actual Japanese-style bar, a garden café, and Nadaman Hakubai, perhaps the most authentic upscale Japanese restaurant in the city. Double rooms begin at $250 but generally cost $460–575 (though weekend Internet specials occasionally drop them as low as $180), while suites start as low as $330 but normally cost more like $700 per night, and can quickly soar to as much as $2,000.

New York Palace (212-888-7000 or 1-800-NY-PALACE; fax 212-303-6300), 455 Madison Avenue at the corner of 50th Street. Subway: E or V train to Fifth Avenue–53rd Street, or B, D, F, or V train to 47th–50th streets/Rockefeller Center. If the arches, marble staircases, and gated courtyard don't capture your heart, the room service (from a world-famous restaurant) will. Originally six town houses built by railroad magnate Henry Villard (the other five were occupied by friends sympathetic to his cause of abolition, friendly journalists, or fellow railroad executives); however, Villard soon went bankrupt and was forced to sell. The buildings variously housed the publisher Random House, the Archdiocese of New York, and Capital Cities Communications for various stretches from the 1940s through the 1990s. New York Realtor Harry Helmsley began advancing the idea of a hotel during the mid-1970s, and in 1981 part of the houses were opened as the 1,000-plus-room Helmsley Hotel. New ownership took over in 1993 and renamed the hotel the New York Palace; today

the combined Main House, Executive Hotel, and towers hold just fewer than 900 rooms.

In wintertime, double rooms (fairly standard, with marble bathroom) come at rates ranging from around $560–699; suites (decorated in both bland, modern hotel style and a more refined classical style) begin at $950 and rise to around $2,000—there are highly exclusive suites costing even more—but be sure to check on weekend packages, which sometimes drop the rate for a double room to "only" about $300. Also, in busy times of year (fall, for example), these rates can go much higher. All rooms come with goose-down comforters, terry-cloth robes, safe, mini bar, ironing board, fax machine/printer/copier, and Floris toiletries. Tower rooms add such extra luxuries as personal phone and fax numbers, Italian linens, umbrellas, *The New York Times* delivered daily, and room service delivery from any of the hotel restaurants, among which is Gilt—presided over by one of New York's most dazzlingly experimental chefs. Did I mention the fitness center with a view of St. Patrick's Cathedral, the complimentary limousine rides to Wall Street, the executive-floor lounge? Or the tower suites' butler service?

St. Regis Hotel (212-753-4500 or 1-800-759-7550; fax 212-787-3447), 2 East 55th Street at the corner of Fifth Avenue. Subway: E or V train to Fifth Avenue–53rd Street. Five stars from Mobil, five diamonds from AAA, a house restaurant (Lespinasse) widely acknowledged as one of the best in the city . . . the St. Regis is, quite simply, one of the top 10 hotels in New York. The building itself is a striking landmark amid Midtown's faceless towers, built in 1904 by John Jacob Astor in Beaux-Arts style—note the fine mansard roof and ornate turrets. Ernest Hemingway, Alfred Hitchcock, and Salvador Dalí all stayed here, as did Joe DiMaggio and Miss Marilyn on their honeymoon; John Lennon and Yoko Ono even occupied suites in the early 1970s. It all comes at a very high price—but is it justified?

Well, for starters each room or suite is furnished in Louis XVI style: Crystal chandeliers hang from ceilings, the roomy and luxurious baths are done in marble, the walls in silk. Some of the chairs and armoires are antiques. Daybeds are de rigueur; some of the king beds are four-posters, and some of those are canopied. Then there's also a fax, VCR, and high-speed Internet access port in each of the units to cater to modern travelers' needs. I mustn't neglect to mention the butler service that comes with each and every room, either. In short, this place piles on the luxury like few others without compromising its superbly elegant setting—and it all happens right at the doorstep of Fifth Avenue's most select shopping. (The famous Tiffany & Co. jewelers, the Japanese department store Takashimaya, the jeweler Harry Winston, and the Sony Wonder store are all within two short blocks of the St. Regis entrance.) When you've tired of strolling from window display to window display, the hotel's refined tearoom and bar (take time to inspect the murals in each) are worth visiting; Manhattan's society types enjoy hobnobbing in both, and you will, too.

EXPENSIVE HOTELS **The Benjamin** (212-715-2500 or 1-888-423-6526; fax 212-715-2525), 125 East 50th Street at the corner of Lexington Avenue. Subway: 6 train to 51st Street, or E or V train to Lexington Avenue–53rd Street. The best of the Manhattan East Suite properties, the all-suite Benjamin exudes class from the really nice lobby to rooms calmly decked out in gold, cream, and taupe tones, mahogany, and big beds with Frette linens and down duvets. One unique touch here is the personal pillow service: You get to select your own head-rest from a choice of 10 (including a water pillow), maintained by the "pillow concierge." If you don't sleep well, you are supposed to get a full refund. Business amenities and services have been loaded up: The concierge, personal shopping service, high-speed Internet access, in-room fax and copier, personal business cards, two-line phones, and true kitchens are nice touches. And the Woodstock Spa offers a full range of treatments. Rates begin around $420 per night, though specials can drop them a bit lower and of course they can go much higher as well.

Millennium Hotel New York U.N. Plaza (212-758-1234 or 1-800-222-8888; fax 212-705-5031), 1 United Nations Plaza (First Avenue) at the corner of East 44th Street. Subway: S, 4, 5, 6, or 7 train to 42nd Street–Grand Central. Outside of diplomats, few visitors know about this no-nonsense business hotel perched way over on Manhattan's East Side right across the street from the United Nations complex. None of the 400 or so rooms (about 30 are suites) is lower than the 28th floor—offices occupy all the lower floors—and all are furnished with lush wall hangings and kitted out with enormous bathrooms, two-line phones, irons, and other business-class amenities such as faxes and safes. CD players show up in certain rooms, and the high floors ensure terrific views from almost all: Some windows actually frame both the Chrysler Building and the Empire State Building.

This is also one of the very few hotels in Manhattan sporting a pool, and this one's huge, with good views from its 27th-floor perch (the gym and health club are welcome extras and also located on this floor). There's even an indoor *tennis court* on the top floor—you might see someone you recognize hitting a ball around. Yes, the hotel's expensive as any other in Midtown, with room rates running from around $250 up to almost $600 per night and more, but specials sometimes drop a room rate in winter down as low as $150 per night—one of the best luxury-hotel bargains I've found in Manhattan given the comfort level and amenities here. Only drawback? It's quite a hike from any subway station, and there aren't any really notable restaurants or sights (except the UN, of course) in the immediate area.

Waldorf-Astoria (212-355-3000 or 1-800-925-3673; fax 212-872-7272), 301 Park Avenue spanning East 49th Street to East 50th Street. Subway: 6 train to 51st Street, or E or V train to Lexington Avenue–53rd Street. Quite frankly, this storied name has seen better days. The majority of the 1,200 rooms in this enormous, block-long art deco doyenne are smaller than many others in Manhattan of similar pricing, and they're looking a bit tired at last check. Still, they're fancy enough for tourists (especially on the club level, with its own private lounge and additional business furnishings such as CD players and high-speed

Internet ports); they're equipped with two-line phone, fax machine, iron, and hair dryer; and the elegant lobby makes a great place to relax to piano music. Guests are also apt to find something to like in the business center, three bars and four restaurants on-site, and fitness and spa services such as a steam room and a cadre of massage therapies. About a quarter of the hotel's rooms are suites—though you likely won't get a look at the ultra-luxe tower wing, where world leaders and presidents regularly lodge when in town. Regular double rooms begin at about $180 per night, with certain rooms costing as much as $500 per night in high season.

BOUTIQUE HOTELS Dylan Hotel (212-338-0500 or 1-866-55-DYLAN; fax 212-338-0569), 52 East 41st Street between Madison and Park avenues. Subway: S, 4, 5, 6, or 7 train to 42nd Street–Grand Central. In its former life as the Chemists' Club, this Beaux-Arts building with its grand staircase was a bar for scientists for more than a century; today it's been reborn, strangely enough, as a boutique hotel. The 100 or so rooms are softly and i ndirectly lit, with ivory, cream, and chocolate interiors, high ceilings, and marble bathrooms fitted with porcelain-and-granite sinks and chrome Italian fixtures. Robes, slippers, classy toiletries, big television, two-line phone, in-room watercooler, newspapers, safe, and high-speed Internet access are standard in each room. The hotel is worth a look just for its famous Alchemy Suite, one of only two suites in the hotel and certainly one of the more intriguing hotel rooms in all Manhattan—it simulates an alchemist's lab with its vaulted ceiling, globular iron overhead lamp,

Gothic columns, and spookily medieval stained-glass window. It's perhaps best to eat out on the town while staying here (though a new restaurant took over in late 2005), but do stay if you can.

Library Hotel (212-983 4500 or 1-877-793 7323; fax 212-499 9099), 299 Madison Avenue at the corner of East 41st Street. Subway: S, 4, 5, 6, or 7 train to 42nd Street–Grand Central. Like books? Then you'll love this clubby place. One of Midtown's newer boutique hotels, this one has what might be the most interesting and unique concept in all New York: 60 rooms arranged and decorated with the corresponding art and books, according to the Dewey decimal system of classification. For the traveler, this means booking into one of 10 theme floors that each precisely matches a library category. (If I'm spoiling the surprise, skip the next few passages.) Third-floor rooms—the first floor of guest rooms—are decorated in social sciences themes such as law, money, and economics; fourth-floor rooms give the feel of various world languages; fifth-floor rooms are designed in math and science themes; and sixth-floor rooms are high on technology. Seventh-floor rooms reflect the arts. Eighth-floor rooms are literary, 9th-floor rooms lean toward the historical, 10th-floor rooms epitomize general knowledge, 11th-floor rooms are philosophically inclined—including the king-bedded Love Room, with a Klimt print, books specially picked by sex expert Dr. Ruth Westheimer, and a balcony overlooking Madison Avenue—and 12th-floor rooms are religiously themed. You can also tell what sort of a room you've got by its "classification number": a room number ending in .001, .002, or .005 contains a queen-sized bed, while one ending in .003 or .004 has a full-sized bed, and .006 rooms have the full monty: a king bed. Rooms are thoughtfully equipped not only with books in the appropriate themes but also with pencils instead of pens, just as a real library is.

The amenities here are considerable—think Belgian chocolates, bathrobes, bottles of complimentary springwater, lovely Natura toiletries from Sweden, two-line phone, a complimentary breakfast, movie channels, VCR with plenty of free videos for loan, and health club privileges at the New York Sports Club. Every room in the place has high-speed Internet access via T-1 lines. There's a second-floor reading room (of course!), stocked with *The New York Times,* the *Wall Street Journal,* and other reading materials—you can also take your included continental breakfast there and stock up on 24-hour free coffee and snacks. Or you might head instead for the quieter 14th-floor Writers Den, a paneled mahogany room with a bar (there's a free wine and cheese reception each weeknight), good views, a huge flat-screen wall television, and a crackling fireplace. The location of this hotel is great, too: You're impressively close to the New York Public Library and the handsome Morgan Library (see *To See—Library*) and Grand Central Terminal's array of eats. Double room rates begin at around $335–425 per night, with suites running $495 per night and family (two-room) units beginning around $920 per night.

Morgans (212-686-0300 or 1-800-334-3408; fax 212-779-8352), 237 Madison Avenue between East 37th and East 38th streets. Subway: S, 4, 5, 6, or 7 train to 42nd Street–Grand Central, 7 train to Fifth Avenue, or B, D, F, or V train to 42nd Street. No sign marks this discreet Madison Avenue boutique hotel behind a solid limestone facade, but New Yorkers in the know have all been here at one time or another thanks to the white-hot restaurant Asia de Cuba (see *Dining Out*) and associated bar in the impressively classy lobby. This was hip-hotel maven Ian Schrager's maiden voyage into the brave new world of stripped-down lodgings—a bit odd, considering that it opened during the heart of the excessive 1980s—but the place caught on. Maybe it was the chic lobby's leather chairs, heavy lamps, and wicker bistro-style tables, or the Escher carpet that first hooked newbies. Regardless, Schrager's signature touches were all here in their infancy, and they remain today: crystal in the bathroom doors, low-slung bedding, steel funnel-shaped sinks that seem more pop-arty than comfortably functional, granite and tile in the bathrooms. Calming color schemes of whites, buttery yellows, and browns, as well as plush fabrics in the halls and seating areas, help soften the effect of all this postindustrial design.

Despite the heavy hipness quotient, many of the 113 rooms do possess modern conveniences such as a small refrigerator, safe, mini bar, and VCR—and the friendly staff, an included continental breakfast, and a health club further enhance the pleasant experience of staying here. If you don't feel like Asian-Cuban fusion cuisine in the restaurant, at least check out the softly lit basement Morgans Bar: It's as good a place as any in these environs for a quiet drink with a companion of business or pleasure. Oh, and the name? It comes from J. P. Morgan, whose mansion (now a library) stands less than a block away. Room rates begin at around $320 per night.

W New York (212-755-1200 or 1-877-946-8357; fax 212-319-8344), 541 Lexington Avenue at the corner of East 49th Street. Subway: 6 train to 51st Street, E or V train to Lexington Avenue–53rd Street, or S, 4, 5, or 7 train to 42nd Street–Grand Central. The original W New York is huge and luxe, from the spacious modern lobby to the in-house spa, from several dining and drinking spaces to plush, comfortable beds. Designer David Rockwell has bathed the 700-plus rooms (of which 60 are suites) in indirect light and decorated them in natural color schemes. Beds in the smallish but sleek rooms are fitted with high-thread-count sheets, goose-down comforters, and pillow-top mattresses; each room also has high-speed Internet access, a CD player and VCR (the hotel maintains a library of CDs and videotapes), two two-line phones, a television with WebTV access, and a box of treats for snacking. The slate-floored bathrooms feature Aveda toiletries. As if that weren't enough, the cool Whiskey Blue bar (see *Entertainment—Bars and Clubs*) is a low-lit power connection scene that doesn't really begin hopping until midnight; the Heartbeat restaurant on the ground floor serves healthy New American cuisine to appreciative guests; and there's also a lobby juice bar serving light fare and a relaxing open lounge for wine and cocktails. The spa and fitness center feature a steam room, sauna, and massage and other therapies and services.

W New York–The Court (212-685-1100 or 1-877-946-8357; fax 212-889-0287), 130 East 39th Street between Lexington and Park avenues. Subway: S, 4, 5, 6, or 7 train to 42nd Street–Grand Central. One of a pair of next-door W hotels on East 39th Street, The Court opened in 1999. It's designed to be classy yet is also super-hip, more so than its calmer cousin hotel; witness the black-clad doormen with earpieces, who likely will ignore your entreaties for a hand. The hotel consists of about 200 rooms (40 of them suites), some with terrace; all are extremely modern—with big wooden desk, high-speed Internet access, CD player—yet it's also homey with its pillowy beds, Aveda bath products, and wine-and-chocolate color schemes. (If you *really* like your room, there's a catalog from which you can order the robes, sheets, toiletries, and even daybeds contained therein.) The lounge (sorry, "living room") has a fireplace and is an outstanding public space for meeting someone. Off the lobby, the Wetbar (see *Entertainment—Bars and Clubs*) is one of the city's hippest upscale lounges. The Drew Nieporent–owned Icon (see *Dining Out*) restaurant serves decent prix fixe meals 7 nights a week.

W New York–The Tuscany (212-779-7822 or 1-800-223-6725; fax 212-696-2095), 120 East 39th Street between Lexington and Park avenues. Subway: S, 4, 5, 6, or 7 train to 42nd Street–Grand Central. The W's other Murray Hill hotel (see above) has bigger, more tranquil rooms and a slightly less see-and-be-seen scene. The spare white units are kitted out in the usual W style—Aveda bath products, CD player in the clock, high-speed Internet access, cordless phone—with oversized beds and bathrooms. The chain's signature "munchie box" of treats makes an appearance here, and the other amenities include a bar (Cherry) and a 24-hour gym on the premises.

BUSINESS HOTELS Jolly Madison Towers (212-802-0600 or 1-800-225-4340; fax 212-447-0747), 22 East 38th Street between Madison and Park avenues. Subway: S, 4, 5, 6, or 7 train to 42nd Street–Grand Central. This Italian-owned hotel isn't top of the line, but it's a fine business-class option with lots of Italian marble, glass, and fabrics throughout. Corners haven't been cut on the business amenities, and you'll find a good Italian restaurant (Cinque Terre) and a massage/sauna facility on the premises as well. Suites are quite nice, and well worth the extra cost. Specials sometimes drop the price as low as $160 per night, dinner included, though they can also go much higher too.

✎ **Shelburne Murray Hill** (212-689-5200 or 1-800-ME-SUITE; fax 212-779-7068), 303 Lexington Avenue near the corner of East 37th Street. Subway: 6 train to 33rd Street. One of the Manhattan East group of suite properties scattered around the city's East Side, the Shelburne Murray Hill has a unique claim to fame and also makes a good choice for families because each room is indeed a suite—which means plenty of room, a full kitchen (including a refrigerator and even a dishwasher), two televisions,

cable Internet access, and a sofa. (You'll feel like you live in the neighborhood with all these amenities.) Some rooms have views of the Empire State Building. If you haven't got one, head for the rooftop—it's a pleasant place to gaze upon the city skyline. And the lobby restaurant has a way with a juicy burger.

That claim to fame? This hotel hosted no less than Cuban dictator Fidel Castro and his entourage for 1 night in 1960 as the young Castro prepared to address the United Nations. Castro left after just one night (his huge group reportedly boned and cooked live chickens in the rooms), believing he was being bugged, and moved uptown to Harlem's Hotel Theresa (see *To See—Historic Sites* in chapter 12). But that's all in the past now. Today the Shelburne is a Murray Hill bargain—and staff are extremely friendly as well.

✳ Where to Eat

Midtown East contains the bulk of the city's most famous restaurants, and if you're staying in this area you will have more trouble *choosing* a fine-dining experience than *finding* one. Consult my listings below, and don't be afraid to ask folks around the city for advice, either; these are New Yorkers, and everyone has an opinion he or she will happily dispense.

Cheap eats aren't all that hard to find, either—the cross streets and avenues here are laced with sushi joints, snack shops, coffee shops, fast-food outlets, French bistros, bars of varying quality . . . a little bit of everything, actually. If you're stumped or in a hurry for something, just make your way to Grand Central Terminal. The food court areas contain several levels

(both literally and figuratively) of options, everything from a grand oyster bar and Charlie Palmer's beautifully designed Metrazur room to quicker and more affordable sushi counters, coffee shops, soup stalls, take-out delis, sandwiches, and dessert shops.

DINING OUT **Asia de Cuba** (212-726-7755), 237 Madison Avenue between East 37th and East 38th streets. Subway: 6 train to 33rd Street. Open Monday through Friday for lunch noon–3:30 PM and dinner 5:30–11 PM, Saturday for dinner only to 12:30 AM, Sunday for dinner only. The fusion of Asian and Latin American cuisine isn't something that has thoroughly worked itself out, yet, but New Yorkers are clearly intrigued at the moment. Around town you'll spot the occasional bewildering restaurant name that's half Chinese, half Spanish—where did this trend start, anyway? No matter; Asia de Cuba is the center of the earthquake right now.

Everything here is cool and white—as befits the unmarked Ian Schrager–Philippe Starck hotel (Morgans) it's located within—and the cuisine is certainly spicy and inventive. Start with shrimp or the excellent oxtail spring rolls, then go with one of the entrées (which don't hold back). The margarita-marinated salmon isn't for everyone, because it tastes strongly of tequila—if it's not to your liking, order up some Chinese boiled and salted pork or a hot-spiced steak with yucca sides. Desserts are sweet and delicious, and there's a full set of designer drinks to match; you can also eat upstairs at the hip bar if you're not interested in one of the tiny tables or the giant communal table.

Brasserie (212-751-4840), 100 East 53rd Street between Lexington and Park avenues. Subway: E or V train to Lexington Avenue–53rd Street, or 6 train to 51st Street. Open Monday through Friday 7 AM–1 AM, Saturday from 11 AM, Sunday 11 AM–10 PM. Alsatian chef Luc Dimnet's simply named brasserie achieves what it reaches for: relatively straightforward food. Begin lunch with onion soup gratinée or escargots, then try seared arctic char, seven-vegetable couscous, or mussels with fries. Dinner offerings are much the same, with the addition of a lobster salad, seared sea scallops with parsnip puree, bouillabaisse, grilled hanger steak, and an over-the-top seafood mixed grill of salmon, shrimp, lobster, sea bass, and scallops. Weekend brunches feature a huge, luxe menu that goes far beyond bacon and eggs to embrace a variety of sushi, foie gras, crabcakes, and the like.

Cinquanta (212-759-5050), 50 East 50th Street between Madison and Park avenues. Subway: E or V train to Fifth Avenue–53rd Street, or 6 train to 51st Street. Open Monday through Saturday noon–midnight, Sunday 5–11 PM. Cinquanta cooks much better-than-average Italian meals, and neighborhood locals appreciate it for doing that. Begin with a carpaccio of fennel-cured salmon, grilled squid, or baby shrimp in white beans; after a first course of pasta—maybe lobster ravioli in pink peppercorns and brandy sauce—move on to reliable main courses such as salmon seared in grappa liqueur and orange sauce, stewed tripe, steak cooked Florentine-style, veal scaloppine, sweet Italian sausages, or braised lamb shank served over fettuccine. There are also wild game dishes, cooked seasonally. You can spend a lot here, but you can also save: The prix fixe (which is the same price at lunch *and* dinner) is an out-standing deal.

Docks Oyster Bar (212-986-8080), 633 Third Avenue at the corner of 40th Street. Subway: S, 4, 5, 6, or 7 train to 42nd Street–Grand Central. Open Monday through Friday 11:30 AM–midnight, Saturday for dinner only 5 PM–midnight, and Sunday 11:30 AM–10 PM. Docks is located very close to the much more famous oyster bar in Grand Central Terminal (see *To See—Big Buildings*), and not nearly as classy looking, yet many patrons who've tried both claim Docks is actually a better place to eat. And they may be right. Inside the huge and fun (in other words, noisy) room, you, too, can down reasonably priced oysters and clams on the half shell at a fraction of the cost you'd pay at that other place. Docks also runs a grill cooking fish dishes, chowders, and shellfish, but stick with the raw stuff—it's the reason to be here. There's a second location on the Upper West Side.

✐ **FiftySevenFiftySeven** (212-758-5757), 57 East 57th Street between Madison and Park avenues. Subway: 4, 5, or 6 train to 59th Street, or N, R, or W train to Fifth Avenue–59th Street. Open daily for breakfast 7–11 AM, lunch 11:30 AM–2 PM, and dinner 6–10:30 PM, Sunday for brunch 11 AM–2 PM. In a beautiful, grandiose dining room featuring high ceilings and onyx chandeliers, the Four Seasons Hotel's restaurant serves rich, fancy meals that manage to be inventive without straying too far off the course. Lunch could start with a light mushroom-shiitake soup, lobster carpaccio, skewers of bison and shrimp, a salad of fresh greens, warm pears, and blue cheese, lobster Caesar salad, or an upscale macaroni and cheese with shrimp; main courses include Maryland crabcakes, salmon, chicken breast with seafood risotto, apple-roasted pork tenderloin, a vegetable-cornmeal cobbler, strip steak, sea bass, salt-and-pepper-crusted tuna, or veal paillard. Dinner could begin with shrimp toast (a Chinatown specialty), crab bisque, salmon terrine, oxtail ravioli, potato pancakes with scallops and salmon, goat cheese ravioli, or truffle salad, then continue with roast lobster, cedar-planked salmon with caviar, seared halibut, grilled bison with a lobster potpie, venison loin with foie gras, filet mignon, or lamb.

The top-rated breakfast, second in New York only perhaps to Norma's, features great lemon-ricotta pancakes, challah French toast with apple-walnut compote and cream, smoked salmon with poached eggs, rhubarb pancakes, Belgian waffles with sausage, and eggs Benedict. There's also a special menu for kids.

Grand Central Oyster Bar & Restaurant (212-490-6650), Lower Level, Grand Central Terminal, East 42nd Street at the corner of Park Avenue. Subway: S, 4, 5, 6, or 7 train to 42nd Street–Grand Central. Open Monday through Friday 11:30 AM–9:30 PM, Saturday from noon. Everybody who's anybody has dined at the raw oyster bar located on the Lower Concourse of Grand Central Terminal. Tiled in gorgeous Guastavino tile and beneath a big vaulted ceiling, this expensive restaurant is a great spot for a sit-down meal of clam chowder, raw oysters, fish or steak, and wine; the menu varies daily according to what's fresh, but generally speaking fish

dishes cost $20–25 each, raw oysters about $2 each. And here's a locals' secret. You don't *have* to drop big bucks in the fancy dining room, because there are several counters and bars where you can just order a bowl of thick white or Manhattan (red) clam chowder and a beer, and get out for less than 10 bucks a head—all the while enjoying the companionable spectacle of the cooks preparing the chowder in special steam-heated metal crocks.

Icon (212-592-8888), 130 East 39th Street at the corner of Lexington Avenue. Subway: S, 4, 5, 6, or 7 train to 42nd Street–Grand Central. Open daily 7–10:30 AM for breakfast, 11:30 AM–2 PM for lunch, and 5–10:30 PM for dinner. The latest in restaurant mini mogul Drew Nieporent's New York offerings, this eclectic restaurant nicely fits in with the W Court Hotel (see *Lodging—Boutique Hotels*) within which it resides. This is one of restaurant maven Nieporent's grandest successes—although those who prefer a quiet night on the town might be surprised by the chic, lively crowd and throbbing music. A luxurious feel pervades the place, of course, and the menu attempts to please all palates from gourmet, to meat-and-potatoes: Rib-eye steaks are served with Yukon potato hash and creamed spinach; thyme-roasted chicken comes with garlic potato puree and roasted vegetables; and the striped black bass is paired with wild mushroom risotto. They also serve burgers and Caesar salads—at lunch only.

La Mangeoire (212-759-7086), 1008 Second Avenue between East 53rd and East 54th streets. Subway: E or V train to Lexington Avenue–53rd Street. Open Sunday through Thursday for lunch noon–2:30, daily for dinner 5:30–10:30 PM. There are tons of restaurants in Midtown East, particularly in the high 40s and mid-50s, but La Mangeoire stands out as a good little midrange restaurant that isn't so well known—yet—that you can't get a table in one of the three intimate dining rooms. The Provençale country cooking here is outstandingly prepared, simple and fresh, by knowledgeable chefs; there's a full wine list, of course, soft French pop playing to set the mood, and a good prix fixe deal (around $22 per person before 6:30 PM, around $26 per person until 7:30 PM).

Starters include a satisfyingly earthy pureed mussel stew with a few whole shellfish tossed in for good measure; entrées include a solid take on coq au vin—the dark-meat chicken is slow-cooked in a deep red wine sauce, flavored with bits of smoky bacon and sautéed country vegetables and sided with thick mashed potatoes. A shepherd's pie of crispy ground lamb, eggplant, and potatoes might be the real star, though. The prix fixe dessert is straightforward but delicious: a simple apple tart composed of thin apple slices and exceptionally buttery crust, served with a dollop of wonderful cinnamon ice cream. Staff are friendlier (and the kitchen more efficient) than at many pricier French places in New York. Word is sure to get out eventually, but for now this is still a bit of a find tucked among some much more famous names.

Le Cirque (212-644-0202), 151 East 58th Street between Lexington Avenue and Third Avenue. Subway: E or V train to 53rd Street, or 6 train to 51st Street. Open Monday through Friday for lunch 11:45 AM–2:30 PM

and dinner 5:30–10 PM Monday through Saturday, Sunday for dinner only 5:30–10:30 PM. This restaurant reopened in May 2006, after relocating to One Beacon Court, a luxury development on East 58th Street. As a second act, Sirio Maccioni and sons have succeeded in topping even themselves. Their Midtown restaurant Le Cirque was for more than 20 years one of the standard-setting places to eat and be seen. But the Maccioni family made a daring move to the plush New York Palace Hotel (see *Lodging—Luxurious Hotels*) from 1997 until 2005, and the results were nothing short of stunning: Adam Tihany's exuberant design retained the Villard Mansion's walnut, oak, marble, art, and chandeliers. Alsatian-born chef Pierre Schaedelin—formerly Alain Ducasse's executive chef in Paris, and thus no slouch—combined French, Italian, and even some Asian influences.

Schaedelin is once again at the helm here, so a meal could start with tuna tartare, a lobster-mango salad, seafood salad, caviar, pumpkin ravioli, smoked salmon terrine, pike quenelles, or seafood stew. The main courses may be similar to what they were before: Dover sole, flounder, tuna steak, *branzino,* or sea bass, in a crispy potato jacket, grilled halibut, roast cod, honey-nut duck breast, a roast venison chop, or top round of lamb. Finish with a rich European dessert such as crème brûlée, an opera cake, a "chocolate extravaganza," vanilla-berry napoleon, soufflé, chocolate cannoli, pineapple-mango "ravioli," or *bombolini*—passion fruit with three kinds of coconut. Also check for daily specials—they might include braised short ribs, osso buco, braised lamb shoulder, bouillabaisse, truffled pork feet, or tripe—three-course prix fixe lunches serving seasonal ingredients, and five-course dinner tasting menus.

March (212-754-6272), 405 East 58th Street between First Avenue and Sutton Place. Subway: N, R, or W train to Lexington Avenue–59th Street, or 4, 5, or 6 train to 59th Street. Open daily for dinner 6–11 PM. March is a great East Side choice for sophisticated New American and fusion food, cooking up chef Wayne Nish's mature menu of lobster, steaks, seafood, and game in a nice space—ask about the small outdoor patio in good weather—and all served by very professional staff. The three-course tasting menu runs $70–100 per person but is divine. While you're waiting, relax with a glass of wine in the front bar or on the recently added rooftop terrace.

Métrazur (212-687-4600), East Balcony, Grand Central Terminal, corner of Lexington Avenue and East 42nd Street. Subway: S, 4, 5, 6, or 7 train to 42nd Street–Grand Central. Open Monday through Friday for lunch 11:30 AM–3 PM and dinner 5–10:30 PM, Saturday for dinner only 5–10:30 PM. Talk about location: Métrazur is found on the East Balcony looking down on Grand Central's busy main concourse. Chef Charlie Palmer, a local legend for his groundbreaking work at Aureole—and also owner of a number of other famous eateries in town—puts together a menu here full of square New American meals and serves it in a big, open room designed to be right in tune with the station's grandiose, stylish update. The famously starred high ceiling of the terminal doesn't hurt the romance of the experience, either. After a first course of salad, herbed spaetzle, baked clams, or duck confit,

dine on such entrées as shrimp ravioli with an orange reduction, smoked tea-encrusted salmon, pork tenderloin, butter-poached lobster, lamb shank with moussaka, or filet mignon. There's a good-value prix fixe dinner between 5 and 6:15 PM, and a $20 prix fixe lunch—of soup or salad, salmon or chicken, and chocolate sorbet or ice cream—from 1:45–3 PM.

Sparks Steakhouse (212-687-4855), 210 East 46th Street between Second and Third Avenues. Subway: S, 4, 5, 6, or 7 train to 42nd Street–Grand Central. Open Monday through Friday for lunch noon–11 PM, Saturday for dinner only 5:30–11 PM. Just a few blocks from Grand Central Terminal, Sparks is one of New York's premier steak houses: a place where the aged prime rib is so good, and the room so grandiose and attractive, that red-meat lovers won't want to pass up the chance to try it while staying nearby. There's really only one thing on the menu: huge slabs of steak, and they don't come inexpensively. You want the basic sliced steak, steak *fromage*, prime sirloin, or filet mignon. That's the beauty of Sparks; they don't fool around here with esoteric sauces, or delicate, unpronounceable salads. (If you simply can't stomach beef, there's veal, lamb, and a surprising choice of seafood—halibut, tuna, sea bass, snapper, salmon, swordfish, crab, scallops, and lobster—though patrons rarely order these.) It's simply the best cut of steak you can get in Manhattan, and the seemingly endless wine list is outstanding as well. You'll almost be able to forget the mob-style assassination that took place outside in the 1980s; you'll almost forget, but you won't, because someone will probably mention it.

❧ **Sushi Yasuda** (212-972-1001), 204 East 43rd Street between Second and Third avenues. Subway: S, 4, 5, 6, or 7 train to 42nd Street–Grand Central. Open Monday through Friday for lunch noon–2:15 PM and dinner 6–10:15 PM, Saturday for dinner 6–10:15 PM. Well liked by the city's Japanese populace, this place now also attracts a healthy number of tourists and locals; the secret is out. The fish is amazingly fresh, served in a modern-looking room and prepared with amazing skill. There are seasonal changes in the menu, including unusual choices such as fugu (a famously poisonous blowfish). Meals are expensive here, but you can save by going for the prix fixe. It's not far from Grand Central Terminal, either.

❧ **Vong** (212-486-9592), 200 East 54th Street at the corner of Third Avenue. Subway: E or V train to Lexington Avenue–53rd Street, or 6 train to 51st Street. Open Monday through Friday for lunch noon–2:15 PM and dinner 5:30–11 PM, Saturday for dinner only, Sunday for dinner only to 10 PM. Hotshot chef Jean-Georges Vongerichten has his hands in a lot of proverbial pies these days, but Vong remains his original creation and a kitchen that is still true to his vision of fusing Thai and French cuisine in high style to good effect. If no longer white hot and host to an A-list crowd, it's still a quick starter kit to Vongerichten's gustatory adventures; the dining room, too, is unusually designed, lit, and spaced, certainly worth a look.

Many diners start with the Black Plate, Vong's mix-and-match taste treat for two of samples and sauces from the kitchen (think lobster, shrimp, crab, and game prepared different ways) on a deep-black-colored plate. Try any combination you think you'll like. Then move on to such fusions as lobster with a selection of Thai curries, squab with an egg noodle pancake, or tamarind-spiced fish. Desserts utilize Asian ingredients such as mango, pear, and rice; the White Plate is a sampler of the best. It's expensive, of course. But don't think you can't eat here affordably— the pretheater prix fixe menu serves full three-course dinners for just $38 per person, and a similar deal at lunch is $28 per person. (Vongerichten's tasting menu, on the other hand, is $72 per person.)

EATING OUT AQ Cafe (212-847-9745), 58 Park Avenue between 37th and 38th streets. Open Monday through Saturday 10 AM–5 PM. Tucked away inside the interesting, often overlooked Scandinavia House Cultural Center, the little AQ is a very interesting and inexpensive lunch bite on the way to Park Avenue or Grand Central Terminal. This place is all about the simplicity and heartiness of Nordic cooking: Swedish meatball sandwiches are accompanied by traditional sides like tangy pickled beets as well as goat cheese and roasted onions; main courses run to heavier items such as a salmon lasagna layered with dill pesto, salsa, and Parmesan béchamel. Smaller, lighter "cold plate" offerings include herring and a smörgåsbord of meats, cheeses, breads, and pickles. Desserts include baked items such as Danish and brownies; wash it all down with Swedish sparkling water or a Danish beer.

Ata-Ru (212-681-6484), 151 East 43rd Street between Third and Lexington avenues. Subway: S, 4, 5, 6, or

7 train to 42nd Street–Grand Central. Open Monday through Friday 8 AM– 8 PM, weekends 10 AM–6 PM. In the heart of a Japanese district around the Grand Central Terminal area, this café cooks up Japanese health foods. But that's far from the only reason to come here. There's also a great espresso machine, a knockout sound system, a high-definition flat-screen television, free high-speed Internet connections for those with laptops equipped to handle them—even a fortune-teller.

Franchia (212-686-4331), 12 Park Avenue between East 34th and East 35th streets. Subway: 6 train to 33rd Street. Open daily 11:30 AM–10 PM. This tiny Park Avenue shop, wedged among soaring apartment buildings and graceful hotels, is related to a vegetarian Korean restaurant in the city. Try anything on the prix fixe, or go à la cart; you'll be eating tofu or other meat substitutes, but the setting, presentation, and accompanying beverages (including sake and a wonderful green tea) are so soothing, you won't even notice.

Junior's (212-692-9800), Lower Level, Grand Central Terminal, Lexington Avenue at the corner of East 42nd Street. Subway: S, 4, 5, 6, or 7 train to 42nd Street–Grand Central. Open Monday to Saturday 7 AM– 10 PM, Sunday 8 AM–8 PM. A satellite operation of the popular Brooklyn deli–lunch counter, this one's just as good, if a little more chaotic. The place is best known for its cheesecakes (you can order single servings, half cakes, or entire cakes), but also go for the thick meat or BLT sandwiches served with delicious pickles and fries on the side or any of a number of other sandwiches, sweets, or treats.

Katsu-Hama (212-758-5909), 11 East 47th Street between Madison and Fifth avenues. Subway: S, 4, 5, 6, or 7 train to 42nd Street–Grand Central, or E or V train to Fifth Avenue–53rd Street. Open Monday through Thursday for lunch 11:30 AM–3 PM and dinner 5–10 PM, Friday 11:30 AM– 10:30 PM, weekends 11:30 AM–9:30 PM. This is a real find, an outstanding and affordable restaurant specializing in *tonkatsu* (incredibly tender pork cutlets), *torikatsu* (chicken cutlets), croquettes, fried shrimp, *ton jiru* (pork-miso stew), and other authentic Japanese cuisine. Wash it down with a cold Sapporo beer. Interestingly, almost all of the staff are Indian— speaking perfect Japanese to the customers. Go figure.

Naples 45 (212-972-7001), 200 Park Avenue at the corner of East 45th Street. Subway: S, 4, 5, 6, or 7 train to 42nd Street–Grand Central. Open Monday through Friday 7:30 AM– 10 PM. Housed inside the distinctive MetLife building that splits up Park Avenue, Naples 45 bakes tremendous upscale pizzas in its venerable wood-burning oven. Sure, they serve vegetable side dishes and a smattering of seafood, sandwiches, and cold-cut plates, but diners come here for the pizza—either individual 10-inch pies (about $12–14 each) or so-called half-meter pizzas better suited to tables of three or four (each costs about $29). Good choices include the four-cheese white pizza, with pecorino, Parmesan, provolone, and mozzarella cheeses; the Vesuvio, with anchovies, olives, capers, and peperoncini; and good old pepperoni or margherita.

Rosa Mexicano (212-753-7407), 1063 First Avenue at the corner of East 58th Street. Subway: 4, 5, or 6 train to 59th Street, or N, R, or W train to Lexington Avenue–59th Street. Open daily 5:30–11:30 PM. A brightly decorated place much improving a somewhat gray stretch of First Avenue, Rosa Mexicano dispenses upscale Mexican—a night here reminds you that this particular ethnic fare doesn't always have to mean just tacos and burritos. Indeed, appetizers include such spirited inventions as flounder taquitos, pickled jalapeños stuffed with smoked trout, and raviolis filled with chicken and poblano-champagne sauce; main courses might run to a spicy lamb shank marinated in hot chile peppers and steamed in parchment paper, or various crêpe creations. The grilled fare includes such choices as shrimp, chicken, beef tenderloin, filet mignon, and pork chops—usually marinated in a mixture of garlic, onions, chiles, and tomatoes prior to cooking. Order a Mexican beer on the side, and finish with cream cheese flan or a chocolate torte flavored with anchos. They deliver, too.

Wu Liang Ye (212-370-9648), 338 Lexington Avenue between East 39th and East 40th streets. Subway: S, 4, 5, 6, or 7 train to 42nd Street–Grand Central. Open weekdays 11:30 AM–10 PM, weekends from noon. This Lexington Avenue winner—one of three in its own little mini chain—cooks up some of the city's most interesting and delicious gourmet Szechuan fare. The chef specializes in seafood, particularly Maine lobster, which you can order stir-fried, sautéed, steamed, or spiced. Fried whole fish is another Szechuan specialty, and there's a surprising number of filet mignon dishes on the menu—try it

seared in a wok and served with mushrooms and spinach. Among the other unusual offerings are the No. 42 (a soup of beef brisket and noodles), several tripe dishes (including shredded tripe paired with a roasted chile vinaigrette), and tangerine prawns: large shrimplike shellfish in a fruit sauce. They're open fairly late for this part of town, too—until 10 PM—and will gladly deliver to hotels in the Murray Hill area.

COFFEE AND SNACKS Buttercup Bake Shop (212-350-4144), 973 Second Avenue between East 51st and East 52nd streets. Subway: 6 train to 51st Street, or E or V train to Lexington Avenue–53rd Street. Open Monday and Tuesday 8 AM–10 PM, Wednesday through Friday to 11 PM, Saturday 10 AM–11 PM, Sunday 10 AM–7 PM. There are two little cupcake shops I love in Manhattan, and this is one of them, parked in a sort-of-drab area of Second Avenue. Once inside, though, all's well—employees set out the hot and fresh cupcakes, cakes, and treats while good coffee brews. You can get a golden, chocolate, red velvet, spice, lemon, or German chocolate cupcake with delicious buttercream frosting for just $1.50, an outstanding bargain in New York. Or go for a muffin, cookie, bar, square, or piece of pie. They also sell entire cakes if you've got room.

🍽 **Cipriani Dolci** (212-973-0999), West Balcony of Grand Central Terminal, East 42nd Street between Lexington and Park avenues. Subway: S, 4, 5, 6, or 7 train to 42nd Street–Grand Central. Open daily 11:30 AM–11 PM. A bakery and café run by the same ownership as the much-higher-profile (and much-more-expensive) Harry Cipriani, this little café in Grand Central Terminal's West Balcony serves outstanding pasta, sandwiches, and coffees to an appreciative Midtown crowd.

Crestanello Gran Caffe Italiano (212-545-9996), 475 Fifth Avenue between 40th and 41st streets. Subway: 7 train to Fifth Avenue, S, 4, 5, or 6 train to 42nd Street–Grand Central, or B, D, F, or V train to 42nd Street. Open Monday through Friday 8 AM–8:30 PM, Saturday noon–7 PM. Right across the street from the famous New York Public Library and just a skip away from Grand Central Terminal, this truly Italian café—it's the first foreign outpost of a Vicenza, Italy, coffee-roasting house—serves great espresso, coffee drinks, sweets, and light pasta meals. The narrow, stylish room hops with business, residential, and tourist traffic all day long; expect a steady stream of Italian between *baristas* and customers. And here's the kicker: They also serve sake (Japanese liquor).

Minamoto Kitchoan Wagashi (212-489-3747), 608 Fifth Avenue near the corner of East 49th Street. Subway: B, D, F, or V train to 47th–50th Streets/Rockefeller Center. For Japanese sweets and baked goods beautifully designed—and even more beautifully wrapped—this is where I'd go first in Manhattan. It's a classy operation through and through, and the confections seem like works of art. You'll pay more than you expect, but you'll also take home a gift or snack you can't find anywhere else between here and Tokyo.

Tea Box at Takashimaya (212-350-0180), 693 Fifth Avenue between 54th and 55th streets. Subway: E or V train to 53rd Street, or 6 train to 51st Street. Open Monday through Saturday 11:45 AM–5:30 PM. Wedged into the basement area of Fifth Avenue's Japanese department store Takashimaya, the Tea Box offers a pleasant alternative to the usual hotel high teas: Here the experience is almost thoroughly Japanese, beginning with the sliding rice-paper screens. Order a pot of green tea for two and share Japanese-style finger sandwiches and snacks. Or you can just sip a single cup and sample one of the store's custom-made chocolate treats or a bento box lunch; afterward, browse the tiny tea shop adjacent.

✴ Entertainment

THEATER Theater at St. Peter's (212-868-4444), 619 Lexington Avenue between East 53rd and East 54th streets. Downstairs in St. Peter's church near the corner of 54th Street, this venue sees such shows as the Jerry Herman retrospective, *Showtune*. Tickets are relatively expensive for an off-off-Broadway show.

FILM AND MOVIES City Cinemas 1, 2, 3 (212-753-6022), 1001 Third Avenue at the corner of 60th Street. Subway: N, R, or W train to Lexington Avenue–59th Street, or 4, 5, or 6 train to 59th Street. Recent films of occasional quality show up here.

Clearview 59th Street East (212-777-FILM, ext. 615), 239 East 59th Street between Second and Third avenues. Subway: 4, 5, or 6 train to 59th Street, or N, R, or W train to Lexington Avenue–59th Street. The single screen at 59th Street shows good second-run films.

Loews Kips Bay Theatre (212-50-LOEWS, ext. 558), 550 Second Avenue between East 31st and East 32nd streets. Subway: 6 train to 33rd Street. Hollywood hits are shown here.

CULTURAL ORGANIZATION Japan Society (212-832-1155), 333 East 47th Street between First and Second avenues. Subway: S, 4, 5, or 7 train to 42nd Street–Grand Central, or 6 train to 51st Street. Open Tuesday through Friday 11 AM–6 PM, weekends until 5 PM. At this center for cultural exchange, the exhibitions area displays both modern and historic objects and objects of art, while the lecture hall sees a regular program of interesting talks on Japanese American topics. Admission costs $5 for adults, $3 for children and senior citizens.

BARS AND CLUBS King Cole Bar (212-339-6721), 2 East 55th Street at the corner of Fifth Avenue. Subway: E or V train to Fifth Avenue–53rd Street. Open daily 11:30 AM–1 AM, Friday and Saturday to 2 AM, Sunday to midnight. Inside the dowdy, expensive St. Regis Hotel, this old-boy's-clubby bar invented the drink known as the bloody Mary. It's a fancy, richly textured place for a drink—dress appropriately.

Monkey Bar (212-838-2600), 60 East 54th Street between Madison and Park avenues. Subway: E or V train to Fifth Avenue–53rd Street, or 6 train to 51st Street. Sometimes a place just drips history. Joe DiMaggio, Marlon Brando, Tennessee Williams, and Tallulah Bankhead have all bent elbows at this fancy bar inside the Hotel Elysée, updated by famed designer David Rockwell. There's very good food and expensive drinks beneath a decor heavy on—you guessed it—monkeys.

Wetbar (212-685-1100), 130 East 39th Street between Lexington and Park avenues. Subway: S, 4, 5, 6, or 7 train to 42nd Street–Grand Central. Open 4 PM–2 AM, weekends to 4 AM. Inside the W Court hotel, this dimly lit, loud bar designed by Rande Gerber throbs to a sensuous beat and a bit too much pretension. The glass walls allow opaque views of street life.

Whiskey Blue (212-755-1200), 541 Lexington Avenue at the corner of East 49th Street. Subway: 6 train to 51st Street, E or V train to Lexington Avenue–53rd Street, or S, 4, 5, or 7 train to 42nd Street–Grand Central. Open 4:30 PM–3 AM weekdays, to 4 AM weekends. An elegant bar inside the W New York hotel, owned by Cindy Crawford hubby Rande Gerber, this low-lit room is *the* place in Midtown East to meet hip singles late-night—or, if you're drinking alone, to be served at the bar by some of the most attractively coutured waitresses in the city.

✳ Selective Shopping

BOOKSTORE Urban Center Books (212-935-3592 or 1-800-352-1880), 457 Madison Avenue at the corner of East 50th Street. Subway: E or V train to Fifth Avenue–53rd Street, or 6 train to 51st Street. Open Monday through Thursday 10 AM–7 PM, Friday to 6 PM, Saturday to 5:30 PM. Inside the fancy New York Palace Hotel is Manhattan's very best architecture bookshop—and how appropriate is that? Perfectly. Its 9,000-plus-title stock is also strong on books related to construction, interior and exterior design, drawing, history, urban planning, and New York City. To find the bookstore, head for the northern wing of the Villard Houses (from Madison Avenue, it's the wing on the left); the store is on the first floor.

FASHION Bergdorf Goodman Men's (212-753-7300), 745 Fifth Avenue at the corner of East 58th Street. Subway: N, R, or W train to Lexington Avenue–59th Street. Open Monday through Saturday 10 AM–7 PM, Thursday to 8 PM, Sunday noon–6 PM. Right across Fifth Avenue from the famously pricey Bergdorf Goodman ladies' shop, this men's store breathes an air that is just as rarefied. It's the best place in Manhattan to pick up superexpensive, custom-tailored suits and clothes in hard-to-find European styles.

Bloomingdale's (212-705-2000), 1000 Third Avenue at the corner of East 59th Street. Subway: 4, 5, or 6 train to 59th Street, or N, R, or W train to Lexington Avenue–59th Street. Open Monday through Friday 10 AM–8:30 PM, Saturday to 7 PM, Sunday 11 AM–7 PM. Not really in the same snooty class as Saks, Bergdorf, and their ilk, Bloomie's—which started out as a hoop skirt store, believe it or not—is actually more fun because everyone feels welcome there. Oh, they've got all the top-name fashion designers, certainly. But they also have racks and racks of sale-priced items (not everything here requires a platinum card). And it's *big*—an entire block, in fact—so you're sure to find something of interest. A new location in the former Canal Jean Co. space in the heart of SoHo is also making waves.

Saks Fifth Avenue (212-753-4000), 611 Fifth Avenue between 49th and 50th streets. Subway: E or V train to Fifth Avenue–53rd Street, or B, D, F, or V train to 47th–50th streets/Rockefeller Center. Open Monday through Saturday 10 AM–7 PM, Thursday to 8 PM, Sunday noon–6 PM. It opened in 1924 and is still, all these years later, the buzzword for "expensive things" and "old money." The name alone inspires awe, and the top-drawer accessories, jewelry, and perfumes will, too, but you can sometimes actually get out of here paying something like moderate prices if you choose carefully. Needless to say, all the top names in fashion—Gucci, Chanel, Armani, Hugo Boss—can be found here (there's an especially strong men's boutique), and Christmas is worth a special visit: The season brings wonderful window displays and special Saks holiday items for sale.

SAKS FIFTH AVENUE, A SHOPPING LANDMARK SINCE 1924

Kim Grant

Takashimaya (212-350-0100), 693 Fifth Avenue between 54th and 55th streets. Subway: E or V train to Fifth Avenue, or N, R, or W train to Fifth Avenue–59th Street. Open Monday through Saturday 10 AM–7 PM, Sunday noon–5 PM. Japanese travelers know all about this spare Fifth Avenue department store, which is a quite famous midpriced chain back in their homeland. The ground floor doesn't really convey the sense of the place, showcasing only a well-known floral boutique and various artistic installations. But upstairs you'll find travel accessories and impossible-to-find-in-America electronics on the second floor, carefully chosen home items on the third floor, women's accessories on the fourth floor, bedroom and infant items on the fifth floor, and cosmetics and salon items on the sixth floor. Don't overlook the basement, either: Down a set of narrow stairs is a specialty tea shop and café known as the Tea Box (see *Where to Eat—Coffee and Snacks*).

FOOD AND DRINK The granddaddy of food shopping in this neighborhood is the **Grand Central Market,** on the Main Level inside Grand Central Terminal at East 42nd Street, Park Avenue, and Lexington Avenue. (Reach it by taking an S, 4, 5, 6, or 7 train to 42nd Street–Grand Central.) The collection of vendors here in Grand Central Terminal is outstanding for both variety and quality; you'll pay more for your picnic than at any of the convenience stores and markets lining Lexington Avenue, but the food is fresher here—often artisanal. The options include **Penzeys** (212-972-2777), a spice vendor; **Greenwich Produce** (212-490-4444), a green-market; the locally based **Oren's**

Daily Roast (see below); **Li-Lac Chocolates** (212-370-4866); not to mention great breads from **Zaro's Bread Basket** (212-292-0160) and **Corrado Bread & Pastry** (212-599-4321), fresh fish and shellfish from **Pescatore Seafood Company** (212-557-4466), cheeses from **Murray's Cheese** (212-922-1540), and German hams from **Koglin** (212-499-0725).

5th Avenue Chocolatiere (212-935-5454), 510 Madison Avenue near the corner of East 53rd Street. Subway: E or V train to Fifth Avenue–53rd Street. Open Monday through Friday 9:30 AM–6:30 PM, Saturday to 6 PM, Sunday 11 AM–6 PM. This unassuming little storefront, snuggled among the heavy-hitting chain and specialty stores along Madison Avenue, actually conceals a pretty good confectionery— the chocolates here are good enough that Japan Air Lines serves them to the big-ticket customers in first class. Drop by for a free sample of the milk or dark chocolate, formed into daisies, fire trucks, and a variety of other shapes.

Oren's Daily Roast (212-388-0014), Main Level of Grand Central Terminal, East 42nd Street at Park and Lexington avenues. Subway: S, 4, 5, 6, or 7 train to 42nd Street–Grand Central. Actually located apart from the main food court in Grand Central, Oren's is a local coffee grinder serving good espresso, Ben & Jerry's ice cream, and those terrific Doughnut Plant doughnuts. There's another outlet on East 58th Street near Fifth Avenue, and three on the Upper East Side.

JEWELRY Tiffany & Co. (212-755-8000), 727 Fifth Avenue at the corner of East 57th Street. Subway: N, R, or W train to Fifth Avenue–59th Street,

E or V train to Fifth Avenue–53rd Street, or F train to 57th Street. Open Monday through Friday 10 AM–7 PM, Saturday 10 AM–6 PM, Sunday noon–5 PM. For all those who thought Tiffany was just a lamp, a visit to the Fifth Avenue headquarters of New York's most important jeweler is a must. The Italian Renaissance design, heavy on the marble and high ceilings, echoes that of Venice's Palazzo Grimani. The busy ground-floor silver section is where you'll find many of Tiffany's finest designs (though I'd avoid buying a bean), and you can look around without being harassed by the staff; for a glimpse of the high life, however, take the elevator—with an attendant—to the second-floor engagement-ring section. Selections here begin at about $1,000, but it's not uncommon to hear visitors chatting with salesclerks about the finer points of a $50,000 ring, then boxing one up in the famous robin's-egg blue boxes. Up early? What about breakfast at Tiffany's? Sorry, I couldn't resist.

TOYS ✍ **F A O. Schwarz** (212-644-9400), 767 Fifth Avenue at the corner of East 58th Street. Subway: N, R, or W train to Fifth Avenue–59th Street. You know Tom Hanks romped all over a huge keyboard here in *Big*. You know that mechanical toys here are big. But did you know that *F. A. O.* stands for "Frederick August Otto," the Schwarz who started it all? The German immigrant to Baltimore moved to New York in 1880 and quickly found a successful formula, moving to Fifth Avenue in 1931 and across the street in 1986. A red toy soldier stands guard outside the General Motors Building; inside, the ground floor features loads of stuffed animals and a disappointingly tiny but well-stocked baby section. Mechanical toys, girls' and boys' rooms, and F A O.'s own lines of plush animals, intelligent games, and toys fill the second-floor and ground-floor levels. There are free video games to play, too, and you can even rent the place— for a cool $17,500 a night—and hold a (supervised) slumber party here. Tired out? Outside, the plaza steps and benches make good places for a rest, a snack, or simply to people-watch.

✴ Special Events

March 17: **St. Patrick's Day Parade,** along Fifth Avenue. This huge, occasionally controversial gathering of Irish and Irish American groups, cadets, pensioners, and high school marching bands (among other folks) proceeds north up Fifth Avenue from approximately 44th Street to 86th Street. Note that police control access to the parade, so you can only view it from certain points. Expect lots of people wearing ridiculously green clothing and shamrocks, and drinking quantities of green-tinged beer.

Midtown West 8

MIDTOWN WEST

Midtown West is, for many visitors and many practical purposes, New York City. Here you'll find some of the enduring symbols of the city: the creative neon and carnival bluster of Times Square, lit like day even at midnight, with the ball descending on New Year's Eve; Rockefeller Center's much-photographed skating rink; Broadway's delis, coffee shops, and gracefully aging theaters (whose marquees gave rise to the name *Great White Way*); Eighth Avenue's mixture of Asian cuisine, newly trendy bars, and scraggly souvenir shops and peep shows; hotels galore; and a pretzel or hot-dog vendor on every corner. It simply must be seen by anyone new to the city, and while coming here isn't exactly "exploring," there are some interesting, lesser-trodden corners.

For example, virtually undiscovered pocket parks sit beneath many big buildings. There's also a higher-than-usual likelihood that you'll come across celebrities in the oddest places. Strolling down Broadway, you might run into Christopher Walken loping gracefully from block to block; hanging out in a deli near the Ed Sullivan Theater or Rockefeller Center, you might catch someone from the Letterman show or *Saturday Night Live* grabbing a bite before taping; and so on.

For the purposes of this book, I have defined Midtown West as everything lying west of Fifth Avenue from West 30th Street (my arbitrary cutoff line, where Chelsea begins) to West 59th Street (the southern boundary of Central Park). Working from north to south, the Pennsylvania Station–Madison Square Garden neighborhood, in Midtown West's southern reaches, is first. It is sometimes referred to on maps as Midtown South—though *MSG* might have been a better moniker, given both the presence of the Garden and the number of cut-rate Chinese restaurants in this area. Where Broadway, Sixth Avenue, and 34th Street converge is known as Herald Square, a now brightly lit district of shops; two blocks south, Little Korea fills a block of West 32nd Street from Broadway to Fifth Avenue.

The blocks north of here around Seventh Avenue and Broadway are variously called the Fashion District or the Garment District, a nod to the days when workers in factories along and between these avenues labored long and hard to produce New York fashions; today the Fashion Institute of Technology's museum in Chelsea (see chapter 6) is the chief reminder of those times, as nearly all the factories long since moved overseas.

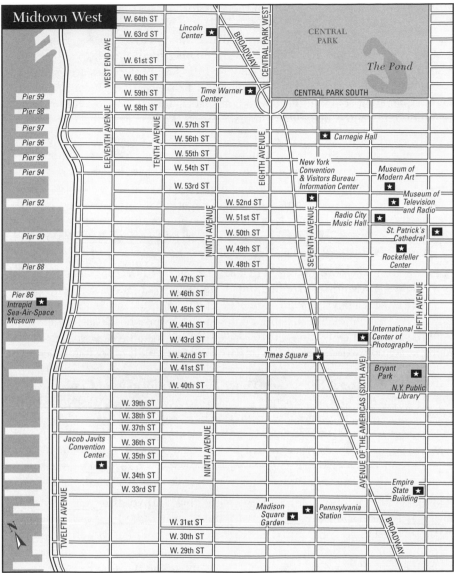

Midtown West

Pier 99
Pier 98
Pier 97
Pier 96
Pier 95
Pier 94
Pier 92
Pier 90
Pier 88
Pier 86 ★
Intrepid
Sea-Air-Space
Museum

Lincoln Center ★
Time Warner ★ Center
CENTRAL PARK
The Pond
CENTRAL PARK SOUTH

★ Carnegie Hall
New York Convention & Visitors Bureau Information Center ★
Museum of Modern Art ★
Museum of Television and Radio ★
Radio City Music Hall ★
St. Patrick's Cathedral ★
Rockefeller Center ★
International Center of Photography ★
Times Square ★
Bryant Park ★
N.Y. Public Library

Jacob Javits Convention Center ★

Empire State Building ★
Madison Square Garden ★
Pennsylvania Station

© The Countryman Press

Times Square, the most famous address in this part of Manhattan, is at the junction of 42nd Street, Seventh Avenue, and Broadway; once, not so long ago, it was a rough-and-tumble district of peep shows, prostitutes, and pickpockets or worse. But Times Square has cleaned up its act and today shines much more brightly. Anyway, the Square is really just a small part of the larger Theater District, which stretches roughly from 42nd Street up to 54th Street and takes in two wide blocks from Sixth to Eighth avenues. There are dozens of Broadway and off-Broadway theater venues packed into this space.

Rockefeller Center lies a bit west of the Theater District, and would be quiet but for the complex of restaurants and shops that have sprung up to service these towering office buildings. Centered around 48th to 50th streets between Fifth and Sixth avenues, the "Rock" and its adjuncts have their own subway station and a cooler sense of elegance, though little foot traffic. This area seems a bit distanced from the common-man bustle of Broadway and Times Square; it leaves some a bit cold, but those who fancy elegant meals, shops, and towering, bland business hotels might enjoy the area.

Finally, the northwestern reaches of Midtown West—say, from Eighth Avenue west to the Hudson River from 42nd up to 59th streets—were once known as Hell's Kitchen; it was a rather tough neighborhood. It has since been rechristened Clinton and is full today of pricey highrises, bistros, bars, ethnic restaurants, and the new Time-Warner megaplex. Eighth and Ninth avenues, part of this area, contain Manhattan's largest concentration of ethnic restaurants—good to know in a pinch when the famous restaurants' tables are all booked up. Many of them are both affordable and delicious.

A few more subdivisions are useful to know. Restaurant Row runs along West 46th Street between Eighth and Ninth avenues; needless to say, it's packed with eateries. Club Row is a block of West 44th Street between Fifth and Sixth avenues occupied by an unusually concentrated number of swanky hotels and private clubs. And the Diamond District doesn't exactly glitter, but its merchants do stretch along a slightly tawdry block of West 47th Street from Fifth to Sixth avenues.

GUIDANCE The popular, high-tech **Times Square Information Center** (212-768-1560), in the thick of the action at 1560 Broadway between West 46th and West 47th streets, distributes visitors information, sells tickets to Broadway events and tours, and dispenses MetroCards for the subway system to the masses. You can also exchange foreign currency for U.S. dollars, take your own digital photo, get money from an ATM, buy (full-price) Broadway tickets, or check e-mail and cruise the Internet for free. The center is open daily from 8 AM until 8 PM.

There's another information booth, the **New York Convention and Visitors Bureau Information Center** (212-484-1222), nearby at 810 Seventh Avenue between West 52nd and West 53rd streets. This one sells tickets, allows limited Internet access, answers queries, and maintains an ATM and a souvenir store with NY-themed gifts. It's open weekdays 8:30 AM–6 PM, weekends until 5 PM.

NEWSPAPERS BUNDLED NEAR TIMES SQUARE

Paul Karr

GETTING THERE You only need to know one thing to get to most points in Midtown West: Times Square. Many of the subway and bus lines run here, so it's easy to reach the giant 42nd Street–Times Square station.

By subway: From Lower Manhattan,

Chinatown, or Fifth Avenue's shopping area, take the N, R, W, or Q train to Times Square. From Greenwich Village, take a 1 train to reach the area; from Tribeca or the Upper West Side, take a 1, 2, or 3 train. You can also take a C train from the Upper West Side or Greenwich Village, or an E train from Fifth Avenue, to the 42nd Street–Port Authority station on Eighth Avenue—there's an underground walkway between the Port Authority and Times Square stations. To reach Rockefeller Center, take a B or D train from the Upper West Side, an F train from the Lower East Side or Upper East Side, or a V train from the Lower East Side or Fifth Avenue shopping area. Finally, if you're on the east side of town, you can take the S shuttle train from Grand Central Station—it runs directly to Times Square several times each hour at least, much more often during peak travel hours.

By bus: City bus lines 6, 7, 10, and 20 run up and down the avenues; the 42 bus runs crosstown (that is, east and west) along 42nd Street. Other bus lines also traverse this area; consult a city bus map (some subway stations post big ones of the area bus lines) for further details.

By car: Do not attempt to drive to the Times Square area. It is hopelessly congested most times of day and often even at night. If you must drive, try to park along one-way Eighth Avenue and walk to your theater or to Times Square; there's metered parking (which becomes free at night) along both sides of the south-traveling avenue. Watch carefully for fire hydrants.

✷ To See

NEIGHBORHOODS **Rockefeller Center** (212-664-3700), West 48th to West 51st streets between Fifth and Sixth avenues. Subway: B, D, F, or V train to 50th Street–Rockefeller Center. Dating from 1933, Rockefeller Center is the acknowledged center of New York's entertainment business and is world famous for both its wintertime outdoor skating rink (anyone can use it) and the Radio City Music Hall music venue. But this huge complex of office buildings and shops contains some secrets, too—including more than 100 art deco works, a set of gardens, the Christie's auction house, television studios, the offices of The Associated Press, and several pocket gardens, among other attractions. John D. Rockefeller commissioned Raymond Hood's massive project to be a new kind of urban center, and it was a huge risk—not only was the Depression ongoing, but at that time there was little of interest between Lower Manhattan and the location he chose. Yet the complex not only succeeded, but also thrived and spiked the boom that created the Midtown we know now; today Rockefeller Center consists of about 20 tall buildings of commercial real estate, shops, and foreign tourist offices, though the public outdoor spaces are much more famous than the center's tenants. Among the most popular spots are the Paul Manship sculpture of Prometheus facing the entrance to Thirty Rockefeller Plaza (sometimes known simply as "30 Rock"); the huge *Atlas* by Lee Lawrie at Fifth Avenue and 50th Street; the famous ice-skating rink and enormous Christmas tree erected there each December; and the NBC studios where *The Today Show* is filmed live each weekday morning. Tours of the center depart from the NBC Experience Store.

Kim Grant

TIMES SQUARE AT NIGHT

New in 2005 is the "Top of the Rock" observation deck, an open-air deck occupying the top of 30 Rock, 70 stories tall above Midtown Manhattan. It offers a nice alternative to the more crowded Empire State Building deck, plus it's outdoors . . . and, of course, you can get something you can't get from the Empire: A view of the ESB itself, decked out in red-white-and-blue, or whatever light scheme happens to be on for the day. Other views face over Central Park and the East River. John D. Rockefeller Jr. first opened a rooftop deck here more than 70 years ago, in an art deco design inspired by ocean liners (there were actually deck chairs up top) and with touches such as cast-aluminum fleur-de-lis. The deck was closed for roughly two decades, but architect Michael Gabellini redesigned the new deck using panels of safety glass; for those unsatisfied with the eye candy outdoors, a crystal geode wall occupies the first level of deck. The entrance is on West 50th Street, between Fifth and Sixth avenues; it's open daily 8:30 AM to midnight, though the last elevator goes up at 11 PM. In bad weather, skip it. Tickets cost $14 per adult, $12 for seniors, and $9 for children.

Times Square, West 42nd Street at Broadway and Seventh Avenue. Subway: N, Q, R, S, W, 1, 2, 3, or 7 train to 42nd Street–Times Square. One of New York City's most photographed—and popular—spots (as you'll discover if you try to loiter here on a Friday or Saturday night in good weather), Times Square is the neon-lit symbol of the new New York. Audaciously commercial, the blocks between Broadway and Seventh Avenue from 42nd to 46th streets explode with high-tech eye candy, while somehow remaining welcoming, visitor-friendly, and surprisingly safe. It's now the crossroads of the city; everyone comes here sooner or later. The former Longacre Square (renamed for *The New York Times* in 1904) has seen both good and hard times, and was in fact extremely seedy by the 1970s and 1980s; however, a firm and focused administrative and police effort to push out crime and pornography has completely remade the district, and for the most part it's no longer seedy. Today high-tech news updates and live television crawl up the sides of skyscrapers. Some of the world's most sophisticated neon advertisements beckon the camcorder. And music and news studios such as MTV regularly broadcast live feeds and concerts from the square. New Year's Eve is more a test of will than an enjoyable party, however—if you enjoy standing packed into a narrow, frigid spot on a sidewalk for hours and hours (you cannot leave, nor are there restrooms) merely to see a glittering ball slowly drop for 1 minute, by all means come. Otherwise, book a table in a nearby hotel bar or restaurant and enjoy the show from a distance.

MUSEUMS International Center of Photography (212-857-0000), 1133 Sixth Avenue at the corner of West 43rd Street. Subway: N, Q, R, S, W, 1, 2, 3, 7, or 9 train to 42nd Street–Times Square. Open Tuesday through Thursday 10 AM– 6 PM, Friday 10 AM–8 PM, weekends 10 AM–6 PM. This good photography museum features exhibits of classic photographs and photography techniques dating back to the birth pangs of the form; exhibitions highlight such holdings as civil-rights-era photographs. Admission costs $10 for adults, $7 for students and senior citizens; Friday nights are by voluntary donation. Children under 12 free.

Intrepid Sea-Air-Space Museum (212-245-0072), Pier 86 at West 46th Street. Subway: C or E train to 42nd Street–Port Authority. Open daily 10 AM–5 PM, weekends to 6 PM in summer. Closed Monday from October to March (closed entirely Oct 6, 2006–May 2008). There's nothing to get the patriotic juices flowing like a look at some of America's air and naval firepower . . . oh, yes, and its prodigious capacity for space exploration, too. Anchored by the aircraft carrier the USS *Intrepid,* which saw heavy action in World War II, the museum also takes in such oddities and intrigue as a nuclear sub, superfast planes (there are some three dozen planes on the *Intrepid's* flight deck), a big chunk of the Berlin Wall outside the museum gates, and Soviet tanks. The museum saw a spike in visits after the 2003 space shuttle disaster; it sees a predictable surge each spring when sailors and ships from around the nation flood the river—and the city—with testosterone for Fleet Week (see *Special Events*). Admission cost $16.50 for adults (less for veterans, seniors, and college students) and $4.50–$11.50 for children.

Museum of Arts and Design (212-956-3535), 40 West 53rd Street between Fifth and Sixth avenues. Subway: E or V train to Lexington Avenue–53rd Street. Open daily 10 AM–6 PM, Thursday until 8 PM. As the name implies, this museum—which changed its name, and its mission, from that of the American Craft Museum—exhibits a range of American arts, crafts, and design in such forms as glass, textiles, metal, clay, and the like. Fashion and architecture also fall under its purview. In the past this museum has organized such shows as an exhibit of recent Danish ceramics, a show of Arline Fisch's jewelry pieces, and a fascinating collection of multimedia responses to the September 11 tragedies. Note that it will be moving to 2 Columbus Circle, home of a controversial conversion project, possibly as soon as by the end of 2006; call ahead to check if it has yet moved. At last check, admission costs $9 for adults, $7 for students and senior citizens, free for children under 12; Thursday night is by voluntary donation.

Museum of Modern Art (MoMA) (212-708-9400), 11 West 53 Street between Fifth and Sixth avenues. Subway: E or V train to Fifth Avenue/53rd Street or B, D, or V train to 47th–50th streets/Rockefeller Center. Open Wednesday to Monday 10:30 AM–5:30 PM, also to 8 PM Friday. MoMA—founded in 1929—moved back to Midtown in 2005 after a hiatus in Queens, and what a reopening it was! The reopening unveiled stunning architectural features; lovely new public sitting areas and gardens; and several excellent new cafés and restaurants created by Union Square restaurant impresario Danny Meyer.

Ah, yes, the museum. This might be the world's best museum of modern art. It contains more than 100,000 paintings, photos, sculptures, and other objects; 4 million film stills; 19,000 films; and many, many books. Too bad it's off the beaten track now, but serious art fans should still make every effort to find a day and get out here if they can possibly find the time. The permanent collection is simply awesome: The painting and drawing section is as outstanding as you would expect, with works by everyone from van Gogh and Seurat to Cézanne, Picasso, Frida Kahlo, and Marc Chagall. Look for special shows such as Matisse Picasso as well. (If there is a particular work that you are very much desiring to see, however, remember to phone the museum to ensure that it is being shown to the public and not in storage.)

There are seminal black-and-white photographs from the likes of Man Ray, Ansel Adams, Paul Strand, and Walker Evans, and plenty of unique objects, prints, posters, and architectural drawings. The film section includes some impressive early films and obscure documentaries. Exhibitions in recent years have included a Munch retrospective, the first to be hung in a major museum in three decades; the first major Dada exhibition in the U.S.; an exhibit on computer animation in motion pictures (*Pixar: 20 Years of Animation*); and a consideration of modern Spanish architecture. Admission costs $20 for adults, $16 for seniors, $12 for students, free for children under 16 except for Friday evenings 4–8 PM, when the museum is free thanks for the generosity of the retail store Target.

🖎 ♿ **Museum of Television & Radio** (212-621-6800 or 212-621-6600), 25 West 52nd Street between Fifth and Sixth avenues. Subway: E or V train to Fifth Avenue–53rd Street, or B, D, or F train to 42nd Street. Open Tuesday to Sunday noon–6 PM. This bicoastal museum (there's an adjunct in Los Angeles) holds a big collection of classic movie and TV reels, which you can view at your leisure once you've gained admission. The fifth-floor listening room is especially interesting: It offers visitors access to a rotating lineup of classic and contemporary radio broadcasts—which might be your only chance to hear Radio Canada, live Sinatra, or a black music history program. Other special exhibitions highlight stars such as Dean Martin and Sammy Davis Jr., and winter Wednesdays bring free lunch-hour screenings of rare, out-of-print television and film projects; on weekends there's a special workshop for kids and their families on the golden age of radio. Admission costs $10 for adults, $8 for students and senior citizens, $5 for children 14 and under.

BIG BUILDINGS **Empire State Building** (212-736-3100), 350 Fifth Avenue at the corner of 34th Street. Subway: B, D, F, N, Q, R, V, or W train to 34th Street–Herald Square. Observation deck open daily 9:30 AM–midnight. King Kong clung to it; Tom Hanks and Meg Ryan were supposed to meet near the top of it. Now once again the tallest building in New York—a title it didn't relinquish until the late 1970s, when the World Trade Center towers were erected—the 1,200-foot-plus Empire State Building rose very quickly in 1930 (a difficult time to raise a building, just a year after the stock crash of 1929). Since the moment it opened, locals and tourists alike have been captivated by the 86th-floor observatory and its 80-mile views; plenty of urban legends, true and untrue, have sprouted up around it. Among those that are true: A U.S. warplane collided with the building in 1945; a woman fell 80 stories in an elevator and survived; the long spire was originally designed to include a spot to hitch blimps, but winds were deemed too strong. The building remains a magnet, and not just for the views; the marble lobby on 34th Street displays murals of the wonders of the world—notice that the ESB has been added as the eighth (a bit of poetic license, there). The exterior is lit with sequences of colors symbolizing holidays, weather, mourning. One of the most romantic traditions involves Valentine's Day, when a group of 15 couples—chosen by competitive essay—marry in 15-minute ceremonies each year on that day. And a bit earlier in February, an annual race pits runners against each other up the stairwells; an Austrian set a new record in 2006 with a time of just over 19 minutes. Tickets to the top cost $10 for adults, $9 for senior citizens and children 12–17, $5 for children 6–11. The building is open daily until midnight—just bear in mind that the last elevator up takes off at 11:15 PM.

Penn Station, Seventh Avenue from West 31st to West 34th streets. Subway: 1, 2, 3, or 9 train to 34th Street–Penn Station. If you're taking an AMTRAK train to New York, your first glimpse of the city will be less than awe inspiring. Penn Station, New York's main long-distance train station, was actually torn down and rebuilt during the 1960s, and the newer version is a lot less impressive than the Beaux-Arts stunner—comparable in beauty to Grand Central—that originally stood where Madison Square Garden now does. But what the station lost in aesthetics, it gained in efficiency. Today more train traffic flows through here than any other station in the country, more than half a million passengers each and every day. If you're looking to get *out* of New York for the day, AMTRAK and the Long Island Rail Road both depart from here rather than Grand Central.

THE EMPIRE STATE BUILDING FROM A DISTANCE

Paul Karr

LIBRARY 🎐 New York Public Library (212-212-930-0830), Fifth Avenue at the corner of 42nd Street. Subway: 7 train to Fifth Avenue, B, D, F, or V train to 42nd Street, or S, 4, 5, or 6 train to 42nd Street–Grand Central. Open Tuesday and Wednesday 11 AM–7:30 PM, Thursday through Saturday 10 AM–6 PM. Nestled snugly between Fifth Avenue and Bryant Park, New York's central public library—technically known as the Humanities and Social Sciences Library—helps anchor Midtown and is one of the city's great free treasures.

Never mind the beautifully designed exterior (something like a Greek temple), or the interior reading rooms (done in marble, with gorgeous lighting fixtures): This library holds a world-class collection of nearly 40 million journals, maps, manuscripts, oral histories, prints, microfilms, and other materials at your disposal—though nothing can be checked out of this branch, so you'll have to do all your work on site. Rotating free exhibits sometimes highlight the library's holdings: The popular New York Eats Out exhibition presented an interesting collection of menus, photographs, and other archives of the city's long-running restaurant scene. Other themed shows have hung the library's prints of Pissarro and Dalí, shown its rare manuscripts (such as a ery rare hand-copy of the Declaration of Independence, and brought together materials chronicling the history of animals within city limits. The library's café—all right, it's a Starbucks—has outdoor seating in summertime, and there's another branch of the city library kitty-corner across Fifth Avenue at 40th Street with large reference and general-interest sections from which books can actually be checked out.

✳ To Do

ICE SKATING Rockefeller Center Ice Rink (212-332-7654), Rockefeller Center at 50th Street near the corner of Fifth Avenue. October through April, open daily 8:30 AM–midnight; closes for half-hour intervals every 2 hours. Subway: B, D, F, or V train to 47th–50th streets/Rockefeller Center. Anyone visiting New York who can skate—and even those who can't—seemingly gives it a whirl here on this small, romantic ice rink set a level down from the street. Admission costs $9–13 for adults, $8–9 for children under 12 (there's a discount on weekends), plus the $7 per person skate-rental fee. They do not take credit cards. There's also a $5 lunchtime skate, and skating lessons (for a fee) too.

SKATERS TAKE A WHIRL AT ROCKEFELLER CENTER.

Kim Grant

✳ Green Space

Bryant Park, West 40th Street to West 42nd Street between Fifth and Sixth avenues. Subway: B, D, F, or V train to 42nd Street. This lovely park is one of my favorite in New York. First off, it has some of the best ground-level views of Manhattan from within the city—that's what a little green space will do for you—and a classy restaurant and boutique hotel right beside it don't hurt, either. Then there's an ice cream kiosk here in summer, statues of Gertrude Stein and the orator William Cullen Bryant, and the New York Public Library backing right up to it—good for reading in any weather. But the park is probably best known among New Yorkers for both the free Wi-Fi Internet access and the popular (and free) series of open-air movies that show here in summer, drive-in-style minus the cars. What else could you want?

✳ Lodging

Nowhere in New York will you find more lodgings than in Midtown West, and weeding through the dozens and dozens of upscale, midscale, and downscale properties can be daunting—particularly since a room rate can vary wildly according to time of year, weather, convention schedules, and many other factors. In general, I don't recommend trying to save money if you want to stay in the Times Square, Theater District, or Midtown West areas; though there are always exceptions, the lower-priced options in these spots are generally much lower in quality than the choices I've listed here. Bottom line? If you want to be close to the action, bite the bullet and pay more.

LUXURIOUS HOTELS **Jumeirah Essex House** (212-247-0300 or 1-888-645-5697; fax 212-315-1839), 160 Central Park South between Sixth and Seventh avenues. Subway: F, N, R, Q, or W train to 57th Street, or A, B, C, D, or 1 train to 59th Street–Columbus Circle. It's not much to look at from the exterior, but the art-deco-styled Essex House—topped with its distinctive neon sign—has got location and amenities to beat those of nearly any other lodgings in New York. Many of the 600 or so rooms (about 80 are suites) overlook Central Park across the street. And you could make a decent argument that the house restaurant Alain Ducasse at the Essex House (see *Dining Out*) is the very best in New York; Mobil's five

stars would seem to concur. But I'm getting ahead of myself. Though no longer part of the Westin family of properties, each room or suite here is still outfitted with famously comfortable beds, pillows, sheets, and duvets, as well as DVD players, Bose wave radios, two-line speaker phones, voice mail, fax machines, and safes. Room rates begin at a lofty $500 for doubles, $625 for suites, and they climb as high as $5,000 for luxury suites.

❦ **The Peninsula New York** (212-956-2888 or 1-800-262-9467; fax 212-903-3949), 700 Fifth Avenue at the corner of 55th Street. Subway: E or V train to 53rd Street–Lexington Avenue, F train to 57th Street, or N, R, or W train to Fifth Avenue–59th Street. This superior luxury hotel, perched at Fifth Avenue very near Central Park since 1905 in a palatial building, gets my vote for one of your best picks if you're packing a platinum card or a company expense voucher. The 239 rooms, decorated in art nouveau style, are all furnished with king beds and filled with state-of-the-art technological touches; some come with great views of the avenue, and all are near the most desirable shopping in the city. This place exudes class from the get-go: Doormen and concierges greet you warmly at the door, front-desk staff are impeccably professional, and you overhear the clinking of glasses in the casual bar-café as you check in.

What's unique here? The business-class amenities go far beyond the call of duty—putting those in many other upscale city hotels to shame. Try a complimentary water bar offering a choice of five bottled waters, complimentary high-speed Internet access, speaker phone and television in the fancy marble bathroom, quiet fax machine (each room gets a personal fax number), mood lighting settings, thermostats, and thermometers and barometers giving the outdoor weather conditions. Many of those controls are operated from a bedside console that will leave you feeling a bit like Captain Kirk on the bridge of the *Enterprise*. Slightly plush furnishings are the equal of those in any other top business hotel in the city (expect Tiffany toiletries in the marble bathroom, among other touches).

The large pool, spa, and health club—35,000 square feet worth, with their own stunning views—further enhance the experience. You can get anything from a facial to a hair coloring to seaweed wraps, shiatsu massages, and Ayurvedic treatments in the spa and salon, while the health club features an indoor pool, Jacuzzi, saunas, steam rooms, and an open-air sundeck framed by the spire of the Fifth Avenue Presbyterian Church; views are knockout. It offers aerobics and Pilates classes, and room service can even be delivered there (though that would seem to be defeating the purpose).

There are no fewer than five dining and drinking areas on the premises—the rooftop open-air bar, when open, is a must-see, while the retooled Fives restaurant replaced the previously French cuisine with a high-tone surf-and-turf menu of "Atlantic Rim" cuisine, served in an elegantly spare room of silver candlesticks and fine carpets. The lobby's Gotham Lounge is a popular spot to partake of afternoon tea or a cocktail.

Add it all up, and the high price tags—rooms begin around $325–585 for a simple king room but rise to as much as $15,000 per night for the two-bedroom Peninsula Suite—suddenly seem justified.

The Plaza Hotel (212-759-3000 or 1-800-759-3000; fax 212-759-3167), Fifth Avenue at the corner of 59th Street. Subway: N, R, or W train to Fifth Avenue–59th Street. Note: This hotel was closed at press time, and will reopen to the public in 2006 or 2007. If you grew up in America, you've seen the Plaza. You've seen it in *Home Alone 2,* when Macaulay Culkin's parents ditched him here. Or you followed every move of children's book heroine Eloise, who lived here. Or you're a classic movie buff who knows that Hitchcock's classic *North by Northwest* was filmed on location here, or an architecture student who knows Frank Lloyd Wright lived here for a few years as he worked on his groundbreaking Guggenheim design and loved the hotel like none other in the city. Yes, there's only one Plaza, at the choice corner of Fifth Avenue and Central Park, and you've got to visit—if not to stay, at least to see. Just be forewarned: It's not the same Plaza you knew of old. That's because in 2005 the hotel closed temporarily, and all but 150 units were in the process of being converted into luxury condominiums—a move that provoked genuine tears and anger among some New Yorkers (others yawned, of course.)

Built in 1907, at a then towering 19 stories (by the same architect who designed The Dakota apartments on Central Park West), the hotel's French Renaissance exterior looks a bit like a castle. There seemingly won't be a bad choice inside among the 280-plus remaining rooms and suites—all have toweringly high ceilings and are beautifully decorated. A giant spa offered sauna, steam, aromatherapy and other treatments, and herbal whirlpools prior to the closure; the good New American bistro, One C.P.S., faced the park; and the Oak Bar and Palm Court bars were both excellent. All this luxury doesn't come cheaply, however—before the closure, double rooms began at $345, suites at $800.

RIHGA Royal New York (212-307-5000 or 1-866-656-1777; fax 212-765-6530), 151 West 54th Street between Sixth and Seventh avenues. Subway: B, D, or E train to Seventh Avenue. Now part of the new upscale Luxury Resorts chain but formerly owned by a Japanese corporation, the RIHGA spares no expense in its stab at being New York's top business hotel—and its famous guests seem to agree that it is. All 500 rooms here are one- or two-bedroom suites, meaning you will always get a separate living room and huge bathroom, sometimes divided by French doors. You will also have a fax machine, VCR, perhaps a small kitchen, and certainly room to roam. Business services include a gym, health club, and babysitting arrangements if needed. Rates range from around $300–600 per night for regular suites, while the most expensive suites—which add CD player, Jacuzzi, printer, and even cell phones to use—go as high as $3,500 per night, though specials occasionally drop the rates as low as $200 a night.

Ritz-Carlton New York (212-308-9100 or 1-800-241-3333; fax 212-877-6465), 50 Central Park South between Fifth and Sixth avenues. Subway: F, N, R, W, or Q train to 57th Street. Until 2002 this hotel was known as the exclusive St. Moritz, but now it's part of the upscale Ritz-Carlton family. No matter; all 277 rooms are still top of the line (which includes the pricing). If you've ever stayed at a Ritz, you know just what to expect— only expect more than usual of it here. Everything's classy, including one additional touch of luxury: If you can't flag a cab, the hotel's limousine service—a Mercedes, not a plain old yellow cab—will whisk you downtown. Double rooms here begin around a cool $560, and suites—well, those start around $1,400 per night.

The Westin New York at Times Square (212-201-2700, 1-866-837-4183, or 1-800-WESTIN-1; fax 212-201-2701), 270 West 43rd Street at the corner of Eighth Avenue. Subway: A, C, or E train to 42nd Street–Port Authority, or Q, R, S, W, 1, 2, 3, or 7 train to 42nd Street–Times Square. The big architectural event in New York in 2002 was the October unveiling of this huge new (863-room) hotel off Times Square in the heart of the Theater District. Its controversial design featured a 45-story tower split in two at night by a moving beam of light—it looks from some angles more like a construction crane than a finished building, or perhaps something from Spain or Hunnertwasser's Vienna—and it's fair to say that it was not well received in all quarters. Gaudy hues are the rule, from bold, irregular swatches of carpet in the lobby to chairs that are almost Klee-Picasso cubist in form. Then again, what else

Paul Karr

THE SLEEK-LOOKING WESTIN NEW YORK, NEAR TIMES SQUARE

would you would expect from Miami's famously colorful Arquitectonica firm?

Rooms are decked out with all the modern conveniences, including the Westin chain's "heavenly bed" and "heavenly bath," cordless phone, hair dryer, and—how about this?—velour bathrobes. Lighting is cool, modern, and indirect as an art gallery's. Work desks are huge, intriguing modern art prints hang on the walls, and some rooms have high-definition television. The open Presidential Suite's living space features a modern sectional couch, Scandinavian-style coffee tables, art on the walls . . . it looks like a Madison Avenue ad shop's waiting area. The valet parking, theater-ticket desk, concierge, currency exchange office, and gift shop are all here and

as professional as expected. All things considered, this is modern luxury at its best with outstanding proximity to Broadway's rich nightlife. The only quibble is that hotel dining is frankly a bit disappointing, with only a chain steak house and a respectable (but also chain) New York sandwich bar from which to choose. Come on, folks, weren't any renegade Alsatian chefs available?

EXPENSIVE HOTELS Algonquin Hotel (212-840-6800 or 1-888-304-2047; fax 212-944-1419), 59 West 44th Street near the corner of Sixth Avenue. Subway: B, D, F, or V train to 42nd Street. Built in 1902, this hotel has long been the hangout of noted writers, from H. L. Mencken to Dorothy Parker, Scott Fitzgerald, and William Faulkner; one particular group's lunchtime meetings in the hotel's Round Room became so famously attended that they spawned a cult following of the Algonquin Club, which lasts to this day. Of out their meeting came *The New Yorker* and many other witty, quality writings. As a hotel, it's got all the right touches—a spa–health club, a pianist in the lounge, a reading room, even a roaming cat. The Oak Room bar-cabaret sometimes sees short theatrical productions, and the hotel restaurant is fine. Though the property was renovated in 1998, rates seem high for what you get; rooms here are a bit small and simple compared with lots of other better choices in Midtown. Then again, nobody else in town has a two-room Dorothy Parker Suite or *New Yorker* clips adorning the walls.

The Iroquois (212-840-3080 or 1-800-332-7220; fax 212-398-1754), 49 West 44th Street between Fifth and

Sixth avenues. Subway: B, D, F, or V train to 42nd Street. A kind of companion to the almost-next-door Algonquin, the Iroquois is a small and elegant luxury hotel often overshadowed by its more famous neighbors. But it does have history: James Dean lived here for a time, and there's a James Dean Suite. Renovated in 1998 to the tune of $10 million, it now sports a Finnish sauna, nice lounge, Italian marble bathrooms, and 114 rooms and nine suites with huge, comfortable beds, CD player, and VCR. Room service is available 24 hours, but so is the health club. Double rooms cost about $385–485, while suites begin at $610 per night and climb to $685. The hotel's excellent French restaurant, Triomphe (see *Dining Out*), opened in 2000.

🐾 **Le Parker Meridien** (212-245-5000 or 1-800-543-4300; fax 212-708-7477), 118 West 57th Street between Sixth and Seventh avenues. Subway: F, N, Q, R, or W train to 57th Street. The Parker Meridien may be my favorite New York hotel. It's not the most expensive place you can book, and it isn't the plushest. But so much thought has gone into this place, and its European cool is so convincing, that it's always on the tip of my tongue when I'm asked for a recommendation. The experience begins in the cool lobby, all marble, columns, tall ceilings, echoes, and mirrors. Then the coolly professional French staff take over, accosting your bags or dealing with reservations. Upstairs, even the simplest room—many with Central Park views—is almost a suite, with the big platform beds divided off from the living room–work area by the huge television (each of which includes a built-in CD/DVD player

and VCR). Those living areas feature blond wood, soft window banquettes, special ergonomic office chairs, mini bar, and modern decor.

The dining choices here are as good as those at any hotel in New York (would the French settle for less?). For breakfast you've got Norma's—the best breakfast in the city—and for lunch the Burger Joint (see *Eating Out*) grills superb patties. Then, at night, Seppi's (see *Dining Out*) serves top-rate French food in a quiet environment with impeccable service. But the real kicker is the rooftop pool—one of New York's very few—and great Gravity fitness club–salon, both with glittering nighttime views of the city as you do your mini laps or weights. There's even a racquetball facility. Double room rates begin around $200 per night, and quickly increase in price.

THE ALGONQUIN HOTEL HAS LONG BEEN THE HAUNT OF FAMOUS WRITERS.
Kim Grant

The Michelangelo (212-765-1900 or 1-800-237-0990; fax 212-581-7618), 152 West 51st Street at the corner of Seventh Avenue. Subway: 1 train to 50th Street, N, R, or W train to 49th Street, E train to Seventh Avenue, or B, D, F, or V train to 47th–50th streets/Rockefeller Center. Possibly the most Italian hotel experience on the East Coast, this outstanding lesser-known hotel sits just north of Times Square. The fabrics, the food, the design, the art . . . the yards and yards of cool white marble . . . practically everything here comes from *la bella paesa.* The huge rooms with coffered ceilings and crown moldings are equipped with cherry furniture, fast-filling deep tub, bidet, and Frette linens. Complimentary international newspapers are dispensed in the lobby; an authentically light Italian breakfast (wolf down an espresso and biscotti to fit in) is served in the breakfast room at no additional. Some business-hotel amenities have been added, too, such as complimentary limousine rides to Wall Street in the morning, VCRs in the rooms, twice-daily housekeeping service, a fitness center, and cell phone and pager rentals. The basement cigar bar is a popular place for a smoke or an informal bite, while the hotel's fine-dining restaurant, Limoncello, serves pricey Italian meals.

☙ **Sofitel New York** (212-354-8844; fax 212-782-3002), 45 West 44th Street between Fifth and Sixth avenues. Subway: B, D, F, or V train to 42nd Street. A cut above the usual Midtown hotels—and situated right on swanky Club Row, a short stretch of 44th Street between Fifth and Sixth avenues—France's 30-story Sofitel offers near-luxury accommodations at almost midrange prices. As befits the French, even standard rooms are designed to be plain yet pleasing, and come with big comfy bed and divan, wall art, WebTV, spacious work desk, and a huge marble-and-tile bathroom with separate tub and shower—the French would never settle for a room without a full bath, after all. Toiletries are French, too, of course. Other thoughtful touches here include candles for taking those baths by candlelight, and vanity mirrors. The 50 suites include an additional room and comforts (with suitably ratcheted-up prices to match, of course).

The hotel restaurant, Gaby, serves good French food (see *Dining Out*) and there's a piano bar as well; the lobby is airy and quite attractive, a good place to meet with friends; and the concierge staff are knowledgeable and useful. Best of all, you're just half a block away from Times Square on one side, half a block from Fifth Avenue on the other (though the best shopping starts about 10 blocks farther north on that avenue). Room rates begin at $269 per night and rise to a high of about $799 per night.

Warwick (212-247-2700 or 1-800-203-3232; fax 212-247-2725), 65 West 54th Street at the corner of Sixth Avenue. Subway: F train to 57th Street. Cary Grant once lived here on the 27th floor, and this was usually the favored hotel of The Beatles when they were in town; is that enough cachet for you? William Randolph Hearst's 1927 construction—and let's be up front about it, he built it for his mistress—saw an upgrade that made the lobby much more pleasant. This isn't exactly the cream of the crop among luxury hotels, but the 426 rooms have been nicely renovated in gold-and-red color schemes with mahogany armoire and marble bathroom, as well as all the usual business-hotel amenities; the 70 suites are especially large, furnished with Regency-type furniture and fireplace, and many also have private terrace. Depending on your room or suite, you might also find a fax machine and/or a CD player; anyone can use the gym and health club, and the bar and restaurant are both quite nice. Double room rates can range anywhere between $300 and $900 per night, though winter rates for standard rooms can dip as low as $180–200 per night, and suites can cost $700–1,200.

BOUTIQUE HOTELS ✿ **The Bryant Park Hotel** (212-869-8100 or 1-877-640-9300; fax 212-869-4446), 40 West 40th Street between Fifth and Sixth avenues. Subway: B, D, F, or V train to 42nd Street or 7 train to Fifth Avenue. This conversion of the dramatic, famous 23-floor American Radiator building into a boutique hotel just across from Bryant Park was unveiled in February 2001 and has won high praise. Hotel owners Brian McNally and Philip Pilevsky commissioned designer David Chipperfield to create and outfit 129 rooms and 20 suites (2 of them are penthouse suites; 11 have terraces overlooking the lovely park). He chose amenities such as Egyptian linens on the beds, cashmere blankets, Tibetan rugs, two-line phones, Bose Wave CD players/radios, fax machines, big televisions with VCRs, and coolly elegant travertine bathrooms. Furnishing is very understated, almost Scandinavian in its simplicity—yet business services such as computers and high-speed Internet access have also been added to the rooms.

Downstairs there's a currency exchange desk, an active concierge, shoeshines, valet parking, and a fitness center with two spa suites. Both the lobby bar and the more chic Cellar Bar are great places to relax with a drink beneath dramatically vaulted brick ceilings, and the hotel's restaurant Koi is excellent. No wonder the place often sees celebrity guests. One additional secret inside this hotel: Beneath the Cellar Bar there's a small, 70-seat theater frequently used as a private screening room by Hollywood types. Add this to a location midway between Fifth Avenue and Times Square, and you've got a winner. Double room rates at the hotel begin at $239 per night but quickly become much higher, especially for suites, which can top $1,000.

Casablanca (212-869-1212 or 1-888-9-CASABLANCA; fax 212-391-7585), 147 West 43rd Street between Times Square and Sixth Avenue. Subway: N, Q, R, S, W, 1, 2, 3, or 7 train to 42nd Street–Times Square. Practically in Times Square, the cozy Casablanca is one of Henry Kallan's growing collection of interestingly themed boutique hotels. This one is an exotically themed little property of 48 rooms, a handful of them suites, loosely based around the classic Bogart film *Casablanca*. That means the units are decorated nicely enough in a sort of North African colonial, rattan-and-ceiling-fan decor; bathrooms are especially well done, and all rooms—which are amazingly quiet, given the proximity to the Square—come with bathrobes, VCR (there's a video copy of the romantic film in every room), two-line phone, CD player, complimentary high-speed DSL Internet access, and mini bar. Suites add a second television as well. The attractive second-floor lounge draws guests in with its relaxed vibe, free chocolate chip cookies, and handy Internet terminal. In fact, nightly wine and cheese, continental breakfast, snacks, and cappuccino are all *also* always free, further ratcheting up the relaxation factor. There may be fancier places in Midtown, but few seem this homey; no wonder Brits love the place. (It's easy to suspend disbelief and feel you've woken up in a laid-back inn in a place like Key West, forgetting that Times Square is beating hyperactively just outside the doors.) The convivial downstairs Italian restaurant serves huge portions, a better place for happy groups than for a quiet romantic dinner. Rates go as low as $160–220 in the off-season; more typically, double rooms cost $200–245 per night in summer, and suites are in the $300–400 range.

Chambers—A Hotel (212-974-5656 or 1-866-204-5656; fax 212-974-5657), 15 West 56th Street between Fifth and Sixth avenues. Subway: F train to 57th Street, E or V train to Fifth Avenue–53rd Street, or N, R, or W train to Fifth Avenue–59th Street. Rooms are certainly plushly equipped at this well-located boutique hotel, with duvet, Frette robes, CD/DVD player, individual library, cordless phone, a supply of bubble bath, and high-speed Internet access all standard. (Some suites even come with a spacious balcony that has potted plants.) Hotel guests get access to the prestigious NY Sports Club gym nearby, they can order room service from TOWN (the excellent hotel restaurant), and there's a concierge, laundry service, maid service, masseuse, computer rentals, spa services—even a

Henri Bendel personal shopper for women should they really need one, as the very upscale women's wear store is close at hand. One more unusual perk: This hotel offers, for about $75 an hour, to bring a personal yoga instructor to your room and work with you one-on-one polishing your chakras. Standard rooms begin at $275–350 per night, while deluxe rooms start at $400, studios at $500, and full suites run $650–1,600 per night.

City Club Hotel (212-921-5500; fax 212-944-5444), 55 West 44th Street between Fifth and Sixth avenues. Subway: B, D, F, or V train to 42nd Street. This former clubhouse was renovated by designer Jeffrey Bilhuber into a plush, exclusive little hotel that opened its doors in early 2002; owner Jeff Klein's creation quickly cultivated a reputation as the lodging of choice for lovely young models and heiresses. It features 65 big rooms in light gold, cream, and chocolate color schemes. Each has a feather bed fitted in Frette linens; original artwork; complimentary bottled water, newspapers, and snacks from the mini bar; a CD/DVD player, with libraries to choose from; and high-speed Internet access. There's a two-line phone in the work area, and another in each marble-and-chrome bathroom—itself loaded up with Hermes toiletries and a pedestal sink. (Some of those bathrooms have even a bidet, if you'd prefer that over a tub.) Three duplex suites are more comfortable still, with 20-foot ceilings and private terraces. Health club access is also included with a night's stay. The hotel restaurant is worth a look all by itself: chef Daniel Boulud's newest project, the red-hot DB Bistro Moderne (see *Dining Out*)—you might see Bob De

Niro or Woody Allen noshing there. (Then again, you might not. Don't blame me.) Rates start at about $300 per night for regular rooms, about $425 per night for the three suites, and escalate from there.

✏ **Flatotel** (212-887-9400 or 1-800-352-8683; fax 212-887-9442), 135 West 52nd Street between Sixth and Seventh avenues. Subway: B, D, or E train to Seventh Avenue. This boxy tower certainly has gone overboard in its attempts to join the raft of modern boutique-style hotels in Midtown. Just check the lobby: Color schemes could have been designed by a child, they're so simple and bright. But it's not a bad place; in fact, it's one of the few hotels in town where you get substantial discounts for long stays. All rooms have family-friendly amenities like ironing board and hair dryer, while most rooms—characterized as "deluxe"— add a vanity, a big platform bed with rich wood headboard, cordless two-line phone, safe, ergonomic work chair, flat-screen TV, VCR, CD player, and small refrigerator and microwave, an outstanding bargain. The huge, modern suites and long-stay one- and two-bedroom apartments add even more—big closet, full kitchen for cooking. There's a small fitness center on the 46th floor and a health club nearby with a big swimming pool; the business center has computers, faxes, and Internet access. And the hotel restaurant, Moda, isn't bad. Rates for double rooms generally hover around $200; suite rates begin around $250–450, though frequent specials make it essential you check by phone for a rate update. Ask about any ongoing promotions. The Flatotel's apartments are charged by the month, and run anywhere from about $4,000 for a

studio to about $8,000 for a two-bedroom apartment.

✏ **The Hudson** (212-554-6000; fax 212-554-6001), 356 West 58th Street between Eighth and Ninth avenues. Subway: A, B, C, D, or 1 train to 59th Street–Columbus Circle. Philippe Starck strikes again, but the Hudson isn't too pricey for a boutique hotel. In a former YWCA building with the fortune (or misfortune) of resting in the shadows of the new AOL-Time Warner complex at Columbus Circle, Ian Schrager's unofficial house designer has outdone himself—at least in terms of decor. This one isn't as minimalist as the rest, and some rooms are more economical than most. After you ride up a green-lit escalator, the lobby is amazing (for Starck): all greenery, glass, dark wood, and brick. Were those French doors? It looks more like Cambridge than something from the year 3000. (And it took 3 years and $125 million to convert it from the Y.) The 1,000 or so (yes, a thousand) rooms are mostly quite small and give an almost cramped feeling, like a train compartment, despite the soft innovative bedside lighting and white colors; beds are not large, either. The trademark steel furniture also makes a comeback, and the showers are a bit too revealing for some critics. Still, there's very high-speed Internet access in the rooms, and a ton of amenities are offered—including video games, coloring books, and board games for kids—so it's worth a look. Double room rates begin around $195.

☸ **The Muse** (212-485-2400 or 1-877-NYC-MUSE), 130 West 46th Street between Sixth and Seventh avenues. Subway: N, Q, R, W, 1, 2, 3, or 7 train to 42nd Street–Times

Square, or B, D, F, or V train to 47th–50th Streets/Rockefeller Center. This relatively new entry in Midtown's crowded boutique-hotel sweepstakes is looking very good so far. All of the 200 or so rooms have CD player, two-line phone, feather bed, hair dryer, iron, and the rest of the comforts you'd expect of a blah business hotel, yet some also have DVD player, and all have been handsomely designed. And the room decor isn't so steely and cold that you'll start looking for reasons to stay out all night. They go the extra mile here with the service, too—the business cards you're issued on check-in with your room's individual number are a very nice touch. The hotel restaurant, District (see *Dining Out*), is excellent as well. Room rates range $250–450 per night.

The Paramount (212-764-5500 or 1-800-225-7474; fax 212-354-5237), 235 West 46th Street between Broadway and Eighth Avenue. Subway: N, Q, R, S, W, 1, 2, 3, or 7 train to 42nd Street–Times Square, or A, C, or E train to 42nd Street–Port Authority. This Theater District entry in the Ian Schrager boutique-hotel chain (which also includes the Hudson, and Miami Beach's famed and chic Delano, among other hotels) must have gotten a lot of word-of-mouth business, because there's absolutely nothing streetside to indicate there's a hotel here within the arched building. No sign, no taxi stand, no bellhops, no nothing—only a softly lit, windowed bar tucked within archways gives a clue that something's going on. Once you're inside, though, it's clear that somebody knows about the place, because this 600-plus-room hotel has been doing plenty of business. Maybe it's the surprisingly affordable prices.

The lobby is typically Schrager big, with a handsome silver-leafed staircase ascending to the second level. Rooms are surprisingly smallish and ultramodern, right down to the oddly conical steel sinks in the bathrooms and the metal furniture in the bedrooms. But they do also have marble desks and beds with gilt-framed headboards—some with Vermeer images, some blank white. Two lobby bars offer a variety of tables, stools, and comfy couches on which to snuggle, snog, or debate: The upstairs Library Bar is more sedate, with mahogany walls, plasma televisions playing arty videos, intriguing restrooms, and a good vibe; the ground-floor Whiskey Bar's bronze tables hop with socializing. There's also a 24-hour fitness room in the hotel for working out. Rates begin at about $200 per night for a double room. Sadly, however, this hotel will close and reopen as a Hard Rock Hotel property, probably by the end of 2006.

☙ **The Royalton** (212-869-4400 or 1-800-635-9013; fax 212-575-0012), 44 West 44th Street between Fifth and Sixth avenues. Subway: B, D, F, or V train to 42nd Street. You can hardly tell this is a hotel from the exterior, which is the idea. Another Ian Schrager–Philippe Starck special, the Royalton was formerly as dowdy as its comrades along West 44th. But Starck has put his indelible stamp on the place, with his characteristically over-grandiose (and slightly mystifying) lobby. Rooms are bigger than those at most Schrager hotels, and packed with extras such as flowers, VCR, CD player, and Dean & DeLuca snacks in the fridge; as usual, however, you might feel a bit put off by the steel, strange sink, ultramodernist furniture, and cool surfaces and decor—it's almost a space-age design. Modern business-hotel amenities such as a new gym and a babysitting service have thoughtfully been added. The 23 suites are enormous, and some have a real fireplace and/or big soaking tub. The lobby bar is a hot gathering spot of music and media types. Double room rates begin around $250 per night.

The Shoreham (212-247-6700 or 1-800-553-3347; fax 212-765-9741), 33 West 55th Street between Fifth and Sixth avenues. Subway: E or V train to Fifth Avenue–53rd Street, or F train to 57th Street. Yet another Midtown boutique hotel, the Shoreham scores as a kind of Starck-Schrager knockoff with 90 modernly designed rooms (they won an award) equipped with real wood closet, sleek surfaces, metal furnishings, VCR, CD player, robes, down comforters, Belgian linens, and Aveda toiletries; complimentary breakfast, espresso, bottled water, and *New York Times;* and original art throughout. Not to mention Jacuzzis, flat-screen TVs, and the like. Plus there's a chic hotel bar, access to a good health club nearby—and Fifth Avenue is only steps away. Regular double rooms start at $320 per night. Suites begin at $390 per night, and can go much higher depending on the comfort level; winter brings deep discounts, however.

The Time (212-320-2900 or 1-877-846-3692; fax 212-245-2305), 224 West 49th Street between Broadway and Eighth Avenue. Subway: C, E, or 1 train to 50th Street. Lots of media attention was piled onto the hip Time when it opened as one of the first true boutique hotels in the city—shutterbugs scrambled to snap the very unusual space-age elevator (check out

the eggshells), sleek rooms, and lobby. It's still a little amazing to find this hotel so close to the overpoweringly bland commercialism of Times Square and its associated chain bars, delis, and hotels. But this place has undeniable character, thanks almost entirely to designer Adam Tihany. Tihany—who also designed Le Cirque 2000, the Jean Georges restaurant in the Trump International Tower/Hotel, and his own restaurant Remi—created rooms that are neutral toned but for one dramatic splash of color in each. Only primary colors (reds, yellows, and blues) have been used, right down to the candy in the dishes, the coffee cups, and the headboards. The fruit in the rooms is the same color as that splash. The toiletries reflect it, too. Tihany's idea was that each room expressed a color's look, smell, taste, and total experience. (If you're still confused, a handy book left in each room explains this colorful idea.) Rooms also contain business-class amenities such as CD player, hair dryer, iron, WebTV, two-line phone, and the like. And the hotel restaurant, 7 Square, is excellent. At press time, this upscale New American restaurant with a New Orleans twist had just changed its concept and menu. Double room rates here range $220–440 per night (as low as $180 per night during certain Internet specials), and suite rates can run anywhere from a sensible $400 up to a stratospheric $5,000 per night—but rates frequently dip with seasonal or Internet specials and deals.

W New York—Times Square (212-930-7400; fax 212-930-7500), 1567 Broadway at the corner of West 47th Street. Subway: N, Q, R, S, W, 1, 2, 3, or 7 train to 42nd Street–Times Square, or 1 or 9 train to 50th Street. You'd expect a W in this high-profile location to be a showpiece, and it is; immediately upon entering, you're confronted by a glass-encased waterfall, part of which you walk beneath en route to the elevator—it feels like you're under the ocean. At the seventh-floor reception desk everyone's dressed stylishly, and the huge, chic lobby area (with a store selling W room amenities) attracts a mixture of the supercool, the dressed-down, and those wanting a drink off street level. You get your key and head for one of more than 500 rooms (about 45 are suites), hoping for one with sleek metallic coffee tables, lighting fixtures, lamps, vases, and maybe a flat-screen television. Rooms aren't huge but they do sport the W's famously comfortable beds, plus high-speed Internet access; the bathrooms feature Aveda products. Double room rates begin at about $340 per night, suite rates at around $400, though frequent Internet and other specials bring those prices down.

BUSINESS HOTELS Hilton New York (212-586-7000 or 1-800-445-8667; fax 212-315-1374), 1335 Sixth Avenue at the corner of West 53rd Street. Subway: B, D, F, or V train to 47th–50th streets/Rockefeller Center, or E train to Fifth Avenue–53rd Street. This hotel is so faceless that you almost could miss it—were it not so huge. The city's largest hotel contains more than 2,000 rooms, all bland but well kept and priced in line with other similar hotels. It's almost like a city here; there are restaurants, food stalls, several bars, a gym, a hair salon, and much more.

Hilton Times Square (212-642-2500; fax 212-840-5516), 234 West 42nd Street between Seventh and Eighth avenues. Subway: N, Q, R, S, W, 1, 2, 3, or 7 train to 42nd Street–Times Square, or A, C, or E train to 42nd Street–Port Authority. This is another Hilton, right in Times Square with about 450 predictable rooms, a handful of suites, and an unbeatable location if you're bent on sampling the neon. In fact, you can experience the neighborhood without ever straying off the property—this hotel has its own huge movie theater, shops, and a wax museum right on the premises. The rooms are nicer than you might think, though—you get a bathrobe and, maybe, a good view. The hotel restaurant has outstanding views of the Square.

Marriott Marquis (212-398-1900 or 1-800-843-4898; fax 212-704-8930), 1535 Broadway between West 45th Street and West 46th Street. Subway: N, Q, R, S, W, 1, 2, 3, or 7 train to 42nd Street–Times Square, or A, C, or E train to 42nd Street–Port Authority. What do you call a tower of nearly 2,000 rooms, stuck right in the middle of the Theater District and taking up a third of a city block? Why, the Marriott Marquis, of course. All of the rooms in this 49-floor monolith have a sameness, but that doesn't stop either the package-tour or the tour-group crowds from booking it almost any time of year; actually, they're quite acceptable business-hotel rooms, and the property tries hard by offering business services such as a limousine, concierge, business center, laundry, and so forth. It's a bit like Biosphere in here at times; so long as distinction isn't a consideration, everything you could possibly need to eat, drink, or buy lies within the complex walls. In fact, you don't even need to wander outside the doors to catch a play at the on-site Marquis Theater. To paraphrase an Eagles song, you can check in, but you might never leave. The hotel's restaurant, The View, offers superlative views from the slowly revolving top floor.

AFFORDABLE HOTELS ✍ **Affinia Manhattan** (212-563-1800), 371 Seventh Avenue at the corner of West 31st Street. Subway: 1, 2, or 3 train to 34th Street–Penn Station, 1 train to 28th Street, or B, D, F, N, Q, R, V, or W train to 34th Street–Herald Square. Practically across the street from both Madison Square Garden and Penn Station, this towering suite hotel (formerly known as Southgate Tower) is certainly well located and professionally staffed. And its rooms are big, clean, and well equipped with kitchenette; some even have the bonus (at no extra charge) of excellent views of the nearby Empire State Building, making it an excellent choice for families with children who want to be close to this part of the city. So why isn't it more famous? Well, it could be the forlorn stretch of Seventh Avenue—extremely busy and noisy, without much of note going on—it stands on. Still, you're just a few blocks from Macy's and Herald Square.

Broadway Inn (212-997-9200 or 1-800-826-6300; fax 212-768-2807), 264 West 46th Street at the corner of Eighth Avenue. Subway: A, C, or E train to 42nd Street–Port Authority. This hotel is a surprising bargain plunked down near Times Square—

especially so given the included breakfast in the nice lobby; unfortunately, it's also parked on a very noisy corner, which means you can sometimes get to experience a little *too* much New York. But for this price, you might not care. The 28 single and double rooms are among the lowest priced I've found among true (and recommendable) hotels in the area. Pay more for one of the dozen or so suites and you'll get a tiny kitchenette with which to prepare your own lunches and dinners, as well as a couch that converts into an extra bed. A couple of rooms even have rudimentary hot tubs. The place is nice enough that people are starting to discover it, which means prices will probably go up someday: doubles $169–299, suites $250–389.

✍ **DoubleTree Guest Suites** (212-921-5212), 1568 Broadway at Times Square and West 47th Street. Subway: N, R, or W train to 49th Street, or N, Q, R, S, W, 1, 2, 3, or 7 train to 42nd Street–Times Square. There's nothing new about this towering hotel right off Times Square (which is hard to find despite its size), but families who've stayed at DoubleTrees previously will love it for the surprisingly spacious one-bedroom suites that are a trademark of this chain. That means a separate living room with a television and couch, and free chocolate chip cookies, too. There are certainly plenty of rooms: 460 in all. Two-line phone, hair dryer, and iron with ironing board are standard. You'll pay extra for high-speed Internet access. Rates for the suites start around $260 per night and go as high as $350 or more, but organizational, seasonal, and other discounts can cut into these prices.

Novotel New York (212-315-0100; fax 212-765-5365), 226 West 52nd Street at the corner of Broadway. Subway: 1 train to 50th Street. It's about as much fun as novocaine, but the Novotel does at least deliver relatively cheap rooms at a very central location. There are absolutely no frills here—the rooms might as well be from some anonymous motel next to some anonymous airport or service road—but they're clean and modern. And the high-rise bar actually has a pretty decent Manhattan view, while drinks are not nearly as highly priced as those in much-more-famous rooftop bars.

Portland Square Hotel (212-382-0600 or 1-800-388-8988; fax 212-382-0684), 132 West 47th Street between Sixth Avenue and Broadway. Subway: B, D, F, or V train to 47th–50th streets/Rockefeller Center, or N, R, or W train to 49th Street. This place, parked on a bland-looking block near the Diamond District, comes off as possibly a bit shabby at first glance. But it's actually not all that bad, so long as you're not expecting luxurious digs. After all, Jimmy Cagney called it home way back when. Note that not all rooms have private bath—make sure to ask about it when you book.

Red Roof Inn (212-643-7100 or 1-800-755-3194), 6 West 32nd Street between Broadway and Fifth Avenue. Subway: B, D, F, N, Q, R, V, or W train to 34th Street–Herald Square, or 6 train to 33rd Street. Don't laugh. Sure, Red Roof is a budget chain everywhere else, but here in New York they've actually managed to build a property that holds up pretty well to some of the other similarly priced options. The fact that the building is new means somewhat big-

ger and better rooms than at similar chain joints—WebTV? Got it. Hair dryer, ironing board, a concierge, a fitness center? Got that, too. There's even a lobby bar. The hotel is plunked down in the middle of Little Korea, which means cheap interesting eats surround you.

Sheraton Manhattan (212-581-3300 or 1-888-625-5144; fax 212-541-9219), 790 Seventh Avenue at West 51st and West 52nd streets. Subway: B, D, or E train to Seventh Avenue, or 1 train to 50th Street. Smaller and less flashy on the exterior than its cousin Sheraton across the street, this one actually offers bigger and newer rooms—at exactly the same rates. Try here first. Room rates start around $200 and go as high as around $400 per night, higher (up to $750 a night) for the suites.

Sheraton New York & Towers (212-581-1000 or 1-888-625-5144; fax 212-262-4410), 811 Seventh Avenue at West 52nd and West 53rd Streets. Subway: B, D, or E train to Seventh Avenue, or 1 train to 50th Street. One of two Sheratons that straddle Seventh Avenue, this is a perfectly good option, if big and bland: It's got 1,750 rooms, which means lots and lots of tourists and conventioneers. But the big, cool public space comes in handy when you're wandering Broadway and don't feel like going all the way back up to your room. Also it's worth noting that this property has five times more suites than its neighbor across the street. Again, room rates are exactly the same as those of the Sheraton listed above.

Wellington Hotel (212-247-3900 or 1-800-652-1212; fax 212-581-1719), 871 Seventh Avenue at the corner of West 55th Street. Subway: B, D, or E train to Seventh Avenue, or N, R, W, or W train to 57th Street. The lobby at this towering hotel is mighty impressive at first glance, and there are plenty of Europeans coming and going. That might give the impression it's a find. Well, the truth is, it's only a middling place due to the inconsistency of the accommodations; rooms vary greatly in quality from floor to floor. You might find an airy, bright one with a great view and big bathroom—or you might find yourself in a noisy, closetlike space next to the elevator. Suites, as a rule, cost a bit more but add space and pullout sofas ideal for a second or third traveler. The location, however, is definitely great—right on Broadway, not far from the theater and dining action—and the rates are comparatively low (about $110–200 per night) for this part of town, especially considering how close it is not only to Broadway but also to Carnegie Hall (just two short blocks away), Central Park, and Times Square. Go ahead and try to beat that price at a predictable hotel.

✳ Where to Eat

Times Square is full of chain restaurants, overpriced steak houses, and middling delis. For a better experience, head east to Rockefeller Center's cafés and fine-dining offerings, or west to Eighth Avenue—it's packed with quality midrange restaurants, including a number of good Asian and French eateries. Ninth Avenue is still more of an ethnic mixed bag; quality and origin swing wildly across the meter at each block. If you're still stumped, think about hitting Restaurant Row, also known as 46th Street between Eighth and Ninth avenues (which is a lot less impressive sounding); pretheater deals abound here, and you can dine on the (relatively) cheap before 6 PM at most of them even if you've no theater plans whatsoever.

DINING OUT Alain Ducasse at the Essex House (212-265-7300), 155 West 58th Street between Sixth and Seventh avenues. Subway: F, N, Q, R, or W train to 57th Street. Open Monday through Saturday for dinner 6:30–9:30 PM, Thursday and Friday also for lunch noon–2 PM. French star chef Ducasse, controversial even in his homeland for attempting to juggle a growing empire of top restaurants and bistros in France, Japan, and now America, made a huge splash—and some say a bigger flop—when he opened this landmark restaurant inside the Westin owned Essex House luxury hotel a few short years back. Critics said ADNY (as it's called in shorthand, and as is stamped on the tableware) was simply charging too much and delivering too little for a meal that began with a complimentary rye bread wafer; after all, this is now among the most expensive restaurants in New York—it's easy to spend $200–400 per person at dinner—and that's a tough act to sustain in tough economic times without world-class chops to back up such bold pricing and flourishes. And now, a succession of two other chefs have taken over the kitchen in the busy Ducasse's stead; critics have begun to wonder if this place will make it for the long haul.

The kitchen has its act together, cooking French meals that read like operatic plays rather than dining cards. Begin with a fine wine and a seafood appetizer, traipse onward to a pasta course, feast on a lamb or duck or whatever else Ducasse has dolled up his special way (he uses vegetables and stocks, rather than loads of cream), then gird yourself for dessert: It goes on and on, with trays of chocolates and cakes and soufflees, a groaning cart offering some of the world's most select, and good-bye gifts. Needless to say, you are going to pay through the nose for this experience—dinner menus range from $150–$225 per person—and, certainly, some things about this experience remain a bit pretentious. (A choice of 20 pens with which to sign the check? Please.) But Ducasse has finally delivered.

✎ **Bryant Park Grill** (212-840-6500), 25 West 40th Street between Fifth and Sixth avenues. Subway: B, D, F, or V train to 42nd Street, or 7 train to Fifth Avenue. Open daily for lunch 11:30 AM–3:30 PM and for dinner 5:30–11 PM. In a fantastic location right on Bryant Park, this expensive restaurant features a host of seafood and other American items—starters like oysters, salmon cakes, calamari salad, and seared sea scallops; lunch and dinner entrées such as grilled pork chops, pastas, stuffed breast of chicken, grilled tuna steak, mahimahi, pan-roasted duck breast, and strip steak with Vidalia onions. It's all served before an entire wall of windows facing the park and the city lights. The food is frankly unspectacular; you come for the view. One nice feature at brunch is a special kids' menu, where kids age 12 and under get a choice of French toast, pancakes, cheeseburgers, grilled cheese sandwiches, and the like along with drinks and pastries.

China Grill (212-333-7788), 60 West 53rd Street between Fifth and Sixth avenues. Subway: Subway: E or V train to Lexington Avenue-53rd Street or B, D, F, or V train to 47th–50th streets/Rockefeller Center. Open Monday to Wednesday 11:45 AM–10:45 PM, Thursday and Friday to 11:45 PM, Saturday for dinner only 5:30–11:45 PM and Sunday for dinner only 5:30–10 PM. It's over-the-top and quite pricey (figure $20–40 per entrée), but I absolutely love this place. Where else in the city can you can sup on plum-spiced lamb chops, lobster pancakes, and Shangai-style lobster over a fabulous curried sauce and noodles, garnished with salty, crisp-fried spinach? Nowhere but here. Lunch is the power meal; try to have dinner, and bring friends when you do. It's traditional here to pass around platters of food and sample all of them, Chinese-style. Tell your server, and they'll help you do just that.

DB Bistro Moderne (212-391-2400), 55 West 44th Street between Fifth and Sixth avenues. Subway: S, 4, 5, 6, or 7 train to 42nd Street–Grand Central. Open daily for dinner 5–11 PM, also Monday only for lunch noon–2:30 PM. A relatively recent addition to the hip 46th Street row of hotels and upscale restaurants, Daniel Boulud's DB Bistro—located inside the hot City Club Hotel—scores spectacularly with its reach and flash. Boulud's two dining rooms are connected by an arched wine bar; the front room, looking out onto the street, is of stone and wood, strikingly decorated by the photographs of Christopher Beane, while the bar is notable for its two large marble tables and chandeliers. The back dining room is more formal.

Lunch could be an appetizer of smoked salmon before a main course of lobster salad with artichokes, endive, and mesclun; curried chicken salad; sirloin steak with fries; or a braised lamb shank with Niçoise olives and rutabaga. Dinner starts with such appetizers as lobster bisque with tarragon flan, artichoke soup, a venison torte with cabbage fondue and glazed turnips, or salmon carpaccio, while the satisfying entrées run to such items as sautéed monkfish with saffron risotto, "old-style" roast lobster, pastas, roast chicken, tuna, cumin-glazed duck, lamb chops paired with a stuffed saddle of lamb. The menu also sports a famous (if slightly ridiculous) $29 hamburger doctored up with truffles, braised short ribs, and foie gras; the price rises to $59 or even $99 when Boulud audaciously adds rare, in-season black truffles to the top. He calls it the best burger in America. Other, more sensible daily specials might include poached capon, venison stroganoff, squab *en croûte,* or bouillabaisse. The dessert choices are just as solid, including a sweet apple rice pudding paired with green apple sorbet, praline parfait (served with pears poached in bergamot tea), peach Melba, cheese plates, and a choice of fig and chocolate creations.

District (212-485-2999), 130 West 46th Street between Sixth and Seventh Avenues. Subway: N, Q, R, W, 1, 2, 3, or 7 train to 42nd Street–Times Square, or B, D, F, or V train to 47th–50th Streets/Rockefeller Center. Open Monday through Friday for breakfast 7–10 AM, lunch noon–2 PM, and dinner 5:30–10 PM, Saturday and Sunday for breakfast 7:30–11 AM and dinner 5:30–10 PM. Inside the hip Muse Hotel, lots of blond wood—courtesy of designer David Rockwell—announces District, a creative fusion restaurant. In June 2006, chef Patricia Williams (formerly of the Morrell Wine Bar) took over, bringing a menu she's calling 'seasonal American cuisine.' Expect her to cook hearty offerings such as Lazy Duck (slowly roasted with spaetzle and carrot puree); grilled Atlantic salmon with fingerling potatoes, braised leeks, and a whole grain mustard vinaigrette; and club sandwiches of grilled shrimp and pancetta. The restaurant's bar is also getting an overhaul, going back to the future with such handcrafted house cocktails such as the Ginger Fizz (ginger vodka with ginger ale and citrus) and the Stormy Weather (vanilla rum mixed with ginger beer). Use them to wash down the bar's mini-burgers.

FireBird Restaurant (212-586-0244), 365 West 46th Street between Eighth and Ninth avenues. Subway: A, C, or E train to 42nd Street–Port Authority. Open for lunch Tuesday through Saturday 11:45 AM–2 PM and dinner 5–11 PM, Sunday 5–8:30 PM for dinner only. Created by American William Holt and his Russian wife (the granddaughter of a former mayor of St. Petersburg), FireBird painstakingly recreates the glory of pre-Revolution Russia—the grand dining room spaces are outfitted in period furniture, actual Russian Ballet costumes, and other touches, while harpists or pianists play background music. There's even a ballroom with a domed ceiling and skylight. The food? Fascinating. The chef gets it just right, balancing heavy flavors with light innovations. The $20 prix fixe lunch is a choice of beef stroganoff, chicken paillard, or salmon *kulebiaka* (a puff pastry), while the full menu expands to offer such appetizers as tea-poached salmon with caviar, herring with potato blini, borscht, and the Zakuska (a combination platter of lamb shank, caviar, roasted beets, smoked salmon, pickled herring) alongside the same main courses (priced $15–20 à la carte).

Dinner might start with vodka-cured salmon, a Russian lobster bisque, veal dumplings, or terrine of foie gras with rhubarb and pistachios, then move on to a part-Russian, part-Continental card of main courses ($30–38): chicken Kiev, tea-smoked duck, lamb loin with goat-cheese-filled gnocchi, filet mignon with stroganoff sauce, lobster risotto, or a grilled pork chop. For $80 per person you can feast like a czar, adding fine caviar in a seven-course orgy of excess that concludes with a shot of honey-flavored vodka. If you're still hankering for a nightcap after all this, there's a piano cabaret downstairs.

Gaby (212-782-3040), 45 West 44th Street between Fifth and Sixth avenues. Subway: B, D, F, or V train to 42nd Street. Open daily 6 AM– midnight. Off the Sofitel hotel's wonderful lobby, this French restaurant treads a line between fancy and casual. The staff come direct from France; the kitchen produces good meals of the sort of Asian-inflected French food that's suddenly running rampant in Manhattan—a vodka-spiked "bloody Mary" soup; crabcakes with pepper aioli; Peking duck over shallots or mixed into risotto. Of course there's a wine list, of course the desserts are rich and good, and of course there's a pianist.

Le Bernardin (212-489-1515), 155 West 51st Street between Sixth and Seventh avenues. Subway: B, D, F, or V train to Rockefeller Center, or N, R, or W train to 49th Street. Open

Monday through Friday for lunch noon–2:30 PM and dinner 5:30–10 PM, until 11 PM Friday, Saturday for dinner only 5:30–11 PM. Le Bernardin has quite a story behind it. Owner Maguy LeCoze opened a Parisian seafood bistro in the 1970s with her brother Gilbert, who had learned to cook from his grandfather—a fisherman in Brittany, France—and their parents, who operated a small inn. The restaurant succeeded beyond their wildest dreams, garnering two Michelin stars, and the LeCozes sold their baby to move abroad and open a New York branch in 1986—again to wide acclaim. (Smaller versions have since opened in Miami and Atlanta.) Gilbert LeCoze passed away in 1994. But Le Bernardin's current chef, Eric Ripert—who worked at some of France's top restaurants, and as a sous-chef in New York with David Bouley—is now one of the city's culinary stars.

Cooking with an attractive philosophy of treating each ingredient as sacred, Ripert begins his seasonally changing prix fixe lunches and dinners with raw or lightly cooked slivers of fish and shellfish, then continues with such meals as roast John Dory, sautéed snapper, poached skate, roast cod, and roast lobster. Meals end with fun French-influenced desserts from pastry chef Oscar Palacios like a stuffed peach, nougat, baked apricots, a cheese plate, or sorbets. The more complex chef's tasting menu costs around $100 per person, perhaps taking in several appetizers, lobster, John Dory, and a chocolate tart or pineapple Charlotte with buttermilk panna cotta . . . but whatever's there, it's worth it. The kitchen will also prepare lamb or pasta on request, and the piano music and extremely strong list of wines only enhance the experience of dining here. This is one of Manhattan's best restaurants, bar none.

Masa (212-823-9800), 10 Columbus Circle (Time Warner Center), 4th floor. Subway: A, B, C, D, or 1 train to 59th Street–Columbus Circle. Open Monday to Friday noon–1 PM for lunch and 6–9 PM for dinner, Saturday for dinner only. It's very difficult to snag a table reservation in this intimate, luxe-priced sushi restaurant on the fourth floor of the Time Warner Center (try the bar instead; see below). Hotshot chef Masa Takayama shuttered his wildly popular L.A. restaurant to open this place instead, where you'll pay upward of $300 (!) per person to sample his *omakase* ("chef's choice" meal). Expect some of the most amazing sushi you'll ever sample, for the highest prices you'll ever pay. The adjacent bar, Bar Masa, is much cheaper (though it's all relative; they're still $20–30 apiece) and you *can* get a table. The bar's menu incorporates Takayama's takes on Japanese street foods, as well as retaining some of the familiar luxury flavorings (truffles, for example) from the main stage.

Morrell Wine Bar & Café (212-981-1106), 1 Rockefeller Plaza at the corner of 49th Street. Subway: B, D, F, or V train to 47th–50th Streets/ Rockefeller Center. Open Monday through Saturday 11:30 AM–10:30 PM, Sunday noon–4 PM. This classy wine bar makes an excellent pause after you've grazed the shops and other attractions in and around Rockefeller Center. Dine from a regularly changing menu of small entrées, or just sip a glass of wine—the selection is excellent, and unusually you can order almost anything by the glass—and snack on smoked salmon, cheeses, and the like. It isn't the sort of place you'd feel comfortable in jeans and sneakers, but if you're dressed to impress, have a look.

Per Se (212-823-9335), 10 Columbus Circle (Time Warner Center), 4th floor. Subway: A, B, C, D, or 1 train to 59th Street–Columbus Circle. Open daily for dinner 5:30–10 PM, also Friday to Sunday for lunch 11:30 AM– 1:30 PM. Thomas Keller's New York venture is an extension of his overwhelmingly famous French Laundry restaurant in Yountville, California (many call it America's best), and this is quite an effort. Despite the high prices, you never wonder why you're paying them: the $125–175 tasting menus, served in a solemn Adam Tihany–designed room, incorporate amazing ranges of artisanal ingredients (ask your server for the details of growing, picking, foraging, and so forth) in stunningly flavored and designed preparations that play with and expand the normal boundaries of such culinary ideas as "mac-and-cheese" and "bacon-and-eggs" in ways far beyond what you thought were imaginable. You can also get quite wonderful versions of more regular fare such as grilled steak or a trussed-up pork loin. You'll battle to even get considered for a table, and you'll spend hours on your meal (figure a half-day: really) should you get a table, but it's all worth it in the end if you succeed. Note that at press time, a 20 percent gratuity was being added automatically to all diners' already-hefty checks; even if service is perfect, be careful not to double-tip.

Redeye Grill (212-541-9000), 890 Seventh Avenue at the corner of 56th Street. Subway: B, D, or E train to

Seventh Avenue, or N, Q, R, or W train to 57th Street. Open daily 11:30 AM–11 PM. Despite all the hype (and it is considerable), this New American–style place serves pretty good upscale seafood. Everyone wants to try the dancing shrimp—jumbo shrimp quick-fried in coconut and inserted into a cut pineapple with a piece of bamboo—and, while they're good, you might do better to move on to main courses such as an outstanding tuna steak, lobster, or sushi, sashimi, and oysters at the big raw bar. There's live jazz on Friday night, and a good weekend brunch as well.

Sea Grill (212-332-7610), 19 West 49th Street. Subway: B, D, F, or V train to 47th–50th streets/Rockefeller Center. Open Monday through Friday for lunch noon–2:30 PM and dinner 5–10 PM, Saturday for dinner only. Designer Adam Tihany—who seemingly created every one of the city's most attractive modern dining spaces—did this one to approximate a maritime theme (a glassed-in private room, bubbles decorating the floors), and the quietly elegant space with low ceilings does indeed feel a bit like a glass-bottomed boat. Except the view is of the fluttering flags and wintertime skaters doing circuits and double axels around the Rockefeller Center ice rink.

Down a private elevator from street level, this top-notch seafood grill features chef Ed Brown's signature fish à la *plancha:* fat squares of grilled-to-crisp mahimahi, red snapper, and the like perched upon beds of wilted spinach flavored delicately with a coral lobster emulsion. Other entrées show more invention: Lump crabcakes are served with snappy mustard, while the salmon roll is a tube of fish

packed inside nut-encrusted nori, flash-fried, cut into quarters, and served end-up between bright dots of miso and wasabi sauce—the crunchy, satisfying taste and texture of the fried nori alone is worth the order. (Landlubbers can go for grilled chicken with a soft polenta cake and wild mushrooms.) A half lobster, oysters, tuna tartare, or the complex and satisfying-tasting seafood chowder are outstanding starters, while dessert options run to key lime pie, fried banana tart in phyllo—or, best of all, a wondrous cakelike steamed chocolate pudding topped with sweet Valrhona chocolate sauce and sided with pistachio ice cream. With quiet piano music tinkling in the background, this unstuffy room's front-row seat on lovers cavorting around the ice to an inner music makes it an outstandingly romantic winter dining spot.

Seppi's (212-708-7444), 123 West 56th Street between Sixth and Seventh avenues. Subway: F, N, R, Q, or W train to 57th Street. Open daily noon–2 AM. One of my favorite underrated French restaurants in New York, Seppi's—a cousin to SoHo's popular Raoul's—opened in December 1998 and has quietly picked up high marks ever since. Executive chef Claude-Alain Solliard has created a menu that leans toward Alsatian cooking, yet is unafraid to experiment with other flavors as well. The lighter "all-day" menu begins serving at midday and includes tasty treats such as a lobster sandwich and Alsatian tart flambé—a kind of thin-crusted French flatbread pizza, topped with caramelized onions and crispy strips of pork. Come dinnertime the menu expands to include one of the city's best grilled peppercorn steaks—cut the French way—plus hearty beef carbonnade cooked in beer, terrific osso buco, and duck roasted in honey and anise sided with sweet potatoes. Appetizers include an inventive crawfish ravioli and a refreshing salad of greens and goat cheese; the dessert list features a signature "Flyer" molten chocolate cake baked crisply on the outside while remaining soft in the center, a marvelous contrast of textures. Sunday brings a special brunch based on chocolate themes. The kitchen's hand with these rich flavors is admirable, while service is friendly and professional; the attached bar makes a great spot for a late-hours drink before retiring, with imported Irish beer on tap—and the unusually late full-kitchen hours mean you may even run across chefs, sous-chefs, and serving staff from some of the city's top restaurants kibbitzing at the bar late-night. The Sunday "chocolate brunch" is popular, and includes such choices as cocoa-inflected steak and a raft of chocolate desserts.

Triomphe (212-453-4233), 49 West 44th Street between Fifth and Sixth avenues. Subway: N, Q, R, W, 1, 2, 3, or 7 train to 42nd Street–Times Square. Open Monday through Friday 7–10:30 AM, 11:45 AM–2:30 PM, and 5:30 PM–10:45 PM; Saturday 7 AM–noon and 5:30–10 PM; Sunday 7 AM–noon. Steven Zobel's small restaurant on the ground floor of the Iroquois Hotel scores with its solid yet inventive upscale French meals—and it added dining space to triple its previously minuscule capacity. Lunch consists of creative salads, grilled salmon, *pappardelle* with duck confit, roast black sea bass, a burger with mustard-pepper sauce and mashed potatoes, a changing daily omelet, and a daily fish special; dinner starts with sweetbreads, chicken livers, or pan-seared sea scallops and continues with such entrées as tuna steak, osso buco, roast pork tenderloin and chicken, grilled strip steak, and lamb chops with port-soaked foie gras. Dessert choices include crème brûlée, a chocolate torte with cherry-port sauce, pear-cranberry *tarte Tatin* with vanilla gelato, and baked caramel apples. There's also a good hotel breakfast of crêpes, French toast, and eggs.

"21" Club (212-582-7200), 21 West 52nd Street between Fifth and Sixth avenues. Subway: B, D, or F train to 50th Street–Rockefeller Center, or E or V train to 53rd Street. Open Monday through Friday for lunch noon–2:30 PM and dinner 5:30–10 PM, Friday to 11 PM, Saturday for dinner only to 11 PM. There's only one "21" Club, and while no longer the bastion of exclusion it once was—the dress code has been relaxed, for example—it certainly still packs a historic punch. (JFK dined here on the evening of his inauguration, after all.) During Prohibition this was the city's most famous speakeasy (an establishment serving illegal liquor)—it featured a hidden wine cellar beneath the house next door, concealed by a wall of smoked hams guarded by a 2-ton door that could be opened only with a meat skewer. (That wine cellar has now been remodeled into a very private dining room where brokers do deals.)

Back in the main dining room good New American meals start with an appetizer such as grilled game sausages with apples and mustards, spicy ahi tuna tartare, Maine crabcakes, or carpaccio of venison, then continue with a lobster and salmon risotto, stuffed veal chops, crisped sea bass with truffled potatoes, or filet mignon. Dessert choices might include rum and chestnut cream on a toasted pecan crisp or a poached pear napoleon with sour cherry mascarpone. If you're hoping simply to sample the place, go for the prix fixe deals: Lunch consists of simple entrées such as angelhair pasta and shrimp or a grilled chicken with goat cheese and pine nuts, while the dinner prix fixe might entail seared salmon steak or butternut squash risotto. A small newer upstairs section serves a different menu at higher prices—it's hard to get in here, but nice for a romantic dinner—and the barroom features walls and a ceiling festooned with an amazing assortment of toys and knickknacks, each with a famous association.

EATING OUT **Brasserie Pigalle** (212-489-2233), 780 Eighth Avenue at the corner of West 48th Street. Subway: C or E train to 50th Street. Open 24 hours. Located right on a busy corner of Eighth Avenue, Pigalle satisfies your need for French fare without paying zillion-dollar prices. The service is good enough and quick enough, and the room's never too smoky to see. Atypically French? Definitely. But the food's the thing here, and Pigalle's kitchen delivers both the expected (*steak frites*, salads) and something a bit more: roast lamb shank with potatoes, grilled monkfish medallions, or a good *demi-poulet au jus* of roast chicken sided with pearl onions. Staff strike a superb balance between professionalism and friendliness, and the place actually feels romantic when they dim the lights—unless you happen to be sitting right next to Eighth Avenue on a warm night when the windows are open. In

that case, find a booth or table deeper within.

Brooklyn Diner (212-977-2280), 212 West 57th Street near the corner of Seventh Avenue. Subway: N, R, Q, or W train to 57th Street. Open daily 8 AM–midnight, Friday and Saturday to 1 AM, Sunday to 10 PM. A popular landmark set above street level near the busy junction of Broadway and West 57th Street, the Brooklyn pulls in visitors with its distinctive neon sign. The interior's sleek black-and-white color scheme and leather booths help set the mood: The place is a bit more upscale than most diners in town. (Waiters are dressed in tails, for instance; there's no dress code, however.) The menu, as you might expect, leans heavily toward American comfort foods—burgers, malts, thick brisket and club sandwiches, egg creams, and the like—but there are also some surprises, such as *steak frites* (a bistro meal of grilled steak accompanied by french fries) and pasta dishes.

The Burger Joint (212-708-7414) 123 West 56th Street between Sixth and Seventh avenues. Subway: F, N, R, Q, or W train to 57th Street. Open daily 11 AM–11:30 PM. You'd never have guessed it, but the chic Le Parker Meridien hotel now conceals one of Manhattan's best burger shops, though this is such an unlikely match that I wonder how long it will last. Hidden in a back room near the reception desk (look for the small neon burger sign and the arrow; that's the only way you'll find it), wood paneling and Yankee clippings tip the place's hand: This is like the lowbrow diner you always expected to find in Manhattan, only to arrive and discover it's become a land of $12 burgers. But not here. Perfectly charred cheeseburgers from the small grill, wrapped in butcher paper, cost $6.50 each; a paper bag of fries run $3; shakes are $4.50; and there's Sam Adams beer on tap (in plastic cups) at a reasonable $4.50. The uptempo soundtrack keeps things moving, as does the New Yawkese banter of the grillmen, but don't expect atmosphere—all you'll find are a few simple booths and tables. This place is a 180-degree U-turn away from the Seppi's restaurant on the other end of the hotel, but sometimes a hamburger is all you want out of life, and The Burger Joint delivers on this promise better than anyone else in the city. Needless to say, they don't take credit cards.

Delta Grill (212-956-0934), 700 Ninth Avenue at the corner of West 48th Street. Subway: C or E train to 50th Street. Open daily noon–3 AM. It's a little surprising to find it here on Ninth Avenue, but this might be Manhattan's best New Orleans–style restaurant. There's no skimping on the food, yet the chef is classically trained and did time in the Big Easy. Expect catfish, jambalaya, po' boys, panblackened fish, and raw oysters. The bar is a fun place to listen to blues or jazz on the weekend. And unlike many other good restaurants, they deliver to hotels in surrounding Midtown, too.

Island Burgers and Shakes (212-307-7934), 766 Ninth Avenue between West 51st and West 52nd streets. Subway: C or E train to 50th Street. Open daily noon–10:30 PM. Look for the COCA-COLA signs on the outside and the stenciled surfboards on the inside. This place completely lacks decor—the tables in its narrow room may be the most tightly packed in Manhattan, and you're sure to

experience moments of leg contact with adjacent diners—but the huge grilled burgers here are among the city's best, and shakes, sodas, and fries are all just right. Don't neglect the fantastic grilled chicken burgers, either—these, too, are among New York's best. It's a wonder more people don't come here. Actually, it's not a wonder; nobody else could possibly fit. Lunchtime is especially busy with the business crowd, so consider coming at off-hours unless you enjoy chaos. A few coveted tables actually have soft chairs and couch seating.

Kum Gang San (2129670909), 49 West 32nd Street between Broadway and Fifth Avenue. Subway: B, D, F, N, Q, R, V, or W train to 34th Street–Herald Square. Open 24 hours. There are precious few Midtown eateries open around the clock anymore, but this one is—which is great if you like Korean food. Huge mirrors make the tall, bi-level space look even bigger than it is; food is served cafeteria-style, and I'd go for Korean barbecue.

L&L Hawaiian Barbecue (212-629-9708), 535 Eighth Avenue between West 36th Street and West 37th Street. Subway: A, C, or E train to 42nd Street–Port Authority. Open daily 10 AM–10 PM. This place really does look Hawaiian inside, including actual newspapers from Honolulu when I last dropped in. And the food is pretty authentic, too: plates of pork and beef wrapped in ti leaves, hamburgers in gravy (a favorite surfer food in the islands), Spam-and-egg sandwiches, barbecued chicken over fries and salad.

Mangia (212-582-5554), 50 West 57th Street between Fifth and Sixth avenues. Subway: F train to 57th Street. Open Monday through Friday

11:30 AM–4 PM. A combination coffee bar, pastry shop, and hot-food bar, this Italian snack shop (open weekdays only, for the business lunch crowd) makes a good quick stop for a bite on the way back to the hotel from a shopping trip on Fifth Avenue. You can sit or stand in front, ordering from a menu of cappuccino, espresso, and other coffee drinks—and delicious pastries such as chocolate *dulce de leche*—or walk to the back, where there's both a hot-food bar in the Italian *tavola calda* tradition and a range of sandwiches made to order (chicken, turkey, and steak).

✎ **Norma's** (212-708-7460), 118 West 57th Street between Sixth and Seventh avenues. Subway: F, N, Q, R, or W train to 57th Street. Open Monday through Friday 6:30 AM–3 PM, weekends 7 AM–3 PM. Manhattan's acknowledged top breakfast spot is this bright restaurant inside the Le Parker Meridien hotel. The inventive, fun menu of breakfast and brunch items (mostly $13–23 each) runs to blueberry pancakes, buttermilk pancakes with peaches and walnuts, banana macadamia nut pancakes, crunchy French toast, Belgian waffles, Alsatian potato pancakes with onions, sour cream, and applesauce, beef hash, waffles, egg dishes, and steak and eggs. Or go light with a baker's basket of breads and doughnuts, a bowl of oatmeal, or fruit or yogurt. The place is so good—kids should love it—that you might forget it's relatively high priced. One caveat: Saturdays and especially Sundays are absolutely crazy; since you can eat a brunchlike menu anytime, try to come during the week.

Pam Real Thai Food (212-333-7500), 404 West 49th Street between Ninth and Tenth avenues. Subway: C or E train to 50th Street. Open daily 11:30 AM–11 PM. Pam Panyasiri gets it just right with the food, and the atmosphere—a brawling, too-tiny place with people waiting in lines out the door for a precious table and holiday trinkets hanging everywhere (even in the dog days of summer)—gets it just right, too. Everything's fruity and just spicy enough, not kill-your-gut spicy. Go for curries, fish, duck, noodles . . . heck, anything . . . and bring your own beer from a bodega around the corner; they don't stock drinks, but you'll want one.

Topaz (212-957-8020), 127 West 56th Street between Sixth and Seventh avenues. Subway: F, N, Q, R, or W train to 57th Street. Open Monday to Friday noon–11 PM, weekends 4–11 PM. The business-lunch crowds like this easy-to-miss Thai eatery, tucked amid office buildings, a bookshop, cof-

SOUP KITCHEN INTERNATIONAL, THE MIDTOWN TAKE-OUT SHOP IMMORTALIZED IN *SEINFELD*

Paul Karr

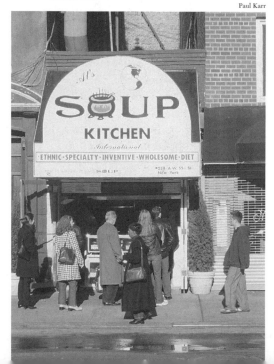

fee shops, and Le Parker Meridien. The kitchen makes a great pad Thai, as well as a range of noodle dishes and red, green, yellow, and massaman curries with shrimp, squid, chicken, or pork. Or try one of the grilled steak dishes or a whole grilled fish.

Virgil's Real BBQ (212-921-9494), 152 West 44th Street between Broadway and Sixth Avenue. Subway: B, D, F, or V train to 42nd Street, or N, Q, R, S, W, 1, 2, 3, or 7 train to 42nd Street–Times Square. Open daily 11 AM–11 PM. Yes, Virgil's is over-promoted, overpriced, and overvisited solely on the basis of its advantageous location just off Times Square. But no, the food isn't bad at all despite the orange-neon hype; using a genuine wood-fired smoker, Virgil's delivers solid, better-than-average ribs, brisket, hot links, catfish, and all the rest of the southern treats you'd expect from a place like this, in an atmosphere to match.

Wondee Siam (212-459-9057), 729 Ninth Avenue between West 52nd and West 53rd streets. Subway: C or E train to 50th Street. Open Monday through Saturday 11 AM–11 PM, Sunday to 10:30 PM. This tiny restaurant of a handful of tables is parked on a nowheres-ville stretch of Ninth Avenue, but its red curries are outstanding for the price. Other dishes—such as pad Thai, sautéed shrimp, a skewer of chicken satay, or *yum ped yang* (roast duck with cashews, onions, and pineapples)—also satisfy. There's also a range of tofu and noodle entrées. Of course, finish with the sweet, refreshing Thai iced tea. There's also a second location just a block north on Ninth, between 53rd and 54th streets.

COFFEE AND SNACKS **Café Edison** (212-840-5000), 228 West 47th Street between Broadway and Eighth Avenue. Subway: C, E, or 1 train to 50th Street. Open daily 6 AM–9:30 PM, Sunday until 7:30 PM. A prominent New York magazine somehow determined that this Polish-Jewish diner in the Edison Hotel was the city's top coffee shop. Though it's kind of a dive, like so many others in the Times Square area it does have its loyal clientele and loads of 1950s-Manhattan atmosphere. There's also standard Jewish deli food, and so-so service. Naturally they don't take credit cards, and you won't need one at these prices.

Columbia Hot Bagels (212-222-3200), West 44th Street between Seventh and Eighth avenues. Subway: N, Q, R, S, W, 1, 2, 3, or 7 train to 42nd Street–Times Square. Open daily 6 AM–11 PM. This tiny shop, originally near namesake Columbia University but now in Times Square due to construction uptown, serves absolutely terrific bagels, with a selection of cream cheese and other toppings, to a packed house. Some locals swear these are the city's best. You can also sometimes find this shop's bagels at the legendary Zabar's food shop (see *Where to Eat—Coffee and Snacks* in chapter 11).

Phillip's Coffee (212-582-7347), 155 West 56th Street between Sixth and Seventh avenues. Subway: F, N, Q, R, or W train to 57th Street. The extremely friendly staff make this tiny space affable; office workers come for terrific espresso, lattes, sandwiches, and smoothies—and some bring packages of the store's custom roast home for their own coffeemakers, too.

✳ Entertainment

MUSIC VENUES Carnegie Hall
(212-247-7800 for tickets, 212-903-9765 for tours), 154 West 57th Street at the corner of Seventh Avenue. Subway: N, R, Q, or W train to 57th Street. How do you get to Carnegie Hall? Practice, man, practice. No, actually you get here by walking a few blocks down Seventh Avenue from Central Park—or taking a handy train right to the famous performance hall's doorstep. It's still going strong after more than 110 years, and has seen some of the world's most famous conductors, orchestras, jazz singers, and even pop musicians take its stage. Tickets for good seats are usually expensive, but your compensation is seats that are luxe and comfortable. Come for top-shelf offerings from classical performers as famous as Midori, the Kodo Drummers of Japan, the Vienna Philharmonic, and the Boston Symphony Orchestra—and sometimes from lesser-known prodigies. Or just take a backstage tour of the hall (on hiatus in summer); tours leave weekdays, three times daily, at 11:30 AM, 2 PM, and 3 PM (note that you can only purchase tickets between the hours of 11 AM and 3 PM); they cost $9 per adult, with discounts for students, seniors, and children. There's also a museum with exhibits explaining the history of the building and commemorating some of the musicians who have passed through it.

Radio City Music Hall (212-247-4777), West 50th Street at the corner of Sixth Avenue. Subway: B, D, F, or V to 47th–50th streets/Rockefeller Center. Tours daily 10 AM–5 PM each half hour. Perhaps the city's best-known music hall, Radio City—like so much else in Midtown—is unabashedly art deco and big, from the instantly recognizable red marquee (it runs a block long), to the gold leaf lining the ceiling, to the cruise-ship design. The hall, seating about 6,000, was built in 1932 by Rockefeller as part of his self-named complex (this was not a modest man).

Of course, most don't come here to study architectural details but rather simply to see the Rockette dancers in action at Christmas or Easter; their chorus lines are New York's most famous. Radio City also sometimes presents theatrical productions, TV specials, and even movie screenings; performers on its stage could include anyone from Tori Amos or Dave Matthews to Luther Vandross, B. B. King, or a revue headlined by that purple PBS dinosaur. You can take a 1-hour backstage tour of the technology behind Radio City's scenes ($10–17 per person), culminating in a visit with one of the real live Rockettes—the famous 175-woman-strong dance troupe.

BROADWAY THEATERS There are dozens of large-capacity Broadway theater houses in Midtown West's Theater District (roughly from Broadway to Eighth Avenue, stretching for about 10 blocks north of Times Square), though only four actually remain standing on Broadway itself. Most have been nicely renovated to something partway between their Roaring '20s grandeur and their later, decaying state. To describe each one—and the plays running therein— would take *another* guidebook. Instead, let someone else do the work: Get your hands on a copy of *Playbill* or any city newspaper such as *The New York Times* or the *Village Voice,* and comb through the listings.

To get tickets, you must phone a theater's box office or its ticket broker; I have provided ticket numbers with the listings below, and newspapers will also list these or other numbers. (Because some theaters cede their box-office operations over to ticket brokers such as TeleCharge or TicketMaster, you may not be speaking with theater staff when you call.) If you've arrived in New York last-minute without tickets for a popular show, you're often out of luck, but always try one of the half-price services in and around Times Square anyway. The most popular is called TKTS (212-768-1818), housed in a kiosk amid the madness at the northern edge of the square at West 47th Street; the service sells last-minute tickets at deep discounts starting at 3 PM (but get there earlier). They don't take credit cards. Failing that, head for the theater itself an hour or two before the curtain opens and inquire about unclaimed tickets.

OFF-BROADWAY AND OFF-OFF-BROADWAY THEATERS In addition to the big-name shows and houses, Midtown West is also rich with smaller off-Broadway and off-off-Broadway theater companies and theaters, in an entertaining variety of spaces; the difference in label (*off Broadway* or *off-off Broadway*) depends merely on the seating size of a venue, not its distance from the famed street. Most of these smaller companies are located just west of the Theater District, between Eighth and Eleventh avenues. Here you'll often find thought-provoking

work at lower ticket prices—locals tend to visit these shows, not tourists—than at the big Broadway houses. The same rules for securing tickets apply: Call the box office or ticket broker in advance, or (failing that) show up at the door early.

COMEDY CLUB Carolines on Broadway (212-757-4100), corner of West 49th Street and Broadway. Subway: 1, C, or E train to 50th Street. This is one of the city's top comedy venues, just north of Times Square, with nightly sets. It's quite popular, so try to book a seat in advance.

FILM AMC Empire 25 Theatres (212-398-3939), 234 West 42nd Street between Seventh and Eighth avenues. Subway: N, Q, R, S, W, 1, 2, 3, or 7 train to 42nd Street–Times Square, or A, C, or E train to 42nd Street–Port Authority. Just off Times Square,

A TKTS DISCOUNT TICKET BOOTH OPERATES AT TIMES SQUARE.

Paul Karr

AMC's monster 25-screen theater shows every big release of the moment.

Clearview Ziegfield (212-777-FILM, ext. 602), 141 West 54th Street at the corner of Sixth Avenue. Subway: F train to 57th Street, E or V train to Fifth Avenue–53rd Street, B or D train to 47th–50th streets/Rockefeller Center, or N, R, Q, or W train to 57th Street. There's just one film playing at a time at this old-timey 54th Street cinema, which seats more than 1,000 viewers. Cinephiles love the huge screen. Usually a recent or second-run flick is showing.

Loews 34th Street Theatre (212-244-8850), 312 West 34th Street between Eighth and Ninth avenues. Subway: A, C, or E train to 34th Street–Penn Station. Hollywood hits are shown here, in the less-than-glorious neighborhood near Penn Station.

AMC Loews 42nd Street E-Walk Theater (212-50-LOEWS, ext. 572), West 42nd Street at the corner of Eighth Avenue. Subway: N, Q, R, S, W, 1, 2, 3, 7, or 9 train to 42nd Street–Times Square, or A, C, or E train to 42nd Street–Port Authority. Right by the Port Authority bus and subway station (and across the street from the Empire 25), Loews's Eighth Avenue cinema shows the usual big releases. It's rumored to be acquired or closing in the near future, however.

Loews State (212-50-LOEWS, ext. 901), 1540 Broadway between West 45th Street and West 46th Street. Subway: N, Q, R, S, W, 1, 2, 3, or 7 train to 42nd Street–Times Square, or 1 train to 50th Street. Recent, medium-quality Hollywood films (the ones that didn't top the box office) seem to be the rule here, at a theater that is located right in Times Square. The former cinema here was destroyed and is now occupied by a huge Virgin Records store; at the bottom level, below all the records and movies, there you find the theater.

🏵 **Paris Theatre** (212-688-3800), 4 West 58th Street near the corner of Fifth Avenue. Subway: N, R, or W train to Fifth Avenue–59th Street. This hip, single-screen cinema across the street from Tiffany, Central Park, and the Plaza Hotel is one of Midtown's best film bargains—if only for the quality of its films. Sadly, the adjacent lounge recently closed its doors.

BARS AND CLUBS B. B. King Blues Club & Grill (212-997-4144), 237 West 42nd Street between Seventh and Eighth avenues. Subway: N, Q, R, S, W, 1, 2, 3, or 7 train to 42nd Street–Times Square. Some pretty decent rock, blues, bluegrass, and even disco acts show up regularly at this Times Square bar-restaurant; in one recent month Pinetop Perkins played one night, a Jimi Hendrix tribute another, Latin Grammy Award winners another, Soul Farm & Moshav Band another (and I'm truly sorry I missed *that* one), and then K. C. & The Sunshine Band on yet another night. If that's not enough incentive to get you here, there's also a very good menu of soul and American food such as blackened catfish, grilled salmon, chicken gumbo, steak, and club sandwiches; the dessert choices include—of course—Mississippi mud pie. And locations don't get much better than this: The club is within a few blocks of countless bars, diners, restaurants, and Broadway and off-Broadway theaters.

Iridium (212-582-2121), 1650 Broadway near the corner of West 51st Street. Subway: 1 train to 50th Street, or N, R, or W train to 49th Street. Open daily 6:30 PM–midnight. A great wine list, combined with smoking jazz, makes this a wonderfully civilized place to hear the genre close to Lincoln Center—and that's even more a surprise when you realize that the Empire Hotel, within which it's housed, is nothing special. But the weird interior, well-dressed jazz aficionados, and triple weekend sets (twice on weekdays) all make this one of Midtown's best bets for hep cats.

Nokia Theatre (212-930-1950), West 44th Street at the corner of Eighth Avenue. Subway: A, C, or E train to 42nd Street–Port Authority. This former Loews movie theater reopened in fall 2005 as an entertainment venue hosting fairly big-name acts like Lynyrd Skynyrd, Social Distortion, and The Pogues.

The Pen-Top Bar (212-956-2888), 700 Fifth Avenue at the corner of East 55th Street. Subway: E or V train to Fifth Avenue–53rd Street. Open Monday to Thursday 4 PM–midnight, Friday and Saturday to 1 AM. One of New York's best lounge views is from the Peninsula hotel's rooftop bar (with a terrace in good weather). No, the drinks aren't cheap, but this view is priceless.

SPECTATOR SPORTS New York Knicks (212-465-6727 for information, 212-465-JUMP for tickets), Madison Square Garden, 2 Penn Plaza at the corners of 33rd Street and Seventh Avenue. Subway: A, B, C, D, E, F, N, Q, R, W, 1, 2, or 3 train to 34th Street. As the only pro sports team playing in Manhattan, the Knicks are understandably in high demand . . . until you look at their dismal record of late; nevertheless, like it or not, tickets cost somewhere between $20 and $1,000 (yes, $1,000)—if you can even get one.

✳ Selective Shopping

BOOKSTORES Gotham Book Mart (212-719-4448), 41 West 47th Street between Fifth and Sixth avenues. Subway: B, D, F, or V train to 47th–50th Streets/Rockefeller Center. Open Monday through Friday 9:30 AM–6:30 PM, Saturday to 6 PM. It just looks like another store selling new and used books, and so it is. But it's much more than that, too. Gotham Book Mart was founded by Ida Frances Steloff, who opened the store in 1920 on a much smaller scale in the Times Square area. As the place grew, moved, and kept growing, Steloff supported and befriended many of New York's struggling and up-and-coming writers—people like Tennessee Williams, James Joyce, Henry Miller, and Anaïs Nin. Steloff lived to the age of 102; her store is still going strong, though many patrons have no idea that this was, for a long time, America's equivalent of Paris's Shakespeare & Co.—a kind of literary salon.

The Mysterious Bookshop (212-765-0900), 129 West 56th Street between Sixth and Seventh avenues. Subway: F, N, Q, R, or W train to 57th Street. Open Monday to Saturday 11 AM–7 PM. Tucked between a luxury hotel and some mighty fine restaurants and coffee shops, this is one of New York's most respected mystery bookstores.

Rizzoli (212-759-2424), 31 West 57th Street between Fifth and Sixth avenues. Subway: F train to 57th Street, or N, R, or W train to Fifth Avenue–59th Street. Open Monday through Friday 10 AM–7:30 PM, Saturday from 10:30 AM, Sunday 11 AM–7 PM. In spring 2001 this Italian publisher closed all but one of its Manhattan stores, but the original remains. Now partly run by the American Institute of Architects, the store still purveys Rizzoli's lush picture books of paintings, photography, architecture, and the like, as well as those of other publishers.

DEPARTMENT STORES Bergdorf Goodman (212-753-7300), 754 Fifth Avenue at the corner of 57th Street. Subway: N, R, or W train to Fifth Avenue–59th Street, or F train to 57th Street. Open Monday through Saturday 10 AM–7 PM, Thursday to 8 PM, Sunday noon–6 PM. This temple to excess sells extremely expensive women's fashions, lingerie, jewelry, cosmetics, accessories, and—especially—shoes. The kitchenware is top rate, too. But don't expect anything resembling a discounted price or a sale; it just isn't that sort of place. Instead, expect completely discreet staff carefully guiding Upper East Side madames and their daughters through life-changing fashion decisions. See also Bergdorf Goodman Men's in "Midtown East," under *Fashion*.

Macy's (212-695-4400), 151 West 34th Street from Broadway to Seventh Avenue. Subway: B, D, F, N, Q, R, V, or W train to 34th Street–Herald Square, or 1, 2, or 3 train to 34th Street–Penn Station. Open daily 10 AM–9 PM, Sunday 11 AM–8 PM. It's hard to believe the self-proclaimed biggest store in the world (which it may or may not be) began as a mariner's little army-navy outlet, but it did. Rowland Macy's shop grew from a tiny store to a chain very quickly; in 1902, after Macy's death, new management moved it to a single huge building at Herald Square, and most of the decorative touches on the exterior remain from that move. (Ironically, Macy didn't live to see the move, and the new owners perished on the *Titanic* just 10 years later.) The store is nationally famous for its sponsorship of New York's big balloon-filled Thanksgiving Parade (see *Special Events*), and New Yorkers know it for the superb flower show it sponsors each spring. Locals and tourists alike flock here regularly for specials and sales on the basement homeware items, to sample from rows and rows of fragrance counters, to check out the affordably priced jewelry or snap up souvenir totes emblazoned with the Macy's logo. There are also extensive clothing sections. One more tidbit: that professional-looking star that adorns the store (and all its ubiquitous print advertising)? It came from—yes—Rowland Macy's tattoo.

FOOD AND DRINK Empire Coffee and Tea Co. Inc. (212-268-1220 or 1-800-262-5908), 568 Ninth Avenue between West 41st and West 42nd streets. Subway: A, C, or E train to 42nd Street–Port Authority. Open weekdays 7:30 AM–7 PM, Saturday 9 AM–6 PM, Sunday 11 AM–5 PM. This purveyor sells just what it says it does: hard-to-find, exotic coffees and teas.

Maison du Chocolat (212-265-9404), 30 Rockefeller Plaza between Fifth and Sixth avenues. Subway: B,

D, F, or V train to 47th–50th streets/ Rockefeller Center. Open Monday to Saturday 9:30 AM–7 PM, Sunday 11 AM–6 PM. These Parisian chocolates are top drawer (and top dollar), displayed like jewels. Try some of the cream or ganache fillings, or sip cocoa at one of the few tables. There's another branch farther uptown, on Madison Avenue between East 78th and East 79th streets (212-744-7117).

JEWELRY **Harry Winston** (212-245-2000), 718 Fifth Avenue at the corner of East 56th Street. Subway: N, R, or W train to Fifth Avenue–59th Street. Open Monday through Saturday 10 AM–6 PM. Harry Winston might not be as big as Tiffany across the street, but it's certainly higher-priced: That's why movie stars are always spotted wearing its diamonds at the big awards. This firm handles some of the largest diamonds in the world, period, as well as a range of other precious gemstones. (And Marilyn Monroe thought it was good enough for her.) The design sense is flawless here, the stones huge, and cutting perfect—and the air thick with the smell of money. What I'm saying is, don't wander in wearing jeans and sneakers.

MUSEUM STORES **ICP Museum Store** (212-857-0002), 1114 Sixth Avenue near the corner of West 43rd Street. Subway: N, Q, R, S, W, 1, 2, 3, or 7 train to 42nd Street–Times Square, or B, D, F, or V train to 42nd Street. Open Tuesday through Thursday 10 AM–5 PM, Friday 10 AM–8 PM, weekends 10 AM–6 PM. The International Center for Photography's store purveys the expected books and catalogs, but also high-end cameras and even regular old photo supplies.

MoMA Design and Book Store (212-708-9700), 11 West 53rd Street between Fifth Avenue and Sixth Avenue. Subway: E or V train to Fifth Avenue–53rd Street or B, D, F, or V train to 47th–50th streets/Rockefeller Center. Open daily 9:30 AM–6:30 PM, Saturday to 9 PM. This museum shop is located inside the newly reopened MoMA on 53rd Street; expect high-quality prints, postcards, art books, and the like, as well as a selection of artfully designed kitchen and office items.

SHOPPING ARCADES **The Shops at Columbus Circle** (212-823-6300), 10 Columbus Circle (Eighth Avenue) between West 58th Street and West 59th Street. Subway: A, B, C, D, or 1 train to 59th Street–Columbus Circle. Mall open Monday to Saturday 10 AM–9 PM, Sunday noon–6 PM; individual shop hours vary. You just knew those two huge towers of the Time Warner Center weren't going to rise above Central Park and forget all about shopping. Three levels of retail shops range from a bookstore to Coach, Godiva, Hugo Boss, Williams-Sonoma, and Armani Exchange . . . among others. (You can also tour CNN's studios here, but that's another matter entirely.) The belowground floor is entirely taken up by a massive Whole Foods store, great for picking up a relatively healthy bite before heading across the circle to Central Park to eat it.

✳ Special Events

May: **Fleet Week** on the Hudson River at Intrepid Sea-Air-Space Museum, Pier 86 at West 46th Street, west of Twelfth Avenue. Subway: C or E train to 42nd Street–Port Authority.

Sailors and their various vessels of war converge on the city for a week of celebration and shore leave.

Late June: **The Annual Lesbian, Gay, Bisexual and Transgender Pride March**. The historic march takes place on the last Sunday in June. Participants march along Sixth Avenue from Columbus Circle to Christopher Street. Whether you're a participant or bystander, it's a lot of fun. The parade is one of four major Gay Pride events in June in NYC—which more than 750,000 people attend—along with Gay Pride week's PrideFest (Greenwich and Washington streets), the rally (Bryant Park), and Dance on the Pier (Pier 54, 13th Street & the Hudson River; you must purchase a ticket to dance, but the gay-themed fireworks above the Hudson can be seen from anywhere along the riverfront).

Late November: **Thanksgiving Day Parade** (212-494-4495), along Broadway. Subway: A, B, C, D, or 1 train to 59th Street–Columbus Circle, N, Q, R, S, W, 1, 2, 3, or 7 train to 42nd Street–Times Square, or B, D, F, N, Q, R, V, or W train to 34th Street–Herald Square. Since 1924 this parade has brought outrageous, oversized balloons to Midtown. The parade begins on Central Park West near the American Museum of Natural History (see chapter 11), then proceeds south along the park to Columbus Circle; from there, it angles down Broadway through Times Square and on to a finish at Herald Square right in front of . . . well, Macy's.

Early December: **Lighting of the Christmas Tree** at Rockefeller Center. Subway: B, D, F, or V train to 47th–50th streets/Rockefeller Center. It's not truly the Christmas season in New York until the lights go up on the specially chosen tree that's hoisted into place each early December in front of Rockefeller Center. Come to see it; lots of other people do.

December 31: **New Year's Eve** in Times Square. Subway: N, Q, R, S, W, 1, 2, 3, or 7 train to 42nd Street–Times Square. Just as the Christmas season is signaled by the lighting of a tree, the end of another year doesn't really sink in until those moments when the brightly lit ball slowly begins sliding down its column in Times Square. If you're actually planning to show up for this spectacle, remember a few things: First, get here early, because half a million other folks have exactly the same idea—and *they* want a front-row spot, too. Second, travel light: New security measures mean tougher searches and more rules about what you can't bring in. Third, you'll have to stand for hours without sitting. And fourth, don't drink much; you cannot leave, even to take refreshment breaks, if you want to be there at the magic moment.

Central Park 9

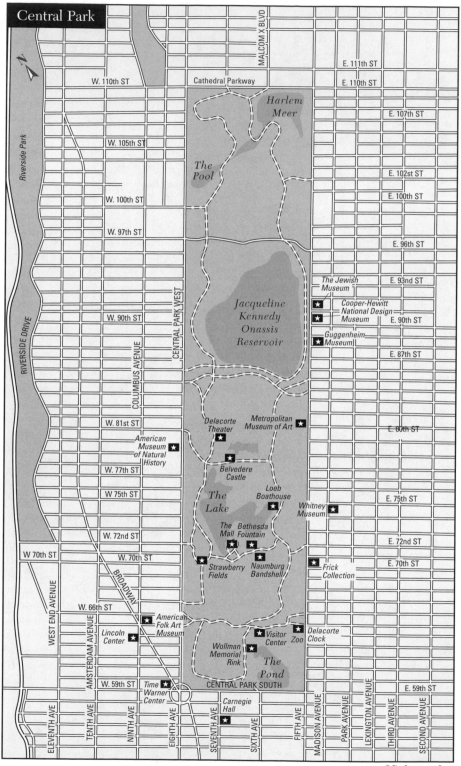

Central Park

W. 110th ST

Riverside Park

W. 105th ST

W. 100th ST

W. 97th ST

W. 90th ST

CENTRAL PARK WEST

COLUMBUS AVENUE

RIVERSIDE DRIVE

W. 81st ST

American Museum of Natural History

W. 77th ST

W. 75th ST

W. 72nd ST

W 70th ST

W. 70th ST

BROADWAY

WEST END AVENUE

AMSTERDAM AVENUE

W. 66th ST

American Folk Art Museum

Lincoln Center

W. 59th ST

Time Warner Center

ELEVENTH AVENUE

TENTH AVENUE

NINTH AVENUE

EIGHTH AVENUE

SEVENTH AVENUE

Carnegie Hall

SIXTH AVENUE

MALCOM X BLVD

Cathedral Parkway

E. 111th ST

E. 110th ST

Harlem Meer

E. 107th ST

The Pool

E. 102st ST

E. 100th ST

E. 96th ST

Jacqueline Kennedy Onassis Reservoir

The Jewish Museum

E. 93nd ST

Cooper-Hewitt National Design Museum

E. 90th ST

Guggenheim Museum

E. 87th ST

Delacorte Theater

Metropolitan Museum of Art

E. 80th ST

Belvedere Castle

The Lake

Loeb Boathouse

Whitney Museum

E. 75th ST

The Mall

Bethesda Fountain

Strawberry Fields

Naumburg Bandshell

E. 72nd ST

Frick Collection

E. 70th ST

Visitor Center

Delacorte Clock

Wollman Memorial Rink

Zoo

The Pond

CENTRAL PARK SOUTH

FIFTH AVENUE

MADISON AVENUE

PARK AVENUE

LEXINGTON AVENUE

THIRD AVENUE

SECOND AVENUE

E. 59th ST

© The Countryman Press

CENTRAL PARK

Central Park is Manhattan's emerald jewel. Stretching some 50 blocks—from the north side of 59th Street all the way north up to 110th Street—and filling everything between Fifth Avenue and Central Park West (Eighth Avenue), the park is many things to many people: bird refuge, memorial, ball field, picnicking ground, dog walk, place for reflection, concert venue, horse path, cross-country ski track . . . and even home.

Touted as a place for uptown's affluent to take Sunday carriage rides, and pushed by the orator-poet William Cullen Bryant, the park was subject to an open design competition. The winners were journalist (and park superintendent) Frederick Law Olmsted and his partner, the architect Calvert Vaux, who together described a "Greensward" vision of the park as a kind of English idyll—rolling meadows, rocky outcrops, and placid pathways. The pair also devised four cross roads (called transverses), along with dozens of bridges, to keep auto traffic as far from the people as possible. Getting the park built proved a bit difficult, however. It took 20 years and $10 million to seize by eminent domain, clear, blast, bulldoze, replant, and landscape 843 acres out of what had been a hodgepodge of swamps, shanties, houses, churches, factories, and pig farms; it took several more decades for all the newly planted trees to grow to maturity and fill out the park, creating what today is a genuinely sylvan—even, in places, semi-wild—place.

Since then the park has taken its place in the heart of New Yorkers—who are fiercely appreciative and protective of it—and also in the lexicon of popular culture. Works of fiction, including James Baldwin's searing *Go Tell It on the Mountain* and the mouse tale *Stuart Little*, all take place in the park; famous residents living beside it have included John Lennon, Madonna (who was famously rebuffed from joining one posh co-op), Jerry Seinfeld, Paul Simon, and many many more—you'll sometimes see them walking or running in the reservoir area. All in all there are few places in New York that are better to see during a short visit. The unique combination of nature, culture, music, scenery, architecture, skyscapes, and real live New Yorkers going about their leisure is simply unbeatable. On a fine-weather day I'd come here—over, say, a walk down Fifth Avenue or a ride to the top of the Empire State Building—without a moment's hesitation.

GUIDANCE There's a visitors center in The Dairy (212-794-6564), on which site there really was a dairy at one time—Manhattanites flocked here for milk. Now it's a kind of chalet where park employees dispense information Tuesday through Sunday 10 AM–5 PM. They will also loan you free chess pieces for a game in the park with a small deposit. Note that the park is officially closed from 1 AM to 6 AM.

GETTING THERE Central Park is so big that it's relatively easy to get to—eventually you're going to run into it one way or another, and most of the hotels in this book are fewer than 20 blocks away. So you'll certainly have a chance to stroll it if you like.

By car: You can drive through the park for a quick visual glimpse, but you can't see it very well by car and you can't park in it. Thus it's a much better idea to drive along the edges, park, and walk in. Try Central Park West, Fifth Avenue (which travels south only), or Madison Avenue (which travels north). Central Park South is a two-way road, but parking is nonexistent.

From the west side of Manhattan, then, take the West Side Highway (Henry Hudson Parkway); I recommend skipping the 56th/57th Street exits and heading to the 72nd Street or 79th Street exits, then driving due east to the park to begin your parking hunt. From the east side of the city, use the FDR (East Side) Drive, taking the 63rd Street exit and heading west to the park.

By subway: There are lots of subway stops surrounding the park, though none in it; which one to take depends on where you're going. To reach the southern edge (the Wollman skating rink, the Sheep Meadow), take an F, N, Q, R, or W train to 57th Street or, farther away, an A, B, C, D, or 1 train to 59th Street–Columbus Circle. To reach the two zoos, take an F train to Lexington Avenue–63rd Street or an N, R, or W train to Fifth Avenue–59th Street. To reach Strawberry Fields, take a B or C train to 72nd Street.

To reach what I consider the nicest walking parts—including the Mall, the Ramble, the Great Lawn, Belvedere Castle, the Delacorte Theater, and the Naturalists' Walk—take a B or C train to 81st or 86th Street. The west side of the big reservoir can be reached by the B or C train to 86th or 96th Street, while the east side is reached by taking the 4, 5, or 6 train to 86th Street, or a 6 train to 96th Street.

Finally, to reach far-northern destinations such as Harlem Meer, the Dana Discovery Center, the Lasker pool and rink, and the Conservatory Garden, take a 2 or 3 train up to 110th Street, or a 6 train to 103rd or 110th Street.

GETTING AROUND The park is huge, and there isn't a single east–west subway line beneath it, so getting around can be a bit of a problem unless you've got a car.

By car: Four major cross streets below ground level cut through the park, connecting the west side to the east: 66th, 81st, 86th, and 96th streets. They are very convenient for getting around quickly, except for occasional closures. If one is closed, simply cut north or south along Central Park West, north along

Madison Avenue (a block east of the park), or south along Fifth Avenue and try the next one.

If you're planning to just drive through, though, note that the park's smaller cross streets—and its network of smaller streets, which offer good views of the meadows, trees, and so forth but are heavily used by kamikaze-like taxis—are closed to vehicles weekdays at midday from 10 AM to 3 PM; from 7 PM to 10 PM at night; and also all weekend from 7 PM Friday until early Monday morning.

By bus: Bus lines crisscross the park, though they don't stop inside it—only at the edges. The 66 and 72 lines cross the park at 72nd Street; the 79 line crosses at 81st Street; the 86 bus crosses at 86th Street; and the 96 and 106 buses cross at 96th Street.

By horse-drawn carriage: Immortalized on *Seinfeld,* horse-drawn carriage rides through Central Park have long been one of the must-do romantic tours of the city. It costs roughly $35 for a 20-minute ride, $55 for a 45-minute tour, and more for longer tours—plus tips, of course. But the romance is undeniable, and the information you'll glean from your tour guide will certainly intrigue. Carriage drivers collect along Central Park South between Fifth and Sixth avenues, across the street from the row of hotels facing the park. Call 212-246-0520 for more information.

✳ To See

MUSEUM The Metropolitan Museum of Art (212-535-7710), 1000 Fifth Avenue at the corner of 82nd Street. Subway: 4, 5, or 6 train to 86th Street, or 6 train to 77th Street. Open Tuesday through Thursday 9:30 AM–5:30 PM, Friday and Saturday to 9 PM, Sunday 9:30 AM–5:30 PM (some galleries open at 11 AM). Though it is technically inside the boundaries of Central Park, I have treated the Met in "Upper East Side" (see chapter 10) alongside the many other museums stretching along Fifth Avenue in the section known as Museum Mile.

SITES ✐ **Belvedere Castle** (212-772-0210), west-central portion of the park near 79th Street. Subway: V or C train to 81st Street. Open Tuesday through Sunday 10 AM–5 PM. Perched on a rock outcropping, this tiny and fanciful stone "castle" is the highest viewpoint in Central Park. Originally designed as a kind of joke or sculpture by Olmsted and Vaux, the structure was later fitted with real doors and windows; today it holds the Henry Luce Nature Observatory, where children can learn about the park's rich bird life, as well as a weather observatory spitting out the very latest data. The castle is also dramatically spotlit at night.

✎ ✐ **Delacorte Clock,** east side of park at Fifth Avenue near East 65th Street. Subway: F train to Lexington Avenue–63rd Street, or N, R, or W train to Fifth Avenue–59th Street. One of my favorite little corners of Central Park is this mechanical clock, which marks each quarter hour with a marvelous little procession of instrument-playing creatures who emerge to one of 32 children's songs programmed into the clock, then dance individual dance steps. (Personally, I like the tambourine-playing bear.)

The Mall, center of park near 72nd Street. Subway: B or C train to 72nd Street. The park's central gathering place is a civilized rectangle of compressed New York life. On a summer weekend street preachers preach, hot-dog, water, and ice cream vendors vend like crazy, in-line skaters check out each other's technique . . . and *everybody's* seemingly there just to look around and see who's still attractive and available.

Down the wide set of stairs, **Bethesda Terrace** is another open plaza. This is the place where, in summer, you'll nearly always find some kind of busker tricking unsuspecting audience members splayed out on the steps, performing some impossible physical feat, or just juggling. It really gets entertaining when one of the buskers tries to draw crowds away from another. This is street theater at its best, in a superb setting with the Bethesda Fountain and the placid lake as backdrop.

The adjacent **Naumburg Bandshell** is the site of summertime concerts (see *Entertainment—Music Venues*).

FOR FAMILIES ♂ ♿ **Central Park Wildlife Conservation Center (Central Park Zoo)** (212-439-6500 or 212-861-6030), on east side of park at 830 Fifth Avenue, from East 63rd to East 64th Street. Subway: F train to Lexington Avenue–63rd Street, or N, R, or W train to Fifth Avenue–59th Street. April through October, open daily 10 AM–5 PM, to 5:30 weekends; November through March, open daily 10 AM–4:30 PM. The 6.5 acres of prime zoo space are one of the park's best places to take children. A tropical rain forest section hosts giant monkeys and other animals; the swimming polar bears and penguins in the Polar Circle are everlastingly popular. A California Coast section has a sea lion pool; feedings three times daily, at 11:30 AM, 2:30 PM, and 4 PM. The adjacent **Tisch Children's Zoo** gets the kids up close and personal with domesticated animals such as a cow, sheep, and Vietnamese potbellied pig, and there are daily environmental education performances to entertain children as well. Tickets get you admission to both; they cost $6 per adult, $1.25 for senior citizens, and $1 for children 3–12.

♂ ♿ **Charles A. Dana Discovery Center** (212-860-1370), Central Park near corner of 110th Street, between Fifth and Lenox avenues (Malcolm X Boulevard). Subway: 2, 3, or 6 train to 110th Street. Open Tuesday to Sunday 10 AM–5 PM, until 4 PM from mid-October until mid-February. Operated by the Central Park Conservancy, the Dana Center at the northeast corner of Central Park isn't the only visitors center in the park—but it's the only one offering programs for kids, and they're offered year-round. If you're really hankering to get some education into your visit, this might be the ticket. Its programs describe the ecology of the park through displays,

KIDS FIND PLENTY TO KEEP THEM HAPPY IN CENTRAL PARK.

Kim Grant

music, and talks. Staff will also loan kids a fishing pole to try their luck at fishing the Meer (lake) in front of the center—encouraging the little ones to toss back all that they hook, of course.

∂ **Swedish Cottage Marionette Theater** (212-988-9093), west side of park near 79th Street. Subway: B or C train to 81st Street. This tiny wood cottage, built as a schoolhouse by the Swedish for an 1876 exposition, is today home to one of America's few remaining puppet theater companies. The company presents *Hansel & Gretel, Cinderella,* and other favorite children's plays throughout the year. Shows usually take place Tuesday through Sunday at 10:30 AM and noon, and Saturday at 1 PM. There are no Saturday shows in summer. Tickets for the puppetry cost $6 per adults, $5 for children.

MEMORIALS *∂* **Balto,** west side of park near 67th Street. This 1925 sculpture commemorates the malamute sled dog who persevered through an Alaska blizzard to help deliver medical supplies to a remote village; his legend grew in the years afterward. Kids love this statue, and often pat it.

Literary Walk, center of park from 65th to 70th streets. Subway: N, R, Q, or W train to 57th Street, F train to 57th Street, 1 or 9 train to 66th Street, or B or C train to 72nd Street. This wide, straight-as-an-arrow walk between several rows of big elm trees leads a walker straight to the Mall. The southern end is flanked by statues of the writers Burns, Shakespeare, and Sir Walter Scott. It's interesting to note that this area, added at the end of the park's construction, contradicted Olmsted's original plan (which was devoid of statuary).

Maine **Memorial,** West 59th Street at Columbus Circle. Subway: A, B, C, D, or 1 train to 59th Street–Columbus Circle. A blockish sculpture by Attilio Picarelli, topped with gilded bronze figures, prominently marks the southwestern gate to the park. It was installed in 1913 to commemorate the battleship *Maine,* which exploded in a Spanish-controlled harbor in Cuba in 1898, killing 260.

Strawberry Fields, west side of park near West 72nd Street. Subway: B or C train to 72nd Street. While former Beatle John Lennon and his wife Yoko Ono resided at The Dakota (see chapter 11) apartment building, they often played in this nearby section of the park with son Sean. After Lennon's assassination in 1980, Ono donated a reported $1 million to restore and preserve the small parcel and landscape into a peace garden. Today the area is shaded by elms and contains a plant species from every nation in the world, including some that bloom quite brilliantly. But the centerpiece is a mosaic crafted in Naples, Italy, that says, simply: IMAGINE. Tourists and devotees alike come here daily in good weather to sit on benches, strum guitars, think about Lennon and his music, stare up at the twin towers of apartments where he was killed, or simply leave small offerings of flowers and notes on the mosaic.

✳ To Do

BASKETBALL There are two places where you can shoot hoops for free in the park. Four half courts—with great views of Midtown—are available next to the Great Lawn, open 9 AM–8 PM. There are several more at the North Meadow

Recreation Center (212-348-4867), on the east side of the park up by 97th Street—the advantage here is that you can borrow a basketball by leaving a piece of photo identification as a deposit. These courts are open 10 AM–8 PM.

BICYCLING There are bicycles for rent at the Loeb Boathouse (212-861-4137). They cost about $10–14 for the first hour, $5–7 for each additional hour—and yes, they have tandem bikes. The best times to cycle are when cars aren't allowed here: 10 AM–3 PM and 7–10 PM weekdays and all through the weekend.

BOATING One of the favorite romantic pastimes in the park during summer is to rent a rowboat and explore the lake with a loved one. Get one at the Loeb Boathouse (212-517-3623), located on the east side of park near East 74th Street, for $9–15 per hour. (You'll also need to place a $30 deposit.) Once on your way, there are four boat landings where you can rest and picnic. You can rent between the hours of 10 AM and 5 PM. There are also gondola rides around the lake, where for a hefty $30 per half hour someone else will do the rowing. Rent these from the Boathouse as well, 5–9 PM weekdays and 2–9 PM weekends.

HORSEBACK RIDING There are more than 5 miles of bridle path along the west side of the park; carriage trails, after all, were one of the park's original planned uses. If you know how to ride, inquire about renting a horse from the stables of the **Claremont Riding Academy** (212-724-5100) at 175 West 89th Street between Amsterdam Avenue and Columbus Avenue. Horse rentals cost about $50 per hour.

ICE SKATING Lasker Rink (212-534-7639), center of park between 106th and 108th streets. Subway: 2 or 3 train to 110th Street, or B, C, or 6 train to 103rd Street. November through March, open daily 11 AM–3 PM and 4–7 PM. This lesser-known park rink, on the park's northern fringe, is equipped for both ice skating and—at certain times—in-line skating. Admission costs $4 per adult, $2 per child under 12.

Wollman Memorial Rink (212-439-6900), central portion of park near 62nd Street. Subway: N, R, or W train to Fifth Avenue–53rd Street, or Q train to 57th Street. October through April, open Monday and Tuesday 10 AM–3 PM, Wednesday through Saturday 10 AM–9 PM, Friday and Saturday to 11 PM. This very popular rink sees plenty of ice skaters in winter—it's a locals' kind of place, as opposed to the much more touristic rink at Rockefeller Center. Admission to the rink costs $3.50, and skate rentals cost an additional $3.50. There are also lockers for rent should you need one.

JOGGING Jogging is extremely popular on the park; there are numerous loops and other places to run—straight up the Literary Walk to the Mall and around the reservoir (it's about 1.5 miles around) is a favorite route, though you can run almost anywhere there's a path. The Great Lawn also maintains a short running track, one-eighth mile in length.

SWIMMING **Lasker Pool** (212-534-7639), central portion of park from 108th to 109th streets. Subway: 2 or 3 train to 110th Street, or B, C, or 6 train to 103rd Street. Open daily 11 AM–3 PM and 4–7 PM. Adjacent to the Lasker ice rink complex, this outdoor public swimming pool is open daily in summer—call for exact opening dates—and quite popular, in part because it is free.

TENNIS There are 30 **tennis courts** (212-316-0800 for information, 212-360-8133 for permits and lessons) just north of the reservoir in the vicinity of West 96th Street at Central Park West (subway: B or C train to 96th Street). Most of them (26) are of clay, but 4 are asphalt; all are open from April through November, daily 6:30 AM–dusk. You must buy a pass to play here; it costs $5 per day, or $50 for an annual adult pass, $20 for an annual senior citizen pass, and $10 for a junior pass (for children under 17). In July, free lessons are offered to children.

✳ Green Space

Central Park is full of green space, obviously—the whole thing is green space. Below I have listed some of my favorite spots, but I've also left out some of my others—the North Meadow, East Meadow, and (Jacqueline Kennedy Onassis) reservoir among them. Get a map at the park information office (see *Guidance*) and go where you like; there really isn't a bad walk in the entire park.

Conservatory Garden, east side of park at Fifth Avenue, from 104th to 106th streets. Subway: 6 train to 103th Street, or 2 or 3 train to 110th Street. Way up at 105th Street, the Conservatory Garden lies behind wrought-iron gates but provides a welcome splash of color with its changing blooms. The beautiful little area includes a pond, flowers, and places to sit; newlyweds are frequently photographed here. There's also a fountain. The free garden is open daily 8 AM–dusk; tours are sometimes offered on Saturday from May through August at 11 AM.

The Great Lawn, center of park between 81st and 85th streets. Subway: B or C train to 81st or 86th Street, or 4, 5, or 6 train to 86th Street. This big, 55-acre meadow was actually once a water reservoir before the city drained and paved it over in the 1930s (employing fill from the excavations for the then-being-built Rockefeller Center complex). Today it's the park's favored location for hanging out. It's also here where the Metropolitan Opera and New York Philharmonic each give two free concerts every summer, and where Simon & Garfunkel played in 1981 and Pope John Paul II presided over Mass in 1995. There's a small set of sports facilities near the expanse of green.

The Lake, central portion of the park from 72nd to 81st Streets. Subway: B or C train to 72nd or 81st Street, or 6 train to 77th Street. One of the park's most distinctive and geographically endearing features is this 22-acre lake, once an impromptu ice-skating rink for New Yorkers that became so popular in the 19th and early 20th centuries that the city eventually built two indoor rinks to handle the load. Since this area was left partly in its original swampy condition (unlike the rest of the park), it has a jagged, unlandscaped quality and many quiet coves to be discovered, some with benches for sitting. Rowboats can be rented at the Loeb Boathouse (see *To Do—Boating*), and drinks or dinner can also be had

Kim Grant

YOU CAN RENT A BOAT TO EXPLORE CENTRAL PARK'S LAKE.

before splendid views. On foot, a stroll over the handsome **Bow Bridge**—it spans a small neck of the lake—is also recommended.

On the lake's western shore, don't miss **Hernshead**—a small outcropping jutting into the lake that was a particular favorite of Olmsted and Vaux. The small loop here culminates with a small semi-enclosed sitting area of cast iron known as the Ladies Pavilion, right on the water; this is one of the park's quietest spots, especially beautiful for contemplation at sunset.

✐ **Naturalists' Walk,** west side of park between 77th and 81st streets. Subway: B or C train to 81st Street. This small, quiet corner of the park features lots of exotic plantings, a nice secluded lawn for picnicking, a double-arched stone bridge, and a delightful wooden bridge, too. It's a good place to bring the kids, and it's near the pleasant **Diana Ross Playground.**

The Ramble, in the heart of the park between 74th and 77th streets, is a slightly more thickly wooded section, with hilly terrain and a network of pathways. It's especially known for the variety and number of birds that return to this part of Central Park each year while migrating north or south along the Atlantic seaboard.

🐑 **The Sheep Meadow,** west-central side of park between 65th and 70th streets, has better views than any other green space in the city, probably, and it's my favorite place for picnics and sunbathing. The bright green expanse once was home to a flock of live sheep; today, it's closed during the wet seasons to protect it from damage, but once summer arrives and the gates come down, it's a free-for-all party of beach blankets, Brie, hacky sacks, and kites.

Shakespeare Garden, west side of park from West 79th to West 80th streets. Subway: B or C train to 81st Street. Climbing the side of the big rock upon which the Belvedere Castle stands, this garden is planted only in flowers that Shakespeare wrote about. There's a mulberry here that's descended from one the Bard himself planted in England.

✳ Where to Eat

DINING OUT Central Park Boathouse (212-517-2233), center of park near 72nd Street. Subway: 6 train to 68th Street, or B or C train to 72nd Street. In summer, open weekdays for lunch noon–4 PM and for dinner 5:30–9:30 PM, weekends for brunch 9:30 AM–4 PM and for dinner 6–9:30 PM. December to March, open daily but no dinner service. Despite complaints about slow service and hit-or-miss food, this place is almost overwhelmingly popular in summer for its tremendous sunset views of the softly lit lake. The combination of straightforward American entrées and fusion twists is unchallenging at best.

Tavern on the Green (212-873-3200), Central Park West at West 67th Street. Subway: 1 train to 66th Street, or B or C train to 72nd Street. Open Monday through Friday for lunch 11:30 AM–3:30 PM and dinner 5–10:30 PM, Friday to 11:30 PM, weekends 10 AM–3:30 PM for brunch and 5–11 PM for dinner. This place is overfrequented by tourists and celebrities, given the middling food, but it's got enough ambience to match anyplace else around here. Formerly the holding pen for Central Park's resident flock of sheep, the building was converted to a restaurant in the 1930s. Restaurant impresario Warner LeRoy refurbished and glitzed up the place with plenty of crystal, mirrors, and stained glass. Five dining rooms overlook two pretty gardens, where waitstaff serve the masses New American meals of steak, seafood, crispy duck inside a pastry shell, and the like. At night the trees outside the windows are either gaudily or beautifully lit, depending on your point of view. Entrées are expensive, but the pretheater dinner is a better deal: just $35 for three courses.

✳ Entertainment

In 1981 the folk duo Simon & Garfunkel played a free show in Central Park to a huge, appreciative crowd. That seemed to spark something, and since then the park has hosted increasing numbers of free concerts and benefit shows (benefiting the park's upkeep, of course). If you're in New York in summer, I can think of no finer way to enjoy a summer evening; for a comprehensive guide to each season's offerings, contact **Central Park SummerStage** (see below), which coordinates most of the shows.

MUSIC VENUES Summertime brings a variety of free and ticketed shows to the park.

The Great Lawn, center of park between 81st and 85th streets. Subway: B or C train to 81st or 86th Street, or 4, 5, or 6 train to 86th Street. This is the site of two annual shows each summer by the New York Philharmonic and the Metropolitan Opera (see *Green Space*).

TAVERN ON THE GREEN

Kim Grant

Naumburg Bandshell, center of park near 72nd Street. Subway: B or C train to 72nd Street. This lovely, classically shaped bandshell, donated to the city in 1983, is the sight of free summertime classical music concerts on Monday and Tuesday evenings. Check the arts pages of *The New York Times* for each summer's schedule.

Rumsey Playfield, center of park near 72nd Street. Subway: B or C train to 72nd Street. SummerStage's summertime program of ticketed shows (see *Special Events*)—anything from jazz to pop—are performed here.

BARS AND CLUBS The Boathouse Bar (212-517-2233), center of park near 72nd Street. Subway: 6 train to 68th Street, or B or C train to 72nd Street. Open to 9:30 PM in-season, call for seasonal opening dates. It's almost impossible to get a seat here on a beautiful summer's day or night— on the weekend, it's standing room only—and the weak drinks and uninspired beers are overpriced. But so what? This bar has the best view in Manhattan, for my money: not of Fifth Avenue or skyscrapers, but rather of the gondolas, rowboats, and lovers cavorting around the lake. It's a happy place for a drink—you'll feel as if you've suddenly landed in Key West or something.

✳ Special Events

June–August: **Harlem Meer Performance Festival** (212-860-1730), Charles A. Dana Discovery Center, Central Park near corner of 110th Street, between Fifth Avenue and Lenox Avenue. Subway: 2, 3, or 6 train to 110th Street. This summer-long music festival, at the Charles A.

Dana Discovery Center (see *To See— For Families*), brings a varied roster of jazz, blues, Latino, and other music to the center's waterside terrace. Also watch for **Dancing on the Plaza** in August, a Thursday-night, August-only series of ballroom dance lessons on the terrace.

June–August: **Central Park SummerStage** (212 360-2756) at the Rumsey Field, in the center of the park just off the Mall near 72nd Street. Subway: B or C train to 72nd Street. This series of mostly free, mostly-on-the-weekend concerts began in 1986 and has since grown tremendously popular. There are now also some ticketed concerts by big-name artists, poetry readings, plays, spoken word, a growing dance series . . . a lot, actually. Check the organization's web site (www.summer stage.com) for a schedule of the summer's performances and, where applicable, ticket prices.

June–August: **Shakespeare in the Park** at Delacorte Theater, near 81st Street. Subway: B or C train to 81st Street. In an open-air theater backed up against a pond, this remarkable free program of Shakespeare plays from the Public Theater has been active ever since theater founder Joseph Papp started it in 1957. Get tickets by arriving a few hours before the 1 PM performance times, or by visiting the Public Theater box office in NoHo (see chapter 3) on performance day.

December 31: **New Year's Eve** fireworks are fired off near Tavern on the Green (see *Dining Out*) around 11:30 PM. Take a 1 train to 66th Street, or a B or C train to 72nd Street, to catch the light show.

Kim Grant

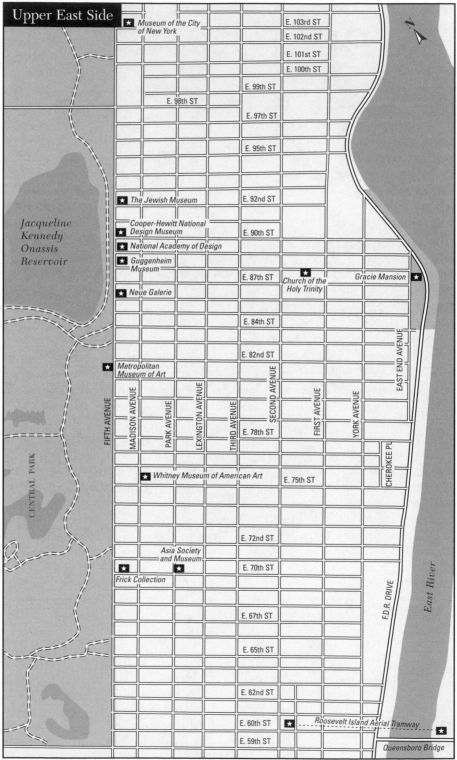

Upper East Side

★ Museum of the City of New York

E. 103rd ST
E. 102nd ST
E. 101st ST
E. 100th ST
E. 99th ST
E. 98th ST
E. 97th ST
E. 95th ST
E. 92nd ST

★ The Jewish Museum

★ Cooper-Hewitt National Design Museum

E. 90th ST

★ National Academy of Design

★ Guggenheim Museum

E. 87th ST

★ Neue Galerie

★ Church of the Holy Trinity

★ Gracie Mansion

E. 84th ST
E. 82nd ST

★ Metropolitan Museum of Art

Jacqueline Kennedy Onassis Reservoir

FIFTH AVENUE
MADISON AVENUE
PARK AVENUE
LEXINGTON AVENUE
THIRD AVENUE
SECOND AVENUE
FIRST AVENUE
YORK AVENUE
EAST END AVENUE

E. 78th ST

★ Whitney Museum of American Art

E. 75th ST

CHEROKEE PL

CENTRAL PARK

E. 72nd ST

Asia Society and Museum

★ ★ E. 70th ST

Frick Collection

E. 67th ST
E. 65th ST
E. 62nd ST

F.D.R. DRIVE

East River

E. 60th ST ★ Roosevelt Island Aerial Tramway ★

E. 59th ST

Queensboro Bridge

© The Countryman Press

UPPER EAST SIDE

The most upper crust of New York's neighborhoods, the Upper East Side stretches—for the purposes of this guidebook—north from East 59th Street (the southern boundary of Central Park) to East 110th Street (the park's northern boundary); it runs from the park to the East River, taking in several smaller neighborhood divisions—notably Yorkville and bits of Spanish Harlem—along the way. (Most cartographers consider the "Upper East Side" designation, with all the cachet it implies, to extend only to East 96th Street or so.)

The neighborhood was once known as Millionaire's Row; today it is still mostly residential, consisting largely of block after block of expensive row houses, town houses, co-ops, apartment high-rises, and very expensive hotels. Surprisingly, there are not a large number of outstanding restaurants, shops, or cultural offerings in this section of the city—with one notable exception, "Museum Mile," a 34-block-long stretch of Fifth Avenue running along Central Park. Many mansions and new structures here hold some of the world's finest art museums, and many visitors to New York City should think hard about making this set of museums their key destination—eschewing, for example, the Empire State Building and Statue of Liberty if necessary—on a very short visit to the city. To come here and not see these treasures would be a shame.

Shopping excellence is mostly confined to the blocks just north of East 59th Street, but what fine names you'll find here—Lauren, Versace, Barneys, and the like.

This is also the section of Manhattan with the thickest concentration of resident celebrities per square mile: The mayor lives here officially, but you might also run into Woody Allen or any number of writers or actors at the corner store or luncheonette.

GETTING THERE Since only one train line runs here—the 4, 5, and 6 trains, long known in Upper East Side lore as the Lexington Line—the subway isn't necessarily always your best choice; it's quite a distance from both Central Park and the easternmost reaches of the area. Buses reach more of the area (and crosstown buses are the only way to get here from the Upper West Side). But the heavy delivery-truck and taxi traffic, coupled with a lack of expressways, means any bus—or the cab you'll occasionally be forced to take—could require an eternity to creep around the neighborhood at the wrong time of day. Parking is similarly very, very difficult anywhere in this neighborhood where important attractions, hotels, or restaurants are located. It's much easier in the less populated upper or eastern reaches.

If you do take the subway, remember that the 4 and 5 trains are express trains, and though they're quicker they stop at only a few stations: 59th Street, 86th Street, and 125th Street.

✳ To See

MUSEUMS 🐾 ♿ **Asia Society and Museum** (212-288-6400; www.asiasociety museum.org), 725 Park Avenue at the corner of East 70th Street. Subway: 6 train to 68th Street. Open Tuesday through Sunday 11 AM–6 PM, Friday until 9 PM. Right here on Park Avenue is New York's most important gathering of Asian resources. The rotating exhibits might include a show of contemporary aboriginal art from Australia organized by the Museum of Contemporary Art in Sydney or a look at Chinese tomb sculptures. Free tours are included with all tickets. Admission costs $10 for adults, $7 for seniors and students, free for children under 16; Friday nights are free of charge.

♿ **Cooper-Hewitt National Design Museum** (212-849-8300; www.ndm.si.edu), 2 East 91st Street at the corner of Fifth Avenue. Subway: 4, 5, or 6 train to 86th Street. Monday through Thursday 10 AM–5 PM, Friday 10 AM–9 PM, Saturday to 6 PM, Sunday noon–6 PM. Inside steel magnate Andrew Carnegie's huge former mansion (it has more than 60 rooms), New York's largest museum of interior design once belonged to Cooper Union; today it is administered by the Smithsonian, its permanent collection divided into four areas. The drawing, prints, and graphic design section features a Michelangelo sketch; the product design and decorative arts section features jewelry, ceramics, glass, porcelain, and ornate furniture; the textiles collection holds 30,000 pieces from as far back as the Han dynasty, especially strong on silks, laces, and costume items; and the wall coverings section shows classic wallpapers from around the world. But perhaps the most interesting room in the museum is the library, with more than 60,000 printed works—some of them quite rare—including large collections of pop-up books, World's Fair material, photographs of Paris in the 1920s and 1930s, and archives of industrial design. Though it may sound a bit stodgy, the exhibitions highlight surprisingly modern and edgy topics such as *New Hotels for Global Nomads,* a fascinating look at the boutique-hotel craze that included an actual room. Other shows have focused on Church's and Homer's landscapes, and the design of wallpapers and staircases. And the summertime Friday-night parties (free with admission) are legend. Admission costs $12 for adults and children 12 and older, $7 for senior citizens and students.

♿ **El Museo del Barrio** (212-831-7272; www.elmuseo.org), 1230 Fifth Avenue at the corner of 104th Street. Subway: 6 train to 103rd Street. Open Wednesday through Sunday 11 AM–5 PM. New York's only Latino museum is this one (usually called simply El Museo), along Central Park on the northern tip of Museum Mile. Founded in 1969 by Puerto Rican artists and educators, it today holds thousands of historical and art objects from Puerto Rican, Caribbean, and Latino history and art history—photos, paintings, sculpture, books, and other items. Rotating exhibitions focus on such topics as Mexican painters, Brazilian art, and new Puerto Rican artists. There is also a permanent exhibition of pre-Columbian artifacts (such as shell and bone tools) from the Taíno people who once roamed the ancient Caribbean creating science and games. Admission is by donation; a contribution of $6 per adult or $4 per student or senior is suggested.

&. **Frick Collection** (212-288-0700; www.frick.org), 1 East 70th Street at the corner of Fifth Avenue. Subway: 6 train to 68th Street. Open Tuesday through Saturday 10 AM–6 PM, Sunday 1–5 PM. What was once the grand home of the notably tightfisted industrialist Henry Clay Frick is now home to his art collection—one that bears the unmistakable stamp of a man who cultivated a special taste for the European master artists, sculptors working in bronze, and other practitioners of decorative arts. Impressionist paintings, French chairs and armoires, Oriental rugs, Limoges enamels, and porcelain abound. There are 16 galleries here in all, each with a distinct personality (though none really seems organized according to a particular theme). The Living Hall is crammed with the work of unrivaled masters—Titian, El Greco, and the like. The Fragonard Room, filled with 18th-century French furniture (including a complicated "mechanical table" with many moving parts from the 18th century), features Jean-Honoré Fragonard's murals of *The Progress of Love.* The Library's Italian bronzes and Chinese porcelain vases lead to the narrow West Gallery, with works of Corot, Velasquez, Rembrandt, and Vermeer. One of the more unusual holdings is Piero della Francesca's painting of St. John the Evangelist in the Enamel Room—Piero's only work in America. If you still haven't had your fill of terrific European art, the East Gallery contains more works by Degas, Goya, Van Dyck, Whistler, and other stars.

This museum's special exhibitions are, for my money, some of the best in Manhattan—they have highlighted such holdings as a set of 17th-century drawings from the École des Beaux-Arts in Paris; the drawings of Jean-Baptiste Greuze; a 15th-century "housebook" (a kind of medieval scrapbook of drawings depicting court life) that gives a unique look inside the late Middle Ages; Gilbert Stuart's portrait of George Washington; the works of El Greco or Vermeer; and a remarkable collection of timepieces running the gamut of the history of time measurement (along with a large number of time-related reference works to accompany it). The Frick also frequently puts on superb exhibitions of loaned works—El Greco and Courbet from the (underappreciated) Toledo Museum of art, the drawings of Cézanne, Degas, de Kooning, Matisse, and van Gogh from the Smith College Museum of Art, and the drawings of Michelangelo, Picasso, and others from the famous Albertina in Vienna, for example. Even if there weren't so many fine pieces of artwork here to contemplate, Frick's house alone would be worth a visit—it's screened from Fifth Avenue's constant dull roar of cabs by an elevated garden and magnolia trees—and there's a wine bar in the peaceful, skylit, and fountained Garden Court, open after 6:30 PM each day the museum is open. Admission costs $15 per person for adults, $10 for senior citizens, and $5 for students; children under 10 cannot enter the museum, while those under 16 must be accompanied by an adult.

♿ **Guggenheim Museum** (212-423-3500), 1071 Fifth Avenue at the corner of East 89th Street. Subway: 4, 5, or 6 train to 86th Street. Open Saturday through Wednesday 10 AM–5:45 PM, Friday 10 AM–7:45 PM. Sol Guggenheim's vision of a modern art museum of a new kind has been spectacularly realized. From the curving, distinctive Frank Lloyd Wright design—which evokes water or a chambered nautilus shell, perhaps, with its sensuous zigguratlike form and leads you past the works through a series of looping circles—to the six collections assembled here, the "Gug" (its full name is actually the Solomon R. Guggenheim Museum) is not to be missed by fans of the nonrepresentational art of Picasso, Kandinsky, Klee, Mondrian, and their ilk.

Formerly housed in an auto showroom on East 54th Street, the museum moved to its Upper East Side space (amid much controversy) in 1959—complete with Wright's oval-shaped columns, huge rotunda, and terrazzo floors inlaid with circular forms. Some neighbors have never really accepted the unusually designed building as their own, but none disputes the very high quality of the art housed within it, which reflects half a dozen tastes. Guggenheim's own collection featured mostly abstract paintings; niece Peggy Guggenheim fancied surrealist and abstract painting and sculpture; German-born Justin K. Thannhauser's collected impressionist and modern art is outstanding, including the work of Cézanne, Degas, Manet, Picasso, Pissarro, and van Gogh, among other leading lights; Karl Nierendorf brought works of German expressionism; Katherine S. Dreier collected avant-garde work; and Giuseppe Panza di Biumo contributed huge quantities of notable minimalist and conceptual art. Changing exhibitions highlight modern work such as Matthew Barney's *Cremaster Cycle* and new film and multimedia work by Pierre Huyghe.

There are additional satellites of this museum in Venice; Berlin; Bilbao, Spain; and now Las Vegas. Never one to rest on its laurels—befitting the art it curates—

THE GUGGENHEIM MUSEUM WAS DESIGNED BY FRANK LLOYD WRIGHT.

Kim Grant

the Guggenheim unveiled the Sackler Center for Arts Education in 2001 to highlight computer and multimedia art (it also contains a theater). And future plans include another yet new exhibition and educational facility, this one perhaps to be located in Lower Manhattan. Admission to the Guggenheim costs $18 for adults, $15 for students and seniors; children under 12 can enter free. There's a museum café on the premises for the parched or hungry.

&. **The Jewish Museum** (212-423-3200; www.thejewishmuseum.org), 1109 Fifth Avenue at the corner of 92nd Street. Subway: 4, 5, or 6 train to 86th Street, or 6 train to 96th Street. Open Sunday through Wednesday 11 AM–5:45 PM, Thursday until 9 PM, Friday 11 AM–3 PM. This museum features exhibits related to the history of the Jewish experience, including the Diaspora and notable Jewish citizens through world history. Exhibits have re-created the Prague of Franz Kafka; a set of light sculptures and other artworks, timed for Hanukkah; and the art of Adolph Gottlieb, for example. Admission costs $10 for adults, $7.50 for students and senior citizens; Thursday nights are by voluntary donation. Note that it's closed on the major Jewish holidays.

&. **The Metropolitan Museum of Art** (212-535-7710; www.metmuseum.org), 1000 Fifth Avenue at the corner of 82nd Street. Subway: 4, 5, or 6 train to 86th Street, or 6 train to 77th Street. Open Tuesday through Thursday 9:30 AM–5:15 PM, Friday and Saturday to 8:45 PM, Sunday 9:30 AM–5:15 PM (some galleries open at 11 AM). Also open on major-holiday Mondays. The grande dame of Manhattan's museums, the Met is simply awesome—as in *awe inspiring*. (The newly scrubbed and restored façade, unveiled in 2006, made it even more so.) And it's big, consisting of more than 1 million square feet of museum space in all—bring walking shoes, obviously—holding some 2-million-plus objects of art that were collected beginning in 1870. At any one time the number of exhibits on display is staggering. You might wander from portraits by the photographer Richard Avedon to objects related to the Asian despot Genghis Khan; from a selection of carefully preserved French fashions from the 1930s to the nature photographs of Vija Celmins; from a show of private-collection impressionist paintings of Monet, Pissarro, Renoir, and the like to sculptures from sub-Saharan Africa, metalwork from the nomadic peoples of Eastern Eurasia, Spanish American art, or cityscapes by the seminal Bauhaus artist Paul Klee. Or simply take in one of the museum's themed exhibitions, such as those collecting arms or armor. Banners above the museum's Fifth Avenue entrance alert viewers to the current exhibitions, which highlight material from the vast collection arranged around such themes as da Vinci's life and drawings; Chinese nature painting and porcelain; Japanese calligraphy; the Silk Road of Asia; and Klee's cityscapes. There's plenty here for obscure tastes, too: Among the more unusual collections are the Costume Institute (on the ground floor), with nearly 50,000 pieces of costume from the past four centuries; an enormous first-floor Egyptian art department; and the oldest surviving piano in the world. Unless you're a specialist, though, don't start on the bottom floor—there's actually very little here except for the Costume Institute (spanning seven centuries and five continents of costumes, accessories, and fashion), an auditorium for lectures and events, and the Robert Lehman Collection of Italian and Northern Renaissance paintings, drawings, and decorative arts.

Instead, things get cooking on the next floor up (the first floor), where the front steps from Fifth Avenue bring you into the museum and its Great Hall. This is the floor where you'll find mostly Western art, even if a right turn does take you to the labyrinthine complex of rooms devoted to Egyptian statuary, jewelry, artifacts, and architecture from prehistoric Egypt to the Roman period. To your left is the main exhibition of Greek and Roman marble, bronze, and terra-cotta sculpture, vases, paintings, jewelry, and other objects; this section also filters into the museum restaurant. Directly in front of you lie stairs to the second floor, and behind them the collection of medieval art: sculpture, tapestries, vessels, and much more from the 4th through 16th centuries (there is much more on display at The Cloisters; see chapter 12). At the back and to the left of the medieval section, you can turn left to find the first of two stories of European art—classic sculptures, decorative arts, furniture, metalwork, textiles, intriguing scientific instruments, and other objects fashioned before 1900 fill period rooms of each major Western European nation. (Directly upstairs hang the paintings of famous masters.) From here you can proceed to a corner room of modern art; again, this is the first of two floors, and features American and European paintings, sculpture, and other forms from all the major artistic movements since 1900—expect to find Picasso, Modigliani, Alfred Stieglitz, art nouveau, and art deco. Directly back from the medieval section you'll find the second level of the Lehman Collection of Italian and Northern Renaissance objects and art. The Arts of Africa, Oceania, and the Americas Wing is also located on this side of the first floor with its objects, monuments, and symbolic personal accessories from the African continent, Central and South America, and many Pacific islands.

At the right-hand back corner of the first floor is the first of two stories that make up the American Wing, which contains some of the Met's finest treasures: decorative arts, furniture in furnished period rooms, and an amazing range of paintings and sculpture. The collection of paintings is almost overwhelming, but especially strong in Hudson River school works—Church, Cole, and their followers—and similar-period American art such as Winslow Homer, James Whistler, and John Singer Sargent. Emanuel Gottlieb Leutze's famous *Washington Crossing the Delaware* is also here. This wing also features the beautiful Charles Engelhard Court, a glassed-in and skylit interior garden decorated with windows and large works of sculpture by the likes of Augustus Saint-Gaudens. Frequent exhibitions—both loaned from other museums and from the huge in-house Henry Luce Center—highlight individual artists, movements, and themes such as American impressionism, images of women, and portraits of artists.

The second floor contains most of the Met's Eastern art but plenty of European and American works as well. The central staircase brings you face to face with the big rooms of European paintings so many come to the Met to see, which run up to the side facing Central Park. (There's also a special set of galleries nearby to highlight 19th-century European paintings and sculpture.) It all comes from a vast holding of French, Italian, Flemish, Dutch, and other masters, and you'll find some of the museum's 37 Monets, 21 Cézannes, and 5 Vermeers on show here, among much else. On this floor you'll also find a small section of Greek and Roman work; a corner wing of modern art; the second floor of the American

Wing, described above; a narrow section of drawings, prints, illustrated books, and manuscripts from the Renaissance forward, as well as photography, prints, and daguerreotypes spanning the entire history of that medium; a delightful hallway of musical instruments (and a violin workshop); rooms of arms and armor; and sections of Islamic, Japanese, ancient Near Eastern, Korean, Chinese, South Asian, and Southeast Asian art. Highlights of these sections alone—which include the largest collection of Asian art in the Western world, some 60,000 objects from as far back as the eighth century BC—could easily fill a book. I recommend the art from the Himalaya region; the works of Chinese calligraphy in the Dillon, Wang, and Young Tang galleries; the Weber galleries of ancient Chinese jade and bronze; the Arts of Japan galleries, with their folding screens, wood-block prints, altar platform (based on a 12th-century example), Neolithic ceramics, and Edo porcelain; the room of Qing dynasty porcelain; and the exceedingly rare Buddhist art from China, Tibet, and Nepal. The Astor Court is a particularly interesting place: It re-creates a Ming-period courtyard from 14th-century Suzhou, China, and is paired with a room of wooden Chinese furniture. Special exhibits along the Great Hall's balcony trace the influence of Chinese and Japanese ceramics on later European work.

In addition to its monumental holdings, the museum offers a wide range of children's and family programs, including short films, tours, discussions, story hours, and sketching classes. (Note that sketching with a pencil or charcoal, and taking still photographs, is allowed—for private use only—except in specially marked areas. But don't try to use a flash, bring in a camcorder, or paint in watercolor, and don't try to sneak in a tripod without clearing it at the information desk first; you won't get in.) If you're hungry, there's an upscale museum café (212-570-3964), which is so popular that the museum actually recommends you make reservations if you want to eat there. It is open 9:30 AM–4:30 PM on Tuesday, Wednesday, Thursday, and Sunday, to 8:30 PM Friday and Saturday. There's also a more downscale cafeteria and an informal bar-café, open slightly longer hours, both on the same side of the museum as the main café—both are near the 81st Street entrance. Then there are the European Sculpture Court Café, a balcony bar in the Great Hall (open Friday and Saturday only, 4–8:30 PM, with music), and a roof garden café open from May through late Fall.

Admission to the Met is technically by donation, with contributions of $20 for adults, $10 for seniors and students recommended; if you enter the Met, you can also enter The Cloisters on the same day (see chapter 12).

The Museum of the City of New York (212-534-1672), 1220 Fifth Avenue at the corner of 103rd Street. Subway: 6 train to 103rd Street. Open Tuesday through Sunday 10 AM–5 PM. Located on the northern edges of Museum Mile in an attractive Georgian Colonial structure, this sleeper of a museum holds quite a lot of material documenting the city's rich history—more than 1.5 million items in all. The collection of Currier and Ives prints is matchless, while the silver collection is also impressive, but many will especially enjoy the toy collection: It showcases dollhouses dating from the 18th and 19th centuries (check out the Florine Stettheimer) and wooden dolls from the same era, among many other toys. The photography section includes half a million prints and negatives, with work from

LOOK magazine, Jacob Riis's seminal photographs of the Lower East Side, almost 3,000 of the Currier and Ives lithographs, and many views of New York from earlier eras. (Also look for the ground-floor Fire Gallery, which features two 1850s-era fire trucks and paintings of famous New York fires.) Certain Sundays are children's days, with plenty of activities, while periodic exhibits focus on such topics as valentines from the 19th century, the Afro-Caribbean roots of Latin music, Hasidic life in Brooklyn, and the construction of the World Trade Center. Admission to the museum costs $15 for families, $7 for adults, and $5 for seniors, students, and children. Free guided tours are offered each Saturday at noon.

National Academy Museum (212-369-4880; www.nationalacademy.org), 1083 Fifth Avenue at the corner of East 89th Street. Subway: 4, 5, or 6 train to 86th Street. Open Wednesday and Thursday noon–5 PM, Friday through Sunday 11 AM–6 PM. Founded in 1825 as a kind of trade association by Thomas Cole and other notable artists of the time, the National Academy is sometimes overlooked by tourists pounding the shoe leather along the Museum Mile. But its holdings are very high quality thanks to the members who have contributed material over the years—Frank Lloyd Wright, I. M. Pei, Frederick Church, Thomas Cole, Jasper Johns, Winslow Homer—and today it holds one of the city's largest collections of 19th- and 20th-century American art, from the Ashcan school to cubist and fauvist material. Exhibitions highlight the work of members, such as a show pairing sculptural works from the academy with those of the nearby Metropolitan Museum of Art (see above), a 6-week annual exhibition on changing topics, a show of work from women members of the academy—women were allowed as members from the beginning—and two centuries of work created by artists in residence in Italy. Admission costs $10 for adults, $5 for students and senior citizens.

Neue Galerie (212-628-6200; www.neuegalerie.org), 1048 Fifth Avenue at the corner of East 86th Street. Subway: 4, 5, or 6 train to 86th Street. Open Friday, 11 AM–9 PM, Saturday to Monday and Thursday 11 AM–6 PM. This distinctive three-story mansion near the Met, where Mrs. Cornelius Vanderbilt III once lived, was converted to a museum in the early 1990s with a specific mission: to show New Yorkers German and Austrian work from a brilliant moment in the early 20th century. (It's no coincidence the museum is named for Vienna's Neue Galerie.) The entire second floor consists of Austrian fine and decorative arts, mostly from Vienna around 1900—there's work from the Vienna Secession (including Klimt's beautiful, Asian-tinged *The Dancer*) and decorative arts such as the jewelry, lighting, and other work of Josef Hoffmann. The third floor is dedicated to German art movements from the same early-20th-century period— it shows Kandinsky, Max Beckmann, the Bauhaus period work of Klee, Mies van der Rohe, and Oscar Schlemmer, and more. The museum café, Café Sabarsky (see *Eating Out*) is a real stunner. Admission to the gallery costs $15 per adult, $10 for seniors and students; children under the age of 12 are not admitted, and those age 12 to 16 must come with an adult.

& **Whitney Museum of American Art** (212-570-3676 for information, 1-877-WHITNEY for tickets; www.whitney.org), 945 Madison Avenue at the corner of East 75th Street. Subway: 6 train to 77th Street. Open Wednesday, Thursday,

Saturday, and Sunday 11 AM–6 PM, Friday 1–9 PM. The Whitney is sometimes maligned for being overly self-important (its grandiose Biennial exhibitions sometimes hit the mark, sometimes miss it, critics claim), but the truth is, this is still a fine repository of artwork—a kind of touchstone for anyone serious about the visual arts in America. The museum was founded in 1931 with about 700 art objects, mostly drawn from Gertrude Vanderbilt Whitney's collections. It was particularly strong on abstract works from the Ashcan school (Sloan, Luks, Everett Shinn); the work of noted realists such as Edward Hopper and Thomas Hart Benton; and early modernists such as Charles Demuth and Max Weber. Though Mrs. Whitney passed away in 1942, collectors have continued to augment the Whitney's holdings ever since with such items as sculptures by Alexander Calder, Claes Oldenburg, and Louise Nevelson, paintings by Georgia O'Keeffe and Fairfield Porter, and 17 works by the energetic coastal painter John Marin.

Today the permanent collection holds more than 12,000 paintings, sculptures, prints, drawings, installations, and photographs from all the leading lights, and it's still growing; this work is displayed on two floors and includes the world's largest collections of Edward Hopper's and Reginald Marsh's work—more than 2,500 Hopper oil paintings and other works, some 200 Marsh pieces. (It's appropriate, because the young painters first showed their work at the Whitney Studio Club, forerunner to this museum.) The collection is also very strong on abstract art and in the work of painters Marsden Hartley and O'Keeffe. The Whitney doesn't skimp on photography, either: You can find the works of Diane Arbus, but also of William Eggleston, Nan Goldin, Garry Winogrand, and many other important photographers. Changing exhibitions showcase an amazing scope and variety of work drawn from these collections, from a small southern town's quilting to John Hedjuk's drawings, video art, meditations on the Internet, a number of short films and gelatin silver prints by photographer Lorna Simpson (such as 31, a daily record of an unknown woman's personal life), and the permanently held collection of Willem de Kooning's work (accompanied by the work of fellow artists such as Jasper Johns and Louise Bourgeois). To name just a few. Then there are the Biennial exhibitions, which began in the 1930s (in odd-numbered years only) as a showcase for recent American art.

Highlights include the third-floor Peter Norton Family Galleries, which also showed the photographs of Ed Ruscha; and the fifth floor's fine Leonard & Evelyn Lauder Galleries are anchored by rooms dedicated to Hopper, O'Keeffe, and Calder. Other galleries at the Whitney include the Ames Family Gallery, which has exhibited paper works of drawing and printmaking from the likes of Christo and Johns; and the Anne & Joel Ehrenkranz Gallery with Mark Hansen's and Ben Rubin's *Listening Post,* an audiovisual work integrating words and sounds based on Internet chat rooms. Friday nights (when admission to the museum is also free) bring SoundCheck, a program of local musicians performing live at the museum. Admission to the Whitney costs $15 for adults, $10 for students and senior citizens; on Friday from 6 to 9 PM it's open by voluntary donation. The popular Sarabeth's bakery (see *Eating Out)* has an outlet here for snacks, coffee, and meals.

NOTABLE HOUSES OF WORSHIP **Central Synagogue** (212-838-5122; www.centralsynagogue.org), 652 Lexington Avenue at 55th Street. Subway: E or V train to Lexington Avenue/ 53rd Street or 4, 5, or 6 train to 59th Street. Built in the mid-9th century by German Reform Jews, the striking Central Synagogue—designed by German immigrant architect Henry Fernbach—began with the so-called Sanctuary building, said to possibly be the oldest Jewish house of worship in New York City. Its most prominent feature, however, is the pair of octagonal towers meant to evoke Solomon's Towers; each is topped with a greenish-colored, onion dome. The structure contains a surprising number of Moorish and Islamic elements, which was the current style of synagogue design in Germany at the time Fernbach designed it. There are worship services in the Blitzer Chapel at 8 AM each weekday morning, as well as Shabbat on Friday at 6 PM and Saturday morning at 10 AM (10:30 AM in winter). Take a free tour of the synagogue Wednesday at 12:45 PM.

Church of the Holy Trinity (212-289-4100), 316 East 88th Street between First and Second avenues. Subway: 4, 5, or 6 train to 86th Street. This Upper East Side church is mostly notable for the pretty garden sporting plantings of seasonal roses, hydrangeas, and other flowers. Concerts are sometimes presented in this space during summer.

Islamic Cultural Center of New York (212-722-5234), 1711 Third Avenue at the corner of East 96th and East 97th streets. Subway: 6 train to 96th Street. This large and relatively new mosque (it was built in the late 1980s, after 20 years of planning and fund-raising) is the center of New York's Muslim culture, plunked down improbably on the Upper East Side; its Skidmore Owings and Merrill design consists of a rather simple cubic form, restrained yet modern in concert with the neighborhood, topped with a striking copper-clad, pre-cast dome. It's the palatial interior that really shines, however—the central prayer space, beneath the dome, almost seems to float. Details include Turkish and Pakistani carpeting, a carved wooden pulpit from India, and Moroccan-style detail work, all donated by Muslim nations. The current Imam, Omar Saleem Abu-Namous, was notable for being one of the very few Muslim leaders to immediately speak out against the September 11 terrorist attacks on New York. Friday prayers (known as Jumu'ah) at the mosque are held each Friday at 1:00 in the afternoon (summer) or 12:30 (winter). Tours are offered daily except Fridays, beginning at 11 AM.

Temple Emanu-El (212-744-1400), 1 East 65th Street at the corner of Fifth Avenue. Subway: 6 train to 68th Street, F train to Lexington Avenue–63rd Street, or N, R, or W train to Fifth Avenue–59th Street. Now the largest synagogue in the world in terms of congregation numbers, Emanu-El began as a congregation in 1845 on the Lower East Side; it later merged with another congregation and began growing steadily in size. This massive Romanesque temple of limestone right across from Central Park was completed in 1929; the arched exterior features detail work symbolic of the twelve tribes of Israel, a giant stained-glass wheel window, and three sets of bronze doors. The interior is even more stunning—amazing stained-glass windows, an ornate bronze ark on the eastern wall fashioned to resemble an open Torah scroll, Guastavino tile, and the

Byzantine-columned Beth-El Chapel with its Tiffany windows are just some of the treats. Tours are available by appointment (call to schedule one); worship services take place Sunday through Thursday in the Greenwald Hall at 5:30 PM, with Friday evening Shabbat services on a changing schedule. These tours are available Sunday to Thursday, and also after Saturday services. There's also a fine little museum (which is also free) on the premises, containing two Bloomingdale Torah crowns among other items.

NEIGHBORHOOD **Yorkville,** East 79th to East 96th streets from Third to York Avenue. Subway: 4, 5, or 6 train to 86th Street, or 6 train to 77th or 96th Street. Now a mixture of medium-rent apartment buildings and restaurants and bars, the Yorkville neighborhood—whose boundaries are hard to define precisely—was once New York's German quarter. Subsequent waves of immigration brought additional Eastern Europeans from Hungary, the former Soviet Union, and what was Czechoslovakia; vestiges of these ethnic influences can still be seen in shops and delis in the vicinity of East 86th Street, though their presence is fading.

✳ Green Space

Carl Schurz Park, East 84th to East 90th streets from East End Avenue to the East River. Subway: 4, 5, or 6 train to 86th Street, or 6 train to 96th Street. The other major park on the Upper East Side, Carl Schurz Park is obviously no match for the one across the way (see below). Still, it's not a bad place to while away a few hours—with views of the East River, plenty of romping dogs, and a summertime jazz series. This park also contains Gracie Mansion, official home to New York's mayors (now media maven Michael Bloomberg, formerly Rudy Giuliani). The mansion, of course, isn't open to the public.

Central Park defines the westernmost boundary of the neighborhood, and most of the park's prime attractions line the park's Fifth Avenue flank. See chapter 9 for more on this fascinating park and its many nooks and crannies.

✳ Lodging

LUXURIOUS HOTELS **The Carlyle** (212-744-1600), 35 East 76th Street at the corner of Madison Avenue. Subway: 6 train to 77th Street. Part upscale apartment co-op and part exclusive hotel, the 34-story Carlyle is one of the city's most exclusive addresses, along with The Pierre and The Mark (see below)—celebrities are often either resident or lodging here. Its 179 rooms and suites are each uniquely decorated in Continental-style furniture and reds and muted oranges; Audubon prints and other fine paintings and drawings hang on the walls, while the furnishings are true antiques. All rooms are fitted out with Frette linens, plush robes, boudoir chairs, fax machine, CD player, and the like; larger corner rooms have a sofa. Nearly all have a king bed. The very luxurious suites add such amenities as separate powder room, private terrace, Steinway or Baldwin grand piano, and views of Central Park and Midtown. There are two restaurants inside, the very expensive Carlyle Restaurant and the equally impressive Café Carlyle, while Bemelmans Bar (see *Entertainment—*

Bars and Clubs) is a popular hangout. Double room rates begin around $300 per night but zoom swiftly upward from there; you'll pay much more, of course, for such extras as a hot tub or pantry and kitchenette—and the most for the newly opened 22nd-floor Royal Suite, a duplex featuring a fireplace, Steinway piano, and plasma TVs. Cost? If you have to ask, you can't afford it.

The Mark (212-744-4300 or 1-800-843-6275; fax 212-744-2749), 25 East 77th Street between Fifth and Madison avenues. Subway: 6 train to 77th Street. This luxury hotel of about 120 rooms (half of them are suites) near Central Park gets my nod as the fanciest of three contenders for the title of king of Upper East Side swank— everyone from the Dalai Lama to Madonna, stayed here—and that feeling begins to sink in the moment you enter the elegant, minimalist lobby. There are plenty of Italian design flourishes and luxurious extras throughout the lobby and rooms, and the fall-over-you-helpful service will knock you out; the concierge and staff here are tops in the city. Twice-daily maid service is standard, and so are a fax machine, a VCR, and high-speed DSL Internet access in every room. Interior decor is marked by lots of marble and floral touches, Frette linens, plants, and Piranesi prints; the bathrooms are huge and luxurious, the furniture antique yet comfortable. Shoeshines are complimentary, as is a copy of *The New York Times* delivered to your door each morning. Cell phones are also available. Of course there's room service around the clock (though some of the rooms also have kitchenette) from the hotel's own Mark's restaurant (see *Dining Out*); it,

too, is suitably grand, serving rich meals and afternoon teas (the tea service is famous citywide). There's even a tea sommelier in the bar, for goodness' sake. Double room rates here mostly range from around $575–695, while suites generally cost $725–1,900 per night.

𝒮 **The Pierre** (212-838-8000 or 1-800-PIERRE-4; fax 212-940-8109 or 212-758-1615), 2 East 61st Street at the corner of Fifth Avenue. Subway: N, R, or W train to Fifth Avenue–59th Street. One of a handful of superluxury boutique hotels clustered near the meeting of Central Park and Fifth Avenue, the castlelike Pierre is famously upper crust (and some very famous faces own co-op units here, too). Audacious enough to have opened in 1929, it has weathered times good and bad by basking unapologetically in its opulence. The 201 units (including about 50 suites) are each decorated with unique interiors of classy silk and marble; you'll find no modern-artsy Ian Schrager–style metal sinks here, but rather ones that seem lifted from the *Orient Express*. And you're pampered beyond belief by trimly attired 24-hour elevator operators and doormen, and service that is refined and professional—all right, it's also a bit fussy, but that's what guests are paying for and expect. (In fact, the amazingly personal and personable service isn't by accident: This hotel has about 650 staff, more than three for every room in the place, the highest ratio I've found.)

Rooms, of course, are comfortable well above the norm. Even the simplest room here is furnished with wingback chair and writing desk, black-and-white marble bathroom, and tiled interiors. So-called boudoir rooms add separate dressing room, mirrored closet, and views of Central Park. Deluxe suites are higher ceilinged, bigger, and furnished with additional armchairs, coffee tables, and desks, while the 10 Grand Suites are more like full apartments—some have an actual dining room, some a terrace, and some have two or even three bedrooms—with private bar, pantry, and spacious living room; these are huge and elegant, with beautiful iron chairs, overstuffed couches, French chairs, and antique armoires. The very topmost floors are occupied by Premier Suites, which have separate parlors. The highest rollers go for the Presidential Suite, which consists of a master bedroom, dressing room, fireplace, living room, and private kitchen, all done up in mahogany and marble.

The hotel is known to be unusually child-friendly among upper-crust city hotels of this sort: Some rooms have been childproofed. Other amenities include the usual fitness center, separate beauty salons for men and women, babysitting services, umbrellas, a cell-phone-rental service, in-house secretaries, all the usual accoutrements you'd expect of a much duller business hotel—and then duvets, terry robes, and video or laser disk players. The beautifully designed hotel restaurant, the Café Pierre, serves very good food in an arched room of well-spaced tables and original art (see *Dining Out*), while the Rotunda bar is worth a look for its weirdly intriguing mural. Afternoon tea service at the hotel is also a big hit. Rates range from around $425–950 and up per day for a double room, around $725–1,300 and up for the suites.

☞ **Plaza Athénée New York** (212-734-9100 or 1-800-447-8800; fax 212-772-0958), 37 East 64th Street between Madison and Park Avenues. Subway: F train to Lexington Avenue–63rd Street, 4, 5, or 6 train to 59th Street, or N, R, or W train to Lexington Avenue–59th Street. The red-awninged, 17-floor Plaza Athénée isn't the most luxurious hotel in the neighborhood—not at this steep pricing—but the service here is excellent. All of the 117 rooms and 35 suites have couches, and business-class touches include two-line phones, CD players, Internet access, fax machines, and the like; maids service all twice daily. Eight of the suites have a separate dining room, terrace, or balcony, and some rooms have a kitchenette. The hotel restaurant Arabelle (see *Dining Out*) is well regarded by guests and locals alike for a romantic dinner, and is especially popular at brunch. This Plaza also scores points for its children's package, which pampers families of four with lots of extras such as tickets to the Central Park Zoo, a Yankees cap, tickets for rowboat rides or ice skating in the park, a VCR, board games—and two connecting rooms for what is essentially the price of one. Double rooms at the hotel normally go for $555–825 per night, though specials sometimes drop the rates as low as $325. The suites begin at $1,200 per night, rising as high as $3,900 for the penthouse.

♣ **The Regency** (212-759-4100 or 1-800-235-6397; fax 212-826-5674), 540 Park Avenue at the corner of East 61st Street. Subway: F train to Lexington Avenue–63rd Street, 4, 5, or 6 train to 59th Street, or N, R, or W train to Lexington Avenue–59th Street. All 265 rooms and 86 suites at this business hotel, now run by the upscale Loews chain, are beautifully appointed in silk, velvet, mahogany, and leather. Little wonder it received four stars from Mobil. Rooms have all the expected amenities—CD player, television even in the bathroom, two-line phone, VCR, *The New York Times* delivered weekdays—though they're at times a bit smaller than expected. Some of the bigger suites add a kitchenette.

Everything else is taken care of as well: A fitness center is equipped with treadmills, cycling machines, free weights, a sauna, and a Jacuzzi. There's a barber and beauty salon on the premises. Feinstein's lounge (see *Entertainment—Bars and Clubs*) is justly renowned around the city, and the hotel restaurant 540 Park (see *Dining Out*) is a power-breakfast scene of hard-charging execs who get up early to wolf down eggs Benedict before morning meetings. And here's a fun fact that also gives you pause: This hotel is particularly known in New York for its designer doggie meals— the French chefs at the hotel restaurant don't even smirk at the thought of preparing a gourmet meal for a pooch, and your canine companion can wash it all down with a bowl of Evian afterward. Room rates (for humans, that is) begin at about $400 for a double room, while suite rates begin at approximately $1,500 apiece.

EXPENSIVE HOTELS The Marmara-Manhattan (212-427-3100 or 1-800-621-9029; fax 212-427-3042), 301 East 94th Street at the corner of Second Avenue. Subway: 6 train to 96th Street. Talk about flying below the radar. You must book an entire month in order to stay at this Turkish-owned

hotel, and the all-suite property is a considerable way uptown from the Fifth Avenue shopping and museum action. Few have heard of it. But if you've got a month (and an expense account) to spare, these luxurious apartments—no more than five to a floor—are excellent. You'd never know at first glance this was a hotel; it looks exactly like a 32-story apartment building, with a doorman just like any other. But it's not. Inside, long-stay guests revel in units that are probably bigger, on average, than any other hotel's in Manhattan. A standard room here consists of a huge bedroom, living room, full kitchen, and marbled bathroom—and that's just for starters. Pay more for a bigger suite and you'll get a second (even a third) bedroom, a washer and dryer, and a Jacuzzi in the bathroom. That's not even to mention the CD player, cordless phones, gourmet food basket awaiting new guests, and (admittedly tiny) gym in the basement.

What price paradise? Aye, there's the rub. The smallest apartment costs a cool $4,500 per month (which is actually only $150 per night). One-bedroom units go for $5,500–7,750 per month—or about $180–250 per night—while two- and three-bedroom apartments cost from $8,600 per month (about $290 per night) up to $19,000 per month, about $630 per night. At least the active 92nd Street Y (see *Entertainment—Cultural Organizations*) is fairly close; the rooftop terrace is ideal during good weather, with expansive views of uptown; and the lobby's art gallery is one of a very few in New York. Only the surrounding neighborhood— which alternates between overpriced eateries and downscale, overpriced bodegas and grocers—is a negative, and if you're keen on taking the subway around town bear in mind that you'll have to hike a few blocks (uphill) to the 96th Street station each time you want to use it. Then, after all that, you might need to transfer to an express train at the next stop.

The Sherry-Netherland (212-355-2800 or 1-877-743-7710; fax 212-319-4306), 781 Fifth Avenue at the corner of East 59th Street. Subway: N, R, or W train to Fifth Avenue–59th Street, or 4, 5, or 6 train to 59th Street. Famously posh and well located, the slim, towering Sherry-Netherland is part residence, part hotel, and all New York—from the big clock over the entrance awning to the grand chandeliered lobby (its art and friezes came from the Vanderbilt mansion), from white-gloved attendants to antique room furnishings. It's almost overkill when you learn this hotel is perched at the corner of Fifth Avenue, simultaneously across from Central Park, the Plaza hotel, *and* the General Motors Building where CBS tapes its live morning programs and toy store FAO Schwarz bewitches children.

You can see the park and the avenue unobstructed from many of the studied 40 rooms and 35 suites, which are each uniquely decorated (as befits its co-op status) but all relatively luxurious. They feature a high ceiling, marble bathroom, and some (nonworking) fireplaces; suites are much bigger and better decorated, recalling the high life in a bygone New York. Breakfast is included each day in the very expensive Harry Cipriani's lobby restaurant, and Godiva chocolates greet each guest. So do fresh flowers, soft drinks, mineral water, robes, a

small library, VCR and fax machine, two newspapers daily, and much more. The barbershop, beauty salon, snack shop purveying treats from around the world, on-call massage therapist, and ticket concierge are just icing on the expensive cake. Since the units are each so different from one another, pricing varies a great deal, but you can probably expect to pay at least $250–300 per night, much more for a large suite; call to inquire about specifics.

Surrey Hotel (212-288-3700; fax 212-628-1549), 20 East 76th Street between Fifth and Madison avenues. Subway: 6 train to 77th Street. This business hotel is nothing special—just an affordable pick in a sea of pricier alternatives, with the majority of the units being suites—but it's quite notable for the dining. Superchef Daniel Boulud has opened Café Boulud inside (see *Dining Out*); if proximity to a hot French restaurant is important to you, you should stay. There are about 40 regular rooms and about 90 one- and two-bedroom suites in the 16-story hotel; prices are surprisingly steep, starting at around $280 per night and rising to more than $400.

BOUTIQUE HOTELS ⊕ The Franklin (212-369-1000 or 1-800-607-4009; fax 212-369-8000), 164 East 87th Street between Lexington and Third avenues. Subway: 4, 5, or 6 train to 86th Street. A surprisingly good value, the uptown Franklin tries hard to compete with the raft of sleek new designer hotels down in Midtown. The simple lobby is the first hint that this place has a different ethos from your everyday bland business hotel—it's modern and spare, a bit like those of, say, the W. Rooms here feature white interiors and bed canopies, with sleek walls, Schrager-esque minimal metal furnishings, fine Belgian linens, cedar closets, VCRs, CD players, and big mirrors, but they are also quite small-ish (and so are the televisions).

Among the nice perks here are a free drink upon arrival, unlimited cappuccino any time of day or night, and a complimentary nighttime fruit bar. A library features an iron clock and room to read; staff are personable, and each member will likely remember your name and face (thus there are lots of repeat customers). Then there are the complimentary bottled water, the European-style light breakfast buffet of pastries, croissants, and coffee, Aveda toiletries, a shoeshine, in-room safe, and access to the respected NYSC gym on 86th Street. You'll forget that the hotel lacks a bar, restaurant, and pool, or that the surrounding area is a bit boring. Double room rates here are highly variable; they might range from around $200–$240 up to around $300, but certain specials occasionally knock them down to as low as an amazing $100 per night.

The Lowell (212-838-1400 or 1-800-221-4444; fax 212-319-4230), 28 East 63rd Street between Madison and Park avenues. Subway: F train to Lexington Avenue–63rd Street, 4, 5, or 6 train to 59th Street, or N, R, or W train to Lexington Avenue–59th Street. About two-thirds of the rooms in the little-known Lowell are suites, and that—among other things—makes it a great under-the-radar choice among the cluster of boutique and grandiose lodgings in this part of the city. This hotel goes a step farther with the European elegance, in terms of both design (it's a kind of big town house) and professional service: Staff are knowledgeable, not cloying or ignorant. All rooms are outfitted with VCR, fax machine, and kitchenette; unusually, however, lots of them also possess a genuine working fireplace stocked with wood, umbrellas to ready for rain, and books to read—some even add a green, private terrace. (One suite even has its own fitness equipment.) The house restaurant, the Post House, is outstanding with grilled meats. Rates are variable; check with hotel staff for an up-to-date quote.

AFFORDABLE HOTELS **The Bentley** (212-644-6000 or 1-888-66-HOTEL; fax 212-207-4800), 500 East 62nd Street at the corner of York Avenue. Subway: 4, 5, or 6 train to 59th Street, or N, R, or W train to Lexington Avenue–59th Street. The sleek, marble-floored lobby of The Bentley seems like that of a boutique hotel, but it really isn't one. The slightly spare (by Upper East Side standards) rooms are certainly affordable, though: Double rooms start at just $135 per night, while suites begin at $235. All are equipped with a CD player, there's a complimentary cappuccino bar in the lobby, and Belgian linens fit the beds. Too bad it's so far east of the most interesting parts of Manhattan: It's practically in the East River. Upper-floor suites aren't half bad, though, and they have amazing views of . . . Queens.

Hotel Wales (212-876-6000 or 1-866-WALES-HO; fax 212-860-7000), 1295 Madison Avenue at the corner of East 92nd Street. Subway: 6 train to 96th Street, or 4 or 5 train to 86th Street. Perhaps the least expensive of the Manhattan East suite-hotel chain—possibly owing to its far-uptown location—the Wales isn't a bad choice for families looking to save a few dollars, and it's got some twee little design touches as well. Rooms are not overly luxurious by New York standards, but all are decorated with fresh flowers and respectably appointed in oak with nice moldings, high ceilings, and (some) VCRs, fireplaces, compact disk players. The open rooftop terrace is nice on a sunny day for gazing at Central Park and the high-rises, and the hotel's off-season "baby package" laudably outfits families with an infant with a king bed plus a crib, a high chair, a baby tub, tub toys, and a stroller.

INN **1871 House** (212-756-8823; fax 212-588-0995), 130 East 62nd Street between Lexington and Park avenues. Subway: F train to 63rd Street–Lexington Avenue, N, R, or W train to 59th Street–Lexington Avenue, or 4, 5, or 6 train to 59th Street. A pretty, shuttered brick town house in a nicely quiet location not far from Fifth Avenue and Central Park, this local secret hides behind ironwork covering the front door. However, it has very recently begun to creep out of the affordable category and into boutique/luxury territory. Inside, hosts Warren and Lia Raum—a financial planner and former antiques dealer—have carefully preserved the home's marble-and-wood fireplaces, moldings around windows, and high ceilings. All give the place an elegant B&B feel, as do the antiques scattered throughout, yet rooms are modernly enough appointed that you won't feel stuck in the 19th century. Each room is small but cozy and country furnished, much as you'd expect to find such a place in, say, Vermont or Maine. There's a

private patio and terrace garden with one of the rooms. Note that the inn is small and thus often booked full; call in advance if you're thinking of coming. Rates range all the way from $235–595 per room.

✳ Where to Eat

DINING OUT Arabelle (212-606-4647), 37 East 64th Street between Madison and Park avenues. Subway: F train to Lexington Avenue–63rd Street, 4, 5, or 6 train to 59th Street, or N, R, or W train to Lexington Avenue–59th Street. Open Monday for breakfast only 7–10 AM, Tuesday through Saturday for lunch noon–2:30 PM and dinner 6–10 PM, Sunday 11:30 AM–2:30 PM for brunch only. The Plaza Athénée hotel's restaurant Arabelle replaces the fancier La Régence—getting a new paint job, floor, makeover, and chef in the process—and it's been a good change. New American fusion fare that's heavy on meats, fish, raw fish, and game. Dinner is expensive but gorgeous among the chandeliers and candles. Lunch and brunch are possibly better times to come, given either a good lunch deal or the outrageous brunch tab (you could spend up to $60 per person) that at least brings you into close contact with monied Upper Easters.

Aureole (212-319-1660), 34 East 61st Street between Madison and Park avenues. Subway: F train to Lexington Avenue–63rd Street, 4, 5, or 6 train to 59th Street, or N, R, or W train to Lexington Avenue–59th Street. Open Monday through Friday for lunch noon–2:30 PM and dinner 5:30–11 PM, Saturday for dinner only 5–11 PM. Charlie Palmer's creation has taken off into the stratosphere inside a brownstone where Orson Welles once lived. Inside an Adam Tihany–designed room—it features art from the respected Pace Prints gallery, huge signature floral arrangements, and a giant two-story window—executive chef Dante Boccuzzi, a Palmer protégé and former top toque at Nobu's Milan outpost (where he worked with Giorgio Armani), delivers tasting menus galore. The lunch could begin with a skate or white bean Parmesan custard appetizer, move on to a garlic-roasted chicken or salmon main course, and finish with banana caramel panna cotta or a chocolate *financière* with pistachio gelato, topped with spiced foam. The market luncheons and dinners change monthly but might feature peppered salmon, roasted garlic soup with Maine crab dumplings, seared scallops with foie gras, a fennel-crusted quail, or a veal pot-au-feu. The prix fixe dinners—$79 per person, $125 with wine pairings—begin with first courses of game bird ravioli and porcini, smoked salmon with a potato doughnut, raw oysters paired with caviar, duck confit, crab salad, or a mixed bag of ocean treats including, perhaps, octopus terrine and truffled scallops. The entrées are often sea based: seared skate, mustard-encrusted scallops with trumpet mushrooms, or lobster fricassee. Landlubbers might go for the pepper-seared venison with chestnut gnocchi, a truffled chicken with polenta, roast Vermont pheasant, fillet and short ribs of beef, or grilled steaks.

Café Boulud (212-772-2600), 20 East 76th Street between Fifth and Madison avenues. Subway: 6 train to 77th Street. Open Sunday and Monday for dinner 5:45–11 PM, Tuesday through Saturday for lunch noon–2:30 PM and dinner 5:45–11 PM. Café Boulud, inside the Surrey Hotel, is a more informal counterpart to Daniel Boulud's famous restaurant Daniel (see below) 10 blocks away. (Of course, that hardly means it's inexpensively priced.) Here Boulud has handed the reins over, but the kitchen is still drawing praise for his treatments of rustic classic French meals. (The café is named for Boulud's grandparents' café outside Lyon, France.) In a room of mahogany walls, nickel sconces, ivory-colored curtains, and other earthy tones, meals are interestingly divided into four categories: Tradition (classical French cooking), Season, The Potager, and The Journey (foods from distant, French-influenced lands). The classical cooking could be a lunch or dinner of pâté or *salade de frisée;* beef à la mode, roast trout, or sole poached in white wine sauce; and savarin, soufflé, or ice cream. The seasonal menu varies, based on what's currently fresh in local markets—winter might find winter greens, sautéed Maine sea scallops, veal shank and tenderloin, or a roast Amish chicken with apples and smoked bacon on the menu, for instance, finished off with a dessert of chocolate mousse or chocolate macaroons with hazelnut cream. The Potager is an exceptional vegetarian menu of beet salads, squash soups, handmade gnocchi, pasta, and fruity soups, crêpes, and sorbets, while the international menu rotates frequently but always intrigues. At press time it listed a Tuscan soup, Vietnamese crispy lobster with green papaya, Thai-style steamed bass, and Creole duck, plus desserts from Provence and Mexico paired with, respectively, almond ice cream and cactus-pear sorbet. Then there are the *plats du* marche, weekly specials such as Kumamoto oysters, Louisiana gumbo (made with rabbit), a truffle dish, a risotto, a fish dish, or a guinea hen stuffed with foie gras. Lunch or dinner, you'll always find something exciting and new to try—great if you can't get a table at Daniel. For either meal, expect to pay about $65 per person, wine and taxes excluded.

Café Pierre (212-940-8195), 2 East 61st Street at the corner of Fifth Avenue. Subway: N, R, or W train to Fifth Avenue–59th Street. Open Monday through Saturday for breakfast 7– 10:30 AM, lunch and Sunday brunch noon–2:30 PM, dinner 6–11 PM. Four stars from Mobil? Well deserved. Right off the main lobby of the sumptuous Pierre luxury hotel, this ultra-classy room of yellow, green, and gold hues—not to mention Italian marble and mirrors, and silk, satin, and bronze—is a stage set with the finest china, chairs, art, and soothing live music every night. You might expect standard French or New American fare, but you might be surprised: The chef takes some chances, and succeeds. Lunch starts with pumpkin soup and chicken liver toast, lobster bisque with a corn flan, ceviche, salad, or one of the inventive pasta dishes such as whole wheat penne with fried chickpeas and chanterelles or perhaps linguine with Dungeness crab, jalapeño peppers, and parsley. For dinner, try a poached lobster salad, grilled halibut, roast cod or chicken, steak mignons with glazed figs and pepper sauce, or grilled lamb chops with asparagus, shaved Reggiano cheese, and balsamic vinegar. Finish with one of the good desserts— flourless chocolate cake sided with pistachio panna cotta and blood

orange sauce, warmed plum cake with ginger ice cream and elderflower syrup, watermelon and lychee soup, a grilled apple Bavarian with apple sorbet and Calvados sauce, or lemon panna cotta with sautéed peaches.

Dinner could start with the equally impressive roast sea scallops, a smoked salmon roulade with lobster, mango, and hearts of palm, pan-seared foie gras with a rhubarb compote, or simply spaghettini with a truffle cream sauce. The entrées run to roasted and grilled snapper, tuna, halibut, and the like, sided with tapenade or a cardamom sauce, perhaps; lobster *Americaine* (sautéed meat, served with brandy and tarragon sauce); roast veal chops; rack of lamb; and beef tenderloin. Accompany it with fine wines or a glass of champagne. The dessert menu is similar to that at lunch, with additional winners such as a warm apple tart with crème Anglaise sauce, a honeydew melon mousse, a daily soufflé, or a piña colada parfait served with macadamia nut crisps. Then there's brunch—it's *much* more interesting than the usual hotel brunch, with starters like crabmeat flan, grilled corn chowder, quail egg and dandelion salads, house-cured salmon, penne with short ribs and chanterelles, and steak tartare. Main courses might include lobster hash cakes, linguine with clam sauce, frittata, apricot-stuffed roast chicken, and French toast made with Italian panettone pastry and served with cherry sauce. Still have room? Finish your brunch with a buttermilk panna cotta and blueberry soup, strawberry sorbet shortcake, a cherry *clafouti* with almond ice cream, a gratin of bittersweet chocolate, or just home-style rice pudding beside some apples poached in rum. You'll even find a full Japanese breakfast and a children's menu—nice unexpected touches. Jackets are required of men at dinnertime, of course—save this place for a grand occasion.

The Carlyle Restaurant (212-744-1600), 35 East 76th Street at the corner of Madison Avenue. Subway: 6 train to 77th Street. Open daily for breakfast 7–10:30 AM, lunch and brunch noon–3 PM, dinner 6–11 PM. The Carlyle hotel's restaurant is an extremely elegant dining room of overstuffed chairs and frilly touches, a good place to savor chef James Sakatos's dependable French fare. Meals run to game, lobster, fish dishes, and chicken and beef in rich sauces, and the kitchen's especially strong on desserts—though a dinner here is really more about the starched-shirt atmosphere than the food. If you're young and hip (or wish you were), you might not like it.

Daniel (212-288-0033), 60 East 65th Street between Madison and Park avenues. Subway: F train to Lexington Avenue–63rd Street, or 6 train to 68th Street. Open Monday through Saturday 5:45–11 PM. Daniel Boulud has taken Manhattan. Where other French chefs have tried and failed to start an empire, Boulud—former chef at the Hotel Plaza Athénée and at famous Le Cirque—has done it. He runs three of the city's most prized eateries today, including this one, his baby, which remains one of the city's undisputed top five restaurants (and occupies the site of the former Le Cirque). Daniel opened in 1993 in a different location as Boulud's first private venture. It moved in 1998 when Le Cirque headed to the New York

Palace Hotel, and has since garnered top honors from the food press, including four stars from *The New York Times.* The multi-course prix fixe menus ($96–$175 per person, depending on the number of courses) that take center stage in a room decorated with Italian touches evocative of the architecture in Boulud's hometown of Lyon, France: 18-foot ceilings, bronze doors, Italian Renaissance lines, and a muted yellow, blue, and wine-red color scheme.

Whether you go à la carte or off the prix fixe menu, meals will be an adventure. Dinner could start with a crab salad, Thai-curried lobster, sea scallops, Jerusalem artichoke soup, pumpkin soup with crispy pumpkin seeds, mussels gratinéed with herbs, almond, ham, and fava beans, toasted lobster, Boulud's house-smoked salmon, Carolina shrimp in curry cream with apple chutney, a creamy shrimp-carrot soup, or a foie gras terrine with apples, shallots, cider, and walnuts. The fabulous main courses might include sea bass cooked in a crispy potato shell and served with a Syrah wine sauce; skate stuffed with chanterelles, served with creamed spinach; pistachio-crusted rack of lamb with a fruit saffron; short ribs braised in wine and sided with a piece of peppery filet mignon; braised cod; roast peppered tuna; or a simply roasted chicken with foie gras—or seasonal specialties such as wild pheasant and other game in winter. Finish with a fruit, cheese, or other desserts such as chocolate-praline millefeuille, grapefruit Melba, *pain perdu* topped with mango (served with orange ice cream and marmalade), a mandarin orange sorbet with ginger meringue and chestnut ice cream, roasted caramelized pineapple with vanilla and piña colada sauce, and a hot chocolate upside-down soufflé with pistachio ice cream. There's also a bar menu that's just as good (and nearly as pricey). There's even a complete vegetarian menu strong on risotto, root vegetables, and salads.

Daniel is open later than most top-rated places, but you should still try to make reservations a month in advance of coming to the city. When you come, remember that there's a dress code; men must wear a jacket, and would feel out of place anyway without one in such a regal space. But that hardly matters. A dining experience in this Venetian Renaissance-style dining room, beneath arched columns and graceful tables, is sublime; don't miss it.

Etats-Unis (212-517-8826), 242 East 81st Street between Second and Third avenues. Subway: 4, 5, or 6 train to 86th Street, or 6 train to 77th Street. Open daily 6–10:30 PM for dinner. This restaurant, pronounced *ay-TAHZ-you-KNEES*—it's French for "U.S.A."—is as much of a family act as you'll find in New York. Owner Tom Rapp (an architect who helped design the romantic, grown-up space) and son Jonathan have created a distinctive room that succeeds at upscale New American cuisine without compromising on price or quality, or attempting to be the least bit showy. The dining room is tightly packed (the only drawback), but the dinner menu is clean and spare: entrées ($20–30 each) of shellfish, lobster, chops, ribs, nothing too frightening to the American palate. But this is no chain steak house; preparations are fresh and

innovative, finished off with outstanding vegetables, sauces, and simple yet creative dessert items. The Rapps couldn't fit a bar in here, so they did the next best thing—created one across the street, another fine place to eat (see Bar@Etats-Unis under *Eating Out*). All in all, this is one of the Upper East Side's nicest surprises, a wonderful dining experience tourists don't know and New Yorkers appreciate. It's just a pity the room is too small to handle more tables.

540 Park (212-339-4050), 540 Park Avenue at the corner of East 61st Street. Subway: F train to Lexington Avenue–63rd Street, 4, 5, or 6 train to 59th Street, or N, R, or W train to Lexington Avenue–59th Street. Open daily 7 AM–1 AM. It's rare that I've recommended a place in this book that doesn't serve dinner, but 540 Park really doesn't—just some of the richest-blood breakfasts in town, plus light lunches and (upscale) bar snacks until late-night. Why come? The rarefied breakfast here at the Regency Hotel is a uniquely New York spectacle. How important is an early bite at 540 Park for the city's movers and shakers? Well, you'll be surrounded by suits you can't afford, the latest cell phones, and maybe even a famous face or two; the air is thick with deals done and to be done. Can't imagine guys in, say, LA getting up this early just to eat and haggle. The food's good, too.

JoJo (212-223-5656), 160 East 64th Street between Lexington Avenue and Third Avenue. Subway: F train to Lexington Avenue–59th Street, or 6 train to 68th Street. Open daily for lunch 11:30–4 PM and dinner 5:30–11 PM; Sunday brunch noon–2:30. This longtime favorite of confident celebrity chef Jean-Georges Vongerichten has new carpets, romantic lighting, a new paint job, and a host of other fixes to two floors of the 64th Street town house it occupies. But the menu, which some food writers have criticized for its stasis over time, didn't change all that much—and no wonder; it remains stellar. Before there was a Vong (see *Dining Out* in chapter 7), Vongerichten was tinkering here with a wondrous, curious fusion of Asian ideas with French ones: blending potatoes, shrimp, duck, steak, tuna, venison, soy sauce, herbs, vegetable stocks, hot spices, and butter in ways nobody had dreamed possible. He's one of the few chefs in town about whom it can be said, without hyperbole, that every bite is an adventure. Desserts are not one bit a letdown, either—the signature molten chocolate cake Vongerichten claims to have invented is one of the stars, but not the only one. The atmosphere here is the final touch; ask to be seated on the bottom level if you're wanting to experience a sublime, romantic dinner.

Mark's (212-879-1864), 25 East 77th Street between Fifth and Madison avenues. Subway: 6 train to 77th Street. Open daily for breakfast 7–10:30 AM, lunch and Sunday brunch 11:30 AM–2:30 PM, afternoon tea 2:30–5:30 PM, dinner 6–10 PM. In The Mark hotel's elegant dining room, the kitchen lays out French-inflected dinners of grilled local foie gras (served with a summery corn relish), cannelloni stuffed with Maine lobster, capped with a lobster foam, and dusted with pepper, or squab roasted on planks of oak and sided with potatoes, chanterelles, and asparagus tips. Or

simply try the warmed Coach Farm goat cheese salad with apples and walnuts. The house "tea master" and wine sommelier can guide you to the proper tea or libation choice to match your meal perfectly, and a skilled pastry chef completes the experience; it's all somehow appropriate in a split-level room of gorgeous woods and leather, with some of the city's best waiters achieving just the right balance of professionalism, respect, and knowledge without crossing the line into fussiness. But bring the platinum card—even a prix fixe "bargain" starts at around $60 per person. Sunday brunches and afternoon teas here are also justly praised, and a good way to experience the kitchen's work less expensively.

Nino's (212-988-0002), 1354 First Avenue between East 72nd and East 73rd streets. Subway: 6 train to 68th or 77th Street. Open Monday through Friday for lunch noon–4 PM and dinner 5 PM–midnight, weekends for dinner only. This fun, upbeat place—there's piano music and much toasting going on—seems like a good-time trattoria, but the food's better and classier than that. Lunch could start with carpaccio of beef, grilled portobello mushrooms, or fresh buffalo mozzarella; a pasta dish such as penne with veal, spinach-ricotta ravioli, or linguine with clams; or gnocchi or duck risotto. Main courses (about $19–25 each at lunch, $25–30 at dinner) are surprisingly sophisticated—salmon, grilled tuna or swordfish, roast chicken, rack of lamb with two sauces, a quail stuffed with shredded duck served with polenta cake, or rack of veal over fried potatoes. There's also a famously huge, spicy lobster for two that you pick from a tank for around $59–69. The excellent waitstaff and masculine, jovial atmosphere enhance the meal.

Payard Bistro (212-717-5252), 1032 Lexington Avenue near the corner of East 74th Street. Subway: 6 train to 68th or 77th Street. Open Monday through Saturday for lunch noon–3 PM, tea service 3:30–5 PM, and dinner 5:45–10:30 PM, weekends to 11 PM. Attached to François Payard's renowned patisserie (see *Coffee and Snacks*), chef Philippe Bertineau's stunning kitchen features a menu of classic French cooking—and he comes by it honestly: He arrived at this post after 4 years of sous-chef time with star Daniel Boulud at Daniel (see above). Lunch might start with duck terrine or a twice-baked cheese soufflé, then continue with salad or a main course (around $23–25 each) of bouillabaisse, risotto, beef tartare, or hanger steak with fries. Dinner adds such items as foie gras, sautéed cod, peppercorn steak, roast venison or chicken, and braised lamb shank but is priced roughly the same as lunch. Finish either meal with pumpkin crème brûlée, chestnut and pear pyramid, passion fruit gratin, or a fruit dish. As a bonus, there's also a surprising afternoon tea service each day ($19–24 per person)—featuring, of course, those scrumptious pastries.

EATING OUT Bar@Etats-Unis (212-396-9928), 242 East 81st Street between Second and Third avenues. Open Monday through Saturday noon–midnight, Sunday 5 PM–midnight. Across the street from the Tom Rapp–owned Etats-Unis (see *Dining Out*), which has no bar of its own, this secret East Side star serves inexpensive meals cooked in the very same kitchen. That's right: The vegetables, sauces, and meats are first prepared at Etats-Unis, then carefully ferried across busy 81st Street in batches, where another cook reconstitutes and assembles them into full, still-fresh meals. Good choices include the Caesar salad, beef stew, terrine, and a daily fish special. There are also lots of wines, served by knowledgeable waiters. It's a great place to go when you're in the neighborhood, need a great bite and a drink, but can't get into popular Etats-Unis.

Café Sabarsky (212-288-0665), 1048 Fifth Avenue at the corner of East 86th Street. Subway: 4, 5, or 6 train to 86th Street. Open Monday and Wednesday 9 AM–6 PM, Thursday through Sunday to 9 PM. Can't make it to Salzburg for that *Sound of Music* package tour this year? Fear not. Housed inside the Neue Galerie (see *To See—Museums*), chef Kurt Gutenbrunner's (of Wallsé; see *Dining Out* in chapter 4) venture succeeds marvelously at giving New York a world-class museum café—and a truly Viennese café—for the first time. And I love the place. Expect terrific Austrian coffee and tortes, plus goulash, schnitzel, and all the rest of the Austrian favorites you only dreamed you might one day sample here in New York. Yet he does it with a lighter touch than his countrymen. Occasionally, the café—which was named for museum cofounder Serge Sabarsky, in case you're wondering—also offers a special dinnertime service that's well worth catching if you can possibly book a table (which is iffy). Even lunch or just a coffee, though, is a calming experience amid furniture by Adolf Loos and the genuine Austrian fixtures and fabrics.

Candle Café (212-472-0970), 1307 Third Avenue at the corner of East 75th Street. Subway: 6 train to 77th Street. Open Monday to Saturday 11:30 AM–10:30 PM, Sunday to 9:30 PM. Normally I steer well clear of places serving drinks with names like Green Goddess, but the Candle Café actually manages to combine a bit of fine-dining ethic with its healthy vegetarian menu. Alongside the juices and smoothies, the café serves dumplings, stir-fries, salads, bean chilis, and fuller entrées (priced $8–16 each) such as a tomatoey lasagna with a tempeh ragout and tofu ricotta. The grilled *seitan* steaks with caramelized onions aren't half bad, either, and there's also a macrobiotic platter of brown rice, vegetables, beans, and sea vegetables; a tofu club sandwich of grilled tofu, tempeh bacon, lettuce, and sprouts; grilled soy burgers; tempeh-portobello *paninis;* or a sandwich of *seitan* and soy mozzarella. You can also order side dishes like basmati rice, roasted potatoes, coleslaw, and blue corn–quinoa corn bread to fill out your meal. Finish with a fruit crumb pie, pumpkin tofu cheesecake, chocolate mousse pie (egg-free, I'm assuming), or soy ice cream sundae and feel smug that you've eaten both healthy *and* well.

Lexington Candy Shop (212-288-0057), 1226 Lexington Avenue at the corner of East 83rd Street. Subway: 4, 5, or 6 train to 86th Street. Open Monday through Saturday 7 AM–7 PM, Sunday 9 AM–6 PM. It's just another tiny corner luncheonette, but it's got more character than most, and local families love the place. Go for the burgers and an egg cream or some other sort of ice cream treat, and don't be surprised by the sticker shock when the tab turns out to be higher than you wish—this is the Upper East Side, after all. At least they still jerk the sodas in the time-tested, right way: at the counter, at the last minute.

♪ **one fish two fish** (212-369-5677), 1399 Madison Avenue at the corner of East 97th Street. Subway: 6 train to 96th Street. Open daily for lunch and dinner. It's nothing fancy, but the Pollak brothers (yes, really) serve fish all ways here; the place resembles nothing so much as a New England seafood chain, with its $3 chowders, burger plates, shrimp dishes, pasta, lobster combinations ($15–24), grilled scallops, fish dishes ($10–14), and kids' menu. Each entrée comes with garlic bread and limitless green salad, a nice touch. You can order milk shakes and choose from a standard list of pies and sundaes for dessert. There's also a cheap, filling brunch, drinks included. Come for quantity.

♦ **Pio Pio** (212-426-5800), 1746 First Avenue between East 90th and East 91st streets. Subway: 4, 5, or 6 train to 86th Street. Open daily 11 AM–11 PM. When you stumble into a nearly unknown place like this and are wowed by the food, you probably think (like I do), "New York should have more of these places." Well, relax; it does. Only trouble is, most of them are buried deep in Queens, the Bronx, or Long Island. That's what happens when anyone sticks around the big city for a little while—sooner or later, they begin tiring of the grind and heading out in search of front yards, fresh air, and half-decent public schools. But Pio Pio, for now, keeps a foothold on the Upper East (with two anchors in Queens, naturally). The specialty is spice-rubbed grilled chickens, served with fries or rice, and that's really all you need to know about the place. This isn't exactly budget eating, though—the decor and food are too good to qualify for hole-in-the-wall status, and that's just one more glorious reason to find the place.

Sarabeth's (212-570-3670), 945 Madison Avenue at the corner of East 75th Street. Subway: 6 train to 77th Street. Open Tuesday 11 AM–3:30 PM, and Wednesday through Friday 11 AM–4:30 PM, weekends 10 AM–4:30 PM. Inside the Whitney Museum of American Art, a branch of this popular West Side bakery-café doles out outstanding brunches and fine-dining lunches and dinners of lamb, steak, fish, and so forth. Brunch is the real star; come early. There's a second Upper East Side location up Madison Avenue at No. 1295, between East 92nd and East 93rd streets (212-410-7335), which is more remote but carries the advantage of opening earlier for breakfast and brunch—at 8 each morning—and also staying open much later (until about 10:30 each night except Sunday, when it closes an hour earlier).

🍴 ✎ **Serendipity 3** (212-838-3531), 225 East 60th Street between Second and Third avenues. Subway: F train to 63rd Street–Lexington Avenue, N, R, or W train to 59th Street–Lexington Avenue, or 4, 5, or 6 train to 59th Street. Open daily 11:30 AM–midnight, Friday to 1 AM, Saturday to 2 AM. There's nothing so New York as a sweets shop, and Serendipity is one of the nicest. They serve meals ($5–17) here such as steaks, chicken sandwiches, a range of interesting burgers—including a caviar burger—salmon, sole, veggie chili, corn and clam chowders, an interesting choice of omelets, French toast, chicken pot-pie, even meat loaf. But almost everyone comes for the sweets, especially the $6.50 signature drink, frozen hot chocolate, as well as hot fudge sundaes, banana splits, pies, and ice cream concoctions. The teas and coffees are top rate as well. Founder and longtime boss Stephen Bruce is legend for his work on charity and benefit events. And talk about star power: This eatery actually had a movie (the John Cusack-starring *Serendipity*) written about it, and it wasn't even terrible; Marilyn Monroe and Andy Warhol were early patrons (it's been here more than 45 years), and fellow diners today might include the likes of Jerry Seinfeld, Cher, Meg Ryan, Yoko Ono, John Travolta, former city mayor Rudy Giuliani, Ron Howard, and/or magician David Copperfield. Try not to gape.

Via Quadronno (212-650-9880), 25 East 73rd Street between Fifth and Madison avenues. Subway: 6 train to 68th or 77th Street. Open weekdays 8 AM–11 PM, Saturday from 9 AM, Sunday 10 AM–9 PM. I'm showing my cards here, but this is one of my favorite midpriced Italian cafés in the city thanks to the right atmosphere and some of the city's best espresso and cappuccino. Owner Paolo della Puppa runs a tight ship of nice tables, good Italian meals and service, and great coffee and sweets. It's also notable for being open three meals a day, plus late at night. Mornings or at lunchtime, order a light Italian breakfast of *bombolone* (a kind of cream doughnut), something from the selection of pressed *panini* sandwiches, a croissant, or even just a plain glass of milk or freshly squeezed orange juice. For dinner, start with antipasti, then try anything from the menu of *primi* (pastas, priced around $18–22 each) or *secondi* (meat, fish, and game dishes, around $30–36 apiece); della Puppa isn't shy about recommending the least-expensive thing on the menu, spaghetti with meat sauce, as the best. Wash it down with a glass of red or white wine. Dessert contains a fuller-than-usual assortment of Italian cookies and sweets, including changing daily specials like an espresso profiterole cake, a pumpkin tart with pumpkin mousse, a Saint-Honoré cake of chocolate, vanilla sponge, and Chantilly cream, a coffee plum cake, the Verona cake (something like a Sacher torte), and one real surprise—the Venetian-style tiramisu di San Dona, which (so far as I can tell) isn't served anywhere else in the United States.

COFFEE AND SNACKS H&H Midtown Bagels East (212-717-7312), 1551 Second Avenue near the corner of East 81st Street. Subway: 6 train to 77th Street, or 4 or 5 train to 86th Street. Open daily. Some of the city's best bagels are served by H&H, which has other outlets in Hell's Kitchen and the Upper West Side. The bagels are puffy and sweet—and most New Yorkers seem to think that's just the way they should be.

Payard Patisserie (212-717-5252), 1032 Lexington Avenue near the corner of East 74th Street. Subway: 6 train to 68th or 77th Street. François Payard's patisserie is the city's best, say Upper East Side devotees. Yes, there's a bistro serving good French meals (see *Dining Out*) and a full selection of mousses, Sachers, madeleines, napoleons, éclairs, millefeuilles, and opera cakes. But Payard's signature patisserie is where the real action is. His creations range from the wild (the Montaigne features a berry mousse sandwiched amid a layer of milk chocolate, chocolate mousse, and Rice Krispies), to the pop-artsy (a Technicolor pistachio creation called the Chinon), to the modern-artsy (the Pont Neuf is an oval of chocolate mousse, topped with a swoosh of brownie and a hazelnut wafer), with some elegantly simple pastry thrown in for good measure: The Notre Dame is a tower of chocolate mousse, vanilla Bavarois, and chocolate biscuit. Notice a theme? Payard plays the texture and mouthfeel of mousse, ganache, and biscuit against each other like a composer, using only the finest French ingredients. All of the desserts are beautifully decorated and tasty.

Via Quadronno (212-650-9880), 25 East 73rd Street between Fifth and Madison avenues. Subway: 6 train to 68th or 77th Street. Open weekdays 8 AM–11 PM, Saturday from 9 AM, Sunday 10 AM–9 PM. Not just a good Italian restaurant, this café also serves dynamite espresso, cappuccino, and a full range of gelati, sorbetti, panna cotta, *semifreddo,* tiramisu, cheese with pear, apple- and raisin-spiked *campagnola* cakes, and fruit tarts. The desserts aren't cheap, but this is the Upper East Side, right? And they're good.

✷ Entertainment

THEATERS Playhouse 91 (212-307-4100 for tickets), 316 East 91st Street between First and Second avenues. Subway: 4, 5, or 6 train to 86th Street. Home to the Jewish Repertory Theatre, this 300-seat house is a good place to settle in for comedic theater such as *Menopause The Musical.*

♿ **Theater Ten Ten** (212-288-3246), 1010 Park Avenue between 84th and 85th streets. Subway: 4, 5, or 6 train to 86th Street. A bit hard to find (it's in the basement of the Park Avenue Christian Church), this theater is said to be the oldest off-off venue in the city. It opened in the 1960s and offers fun, serious, and thought-provoking fare—or sometimes all three at once, as in the case of *The Two Gentlemen of Verona,* a 1950s beach-blanket update of Shakespeare.

FILM City Cinemas 86th Street East (212-777-FILM, ext. 763), 219 East 86th Street between Second and Third avenues. Subway: 4, 5, or 6 train to 86th Street. Straightforward hit movies are screened here.

♿ **Clearview 62nd & Broadway** (212-777-FILM, ext. 864), 400 East 62nd Street at the corner of First Avenue. Subway: 4, 5, or 6 train to 59th Street, or N, R, or W train to Lexington Avenue–59th Street. All the expected big releases are shown at this theater—and it's handicapped-accessible.

Loews 72nd Street East (212-50-LOEWS, ext. 704), 1230 Third Avenue near the corner of East 71st Street. Subway: 6 train to 68th Street. This single-screen cinema close to the main artery of 72nd Street shows decent midlist Hollywood releases.

UA East 85th Street (212-249-5100), 1629 First Avenue at the corner of East 85th Street. Subway: 4, 5, or 6 train to 86th Street. This single-screen cinema shows second-run films from Hollywood; somehow it hangs on, as other cinemas get demolished all over town.

UA 64th Street and Second Avenue (212-832-1671), 1210 Second Avenue at the corner of East 64th Street. Subway: F train to Lexington Avenue–63rd Street, 4, 5, or 6 train to 59th Street, or N, R, or W train to Lexington Avenue–59th Street. Big Hollywood hits and new releases are featured here.

CULTURAL ORGANIZATIONS ♞ Asia Society and Museum (212-288-6400), 725 Park Avenue at the corner of East 70th Street. Subway: 6 train to 68th Street. Open Tuesday through Sunday 11 AM–6 PM, Friday until 9 PM. Frequent lectures and other programs introduce Asian cultures to New Yorkers and tourists alike. Admission costs $10 for adults, $7 seniors and students.

♞ ♿ **92nd Street Y** (212-415-5500; www.92Y.org), East 92nd Street at the corner of Lexington Avenue. Subway: 4, 5, or 6 train to 86th Street, or 6 train to 96th Street. Box office open Monday through Thursday 9 AM–7 PM, Friday 9 AM–5 PM, Sunday 10 AM–8 PM, Saturday only before performances 6–9 PM. One of New York's most active cultural organizations is—surprise—this huge Y tucked way uptown at Lex and 92nd. (There's also an adjunct at 35 West 67th Street near Lincoln Center, since the Y joined hands with the excellent Makor arts center; see *Entertainment* in chapter 11 for more details.) Founded in 1874 as the Young Men's and Young Women's Hebrew Association, the Y is famous throughout the city for its varied program of lectures—by writers, heads of state, celebrities, scholars, scientists, television personalities, and others—and affordable classes in art, music, writing, business, dating, nutrition, health, religion, and just about anything else you can imagine. The Y even arranges day hikes of surrounding mountains and travels to foreign lands. There's so much going on here that it's almost impossible to keep a handle on it; check local newspapers such as the *Village Voice* or *The New York Times* for the latest schedule of events. Note that the Y is closed on Jewish holidays such as the first 2 and last 2 days of Passover (usually in April).

BARS AND CLUBS ❧ **Bemelmans Bar** (212-744-1600), 35 East 76th Street at the corner of Madison Avenue. Subway: 6 train to 77th Street. Open daily, noon–1 AM. Named for the muralist and book illustrator (of *Madeline*) whose work graces its walls, the posh Carlyle hotel's other piano bar—a good deal less expensive than the adjacent Café Carlyle (see below)—is one of the East Side's nicest places to take a loved one for a quiet cocktail or celebratory glass of something bubbly. The cover is usually around $10 per person.

Café Carlyle (212-744-1600), 35 East 76th Street at the corner of Madison Avenue. Subway: 6 train to 77th Street. Open Monday through Wednesday 6:30–10 PM, Thursday through Saturday 6:30 PM–midnight. The Carlyle hotel's café featured pianist Bobby Short for more than three decades until he passed away in 2005. Other

luminous performers have taken over, and even Woody Allen drops in often to play clarinet. Really (see www.woodyallenband.com for schedule). Dress nicely and bring your wallet.

Feinstein's at the Regency (212-339-4095), 540 Park Avenue at the corner of East 61st Street. Subway: F train to Lexington Avenue–63rd Street, 4, 5, or 6 train to 59th Street, or N, R, or W train to Lexington Avenue–59th Street. Open Tuesday through Saturday at 6 PM, first show at 8:30 PM, later show Friday and Saturday at 11 PM. By day a power-breakfast restaurant, this space becomes at night one of the more popular cabaret spaces on the east side of the city. Cover charges are steep, however.

✳ Selective Shopping

FASHION **Michael's** (212-737-7273), 1041 Madison Avenue (second floor) between East 79th and East 80th streets. Subway: 6 train to 77th Street. Open Monday through Saturday 9:30 AM–6 PM, to 8 PM Thursday; closed weekends in July and August. Yes, it's a consignment store—but this place, which has been around for almost 50 years now, is about as far away from the East Village's recycled vintage jeans and cowboy shirts as you could possibly get. Instead, look for barely worn women's wear of the highest pedigree: dresses and accessories from the likes of Armani, Chanel, Hermes, Prada, Valentino, and Gucci. This store is especially renowned for its selection of (presumably once-worn) wedding gowns.

MUSEUM STORES **AsiaStore** (212-327-9217), 725 Park Avenue at the corner of East 70th Street. Subway: 6 train to 68th Street. Open daily

11 AM–6 PM, Friday until 9 PM. The museum store of the respected Asia Society is a sleek, modern showroom of Asian books, CDs, furnishings, and gift items. It's a great place to browse for a unique teapot, print, decorative item, hard-to-find volume, or distinctive piece of jewelry. The store is located in the lobby of the Park Avenue museum.

Guggenheim Museum Store (212-423-3615), 1071 Fifth Avenue at the corner of East 89th Street. Subway: 4, 5, or 6 train to 86th Street. Open Saturday through Wednesday 9:30 AM–6:15 PM, Thursday 11 AM–6 PM, Friday 9:30 AM–8:30 PM. This is the museum store for the distinctively curvilinear modern art museum.

The Met Store (212-570-3894 or 1-800-468-7386), 1000 Fifth Avenue at the corner of 82nd Street. Subway: 5 train to 77th Street, or 4, 5, or 6 train to 86th Street. Open Tuesday through Thursday 9:30 AM–5:30 PM, Friday and Saturday to 9 PM, Sunday 9:30 AM–5:30 PM. No, it's not the New York Mets store. Located just off the vast Museum of Metropolitan Art's Great Hall—with additional branches elsewhere in the museum—the Met's popular museum store sells prints, books, photos, and other gift items.

National Academy of Design Museum Shop (212-369-4880), 1083 Fifth Avenue at the corner of East 89th Street. Subway: 4, 5, or 6 train to 86th Street. Open Tuesday through Thursday 10 AM–5 PM, Friday to 6 PM, Saturday and Sunday 11 AM–6 PM. The National Academy's in-house store is open even when the museum isn't (Monday and Tuesday), offering gifts, cards, the academy's own books and catalogs, and even some original works by academy members.

Neue Galerie Bookstore/Design Shop (212-628-6200), 1048 Fifth Avenue at the corner of East 86th Street. Subway: 4, 5, or 6 train to 86th Street. Open Wednesday through Monday 11 AM–6 PM, Friday to 9 PM. The Neue Galerie's shop sells more than books—you can also pick up Austrian- and German-designed gift items.

Whitney Museum Store (212-570-3614), 945 Madison Avenue at the corner of East 75th Street. Subway: 6 train to 77th Street. Open Tuesday 11 AM–4:30 PM, Wednesday and Thursday 11 AM–6 PM, Friday 1–9 PM, Saturday and Sunday 11 AM–6 PM. The impressive Whitney Museum's store is the place to pick up calendars, prints, and other gift items related to the museum's holdings of American art.

UPPER EAST SIDE STREET CORNER
Paul Karr

✳ Special Events

January: **Winter Antiques Show,** Park Avenue at the corner of East 67th Street. Subway: 6 train to 68th Street. This charity show brings some of the nation's top dealers to the Seventh Regiment Armory and takes a bit of the chill off the Manhattan winter. Admission costs $20, but includes a nice catalogue.

🌹 *June:* **Museum Mile Festival** (212-606-2296), Fifth Avenue. Subway: 4, 5, or 6 train to 86th Street. This unbeatable combination of free events and free admission to all of the big Fifth Avenue museums happens only once a year, and it's always on a Tuesday in June, but if you're in town it's a must-attend.

July: **Music in the Garden** (212-289-4100), 316 East 88th Street between First and Second avenues. Subway: 4, 5, or 6 train to 86th Street. This garden concert series takes place at the Church of the Holy Trinity on Wednesday nights in July, beginning at 7:15 PM. Usually it consists of chamber music.

Upper West Side 11

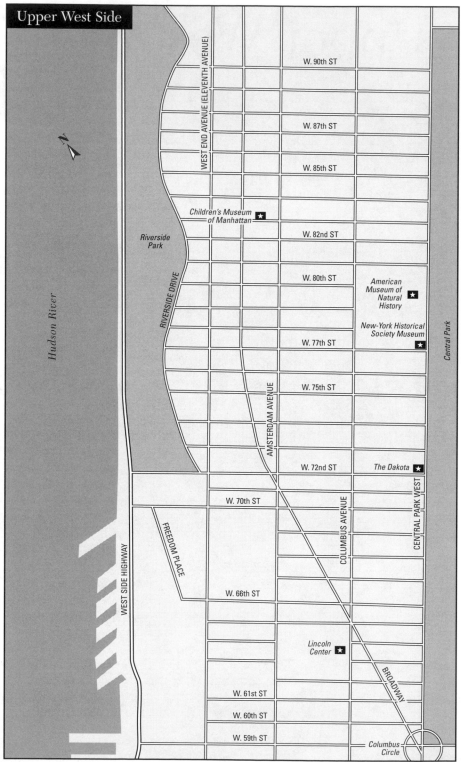

Upper West Side

W. 90th ST
W. 87th ST
W. 85th ST

WEST END AVENUE (ELEVENTH AVENUE)

Children's Museum of Manhattan

Riverside Park

W. 82nd ST

RIVERSIDE DRIVE

W. 80th ST

American Museum of Natural History

New-York Historical Society Museum

W. 77th ST

W. 75th ST

AMSTERDAM AVENUE

Hudson River

W. 72nd ST

The Dakota

W. 70th ST

COLUMBUS AVENUE

CENTRAL PARK WEST

Central Park

FREEDOM PLACE

W. 66th ST

WEST SIDE HIGHWAY

Lincoln Center

W. 61st ST
W. 60th ST
W. 59th ST

BROADWAY

Columbus Circle

UPPER WEST SIDE

Running from the southern edge of Central Park, at 59th Street, up to the park's northern boundary at 110th Street, the Upper West Side is perhaps New York's most interesting neighborhood. Why? I'm not exactly sure. It's a place characterized by sprawling green space, distinctive and diverse ethnic populations, fine residential architecture, a selection of restaurants (both highbrow and lowbrow), outstanding specialty markets and gourmet food shops, some of the city's finest bagels, and much more. This isn't a district of haute couture or haute cuisine, not exactly: Rather, it's a mostly residential place where people love to prowl the wide sidewalks and cross streets, eating anything and everything from knishes to hot dogs to pad Thai.

The neighborhood's boundaries expand depending on whom you ask; some residents of the Columbia University neighborhood, more than 50 blocks north, count themselves West Siders, though that's probably stretching things a bit. Nobody argues over its other borders, however: the Hudson River to the west and Central Park's lush expanse to the east form distinct, attractive bookends for the district. Hard though it may be to believe, this was once entirely farmland—and, before that, contested woodland. Native American tribes scuffled with Dutch settlers for a time over control of the area; by the early 18th century the Dutch had begun systematically clearing and planting the area, then called Bloomingdale—a British adaptation of "flowery valley" in Dutch. They laid out a several-mile-long road (now known as Broadway) to connect the thriving mercantile district of Lower Manhattan with their farms, and within a century downtown merchants were building summer homes in the neighborhood as well.

Two moments shaped the area's geography most decisively. The first was the creation of Central Park in 1853 by the architect Frederick Law Olmsted (see chapter 9). An uncoordinated patchwork of farmland, woods, shacks, homes, and churches was cleared away—not without some controversy—and replaced by one of the world's largest and most intriguing urban parks, which rambles some 60 blocks north from 59th Street (renamed Central Park South for the brief stretch where it bounds the park). The second moment was the subsequent extension, in 1870, of New York's elevated subway tracks to the neighborhood. The addition of public transit drew the Upper West Side even closer to the city, both physically and emotionally, and grandiose high-rise apartment buildings in art deco style soon began shooting up both along the park and the other avenues of Amsterdam, Columbus, West Side, and Riverside.

In the 1890s Columbia University relocated from the East Side to Morningside Heights, taking over the grounds of the Bloomingdale Lunatic Asylum and injecting a much-needed vitality into the district. Much later some of the city's richest offerings were concentrated under one complex when Lincoln Center was unveiled in the 1950s, again replacing a downtrodden neighborhood (and once again ruffling feathers).

Walking the streets, it quickly becomes apparent that Jewish residents form the backbone of the neighborhood: You're never far from a bagel shop or synagogue. (Stand-up comedian Jerry Seinfeld has long called the Upper West Side his turf, drawing his pointed observations of the banal mostly from, in his words, walking up and down Columbus and Broadway.) Yet the neighborhood also contains large numbers of Eastern European, Russian, and Hispanic residents.

GETTING THERE *By car:* Reach this neighborhood from the north by using the West Side Highway (an extension of the Henry Hudson Parkway); get off at the 79th Street–Boat Basin exit. Parking here is difficult but not impossible, though you must check signs on residential streets carefully to avoid a ticket on street-sweeping day. At the right times you can find open meters along Amsterdam and Columbus avenues. Weekends are very tight.

By subway: The fastest way to get here from downtown by subway is to take an express 2 or 3 train to 72nd or 86th Street; you can reach many of the places listed below from these stations. You will need to take a local 1 train for certain destinations such as Lincoln Center. Two important hub stations near the Upper West Side are 42nd Street–Times Square and 59th Street–Columbus Circle; if you can reach one of those, you're almost home. Remember that, from the A, B, C, or D trains, you can change at the circle to a 1 train.

By bus: There are several useful routes, including the handy 5 bus up and down Riverside Drive (it runs from Harlem to Greenwich Village), the trusty 10 bus up and down Central Park West (running from Harlem to Penn Station), the popular 104 bus heading up and down Broadway to and from 42nd Street, and the one–two punch of the 7 and 11 buses running north along Amsterdam and south along Columbus to and from, respectively, Union Square and Chelsea.

✳ To See

MUSEUMS ✎ ♿ **American Museum of Natural History** (212-769-5100; www.amnh.org), Central Park West at West 79th Street. Subway: B or C train to 79th Street. Open daily 10 AM–5:45 PM. This huge museum may seem a bit outdated in places, but it's undeniably attractive to kids—exhibitions like a 94-foot blue whale model, skulls, skeletons, meteorites, simulated tropical forests and oceans, and the like. It is certainly diverse in its science and environmental exhibits, easily worth half a day if you've brought the kids. Among the highlights: great gemstone collections and fossilized dinosaur bones reconstructed into impressive mockups of what those roaming giants must have looked like. Other exhibits play up the interactive angle, albeit in old-fashioned style.

For my money, though, the rotating exhibitions here are far more interesting than the diorama-based permanent collection rooms. Recent exhibits have highlighted the lives and work of Darwin and Einstein, the history of baseball, landscape photography, and Vietnam, among other topics. The Rose Center for Earth and Space, featuring the Hayden Planetarium, is also interesting—it features space shows narrated by Tom Hanks and Harrison Ford, and in 2003 presented an exhibit of striking Apollo mission photographs. There's one entrance on the Central Park side, with stairs that are popular for hanging out and chatting in nice weather, and a second smaller entrance (with shorter lines) at 77th and Columbus. Admission here is by donation; the suggested contribution is $14 for adults, $10.50 for students and senior citizens, and $8 for children ages 2 to 12. Combination tickets allowing admission to the planetarium's popular space shows or IMAX films are also available, costing more.

✂ ᜪ **Children's Museum of Manhattan** (212-721-1234; www.cmom.org), 170 Central Park West, between 76th and 77th streets. Subway: B or C train to 81st Street, or 1 train to 79th Street. Summer, open Tuesday through Sunday 10 AM–5 PM; closed Tuesday from mid-September to June. Easy to miss down a side street a few blocks off Central Park, this kids' museum offers five floors of exhibits and special programs focusing on books, basic science, and the arts for both infants and children. Recent additions include a theater space and an expanded ecology area outdoors. Even grown-ups might learn something from exhibitions such as Chagall for Children or in the live television studio. Admission to the museum costs $8 for adults and children, $5 for senior citizens.

🏛 ✂ ᜪ **New-York Historical Society Museum** (212-873-3400), 2 West 77th Street at the corner of Central Park West. Subway: B or C train to 77th Street, or 1, 2, or 3 train to 72nd Street. Open Tuesday through Sunday 10 AM–6 PM. New York's self-proclaimed oldest museum, the New-York Historical—the name is still hyphenated because the city and state names in fact once both were— resides in a solid, columned Greek Revival–style building facing Central Park. It's a smallish museum, one that can be capably visited in an hour or two, yet it holds surprisingly rich collections (more than 100 Tiffany lamps, for example); as such, this makes a great half-day stop when there isn't time to see the city's larger museums or the weather's not cooperating with plans for a picnic in the park.

THE AMERICAN MUSEUM OF NATURAL HISTORY'S FAMOUS *T. REX*

Kim Grant

The main floor is dominated by the open Great Hall and four galleries of various shapes and sizes, hosting rotating special exhibits; in 2002 the museum presented the first in a series of shows that will explore the impact of September 11 on New York's cityscape. This exhibit featured powerful, never-before-seen video footage of the attacks and their aftermath, as well as an extensive series of photographs from the Magnum photographers group documenting subsequent recovery efforts. An adjacent room held a history of the towers' construction, featuring period black-and-white photographs and architects' drawings paired with the museum's decades-old scale model cityscape of Manhattan—a model that could not be altered to remove the towers without damaging its integrity. The exhibit, then, was created as a kind of apologia.

Other bottom-floor rooms hold other rotating exhibits, such as a history of the Macy's parade and its floats (a lighter touch in a somber moment) or the work of social activist–folk artist Ralph Fasanella, a New York native whose Howard Finster–like paintings of northeastern baseball stadiums, mills, newspaper presses, and other workplaces speak powerfully and critically to the plight of the American working class. The second-floor research library, much beloved by area history scholars, is free and open to the public. It holds some 350,000 books; 2 million manuscripts; long-defunct city newspapers; and thousands of obscure maps and rare photographs documenting New York's changing urban landscapes, construction and restoration projects, and other spaces, plus much more. No space is wasted: Even this level's central corridor is hung with interesting exhibits, such as one tracing the history of neighborhood businesses (an Italian café, a sporting goods store, a linen firm, an engraver, and so forth).

Keep climbing, because the top level—officially known as the Henry Luce III Center for the Study of American Culture—holds some of the museum's finest treasures. It's here that the society shows, on a rotating basis, prints from its original (as in, *the* original) edition of John James Audubon's *The Birds of America.* You might find a gray jay holding court one month, a red-cockaded woodpecker the next; the museum has recently trimmed the number of Audubons it places on display at one time, however, for conservation purposes—the works are very sensitive to light—so you're unlikely to see more than four or five of Audubon's panels during any single visit to the city. Still, they're well worth a jaunt upstairs. That's not nearly all you'll find on this top floor, however; the meat of the museum's vast public holdings is also carefully archived here. There's a good collection of work by some of the Hudson River school painters, for instance, as well as historical portraits and extensive collections of buttons, coins, and military and fire-fighting memorabilia, among many other objects—all housed in a special series of cabinets. Overwhelmed by so much history crammed into one floor? Audio tours and a computer kiosk help orient you; inquire at the information desk.

There's also a small children's area in the basement known as Kid City, and a good little museum store. Admission costs $10 for adults, $5 for students and seniors; children under 12 enter free.

HISTORIC SITE **The Dakota,** Central Park West at the corner of West 72nd Street. Subway: B or C train to 72nd Street. This towering apartment building was constructed in the late 19th century, and was pathbreaking for its time—it was the first large uptown structure in what was then largely countryside. Many celebrities have lived there since, but the building is best known for the assassination of John Lennon at the gates to the building's 72nd Street parking lot in 1980; he is commemorated by his wife Yoko Ono in Central Park's Strawberry Fields section nearby (see chapter 9). By the way, The Dakota's equally grandiose neighbor, the San Remo, has been home to an equally awesome star list, including—but certainly not limited to—Apple computer cofounder Steve Jobs, U2 singer Bono, and actors Demi Moore, Bruce Willis, and Dustin Hoffman.

✳ Green Space

Central Park is perhaps the most interesting destination on the Upper West Side—and it's the Upper West Side's playground. This park is so big and wonderful that I have described it in its own chapter. See chapter 9 for a full discussion of the park's history, activities, and secrets.

Riverside Park (212-408-0264), between Riverside Drive and the Hudson River. Narrow, green River-

Kim Grant

THE DAKOTA

side Park stretches along the Hudson River's bank from West 72nd to West 155th Street. Park designer Frederick Law Olmsted laid out the park's design, which incorporates plenty of green space, trees, public sculpture, and recreational areas; scenes from the Tom Hanks–Meg Ryan film *You've Got Mail* were shot here to take advantage. There are volunteer-kept gardens at West 83rd Street, dog runs at West 72nd and West 87th streets, and a Cherry Walk north from West 100th Street. The park extends to Harlem; see the listing in Chapter 12 for further information.

✳ Lodging

LUXURIOUS HOTEL **Trump International Hotel** (212-299-1000 or 1-888-44-TRUMP; fax 212-299-1150), 1 Central Park West at Columbus Circle. Subway: A, B, C, D, or 1 train to 59th Street–Columbus Circle. Donald Trump's high-rise hotel may be the most luxurious lodging experience in New York, making up for its foreboding slablike exterior with unmatched service, amenities, dining . . . and prices. The 170 rooms and suites are incredibly spacious, and they're decked out like a millionaire's city pied-à-terre—fresh flowers, wooden armoire, work desk with fax machine and complimentary computer if you ask for one, hot tub in the marble bathroom, granite-countered kitchen with china and silver, even a small stocked bar. Big windows look out on Central Park across the street and the city skyline. The living room has an entertainment center with CD, DVD, and VCR player for guests' leisure, and the hotel issues you a cell phone, stationery with your name on it, and business cards for the duration of your trip. Bathrooms come equipped with bath salts; closets hold umbrellas and shopping bags; and naturally, the building also has a 55-foot lap pool, a health club with the very latest in high-tech fitness gear (such as an in-line skate trainer, weights, and resistance equipment), and a salon offering massage services, manicures, and a steam room.

But the real kicker here is the personal butler service. At least one staffer (known as your Trump Attaché) personally cleans your (and only your) room and Jacuzzi, sets out your (and only your) meals, and adjusts the telescope set out for your star- or park-gazing. The turndown service is so much more than chocolates on the pillow—your attaché lays out slippers and a robe on the bed, mineral water and crystal on a silver tray. And you simply cannot get better room service anywhere in New York than you can here: The hotel restaurant, Jean Georges, is already one of New York's four or five best (see *Dining Out*). But when one of the restaurant's chefs will actually come to your room and cook for you, 24 hours a day, whenever you pick up the phone . . . well, that is almost too much. All of this comes very, very expensively, of course. Weekday rates start at $525–575 per night for a standard or deluxe room, $800–1,650 for the one- and two-bedroom suites. Weekend rates are lower, though, and wintertime

might see the rates "dip" as low as $325–395 per night for a regular room or $500–950 per night for the suites. Special deals include honeymoon and romance packages.

BOUTIQUE HOTEL 🗝 🐾 **On the Ave.** (212-362-1100 or 1-800-497-6028; fax 212-787-9521), 2177 Broadway at the corner of West 77th Street. Subway: 1 train to 79th Street, or 2 or 3 train to 72nd Street. The "Ave." in question must be Broadway, because there isn't actually a named avenue until you get to Columbus and Amsterdam. Still, that's a minor quibble. This ultramodern hotel, right around the corner from Broadway, is easy to miss with its sleek exterior—but if you love modern design, you should consider it. Inside, it's somewhat like the minimalist boutique hotels of Midtown, only hewing to a bit more relaxed, more self-serve, less elaborate ethos. The cool delightful lobby is just like an art gallery, with square banquettes, original art on the softly lit walls, and not a rug or carpet in sight.

Regular double rooms are rather stripped down—think metal fixtures and furniture, polished floors, sleek surfaces, and furniture that looks like it came from a modern art design show. The penthouse-level rooms and suites are bigger and better, with Godiva coffee products and private balcony. (There's also a communal tiled balcony with potted plants and Adirondack chairs that everyone in the hotel can enjoy.) Business-class amenities have been added to all 200-plus rooms and 23 suites as well, such as high-speed Internet access, complimentary copies of *The New York Times,* good-quality toiletries, ironing board, and terry-cloth bathrobes.

Unusual for New York, pets and kids are both very welcome here (the hotel will provide babysitting on request). And some upper-floor rooms actually have glimpses of Central Park. Given the interesting decor of the place, and its unusually neighborhoody location, I'd rate this as a dark horse in Manhattan's lodging derby. Rooms used to be cheap, but today double room rates are now $300–425; the penthouse suites go for $495–995 per night, depending on room and time of week or year.

BUSINESS HOTEL 🐾 🐕 **The Phillips Club** (212-835-8800 or 1-877-854-8800; fax 212-835-8850), 155 West 66th Street between Broadway and Amsterdam. Subway: 1 train to 66th Street. An all-suite hotel of clean, modern lines just steps from Lincoln Center, the Phillips Club caters mostly to the upper-crust arts crowd—and that sometimes includes the world-renowned artists who perform at the center. (Half the 90 or so suites look out on the Juilliard School of Music, if that gives you some idea of the clientele, and more than half the guests here are long-stays.) Upstairs from the minimalist lobby, suite units are divided in half, each containing a narrowish living room, fully functioning marble-countered kitchen—a big bonus, and they've even thought to build in a working dishwasher—and an equally narrow bedroom. The big marble bathroom somewhat compensates. It really is like renting an expensive apartment in the city: There's a washer and dryer on each floor for doing laundry; you can bring your pet; pastas, ready-made meals, and other groceries can be delivered from the pricey Balducci's gourmet food store downstairs; and there's a

big-screen television with VCR, a CD player, and two-line phone. Downstairs you'll find the business center and several meeting rooms. One of the nicest perks here is entry to the chic Reebok Sports Club nearby, with its rock-climbing wall, three-lap pool (with underwater music), and spa. Rates begin at $400 per night for a small suite, $500 per night for a one-bedroom suite, and $1,000 per night for a two-bedroom suite, less in winter.

INNS **Country Inn the City** (212-580-4183; fax 212-874-3981), 270 West 77th Street between Broadway and West End Avenue. Subway: 1 train to 79th Street. Who would have guessed that New York boasted a top-flight bed & breakfast, plucked out of Vermont and tucked into an attractive residential pocket just steps from Lincoln Center? Yet it's true. This late-19th-century West Side brownstone conceals four one-room apartments furnished with four-poster queen bed, bright rugs, kitchenette, art prints, high-speed Internet access, and small living and dining areas. It's all simple, polished, and tasteful in an appealing, summer-home way—and with three of the city's top gourmet grocers (see *Selective Shopping*) just a few blocks away, you'll use that kitchen. The fridge is stocked for breakfast, phones have answering machines, and ceilings are high and airy; there is no nightly cleaning service, however, unless you stay at least 4 nights. (Unless you snag a last-minute opening, there's always a 3-night minimum stay here.) Rates here are very affordable given the quality of the accommodations, running $150–300 per night, and last-minute specials sometimes cut rates even further.

🏅 **Inn New York City** (212-580-1900 or 1-800-660-7051; fax 212-580-4437), 266 West 71st Street between Amsterdam and West End avenues. Subway: 1, 2, or 3 train to 72nd Street. No sign marks the spot, but New York's premier B&B awaits down another Upper West side street. Owner Ruth Mensch and daughter Elyn have designed an amazing Victorian wonderworld of period antiques, screens, art, pianos, whirlpools, and other surprises. Each of the four suites here is formal and crisp—you'll want to tread lightly on the furniture, antiques, and knick-knacks while staying, and families with children should stay elsewhere. For adults, though, it's pure indulgence. The long, narrow ground-floor Opera Suite contains a baby grand piano in the front (and they keep it tuned, too), plus fancy furnishings such as a bed with a stained-glass headboard, wood-burning fireplace, and flowery design touches—and French doors leading onto a private terrace. The second-floor spa suite is the most beautiful, featuring a cushy king bed, a walk-up hot tub in its own little windowed alcove, and a sauna; chestnut armoires, a barber's chair, a wicker lounge, cabinets of dolls, and a fireplace complete the experience.

There are two more suites as well, the homey Vermont on the ground floor—it has a private entrance, plus lots of oak and pine—and the big, skylit, high-ceilinged Library on the third floor with exposed brick and a comfy leather sofa. All rooms have modern conveniences, including phone, bathrobes, furnished galley kitchen, CD player, and VCR, and the fridge is stocked with wine, quiche, breakfast items, and other gourmet treats from Zabar's. Maids service the rooms daily, and newspapers are delivered each morning. The elaborate brass-and-marble bathrooms seem a bit tiny, but that's a small matter when you're staying in what is almost a country estate just steps from the only-in-New-York madness and wonder that is 72nd Street. Rates at the inn range from $375 to $475 per night for double occupancy of the Vermont Suite (curiously, fall and winter rates are highest) to $475 to $575 per night, double occupancy, for the other three suites. (Note that they tack on a $100 surcharge if you book only 1 night's stay, though.) It's truly one of the most remarkable lodging experiences in all New York.

AFFORDABLE HOTELS Comfort Inn Central Park West (212-721-4770; fax 212-579-8544), 31 West 71st Street between Central Park West and Columbus Avenue. Subway: B or C train to 72nd Street, or 1, 2, or 3 train to 72nd Street. If the Excelsior and Beacon hotels (see below) are a revelation to most tourists, this Comfort Inn—somehow built in the middle of a pretty residential street just half a block from Central Park (who approved this zoning-board deal?)—is so little known that I'd wager most Upper West Side *residents* don't even know it's here. Rooms are nothing to write home about; they're bland, with undersized televisions. Still, the price is very low for this neighborhood—double room rates mostly range $100–160 per night—and the quiet, cross-street location is ideal for those fed up with the honking of downtown cabs and buses.

Excelsior Hotel (212-362-9200 or 1-800-368-4575; fax 212-721-2994), 45 West 81st Street between Central

Park West and Columbus Avenue. Subway: B or C train to 81st Street. This West 81st Street sleeper, inside a tall high-rise that holds its own with the luxury apartment buildings along the block, must have been one of the better-kept lodging secrets in town. Set just half a block off Central Park and directly across the street from the popular American Museum of Natural History (see *To See—Museums*), it offers upscale rooms and service at a midrange price. And while it might seem remote from New York's major attractions, there are plenty of shops and restaurants nearby—and you're always just a short cab ride from Midtown. The gorgeous open lobby features a daytime concierge and gift shop; its leather couches are ideal for relaxing. They've even added high-speed Internet access for a small fee.

Standard rooms here are fine, but the two-room suites are really wonderful—a particularly good value considering the ace location. They're spacious and well adorned, with pull-out couch, dual televisions, and extra touches like romantic French doors separating the bedroom from the living room, a kit of good toiletries, and a tub that's actually deep enough to bathe in. All rooms feature beautiful king and queen beds with plush duvets that feel like they were plucked out of a fine country resort, and some come with views of the museum across West 81st Street (the rest have "city views" north toward Harlem). Some also are fitted with computer and T-1 Internet lines; anyone can use the small fitness room. Rates for double rooms range from around $130 to $230 (you pay more for park views), while those one-bedroom suites cost $240–440 per night

and two-bedroom suites cost upward of $360–550. Internet specials frequently drop those rates, though.

Hotel Beacon (212-787-1100 or 1-800-572-4969; fax 212-724-0839), 2130 Broadway at the corner of West 75th Street. Subway: B, C, 1, 2, or 3 train to 72nd Street. Close to both Central Park and Lincoln Center, the Beacon was long one of my favorite midpriced hotels in Manhattan, hands-down, and I'll tell you why. It's not the luxury; rooms here are standard issue. Rather, the Beacon's charm is all about location, convenience, and space—lots of space—and this combination makes the place one of the city's better hotel deals for the price in my book. Begin with the location: The hotel is right on Broadway, the heart of the West Side's restaurant bounty spread out before it. Outstanding food shops, including Fairway and Citarella, lie directly across the street, with venerable Zabar's (see *Selective Shopping*) just a couple of short blocks away. Since rooms—all rooms—have kitchenette (with real oven), this turns out to be a major bonus. Don't feel like cooking? Dozens of restaurants, in all price ranges, clamor for your attention along Broadway, Amsterdam, and Columbus.

The 200-plus rooms and one- and two-bedroom suites aren't bad, either—suites, in fact, consist of two downright huge rooms separated by doors. The suites sport not only a kitchenette but also several phones, two televisions, an ironing board, a big sofa, and deep closets. Lower-floor rooms look out on Broadway's human circus, while higher floor rooms look out on New Jersey. Doesn't sound exciting, but actually it isn't bad: Sunsets against the cityscape are attractive. The downstairs Beacon Theatre hosts a surprising variety of quality music events (you'll know something's up if there are lots of people lined up outside the hotel in the early evening). Only drawback I can think of? Some serious inflation has set in for the suites during recent years; in other words, now you're paying for those kitchens, though these aren't luxury units. Still, it's a good deal. Rack rates range $195–240 for a double room, $255–650 for the suites.

BED & BREAKFAST Holmes Bed and Breakfast (917-838-4808; fax 212-769-2348), West 91st Street between Amsterdam Avenue and Central Park West (call for exact address). Subway: B or C train to 86th or 96th Street. Since 1995 artist Marguerite Holmes has operated this small B&B just a block from Central Park. Decorated with the friendly hostess's original art, the brownstone feels like a home rather than a hotel. All rooms are named for fruit. The Blueberry and Cranberry rooms each come with a private bathroom, nice drapes, and plush chairs (the Cranberry Room adds a private terrace), while the Orange and Banana rooms share a hall bathroom but have kitchenette and exposed brick walls or a fireplace. All four rooms have television (some with VCR), phone, answering machine, and refrigerator; breakfast is self-serve, from a pantry. The rates are just $90 per night for the two rooms that share a bathroom, $100 per night for the two that don't.

✳ Where to Eat

DINING OUT Aix (212-874-7400), 2398 Broadway at the corner of West 88th Street. Subway: 1 train to 86th Street. Open daily 5:30–10:30 PM for dinner, Friday and Saturday to 11 PM, also Sunday 11:30 AM–2:30 PM for brunch. French chef Didier Virot, former top dog at highly rated Jean Georges and JoJo (as well as his own brief venture in the Dylan hotel), has gone Provençale—with both the food and the decor—at this West Side star; it's a daring attempt to pick up the pieces and try again. You'll feel as if you've stumbled into a bright van Gogh of yellows and oranges, but this is no rural corner café: Three floors of Oriental carpets, rich booths, and showy little mezzanine levels see to that. You then sit down to brightly colored meals of lamb, roast squab, venison with a quince-beet strudel dolled up in cocoa-coffee sauce, and pastas with inventive French-country-influenced sauces, most of them served on arty glass plates.

Starters are fairly straightforward and good whatever they are, from truffle gnocchi to good pistachio-encrusted foie gras to tomato tarts; the main-course combinations of main ingredient, sauce, and side dish are at times unsettling, at times revelatory, but it's Jehangir Mehta's dessert list that *really* raises the eyebrows. It features intriguing choices such as licorice-flavored panna cotta, nut soufflés and crème brûlées, an apple-herb brioche, pineapple sorbet with pineapple cake, and a signature "Provençale salad"—a kind of fruit-and-vegetable salad served with candy and mint ice cream. His experimentation seemingly never stops. The long wine list here contains hundreds of choices, including more than a dozen wines by the glass. Aix is often booked full, though, so call ahead rather than just showing up.

Compass (212-875-8600), 208 West 70th Street between Amsterdam and West End avenues. Subway: 1, 2, or 3 train to 72nd Street. Open Monday through Saturday for dinner 5–11 PM, Sunday also for brunch 11:30 AM–2:30 PM and to 10 PM for dinner. Right in the same space, and with the same chef, as the crash-and-burn eatery known as Marika that floundered here not long ago, this effort stands a good chance at succeeding despite a history of failed restaurants in the space. Dine on sophisticated—yet not completely avant-garde—New American–French fusion cuisine from a seemingly endless parade of chefs in a sedate, upscale-bistro environment. The $35 prix fixe dinner is a great deal with its choice of whatever the current chef's serving: maybe chopped salad, shrimp-corn soup, or saffrony risotto fritters to start; calf's liver, roasted hanger steak, or Parmesan-encrusted cod for the main course; and basil cake with mint sorbet or lemongrass panna cotta to finish. The à la carte menu choices rotate—starters often come from the sea, such as citrus-cured salmon with fried oysters, a peekytoe crab gazpacho, tuna carpaccio salad, or Maine sea scallops in a lobster-carrot broth. Main courses could run to monkfish paired with lamb, red snapper with tapenade, a honey-glazed pork loin with roasted Vidalia onions, lemon sole with caramelized cauliflower, or soft-shell crabs fried in tempura batter; you can also get standard tuna steaks, veal chops, and steaks off the grill, as well as halibut, roast chicken, or duck. Mouthwatering dessert choices might be a cheese plate or three-layer dessert of chocolate, hazelnuts, cream cheese, coffee oil, and nutmeg ice cream. The more

informal lounge area serves cocktails and a short menu of salads, bar snacks, and other good things.

Jean Georges (212-299-3900), 1 Central Park West at Columbus Circle. Subway: A, B, C, D, or 1 train to 59th Street–Columbus Circle. Open noon–3 PM for lunch and 5:30–11 PM for dinner, Saturday for dinner only. One of New York's top restaurants is this Trump hotel stunner right across from Central Park. Five-star chef Jean-Georges Vongerichten weaves Asian, American, and Alsatian influences into his food, producing meals of beauty and complex flavoring. Begin with grapefruit-mint salad, a porcini tart, scallops with caper-raisin sauce, a beautiful checkerboard of tuna and *hamachi,* or toasted foie gras brioche, then continue on to halibut in mustard, baked Maine char with chanterelles, pistachio-crusted sea bass, lobster tartine with a fenugreek broth, a spiced duck steak, or mushroom-dusted lamb. Dessert choices might run to a roasted pear sided with licorice ice cream, chocolate soufflé, a chestnut ice cream, or fruit tarts. The prix fixe lunch is a relative bargain, given that entrées cost $30–40 each and dinners are prix fixe only, at around $85–115 per person; the lunch could begin with fish stew and continue with grilled lobster, baked salmon, lamb shank, or roast squab, then finish with chestnut crème Anglaise or a chocolate napoleon. Tasting menus incorporate seasonal items such as sour cherries and pumpkin seeds.

La Boite en Bois (212-874-2705), 75 West 68th Street between Central Park West and Columbus Avenue. Subway: 1 train to 66th Street, or B or C train to 72nd Street. Open daily for lunch 11:30 AM–3 PM and for dinner 5–10 PM, except no lunch Monday. This tiny, narrow West Side restaurant close to Lincoln Center really hasn't garnered the attention it should. This is French country cooking of a very high caliber, yet the room is relaxed enough that you don't necessarily need to wear pretheater tails and tux. Try a beautiful appetizer of smoked trout (the portion is huge and delicious), then dive into the specials menu. Duck stewed in red wine sauce is one very good choice, as is the swordfish, but anything's good—all typically French bistro food. Plan on sitting very close to other parties, however, as this place is definitely not for the claustrophobic. (And, because it's so tiny, reservations are required of all diners.) Don't neglect the outstanding prix fixe deals for dinner before theater time.

Ocean Grill (212-579-2300), 384 Columbus Avenue between 78th and 79th streets. Subway: B or C train to 81st Street. Open daily noon–4 PM and 5–11 PM, weekends to 11:30 PM, Sunday from 10:30 AM. One of the nicer sit-down spots on the Upper West Side is this upscale seafood grill, located across Columbus Avenue from the peaceful American Museum of Natural History. The crowd is attractive and appreciative, and the food's very good—almost all fish and shellfish dishes, obviously, such as blackened swordfish, crab hash, lobster bisque, or peppered scallops. Weekend brunch is also a scene worth catching.

Ouest (212-580-8700), 2315 Broadway near the corner of West 84th Street. Subway: 1 train to 86th Street. Open Monday through Saturday 5–11 PM, Friday and Saturday to midnight, Sunday to 10 PM and also for brunch 10 AM–2 PM. Tom Valenti's latest venture is as dynamic as it is popular. The chef has brought his philosophy of New American cooking, which is curiously heavy on bacon and refreshingly unpretentious for a New York chef, to dishes such as pork chops, tripe, meat loaf (made rich with eggs, saltine crackers, and Tabasco sauce), grilled salmon with Yukon potatoes, linguine with tuna, and the like. Roast chicken with mashed potatoes and short ribs with fava beans are two more solid choices. Of course, this isn't to imply these meals are simple—Valenti uses the finest, freshest ingredients he can get his hands on and careful cooking technique; the results are a lot more complex than your mom could turn out with her Kenmore. Finish with a chocolate hazelnut cake or a delightful plum crisp, and—if you were hungry beforehand—be glad you booked a table here, rather than at one of those minimalist places serving you a teaspoon of pâté on the center of a square plate and charging 50 bucks for it.

EATING OUT **Artie's New York Delicatessen** (212-579-5959), 2290 Broadway at the corner of West 83rd Street. Subway: 1 train to 79th Street. Open daily 9 AM–11 PM. This Upper West Side deli isn't the biggest name in town, but local connoisseurs claim that it's serving food as good as Carnegie, Second Avenue, Katz's, and the other heavyweights. That's a remarkable claim, given that Artie's opened in the fall of 1999. But they've gotten the decor right—salamis and cured meats hang from the rafters, tables are deli-simple. And there's a predictable, well-done menu of Jewish comfort foods being served—think tongue, brisket, bagels with lox, grilled hot dogs, egg salad, matzoh ball soup, chopped liver, a multitude of pastrami and corned beef sandwich combinations, even an entire menu subsection dedicated to Reubens—as well as a few hot entrées such as sliced steak, served on an onion pocket roll and sided with mashed potato. Skip the "Thanksgiving dinner," though; it's nowhere near as good as the other entrées.

Big Nick's (212-362-9238), 2175 Broadway between West 76th and West 77th streets. Subway: 1 train to 79th Street, or 2 or 3 train to 72nd Street. Open 24 hours. I've never seen a place quite like this one: a Greek coffee shop–burger joint where chaos rules as the servers rapidly take orders for everything from a fruit smoothie to blintzes to burgers to omelets to milk shakes. They'll cook anything and everything here, and they do it all with a smile, well into the wee hours. The specialty is the huge delicious grilled burger, served with fries and lettuce in a combo plate for $5–9; there's a seemingly endless choice of burger styles, including ones with blue cheese, olives, and garlic sauce.

But they cook much more than diner food here. You can also order pasta, veal, barbecued chicken, fried clams, fish, teriyaki, casseroles, pizzas, an omelet, a pastrami sandwich, even a tofu pizza. (They'd probably whip up a leg of lamb and side it with a bowl of cereal if you asked 'em.) This place is just plain fun. There are plenty of cakes, pies, and pieces of sweet

baklava for dessert, too, and this is also one of the best spots in the neighborhood—maybe in town—to get a fresh-squeezed carrot juice or smoothie when you're run down. The staff actually seem to care about your personal well-being when they're making it.

Don't come expecting a quiet dinner; this is a diner, after all, with all the hectic to-and-froing that implies. But if the indoors seating seems a bit too claustrophobic, head outdoors for the sidewalk seating beneath omnipresent scaffolding. You might be joined by cabbies, newsstand vendors getting off late at night, or someone just drifting in to take a load off, but—even if you are, psychologically speaking, miles away from the neighborhood's froufrou French restaurants—you'll definitely know you've landed squarely in New York.

✔ **Brother Jimmy's** (212-501-7515), 428 Amsterdam Avenue between West 80th and West 81st streets. Subway: 1 train to 79th Street, or B or C train to 81st Street. Open daily 5 PM–midnight, Friday and Saturday to 1 AM. The closest thing the Upper West Side's got to a down-home southern barbecue pit, this growing chain glories in its (put-on) redneckness. Think Elvis, big plates of ribs, a Bud Light–swilling football crowd focusing rapt attention on the big-screen television, and all the rest. North Carolina–style 'cue and ribs feature prominently (the owner is a native), and so do Carolina hoops and gridiron action. The Wednesday-night special is just crazy: all you can eat of a buffet of ribs, meat loaf, mac and cheese, and fried chicken for just $10, and residents of the South get an extra 25 percent off that. Tuesday brings a similar $11 all-you-can-eat special from burgers, hot dogs, slaw, beans, ribs, and chicken . . . and awful Southern karaoke afterward. Sandwiches are also a good bet. But then, there's also this: Children under 12 eat here free. Free! Believe it? It's true.

Good Enough to Eat (212-496-0163), 487 Amsterdam Avenue between West 83rd and West 84th streets. Subway: 1 train to 86th Street, or B or C train to 86th Street. Open Monday through Friday 8 AM–4 PM and 5:30–10:30 PM, Saturday and Sunday from 9 AM. This down-home eatery serves breakfast, lunch, and dinner much like a New England roadside diner might—right down to the bad country-Gothic-style decorations. But oh, the food! They actually do a Thanksgiving dinner every day, with turkey and cranberry sauce and all the fixin's, and that fact alone is reason enough to come. If you need more reason, they've got the same sort of meat loaf, pancakes, and pies your mother made—and they don't fancy them up here with bits of jalapeño pepper, whole wheat crust, or any such thing. Weekend brunches are an event that spills out onto the sidewalk; expect a wait.

🍴 **Gray's Papaya** (212-799-0243), 2090 Broadway at the corner of West 72nd Street. Subway: 1, 2, or 3 train to 72nd Street. Open 24 hours. The "recession-buster special" has perplexingly crept *up* in price in recent years, even as the economy has gotten worse, but you still can't beat this deal for a quick New York street meal— two delicious grilled all-beef dogs and a cup of sweet papaya or a pineapple-coconut juice for just $2.55. Don't

forget to ask for onions, barbecue sauce, and sauerkraut: "One special with everything" should do it. The 72nd Street location of this growing mini chain has less atmosphere than almost anyplace else I've ever eaten in New York—dirty floors, narrow sticky stand-up counters, an unending stream of stragglers and foot traffic, mustard spilling from the too-big vats and the overloaded dogs. But still I keep coming back. Why? Because it's real. And when you're in a hurry, the food is just right. Case closed.

La Caridad 78 (212-874-2780), 2199 Broadway near the corner of West 78th Street. Subway: 1 train to 79th Street. Open daily 11:30 AM–midnight, Sunday to 10:30 PM. I just don't get it. This curious amalgam of Cuban and Chinese cuisine is wildly popular among the Upper West's locals, few of whom are either Chinese or Cuban. Why? Maybe it's the rock-bottom prices. Maybe it's the incredibly happy vibe of the place, which is often packed with locals at odd hours. Maybe it's the succulent black beans, Cuban bread, tamales, and chicken with rice. Or maybe it's the option of calling a last-minute audible and ordering the (so-so) Chinese cuisine when the munchies have struck and only dumplings will do. Whatever the reason, though, this inexpensive diner with the big windows looking out on Broadway is as neighborly and neighborhood a place as you can find.

Patsy's Pizzeria (212-579-3000), 61 West 74th Street near the corner of Columbus Avenue. Subway: B or C train to 72nd Street, or 1, 2, or 3 train to 72nd Street. Open daily noon– 11 PM, Friday and Saturday to midnight. There are plenty of great pies and pizzerias in New York City, but when push comes to shove I always vote Patsy's as my favorite. I don't know why; could be the delicious, naturally sun-sweetened San Marzano tomatoes they use for sauce. Or it could be the lovely crusts, perfectly charred in Patsy's wood-fired ovens. Or the simple, quality pepperoni they toss on top; the good beers on tap in the tiny bar area; the pleasant dining room, which has a laid-back neighborhood feel and distances itself from the drab Formica tables of your neighborhood pizza joint. There's another location in Murray Hill, and others on the Upper East Side and in Harlem; I like this one best.

✔ **Popover Café** (212-595-8555), 551 Amsterdam Avenue between West 86th and West 87th streets. Subway: 1 train to 86th Street, or B or C train to 86th Street. Open daily 8 AM–10 PM, weekends from 9 AM. This is a café like many others in New York—serving a good menu of soups, salads, and slightly fancy sandwiches—but for its signature item. That signature item, of course, is a popover: a big, eggy puff buttered up with the legendary strawberry butter. It's the perfect side to your sandwich, your salted-and-peppered eggs, smoked salmon scramble, or big waffles. Are you sensing a theme here? Weekend brunch is the best time to come, and as a result lines get long; expect to wait, perhaps browsing through the gift shop next door to pass the time while you do.

Sarabeth's West (212-496-6280), 423 Amsterdam Avenue between West 80th and West 81st streets. Subway: 1 train to 79th Street. Open Monday through Friday 8 AM–11 PM, weekends to 10 PM. Sarabeth's is another of the West Side's primo brunch spots; this one features terrific waffles and egg dishes, and is true to founder Sarabeth Levine's vision of a place to taste great jams on top of quality hotcakes and baked goods. It's in the original bakery space of what soon became a trio of popular eateries. It's better to stick with brunch or breakfast, which also runs to homemade porridges and granolas, country bacon, home fries, and French toast; however, the weekday lunch menu here is of slightly twee (but tasty) salads, sandwiches, and the like on good bread and isn't anything to sneeze at.

COFFEE AND SNACKS H&H Bagels (212-595-8000 or 1-800-NY-BAGEL), 2239 Broadway at the corner of West 80th Street. Subway: 1 train to 79th Street. Open 24 hours. On the television program *Seinfeld,* Jerry's friend Kramer worked at this bagel shop years ago—only to go on strike. For more than a decade. From the only job he apparently ever held. In any case, everybody on the Upper West Side knows this place: Its doughy bagels are a little expensive, but sweet enough that you don't need anything to accompany them.

The Sensuous Bean (212-724-7725 or 1-800-238-6845), 66 West 70th Street between Central Park West and Columbus Avenue. Subway: B or C train to 72nd Street, or 1, 2, or 3 train to 72nd Street. Open Monday through Friday 8:30 AM–6:30 PM, Saturday to 6 PM, Sunday 9:30 AM–6 PM. This tiny coffee shop is really more of a coffee and tea retailer—you can get just about anything—but they also brew up small cups of coffee and espresso for an appreciative daily parade of locals.

Kim Grant

ZABAR'S

Zabar's Café (212-787-2000), 2245 Broadway at the corner of West 80th Street. Subway: 1 train to 79th Street. Open Monday through Saturday 7:30 AM–7 PM, Sunday to 6 PM. The café associated with the great Zabar's specialty food shop is an excellent place for a quick juice, doughnut, sandwich, pastry, or my favorite quick lunch in New York—a $3.50 bagel stuffed with cream cheese and smoked salmon. They also sell excellent iced house-brand coffee.

✳ Entertainment

Lincoln Center

🎭 ♿ **Lincoln Center** (www.lincoln center.org) is a world unto itself, a concentration of fine arts that rivals any in the world. The 12 resident performing companies here—each an independent entity—and the visiting artists represent some of America's very finest dance, opera, jazz, puppetry, and classical music. To get here, just take the 1 train to 66th Street; the center (practically) has its very own stop.

All told the center presents approximately 350 live performances each year, everything from free outdoor concerts on the plaza to top-drawer classical and jazz. The new Lincoln Center complex opened in 1959, controversially replacing housing projects that previously stood on the site; most of its facilities are wheelchair accessible, and the central plaza marked by a large fountain makes for superb people-watching—and even some organized dances—during the summer weather.

BALLET Each spring the touring **American Ballet Theatre** (212-477-3030 for information, 212-361-6000 for tickets; www.abt.org)—founded in 1939, it's one of the world's most important ballet companies—dances for 2 months at the Metropolitan Opera House. ABT normally performs the work of top choreographers such as Tharp, Robbins, and Balanchine. Tickets cost anywhere from $26 to $93 per person.

The School of American Ballet (212-769-6600; www.sab.org), the nation's top-rated ballet school, opens its springtime workshops and performances to the public, all held at the Juilliard Theater at 155 West 65th Street (the box office is at street level) between Amsterdam Avenue and Broadway. Tickets cost $35 per person but are extremely hard to get.

The New York City Ballet (212-875-5000 or 212-870-5570 for tickets; www.nycballet.com) trains its own dancers and creates all its own choreography. Performances take place 23 weeks each year in the New York State Theater at Columbus Avenue and West 63rd Street (beside the great fountain). The winter season brings 6 weeks of company founder

George Balanchine's *The Nutcracker* in a famously elaborate production—including some very talented children in the cast—to the stage during November and December. Call ahead about these tickets, because New Yorkers and tourists alike will be clamoring for them in October and November. The rest of the season might find the NYCB's own *A Suite of Dances* or *Serenade,* or perhaps *Swan Lake* or one of the dozens of other repertory, "Master's Choice," and classic matinee performances. Tickets generally cost about $30–75 per person.

CLASSICAL MUSIC The Chamber Music Society of Lincoln Center (212-875-5775) presents a range of classical work at Alice Tully Hall, including the *Live from Lincoln Center* public television series. New artistic directors David Finckel and Wu Han took over the reins for the 2006–2007 season.

Founded in 1842, the **New York Philharmonic** (212-875-5000 or 212-875-5709 for information, 212-875-5030 or 212-875-5656 for tickets) is the nation's top orchestra, currently directed by Lorin Maazel. Its 106 players perform approximately 170 concerts annually: not only in Avery Fisher Hall at Broadway and West 65th Street, but also free shows in Central Park and other parks, a series of shows for young people, lower-priced matinee and rush-hour shows, and special holiday programs. The orchestra's rehearsals are also sometimes open to the public; tickets cost just $15 per person.

JAZZ ♪ Artistic director (and world-class player) Wynton Marsalis directs the house band and helps schedule the **Jazz at Lincoln Center Presents** (212-258-9800 or 212-721-6500 for tickets) series, held from September through June at its new homes in Frederic P. Rose Hall and Dizzy's in the Time Warner Center at Columbus Circle, just seven blocks south from Lincoln Center. There's a special effort made to bring jazz to young listeners. Note that the box office is located at the corner of Broadway and West 60th Street; it's open daily 10 AM–8:30 PM, except Sunday when it opens an hour later.

FILM Since 1969 **The Film Society of Lincoln Center** (212-875-5600 or 212-875-5601 for tickets) has screened a striking range of work at the Lincoln Center's movie house, the Walter Reade Theater at 70 Lincoln Center Plaza and Columbus Avenue (take a 1 train to 66th Street). Both its international and domestic offerings make a nice contrast with the bland fare purveyed across Broadway at the unabashedly commercial Sony multiplex. You might catch anything from classic 1930s and 1940s films to the newest independent import fresh off the plane from Latin America. Despite the pricey tickets, this is a terrific place to discover brand-new films by good directors you've never heard of before—and wouldn't find anywhere else in town. This society also runs the New York Film Festival.

OPERA The Metropolitan Opera (212-362-6000), usually known simply as The Met, may be the world's preeminent opera company—and has been so almost since the moment of its founding in 1883. Inside the grandly arched, columned, and stained-glass Metropolitan Opera

House standing behind the great fountain between Amsterdam and Columbus avenues (it opened in 1966, replacing the original Times Square opera house), you can see *Faust, La Bohème, Otello, Don Giovanni, Tristan und Isolde,* and other great works in the form, often (but not always) sung in their original languages. Devices on the backs of seats provide instantaneous translations for those who do not speak German or Italian. There are seven performances each week during the opera season from September through April, and guest conductors and performers might include the likes of Pavarotti. Some of the performances are also broadcast live to television and radio audiences each season. Ticket prices can range $25–295 depending on time of week, performance, and seat location.

The New York City Opera (212-870-5570 for tickets) presents performances at the New York State Theater on Columbus Avenue at West 63rd Street, offering a varied card of both well-known and lesser-known works from classic composers such as Verdi, Handel, Puccini, and Monteverdi. But there are also such wild cards as Stephen Sondheim's *A Little Night Music* and a specially commissioned trio of works from contemporary composers called *Central Park.* City Opera has always prided itself on keeping ticket prices low and opera accessible to the masses—it was first to offer subtitles to foreign-language operas, before The Met, and its Showcasing American Composers series introduces a dozen works to the public absolutely free each year. Tickets usually range from $25 to $110 per person.

THEATER The **Lincoln Center Theater** (212-362-7600), a nonprofit organization, has been called the finest theater in America by no less than *The New York Times.* LCT produces interesting work at affordable prices, usually in one of two venues—the 1,000-plus-seat Vivian Beaumont Theater and the lower-level 300-seat Mitzi E. Newhouse Theater, both at 150 West 65th Street in Lincoln Center—or occasionally the John Golden Theater at 252 West 45th Street (near Times Square). Recent plays have included *Awake and Sing!, The Light in the Piazza,* and *The House in Town,* a World War I piece set in the north of France, Tony Award–winning composer William Finn's song cycle *Elegies,* and *Vincent in Brixton,* a play about van Gogh's early time in London.

Beyond Lincoln Center

THEATERS **Promenade Theater** (212-580-1313 for information, 212-239-6200 for tickets), 2162 Broadway between West 76th and West 77th streets. Subway: 1, 2, or 3 train to 72nd Street or 1 train to 79th Street. Ironically, this 400-seat theater is small enough that it's considered "off Broadway." Yet it's *on* Broadway, inside a renovated church. Anyhow, there are fine productions here such as *Tea at Five,* with Kate Mulgrew starring as Katharine Hepburn in a play about the great actress's life, and then there was *Almost Heaven*—a musical based loosely on some unusual arrangements of singer John Denver's songs.

✪ **78th Street Theatre Lab** (212-873-9050), 236 West 78th Street between Amsterdam Avenue and

Broadway. Subway: 1 train to 79th Street. This tiny, third-floor off-off-Broadway theater is great simply because its productions, while way under the radar, are inexpensively priced and fresh—such as a Tex-Mex take on *The Taming of the Shrew* and a rock-and-roll, uptempo *Dracula*. Tickets often cost as little as $10 per person.

MUSIC VENUES Also see *Lincoln Center* for information about Alice Tully Hall, Avery Fisher Hall, the Metropolitan Opera House, and the New York State Theater.

Beacon Theatre (212-496-7070), 2124 Broadway between West 74th and West 75th streets. Subway: 1, 2, or 3 train to 72nd Street. Box office open Monday through Friday 11 AM–7 PM, Saturday noon–6 PM. This gracefully aging art deco theater, in the same toweringly high West Side structure as the good Hotel Beacon (see *Lodging—Affordable Hotels*), showcases an appealing variety of performers: anything from jazz or blues to a Cuban pianist, Indian sitar master, the Allman Brothers, Def Leppard, or rising American star Ryan Adams and Grammy-winning singer Norah Jones. It's amazing how many big names play this intimate venue, too—Jerry Seinfeld recently did stand-up here, for instance—considering that it seats less than 3,000.

Cleopatra's Needle (212-769-6969), 2485 Broadway between West 92nd and West 93rd streets. Subway: 1, 2, or 3 train to 96th Street. This is one of the best unknown jazz clubs in the city—though connoisseurs know it very well. There's no cover charge (each table must merely buy at least $10 worth of drinks during a set), and

if you like piano music you'll find it here every night. Pianists and vocalists in the regular rotation are quite good, as well.

Triad Theater (212-362-2590), 158 West 72nd Street between Amsterdam and Columbus avenues. Subway: 1, 2, or 3 train to 72nd Street. Upstairs from a club, this tiny cabaret venue puts on various revues such as a Grammy tribute and *Who Killed Woody Allen?* There's a two-drink minimum.

FILM Also see *Lincoln Center,* above.

Clearview 62nd and Broadway (212-777-FILM, ext. 864), 1871 Broadway at the corner of West 62nd Street. Subway: 1 train to 66th Street. One screen presents midlist films.

Lincoln Plaza Cinemas (212-757-2280), 1886 Broadway at the corner of West 62nd and West 63rd streets. Subway: 1 or 9 train to 66th Street, or A, B, C, D, 1, 2, or 3 train to 59th Street–Columbus Circle. A wonderfully eclectic selection of films—with nary a box-office smash among them—is screened here, belowground at Lincoln Plaza.

Loews 84th Street (212-50-LOEWS, ext. 701), 2310 Broadway at the corner of West 84th Street. Subway: 1 train to 86th Street. This theater is wildly popular with Upper West Side residents, who come with their families for Hollywood smashes.

Loews Lincoln Square 12 & IMAX (212-336-5020), 1998 Broadway at the corner of West 68th Street. Subway: 1 train to 66th Street. Lines can get long at this multiplex theater, which screens blockbuster movies just two blocks from Lincoln Center to huge, appreciative crowds of Upper West Siders. The IMAX theater upstairs shows really-big-screen stuff like the fascinating *Roving Mars.*

Makor (212-601-1000), 35 West 67th Street between Central Park West and Columbus Avenue. Subway: 1 train to 66th Street. Now part of the Upper East Side's active 92nd Y (see chapter 10), Makor screens unusual films of quality, such as a reshowing of the original *The Producers,* which spawned the phenomenally successful Broadway play; a documentary about homeless children in post-Ceausescu Romania; and a film about Bedouin social structures. It all happens on a single screen, but at least there are multiple showings nightly. There are also juried film competitions here.

BARS Dive 75 (212-362-7518), 101 West 75th Street between Amsterdam and Columbus avenues. Subway: B, C, 1, 2, or 3 train to 72nd Street. Open Monday through Friday 5 PM–4 AM, weekends from noon. This bar isn't exactly a dive—it's in the Upper West Side, after all—but it's fairly close. Call it a safe dive. Sports are featured on the television (it's a great place to catch a baseball game or the Super Bowl, for example), and the crowd runs the gamut from sports nuts to artsy, well-heeled locals just wanting to have a bottle of beer without paying an arm and a leg and don jacket and tie for it.

✴ Selective Shopping

FOOD AND DRINK 🐟 **Barney Greengrass, The Sturgeon King** (212-724-4707), 541 Amsterdam Avenue between West 86th and West 87th streets. Subway: B, C, or 1 train to 86th Street. Open Tuesday through

Sunday 8:30 AM–4 PM, weekends until 5 PM. I love this place. I love the name, I love the lettering, I love the simple tables they've set up right in the middle of the shop, I love the friendly staff behind the fish bar. But most of all I love the cured salmon. You can buy it and take it home like a local, but if your hotel doesn't have a fridge, fear not—come for brunch and order an egg dish or a bagel with the gorgeous smoked fish. Assuming you like it as much as I do, you'll go home happy.

Citarella (212-874-0383), 2135 Broadway at the corner of West 75th Street. Subway: 1, 2, or 3 train to 72nd Street. Open Monday through Saturday 7 AM–9 PM, Sunday 9 AM–7 PM. Citarella completes New York's single greatest stretch of specialty food shops, helping anchor the seven-block-lock Fairway–Zabar's axis that runs along the west side of Broadway from 74th to 81st streets. It specializes in great cuts of meat and fish, Italian cheeses and mineral waters, imported chocolates, and premade meals. A warning: It's probably the most expensive, per pound, of the shops along this little gourmet row of Broadway.

Fairway (212-595-1888), 2127 Broadway at the corner of West 74th Street. Subway: 1, 2, or 3 train to 72nd Street. Open daily 6 AM–1 AM. I could write a book about this place. Maybe someday I will, but in the meantime suffice it to say that this is organized chaos—a giant warehouse of hard-to-find and high-quality condiments, specialty foods, ice creams, coffees, chocolates, cookies, chutney, fruit, bagels, sushi, and so much more. Go on a Friday night or a Sunday afternoon and you're taking your life into your hands: The deli resembles a street fight, except all the participants are female and between the ages of 45 and 90. Nevertheless, I'd never visit this part of town without dropping in to see what's on the shelves. One more warning: Don't cut in the lines (which break in two to allow cross traffic). People don't like it.

Zabar's (212-787-2000), 2245 Broadway between West 80th and West 81st streets. Subway: 1 or 9 train to 79th Street. Open Monday through Friday 8 AM–7:30 PM, Saturday to 8 PM, Sunday 9 AM–6 PM. New York's most amazing gourmet food store can get pretty claustrophobic when local grandmothers are out shopping for lox and nothing will stand in their way. Still, this is a must-visit for great fresh-ground coffees, cheese, imported chocolate milk from Denmark, local sodas, smoked fish, Doughnut Plant doughnuts, and ready-made meals of chicken, fish, ribs, potpies, and steak.

✳ Special Events

July: **Lincoln Center Festival** at Lincoln Center. Subway: 1 train to 66th Street. This annual July event highlights the various cultural and arts offerings of the center, including ballet, theater, Noh plays, and a whole lot more; many guest performers are brought in to boost the quality even higher.

Late September–early October: **New York Film Festival** at Lincoln Center. Subway: 1 train to 66th Street. The Film Society of Lincoln Center puts on this annual festival of world films, usually with a documentary or otherwise thoughtful bent.

November to December: **The Nutcracker** at Lincoln Center. Subway: 1 train to 66th Street. The New York City Ballet presents this timeless classic with the dancing toys each November and December. Try to get tickets in advance, because they're a hot property.

North of Central Park

HARLEM

MORNINGSIDE HEIGHTS

WASHINGTON HEIGHTS

Kim Grant

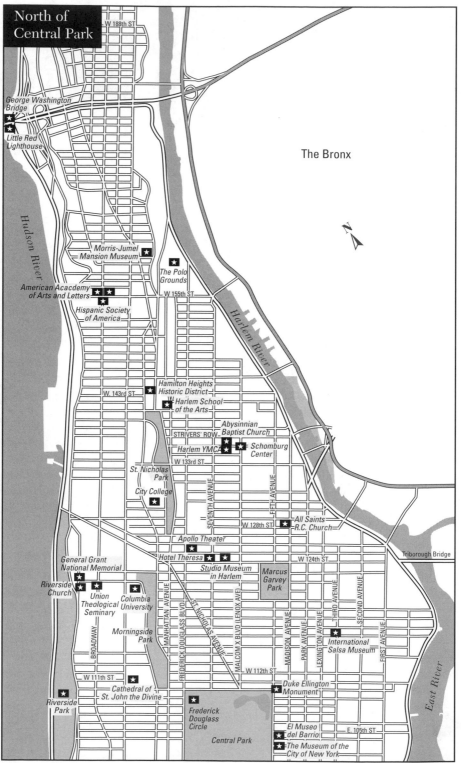

North of
Central Park

George Washington
Bridge

Little Red
Lighthouse

Hudson River

The Bronx

W 188th ST

N

Morris-Jumel
Mansion Museum

The Polo
Grounds

American Acacdemy
of Arts and Letters

W 155th ST

Hispanic Society
of America

Harlem River

Hamilton Heights
Historic District

W. 143rd ST

Harlem School
of the Arts

Abysinnian
Baptist Church

STRIVERS' ROW

Harlem YMCA

Schomburg
Center

W 133rd ST

St. Nicholas
Park

City College

SEVENTH AVENUE

FIFTH AVENUE

All Saints
R.C. Church

W 128th ST

Apollo Theater

Hotel Theresa

W 124th ST

Triborough Bridge

General Grant
National Memorial

Studio Museum
in Harlem

Marcus
Garvey
Park

Riverside
Church

Union
Theological
Seminary

Columbia
University

BROADWAY

Morningside
Park

MANHATTAN AVENUE

FREDERICK DOUGLASS BLVD

ST NICHOLAS AVENUE

MALCOM X BLVD (LENOX AVE)

SEVENTH AVE

MADISON AVENUE

PARK AVENUE

LEXINGTON AVENUE

THIRD AVENUE

SECOND AVENUE

FIRST AVENUE

International
Salsa Museum

W 111th ST

W 112th ST

Duke Ellington
Monument

Cathedral of
St. John the Divine

Riverside
Park

Frederick
Douglass
Circle

East River

El Museo
del Barrio

E. 105th ST

Central Park

The Museum of the
City of New York

© The Countryman Press

HARLEM, MORNINGSIDE HEIGHTS, AND WASHINGTON HEIGHTS

Ah, Harlem, we hardly knew ye. You touched a nation, carved out an identity, brought us life-changing music, and saw such hard times. And yet the Harlem of today is neither the Harlem of the heyday 1920s—nor the poverty-stricken slum so often portrayed in film and television.

To be sure, this neighborhood remains scruffy around the edges—some blocks still seem to consist entirely of fading fried chicken and check-cashing establishments—and there is still not nearly enough green space. But the unique culture and history here are undeniable, and new blood is slowly bringing a wave of more interesting restaurants, museums, and cultural offerings.

There are fewer jazz clubs—the original Big Apple club, from which the city took its name, was here on 135th Street but is now closed—yet more retail stores; the church community remains tight knit and active. As the neighborhood slowly upscales and becomes more ethnically diverse, change is definitely afoot. It's even possible this might one day become the next hot neighborhood for young hip Manhattanites looking to escape their tiny downtown apartments, buy a row house, and jazz it up with the latest wireless gadgets.

Before this happens, though, an ode to the Harlem that was. The blocks north of Central Park, originally Native American lands, were colonized by the Dutch—hence the name; Haarlem is a small, attractive city in the Netherlands—and their African laborers not long after the Pilgrims landed on Plymouth Rock. For the next 200 years it remained largely rural—wealthy New Yorkers such as John James Audubon carved out massive estates from the green expanses that once covered the area—but New York's explosive growth and progress eventually pushed north to here; the extension of subway tracks spelled a new era for Harlem, and it knew a brief heyday as a center of Manhattan high society.

This moment of prosperity was not to be sustained, however, and as local real estate prices plunged back to earth, African Americans from New York and the southern states began pouring into the district in great numbers; by the 1920s this was the single most vibrant and concentrated expression of their culture in America, a decade known as the Harlem Renaissance. The 1930s, 1940s, and 1950s saw that moment in the sun extend itself: Jazz legends such as Louis Armstrong, Count Basie, Cab Calloway, Duke Ellington, Coleman Hawkins, Charles Mingus, and Charlie Parker, and poets such as Langston Hughes, all found a voice—and an appreciative audience—here, filling such venues as the Apollo Theater to the maximum night after night. Sadly, some of the old hot spots are now gone. The Cotton Club, for one, is no longer; once located at 644 Lenox Avenue and West 142nd Street (and featured in the 1984 Francis Ford Coppola film of the same name), it moved downtown in the 1930s before swiftly closing. During its short incarnation as a gathering place for Harlem's African American movers and shakers, Cab Calloway led the club's house band; and such jazz superstars as Ellington, Armstrong, and Ethel Waters all played extended engagements here.

As went the Cotton Club, so went Harlem: The good times were not to last very long, and the 1960s and 1970s brought yet another ebb in the area's fortunes. Racial tensions began to boil over. The assassination of controversial civil rights activist Malcolm X in Harlem's Audubon Ballroom in 1965 sent a chilling message to the local black community, itself already beginning to feel the effects of unemployment, rising drug use and crime, and the construction of huge, substandard housing projects under the guise of "urban renewal." All these forces began sapping the neighborhood's spirit; for the first time, African American families began to move *out* of Harlem in numbers, and its population began to dip.

But the past 20 years have seen a reversal in Harlem's fortunes once more, most dramatically in the past decade. New money and energy are flowing back into the neighborhood—witness basketball star Magic Johnson's successful new movie megaplex and former president Bill Clinton's decision to locate his office here. Rap and R&B music pulses in the streets; upscale restaurants are flourishing; soul food dives are seeing busloads of middle-American tourists. The streets feel safer than they have in decades, and there is renewed pride in the history, architecture, and tremendous artistic heritage that once thrived here . . . and could again. The neighborhood's many fine town houses (which can be found along Riverside Drive, Strivers' Row, and other pockets), museums, music clubs, shops, restaurants, and other cultural offerings—focused on the central artery of 125th Street—are definitely well worth a full day of your time.

A MURAL IN HARLEM

Paul Karr

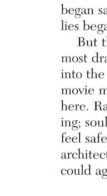

To the south of Harlem, bordering the northern edges of Central Park and the Upper West Side, Columbia University's neighborhood is another pocket of culture worth exploring. The neighborhood, known as Morningside Heights, is largely residential—and as a place where people live and breathe (rather than have a good time), that means a lot of apartment buildings, brownstones, shoe repairmen, dry cleaners, grocery stores, and mediocre shopping at best. Don't plan to spend more than half a day here, time best spent touring Columbia and the huge Cathedral of St. John the Divine that looms over it and everything else in the surrounding neighborhood. If you really do want to explore the district, there are a number of other small museums and churches, such as Union Theological Seminary, Riverside Church, the American Numismatic Society, and the like.

East Harlem (also known as Spanish Harlem) is just what it sounds like: a thoroughly Spanish neighborhood. Again, this is a residential area of blocks and blocks of apartment buildings and essential services, and frankly isn't worth your time on a short visit to New York. But if you're particularly interested in Hispanic history, there is one excellent resource worth seeking out—the superb El Museo del Barrio.

To the north of Harlem, at the very northern tip of the island of Manhattan, lies Washington Heights. You can find the neighborhood by looking for the pretty George Washington Bridge spanning the Hudson. Here, there's a world-class museum experience (The Cloisters) and some serious green space, and you can actually come by subway if you don't mind riding for a while.

GETTING THERE *By train:* Harlem and the surrounding area are mostly easily reached via the A train, an express train that stops at various points in Midtown, Greenwich Village, and Lower Manhattan. Heading north, it whizzes very quickly from 59th Street to 125th Street, and then to 168th Street—in just two stops, the longest stretches of express passage in the city. The B and C trains stop at all the local stations between those points, and thus are useful for reaching other Harlem-area destinations. You can change to a local B or C train at either 125th Street or 168th Street. You can also take the express D train, which is a very quick ride from Midtown, but its only stop in Harlem is at 125th Street; miss it, and wind up deep in the Bronx.

For attractions nearer the Hudson River, such as Columbia University and Riverside Church, use the local 1 train line.

By car: A car can be useful in Harlem, because parking is plentiful and the many parks here are not always easily reached by public transit. To reach Inwood Hill Park, Fort Washington Park, and other destinations at the northern tip of Manhattan, take the Henry Hudson Parkway to 178th Street. To reach The Cloisters, take the Dyckman Street–Riverside Drive exit near the Henry Hudson toll bridge. To reach Sugar Hill or Riverside Church, take the 158th Street exit. To reach the 125th Street area, take the 125th Street exit. To reach Columbia University and the Cathedral of St. John the Divine, it's usually best to take the 96th Street exit, then Riverside Drive north to 110th Street. Riverside Drive is a very convenient way of getting north and south quickly, while traveling east and west is more troublesome—avoid major cross streets such as 96th and 125th streets, which are constantly full of bus, taxi, and commercial traffic.

By bus: Many city bus lines also travel to and through Harlem along major north–south avenues, including the 2, 3, 4, 5, 7, 10, 11, and 18 buses.

GETTING ORIENTED In July 2003, the city's official tourism office opened a **Harlem Visitor Information Kiosk** on 125th Street, just east of Seventh Avenue (Adam Clayton Powell Jr. Boulevard). Located in the Adam Clayton Powell State Office Building plaza at 163 West 125th Street, it's open 7 days a week and dispenses information not only about Harlem but also attractions city-wide. Weekdays, the kiosk opens from 9 AM to 6 PM; weekends, it opens an hour later, at 10 PM. Subway: A, B, C, D, 2, or 3 train to 125th Street.

✳ To See

MUSEUMS American Academy of Arts and Letters (212-368-5900; www.arts andletters.org), 633 West 155th Street (Audubon Terrace) at Broadway. Subway: B, C, or D train to 155th Street, or 1 train to 157th Street. Open Thursday through Sunday, during exhibitions only, 1–4 PM. This handsome landmark uptown building honors the work of American writers and artists with a collection of books, manuscripts, photographs, and original notebooks and musical scores relating to leading lights such as William Faulkner, Duke Ellington, Toni Morrison, Susan Sontag, and Dizzy Gillespie. Admission is free.

The Cloisters (212-923-3700; www.metmuseum.org), Fort Tryon Park at 190th Street. Subway: A train to 190th Street. Open March through October, Tuesday through Sunday 9:30 AM–5:15 PM, November through February 9:30 AM–4:45 PM. This is one of New York's best museum bargains, an outstanding collection of art in a setting so fanciful you'll forget you're in New York for a day. Owned and operated now by the Metropolitan Museum of Art, the museum opened in 1938 with financing from the Rockefeller family in Fort Tryon Park (see *Green Space*). The layout presents a hodgepodge of architectural styles, unified by the cloisters (quadrangles covered by some sort of roof). Inside, you'll find some of the most spectacular medieval European holdings of the Met, including ornate tapestries; pieces of ancient column work and other architectural sculpture, such as a 13th-century limestone door from a French monastery; delicate illuminated manuscripts; enamel and ivory works; a 13th-century section of stained glass that is probably from France's famous cathedral in Rouen; and much

THE CLOISTERS HOUSES A VAST COLLECTION OF MEDIEVAL ART

Kim Grant

more—more than 5,000 works of art in all. Much of it is thanks to the early collecting efforts of sculptor George Gray Barnard, who traveled the back roads of France for years seeking out and acquiring forgotten treasures. The gardens here are also unique, having been planted according to medieval-era herbal and literary publications—keep an eye out for plants such as mandrake that you never imagined still existed. There's also a small café on the premises, open daily. Admission to The Cloisters is by donation, so you can pay what you wish, but the museum suggests $15 for adults, $10 for senior citizens and students. There is no sur-charge for any special exhibitions. If you are taking the subway, note that you'll need to walk perhaps half a mile through the park from the subway station eleva-tor to reach the museum. If you're driving, parking is free.

El Museo del Barrio (212-831-7272), 1230 Fifth Avenue at the corner of 104th Street. See chapter 10.

Hamilton Grange National Memorial (212-283-5154; www.nps.gov/hagr), 287 Convent Avenue between West 141st and West 142nd streets. Subway: 1 train to 137th Street, or A, B, C, or D train to 145th Street. Open Wednesday through Sunday 9 AM–5 PM; temporarily closed in summer 2006. The former home of important Constitution crafter Alexander Hamilton, this 1802 Federal-style home once presided over a 32-acre estate. Hamilton was actually born in the West Indies before moving to New York, attending the young Columbia Uni-versity (see *Higher Learning*), becoming General Washington's right-hand man during the American Revolution, then joining Congress. Hamilton helped craft the important *Federalist Papers* and was selected as first secretary of the Trea-sury, a difficult position that entailed creation of a federal bank, establishing credit, and creating a debt system for the new nation's government. The period furniture is augmented by regular programs of music, lectures, and children's education. Admission is free.

Hispanic Society of America (212-926-2234; www.hispanicsociety.org), 633 West 155th Street (Audubon Terrace) at Broadway. Subway: B, C, or D train to 155th Street, or 1 train to 157th Street. Museum and library open Tuesday through Saturday 10 AM–4:30 PM; museum also open Sunday 1–4 PM. The His-panic Society's museum holds Spanish art from the Middle Ages to the present, and it's very impressive for such a little-known museum. The museum's collec-tion includes Juan Vespucci's *Map of the World* and Goya's *The Duchess of Alba*. There's also a top collection of earthenware and porcelain from Europe and Latin America. But textiles are the real star here—if you're interested in Mus-lim-influenced work from the Iberian Peninsula (these designs often featured lions, floral patterns, and inscriptions), or perhaps something woven of silver or gold, this is the place to come. The library adds historical archives, letters, and illuminated manuscripts, among other treasures. Admission is free.

Morris-Jumel Mansion Museum (212-923-8008; www.morrisjumel.org), 65 Jumel Terrace at 160th Street and Edgecombe Avenue. Subway: C train to 163rd Street. Open Wednesday through Sunday 10 AM–4 PM. Built in 1765 as a summer house for a British colonel and his wife, this Palladian-style mansion is now the oldest home in New York. Its two-story portico features four high columns, while one wing is octagonal—the first residence in America to incorpo rate such a design—and the kitchen features another possible first in American architecture, an alcove. Colonel Roger Morris and his family were forced to abandon the mansion during the American Revolution, however, and George Washington commanding the Continental army—occupied it for 3 months dur ing the war, using it as headquarters for his victory at Harlem Heights. Later it was purchased by the Frenchman Stephen Jumel.

Today the mansion features nine rooms of lavish Empire furnishings from the 18th and 19th centuries—more than 1,000 objects in all, such as a Chippendale table, a British harpsichord from 1776, a 1795 piano from pioneering American piano builder Benjamin Crehore, a bed said to have once belonged to Napoleon (who knew Jumel's wife), and chairs that once belonged to the queen of Holland. The neighborhood's history is also archived in detail, and in the basement—formerly the servants' kitchen—additional exhibits explain slave and servant life from the period. Admission costs $4 for adults, $3 for seniors and students. The nearby street known as Sylvan Terrace is notable for its fine row houses, and an old milepost behind the mansion is worth a look as well.

The Museum of the City of New York (212-534-1672), 1220 Fifth Avenue at the corner of 103rd Street. See chapter 10.

The Studio Museum in Harlem (212-864-4500; www.studiomuseum.org), 144 West 125th Street between Adam Clayton Powell Jr. Boulevard (Seventh Avenue) and Lenox Avenue (Malcolm X Boulevard). Subway: 2, 3, 4, 5, 6, A, B, C, or D train to 125th Street. Open Wednesday to Sunday noon–6 PM, except Saturday from 10 AM. The Studio Museum, founded in 1968 to highlight the work of artists of African descent, features two floors of galleries, a garden, and a gift shop. Exhibitions here have included a show of drawings by Gary Simmons; a show highlighting Harlem postcards through history; a show of black abstract artists; and a photography show curated by the editor of *Aperture* magazine. Admission is by donation, and the suggestions are $7 for adults, $3 for seniors and students.

HISTORIC SITES Apollo Theater (212-749-5838 for tickets, 212-531-5300 for information; www.apollotheater.com), 253 West 125th Street between Adam Clayton Powell Jr. Boulevard (Seventh Avenue) and Frederick Douglass Boulevard (Eighth Avenue). Subway: A, B, C, or D, 2, or 3 train to 125th Street. The famous Apollo still hosts weekly Wednesday amateur nights (see *Entertainment—Music Venues*), as well as a long-running musicals and occasional jazz and gospel. Call for event schedules.

Dyckman Farmhouse Museum (212-304-9422; www.dyckmanfarmhouse.org), 4881 Broadway at West 204th Street. Subway: A train to 207th Street. Open Wednesday through Sunday 11 AM–4 PM, except Sunday from noon. One of the few true remaining vestiges of the original colonial Manhattan, the handsome Dyckman farmhouse dates back to 1784, when it was built to replace an earlier home burned by the British. The fieldstone-and-wood house stood at the center of enormous farms and orchards, and was used for a time as an inn after the war; today the museum here consists of six rooms of exhibits (mostly period furniture) and one room of Revolutionary War memorabilia. Admission costs $1 for adults and children over the age of 10; tours must be reserved for groups of 10 or more.

General Grant National Memorial (212-666-1640; www.nps.gov/gegr), Riverside Drive at West 122nd Street. Subway: 1 train to 116th Street. Open daily 9 AM–5 PM. This small, domed memorial—it looks a bit like the U.S. Capitol—holds the twin tombs of Union general Ulysses S. Grant and his wife, Julia. Constructed of granite and marble in 1897, it is still the largest mausoleum in the United States. Exhibits at the visitors center discuss Grant's life and, of course, his victory in the Civil War—there are several large maps of the war's theaters here. But some visitors remember the place less for its history than for the folksy, crazy-quilt pop art bench that stretches seemingly forever along one side of the memorial; the bench is nothing if not incongruous, but it does provide a place to sit when weary. There's also a small bookshop on the premises. Admission to the memorial is free of charge.

Harlem YMCA (212-281-4100), 180 West 135th Street between Adam Clayton Powell Jr. Boulevard (Seventh Avenue) and Lenox Avenue (Malcolm X Boulevard). Subway: B, C, 2, or 3 train to 135th Street. Much more than just a health club, the Harlem Y has long been a center of art, culture, and faith in the neighborhood. Its members have included Jesse Owens, George Washington Carver, Langston Hughes (who read here), Sidney Poitier, Danny Glover, and Joe Louis, among many others.

Hotel Theresa, Adam Clayton Powell Jr. Boulevard (Seventh Avenue) between West 124th and West 125th streets. Subway: A, B, C, D, or 1 train to 125th Street. This tall, blocky office building was originally the site of a fancy hotel where Harlem celebrities such as Lena Horne, Joe Louis, and Malcolm X often hobnobbed and conducted meetings. The hotel became world famous when it hosted Cuban dictator Fidel Castro during his 1960 visit to address the United Nations. Castro, who quartered here in the (by then threadbare) hotel in a poor neighborhood as a not-so-subtle dig at crass American capitalism (read: Midtown's luxury hotels), chatted with Malcolm X and Nikita Khrushchev, then spoke from a balcony to a cheering crowd about the oppressive American government. The building was converted into office space in the early 1970s; although designated as a city landmark in the 1990s, it is not open to the public.

The Polo Grounds, from 155th to 159th streets between Harlem River Drive and Frederick Douglass Boulevard (Eighth Avenue). Subway: B or D train to 155th Street. It's just a huge, drab complex of apartment houses now, but the land beneath once contained Gotham's most hallowed sporting grounds. Originally built for polo, hollowed out by geography and oddly U shaped because of the strange housing lot sizes in this part of the island, the Polo Grounds found fame as quirky home to the New York Giants from 1890 until 1957, when the club left for San Francisco. The New York Yankees also played home games here from 1913 until 1922, when a new slugger named Babe Ruth sold so many tickets that the team was able to build Yankee Stadium and move to the Bronx. (So did the worst team in baseball history, the 1962 New York Mets, but that's another matter.) Willie Mays's amazing over-the-shoulder World Series catch of Vic Wertz's long fly ball was made in these grounds in 1954—in deep, deep center field—and Bobby Thomson's famous "shot heard 'round the world" home run was hit here, too, in 1951. Fourteen Series in all took place here. A small plaque in the housing complex commemorates the location of home plate when Thomson struck his blow.

FOR FAMILIES ✐ **Little Red Lighthouse** (212-304-2365), west of Henry Hudson Parkway and West 178th Street. Subway: A train to 175th or 181st Street. Unless you've driven the big George Washington Bridge eastbound from New

Jersey, you probably wouldn't know that Manhattan possesses a cute-as-a-button lighthouse right beneath the supports of this bridge. But it does. Officially called Jeffreys Hook Lighthouse, it's a squat, bright reminder that the Hudson was once one of the world's most important shipping lanes. The lighthouse was first lit in 1881 and moved from southern New Jersey to Manhattan in 1921, where it remained actively lit by the Coast Guard for more than a decade afterward; a campaign by New Yorkers—aided by a children's book writer, who penned *The Little Red Lighthouse and the Great Grey Bridge*—then saved it from demolition in the nick of time. You cannot drive here, but you can take the subway to Riverside Park and walk or bike the path to its foot (there is a pedestrian walkway over the expressway near West 181st Street). Public tours of the lighthouse interior are given spring through fall, and a fall festival highlights its history.

CHURCHES Abyssinian Baptist Church (212-862-7474), 132 West 138th Street between Adam Clayton Powell Jr. Boulevard (Seventh Avenue) and Malcolm X Boulevard (Lenox Avenue). Subway: 2 or 3 train to 135th Street. This ornate Baptist church, which dates back to the early 19th century (it was founded as a reaction to segregated houses of worship), features a terrific choir that belts 'em out year-round on Sunday to an enthusiastic, mixed crowd of churchgoers—the congregation is huge—and global tourists seeking a bit of the local gospel experience. Harlem congressman Adam Clayton Powell Jr. and his father both preached here. The church remains very, very active in the surrounding community as well: This is one place in Harlem where history still lives, and is being made anew. Explorer's tip: If you can't get up here to hear the choir—Sunday services begin at 11:30 AM, but you'll want to arrive a little early for a good seat—remember that the same vocal group occasionally performs at the Metropolitan Museum of Art on Fifth Avenue (see chapter 10) during the holiday season. Admission is free.

THE CATHEDRAL OF ST. JOHN THE DIVINE— STILL UNFINISHED—IS THE LARGEST GOTHIC CATHEDRAL IN THE WORLD.

Kim Grant

The Cathedral Church of St. John the Divine (212-316-7540 for information, 212-932-7347 for tours, 212-662-2133 for event tickets), 1047 Amsterdam Avenue at the corner of West 112th Street. Subway: 1 train to 110th Street. Open to the public daily

DIVINE INTERSECTION

St. John the Divine is a world unto itself, and—as with the Met—you could easily spend an entire day poking around here. My top choices for must-sees while walking around the place include these hidden gems:

- The American Poets' Corner of stones incised with the names of famous poets (each must be elected to enter), and the much less famous poetry wall in the ambulatory—where every poem mailed or brought to the cathedral is hung, regardless of quality.
- The bronze lamps from the original Pennsylvania Station gracing the front steps.
- The two aging peacocks roaming the grounds and gardens, the only living descendants of chicks brought here in 1973.
- Greg Wyatt's, er, interesting large *Peace Fountain* sculpture.
- An AIDS chapel, which contains the famous AIDS Quilt stitched together from the stories of those who perished of the disease, and an altarpiece by Keith Haring.
- An herb garden.
- The handsome dean's house, which is not open to the public.

7 AM–6 PM, until 7 PM Sunday. Believe it or not, this gargantuan Episcopal cathedral begun in 1892 is still unfinished—in fact, it's not anywhere near finished. Even more remarkable, the craftsmen working the construction project have been charged with using only traditional methods (such as cutting stone by hand) in the construction; you can actually visit a yard where stone is cut. This church is simply awesome in scale—the biggest true cathedral in the world, for those who care, though a discussion of why St. Peter's in Rome is not technically classified as a cathedral will have to wait for another time. St. John's massive dome thrusts 162 feet into the sky—the Statue of Liberty would fit easily inside it—and the towers rise 125 feet at the nave; the entire cathedral measures approximately 600 feet long by 145 feet wide (about two football fields). Its west-entrance doors weigh 3 tons each. It contains seven chapels. It's so big that it maintains a visitors center for the befuddled and disoriented.

From its huge ornate rose window to the flying buttresses topped with angels (Gabriel is facing due east to the huge pulpit) and massive organ pipes, everything is oversized—yet somehow retains a note of grace. You'll easily discover the cathedral's more obvious treasures, such as the interior done in tilework by the famed mason Rafael Guastavino, but also try to take a tour to get insight into the cathedral's most interesting nooks, crannies, and gargoyles. (If you're short on time, see the box for some of my top picks of what to see.) The church's very interesting "vertical" tours have recently been reinstated (they'd been on hiatus since a December 2001 fire seriously damaged significant portions of the church interior and its two precious 17th-century tapestries). These special tours cost

$15 per adult, $10 per student and senior, and take place only on Saturday at noon and 2 PM; bring a flashlight. The fire also silenced the cathedral's huge Aeolian Skinner organ, which is sensitive to soot, but the stained-glass work was saved by careful firefighters. General-interest tours of the cathedral are still offered to the public once daily, however; they begin at 11 AM sharp, Tuesday through Saturday, and Sunday at 1 PM. They ask a donation of $5 per person, $4 for students or seniors. Special events held at the cathedral might include choral music (Handel's *Messiah* in the Christmas season, of course) or chamber music, but also anything from origami and wool-spinning workshops to art tours of the interior and dance classes. Phone the cathedral staff for further information.

Riverside Church (212-870-6700), 490 Riverside Drive between 120th and 122nd streets. Subway: 1 train to 116th Street. Open to the public daily 7 AM– 10 PM, visitors center open Wednesday 10 AM–7 PM. Tall and slim, nondenominational Riverside Church was built on a height-of-land by John D. Rockefeller in the 1930s as a backlash against St. John the Divine's exclusionary policies. Its Gothic design is said to derive from that of Chartres Cathedral in France and features a soaring, 24-story central bell tower reaching a height of nearly 400 feet—instantly recognizable even across the river in New Jersey. Inside, the nave features a small floor labyrinth copied from a maze at Chartres; the stained-glass window of Christ's life is of Flemish design, probably from the 16th century and France; and tapestries date from the same era. The pipe organ is especially attractive. Martin Luther King Jr. once preached from the pulpit here (opposing Americans' involvement in the Vietnam War, for example), and other world figures such as freed South African leader Nelson Mandela have since taken it to speak of peace, tolerance, and other issues of social justice. The church even hosts special popular music, chamber music, gospel, dance, theater, and puppetry events—beyond the usual choral fare, which it also hosts—such as a famous onetime benefit concert in honor of the late Linda McCartney and occasional AIDS benefits. Admission to the church is free; event ticket prices vary.

LIBRARY ♿ **Schomburg Center for Research in Black Culture** (212-491-2200), 515 Malcolm X Boulevard (Lenox Avenue) at the corner of 135th Street (temporary entrance at 103 W. 135th Street). Subway: 2 or 3 train to 135th Street. General-reference section open Tuesday and Wednesday noon–8 PM, Thursday and Friday noon–6 PM, Saturday 10 AM–6 PM. Motion-picture and recorded sound section open Tuesday through Saturday 10 AM–5 PM, Photographs and Prints section open Wednesday through Friday noon–5 PM, SATURDAY 10 AM–5 PM. Hours for other sections variable. The Schomburg research library, part of the New York Public Library, is incredibly rich in African American historical holdings: There are 5 million pieces in all at present. The archives' most significant collections were assembled by the Puerto Rican–black scholar Arturo Alfonso Schomburg. The Art and Artifacts Division holds a number of rare items from African nations, including weaponry, documentaries, anti-apartheid posters, and much more. The General Research and Reference Division holds plenty of African American literature, as well as periodicals from Africa and the Caribbean. The Manuscripts, Archives and

Rare Books Division gathers rare jazz sheet music, historical documents, and the like. The popular Moving Image and Recorded Sound Division (which maintains separate hours from other sections of the center) hosts television broadcasts, music collections, and early jazz and tap dance films. Finally, the Photographs and Prints Division is especially strong on material related to the Civil War, slavery, and Harlem history (including good material on the Harlem Renaissance). Recent special exhibitions have included In Motion: The African-American Migration Experience, Through the Eyes of the Gods: An Aerial View of Africa, and Malcolm X: A Search for Truth. And the concert program is outstanding, as well. Admission is free, while event prices vary.

NEIGHBORHOODS Strivers' Row (St. Nicholas Historic District), West 138th and West 139th streets between Adam Clayton Powell Jr. Boulevard (Seventh Avenue) and Frederick Douglass Boulevard (Eighth Avenue). Subway: B or C train to 135th Street, or A or D train to 145th Street. This is one of the most attractive sections of Harlem, notable as much for the unusual, European-style alleys behind the row houses and brownstones as for those buildings' attractive facades. Middle- and upper-class African Americans filled these houses—some Georgian in style, some neo–Italian Renaissance—during the 1920s, and today they attract a mixture of businessmen, university professors, and actors and musicians.

Sugar Hill, Edgecombe Avenue between West 145th Street and West 155th Street. Subway: A, B, C, or D train to 145th Street, or C train to 157th Street. An honest-to-goodness hill rising above Harlem, and the center of a neighborhood from which many famous locals sprung. To see it, stroll Edgecombe Avenue, especially the blocks in the 150s: These row houses were once home to many of the musicians and other leading lights who fueled the so-called Harlem Renaissance. The apartment building at 409 Edgecombe Avenue was surely among the swankiest in these parts—its residents included W. E. B. DuBois and Thurgood Marshall—and many of the town houses here are quite attractive as well.

HIGHER LEARNING The City College of New York (212-650-7000), West 138th Street and Convent Avenue. Subway: 1 train to 137th Street. Founded back in 1847, City College moved uptown in the early 20th century and today sits inside four arched entrances in the St. Nicholas Heights neighborhood on a small spur of land poking above most of Harlem. The campus was built around the North Campus Quadrangle; a short walk shows off some fine buildings, most of which were built around the same time, such as massive Shepard Hall—it features a Gothic tower of local schist and contains an enormous Great Hall. (It is also home to both the city's only school of architecture and the Colin Powell Center for Policy Studies, which was named for one of the college's most famous alumni.)

Columbia University (212-854-1754), West 116th Street and Broadway. Subway: 1 train to 116th Street. An Ivy League university of nearly 20,000 graduate and undergraduate students, Columbia is New York's largest-campus institute of higher learning and makes a fine stroll. The university was actually founded in

Lower Manhattan—adjacent to Trinity Church (see chapter 1)—back in 1754 by King George II; it was called King's College then, and was the fifth such institution to be formed in the United States. The eight students in the inaugural class met for instruction in a simple two-story schoolhouse; by 1767 the college was offering North America's first medical degree. From 1776 until 1784 revolution closed the university down, and when it emerged it was with a new name and scope. Enrollment grew steadily, forcing a move in 1849 to a Midtown East location that suited Columbia's purpose for the subsequent five decades. During this time a law school and engineering school were both incorporated, and the university became one of the first to stress graduate education and research. Around the turn of the 20th century Columbia moved again, this time for the final time—its campus plans specially drawn up by renowned architect Charles McKim and his firm, whose design emphasized large Greek-style public spaces, domes, and Italian Renaissance architecture. The sciences began to flourish in this new home, as did the social sciences, the arts, journalism, and literature; the medical school formed a pioneering partnership with a hospital in the Washington Heights area of Harlem; Dwight D. Eisenhower served as president for a time. Pathbreaking work in physics, international relations, economics, and other fields would soon follow.

Even half an hour strolling the central pedestrian artery through campus (College Walk) offers a good taste of what's here. From Broadway, enter the college outside the 116th Street subway station on Broadway—passing the Miller Theater—and walk east along College Walk. About halfway between Broadway and Amsterdam Avenue, you'll spy the impressively domed and columned Low Memorial Library to your left. The cruciform library was built in 1895, designed as a nod to both the Pantheon and the Parthenon. Walk up the broad stairs for a better view of things—this is still the largest granite dome in America—then proceed indoors: The campus visitors center is located here to guide you to specific sights, and the interior's fine marble work and bronze and marble busts are also worth a look. (Though you can't tour it, the president's office is located here, and the annual Pulitzer Prizes are handed out in the building's rotunda.) Beside the library, directly to the east, stands little brick St. Paul's Chapel, its design featuring a central rotunda with stained glass, and columns on the reverse side; the interior is done in Guastavino tile. Directly across the green and College Walk, Butler Library is also distinctive for its long row of columns; the facade is inscribed with the names of famous writers.

Union Theological Seminary (212-662-7100), 3041 Broadway between West 120th and West 121st streets. Subway: 1 train to 116th Street. Originally located in the New York University neighborhood much farther downtown, UTS—a graduate school in theology, with a relationship to many of the surrounding houses of faith and institutes of higher learning—today occupies an attractive, quiet campus. The centerpiece is a lovely Gothic tower. The seminary's campus is not technically open to tourists, but visitors are not unwelcome, either; call ahead if you're very much wanting to drop in. There's also a pretty courtyard that somehow creates an oasis right off Broadway, and the students often relax here in surprisingly casual fashion.

BRIDGE **George Washington Bridge.** Fort Washington Avenue at West 178th Street. Subway: A train to 175th or 181st Street. This solid-looking steel suspension bridge, crossing from the Bronx to New Jersey, has been one of the Hudson River's most dramatic crossings since it opened in 1931—and at night during certain times of the year, when it's lit up, is extremely attractive. During daytime some souls do brave the pedestrian walk, though midriver the winds can be fierce and the 14 lanes of traffic are daunting. Even some New Yorkers don't realize that there's a red lighthouse—and a fort—beneath the New York–side supports (see *For Families*).

☀ To Do

The recreation area in **Riverside Park** between West 101st and West 111th streets features basketball courts, playing fields, volleyball courts, and now a skateboard park.

BIRD-WATCHING A bird sanctuary runs between West 116th and West 124th streets.

BOATING There's a kayak launch in **Riverside Park** at West 148th Street.

TENNIS There are tennis courts at West 119th Street. Call 212-360-8133 about tennis permits.

☀ Green Space

Central Park touches the southern reaches of Harlem. This wonderful park is well worth its own chapter; see chapter 9 for a full treatment of its treasures.

Fort Tryon Park (212-360-1311), 741 Fort Washington Avenue at West 193rd Street. Subway: A train to 190th Street. Thanks to a recent sprucing up and increased security, the surprisingly high and wild bluffs of this park overlooking the Hudson River make a fine green sanctuary for a walk when you're tiring of downtown. John Rockefeller commissioned noted park designer Frederick Law Olmsted—he of Central Park fame—to landscape this piece of terrain into a public space, then donated it to the city. The Heather Garden is well loved by locals, and the boats on the Hudson below present a calming counterpoint. During summer there are live jazz and chamber music concerts here; fall brings foliage. This is also the site of the expensive New Leaf Café (see *Dining Out*); sunsets over the New Jersey Palisades are especially scenic.

Fort Washington Park, along the Hudson River west of the Henry Hudson Parkway from West 155th to West 179th streets. Subway: A, C, or 1 train to 168th Street–Washington Heights, or A train to 175th Street. Fort Washington Park is notable mostly for its striking views of the Palisades hills of New Jersey, across the Hudson. The park also contains Manhattan's cutest lighthouse, known simply as the Little Red Lighthouse (see *To See—For Families*).

✐ **Inwood Hill Park,** west of Broadway from Dyckman Street north to the Harlem River. Subway: A or 1 train to 207th Street, or 1 train to 215th Street.

Some of the most lovely, thickly wooded acres in all Manhattan lie here in Inwood Hill Park, at the tip of the island where the Hudson River meets the smaller Harlem River (the dividing line between Manhattan Island and the Bronx). There's actually virgin forest here—that means no human hands have supposedly ever cut, logged, cleared, or grazed these woods, and if you've never seen them they're eye-openingly different from the Christmas tree plantation groves of suburban America. There's an ecology center explaining why. Baker Field, Columbia University's waterfront football stadium (and the site of many, many losing seasons)—its official name now is Lawrence A. Wien Stadium—is located in the 196-acre park at West 218th Street alongside a boathouse, field-house, baseball field, and tennis center. So is Manhattan's last remaining salt marsh as a marine sanctuary on the Hudson (at the bottom of Dyckman Street).

If you do come here, above all remember that you're standing on colonial history: This is supposedly the spot where Native Americans living on the island of Manhattan sold it to Dutch traders, led by Peter Minuit, beneath a giant tulip-tree for the total sum of 60 guilders (about $25) in 1626. Tiny, one-way Indian Road near the Columbia boathouse—the only roadway officially called a *road* in Manhattan—and a rock with a plaque affixed to it somehow attempt to commemorate this transaction, but the bald eagles you'll occasionally see high above (there's a nesting box in the park) are much more impressive than this token gesture.

Riverside Park, between Riverside Drive and Hudson River from West 72nd to West 155th Streets. Subway: 1 train to 110th, 116th, 125th, 137th, 145th, or 157th Street. Riverside Park stretches along the Hudson River's bank from 72nd to 155th Streets; the Harlem stretch is particularly rich with recreational opportunities (see *To Do*). Besides the park's famous—and rare—canopy of elms, there are also a row of plane and sycamore trees from West 101st to West 110th Streets; a Cherry Walk, which runs from West 100th to West 124th Streets; a community garden at West 138th Street; and a handy dog run at West 105th Street. Best of all, a green lawn runs right down to the riverside between West 147th and West 152nd Streets.

✳ Lodging

AFFORDABLE HOTEL International House (212-316-8473), 500 Riverside Drive at the corner of Claremont Avenue. Subway: 1 train to 125th Street. A kind of massive, two-building dormitory for Columbia, Barnard, and other visiting graduate students—usually students visiting from abroad—the blocky art-deco-style I House was originally built by the Rockefellers to foster international exchange and goodwill. Today it also opens 11 hotel rooms and suites to travelers year-round, all costing from around $125 double occupancy (there's an additional charge for extra guests). Single rooms are also occasionally available in summer or during winter break, for around $45 per person. All rooms here come with two twin beds and air-conditioning; the slightly more expensive deluxe guest rooms add a small refrigerator and more space, while suites add a pull-out sofa in a living-room area for a bit more money. Some rooms face pleasantly out onto green Sakura Park, and attractions such as Grant's Tomb, Riverside Park, and Columbia itself lie just steps away. There's also a pub on the premises, 24-hour security downstairs, a laundry room, and assorted internationally flavored activities running almost year-round. (There's a surprisingly beautiful auditorium.) Nothing here is fancy, but if you've got business or pleasure in the Columbia area, this is your best—actually your only—bet.

BED & BREAKFASTS **Bed and Breakfast Mont Morris** (917-617-4354), 56 West 120th Street between Lenox Avenue (Malcolm X Boulevard) and Morris Park West. Subway: 2 or 3 train to 116th Street. There are four rooms in this four-story brownstone on a quiet street in Harlem's Mount Morris neighborhood, and they're quite affordable—$89–99 per night for double occupancy—although very simply decorated. (There's no air-conditioning, for example.) But each room does have a private bath. The ground floor consists of two apartments, one a small studio with a tiny bathroom and one more conventionally sized, with a full kitchen; both have telephone and ceiling fan, as well as a simple queen bed, twin bed, and furnishings. The second-floor room, also with both a queen and a twin bed, has a fireplace and a small fridge. The third-floor room has two full-sized beds and a private bathroom on the hall. All guests here get continental breakfast at a bakery just down the block, and you're just half a block from Marcus Garvey Park, site of music in the summer.

Harlem Flophouse (212-662-0678), 242 West 123rd Street between Adam Clayton Powell Jr. Boulevard (Seventh Avenue) and Frederick Douglass Boulevard (Eighth Avenue). Subway: A, B, C, or D train to 125th Street. Despite the name, this refurbished town house of three rooms provides an inexpensive option for staying close to 125th Street's prime dining, shopping, and people-watching. The place was opened to fill a dearth of lodging in Harlem; each of the wood-floored rooms is named for a famous Harlem artist or musician. All of them—from the Corky Hale, with its Capodimonte lamps, to the tin-ceilinged, wooden-shuttered Chester Himes, to the walnut-manteled Cozy Cole—are very simply furnished with lighting, bedding, and furniture either custom-made or salvaged from markets or the street. Double rooms here cost about $125 per night, while the single occupancy rate is around $100. The included breakfast is hearty southern: eggs, sausage, and crackers.

Urban Jem Guesthouse (212-831-6029), 2005 Fifth Avenue between 124th and 125th streets. Subway: 4, 5, or 6 train to 125th Street. Tucked inside a 19th-century brownstone near Marcus Garvey Park, Urban Jem offers a rather unique way to live like a local for a few days in Harlem. It's centrally located—within three blocks of the Apollo Theater, shopping, restaurants, and the like—and homey, with two studio apartments (each with private kitchen and bath) and a third, larger room that can either be rented as a suite or split into two separate, bathroom-sharing rooms; all are nicely appointed, with marble fireplace. Continental breakfast is served in the dining room, which overlooks Fifth Avenue. Rates range $90–200 per double room; there's a 2-night minimum stay on weekends.

✳ Where to Eat

DINING OUT **Bayou** (212-426-3800), 308 Lenox Avenue (Malcolm X Boulevard) between 125th and 126th streets. Subway: 2 or 3 train to 125th Street. Open Monday through Friday for lunch 11:30 AM–4 PM and 6–10 PM for dinner, Saturday 6–11 PM for dinner, Sunday noon–4 PM for brunch. Chef Steven Manning's Creole cooking is served in an attractive room decorated with classy black-and-white photographs, right above his Slice of Harlem pizzeria (see *Eating Out*). Lunch here might start with barbecued shrimp or fried eggplant with powdered sugar, then continue with shrimp Creole, jambalaya, deep-fried catfish with rémoulade sauce, crawfish étouffée, or a thick po' boy; side dishes like a sweet yellow corn bread never fail to impress, either. The dinner menu is much the same, only it adds a bit more cachet in the form of turtle soup, rack of lamb, double-cut pork chops, and steak au poivre. (In the interest of full disclosure, it also adds fried oysters and sautéed chicken livers.) Entrées here are very reasonable, most of them costing around $13–22 apiece; try a pecan brownie or the bread pudding for dessert.

🍲 **Copeland's Restaurant** (212-234-2357), 547 West 145 Street between Amsterdam Avenue and Broadway. Subway: A, B, C, D, or 1 train to 145th Street. Open Tuesday through Saturday for dinner 4:30–11 PM, until midnight Friday and Saturday, Sunday noon–9 PM. Serious foodies count

this as one of the top two or three southern-cooking eateries in all Harlem (Amy Ruth's and Charles' are the other two that always seem to get a vote). The restaurant's interior decor pays homage to the heroes of Harlem in the form of portraits, and the meals—influenced by the Deep South, Louisiana, even Europe—certainly don't do anything to let down their memory. For dinner (costing around $10–25 per entrée), start with some of owner Calvin Copeland's gumbo, shrimp, or (if you're feeling adventurous) the chitterlings vinaigrette. The main course has to be fried chicken with gravy, fritters, and honey, or else barbecued spare- or short ribs, or maybe fried pork chops sided with a plate of pan-fried apples. If you're hankering for Cajun cooking, there's jambalaya, shrimp Creole, and étouffée. The kitchen also serves fancier, more expensive seafood dishes like braised lobster tails and sea scallops, but I'd stick to the lowbrow southern entrées, which are top notch—and can always be accompanied with great side dishes such as candied yams, macaroni and cheese, or collard greens. On Sunday, of course, there's a gospel brunch with a fine-looking crowd of after-church locals and their kids happily taking in the food and music. Note that reservations are absolutely necessary on weekend nights, when live music takes over, and for the Sunday brunch as well. The cafeteria next door is also operated by the same ownership, though it's considerably less upscale—actually, it reminds me of a school cafeteria with its 20-year-old furniture.

Londel's Supper Club (212-234-6114), 2620 Frederick Douglass

Boulevard (Eighth Avenue) between 139th and 140th streets. Subway: A, B, C, or D train to 145th Street, or 2 or 3 train to 135th Street. Open Tuesday through Saturday for lunch noon–4 PM and for dinner 5–11 PM, Sunday for brunch noon–5 PM. A cut above some of the other soul food joints in Harlem—the moment you pass muster at the velvet rope and stroll into the classy little dining room, you'll know this is a different sort of place. Londel's (technically a "supper club") serves great fried chicken, with or without waffles. Good barbecue and great macaroni and cheese are also smart choices. Or if those don't tickle your fancy, try one of the fancier dishes, such as pork chops, shrimp, or catfish. Entrées mostly cost $12–20 each here, and there's live music on weekend nights (Friday is jazz night). Buffet brunches are outstanding as well—choices include pork, smothered chicken, and plenty of side dishes—and afterward you can wander around the lovely neighborhood known as Strivers' Row (see *To See— Neighborhoods*).

& **New Leaf Café** (212-568-5323), 1 Margaret Corbin Drive in Fort Tryon Park. Subway: A train to 190th Street. Open Tuesday to Saturday for lunch noon–3 PM and dinner 6–10 PM, Sunday for brunch 11 AM–3 PM and for dinner 5:30–9:30 PM. Operated by Bette Midler's nonprofit New York Restoration Project, the New Leaf serves some decent uptown meals— though few know it, because the café is hidden within a stone house in pretty Fort Tryon Park, miles north of Midtown's hubbub. Whether you eat on the patio or inside, you'll have good views of park or river. The dish-

es are straightforward American fare: roast chicken, steak, tenderloin, changing fish dishes, and predictable brunches. The oak bar is a nice place for a drink. Prices run $10–18 for lunch entrées, $20–30 for dinner.

Rao's (212-722-6709), 455 East 114th Street at the corner of Pleasant Avenue. Subway: 6 train to 116th Street. Open by appointment only, weekdays only, 1 seating nightly. I'm certainly not going to be the one who recommends you make your way over to Spanish Harlem during a short trip to Manhattan. On the other hand, anyone craving a true taste of Italian New York just might make this journey— by car, preferably—because Rao's (say *RAY-ohs*) is the best. Unfortunately for you, it *knows* it's the best, and so you have to reserve every single meal here (there are just 10 tables, highly coveted by powerful New Yorkers)— and they might not take your reservation at all. Even if they do, they won't take your credit cards. It's almost like belonging to a private supper club . . . in Sicily. Anyhow, the delicious meals keep it simple: unadorned southern-Italian-style pastas, meat, and fish washed down with strong drinks from a personable bartender. It's atmosphere you come here for (and the conviviality among the patrons). If you can't get in, visit a gourmet supermarket somewhere in the city: Rao's jars and sells its pasta sauce for about $9 per throw.

Terrace in the Sky (212-666-9490), 400 West 119th Street between Amsterdam Avenue and Morningside Drive. Subway: 1 train to 116th Street. Open Tuesday through Friday for lunch noon–2:30 PM and dinner 6–10 PM, until 11 PM Friday and

Saturday, Sunday for brunch only 11 AM–3 PM. This 16th-floor restaurant with splendid views is the best place to dine in style after touring Columbia University—in fact, it's one of uptown's best fine-dining experiences—but dress up and bring plenty of cash or credit if you do; it's very expensive and classy. The seasonally changing menu here is outstandingly crafted. Lunch might start with a wild game pâté, pumpkin bisque, wild mushroom and cauliflower polenta, or small bouillabaisse; main courses run to pan-seared salmon and skate, hanger steak, pork medallions with quince puree, and the like. Dinner adds such appetizers as potato blinis, poached lobster, and peekytoe crab salad, along with main courses (priced around $32–39 each) such as risotto of duck confit, roasted squash, and wild mushrooms; grilled tuna with leeks, salsify, and chard; osso buco and tenderloin venison with squash gnocchi; a two-lamb sampler; grilled sirloin; and roast Muscovy duck breast with dumplings and bok choy. The prix fixe dinner offers diners a choice of braised short ribs of beef or crispy cod. Dessert options could include such treats as a cheese plate, *tarte Tatin,* five-spice crème brûlée, chocolate peanut butter mousse cake, roasted pear turnover, banana mousseline tart, or a whimsical four-pack of pumpkin sweets (crème brûlée, cheesecake, pie, and scone with chutney). All on fine china and crystal. Are you getting the picture? This is a sophisticated place, for sophisticated palates, and chef Jason Patanovich (previously of Virginia's Kingsmill resort and New York's Picholine) rarely lets them down. Lunch entrées cost around $18–24 each, and there's a prix fixe Tuesday through Thursday.

Note that there's open-air rooftop dining in summer, and glass-enclosed greenhouse dining in winter, both with views of surrounding parks, buildings, and the cliffs of New Jersey.

EATING OUT Africa Kine (212-666-9400), 256 West 116th Street between Adam Clayton Powell Jr. Boulevard (Seventh Avenue) and Frederick Douglass Boulevard (Eighth Avenue). Subway: B or C train to 116th Street. Open daily 12:30 PM–2 AM. If you're in the mood for Senegalese cooking, all you need to do is wander along West 116th in Harlem and you'll find plenty of options. Africa is one of the best, serving dishes such as lamb *mafe* (a kind of peanut butter stew), grilled chicken, and couscous, all washed down with refreshing juice drinks. Note that this restaurant now accepts credit cards.

Amy Ruth's Homestyle Southern Cuisine (212-280-8779), 113 West 116th Street between Malcolm X Boulevard (Lenox Avenue) and Adam Clayton Powell Jr. Boulevard (Seventh Avenue). Subway: B, C, 2, or 3 train to 116th Street. Open 24 hours on weekends, Sunday to Thursday 7:30 AM–11 PM. Amy Ruth's—named in memory of owner Carl Redding's grandmother—hasn't been in Harlem long, but the newcomer is already grabbing loads of attention for its great soul food. Fried chicken, sweetened with honey (reportedly Redding even keeps a beehive on the premises for the freshest possible honey), is the star here, and locals order it paired with crunchy waffles. But there are also outstanding daily specials; order whichever looks best—whether you choose the fried catfish, the smothered chicken, the ham hocks, or something else, you will be happy you made the trek. Most entrées cost just $9–12, and Redding isn't afraid to experiment: The jury's still out on his "soulvioli," or "soul food ravioli."

❧ Charles' Southern Style Kitchen (212-926-4313), 2839 Frederick Douglass Boulevard (Eighth Avenue) between 151st and 152nd streets. Subway: B or D train to 155th Street. Open Monday to Saturday, 8 AM– 1 AM, Sunday 8 AM–9 PM. Charles Gabriel, the legend goes, learned to cook beside his mother in the cotton fields of North Carolina. Today his tiny take-out operation and sit-down eatery draw legions for what might be the top fried chicken in New York, as well as hefty portions of chops, chicken, and wonderful southern side dishes like black-eyed peas. The inexpensive all-you-can-eat buffet is very deservedly popular.

La Marmite (212-666-0653), 2264 Frederick Douglass Boulevard (Eighth Avenue) at the corner of West 121st Street. Subway: A, B, C, or D train to 125th Street. Open Monday to Saturday 8 AM–10 PM, Sunday to 10 PM. There are plenty of Senegalese restaurants in this neck of Harlem, but La Marmite (along with Africa Kine, above) is among the better of them. Specialties include stews, fish, and fried rice; all are inexpensively priced.

M & G Soul Food Diner (212-864-7326), 383 West 125th Street at the corner of Morningside Avenue. Subway: A, B, C, or D train to 125th Street. Open daily 8 AM–midnight. Manhattan's best soul food diner is its only soul food diner, but the M & G could hold its own anywhere. What do you want? Fried chicken, of course, which seems to be turned out practically around the clock. Ribs, greens,

and other soul food staples can't miss, either. They don't take credit cards.

Miss Mamie's Spoonbread Too (212-865-6744), 366 West 110th Street between Columbus and Manhattan avenues. Subway: B, C, or 1 train to 110th Street. Open daily 11 AM–10:30 PM, Sunday to 9 PM. For a moment you might feel like you've stepped into a Fannie Flagg book when you find Miss Mamie's. Exemplary catfish, barbecue, vinegary North Carolina–style ribs, and fried chicken are among the stars at this cafeteria-style eatery, operated by the same owner as Miss Maude's (see below) and named for her mother. A distinctive red-and-white-checkerboard floor and cute curtains set the

PIZZA NEAR COLUMBIA UNIVERSITY

Paul Karr

homey experience, which side dishes like grits, corn bread, and candied yams complement. But why pick and choose? Go for an $18 sampler and try a little bit of everything the kitchen will roll out to you. Entrées cost $13–18 each, and the desserts—including peach cobbler, apple pie, and banana bread pudding—are sweet and especially good. Former president Clinton is said to be a big fan of the place.

Miss Maude's Spoonbread Too (212-690-3100), 547 Malcolm X Boulevard (Lenox Avenue) between 137th and 138th streets. Subway: B or C train to 135th Street. Open daily 11:30 AM–10 PM, Sunday from 10:30 AM. Yet another Harlem eatery named for a matron of the owner—this time it's an aunt of Norma Jean Darden, the former model and actress who owns two Harlem restaurants—Maude's is a bit less famous than its cousin restaurant, Miss Mamie's (see above). But it shouldn't be. The dining room looks just right, with nice old-fashioned photos and trimmings, and the food tastes finger-licking good, too. Anything is delicious, especially the excellent meat-and-two plates—go for meat loaf, catfish, or a bowl of gumbo, and remember to try the great side dishes such as the usual macaroni and cheese and candied yams. Many of these dishes are the same as those at the sister restaurant, just a bit better; also, there are a few choices, like oxtails and jerk chicken, you can't find at Mamie's. Prices are similar ($10–15 per entrée), and Maude's kitchen offers the same $15 sampler platter that Mamie's does.

🍴 **Patsy's** (212-534-9783), 2287–2291 First Avenue between 117th and 118th streets. Subway: 6 train to 116th Street. Open daily 11 AM–11 PM. Pizza experts in New York claim this out-of-the-way pizzeria in Spanish Harlem, the original Patsy's (dating way back to 1933), cooks New York's best pizza in a legendary coal oven that's been pleasing generations of locals for decades. The thin crusts here are charred to perfection inside the oven, then topped with tomato sauce (which is amazingly fresh and good) and mozzarella (which is the same). Pies cost about $12–15 each. You can also order by the slice, an unbelievable bargain for which you'd expect to pay two or three times the cost, but they *don't* accept credit cards. They do, however, serve surprisingly hoity-toity desserts too. Make the journey. Also see Patsy's Pizzeria in chapter 11.

Perk's (212-666-8500), 553 Manhattan Avenue at the corner of West 123rd Street. Subway: A, B, C, or D train to 125th Street. Owner Hank Perkins's newish eatery, just a couple of minutes' walk from Harlem's main artery (125th Street), serves a dinner menu featuring fillet of catfish, crabcakes, baby back ribs, steaks, fried and chili-grilled shrimp, and linguine. There's also a bar menu of chicken wings, burgers, lobster bisque, chicken livers with sautéed onions, and some of the dinner items.

Slice of Harlem (212-426-7400), 308 Malcolm X Boulevard (Lenox Avenue) between 125th and 126th streets. Subway: 2 or 3 train to 125th Street. Open daily 11 AM–10 PM. Downstairs from co-owned Bayou (see *Dining Out*), this place offers just what it says it does—plenty of slices and whole pies. The quality's good, though the pizza is no match for Patsy's (see above).

❧ **Sugar Shack Café** (212-491-4422), 2611 Frederick Douglass Boulevard (Eighth Avenue) at the corner of 139th Street. Subway: B or C train to 135th Street. Open daily 5 PM–midnight, weekends later. A great Harlem find, the Sugar Shack—inside a renovated brownstone perched on a corner near Strivers' Row—deliver good food, live jazz once a week, and lots of poetry readings. Decor is more interesting than at most Harlem joints, and the ground-floor bar is especially atmospheric. The food is what you would expect it to be: filling portions of catfish, fried chicken, barbecue, and the like, with sides of macaroni or greens. But there are also a few surprises such as scallops and spring rolls. Friday night brings live music and gets the joint jumping, while the Sunday brunch is a very good deal.

Sylvia's (212-996-0660), 328 Malcolm X Boulevard (Lenox Avenue) between 126th and 127th streets. Subway: 2 or 3 train to 125th Street. Open Monday through Saturday 8 AM–10:30 PM, Sunday 11 AM–8 PM. Much hyped and tour bus inundated, Sylvia and Herbert Woods's Lenox Avenue eatery is probably the most famous in Harlem. The Woods met in a bean field when they were just 11 and 12 years old, the story goes, and have now been married for 60 years. Their restaurant—which opened in 1962—has blossomed into a full-fledged media star. What keeps diners coming back? Great barbecued ribs, salmon croquettes, chops, and southern desserts. Sunday gospel brunch, as with any other in Harlem, gets quite packed; if you don't want those crowds, try for the Saturday-afternoon brunch, when jazz prevails. The quality of the meals here can sometimes waver, but if you like following the masses, have a look.

Tom's Restaurant (212-864-6137), 2880 Broadway at the corner of 112th Street. Subway: 1 train to 110th Street. Open Monday through Wednesday 6 AM–1:30 AM, Thursday

SYLVIA'S MAY BE HARLEM'S BEST-KNOWN EATERY.

Kim Grant

through Saturday 24 hours, Sunday noon–1:30 AM only. If you owned a television set anytime during the 1990s, you will instantly recognize the facade of this Columbia University–area diner—it appeared, early and often, as the exterior shot for the ubiquitous coffee shop on the hilarious TV series *Seinfeld.* They've paid homage with a wall of memorabilia related to the show, and the famous red neon sign stretching around the corner remains. The food here isn't half bad, either: cheap burgers, fries, grilled cheese sandwiches, BLTs, lunch and dinner plates, shakes, and more cooked up by the longtime Greek owners. Quite frankly it's nothing special, but—like a true diner should be—it's open 24 hours much of the week, attracts a varying cast of characters depending on the time of day or night (Columbia University students are your most likely cohorts), and does offer a slightly *Seinfeld*-ian experience. Everything here is priced inexpensively.

COFFEE AND SNACKS Hungarian Pastry Shop (212-866-4230), 1030 Amsterdam Avenue at the corner of West 111th Street. Subway: B, C, or 1 train to 110th Street. Open daily 7:30 AM–11:30 PM, from 8:30 weekends and until 10 PM Sunday. A cute little Eastern European café situated right across the street from the massive Cathedral of St. John the Divine, this pastry shop is a great place to take a break after touring nearby Columbia. You might feel like you're in Vienna as you nurse your single cup of coffee for hours, slowly devour something sweet (everything here's good, especially the cakes, tortes, tarts, and croissants), and try unsuc-

cessfully to catch the eye of an attractive waitress. They don't take credit cards, and they don't serve meals, but this place is well worth a detour of a few blocks. Movie buff note: Woody Allen's film *Husbands and Wives* shot a scene here, and famous faces are occasionally seen among the erudite.

✳ Entertainment

MUSIC VENUES Aaron Davis Hall (212-650-7100 for tickets, 212-650-6900 for information), City College of New York campus, 138 Convent Avenue at West 135th Street. Subway: 1 train to 137th Street, or A, B, C, or D train to 125th Street. Part of the City College of New York, whose towers loom over Strivers' Row in the northern reaches of Harlem, ADH (as it's known) puts on a varied annual program of performances. Events in a typical season might include a dance performance by the Forces of Nature Dance Company; a benefit performance by the husband-and-wife duo of Ashford & Simpson; a concerto by the woodwinds quintet Imani Winds; actor Avery Brooks's portrayal of Paul Robeson; the salsa entourage Manny Oquendo Y Libre; the eclectic SYOTOS band; or a performance of the play *Godmother,* about Harlem poet Langston Hughes's relationship with his patron Charlotte Mason. Ticket prices vary with the performance.

& **Apollo Theater** (212-749-5838 for tickets, 212-531-5300 for information), 253 West 125th Street between Adam Clayton Powell Jr. Boulevard (Seventh Avenue) and Frederick Douglass Boulevard (Eighth Avenue). Subway: A, B, C, D, 2, or 3 train to 125th Street. This is it: The center of Harlem. The three-story Apollo with the famous vertical sign is most famous for its live television program *Showtime at the Apollo*—a produced segment based on the lively weekly amateur competitions that have occurred Wednesday night since the mid-1930s. Ella Fitzgerald, Michael Jackson, Sara Vaughn, and James Brown are among the young talents who were first "discovered" at these live Wednesday events, which invariably begin at 7:30 PM and follow a time-tested format of live music, humor, prize giveaways, and then a spirited competition before a wildly appreciative—and sometimes brutally honest—audience. Things get festive here. ("If they're singing Jesus songs bad," cries one night's hostess with gospel zeal, "and you don't like the way they're singing, boo 'em! Jesus knows they can't sing!") The Apollo's colorful stage also sees a changing schedule of other presentations, such as the Temptations, George Clinton, a Latin music festival, Sweet Honey in the Rock, *Jazz at Lincoln Center* programs, benefits, and the Harlem-centric musical *Harlem Song*. Recent renovations have spruced up the theater's lighting, sound system, and wheelchair accessibility; event tickets generally cost $10–30 per person.

Copeland's Restaurant (212-234-2357), 547 West 145 Street between Amsterdam Avenue and Broadway. Subway: A, B, C, D, or 1 train to 145th Street. This Harlem standard features jazz piano most nights, plus singers on weekends and gospel on Sunday.

 Jazzmobile (212-866-4900), 154 West 127th Street. Performances at various locations. Since 1964, Jazz-mobile has brought a roving program of free jazz to various high-profile locations, including the General Grant National Memorial (see *To See—Historic Sites*), over the course of the summer. There are also free Saturday jazz workshops at public schools in Harlem with master jazz artists, and wintertime lectures to schoolkids.

Lenox Lounge (212-427-0253), 288 Lenox Avenue (Malcolm X Boulevard) between 124th and 125th streets. Subway: 2 or 3 train to 125th Street. Open daily noon–4 AM. Harlem's second most famous performance venue (the Apollo still takes the prize as best known) opened in 1939, and its Zebra Room quickly became a focal point for jazz stars such as Billie Holiday, Miles Davis, and John Coltrane. A tiny red lounge with art deco lettering, facade, and interior, it's still going strong today—a 1999 renovation helped matters greatly, giving the fading facility a retouch. Now the place is once again a kind of hot spot for Harlem's elite; there's jazz 6 nights a week (Thursday is R&B night), with weekends bringing free-form jazz—vocalists take over Sunday night—while Monday night sees extended jam sessions fill the room. Cover charges range from free up to around $10 or $20 per person. There's also a menu of barbecued chicken, fried chicken, crabcakes, luscious ribs, fish, and the like to accompany the music.

Londel's Supper Club (212-234-6114), 2620 Frederick Douglass Boulevard (Eighth Avenue) between 139th and 140th streets. Subway: A, B, C, or D train to 145th Street, or 2 or 3 train to 135th Street. Friday is jazz night at this popular buffet-style eatery.

Miller Theater (212-854-7740 for information, 212-854-7799 for tickets), campus of Columbia University, 2960 Broadway at the corner of West 116th Street. Subway: 1 or 9 train to 116th Street. Columbia's Jazz Composer Portraits series brings the work of important jazzmen to the Miller Theater, as interpreted by combos— usually house pianist Eric Reed (artistic director of the series) and his big band. Past performances have featured the work of the late Billy Strayhorn ("Take the A Train") as well as contemporary stars Ben Wolfe and Donald Brown. Tickets for these performances, which usually begin at 8 PM, cost up to about $30 per person.

☙ **Parlor Entertainment** (212-781-6595), 555 Edgecombe Avenue at the corner of West 160th Street. Subway: C train to 155th Street, or 1 train to 157th Street. This is the ultimate locals-only jazz spot—a Harlem apartment. Each Saturday and Sunday afternoon, talented local jazz players and Juilliard jazz hopefuls assemble in noted New York jazz singer Marjorie Eliot's big living room and play free sets to the first 40 who show up to fill the folding chairs. Eliot even offers punch and cookies. This is not an event to be abused; don't come with a tour group, and don't come at the wrong time. But if you're in the neighborhood and you absolutely love real jazz, think about stopping by. (And please donate generously, if you enjoy the music.)

Perk's (212-666-8500), 553 Manhattan Avenue at the corner of West 123rd Street. Subway: A, B, C, or D train to 125th Street. A soul food eatery with music at night, Perk's hosts Wednesday- and Thursday-night jazz jams, beginning at the welcome early hour of around 7 or 7:30 PM, in its second-floor lounge. Wynton Marsalis has been sighted sitting in here.

St. Nick's Pub (212-283-9728), 773 St. Nicholas Avenue near the corner of 149th Street. Subway: A, B, C, or D train to 145th Street. Closed Tuesday. Once more colorfully known as Luckey's Rendezvous, local jazz diva Berta Alloway's venue is well known in Harlem for combos such as the Sugar Hill Jazz Quartet. The music starts at 9:30 six nights a week; Monday is famous for some of Harlem's best instrumental jazz jams, while on Wednesday and Sunday the singers take over the jamming and scatting. Cover charge for the jazz ranges $12–40, depending on where you sit.

THEATER The National Black Theatre (212-722-3800), 2031–2033 Fifth Avenue between 126th and 127th streets. Subway: 2, 3, 4, 5, or 6 train to 125th Street. Opening hours vary; call. Located inside a former jewelry factory, this cultural organization—which formed in 1968 but is no longer just a performing arts group—focuses on cultural change and on fostering artists who are also entrepreneurs. Tours of the facility include a look at the largest Yoruba art collection in the Western world and Ancestral Hall, with its exhibits chronicling the lives of 75 famous African Americans.

FILM & AMC Magic Theatres (212-665-8742 or 212-665-5923), 300 West 125th Street at the corner of Frederick Douglass Boulevard (Eighth Avenue). Subway: A, B, C, or D train to 125th Street. This 10-screen movie theater right on Harlem's main drag is the place in Harlem to see first-run

Bond, Harry Potter, Austin Powers, Adam Sandler, and other Hollywood flicks; it has already become something of a local magnet. Seats are supercomfortable. (They even have some rocking chairs and love seats!) Tickets are steep, though.

READINGS **Sugar Shack Café** (212-491-4422), 2611 Frederick Douglass Boulevard (Eighth Avenue) at the corner of 139th Street. Subway: B or C train to 135th Street. Poetry readings from local residents are featured at this good soul food restaurant around the corner from the pretty town houses of Strivers' Row. Note that it's closed Monday.

BARS AND CLUBS **The West End** (212-662-8830), 2911 Broadway between 113th and 114th streets. Subway: 1 train to 110th Street. Open daily to 4 AM. A former serious Beat stronghold where the likes of Ginsberg and Kerouac hung out and philosophized, The West End is today a very normal restaurant, though prices are higher than they once were and karaoke rules the roost (oh unhappy day). But it's still worth a look if you worship—or once worshiped—the Beats.

✴ Selective Shopping

The **Malcolm Shabazz Harlem Market** (212-987-8131), on Lenox Avenue (Malcolm X Boulevard) between West 115th and West 116th streets (subway: 2 or 3 train to 116th Street) is Harlem's most interesting street market. It is extremely international—mostly African—in flavor, with a wide variety of carvings, jewels, cloth, and other crafts purveyed in stall after stall. If you're

wanting a real slice of life and some extremely interesting people-watching, this is the place to come. It's open daily from 10 AM until 9 PM.

Though there's nothing particularly selective about it, the mere presence of the relatively new but firmly established **Harlem USA** mall at the corner of Frederick Douglass Boulevard (Eighth Avenue) and West 125th Street cheers some locals. Subway: A, B, C, or D train to 125th Street. Corporate and controversial though it may be (it was built after a study showed Harlem residents possessed more disposable income than expected), this colorful glass six-level mall—right smack on 125th Street—has been heralded by some as the signal of a second Harlem Renaissance. That might be a bit of a stretch; still, it's undeniable that you can now satisfy a sudden urge to pop into HMV Records, Old Navy, or other name-brand retailers for a quick shopping or souvenir fix. There's also a 10-screen multiplex cinema (see *Entertainment—Film*) in the $65 million complex, which was designed without central corridors for milling around inside; instead, each store opens out onto the street. A New York Sports Club branch allows for pumping iron, while a Chase Manhattan Bank branch supplies the necessary funds.

ARTS AND CRAFTS **Xukuma** (212-222-0490), 183 Lenox Avenue (Malcolm X Boulevard) between 119th Street and 120th Street. Subway: 2 or 3 train to 116th Street. A store selling gifts with African American themes, such as soaps, bath and body items, garden supplies, stationery, and T-shirts. The store also sometimes hosts music and other events.

BOOKSTORE **Hue-Man Bookstore** (212-665-1033), 2319 Frederick Douglass Boulevard (Eighth Avenue) at the corner of 125th Street. Subway: A, B, C, or D train to 125th Street. By far the most interesting of the shops in the Harlem USA mall (see above), Hue-Man opened in 2002 and now purveys an extensive selection of African American and other titles; it's owned by three noted black business-women.

MUSEUM STORE **The Met Store** (212-923-3700), in The Cloisters in Fort Tryon Park at West 190th Street. Subway: A train to 190th Street. At The Cloisters, a branch of the popular Met Store features publications and reproductions produced by the museum, as well as other books and merchandise, with an emphasis on the art of the Middle Ages.

✴ Special Events

Early January: **Three Kings Day Parade** (212-660-7144). This fun Spanish Harlem event in the first week of January puts on a colorful annual parade along East 106th Street and then north 10 blocks into Spanish Harlem.

Late July–early August: **Harlem Jazz & Music Festival** (212-862-7200), various locations. This monthlong series of events, beginning in late July and continuing into August, has occurred around Harlem—and in other parts of Manhattan, as well—since 1991. There are jazz-history walking tours beginning at the Schomburg Center and The Studio Museum in Harlem (see *To See*); free concerts and theater; and a closing concert at Riverbank State Park.

August: **Harlem Week,** various locations. Actually an August-long celebration, Harlem Week features Monday-night plays, Tuesday-night walking tours, poetry readings, out-door jazz concerts, art exhibits, basketball tournaments—mostly along West 135th Street.

Late August: **Charlie Parker Jazz Festival,** Marcus Garvey Park near the corner of West 122nd Street and Fifth Avenue. Subway: 2, 3, 4, 5, or 6 train to 125th Street. One Saturday in late August, a jazz player or combo takes the stage at Marcus Garvey Park's bandshell for a 4- or 5-hour jam beginning at 3 PM. There's also a concert the next day in the East Village's Tompkins Square Park (see *Green Space* in chapter 3).

The Outer Boroughs

13

THE BRONX

BROOKLYN

QUEENS

STATEN ISLAND

THE OUTER BOROUGHS

Locals know that New York City is more than just Manhattan. They know because an awful lot of locals who work on that glittering isle actually *live* in one of the so-called Outer Boroughs: Brooklyn, the Bronx, Queens, Yonkers, and Staten Island. They live there because they can't afford to live in Manhattan, or simply choose not to do so; maybe they value lawns and breathing space over proximity to the hustle and bustle (and their jobs). Maybe they're artists in search of affordable studio and gallery space, filling in neighborhoods like Fort Greene or Williamsburg in Brooklyn. Maybe they're families fleeing the claustrophobia of the city's dense central island. Maybe they're descendants of immigrants who landed on Ellis Island long ago, found cheap digs in the boroughs, and never left.

In any case, these are places filled with real New Yorkers, trees, accents, and flavors. They're not always pretty, but they're unfailingly interesting—and authentic—if you know where to look.

Longtime ethnic pockets such as Brooklyn's Russian and Polish quarters, Queens's deep-rooted Chinese community, or the Bronx's Italian neighborhoods offer a number of quietly good eateries and cultural attractions—though you often have to be a local resident to know they exist. (I have saved you the work of relocating by tipping you off to some of the best.) A number of the city's most entertaining and venerated attractions—places like the Bronx Zoo, the Brooklyn Art Museum, and Yankee Stadium—also lie outside Manhattan's boundaries. And some mighty fine restaurants, specialty shops, art galleries, clothing boutiques, and other intriguing places have also slowly sprung up around the Outer Boroughs to follow a new wave of creative Manhattanites moving here in search of lower rents, trendier digs, or a new artistic challenge.

The lesson? You can't learn everything about New York simply standing on Fifth Avenue or gawking at Times Square's bright lights. So pack your subway pass and head for the boroughs to get another angle on the "real" New York.

THE BRONX

Da Bronx" is without question the city's most often snubbed, roasted, and reviled borough. Locals poke fun at the tenements, the crime, the accent, and just about everything else. And it's certainly true that vast sections of the borough are blighted. Yet there are also some merits to be found here, way uptown. (And it *is* uptown: Parts of the Bronx lie so far north that you must travel several miles *south* just to get to Harlem, a neighborhood that itself already lies far north of a comfortable orientation point such as the Empire State Building.) Witness a world-class zoo and perhaps the most famous baseball stadium in the world, for starters.

The Bronx was named for Jonas Bronck, the Swedish explorer who first settled the area during the 1630s. A major landmark was erected in 1748 when Frederick Van Cortlandt built his Van Cortlandt House (see *Green Space*); at the end of the American Revolution, Washington's troops garrisoned at the house before marching on New York to take the British. The area steadily expanded, for better and worse, and in 1904 the metropolitan subway system came to the borough. Yankee Stadium opened in 1923, and a series of bridges and expressways unveiled during the 1930s draw the borough even closer to Manhattan. But with this new accessibility came very rapid growth, not without consequence; immigrant populations sought out the Bronx's cheaper rents, and by the 1970s the borough's crime, poverty levels, and substandard housing had become extremely serious problems, serious enough to merit a personal visit by U.S. president Jimmy Carter.

The area has begun a slow recovery from those dark days, and today Latin and Italian cultures are the two primary influences here. You shouldn't budget more than a half or full day for activities here, because the prime attractions are scattered quite far apart from each other. I also don't recommend staying or eating here, especially if you're on a tight schedule. But it might be interesting to sneak a peek at a real working-class neighborhood whose current pride and joy is local girl Jennifer Lopez, now quite famous as an actress and singer; her first musical album was called *On the 6* as homage to the long, long subway ride she once made daily from her Castle Hill neighborhood into Manhattan

GETTING THERE The Bronx is a bedroom community, and thus fairly well served by subway lines. The commute, however, is a long one. It's easiest to reach the prime attractions by car.

By car: The Henry Hudson Parkway (an extension of the West Side Highway) reaches the western Bronx, and clearly marked exits indicate Van Cortlandt Park. To reach the Bronx Zoo, get to the Cross Bronx Parkway—again, reached via the Henry Hudson Parkway on the west side of Manhattan—get onto it, and then change to the Bronx River Parkway. Yankee Stadium is trickier to find; use the subway (see below).

By subway: I don't recommend taking a bus to the Bronx, but you can get here by subway in easy, if time-consuming, fashion. To reach Yankee Stadium, take the 4, B, or D train to 161st Street. (Note that B trains only run weekdays, and some D trains at rush hours skip local stops such as Yankee Stadium; on game days, however, there are extra trains stopping here.) To reach the Bronx Zoo, take the 5 express train uptown from an express station such as those at Grand Central or Union Square; from the west side, you can also take the 2 train, though this takes a while to get there. To reach Van Cortlandt Park, take either the 1 or 9 train uptown to the very last stop on the line.

GETTING AROUND The Bronx's attractions are all so far apart that you'll need a car to get from point to point. There is simply no other convenient way to connect those dots.

✳ To See

FOR FAMILIES 🥾 **Bronx Zoo** (718-367-1010), Fordham Road at Bronx River Parkway. Subway: 2 or 5 train to Bronx Park East. Open daily 10 AM–5 PM, to 5:30 PM spring and summer weekends, to 4:30 PM winter. Everyone has heard of the Bronx Zoo. (No, I'm not talking about the New York Yankees; see below for details on that successful baseball club.) But few have been there. Now here's your chance to visit the biggest city zoo in the United States (and one of the best run). There are more than 6,000 species here in all, including some rather unusual ones: More than 80 rare snow leopards have been bred here, for example. To run the world faunal gamut while keeping some semblance of order, the giant zoo is broken up into self-explanatory sections such as African Plains, an Aquatic Bird House, the World of Birds, Wild Asia, Himalayan Highlands, JungleWorld, and World of Reptiles. One of the

SOME RESIDENTS OF THE BRONX ZOO

Kim Grant

most interesting additions, however, is the Congo Gorilla Forest, 6.5 acres of re-created African rain forest habitat containing more than 300 animals including monkeys, pythons, wild hogs, assassin bugs, Nile monitors, and—of course—a population of about two dozen lowland gorillas. At holiday time watch for Holi-day Lights, a nightly program of pathways, artful ice-carving demonstrations, lighted animal sculptures—some of them animated—and nighttime sea lion feedings. There's a slight extra charge for these exhibits, which are open 5 PM–9 PM weekends from Thanksgiving through mid-December, then daily 5–9 PM until early January (but closed on Christmas Eve). Admission to the zoo costs $11 for adults, $8 for seniors and children 2–12, discounts in winter; parking costs $8 per car. (Wednesday is free, but a donation of the usual admission amount is strongly suggested.)

🍴 🖊 ♿ **Wave Hill** (718-549-3200), 675 West 252nd Street at Independence Avenue. By car: Henry Hudson Parkway to Exit 21 or 22. By train: MetroNorth commuter line from Grand Central Terminal to Riverdale station. Open Tuesday through Sunday 9 AM–5:30 PM, winter to 4:30 PM; greenhouses open shorter hours. One of New York's best places to take the kids is, unfortunately, quite dis-tant from the central attractions of the city. If you're driving, though, Wave Hill is a must-see—a peaceful mansion on the placid banks of the Hudson that once housed famous residents but has since been turned into an environmental edu-cation center. The centerpieces include extensive, carefully landscaped gardens (some of Great Manhattan's very best—with outstanding views as a welcome bonus) and a greenhouse of rare flowers and plants; the rotating programs of art, literature, horticulture lectures, kids' activities, and gardening classes mean there's usually something going on here. Even if there isn't, this is a splendid place for a stroll and a picnic. From mid-March through mid-November, admis-sion costs $4 per adult, $2 for students and senior citizens, and Tuesdays and Saturday mornings are free; Wave Hill is also completely free to visit during the winter months.

🍴 🖊 ♿ **Yankee Stadium** (718-579-4531), River Avenue at 158th Street. Subway: 4, B (weekends only), or D train to 161st Street–Yankee Stadium. Tours are given 10 AM–4 PM weekdays and 10 AM–noon weekends during the off-season and when the team isn't playing home games. Love 'em or hate 'em (and if you're not from New York, you probably grew up hating 'em), the New York Yankees epitomize Big Apple sports. This club has lived larger than any in pro-fessional sports, perhaps, claiming a record 26 world championships and—in the process—retiring the uniform numbers of some of the game's greatest legends, guys with names like Mantle, Ruth, and Gehrig. Apple shaped and triple tiered, Yankee Stadium—built in 1921 on lands purchased from the Astor family—is not the only home field the Yankees have ever known. But it does contain most of their significant history. Although you cannot tour the stadium on game days during the professional baseball season running from April through the playoffs in late October—you will need a game ticket to get in at those times (see *Enter-tainment*)—you *can* tour it when the team is playing away from home or during the off-season. A tour takes approximately 1 hour and costs $14–$25 for adults, $7–$17 for seniors and children 14 and under; while learning about Yankee

Kim Grant

NEW YORK YANKEES FANS

history you'll visit the field, dugout, press box, Monument Park (statues are erected here, commemorating the team's greatest stars), and in the off-season the players' private clubhouse. Though the stadium is way way uptown, a long subway ride or drive from Manhattan, a trip here is practically a trip to the Hall of Fame; if you're nuts about baseball, don't miss it. Note that you can also purchase tour tickets at any of the Yankee stores around Manhattan—there's one in Times Square and another on Fifth Avenue in the 30s, for example.

✳ To Do

GOLF **Van Cortlandt Golf Course** (718-543-4595), Van Cortlandt Park South at Bailey Avenue. Subway: 1 train to 242nd Street–Van Cortlandt Park. If you're seriously into golf history, a visit to this course—one of the oldest in America—might be in order. Truth be told, the course isn't entirely attractive today (housing projects overlook a couple of holes, and waterbirds sometimes run riot over the place), but there are still some relatively graceful views to be had and a few challenging holes toward the finish. Green fees run about $25–30 per person.

✳ Selective Shopping

HOME FURNISHING STORE **ABC Carpet & Home Warehouse Outlet** (718-842-8772), 1055 Bronx River Avenue. Open daily 10 AM–7 PM, Sunday 11 AM–6 PM. This newest outpost of the luxe Manhattan furnishings store ABC Carpet & Home offers lower-priced (but still great) stuff. Expect lots of high-quality imported carpets, furniture, decorative lighting, and other hard-to-find items—a piece of statuary for the estate garden, perhaps?

✳ Green Space

Van Cortlandt Park (718-430-1890), Broadway at West 240th Street and Birchall Avenue. Subway: 1 train to 242nd Street–Van Cortlandt Park. The city's third largest park, Van Cortlandt contains more than 1,100 acres of greenery and plenty of fields, woods, ball fields, playgrounds, a lake, even a golf course. This was originally part of the estate of the powerful Van Cortlandt family, which farmed the property and built power-generating mills on it for nearly two centuries beginning in 1699; New York assumed control of the park in 1888, and Van Cortlandt's stone house is now a museum.

✍ **Wave Hill** (718-549-3200), 675 West 252nd Street at Independence Avenue. Subway: 1 train to 231st street, then Bx7 or Bx10 bus to 252nd Street. Or Metro-North commuter rail to Riverdale Station. This environmental education center (see *To See—For Families,* above)—also once the retreat of great artists and composers—features great views of the Hudson and the New Jersey Palisades, and it's especially strong on kids' programs, art shows, and summer concerts. The gardens and enclosed greenhouses are wonderful to view, as well. Begin at the visitors information enter, housed inside a stone mansion.

✳ Where to Eat

DINING OUT **The Black Whale** (718-885-3657), 279 City Island Avenue at the corner of Carol Street. Subway: 6 train to Pelham Bay Park, then Bx29 bus. Open Tuesday to Friday 4 PM–midnight, Saturday from noon, Sunday 10 AM–10 PM. This City Island legend from the '60s and '70s reopened in 1998 and again serves family-friendly meals of pasta, meat, and seafood. You can go simple at "the Whale" (meat loaf with mashed potatoes, baby back ribs, grilled sirloin) or slightly fancier (seared, sesame-encrusted tuna with a ginger-orange sauce, pan-roasted scallops with onion-basil relish, grilled swordfish with coconut rice, grilled pork chops with Calvados sauce and grilled peaches). The big Sunday brunch buffet remains everlastingly popular—cooks whip up omelets right in front of your nose—as do wonderful desserts like warmed apple crisp, chocolate layer cake, and an orange "frizz" (a lot like a Creamsicle). The outdoor patio, with its fountains and garden, is one of the most romantic places to eat for miles. And the Tuesday night "Dinner and a Movie" deal is unique and satisfying to both mind and palate.

Dominick's (718-733-2807), 2335 Arthur Avenue between Crescent Avenue and East 187th Street. Subway: B, D, or 4 train to Fordham Road; then take Bx12 bus to Arthur Avenue. Open Monday to Thursday, noon–10 PM, Friday and Saturday to 11 PM, Sunday 1–9 PM. Make your way to Dominick's and you've found New York's red-sauce nirvana, much better and more authentic than anything you'll find in Manhattan's Little Italy. Extremely popular, the restaurant is perhaps locals' favorite Italian eatery of all the many choices strung out along Arthur Avenue. It's strictly no frills: they take no reservations, credit cards, or nonsense. Heck, there isn't even a menu to speak of, really. Instead, a family feel predominates as you stand on line with congenial strangers waiting to get in, then belly up to communal tables and wolf down one of the huge plates of pasta or seafood.

Le Refuge Inn (718-885-2478), 620 City Island Avenue at the corner of Sutherland Street. Subway: 6 train to Pelham Bay Park, then Bx29 bus to Sutherland Street. Open for dinner Tuesday to Sunday 6–10 PM. Le Refuge is a remarkable hideaway, which also serves as a bed & breakfast in the unlikely location of City Island (if you're truly enchanted, double rooms cost about $135 per night). For more than a quarter century Pierre Saint-Denis has operated the discreet establishment overlooking City Island's harbor, perfect for a quiet getaway from the city. Though difficult to reach by public transit, it's well worth seeking out if you're driving to Manhattan. For around $45 per person, you can experience a three-course prix fixe French meal that begins with salad, duck liver mousse, escargots in puff pastry, gratin, crabcake, or lobster ravioli, then moves on to entrées such as grilled salmon, duck in brandy sauce, grilled chicken, filet mignon, loin of lamb, or bouillabaisse; finish sweetly with opera cake, chocolate mousse, crème brulée, or profiteroles. Sunday brunch is $25 per person, lunches are $35 apiece, and there are occasional concerts here as well.

Mario's (718-584-1188), 2342 Arthur Avenue between Crescent Avenue and East 186th Street. Subway: B, D, or 4 train to Fordham Road; then take Bx12 bus to Arthur Avenue. Open Tuesday to Sunday noon–11 PM. This family joint feels like it has been here forever (actually, it's been here more than 80 years), serving southern Italian fare such as veal saltimbocca, osso buco, seafood, pastas, good pizzas, and the like. It's definitely a cut above the others along Arthur Avenue in terms of fine-dining atmosphere and price. A *Sopranos*-like cast of regulars adds a touch of authenticity, and afterward the *dolce* (sweets) are pretty good, too.

EATING OUT **Lobster Box** (718-885-1952), 34 City Island Avenue. Subway: 6 train to Pelham Bay Park, then Bx 29 bus. Open daily 11:30 AM–11:30 PM, weekends to 1 AM. Manhattan couldn't feel farther away here way down at the tip of City Island, beside Johnny's Reef, operated by the same ownership. This salty little fried-food emporium serves cheap seafood cafeteria-style to appreciative crowds of locals. They also do pasta and lobsters stuffed with cheese (ownership is Italian), but I'd stick to fried fish and shellfish and the cheap beer. Eat outside: You're looking right at (and smelling) the islands and boats of Long Island Sound.

✳ Entertainment

SPECTATOR SPORTS ⚾ **New York Yankees** (718-293-6000), Yankee Stadium, River Avenue at 158th–161st streets, the Bronx. Subway: 4, B (weekends only), or D train to 161st Street–Yankee Stadium. The ticket office opens weekdays 9 AM–5 PM. The Yankees are, quite simply, one of the most successful pro sports teams in the world. This team seems to win the American League East division every single year (though the Red Sox toted off the World Series trophies in 2004), and has amassed 26 world championships in all. To see stars like Jeter, Mussina, and Rivera in action, buy a ticket and a hot dog and hang out like a local for a day. If you get here very early, try to wander over to Monument Park (it's in Section 35, between the bullpens), which closes to the public about 45 minutes before game time. Here you'll find statues, plaques, and a walk honoring the team's top stars; major-league players love this area. (Note that bleacher-seat ticket holders cannot visit the park—their tickets don't allow access to this level of the field.)

BROOKLYN

Brooklyn (the word meant "broken land" in Dutch, a nod to the once rolling geology and topography of the area) is undoubtedly the best known of New York's satellites. Located directly across the East River from some of Manhattan's most impressive buildings—and connected to that island by the graceful Brooklyn Bridge—this huge borough likes to brag that it's America's fourth largest city. It has always been closely tied to Manhattan, yet a little different, too.

It started out, like Manhattan, as a Native American and then Dutch stronghold. Later waves of immigration and annexation helped swell its size to the present 2.5 million, a third of New York City's total population; Brooklyn's known for harboring the city's largest Jewish, Russian, and Polish populations. Many famous entertainers were born here, including Neil Diamond, Barbra Streisand, Spike Lee, Eddie Murphy, Mary Tyler Moore, and lots more.

The borough's various neighborhoods have each hammered out their own distinct personalities. Artists and musicians have been decamping in Carroll Gardens, Fort Greene, DUMBO, and Victoria Terrace in recent years; Brooklyn Heights' fantastic views and pretty town houses have long attracted wealth; Borough Park is famous for its concentration of Hasidic Jews; Brighton Beach's "Little Odessa" Russian community is the nation's largest; Flatbush Avenue was once a street of Jewish butchers and bakers; and Smith Street, running through Boerum Hill and Carroll Gardens, has found surprising new life as a center of haute cuisine.

All in all this is easily the most interesting of the Outer Boroughs, with the best shopping, restaurants, and sights; I could easily have written an entire book on it—walking you through every last Russian deli of Brighton Beach, every carnival ride at Coney Island, every boutique shop in Brooklyn Heights, and so forth. If you've got time for just one off Manhattan trip, catch a train—you've got lots of choices; see below for more information—and come to Brooklyn.

GETTING THERE Brooklyn is very easy to reach by subway, and frustrating to reach by car. Of course, some destinations (such as the Brooklyn Brewery) *must* be reached by car.

By car: If you must drive, then, use the Brooklyn–Battery Tunnel to get from Lower Manhattan to Carroll Gardens; the Brooklyn or Manhattan bridges from

Chinatown to Brooklyn Heights and DUMBO, Fort Greene, and Park Slope; and the Williamsburg Bridge from the Lower East Side to Williamsburg. Coney Island takes quite a bit of time to reach by car.

By subway: Many lines travel here from Manhattan. Brooklyn Heights is best reached by the 2 or 3 train to Clark Street, or the A or C train to High Street (the heart of DUMBO). Prospect Park, the Brooklyn Academy of Music, the Brooklyn Museum, and the Park Slope neighborhood are all very easily reached—the Q train from Manhattan stops right at the park, as do the F, 2, and 3 lines. Carroll Gardens is reached by taking the F train to Bergen Street or Carroll Street. Williamsburg lies along the J, M, and Z subway lines; get off at Marcy Avenue. Fort Greene is not conveniently served by the subway, but the F train stop at York Street comes fairly close. Coney Island is the very last stop on the W line, which stops on Canal Street (in Chinatown); in SoHo; and in Times Square, among other locations in Manhattan.

✳ To See

MUSEUMS ♿ **Brooklyn Museum of Art** (718-638-5000; www.brooklynmuseum.org), 200 Eastern Parkway at Prospect Park (in Prospect Park). Subway: 2 or 3 train to Eastern Parkway, or B, D, N, R, or Q train to Atlantic/Pacific Street. Open Wednesday through Friday 10 AM–5 PM, Saturday and Sunday 11 AM–6 PM, first Saturday of each month until 11 PM. Right on Prospect Park, and beside the Botanic Garden (see *Green Space*), this museum is just enormous—not as big as the Met, but still impressively full of modern art and historic archaeology. Its permanent collections include the work of such American painters as Frederic Church, Georgia O'Keeffe, Winslow Homer, Marsden Hartley, and Mark Rothko; work by Degas, Pissarro, and Matisse; and nearly 60 sculptures by Auguste Rodin. A set of a dozen very old Assyrian reliefs has been placed back on display after a period of conservation. The museum's Egyptian section (which includes a 2,600-year-old mummy) has been vastly enlarged. Saturdays bring special programs such as films, talks, and music. Asian holdings include a significant collection of Korean art and a full set of Hiroshige's *100 Famous Views of Edo* woodblock prints. Rotating exhibits have recently showcased Victorian nudes, cutting-edge video art, a Persian manuscript, and African artwork. Admission costs $8 for adults, $4 for students and seniors, free for children under 12.

New York Transit Museum (718-694-1600), Boerum Place at Schermerhorn Street. Subway: 2, 3, or 4 train to Borough Hall, or M or R train to Court Street. Open Tuesday to Friday 10 AM–4 PM, weekends noon–5 PM. Housed in a historic 1936 IND subway station in Brooklyn Heights, and easily accessible by subway, the New York Transit Museum is the largest museum in the United States devoted to urban public transportation history, and one of the premier institutions of its kind in the world. The museum explores the development of the greater New York metropolitan region through the presentation of exhibitions, tours, educational programs and workshops dealing with the cultural, social and technological history of public transportation. Go to www.mta.info for details of current exhibits and programs, or to shop the museum's online store. Admission costs $5 per adult, $3 for seniors and children age 3 to 17 (seniors enter for free on Wednesday. There's also a gallery annex and store in Grand Central Terminal's main concourse (in the Shuttle Passage)—call 212-878-1016 for details.

HISTORIC SITE Brooklyn Bridge, between Brooklyn Heights and Chinatown. Subway: 4, 5, or 6 train to Brooklyn Bridge–City Hall (for New York side); 2 or 3 train to Clark Street, or A or C train to High Street (for Brooklyn side). It's difficult to deny that this is one of the world's most famous bridges, pleasing in structure and scale, and accommodating enough to admit automobile, bicycle, and pedestrian traffic with (nearly) equal ease. Designed by bridge engineer John Roebling in the 1860s, this one suffered tragedy before it was even begun: Roebling was killed in a freak accident prior to construction (26 more would die during the 13 years of construction), and his son Washington was forced to assume management of the project. But the younger Roebling soon took severely ill from spending too much time belowground supervising the digging for supports, and his wife, Emily, took over—learning engineering on the spot, coached by her bedridden husband. Many cutting-edge techniques were tried out during the bridge's construction, including dynamite for blasting and the use of steel suspension strands; when the bridge finally opened in May 1863, arc lamps lighting the pedestrian walkway (and a one-cent toll in force), it was widely acclaimed. Circus mogul P. T. Barnum walked 21 of his elephants across in 1884 to prove its sturdiness.

A walk across the four-cabled, 1,600-foot-long bridge—above (not beside) six lanes of traffic, for a change, and beneath the two famously arched support towers—is still a fine way to spend a spring or summer morning; you'll be treated to terrific views of both Manhattan and its harbor if you do. If you mind heights or proximity to auto exhaust, however, you might think twice about making the stroll. In that case, take the subway to Brooklyn Heights and walk the Promenade (see *Neighborhoods*) for exquisite views of the bridge. There are several good restaurants at its base on both ends as well, and a park is slowly being constructed around the bottom of the Brooklyn side.

FOR FAMILIES *✐* **Astroland Amusement Park** (718-265-2100), 1000 Surf Avenue at the corner of West 10th Street (on Coney Island). Subway: W train to Coney Island. Spring, open weekends noon–closing time (depends on weather, generally begins operation late March); mid-June through Labor Day, open daily noon–midnight; September, open weekends noon–closing time. Got little ones? Bring 'em here to Coney Island's boardwalk and a monster ride. Astroland is mostly known for its 75-year-old Cyclone roller coaster, a loopy, wooden-tracked thrill ride that's steeper, and more frightful, than most—aficionados say it's one of the best (that is, scariest) in the world. After departing from an old-style station, the track drops a dozen times in all during the 2-minute ride, hitting speeds of 60 miles per hour as it goes through six stomach-churning 180-degree turns. If you can get through the first drop, 85 feet at a steep 60-degree angle, you might hold down your lunch through the ride. Other Astroland attractions include a

Kim Grant

ASTROLAND AMUSEMENT PARK ON CONEY ISLAND

water flume ride, a pirate ship, a "scrambler" ride, a Tilt-A-Whirl, and the usual assortment of games of skill and chance. Admission to the park and boardwalk are free; ride tickets cost $2–5 each, or a day pass—known here as a P.O.P. (Pay One Price) ticket—costs $21.99 per person. You can also purchase a packet of 10 kiddie ride tickets for about $15. The Cyclone costs $5 per run.

𝒮 **Deno's Wonder Wheel Park** (718-372-2592), 1025 Boardwalk at West 12th Street (on Coney Island). Subway: W train to Coney Island. Open Memorial Day through Labor Day, daily 11 AM–midnight; April, May, September, and October, open weekends only noon–9 PM (weather permitting). Another attraction right on the Coney Island boardwalk, this amusement park opened in 1920 and features as its centerpiece a graceful 150-foot-high Ferris wheel known simply as the Wonderwheel. If you crave Ferris wheels, don't miss it; it's just $5 a whirl. There are 24 other rides here as well, some costing less; a 5-ride pack of tickets costs $20. Kids ride for $2, or ride 10 times for $18.

𝒮 **New York Aquarium** (718-265-FISH), Surf Avenue at West Eighth Street (on Coney Island). Subway: W train to Coney Island. Spring and fall, open weekdays 10 AM–5 PM, weekends to 5:30 PM; summer, open 10–6 PM weekdays, to 7 PM weekends; winter, open daily 10 AM–4:30 PM. New York City's lone aquarium (and the nation's oldest) takes some traveling to reach, but once you're here it's well worth a visit despite the somewhat high price of a ticket and parking. The aquarium opened in 1896 in Manhattan's Battery Park, then closed during World War II (the denizens temporarily swam their laps at the Bronx Zoo); it reopened here across from the Coney Island boardwalk in 1957, and now houses some 8,000 specimens of 350 or so aquatic species under the auspices of the Wildlife Conservation Society. Highlights include such sea mammals as dolphins, beluga whales, and walruses. A sea horse exhibit was added to the Sea Cliffs section in 2000 to showcase these intriguing masters of disguise, and an even newer "stingers" exhibit currently features lovely but venomous ocean species such as jellyfish (which are composed of a remarkable 95 percent water), sea wasps, and anemones. Admission costs $12 for adults, $8 for children 2–12 and seniors; parking costs an additional $8 per car.

NEIGHBORHOODS Brooklyn Heights Promenade, along Hudson River between Middagh and Montague streets (in Brooklyn Heights). Subway: 2 or 3 train to Clark Street, M, N, R, or W train to Court Street, or A or C train to High Street. There's no better view of Manhattan than the one from this brownstone-lined boardwalk; it faces the East River, Brooklyn Bridge, Ellis Island, and the Statue of Liberty, not to mention the Manhattan skyline—you'll easily pick out the Empire State Building and the Chrysler Building. (Local residents and photographers got a terrifyingly clear view of the collapse of the World Trade Center towers in September 2001.) It also frames perhaps Brooklyn's prettiest neighborhood, Brooklyn Heights. To explore the area, begin at Montague Street, then walk down to the promenade, detouring to stroll Orange, Cranberry, Pine-apple, and other cutely named side streets.

Coney Island Boardwalk (on Coney Island). Subway: W train to Coney Island. The most famous boardwalk in New York takes a long subway ride or drive to reach—it's at the very last stop of the W line—but rewards the hot or hungry traveler with a decently clean beach, amusement park rides, and enough honky-tonk to feel you're partaking of a uniquely American escape from the city. Not to mention all the taffy, soft-serve ice cream, all-beef hot dogs, and lime rickeys you could want. (Also see *For Families* for more on Coney Island.)

DUMBO (beneath the Brooklyn Bridge, just downhill from Brooklyn Heights). Subway: A or C train to High Street. This neighborhood, which falls literally beneath the Manhattan and Brooklyn bridges, was coined not for a flying ele-phant, but for being Down Under the Manhattan Bridge Overpass. Clever, isn't it? And hip, too: Though small, this neck of the woods packs a touristic punch all out of proportion to its size. You'll find some of New York City's best ice-cream parlors, pizza joints, classy restaurants, and chocolate emporia, not to mention artists' lofts and boutiques.

✳ Green Space

🐾 ♿ **Brooklyn Botanic Garden** (718-623-7200), 1000 Washington Avenue at Eastern Parkway (in Park Slope). Subway: 2 or 3 train to East-ern Parkway, or B, D, N, R, or Q train to Atlantic/Pacific Street. In summer (April through September), open Tuesday through Friday 8 AM–6 PM and weekends 10 AM–6 PM; the rest of the year, open same days but open to 4:30 PM daily. The best arbor-etum in New York isn't in Manhattan,

THE BROOKLYN HEIGHTS PROMENADE OFFERS SPECTACULAR VIEWS OF MANHATTAN.

Paul Karr

but rather this vaguely Birkenstock-shaped parcel adjacent to Brooklyn's Prospect Park. The garden was created back in 1897 by state legislators. Beginning around 1911, flowers and plants were installed. Both Japanese Hill-and-Pond Garden and the very important collection of bonsai trees were soon added, then a rose garden and a children's garden. Eventually a research program was begun to develop new plants.

Among the garden's many highlights are the Shakespeare Garden, a Celebrity Path naming some of the many celebrities born in this borough (Sandy Koufax, Woody Allen, Arthur Miller, and Neil Diamond, to name just a handful), the Cranford Rose Garden—containing some 5,000 bushes and more than 1,000 varieties—and the Japanese Garden (note the 500-year-old lantern). Magnolia Plaza, dating from the 1930s, is best in April and May when up to 17 varieties blossom. Cherries are another specialty here: One highlight is the annual Sakura Matsuri (Cherry Blossom Festival) in late April, when the 76-tree Cherry Esplanade and adjacent Cherry Walk and pond explode in a blizzard of white and pinkish petals. Here's a tip for if you happen to be visiting New York during frigid weather: The garden is great for a winter visit, because parts of the greenhouse complex—which includes desert, aquatic, bonsai, and tropical areas—are kept constantly heated at comfortable temperatures. And the first of what will be about 80 scarlet oak trees in a grove have been planted to commemorate the events of September 11, 2001. Admission to the garden costs just $3 for adults, $1.50 for seniors and students, except free Tuesdays and Saturday mornings.

&. **Prospect Park** (718-965-8951), at Prospect Park West, Parkside Avenue, and Washington Avenue. Subway: F or Q train to Prospect Park, or 2 or 3 train to Eastern Parkway–Brooklyn Museum or Grand Army Plaza. A huge (500-plus-acre) park designed by the team of Frederic Law Olmsted and Calvert Vaux, the same duo responsible for Central Park's unique expanse of greenery. It possesses a similar mixture of open fields and surprisingly wooded natural groves of trees—and as in Central Park, in summer you can pedal a boat on a pond while in winter you can skate on the Wollman Rink. Summer offerings here in the park are prodigious, free, and fun, including an amazing variety of quality music acts; bring a blanket. There's also a small, 11-acre zoo on the premises, run by the prestigious Wildlife Conservation Society; some 400 animals are housed here in three exhibit areas (World of Animals, Animal Lifestyles, and Animals In Our Lives). The zoo phone is 718-399-7339; its doors are open daily 10 AM–5 PM (to 4:30 PM in winter), and admission costs $5 for adults, $1.25 for seniors, and $1 for children ages 3 and up.

✳ Lodging

Brooklyn is surprisingly slim on accommodations, but still a better bet than any of the other Outer Boroughs. What there is, mostly, is a handful of chain hotels and a couple of medium-grade (though interesting) bed & breakfasts.

BUSINESS HOTEL **Brooklyn Marriott** (718-246-7000 or 1-888-436-3759), 333 Adams Street (in Boerum Hill). Subway: M, N, R, or W train to Court Street, or 2, 3, 4, or 5 train to Borough Hall. This huge chain hotel—huge for Brooklyn, anyway—

opened in 2002 on seven floors in a sleek downtown location that's already proving popular. The 375 rooms include 75 specially designed rooms for business travelers; each contains a work desk, lamp, two-line speaker phone, voice mail, and high-speed Internet access, in addition to the usual television, newspapers, mini bar, and complimentary coffee. Room decor is about what you'd expect: business-class fittings. There's a big health club here with a big indoor pool—downright enormous by New York standards, actually, and a good reason to stay here if you (or your kids) will enjoy that. Other hotel services include a barber, concierge, laundry service, room service, lounge, restaurant, business center, and small rental car desk. Double room rates range from around $150–310 and up per night; parking costs an additional $10–15 per night. It's quite nicely located for strolling Montague Street's shopping and dining, walking to the Promenade, catching a movie, or just hanging out on the big open plaza at midday watching locals chatting and chewing. The hotel is currently embarked on ambitious expansion plans, too, so more and newer rooms will be coming in the near future.

AFFORDABLE HOTELS ✿ **Avenue Plaza Hotel** (718-552-3300 or 1-877-4-PLAZA-9; fax 718-552-3201), 4624 13th Avenue (in Borough Park). Subway: M or W train to Fort Hamilton Parkway. Located in south-central Brooklyn, this business hotel features a balcony and kitchenette in the rooms, and offers good value if you're looking to see the borough with the family—although you'll need to take the train to see anything of note. (Coney Island is fairly close, how-

ever.) The standard rooms here are rather cookie cutter—they do come equipped with safe, coffeemaker, hair dryer, and two-line phone—while suites are nicer, adding more room and plush drapes, duvets, and couch. Four also have Jacuzzi tub. There's an indoor shopping mall on the ground level, with a jewelry store, florist, and clothing shops; you can rent a cell phone there as well. The hotel also maintains a restaurant. Rates range from around $160 for a standard, lower-floor room to $450 for the Presidential Suites containing two Jacuzzis each; all rates include breakfast.

Comfort Inn–Brooklyn (718-238-3737 or 1-800-228-5150), 8315 Fourth Avenue at 83rd Street (in Bay Ridge). Subway: R train to 77th Street. It's a little unlikely that you'll want or need to stay all the way out in Bay Ridge, which is quite far from Manhattan, near the Verrazano-Narrows Bridge, and thus not quickly or easily reached. But if for some reason you do, this pinkish four-story chain hotel offers you a decent option. Once the Hotel Gregory (which dated from the 1920s), the hotel has been upgraded and renovated to midrange chain standards. Some of its suites contain Jacuzzi, continental breakfast is included with every room, and there's a café on-site. Rates start at around $140–180 per night for a double room; parking costs an additional $6.50–15 per night.

BED & BREAKFASTS **Awesome Bed and Breakfast** (718-858-4859 or 646-369-7272; fax 718-528-8492), 136 Lawrence Street at Willoughby Street (near Brooklyn Heights). Subway: M, N, R, or W train to Court Street or

Lawrence Street. The cheapest of the accommodations I list here, the Awesome is serviceable but nowhere close to fancy—it's more like a friendly youth hostel, with a youngish crowd to match. At least the place is close to Brooklyn Heights and just six blocks from the Brooklyn Bridge (and above a chicken shop). Also, it's less likely to be fully booked than other B&Bs in Brooklyn, because it's larger. Decor is zany and unpredictable (one room's walls are described as "smoky mustard," and they make an interesting contrast with the zebra-print bedspreads); bathrooms are shared but local calls are free, and a small continental breakfast is served, too. Bear in mind that this is not the quietest place, and that bathrooms are shared. Rates range $89–135 double, about $35 extra for a third person. Weekly and monthly rates are more economical.

Baisley House (718-935-1959; fax 718-935-1959), 294 Hoyt Street (in Carroll Gardens). Subway: F or G train to Carroll Street. You'll either chuckle or gasp at the interior decor when you walk into the drawing room of this little three-room B&B, tucked into the hot and hip Carroll Gardens district; it's wild, with a profusion of statues and paintings. Rooms inside the Victorian brownstone are much plainer, and bathrooms are shared, but owner Harry Paul has remodeled the 19th-century home to present a European-style experience, and the rose garden benefits from his gardening expertise. Interestingly, a program of spa treatments and overnight packages is now also being offered at the house, with facials, massages, and other treatments available either in a treatment room or in individual

rooms. Room rates range from $134 single to $190 double; a plentiful breakfast is included, served in the dining room and library. But remember that a 2-night minimum stay is required; if you really can only stay 1 night, you'll pay 50 percent extra.

Bed & Breakfast on the Park (718-499-6115; fax 718-499-1385), 113 Prospect Park West (in Park Slope). Subway: F train to Seventh Avenue or 15th Street–Prospect Park, or 2 or 3 train to Grand Army Plaza. Of all Brooklyn's bed & breakfasts, this one is probably the best—and it's located steps from big Prospect Park, a real plus for morning walks and access to the museums and arts facilities bordering the pretty park. The B&B's front parlor features a mixture of Victorian antiques, and rooms lean toward the frilly—you'll feel like you're in England (or maybe Connecticut). Though there are a few shared baths, even those rooms are quite appealing. Bird's Eye View has two twin beds and a writing desk; top-floor Lady Liberty's canopy bed is enhanced by its own private rooftop garden and a private bath; the Garden Suite comes with working fireplace, a big king bed, and its own bath as well. The more elaborate suites, such as Grand Victorian (it comes trimmed with French lace, down comforters, Oriental rugs, and a fine tub), are all equipped with private bath and sitting area, and cost more. Breakfast, featuring homemade pastries and freshly grilled hotcakes and other entrées, is served in a handsome dining room on Royal Crown Derbyware. The seven rooms range from around $125–300 each.

Garden Green Bed & Breakfast (718-783-5717; fax 718-638-7854), 641 Carlton Avenue between Park

Place and Prospect Place (in Prospect Heights). Subway: Q train to Seventh Avenue, or 2 or 3 train to Bergen Street. This three-room brick guesthouse isn't actually a bed & breakfast; there's no breakfast service at all. But the location is very good—it's fairly close to huge Prospect Park, the famous Brooklyn Museum, and other attractions—and the place is a cut above the other moderately priced B&B choices I've listed here. There are two guest rooms, with single and double beds, and a "garden apartment" with full kitchen and view of the pleasant interior garden. Hosts Laura and Robert Keith have filled the rooms with antiques, art, and greenery. Rates range from $100 to $125 for single rooms to $120 to $150 for doubles.

✻ Where to Eat

DINING OUT al di là (718-783-4565), 248 Fifth Avenue at the corner of Carroll Street (in Park Slope). Subway: M, N, or R train to Union Street. Open Monday to Thursday 6–10:30 PM, Friday and Saturday to 11 PM, Sunday 5–10 PM. Opinions of this smallish Venetian-style trattoria vary, but I'm including it here because it's absolutely unique—and enough Brooklynites are crazy about it to make it worth a close look. In any case, there are few other places in North America where you can sample authentic Venetian cooking like this. Depending on your opinion, it's either a great family-style place serving amazing portions of mussels, clams, and pastas, or an overly stuffy place where the food's only so-so. Walking in, you'll be staggered by the decor: gorgeous red drapes, fancy fixtures mixed with plain ones, and some communal-style

seating for large groups (or for strangers who don't want to eat alone). The menu is heavy on seafood (that's what people eat in Venice), but also concoctions of amusing pasta and earthy liver you won't see elsewhere around town. Of course, you could just opt for the delicious seared hanger steak, too. Entrées cost $15–20.

Chez Oskar (718-852-6250), 211 DeKalb Avenue at the corner of Adelphi Street (in Fort Greene). Subway: C train to Lafayette Avenue, M, W, or R train to DeKalb Avenue, or G train to Fulton. Open daily 11 AM–midnight, weekends to 1 AM. This is the sort of French bistro that's already taken Manhattan by storm, and now appears to be conquering and re-invigorating Brooklyn, starting here in burgeoning Fort Greene; all the decorative touches have been done right, from the rows of gold mirrors up to the tin ceiling and down to the absolutely essential bar. The kitchen turns out just what you'd expect—good mussels with fries, steaks, risotto, plenty of seafood entrées—and decently affordable (they cost about $9–20 apiece). Desserts are very well done; there's a weekend brunch and sometimes live music, too.

Convivium Osteria (718-857-1833), 68 Fifth Avenue between Bergen Street and St. Marks Place (in Park Slope). Subway: 2 or 3 train to Bergen Street, or Q train to Seventh Avenue. Open daily for dinner 6–11 PM, weekends to 11:30 PM, Sunday 5:30–10 PM. This place is for real: The owners have created a combination of Spanish, Portuguese, and Italian tastes that never bows to a conventional, lowest-common-denominator mentality. What might have become a circus—a Roman theme park, toga-wearing or red-cape-waving waiters dashing about and the like—instead is perfectly executed: muted wood, candlelight, graceful decorative posters, and other touches. The food is terrific and straight-ahead regional; think antipasto, tapas, tuna tartare, lamb, steaks, orange duck, frisée, grilled chicken, and well-loved braised artichokes. Latin cooking doesn't get more authentic than fried *bacalhau,* a dish of salted cod that the Portuguese are mad for, or the Tuscan-style white bean salad. But the true star on the menu here is the huge seafood couscous for two, a dish packed with shrimp, lobster, squid, and raisins (among other things) then poured over the toothsome and tasty couscous grains. Entrées cost about $15–22; the seafood couscous costs $42 for two. No credit cards are accepted.

Henry's End (718-834-1776), 44 Henry Street between Cranberry and Middagh streets (in Brooklyn Heights). Subway: A or C train to High Street, or 2 or 3 Street to Clark Street. Open daily 5:30–10:30 PM, Saturday until 11:30 PM, Sunday to 10:30 PM. A classy place serving a masculine menu, Henry's End—located at the end of Henry Street, hence the name—plates up big food: lamb steaks, soft-shell crabs, veal, steak au poivre, steak Diane, fried chicken, and the like. From fall through winter, a "game festival" menu takes over the proceedings, and that means you can order venison, turtle soup, and much more that you can't get during the rest of the year. Most entrées cost about $17–23 each.

Liquors (718-488-7700), 219 DeKalb Avenue between Adelphia and Claremont avenues (in Fort Greene). Subway: C train to Lafayette Avenue, or G train to Washington–Clinton. Open Tuesday through Saturday for dinner 6 PM–midnight, to 1 AM weekends. Another new place along suddenly hot DeKalb Avenue, Liquors transforms a former liquor store into a very good restaurant serving an extremely eclectic menu that ranges from Asia to the Caribbean to northern Italy and beyond. Try something daring like wasabi salmon or pad Thai. There's also live music some nights.

Locanda Vini & Olli (718-622-9202), 129 Gates Avenue at Cambridge Place (in Clinton Hill). Subway: C train to Clinton–Washington. Open Tuesday through Sunday for dinner 6–10:30 PM, weekends to 11:30 PM, Sunday to 10 PM. Operated by husband-and-wife Italian owners with a real live Italian chef, this place in pretty Clinton Hill is already bringing in loads of repeat customers for its Tuscan and northern Italian fare. Housed in a former pharmacy (and many of the old-fashioned fixtures remain), the kitchen serves something for everyone: Appetizers are country-simple and satisfying, such as tongue in parsley sauce; the bread is top rate; and main courses such as pork loin, lamb, venison, and pasta never disappoint. There are plenty of unusual pastas with interesting sauce combinations (ever tried pici? in a porcini sauce?), as well as good desserts and a cheese plate. Entrées go for $5–15 each, though you might want to try at least two courses.

The Minnow (718-832-5500), 442 Ninth Street between Sixth and Seventh avenues (in Park Slope). Subway: F train to Seventh Avenue. Open Monday and Wednesday through Saturday for dinner 5:30–10 PM, Sunday for brunch 11:30 AM–2:30 PM and dinner 5–10 PM. Trivia note: Owner

Aaron Bashy nearly called this restaurant the Pickled Mackerel instead. What was he thinking? Anyhow, as burgeoning Park Slope continues to upscale itself, this tiny place has carved out its territory as one of *the* places for a power dinner. Seafood is king here: Try a blue crab feast, a whole roast fish (it changes nightly) with sauce and side dishes, or even a nonseafood item such as lamb. Entrées cost $15–20 each.

Nick's Lobster Restaurant (718-253-7117), 2777 Flatbush Avenue near the Belt Parkway. Open daily noon–10 PM, until 11 PM weekends. You don't come all the way out here to waterside Brooklyn for decor, you don't get here by public transit, and—once here—you don't come to eat steaks or even fish. It's all about lobster at Nick's, boiled up red and right and not exorbitantly overpriced. If you're on a tight schedule in the city, you likely won't have time to make a foray. (Then again, you can't get to New England by subway, either.)

Peter Luger (718-387-7400), 178 Broadway near the corner of Driggs Avenue (in Williamsburg). Subway: J, M, or Z train to Marcy Avenue. Open Monday to Thursday 11:30 AM–9:45 PM, Friday and Saturday to 10:45 PM, Sunday 1–9:45 PM. Nowhere near anything of note (except the Williamsburg Bridge, and that's hardly notable), this is the premier off-Manhattan steak house; in fact, most who've eaten here believe it's the top steak house in New York, bar none. Some think it's among the *world's* finest, despite occasionally grating service and a complete lack of frills or grace. Is the superlative food alone enough incentive to get you out here to a remote corner of Williamsburg?

If it is, there's only one thing you want when you get here, so don't bother asking the potentially chilly waiter to see the menu: Porterhouse steak for two, well aged and very carefully selected, sliced at the table and topped with a buttery sauce is all you need. Simple side dishes might include some German fried potatoes and a pile of creamed spinach. They've got rich desserts like chocolate mousse, tarts, and cheesecake, too, and lunch has been added (a hamburger with fries here is much better than at your average eatery), but steak dinners will always be the star. Lunch entrées cost $5–30 (for a steak meal), dinner items $30 and up.

Pete's Downtown (718-858-3510), 2 Water Street at Old Fulton Street (near Brooklyn Heights and DUMBO). Subway: A or C train to High Street. Open Tuesday through Thursday noon–10 PM, Friday until 11 PM, Saturday for dinner only 5–11 PM, Sunday 2–9:30 PM. Right next to Grimaldi's, with a tremendous view of the Brooklyn Bridge, this straight-ahead Italian American place is ragged around the edges—and Brooklynites like it that way. After starting with antipasto, clams, or calamari, lunch might consist of chicken mozzarella sandwiches on *ciabatta* bread, a variety of gnocchi, cooked or baked pasta, or a chicken, shrimp, or veal dish such as scampi, veal Marsala, or chicken parmigiana; entrées cost $10–13. Dinnertime adds fancier presentations. Chicken *scarpariello* is cooked with sauce, garlic, wine, and basil, and served with potatoes, for example, while a host of seafood entrées is offered—mixed seafood is served on linguine with spicy *fra diavolo* sauce, while tilapia is simmered in tomato sauce with capers and black olives, then topped with mussels and clams. There's also prime sirloin steak, grilled salmon, and stuffed pork chops at night. Dinner entrées are priced at $17–22. Salads and a children's menu are also offered.

River Café (718-522-5200), 1 Water Street at Old Fulton Street (near Brooklyn Heights and DUMBO). Subway: A or C train to High Street. Open daily for lunch noon–3 PM and for dinner 6–11 PM, from 11 AM for Sunday brunch. One of the most famous—and doubtless the best— restaurants in Brooklyn; this restaurant's kitchen could hold its own with the best on the Upper East Side. What they can't offer, however, is a view like this matchless one. You're right on the river, beneath the Brooklyn Bridge, nothing but boats between you and the Manhattan skyline. And the dining room is as classy as the view, so be sure to order a cocktail for starters while you take in the ambience—hopefully at sunset. But let me get back to the food, because it's divine. Start with smoked salmon and caper mousse, truffle-stuffed sea scallops, or grilled squab, then move onward and upward to grilled tuna, seared salmon paired with fried oysters, grilled swordfish with bone-marrow-stuffed raviolis, or roast rack of lamb. Finish happily with napoleons, warm carrot cake with cream cheese soufflé, a hot strawberry tart, or something else sweet. This perfection does not come cheaply—you can only order a prix fixe at dinner. Expect to pay upward of $85–100 per person for the privilege. (For a bargain, come at lunch instead, where entrées are "only" $25–28 apiece.)

Robin des Bois/Sherwood Café (718-596-1609), 195 Smith Street between Baltic and Warren streets (in Boerum Hill near Carroll Gardens). Subway: F or G train to Bergen Street. Open daily noon–midnight, from 11 AM weekends. This French restaurant features an outstanding back patio area, with garden and upscale-kitschy furnishings; the dining room and indoor bar are pretty wild, too. But the food's good and the beer's cold. The Gothic-type menu features hearty meals of onion tart, *croque-monsieur* sandwiches, goat cheese and tapenade sandwiches, smoked duck breast plates, roast chickens, and steak tartare served on groaning wooden boards. The weekend brunches are a delight, and the fixtures are for sale. Meals are $8–20.

Rose Water (718-783-3800), 787 Union Street between Fifth and Sixth avenues (in Park Slope). Subway: Q train to Seventh Avenue, or 2 or 3 train to Bergen Street. Open daily for dinner 5:30–11 PM, also for brunch 11 AM–3 PM weekends. Park Slope residents are known to hit friendly Rose Water for exemplary upscale fusion fare that includes Middle Eastern staples such as hummus and baba ghanouj, but also goes far beyond the call of duty to experiment with seared diver scallops, grilled lamb, pork chops, and skate. Ingredient are fresh and often organic, and there's an interesting use of roses in the dessert items.

EATING OUT Brawta Café (718-855-5515), 347 Atlantic Avenue at the corner of Hoyt Street (in Boerum Hill). Subway: A, C, or G train to Hoyt–Schimmerhorn, or F or G train to

Bergen Street. Open Monday to Saturday noon–11 PM. Some of the best jerk chicken and pork in the city are served at this café, to the tune of almost hypnotic reggae music; bring your young 'uns, who might appreciate the Bob Marley groove. Whether you fancy an authentic Jamaican plate of ackee and cod, Ital vegetable stew, Red Stripe–cooked chicken, curried goat, oxtail stew, pan-fried porgy, or just pieces of jerk chicken, this is the place to find it. A warning to the wise: Some of these items are very, very spicy; check with your server before ordering if this might be a problem for you. Main courses—referred to as "Big Tings" on the menu—are priced $7–16 each. There's also a juice bar and dessert menu ("Sweet Tings").

Café LULUc (718-625-3815), 214 Smith Street between Baltic and Butler streets (in Carroll Gardens). Subway: F or G train to Bergen Street. Open daily 8 AM–midnight. French bistro meets all-day brunch hot spot at this Carroll Gardens favorite. The daytime offerings include salads, pancakes, eggs, sandwiches, and pasta. Dinner consists of much more imaginative items, starting with appetizers such as a grilled swordfish Niçoise salad or grilled lobster and chorizo salad, then moving on to penne, fusilli, pistachio-encrusted cod, oven-roasted salmon, lamb brochette, and grilled hanger steak.

☙ **Ferdinando's Focacceria** (718-855-1545), 151 Union Street between Columbia and Hicks streets (in Cobble Hill). Subway: F or G train to Carroll Street. Open Monday through Thursday 11 AM–7 PM, Friday and Saturday to 9:30 PM. A little hard to find, but worth it, Ferdinando's is one of Brooklyn's best lowbrow Italian bites and is exceptionally easy on the pocketbook, too. This place has been here forever, it seems. Sip a glass of good wine and munch on snacks such as fried eggplant, complex pasta dishes, and fish, or just go for one of the signature sandwiches such as the sinfully good one stuffed with a potato croquette and *panelle* (chickpea fritters and ricotta). It's great eating at a pittance.

Grimaldi's (718-858-4300), 19 Old Fulton Street between Front and Water streets (near Brooklyn Heights and DUMBO). Subway: A or C train to High Street. Open weekdays 11:30 AM–10:45 PM, Friday and Saturday to midnight, weekends from noon. Lately everyone seems to feel that this place, wedged almost right beneath the Brooklyn-side supports of the Brooklyn Bridge, is the top pizza joint in New York. I remain firmly convinced, after repeat tastings, that it isn't so: My vote still goes to Patsy's, in a slim margin over John's, Ray's, Lombardi's, and this place, which I frankly don't find overwhelmingly terrific. Oh, the crust is superb and the atmosphere is red-and-white-checkered-tablecloth right. Yet the cheese and sauce are just as good as other top places, not head-and-shoulders better. In any case, views of the Brooklyn Bridge are terrific, and the pizzas are still very good. Note that no slices are sold, but there is a wine list.

Junior's (718-852-5257), 386 Flatbush Avenue Extension at the corner of DeKalb Avenue (in Fort Greene). Subway: M, N, Q, or R train to DeKalb Avenue. Open daily 6:30 AM–12:30 AM, later on weekends. The food at this Brooklyn deli isn't consistently top notch—it's the usual assortment of soups and thick sandwiches, burgers, bagels with lox, and the like—but regulars don't care, because they know they will get through the main meal. They're here for the ending anyway, the best cheesecake in New York: dense, sweet, and cheesy, yet still light. Try a lime cheesecake if you're tired of the regular flavor. There's a smaller branch of Junior's inside Manhattan's Grand Central Terminal as well.

Panino'teca 275 (718-237-2728), 275 Smith Street between DeGraw Street and Sackett Street (in Carroll Gardens). Subway: F or G train to Carroll Street. Open Tuesday to Saturday noon–11 PM, to midnight weekends. For glasses of Italian wine and true-blue bar snacks such as pressed panini, good bruschetta, and tiny fingerlike sandwiches, this Smith Street wine bar is fast becoming a sure bet. Very few items cost more than $9, and many of the items cost less. Think of the place as a kind of Italian tapas bar perfect for grazing or making a delicious, varied little meal, and you won't go wrong. Note that the establishment doesn't take credit cards.

COFFEE AND SNACKS Brooklyn Ice Cream Factory (718-246-3963), 1 Old Fulton Street at Water Street (near Brooklyn Heights and DUMBO). Subway: A or C train to High Street. Open daily noon–10 PM. Opened by the adjacent (and top-rank) River Café (see *Dining Out*), this ice cream joint is my favorite in the New York metro area. How do I love thee? Let me count the ways. The location (it's housed within a former fireboat house, and views of the Manhattan skyline are matchless).

The ice cream (supercreamy, without being cloying). The hot fudge and syrups (created by the River Café's pastry chef). The fact that they make malts. The fact that they don't take credit cards. The fact that they serve espresso. The fact that they have restrooms. All in all, this is a perfect summertime ice cream experience—I'd take the train over here just to get a coffee milk shake anytime, and you should, too. Cones, dishes, and shakes cost $3–5 each.

🕊 Jacques Torres Chocolate (718-875-9772), 66 Water Street (in DUMBO) between Dock Street and Main Street. Subway: A or C train to High Street, or F train to York Street. Open Monday to Saturday 9 AM–7 PM, Sunday 10 AM–6 PM. The most famous chocolate maker in New York is Jacques Torres, who was until recently known only as the award-winning pastry chef at Le Cirque 2000 (he had been there since 1989). In late 2000, however, Torres unveiled his latest project, a factory for making treats out of imported Belgian chocolate—and it's since taken over his life. Torres built the factory himself—he helped install the copper lighting, cut the marble for the worktables and the glass for the shelving—and now supervises the baking of pastries and the tempering of the chocolate, the dipping of bonbons and coconut bars, the filling of cream centers, and all the rest. The handful of small tables here is the only place you can sample the goods and drink Torres's Mexican-spiced hot chocolate; on weekends it is crazy-busy, with lines spilling out the door, but it's all worth it once you've tasted the chocolate. There's now a popular second location in SoHo, too.

🦐 🐚 **Nathan's Famous** (718-946-2202), 1310 Surf Avenue at Stilwell Avenue (on Coney Island). Subway: W train to Coney Island. Open daily 8 AM–1 AM. Some of the best hot dogs in New York are served way out here on Coney Island, right beside the beach: delicious all-beef concoctions, grilled to perfection. They do more than just dogs here, however; they also serve great clams, burgers, fries, sodas, and homemade lemonade. You'll pay more than the original nickel a hot dog, but everything important still does cost less than $5. (Note that you can also find Nathan's outlets in various food-court-type venues, such as one near Borough Hall, because the owners have sold out the name—in fact, you'll find it at rest areas across America now—but this is the original, and a much better bite.)

BREWERY Brooklyn Brewery (718-486-7422), 79 North 11th Street between Berry and Wythe streets (in Williamsburg). Subway: L train to Bedford Avenue. Open to the public Friday night (6–11 PM) and Saturday afternoon (noon–5 PM) only. Brooklyn Brewery took root in the late 1980s when a former Middle Eastern wire-service correspondent returned to Brooklyn and quit writing to try to revive the borough's former tradition of craft brewing. After a rocky start, the venture has turned out to be a ringing success; today you'll see this brewery's logo anywhere hip—with a beer from virtually all the major beer types represented in a bottle or on tap somewhere in the city—but did you ever want to go to the source? You can, though you do have to plan ahead. Tours are given Saturday only (and then only noon–5 PM), so book early if you want to visit; Friday night

Kim Grant

NATHAN'S FAMOUS SERVES HOT DOGS AND MORE.

also brings tasting events in a specially constructed room 6–10 PM. Then there are additional special events such as comedy nights, theater, and beer release parties. Believe it or not, families love this place. And don't miss the annual Brooklyn BeerFest when, late each September, the brewery throws an open-air bash to kick off the Oktoberfest season.

✳ Entertainment

MUSIC VENUES BargeMusic (718-624-2083), Fulton Ferry Landing at East River (near Brooklyn Heights and DUMBO). Subway: A or C train to High Street, or 2 or 3 train to Clark Street. Concerts Thursday through Saturday at 7:30 PM, and Sunday at 4 PM. What a wild idea this is: Take a former barge, moor it in the East River at the scenic foot of the Brooklyn Bridge, then place a classical chamber music ensemble on top of it. Stir well; instant success story. Created in 1977 by violinist Olga Bloom, this remarkable experiment brings classical music to the masses year-round (not in a seasonal format), with four performances each and every week to a grateful audience of 125. (Performances are not open-air atop the 100-foot barge, but rather inside a small concert hall made cozy by a fireplace and wooden paneling.) BargeMusic's reputation for exposing new emerging talent has slackened somewhat in recent years, and the program now presents a more regular cast of performers, but you can still hear an ear-opening range of soloists and works during any given week. Tickets cost $35–$40 for adults, $25 for full-time students, and $30 for seniors (on Thursday only).

Brooklyn Academy of Music (BAM) (718-636-4100), 30 Lafayette Avenue at Ashland Place (in Fort Greene). Subway: Q, 2, 3, 4, or 5 train to Atlantic Avenue, or M, N, R, or W train to Pacific. BAM is Brooklyn's answer to Lincoln Center, offering a full and impressive program of films, dance performances, theater, and other entertainment. And it's been doing so since 1861—which may make it the oldest continually operating performing arts institute in the United States—although the original theater burned in 1903; the present main facility opened its doors 5 years later, in high fashion (Enrico Caruso performed *Faust* with the Metropolitan Opera). Since that time, an opera house, theater, cinemas, a restaurant, a bookstore, and a café have all been added. The night's typical program nowadays might include anything from a performance of *Medea* or a concert

by the Brooklyn Philharmonic to appearances by the likes of Tom Waits and modern dancers from Japan and Europe. The annual Next Wave Festival showcases cutting-edge work in a variety of genres from September through November. Films cost $10 each for adults, less for children, students, and seniors. Note that there is now a shuttle bus from Manhattan, known as the BAMBus, departing Park Avenue and 42nd Street in time for all musical performances; it costs $10 round-trip, $8 for students, but reservations must be made 24 hours in advance (call 718-636-4100).

FILM **BAM Rose Cinemas** (718-623-2770 or 718 636-4100 for information, 718-777-FILM for tickets), 30 Lafayette Avenue at Ashland Place (in Fort Greene). Subway: Q, 2, 3, 4, or 5 train to Atlantic Avenue, or M, N, R, or W train to Pacific. Looking to see that hard-to-find documentary, avant-garde short, independent production, or foreign film? This is by far the best place in the Outer Boroughs (and one of the best in New York) to catch a flick—usually something really thought provoking, say a new print of the original *Solaris*, a first-run of Al Gore's *An Inconvenient Truth*, or a Ukrainian film festival with atmospheric live piano music accompanying during some of the films. Part of the Brooklyn Academy of Music (see above), the cinema complex consists of four theaters, each with great sound and outstanding sight lines; the cinématek division offers particularly stimulating fare. General-admission tickets cost $10 per film for adults; there's a $3 discount if you belong to BAM's Cinema Club, are a student with ID (except on weekends), a child under 12, or a senior.

Cobble Hill Cinema (718-596-9113), 265 Court Street at the corner of Butler Street (in Cobble Hill). Subway: M, N, R, or W train to Court Street. The biggest Hollywood hits are screened here on five screens.

Pavilion Brooklyn Heights Cinema (718-369-0838), 70 Henry Street at the corner of Orange Street (in Brooklyn Heights). Subway: 1 or 2 train to Church Street, or A or C train to High Street. There are only two screens at this tiny Brooklyn Heights theater, but it's a good place to catch a new release or just-finished-its-run flick of particular interest on a rainy day.

UA Court Street 12 (718-246-8170), 106 Court Street near the corner of State Street (in Boerum Hill). Subway: A, C, or F train to Jay Street–Borough Hall, M, N, or R train to Court Street, or 2, 3, 4, or 5 train to Borough Hall. Opened in July 2000, this United Artists multiplex cinema battled Boerum Hill neighborhood opposition to bring the latest Hollywood hits to the area.

SPECTATOR SPORTS ❧ **Brooklyn Cyclones** (718-449-8497), KeySpan Park, 1904 Surf Avenue between West 17th and West 19th streets (on Coney Island). Subway: W train to Coney Island. A farm team of the Queens-based New York Mets, Brooklyn's minor-league baseball team toils in the New York–Penn League, playing 38 home games each summer just a few blocks from the Coney Island boardwalk in 7,500-seat KeySpan Park. In 2001, with views of ocean and amusement parks, they took the league title. Can't get tickets? The team reserves a few hundred for last-minute arrivals; line up after 10 AM for a shot at some. It costs just $5–12

a seat; at these prices, you can't afford *not* to come.

❋ **Selective Shopping**

FOOD AND DRINK **Jacques Torres Chocolate** (718-875-9772), 66 Water Street (in DUMBO) between Dock and Main Streets. Subway: A or C train to High Street, or F train to York Street. Open Monday to Saturday 9 AM–7 PM. Chocolate master Torres's Brooklyn factory isn't open for tours, but you can see some of the magic through glass windows while they're boxing up some of the delicious gourmet chocolates created there. (Also see *Where to Eat—Coffee and Snacks.*)

MUSEUM STORE ♿ **BMA Museum Shop** (718-638-5000), 200 Eastern Parkway at Prospect Park (in Prospect Park). Subway: 2 or 3 train to Eastern Parkway, or B, D, N, R, or Q train to Atlantic/Pacific Street. Open Wednesday through Friday 10:30 AM–5:30 PM, Saturday and Sunday 10:30 AM–5:30 PM, first Saturday of each month until 11 PM. The Brooklyn Museum of Art's museum store is a good place to pick up a souvenir of one of New York City's better unknown art museums.

❋ **Special Events**

April–May: **Cherry Blossom Festival** (718-623-7200), Brooklyn Botanic Garden, 1000 Washington Avenue at Eastern Parkway (in Park Slope). Subway: 2 or 3 train to Eastern Parkway, or B, D, N, R, or Q train to Atlantic/Pacific Street. The annual Sakura Matsuri (Cherry Blossom Festival) in late April sees the botanical garden's 76-tree Cherry Esplanade and adjacent Cherry Walk and pond erupt in brilliant white and pink. In 2006, the festival celebrated its 25th anniversary; this is now one of the largest such festivals in the Northeast, with a full weekend of flower-arranging classes, haiku readings, dance, calligraphy, drumming, and tours of both the cherry blossoms and the famous collection of bonsai trees.

Late June: **Mermaid Parade** along the Coney Island boardwalk. Subway: W train to Coney Island. The city's craziest parade—think Mardi Gras, without the booze—takes place out here in Brooklyn late each June. Expect to see something you've never seen before, and think about leaving the kids back at the hotel.

QUEENS

The huge borough of Queens was named for the queen of England and, until 100 years ago, still looked more like upstate New York than a thickly populated suburban escape hatch across the famous-in-song 59th Street (Queensboro) Bridge. Though there's little regal about Queens today—it's almost entirely residential (with an especially heavy concentration of Chinese residents seeking more light and space than Manhattan's Chinatown can offer) and is home to both of New York's major airports—it certainly contains a lot of life. From Rockaway's middle-class beach houses to Astoria's close-knit Chinese community, from Long Island City's suddenly arty makeover to the sports stadiums in Flushing, this is a good place for residents of its almost endless suburban blocks (in neighborhoods with names like Kew Gardens, Corona, Jackson Heights, Astoria, and Forest Hills) to have plenty of low-key fun.

As a visitor, however, it's a different story: You'll have to work to get here, then work to get from point to point. Don't plan on staying or spending much time out here. If you're specifically interested in modern art, baseball, or tennis, however, it's worth a visit for these diversions—and to cross the borough off your "life list."

GETTING THERE *By car:* From Manhattan, take the Queens–Midtown Tunnel from East 42nd Street to the Long Island Expressway and proceed from there to whichever expressway you need to use next.

By subway: You can also reach Queens via public transit. The multicultural 7 subway line ends at Flushing Meadows and Shea Stadium, while the E and F trains go through Jackson Heights and on to Forest Hills.

✳ To See

MUSEUMS ❦ **The Isamu Noguchi Garden Museum** (718-204-7088), 9-01 33rd Road (at Vernon Boulevard) in Long Island City. Subway: N or W train to Broadway or F train to Queensbridge–21st Street. Open Wednesday through Friday 10 AM–5 PM, weekends 11 AM–6 PM. This museum, inside Noguchi's home (ignore the surrounding blight), is one of the more interesting and little-known art experiences of the Outer Boroughs: Noguchi's art, architecture, furniture, and interiors and exteriors continue to play an important role in modern design.

Born in Los Angeles in 1904 to an American mother and a Japanese father (both were writers), Noguchi grew up in Japan, Indiana, and New York City; his star as a sculptor quickly rose, and he would remain a fixture of the New York art scene—while traveling the world to design plazas, parks, playgrounds, gardens, buildings, and to sculpt—ever after. In 1961 he moved to Long Island City, gradually building a museum to house his work; the annex now contains nearly all of it, including examples of his Akari light sculptures, masks, furniture, and distinctive paper lanterns. There's a café and museum shop as well. Free tours are offered at 2 PM daily. Admission costs $10 for adults, $5 for seniors and students; children under 12 enter for free.

P.S. 1 Contemporary Art Center (718-784-2084), 22–25 Jackson Avenue at 46th Avenue in Long Island City. Housed within a former public school, P.S. 1 is affiliated with the Museum of Modern Art (see "Midtown East"). Its recent exhibitions have included works of video art, multimedia sculpture, photographs of Vietnam, art based on FBI files, art from Mexico City, and much more. Reach the center by taking the E or V (weekdays only) train to 23rd Street, 7 train to 45th Road, or G train to 21st Street or Court Square. Opening hours are Thursday through Monday noon–6 PM; admission is by suggested donation of $5 per person, $2 per student and seniors.

FOR FAMILIES ✑ **New York Hall of Science** (718-699-0005), in Flushing Meadows/Corona Park at the corner of 111th Street and 46th Avenue. Subway: 7 train to 111th Street. Summer, open weekdays 9:30 AM–5 PM and weekends 10 AM–6 PM; rest of the year, open Monday to Thursday 9:30 AM–2 PM, Friday to 5 PM, and weekends 10 AM–6 PM. One of New York's best science museums is awfully hard to find, out here in Flushing Meadows, but well worth a trip with the kids if you're looking to catch a Mets game and make a day of it. It's strongest on interactive exhibits. Admission costs $11 for adults and $8 for children, but is waived on Friday afternoon and the first hour of the day Saturday morning.

✑ **Queens County Farm Museum** (718-347-3276), 73-50 Little Neck Parkway, Floral Park (Queens). By car: From Manhattan, take the Queens–Midtown Tunnel at East 42nd Street to the Long Island Expressway, then Grand Central Parkway Exit 24 (Little Neck Parkway), then continue three blocks to the museum. Open Monday through Friday 9 AM–5 PM (outdoor portions only), weekends 10 AM–5 PM. Of course you don't come to New York City to experience farm life, but it's fascinating to realize that the vast majority of the city above Lower Manhattan once consisted almost entirely of farmland, even into the 1800s. The city's sole remaining working farm dates to 1697, and it still encompasses 47 acres—albeit just off the roaring Grand Central Parkway. If you visit, you'll find farm buildings, a greenhouse, cows, merino sheep, an herb garden, an orchard, and plenty of vegetables. (Produce is sold at the farm's stand from July through October.) In spring there's an Easter egg hunt, auto show, and more. In fall, of course, there are plenty of crops being harvested and occasional events—and hayrides—to highlight the pumpkins, apples, and other produce; the Queens County Fair is also held here at that time. The farm is free except during special events.

Kennedy International Airport. Subway: A train to Broad Channel. One of the
highlights in a tour of Quirky Queens would have to be little Broad Channel,
which is truly worth a look if you're out this way. It's a transplanted Massachu-
setts- (or maybe Louisiana-) style fishing village, complete with weathered boats,
bleached piers, houses on stilts, and a downright slow pace of living. Unfortunately, the din of airplanes taking off and landing at nearby Kennedy Airport frequently disturbs the peace and quiet of what otherwise might be a genuine oasis.
Be that as it may, it's still an amusing place to stroll for a few hours with a cam-
era forgetting the hubbub of cabs and sirens a few miles away. To get here, take
the A train—yes, the same one that shoots you north to Harlem going the other
direction—out of the city toward Brooklyn, Queens, and Rockaway nearly to its
end. Get off at the Broad Channel station and simply begin wandering.

✳ Green Space

✐ **Flushing Meadows–Corona Park** (718-699-4209), between Jewel Avenue,
111th Street, and Roosevelt Avenue. Subway: 7 train to 111th Street or Willets
Point–Shea Stadium, or, from Penn Station, Long Island Rail Road (Port Washington branch) to Shea Stadium. Weighing in at a total of more than 1,250 acres,
this huge park out in Queens would be much better known if it weren't parked
on the back side of LaGuardia. Besides a truckload of impressive attractions—
including a pro baseball stadium (see Shea Stadium under *Entertainment—
Spectator Sports*), the USTA Tennis Center, host to the annual U.S. Open
tournament (again, see *Spectator Sports*), a two-time World's Fair site, a science
museum, an ecology center, and a good little museum of art, among others—the
park contains oodles of green space and two big freshwater lakes. The carousel
and playground are great for kids. There's also a top-notch Latin American festival in early August, and a mini golf course for testing your short game. As if all
this weren't enough (it is), a pool and ice skating rink have been added as well. If
you've got time to make it out here, it's a fantastic place, but—as with any large
city park—please be extra careful at night.

✐ **Jamaica Bay Wildlife Refuge** (718-318-4340), in Jamaica Bay between
Howard Beach and the Rockaways. Subway: A train to Broad Channel. You'll
feel far, far from Manhattan in this pocket of wetlands tucked among rivers and
roads—it's especially noted for the bird life alighting here twice annually on
migrations north and south. There's a short trail and an interpretative center to
explain the local ecology; some quite fascinating tours focusing on specific wildlife are offered. Admission is free, and the park is open daily from sunrise to
sunset. The interpretative center opens daily from 8:30 AM to 5 PM.

✳ Where to Eat

EATING OUT ✐ **Mardi Gras** (718-
261-8555), 70-20 Austin Street
between 70th Avenue and 70th Road.
Subway: E, F, G, or R train to 71st
Avenue–Forest Hills. Open daily

noon–midnight, weekends to 1 AM. It's
got a slightly chain-restaurant feel, but
there's no denying that this place in
Queens's slightly swanky Forest Hills
area does convey an experience that

could only be New Orleans. Start with bottomless glasses of sweet tea and second-floor seats with open views of the place. (The ground floor, where the bar is, is noisier.) Crawfish is good, and voodoo chicken (which is not exactly the superspicy bird that the name implies) might be the best thing on the menu, though the decent jambalaya—which can be ordered as an entrée (the appetizer is plenty big enough for one)—puts up a fight, too. Menu portions here are *huge,* if uneven; you can't possibly go hungry on all the Cajun and Creole offerings here, even if you're not fully satisfied with the results.

Nick's Pizza (718-263-1126), 108-26 Ascan Avenue between Austin and Burns streets. Subway: E, F, G, or R train to 71st Avenue–Forest Hills. Open daily 11 AM–11 PM. Queens' best pizza joint is this one in Forest Hills, which scores near pizza perfection despite the bland exterior and workaday interior. The pizzeria doesn't appear to possess a coal-fired or brick oven but still miraculously manages to produce terrific, charred thin crusts adorned with simple tomato sauce, fresh basil and mozzarella, and quality toppings. Nick's serves wine and desserts. Most pizzas cost $11–16.

Q, A Thai Bistro (718-261-6599), 108-25 Ascan Avenue between Austin and Burns streets. Subway: E, F, G, or R train to 71st Avenue–Forest Hills. Open daily for lunch noon–3 PM and dinner 5–10:30 PM, to 11:30 PM weekends. One of Queens's best Asian eateries is this bandbox-sized Thai operation in Forest Hills, serving all the usual suspects—pad Thai, fish, crabs, chicken in peanut sauce, Thai iced coffee—but just a little bit better than almost everyone else does. The

owners (who aren't Thai) decided to riff on the Thai concept, with unexpectedly wonderful flavor experiments such pasta fish with Thai influences; they also riffed on interior design—check out the walls to see what I mean. The wine bar is a nice place to sip and think about it all.

❧ **Tibetan Yak** (718-779-1119), 72-20 Roosevelt Avenue between 72nd and 73rd streets. Subway: E, F, G, R, or V train to Jackson Heights. Open daily noon–11 PM. There are just a handful of Tibetan places in New York, and this one—in extremely multiethnic Jackson Heights—scores with good lunch specials, reasonable prices, and tasty meals of Chinese-style beef dumplings, stir-fried rice dishes, vegetarian offerings, lamb curry, and some more unusual selections as well.

✳ Entertainment

SPECTATOR SPORTS **Shea Stadium (New York Mets)** (718-507-METS), 123-01 Roosevelt Avenue between the Grand Central Parkway and the Van Wyck Expressway. Subway: 7 train to Shea Stadium or Long Island Rail Road to Shea Stadium. The Mets (sometimes dubbed the Mutts in bad years, the Amazin' Mets in good ones) have played some colorful ball at this field. In 1969 they were the toast of baseball, improbably thumping a tough Orioles team to win their first world championship behind the arms of Tom Seaver, Tug McGraw, and Nolan Ryan, among others. In 1986 the Mets won a second world title, breaking the hearts of the Boston Red Sox and their fans. Shea, opened in 1964 for the Mets' inaugural season, is famous for the sonic booms of aircraft taking off and landing at nearby

LaGuardia Airport—but it's also still a decent place to catch a game and munch hot dogs. At press time the club had been revitalized by a series of recent acquisitions: Tom Glavine, Pedro Martinez, Carlos Beltran, and Carlos Delgado among the biggest—making a world of difference.

USTA National Tennis Center (718-760-6200 for information, 1-888-OPEN-TIX for U.S. Open tickets), Flushing Meadows–Corona Park. Subway: 7 train to Shea Stadium or Long Island Rail Road to Shea Stadium. Swivel-headed tennis fans will absolutely want to make a visit out here to Arthur Ashe Stadium, where the U.S. Open reigns supreme for 3 weeks each late August and early September. The world's top stars are always here. You won't be alone, though—this is reputedly the world's best-attended annual sports event, with more than 600,000 watching at least one match—and entertainment celebrities are known to frequent the Open.

STATEN ISLAND

S taten Island gets very short shrift from most travelers, not surprising given its position—it is much closer to New Jersey than to Central Park. Yet lots of Lower Manhattan financial types happily make a regular commute to and from this island, which actually boasts a lot of history. There's plenty of wild parkland, a tiny railroad, attractive and historic architecture, a lighthouse, good restaurants—after all, the island is bigger than Manhattan. Add in the free ferry service and terrific views of the Statue of Liberty en route, and this can be a quite enjoyable day or half-day trip.

GETTING THERE *By ferry:* To get here from Manhattan, it's best to take the free Staten Island ferry (see *To See—Scenic Ride*), which departs from South Ferry in Manhattan—reached via the 1 train to South Ferry, the 4 and 5 trains to Bowling Green, and the N and R trains to Whitehall Street.

By car: From Manhattan, it's easy to get here—if you don't mind driving all the way to Brooklyn or New Jersey. From Brooklyn, you can get to the island by driving over the Verrazano-Narrows Bridge (the toll is expensive, however) or taking an express bus. Once you're on the island, the roads are fine.

By bus: Amazingly, you can take a fast express bus from downtown Manhattan and be on Staten Island in half an hour—as fast as, or faster than, getting to Battery Park and taking the ferry. Though less scenic, these express buses do pass over several famous bridges with good views of Lower Manhattan en route to the island. Catch an express bus such as the X1 from Fifth Avenue or Union Square; the fare is $5 per person, one-way.

GETTING AROUND Once you're here, the Staten Island railroad transports you from one end of the island to the other, though there's only one line; it begins at St. George station, next to the ferry docks on the island's northern tip, and terminates in Tottenville at the southern end.

✳ To See

MUSEUMS Jacques Marchais Museum of Tibetan Art (718-987-3500), 338 Lighthouse Avenue at St. George Road. By car: Take the Staten Island ferry to the island, taking Richmond Road 5 miles to Lighthouse Avenue; turn right and continue uphill to No. 338. Open Wednesday through Sunday 1 PM–5 PM. This is a museum Richard Gere could love, built in the 1940s to drum up awareness of the exiled Tibetan Buddhist culture and also to support Tibetans living in exile. In a Himalayan-style *gompah* (temple building) parked in a hilly residential neighborhood of the island, the Western Hemisphere's only museum of Tibetan art (so far as I know, anyhow) holds more than 1,200 items such as an 18th-century Chinese Buddha, a painted clay statue that may date to the 14th century, and an altar that's over the top with dozens of bronze Bodhisattva statuettes, *thangka* paintings, and authentic wall hangings; you will learn more about Tibet, Mongolia, and Nepal than you ever thought you could. Outdoors lie peaceful gardens. Strange fact: The museum is named for Jacques Marchais, but that person doesn't exist; it's a pseudonym for the art dealer Jacqueline Klauber, who collected the art here with her husband and built the museum with the proceeds from it. Sunday brings lectures on related topics to the museum, while October brings a Tibetan festival. Admission to the museum costs $5 for adults, $3 for senior citizens, and $2 for children under 12. The museum shop's handcrafted gifts are deliberately simple—incense, books, jewelry, art, and CDs of sacred Tibetan music—and are priced as low as just 46 cents.

Staten Island Museum (718-727-1135), 75 Stuyvesant Place at Wall Street. Museum open Tuesday to Saturday 9 AM–5 PM, Sunday 1–5 PM, archives open Tuesday to Thursday only, 10 AM–4 PM. Located at the Staten Island Institute of Arts and Sciences just two blocks away from the ferry terminal, this little museum stocks a collection of portraits, ecology exhibits, and the like—including a particular focus on landscape art related to the island. New as of fall 2005, an exhibit of photographs, ship models, and the like commemorates the 100-year anniversary of ferry service between Staten Island and Lower Manhattan. Donations for $2 per adult and $1 per student or senior are suggested.

HISTORIC SITE ✐ **Historic Richmondtown** (718-351-1611), 441 Clarke Avenue between St. Patrick's Place and Arthur Kill Road. By car: Take the Staten Island ferry to the island, taking Richmond Road 5 miles to St. Patrick's Place. By bus: From the ferry, take the S74 bus to Richmond Hill Road. Open Wednesday through Sunday 1–5 PM, summertime Wednesday through Saturday from 10 AM. More than 25 buildings fill this peaceful 100-acre site, which explains the history of the town—and the island—in carefully interpreted detail, recalling a time when most of New York was rural and Richmondtown was a major transit hub between New Jersey and Manhattan. Highlights of the tour include a 17th-century elementary school (the oldest remaining in the United States) and a general store. Throughout, interpreters faithfully bake bread, spin yarn, weave clothing, hammer tin, and reenact other pioneer tasks. Admission costs $5 for adults, $3.50 for senior citizens and children 5–17.

SCENIC RIDE ✿ ✐ **Staten Island Ferry** (212-225-5368), at the waterfront in St. George. Staten Island residents depend on this ferry to get to work, but you can use it—for free—to escape Manhattan to a smaller island for a day, taking in scenic views of the skyline and Lady Liberty (and ocean breezes) along the way.

This has been called one of the world's greatest boat journeys thanks to the striking scenery. The ferry runs 24 hours, most frequently during rush hour (four times hourly), least frequently at night (just once per hour); the ride takes about 25 minutes.

✳ To Do

GOLF **La Tourette Park Golf Course** (718-351-1889), 1001 Richmond Hill Road. By car: Take the Staten Island ferry to the island, taking Richmond Road 5 miles to St. Patrick's Place. From the ferry landing, take the S74 bus to Richmond Hill Road. Located inside La Tourette Park (see *Green Space*), this par-72 course is widely considered one of the best public links in the five boroughs. There's a clubhouse and a restaurant.

✳ Green Space

La Tourette Park, west of Richmond Road. By car: Take the Staten Island ferry to the island, taking Richmond Road 5 miles to St. Patrick's Place. From the ferry landing, take the S74 bus to Richmond Hill Road. It's difficult to believe such a thickly forested, large park could exist so close to the towers of Manhattan, but it does—and, in fact, this U-shaped, 600-acre park is big enough and wild enough that you could easily get lost here. A greenbelt trail makes a loop of the park, with trailheads at St. Andrew's Church on Richmond Road and the Seaview Hospital on Brielle Avenue. It traverses thick woods, a hill with but a single abandoned dwelling and expansive views, and a deep hollow before returning to civilization; if you look hard, you'll find trees and herbs not normally found in northeastern climes such as hickories and cicely. Historic Richmondtown (see *To See—Historic Site*) is also located here.

✳ Where to Eat

DINING OUT **Aesop's Tables** (718-720-2005), 1233 Bay Street at the corner of Maryland Avenue. From the ferry terminal, take the S51 bus to Bay Street and Highland. Open Tuesday through Saturday for dinner 5:30–10:30 PM, Sunday for brunch 10:30 AM–3:30 PM and dinner 4:30–8:30 PM. Possibly the best restaurant on Staten Island, whimsically named Aesop's Tables features a great back garden, a beautiful interior, and solid New American cooking—anything from grilled smoked fish and pan-seared trout or duck breast to meatless risotto and meat loaf appears on the frequently changing menu. The weekend brunches are outstanding, the wine list is competent, and throughout staff strive to make this a classy, potentially romantic dinner. Great desserts complete the experience. Main courses cost $15–30 each.

EATING OUT ☯ **Denino's Pizzeria** (718-442-9401), 524 Port Richmond Avenue between Hooker Place and Walker Street. From the ferry terminal, take the S44 bus to Hooker Place. Open Monday to Thursday noon–10:30 PM, weekends to 11:45 PM. Staten Island's most famous pizza pie parlor holds its own against all Manhattan, Brooklyn, and Jersey comers.

Sure, the place has no atmosphere to speak of, and the most popular pizza is a truly puzzling pie of meatballs, onions, and ricotta, but hey—calcium and dairy helps you burn fat, right? Pizzas here are surprisingly inexpensive, most costing $8–13 each, and they're quite good. Crusts are thin and tasty; toppings are unfancy, as they should be. Note that Denino's does not accept any credit cards. A bonus: Ralph's Famous Italian Ices (see *Coffee and Snacks*, below) is right across the street.

Killmeyer's Old Bavaria Inn (718-984-1202), 4254 Arthur Kill Road at the corner of Sharrotts Road. From the ferry terminal, take the S74 bus to Sharrotts Road. Open Monday to Thursday 11 AM–10 PM, Friday and Saturday to 2 AM, Sunday noon– 10 PM. More a bar than a restaurant— and a German beer hall, at that— Killmeyer's does deliver good fun and suitably Teutonic bar snacks and meals such as wurst, sausages, and chops. The beer offerings (there are almost 100 in all) feature Germany, of course; the brews from Deutschland include top brands such as Ayinger, Erdinger, Hacker-Pschorr, and Paulaner. Explorer's tip: On Monday and Tuesday the restaurant serves an all-you-can-eat buffet.

COFFEE AND SNACKS 🍧 **Ralph's Famous Italian Ices** (718-273-3675), 501 Port Richmond Avenue at the corner of Catherine Street. From the ferry terminal, take the S44 bus to Port Richmond Avenue. Open April through mid-October, daily noon– 11 PM. One of New York's top Italian ice makers, Ralph's began as a family business started by Italian immigrant Ralph Silvestro way back in 1928. It has since franchised itself, with the result that you can now find it in Long Island, New Jersey, and even North Carolina. They still don't take credit cards, though, and they still make top "water ices" and sherbets in a fun variety of sweet and fruity flavors at this corner shop with the throwback-style carnival signs. Cannoli? Root beer? Cotton candy? Mai tai, mud slide, peppermint patty, coconut raspberry tart? Honeydew? They're all here. Try 'em.

✳ Entertainment

ARTS VENUE 🎭 **Snug Harbor Cultural Center** (718-448-2500), 1000 Richmond Terrace. From the ferry landing, take the S40 bus to New Brighton. Opening hours vary by venue, call for information. This amazing and attractive 85-acre waterside complex of buildings was once used as housing and a hospital for ill or aging mariners; the arts venue today encompasses artists' studios, a summertime sculpture competition, musical performances by New York's famous opera company and philharmonic orchestra, and much more. This is one of the Northeast's more amazing assemblages of Greek Revival architecture in one place; in fact, a Greek Revival temple houses the Newhouse Center for Contemporary Art's gallery and exhibition spaces and studios; a Beaux-Arts vaudeville theater is now the music hall. You'll also find a children's museum, a kids' maze, maritime museum, and botanical garden on the premises. Admission to the building is free, though certain performances, exhibitions, and special events do carry ticket prices:

The Children's Museum is $5, for instance, and the Newhouse Galleries cost $3 per adult.

SPECTATOR SPORTS 🏵 **Staten Island Yankees** (718-720-9265), 75 Richmond Terrace at Wall Street near the ferry landing in St. George. As if the Mets–Yankees rivalry weren't enough, now there's a minor-league version of it, too. In 2001 this new baseball franchise—a farm team of the estimable uptown Yankees—unveiled Richmond County Bank Ballpark, where the club plays the Mets-affiliated Brooklyn Cyclones each summer before usually packed houses.

INDEX